WESTERN
CIVILIZATIONS

WORLD · POLITICAL

NATIONAL BOUNDARIES

Winkel Tripel Projection

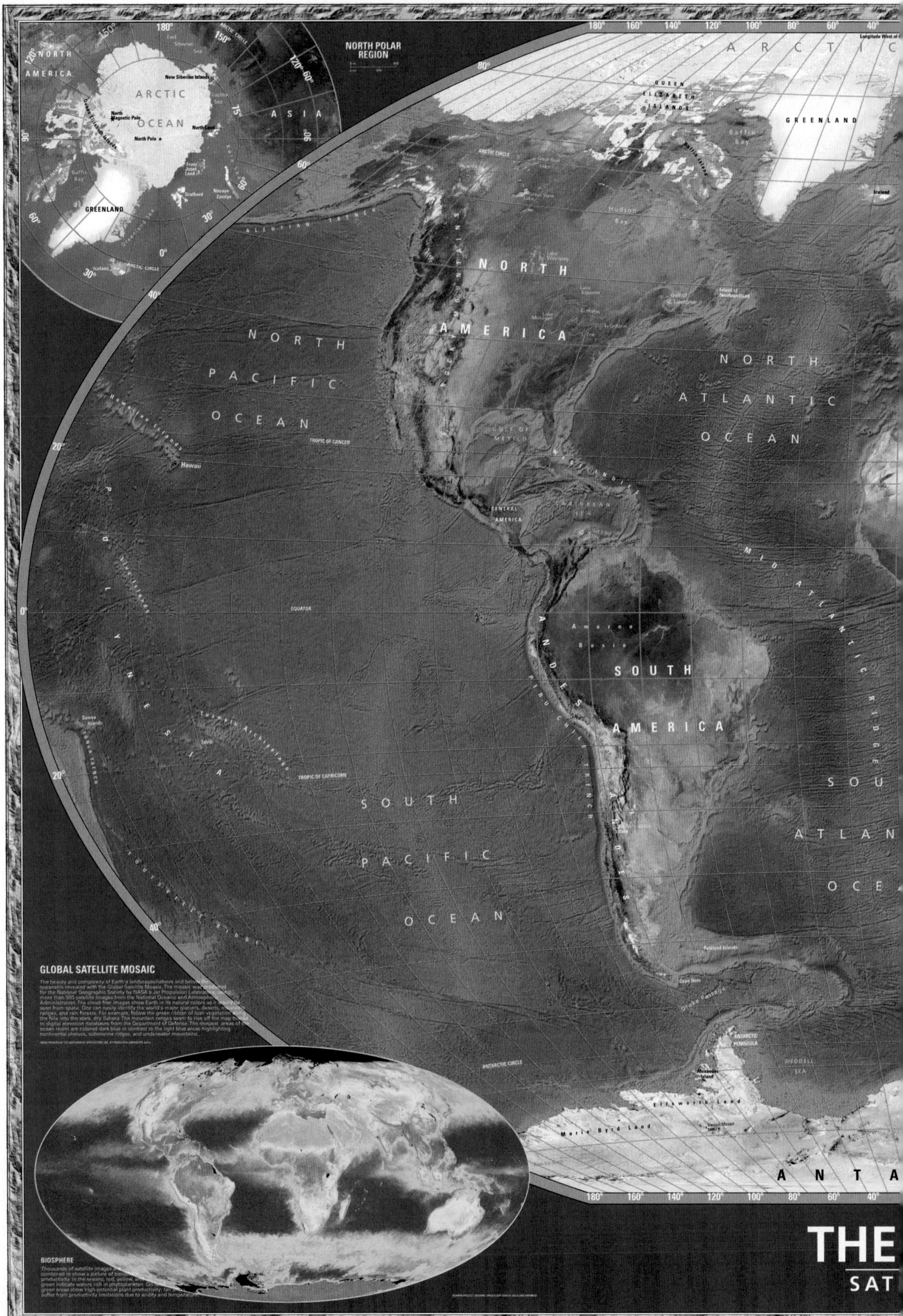

NORTH POLAR REGION

ARCTIC OCEAN

NORTH AMERICA

ASIA

GREENLAND

New Siberian Islands

North Magnetic Pole

North Pole

North Land

Franz Josef Land

Svalbard

Novaya Zemlya

Baffin Bay

Iceland

ARCTIC CIRCLE

QUEEN ELIZABETH ISLANDS

GREENLAND

Iceland

ARCTIC CIRCLE

NORTH AMERICA

NORTH PACIFIC OCEAN

Hawaii

TROPIC OF CANCER

GULF OF MEXICO

CARIBBEAN SEA

CENTRAL AMERICA

NORTH ATLANTIC OCEAN

MID ATLANTIC RIDGE

Hudson Bay

Lake Winnipeg

Lake Superior

EQUATOR

POLYNESIA

Samoa Islands

SOUTH AMERICA

Amazon Basin

ANDES

PERU CHILE TRENCH

TROPIC OF CAPRICORN

SOUTH PACIFIC OCEAN

SOUTH ATLANTIC OCEAN

Falkland Islands

Cape Horn

Drake Passage

ANTARCTIC PENINSULA

WEDDELL SEA

Alexander Island

Ellsworth Land

Marie Byrd Land

ANTARCTIC CIRCLE

ANTARCTICA

GLOBAL SATELLITE MOSAIC

The beauty and complexity of Earth's landscapes ashore and below the oceans is revealed with the Global Satellite Mosaic. The mosaic was produced for the National Geographic Society by NASA's Jet Propulsion Laboratory, using more than 500 satellite images from the National Oceanic and Atmospheric Administration. The cloud-free images show Earth in its natural colors as it would be seen from space. One can easily identify the world's major glaciers, deserts, mountain ranges, and rain forests. For example, follow the green ribbon of lush vegetation as it falls into the stark, dry Sahara. The mountain ranges seem to rise off the map thanks to digital elevation databases from the Department of Defense. The deepest areas of the ocean realm are colored dark blue in contrast to the light blue areas highlighting continental shelves, submarine ridges, and underwater mountains.

BIOSPHERE

Thousands of satellite images combined to show a picture of biological productivity in the oceans, red, yellow, and green indicate waters rich in phytoplankton. On land, green areas show high-potential plant productivity; tan areas suffer from productivity limitations due to aridity and temperature.

THE
SAT

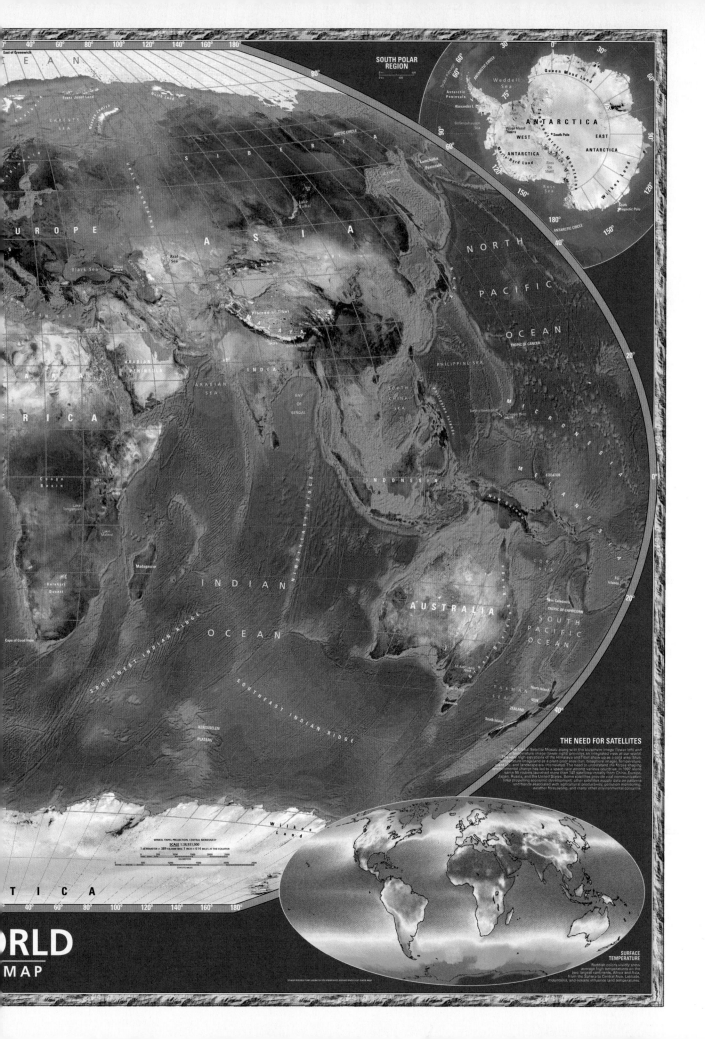

VOLUME A/SIXTEENTH EDITION

JUDITH G. COFFIN

ROBERT C. STACEY

BASED ON *WESTERN CIVILIZATIONS*
BY EDWARD McNALL BURNS

ROBERT E. LERNER

STANDISH MEACHAM

W · W · NORTON & COMPANY · NEW YORK · LONDON

WESTERN
CIVILIZATIONS

THEIR HISTORY
& THEIR CULTURE

W. W. Norton & Company has been independent since its founding in 1923, when William Warder Norton and Mary D. Herter Norton first published lectures delivered at the People's Institute, the adult education division of New York City's Cooper Union. The Nortons soon expanded their program beyond the Institute, publishing books by celebrated academics from America and abroad. By mid-century, the two major pillars of Norton's publishing program—trade books and college texts— were firmly established. In the 1950s, the Norton family transferred control of the company to its employees, and today—with a staff of four hundred and a comparable number of trade, college, and professional titles published each year—W. W. Norton & Company stands as the largest and oldest publishing house owned wholly by its employees.

Composition: TSI Graphics
Manufacturing by R. R. Donnelley & Sons—Willard Division
Book design by Antonina Krass
Layout artist: Paul Lacy
Production manager: Ben Reynolds
Editor: Karl Bakeman
Associate Director, Electronic Media: Steven S. Hoge
Copy Editor: Candace Levy
Project Editor: Lory A. Frenkel
Editorial Assistants: Rebecca Arata, Kate Feighery

The Library of Congress has cataloged the one-volume edition as follows.

Coffin, Judith G., 1952–
    Western civilizations: their history & their culture / by Judith G. Coffin and Robert C. Stacey.—16th ed.
        p. cm.
    Includes bibliographical references and index.
    ISBN 978-0-393-93099-3 (hardcover)
    1. Civilization, Western—Textbooks. 2. Europe—Civilization—Textbooks. I. Stacey,
Robert C. II. Title. III. Title: Western civilizations, their history and their culture.

CB245.C65 2008
909'.09821—dc22   2007042776

ISBN 13: 978-0-393-93100-6 (pbk.)
W. W. Norton & Company, Inc., 500 Fifth Avenue, New York, N.Y. 10110
www.wwnorton.com

W. W. Norton & Company Ltd., Castle House, 75/76 Wells Street, London W1T 3QT
1 2 3 4 5 6 7 8 9 0

To our families—Robin, Will, and Anna Stacey, and Willy, Zoe, and Aaron Forbath—for their patience and support. They reminded us that books such as this are worth the work, and also that there are other things in life.

To Robert Lerner, Standish Meacham, Edward McNall Burns, and Marie Burns, our predecessors who successfully guided *Western Civilizations* for thirteen editions, spanning six decades.

ABOUT THE BOOK

Used by over 1,000,000 students *Western Civilizations* is renowned for its balanced presentation, clear prose, and exceptional treatment of cultural history. Originally published in 1942, the book began as an outgrowth of Edward McNall Burns's Western civilizations course at Rutgers University. Robert Lerner (Northwestern University) and Standish Meacham (University of Texas at Austin) took over authorship in the ninth edition and extended the book's traditional strengths to include the new social history. Beginning with the fourteenth edition, Judith Coffin (University of Texas at Austin) and Robert Stacey (University of Washington) debuted as the third generation of authors to lead this book. While Coffin and Stacey maintain the balanced presentation of *Western Civilizations*, they have enlarged the conception of "Western Civilization" to take in the diversity of the European world.

ABOUT THE AUTHORS

JUDITH G. COFFIN received her Ph.D. in modern French history from Yale University. She has taught at Harvard University and the University of California, Riverside, and is currently associate professor of history at the University of Texas at Austin, where she won a 1999 University of Texas President's Associates' Award for Teaching Excellence. Her research interests focus on the social and cultural history of gender, mass culture, slavery, race relations, and colonialism. She is the author of *The Politics of Women's Work: The Paris Garment Trades, 1750-1915.*

ROBERT C. STACEY is Dean of Humanities and Arts and Professor of History and Jewish Studies at the University of Washington in Seattle. A long-time teacher of western civilization and medieval European history, he has received Distinguished Teaching Awards from both the University of Washington and Yale University, where he taught from 1984 to 1988. The author or coauthor of four books, he is a Fellow of the Royal Historical Society and has held awards from the American Council of Learned Societies and from the Guggenheim Foundation. His current research deals with the history of Jews in medieval England.

CONTENTS

PART II   THE GREEK AND ROMAN WORLDS

PART III  THE MIDDLE AGES

CHAPTER 7 ROME'S THREE HEIRS: THE BYZANTINE, ISLAMIC, AND EARLY MEDIEVAL WORLDS 244

CHAPTER 8 THE EXPANSION OF EUROPE: ECONOMY, SOCIETY, AND POLITICS IN THE HIGH MIDDLE AGES, 1000–1300 286

CHAPTER 9 THE HIGH MIDDLE AGES: RELIGIOUS AND INTELLECTUAL DEVELOPMENTS, 1000–1300 330

PART IV FROM MEDIEVAL TO MODERN

Maps

CHRONOLOGIES

Documents

PREFACE

Since the 1920s, the western civilization survey course has held a central place in the curricula of American universities and high schools. Yet the concept of "western civilization" remains both elusive and controversial. It seems appropriate, therefore, that we begin by defining our terms. How do we, as authors, conceive of our subject?

During much of the twentieth century, "western" civilization meant "the civilization of western Europe," to which the history of the Ancient Near East was somewhat arbitrarily attached. Western civilization was therefore presented as beginning at Sumer, developing in Egypt, and then flowering in Greece. From Greece it spread to Rome, then made its way to France, Germany, England, Italy, and Spain, whose emigrating colonists brought it to the Americas after 1492. Rather like a train passing through stations, western civilization was thus conceived as picking up "cargo" at each of its stops, but always retaining the same engine and the same baggage cars.

This vision of western civilization was not only selective, it was often tied to a series of contentious assumptions. It cast the worldwide dominance of the European imperial powers between roughly 1800 and 1950 as the culmination of several thousand years of historical development, which it was the obligation of historians to explain. It also tended to presume that European global dominance in the nineteenth and twentieth centuries reflected and demonstrated the superiority of western European civilization over the African, Asian, and Native American civilizations the Europeans conquered during the heyday of their imperial expansion.

Historians today are keenly aware of how much such an account leaves out. It slights the use of force and fraud in European expansion. It also ignores the sophistication, dynamism, and humanity of the many cultures it sidelines. By neglecting the crucial importance of Byzantium and Islam, it even gives a misleadingly narrow account of the development of European civilization. It also misleads us about the civilizations created in North and South America after 1492, which were creole, or hybrid, cultures, not simply European cultures transplanted to other shores. This is not to argue that a study of western civilizations must give way to a study of world civilization. It is merely to insist that understanding the historical development of the West requires us to place our subject in a geographical and cultural context that is wider than western Europe alone; and that, shorn of its triumphalism, the history

of these various and differing western civilizations becomes vastly more interesting.

Therefore, we mean for the plural in our title, *Western
Civilizations*, to be taken seriously. The West cannot be
understood as a single, continuous historical culture.
Rather, there have been a number of western civilizations whose fundamental characteristics have changed
markedly over time. We treat "western" as a geographical designator referring to the major civilizations that
developed in and around the Mediterranean Sea between 3500 B.C.E. ("Before the Common Era," equivalent to the Christian dating system B.C., "Before
Christ") and 500 C.E. ("Common Era," equivalent to the
Christian dating system A.D., "Anno Domini," "the Year
of the Lord"). We also treat as "western" the civilizations that emerged out of the Mediterranean world in
the centuries after 500 C.E., as the Greco-Roman world
of antiquity divided into Islamic, Byzantine, and Latin
Christian realms. The interdependence and mutual influences of these three western civilizations upon each
other will be a recurring theme of the first half of this
book. We take the same approach to describing the
complex relationships between Europe and the other
world civilizations with which it came into contact
after 1500.

Western Civilizations rests on the efforts and learning
of three generations of historians. Edward McNall
Burns, Robert Lerner, and Standish Meacham constructed a textbook that combined a vigorous narrative
style with attention to the diverse ways in which ordinary people responded to changing environments, societies, and cultures. In building upon their work, we
have tried to retain these traditional strengths by remaining attentive to narrative, by aiming for clarity
and accessibility without compromising on accuracy
or ignoring complexity, and by presenting politics and
culture as part of a single, shared world of historical experience.

We have also made significant changes to the book
that reflect the changing historical interests of teachers, students, and scholars. In keeping with our broadened understanding of western civilizations, we devote
much more attention to the world outside western Europe. We continue to integrate new scholarly work in
social and cultural history and the history of gender
into our narrative, but we have also substantially increased the attention we pay to economic, religious,
and military history. We also pay particular attention
to the varying ways in which these different western
civilizations sought to govern themselves and the territories they conquered. "Empire" has been a consistent

theme in the history of the West for more than four
thousand years. In revising this book, we have tried to
do justice to its importance.

CHANGES TO THE SIXTEENTH EDITION

Throughout, we have worked to integrate the text, visual material, and pedagogy. That has meant bringing
in different images, rewriting focus questions, and
adding study questions to the documents as well as up-
dating the text. These changes make the text more
user-friendly while still allowing professors and students alike to tailor it to their particular course and
interests.

Part I, "The Ancient Near East," was completely reorganized and rewritten for the fifteenth edition.
However, we have made a number of changes to the
text as well as to the artwork and document selections.
In Chapter 1, the discussion of prehistory and the
emergence of the earliest towns and villages have been
updated, with particular attention to the exciting archaeological work currently underway at Çatal
Höyük. We have also revised the presentation of
Sumerian religion and added a discussion of Enheduanna, high priestess and daughter of Sargon I of
Akkad. In Chapter 2, we have revised the discussion of
Hatshepsut's role as a female pharaoh and added many
new illustrations, including Hatshepsut's mortuary
temple, one of the glories of ancient Egyptian architecture.

In Part II, readers will find a much-improved program of illustrations in all the chapters. Chapter 4 includes a revised account of Hellenistic religions,
especially the so-called "mystery cults." Reflecting the
consensus of recent scholarly work, Mithraism is now
discussed only in Chapter 5, as an example of the new
religious devotions that swept through early imperial
Roman society. Readers will also find in Chapter 5 a
new treatment of the economy of the Roman empire.
Chapter 6 offers a completely new account of the fall
of the western Roman empire during the fifth century
C.E., emphasizing the suddenness of Rome's collapse
and the profound consequences this collapse had for
the Roman economy and for standards of living within
the western Roman empire. Here too, as throughout
the book, we are trying to reflect the current balance
of scholarly opinion.

In Part III, "The Middle Ages," Chapter 7 now includes a separate section on the Vikings with several
new accompanying illustrations. This chapter also features a revised explanation of the split between Shi'ite

and Sunni Islam, a revised assessment of the influence of early Islamic civilization on Europe, and a new document box pairing passages from the Qur'an on Jews and Christians with the "Pact of Umar." Chapter 8 features another new document box, on the summoning of the First Crusade in 1096. A number of new illustrations have been added to Chapter 8 to give more students a better sense of daily life during the high middle ages. Readers will also find an improved discussion of climate change during this period. Chapter 9 includes a new document box on kingship as a religious office, which we hope will make it easier for students to grasp the issues at stake in the Investiture Conflict.

Part IV, "From Medieval to Modern," begins with a completely new chapter (10) on the later middle ages, which emphasizes the remarkable resilience and creativity that characterized European responses to the Black Death. The far-reaching consequences of the plague upon social, economic, and religious life are the central themes of this chapter. Interestingly, however, there is now considerable doubt among historians and epidemiologists as to whether the Black Death was in fact an outbreak of bubonic plague, or whether it may have been some other disease entirely. This new chapter includes an up-to-date discussion of this controversy, which remains unresolved as this book goes to press.

In Chapter 13, "Reformations of Religion," readers will find a new section on "Reform and Discipline," and a new selection of paired documents, contrasting Lutheran and Catholic positions on marriage and celibacy.

In Part V, we have rewritten Chapter 16, "The New Science of the Seventeenth Century," to make it clearer and more accessible. It emphasizes the transformation of scientific knowledge, practice, and institutions. Here as in all our discussions of intellectual history, we foreground the context in which new ideas emerged and how those ideas came to matter for a range of people, from philosophers, rulers, and bureaucrats to explorers, artists, and artisans.

In Part VI, we have expanded discussion of Napoleon's empire and its legacy to Europe and the world. We have added to Chapter 21 an extended discussion of slavery and its abolition in the Americas which follows up on the treatment of the Haitian revolution in Chapter 18. Coming as it does before the section on the American Civil War, it places developments in the United States in a larger, comparative perspective. No course can be comprehensive, especially one dealing with a topic as hard to define as the West, but we have chosen to touch down on a few topics, like the politics of abolition, with an eye to highlighting comparisons and global connections. We have expanded the treatment of U.S. imperialism in Chapter 22 for the same reason.

Part VI continues to be organized thematically. Chapter 19, on industrial society, focuses on the relationship between social, economic, and cultural change—or on industry as a way of life. Chapters 20 and 21 break the tumultuous history of the mid-nineteenth-century revolutions into two parts, to make themes easier to follow. Chapter 20 goes from the reaction against the French Revolution of 1789 to the renewed outbreak of revolution in 1848, and includes a discussion of nineteenth-century political ideologies and cultural movements. Chapter 21 begins with the revolutions of 1848 in central and eastern Europe and then focuses on the issues those revolutions raised, nation and state building, as they played out elsewhere.

In Part VII, we have revised Chapter 24, on World War I. Readers will find more material on the long-term evolution of warfare and the emergence of total war. We have also expanded the treatment of the Paris Peace Conference, another important global moment. The new scope of war summoned global institutions to contend with the war's ramifications. Whether or not those international concerns could be compatible with national interests was an open question, and would become a theme of the history of the twentieth century. So would other issues central to the Peace of Paris, such as the expansion of empire, the mobilization of movements for national self determination, and the protection of minorities within new nation states.

In Part VIII, which was almost entirely rewritten for the previous edition, we added discussion of the history of human rights to conclude the chapter on globalization. Why, suddenly, is the language of human rights so familiar? The change highlights the dramatic political transformation wrought by the end of the cold war; it also reflects the new horizons of a rapidly globalizing world, with all their potential and peril. Finally, a history of human rights provides the occasion to review some of the central debates of the Western political tradition.

INNOVATIVE PEDAGOGICAL PROGRAM

Western Civilizations, Sixteenth Edition, is designed for maximum readability. The crisp, clear, and concise narrative is also accompanied by a pedagogical program to help students study while engaging them in the subject matter. Highlights of this innovative program include:

- **New "Transformations" feature provokes students to consider the implications of major historical events.** Throughout the Sixteenth Edition, we have inserted new material on important "transformations" in the history of western civilizations. Highlighted with an icon, these sections ask students to reflect on the larger political, social, or cultural consequences of major turning points in history. Frequently, they draw on cutting-edge scholarship that has transformed our understanding of these events. New "Tranformations" include:

- Chapter 1: "The Origins of Food Production in the Ancient Near East." This rewritten and expanded section focuses on the disadvantages and the advantages of agriculture.

- Chapter 6: "The German Invasions and the Fall of the Western Roman Empire." The new material on the German-Roman relations elaborates on the economic collapse of western Rome in the fifth century, and explains how aspects of Roman life—the tax and administrative system, agricultural systems, and city life—persisted.

- Chapter 10: "The Black Death." The effects of the plague rippled across Europe. It affected every aspect of life. For example, fewer people were available to work the fields, but there were also fewer people to feed. Prices of grain went up, but because there were fewer people competing for jobs, wages did, too. Consequently, ordinary people could now afford not only to buy more bread, they could also purchase dairy products, meat, fish, fruits and wine on a more regular basis. As a result, the people of Europe in the later middle ages ate a more balanced diet, and were consequently better nourished than they had been for centuries, or than some are today.

- Chapter 16: "Science and Cultural Change." This new "transformation" section deals with the cultural shifts that arose from the Scientific Revolution. Beginning in the 17th century, embracing science and the scientific method was at the heart of what it meant to be "modern." This has implications for the Enlightenment, but it also became the justification for new technologies and for new empires.

- Chapter 24: "The Peace Settlement at Versailles." The Treaty of Versailles marks the emergence of the United States as a world power. But it also represents the first time so many countries were involved in a peace settlement and marks the scope of the war, the growing national sentiments and aspirations, and the tightening of international communication and economic networks.

- **NEW Document Questions.** Professors requested questions for the documents in the book. We have added questions at the bottom of each box that ask students to engage the primary source or connect it to the larger issues in the chapter.

- **End-of-Chapter Key Terms.** In response to requests from professors, each chapter includes a list of key terms to help students focus on the key ideas, events, or people in the chapter.

- **In-Text Documents.** To add depth to the more focused narrative of *Western Civilizations*, each chapter contains an average of four primary sources, two of which are paired to convey a sense of historical complexity and diversity.

- **Map Program with Enhanced Captions.** Over 130 beautiful maps appear throughout the text, including twenty-five new maps, each accompanied by an enhanced caption designed to engage the reader analytically while conveying the key role that geography plays in the development of history and the societies of the world.

- **In-Chapter Chronologies.** Several brief chronologies built around particular events, topics, or periods appear in each chapter and are designed to provide road maps through the narrative detail.

- **Focus Question System.** To ensure that students remain alert to key concepts and questions on every page of the text, focus questions guide their reading in three ways: (1) a focus question box appears at the beginning of each chapter to preview the chapter's contents; (2) relevant questions reappear at the start of the section in which they are discussed; and (3) running heads on the righthand pages keep these questions in view throughout the chapter.

- **Pull Quotes.** Lifted directly from the narrative, pull quotes appear throughout each chapter to highlight key thoughts and keen insights while keeping students focused on larger concepts and ideas.

RESOURCES FOR STUDENTS

StudySpace
wwnorton.com/studyspace

This student website provides a rich array of multimedia resources and review materials within a proven, task-oriented study plan.

Each chapter is arranged in an effective *Organize, Learn, and Connect* pedagogy:

Organize
In this section, students can work through Focus Questions, print out Chapter Outlines and summaries, or check in with Progress Reports that help them focus their studies.

Learn
This section encourages active learning with:
- **iMaps and GeoQuizzes that engage and test students' geographic knowledge** with map review worksheets and maps with zoom functions, highlighting, and labels.
- **Multiple-choice quizzes for each chapter.**
- **FlashCards** with audio pronunciations.
- **Interactive Chrono-Sequencers** that challenge students to reassemble sequences of events, reinforcing their understanding of the flow of history.
- **NEW! Document Quizzes** provide a form for students to answer the questions about the in-text documents.

Connect
In this section, students are reminded to connect to additional resources that include:
- **250 additional primary source documents**
- **Research Topics** that combine a writing prompt, documents, headnotes and sample questions.
- **NEW Interactive MapPlayer** with audio introductions, transitions, and conclusions, along with a suite of interactive functions to examine individual maps as they are presented in a progressive sequence.
- **Audio Glossary**

Study Guide
Margaret Minor and Paul Wilson, *Nicholls State University*

The *Study Guide* gives students a comprehensive means for review and self-assessment. Each chapter contains a chapter outline, identifications, multiple-choice questions, matching, and true/false questions, chronologies, and short-answer and essay questions.

RESOURCES FOR INSTRUCTORS

Norton Media Library
This newly expanded resource for multimedia lectures offers:
- PowerPoint presentations for each chapter
- Hi-resolution maps and graphics files from the book
- Art from the book
- Questions for Classroom Response PowerPoints (Clicker Questions)

Instructor's Manual
Steven Kreis, *American Public University*

Each chapter in the *Instructor's Manual* includes lecture outlines, key lecture topics, suggested films, and suggestions for integrating media into the classroom and using media as homework assignments.

Test Bank
April Harper, *State University of New York, Oneonta*

This vastly expanded test bank includes 60% more questions, including true/false and essay questions. It is available in *ExamView® Assessment Suite*, WebCT, and Blackboard formats.

Blackboard and WebCT Coursepacks offer study plans that integrate review materials for each chapter, as well as ready-to-use test banks, maps, PowerPoint lecture presentations, and practice quizzes.

Map Transparencies

ACKNOWLEDGMENTS

The drafts of the manuscript have benefited from careful reading by and suggestions from a group of professors to whom we are greatly indebted. Our sincere thanks to:
- Eric Ash, Wayne State University
- Sacha Auerbach, Virginia Commonwealth University
- Ken Bartlett, University of Toronto
- Benita Blessing, Ohio University
- Chuck Boening, Shelton State Community College
- John Bohstedt, University of Tennessee–Knoxville
- Dan Brown, Moorpark College
- Kevin Caldwell, Blue Ridge Community College
- Jodi Campbell, Texas Christian University
- Annette Chamberlain, Virginia Western Community College
- Jason Coy, College of Charleston
- Benjamin Ehlers, University of Georgia

- Maryann Farkas, Dawson College
- Gloria Fitzgibbon, Wake Forest University
- Tina Gaddis, Onondaga Community College
- Alex Garman, Eastern New Mexico State University
- Norman Goda, Ohio University
- Andrew Goldman, Gonzaga University
- Robert Grasso, Monmouth University
- Sylvia Gray, Portland Community College
- Susan Grayzel, University of Mississippi
- Hazel Hahn, Seattle University
- Derek Hastings, Oakland University
- Dawn Hayes, Montclair State University
- John Houston, Fordham University
- Michael Hughes, Wake Forest University
- Bruce Hunt, University of Texas–Austin
- Ahmed Ibrahim, Southwest Missouri State University
- Kevin James, University of Guelph
- John Kearney, Cy Fair Community College
- Elizabeth Lehfeldt, Cleveland State University
- Thomas Maulucci, State University of New York–Fredonia
- Amy McCandless, College of Charleston
- Nicholas Murray, Adirondack College
- Charles Odahl, Boise State University
- Bill Olejniczak, College of Charleston
- Jeffery Plaks, University of Central Oklahoma
- Peter Pozesky, College of Wooster
- Rebecca Schloss, Texas A&M University
- Patrick Speelman, College of Charleston
- Paul Teverow, Missouri Southern State University
- James Vanstone, John Abbott College
- Kirk Willis, University of Georgia
- Ian Worthington, University of Missouri–Columbia
- Margarita Youngo, Pima Community College

We want to thank Steve Forman and Jon Durbin at W. W. Norton & Company for their faith in this project; Karl Bakeman for his intelligent editing, consistent support, and exceptional good cheer; and Rebecca Arata, Kate Feighery, Ben Reynolds, and Lory Frenkel for their help with all aspects of the production process.

Robert Stacey is principally responsible for Chapters 1–15. He owes special thanks to Jason Hawke of Northern Illinois University for his extraordinary help in drafting Chapters 1–5. He would also like to acknowledge the assistance of a large number of friends and colleagues around the country who have taken the time to answer queries and offer suggestions: Jon Crump, Gerald Eck, Sandra Joshel, Mary O'Neil, Ben Schmidt, Julie Stein, Carol Thomas, Joel Walker, and Dan Waugh of the University of Washington; Michael Halvorson, University of Puget Sound; Michelle Ferry, University of California, Santa Barbara; Byron Nakamura, Southern Connecticut State University; Lawrence Duggan, University of Delaware; and Robert Stiefel, University of New Hampshire.

Judith Coffin is principally responsible for the revisions to Chapter 16–29. Many colleagues have supplied expertise and references, particularly Caroline Castiglione, David Crew, Paul Hagenloh, Tony Hopkins, Bruce Hunt, Standish Meacham, John Merriman, Gail Minault, Joan Neuberger, Paula Sanders, Daniel Sherman, James Sidbury, Robert Stephens, Michael Stoff, and Charters Wynn. Patrick Timmons, Marion Barber, Cori Crider, April Smith, and, especially, Michael Schmidt were terrific research assistants. Special thanks to Dinah Chenven and Norman Chenven who drafted Chapter 16, to James Brophy for his consistently excellent advice, to Geoffrey Clayton and Justin Glasson, who have researched, edited, and written many chapters, and to the students in Western Civ at the University of Texas, Austin.

WESTERN
CIVILIZATIONS

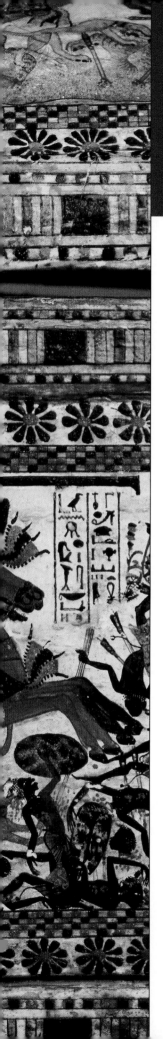

PART I

THE ANCIENT NEAR EAST

THE STORY OF Western civilizations begins in the Near East about 13,000 years ago. As the glaciers slowly receded, a new ecological world of marshes, grasslands, and domesticable animals emerged at the eastern end of the Mediterranean Sea. In this new world, humans made a momentous transformation from small hunting-gathering bands to larger, agriculturally based communities. A second great leap forward occurred around 5,000 years ago when the first true cities appeared, first between the Tigris and the Euphrates rivers, and then throughout the Near East.

Traditions of urban independence and autonomy soon gave way to larger political configurations. In Old Kingdom Egypt, the pharaohs ruled an integrated realm that stretched for hundreds of miles along the Nile River. In Mesopotamia, Sargon of Akkad created an empire that would inspire imitators for 1,500 years. By 1500 B.C.E. (Before the Common Era; equivalent to the Christian dating system B.C., meaning "Before Christ"), an international system of trade and diplomacy encompassed the entire eastern Mediterranean world.

Around 1200 B.C.E., however, this international system collapsed in cataclysm, taking with it most of the established empires of the era. The resulting power vacuum made space for new states to emerge, particularly in the Middle East. But the imperial hiatus proved temporary. As iron slowly replaced bronze as the essential raw material for tools and weapons, new, more powerful Near Eastern empires emerged: larger, better armed and organized, and more aggressively expansionist than the Bronze Age empires that preceded them. By 500 B.C.E., the largest of these empires, Persia, was the undisputed master of the Near Eastern world.

Equally dramatic developments were occurring in religious and cultural life. The pyramids of Egypt, the *Epic of Gilgamesh,* the works of Homer, and the religious traditions of Zoroastrianism and Judaism had all taken shape by the time this period closed around 500 B.C.E. On these foundations, all the subsequent civilizations of the western (i.e., the Mediterranean) world have continued to rest.

	POLITICS	SOCIETY AND CULTURE	ECONOMY	INTERNATIONAL RELATIONS
B.C.E. 40,000		Paleolithic Era (40,000–11,000 B.C.E.)		
		End of the Ice Age, beginning of the Neolithic Era (11,000 B.C.E.)		
10,000	The Predynastic Period in Egypt (c. 10,000–3100 B.C.E.)	Settled agriculture in Fertile Crescent (8500 B.C.E.)	Grain storage begins (9500 B.C.E.)	
8000		Stone walls and tower of Jericho (8000 B.C.E.)	Emergence of pottery in Jericho (8000–7000 B.C.E.)	
			Domestication of animals, raising of crops (7000 B.C.E.)	
6000	Ubaid culture governed by priestly class (5900 B.C.E.)		Copper tools appear (6000 B.C.E.)	Ubaid culture (Mesopotamia) (5900 B.C.E.)
			Ubaid culture builds irrigation channels of stone (5900 B.C.E.)	
		Agriculture established in Egypt and the Balkans (5000 B.C.E.)	Long-distance trade emerges (5000 B.C.E.)	
		Increased trade engenders social stratification (5000 B.C.E.)		
		First known settlement in Egypt (4750 B.C.E.)		
4000		Uruk Period (4300–2900 B.C.E.)		
		End of the Stone Age (4000 B.C.E.)		
		Cities form in fertile Mesopotamia (3500–3000 B.C.E.)	Building of the White Temple at Uruk (3500–3300 B.C.E.)	
			Pottery-throwing wheels (3500 B.C.E.)	
			Ubaid/Sumerians begin inscribing symbols on tablets (3300 B.C.E.)	
			Wheeled chariots (3200 B.C.E.)	
			Egyptians build fortifications, temples, settlements (3200 B.C.E.)	
			Appearance of cuneiform script (3100 B.C.E.)	Sumerian civilization (3100 B.C.E.)
3000	The Archaic Period in Egypt (3100–c. 2686 B.C.E.)	Beginning of the Bronze Age (3000 B.C.E.)	Discovery of bronze (3000 B.C.E.)	
		Egyptians develop hieroglyphs and hieratic script (3000 B.C.E.)		
	Emergence of lugal leadership in Mesopotamia (2900–2500 B.C.E.)			
	Early Dynastic Period (I & II) (2900–2500 B.C.E.)			
	The Old Kingdom in Egypt (c. 2686–2160 B.C.E.)	Great Pyramids of Giza (2640–2510 B.C.E.)		
		Royal Tombs of Ur (2550–2450 B.C.E.)		
	Early Dynastic (III) (2500–2350 B.C.E.)	*Epic of Gilgamesh* (2500 B.C.E.)		
	The Akkadian Period (2350–2160 B.C.E.)			Sargon of Akkad conquers Mesopotamia (2360 B.C.E.)
	Sargon organizes Mesopotamia (2350 B.C.E.)			
	First Intermediate Period (2160–2055 B.C.E.)			Gutians conquer Sumer and Akkad (2160 B.C.E.)
	Unity of Egypt dissolves (2150 B.C.E.)			
	Ur Dynasty III (2100–2000 B.C.E.)			

POLITICS	SOCIETY AND CULTURE	ECONOMY	INTERNATIONAL RELATIONS	
				B.C.E. 2000
e Middle Kingdom in Egypt (2055–c. 1650 B.C.E.)	Indo-European linguistic forms appear (2000 B.C.E.)	Horses introduced to Near East (2000–1700 B.C.E.)		
e Palace Age in Minoan culture (1900–1700 B.C.E.)		Major expansion of trade (1900–1700 B.C.E.)	Minoan civilization flourishes in Crete (1900–1500 B.C.E.)	
ammurabi unifies Sumero-Akkadian rea (1792–1750 B.C.E.)	Code of Hammurabi (1750 B.C.E.)			
		Minoan trade with Egypt, Anatolia, and Cyprus (1700 B.C.E.)		
cond Intermediate Period c. 1650–1550 B.C.E.)			The Hyksos overrun Egypt (1650–1550 B.C.E.)	
			Hittites capture Babylon (1595 B.C.E.)	
e New Kingdom in Egypt 550–1075 B.C.E.)	Appearance of Linear B in Mycenaean Greece (1500 B.C.E.)	Trade surges with new international-ism (1500 B.C.E.)	The Mitannians adopt cavalry and chariot technology (1500 B.C.E.)	1500
			Mycenaean civilization established (1500 B.C.E.)	
utmosis III and Hatshepsut take he throne (1479 B.C.E.)			Age of internationalism begins (1500 B.C.E.)	
			Hittite Empire (1450 B.C.E.)	
			Mycenaeans subjugate Crete (1400 B.C.E.)	
ign of Amenhotep III, the Magnifi-ent (1387–1350 B.C.E.)			Complex societies developed at Mycenae, Thebes, Athens, etc. (1400–1200 B.C.E.)	
ddle Assyrian Period 362–859 B.C.E.)				
nenhotep IV, later Akhenaten, takes he throne (1350 B.C.E.)	Rise of Amon as Egyptian national god (1350 B.C.E.)			
			Treaty between Egypt and Hittite Empire (1286 B.C.E.)	
			Rise of Phoenicians (Canaanites) (1200 B.C.E.)	
			Mycenaean civilization implodes (1200 B.C.E.)	
			Sea Peoples ravage Near East (1200–1179 B.C.E.)	
			Ramses III defeats Sea Peoples (1179 B.C.E.)	
		Philistines introduce vine and olive tree to the Levant (1050 B.C.E.)	Philistine preeminence in the Levant (1050 B.C.E.)	
ul becomes first Hebrew king 025 B.C.E.)			Egypt collapses (1000 B.C.E.)	1000
ign of King David 000–973 B.C.E.)				
brew Kingdom splits upon death f King Solomon (c. 933 B.C.E.)				
o-Assyrian Empire 359–627 B.C.E.)			Phoenicians establish Carthage (800 B.C.E.)	
			Assyrian Empire expands (800–700 B.C.E.)	
ign of Sargon II (722–705 B.C.E.)		Assyrians master iron smelting (700 B.C.E.)		700
	Zoroaster, founder of Zoroastrianism (600 B.C.E.)		Hebrew captivity in Babylon begins (587 B.C.E.)	
ign of Darius I of Persia 521–486 B.C.E.)			Athens defeats Darius I at Battle of Marathon (490 B.C.E.)	
			Alexander the Great invades Persia (334 B.C.E.)	

Chapter ONE

THE ORIGINS
OF WESTERN
CIVILIZATIONS

The human history of the Mediterranean world begins only about 40,000 years ago with the completed evolution of *Homo sapiens sapiens*, the modern human species to which we all belong. Civilization is an even more recent development. To the peoples of the ancient world, the characteristic manifestations of civilization—government, literature, science, and art—were necessarily products of city life. Cities, however, became possible only as a result of the agricultural and technological discoveries that emerged between the end of the last Ice Age, about 13,000 years ago, and the appearance, in Mesopotamia, of the first true cities approximately 5,000 years ago. The story of Western civilizations is thus a short one. In geological time, it is merely a blip on a radar screen.

Why the world's first cities should have developed in the inhospitable region between the Tigris and the Euphrates rivers in modern-day Iraq is a question for which historians do not have a convincing answer. Once developed, however, the basic patterns of urban life quickly spread to other parts of the Near Eastern world. A steadily widening network of trading connections developed among these early cities; but so too did an intense competition for control over people and resources. Attempts during the third millennium B.C.E. to forge lasting empires out of these fiercely independent city-states did not succeed. By the middle of the second millennium B.C.E., however, it was becoming clear that the future of the ancient Near Eastern world would be determined not by the internecine struggles of the Mesopotamian cities but by the competition between the emerging imperial powers of Anatolia (modern-day Turkey) and Egypt.

FOCUS QUESTIONS

• What were the consequences of hunting and gathering for early human societies?

• What changes allowed the transition from hunter-gatherer to sedentary societies?

• What were the principal influences behind the early emergence of urban life in Mesopotamia?

• Why did a common religion not create peace among the Sumerians?

• How did Hammurabi bind his empire together?

• In what ways did patterns of development in early Egypt differ from those in Sumer?

More than 9,000 years ago, one of the earliest towns in human history began to develop at Çatalhöyük (*shatal-HOO-yuk*) in south-central Turkey. Over the next 2,000 years the town grew to cover an area about the size of thirty American football fields—about thirty-three acres—in which some 8,000 inhabitants lived in more than 2,000 separate houses. Yet there were hardly any streets in Çatalhöyük. Each house was built immediately next to its neighbor and generally on top of the ruins of a previous house. People entered their houses by walking across their neighbors' rooftops and then climbed down a ladder dropped through a hole in their own roof.

Despite (or perhaps because of) their beehive-like residential patterns, the people of Çatalhöyük lived in an elaborately organized and technologically sophisticated society. They wove wool cloth; made kiln-fired pottery; painted elaborate hunting scenes on the plaster-covered interior walls of their houses; and made sickles, knives, spears, arrows, and other tools from razor-sharp obsidian that they imported from the nearby Cappadocian mountains. They honored their ancestors with religious rites and buried their dead beneath the floors of their houses. These people were also accomplished sculptors, whose full-figured, carved female figurines may have had religious significance or could simply be evidence for Stone Age eroticism.

As settled agriculturalists, the people of Çatalhöyük grew grains, peas, and lentils and tended herds of domesticated sheep and goats. Like their nomadic ancestors, they also gathered fruits and nuts and hunted wild

Female Figurine from Çatalhöyük. This female figurine was found in a grain storage area at Çatalhöyük. Its significance has been much debated but remains uncertain.

cattle, horses, and pigs. Comparisons of male and female skeletons suggest that there were few differences in occupation or diet between men and women. But despite their relatively healthy diets and their numerous possessions, life expectancy at Çatalhöyük was short, shorter in all likelihood than it was among the nomadic hunter-gatherer bands that surrounded them. At Çatalhöyük, men died, on average, at the age of thirty-four. Women, who bore the additional risks of childbirth together with the common threats of accident, smoke inhalation, and infectious disease, died around the age of thirty.

Towns like Çatalhöyük are very recent developments in human history, but they are the foundation on which all subsequent human civilizations have rested. How, when, and why, then, did such towns emerge?

THE STONE AGE BACKGROUND

What were the consequences of hunting and gathering for early human societies?

Prehistory, the era before the appearance of written records around 3000 B.C.E., is a period of much greater duration than recorded history, but it is only through archaeological discoveries that we can learn anything at all about the important developments that occurred during these years. Archaeologists generally agree that primates with some human features first appeared in Africa 4 to 5 million years ago, and that tool-making hominids (species belonging to the genus *Homo*, to which we as *Homo sapiens sapiens* also belong) evolved approximately 2 million years ago. Because early hominids made most of their tools out of stone, all human cultures down to the fourth millennium B.C.E. (the 1,000-year period ending in 3000 B.C.E.) are referred to as belonging to the Stone Age. Scholars generally divide this vast expanse of time into the Paleolithic ("Old Stone") and the Neolithic ("New Stone") Eras, with the break between them falling around 11,000 B.C.E.

Specifically human traits evolved gradually during the Old Stone Age, even before our modern human species made its first appearance in Africa some 50,000 to 100,000 years ago. For example, a burial site discovered near Burgos in Spain revealed that an early

WHAT WERE THE CONSEQUENCES OF HUNTING AND GATHERING FOR EARLY HUMAN SOCIETIES?

THE STONE AGE BACKGROUND   9

Neanderthal. This computer-generated model is based on a skull dating from approximately 40,000 B.C.E.

hominid species known as *Homo heidelbergensis* (sometimes called Heidelberg Man) deliberately buried its dead with valuable grave goods some 350,000 years ago, suggesting that these hominids had already developed some conception of burial as a symbolic rite. Neanderthals, a later hominid species that lived 30,000 to 200,000 years ago, left even clearer evidence of artistic, musical, and spiritual capacities. Among many other recognizably human characteristics, Neanderthals produced (and presumably wore) jewelry; painted on the walls of caves; and buried their dead in standardized, oval-shaped graves with symbolic objects such as goat horns and, in one case, flowers. But could Neanderthals speak? Did they have a language? At present there is no way that archaeology can answer such questions.

Around 40,000 B.C.E., however, at the beginning of the Upper Paleolithic Era, the pace of human development began to accelerate dramatically. *Homo sapiens sapiens* began to produce more effective and finely crafted tools such as fishhooks, arrowheads, and sewing needles made from organic materials such as wood, antler, and bone. The most dramatic visual evidence of the change is, however, the famous cave paintings at Lascaux in France (see illustration below). Although these paintings were discovered in 1940, archaeologists have only recently realized that these extraordinary hunting scenes were painted in the dark recesses of caves in areas where the acoustical resonance was greatest. These paintings must, therefore, have been part of a set of ritual observances that also involved sound and perhaps even music. They are thus almost certain evidence for the development of language as well as of artistic and religious ideas in the Upper Paleolithic Era.

But despite these important developments, the basic patterns of human life changed little during the Upper Paleolithic Era. Virtually all human societies before 11,000 B.C.E. consisted of small bands of hunter-gatherers, probably never exceeding more than a few dozen individuals, that moved incessantly in search of food. Because they could not stay in any one location for long, these people left no continuous archaeological record whereby we might trace the development of their culture. Our knowledge of them is therefore very limited.

The social, economic, and political consequences of Paleolithic hunting and gathering were profound. Because early humans had no domestic animals to transport their goods, they could have no significant material possessions—wealth—aside from basic tools they could carry with them. And because humans could not accumulate goods over time, disparities in individual wealth, with their attendant distinctions of rank and status, were unlikely to develop. These

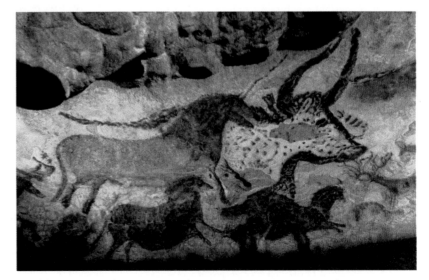

Cave Paintings from Lascaux, France. These paintings, which date to between 10,000 and 15,000 B.C.E., show several of the different species of animals that humans hunted during the Ice Age. The largest of the animals shown here is a now-extinct species of long-horned cattle known as aurochs.

societies may well have been highly organized—it is a gross error to presume that early societies were necessarily primitive—but hierarchical structures of leadership were uncommon and possibly unknown. When conflicts arose within a group, the usual solution was probably to divide and separate—a process that also kept the total numbers in the band in balance with what the natural resources of the area could support.

We do not know how labor was divided among the members of these Paleolithic bands. Although scholars once assumed that men did the hunting and women the gathering, such gendered presumptions do not reflect the complex realities of modern hunter-gatherer societies, and they are probably not applicable to the Paleolithic Period either. It is more likely that all members of a Paleolithic band (except for the very young and the very old) engaged to some extent in all the basic activities of the group. Acquiring food and tools must have been the first concern of nearly everyone. Specialization—the process by which some members of the group are freed up to engage in activities other than food acquisition—was nearly impossible. Specialization requires the accumulation of storable surpluses, and this was something Paleolithic people lacked the technology to accomplish.

THE NEOLITHIC REVOLUTION

What changes allowed the transition from hunter-gatherer to sedentary societies?

Fundamental changes in human life began to take shape around 11,000 B.C.E., the dawn of the Neolithic Era, or New Stone Age. These breakthroughs included the development of managed food production, the beginnings of semipermanent and permanent settlements, and the rapid intensification of trade, both local and long distance. For the first time, it now became possible for individuals and communities to accumulate and store wealth on a large scale. The results were far reaching. Communities became more stable, and human societies more complex. Specialization developed, along with distinctions of status and rank. The revolution brought about by the innovations of the Neolithic Era was a necessary step before cities in the truest sense could appear toward the end of the fourth millennium B.C.E.

THE ORIGINS OF FOOD PRODUCTION IN THE ANCIENT NEAR EAST

 During the Upper Paleolithic Ice Age (c. 40,000–11,000 B.C.E.), daytime temperatures in Mediterranean Europe and Asia averaged about 60°F (16°C) in the summer and about 30°F (–1°C) in the winter. Cold-loving game species such as reindeer, elk, wild boar, bison, and mountain goats roamed the hills and valleys. But as the glaciers receded northward such species retreated with them. Some humans moved north with the game, but others stayed behind to confront and create an extremely different sort of world.

Specifically, within about 3,000 to 4,000 years after the end of the Ice Age, the peoples living at the eastern end of the Mediterranean Sea accomplished one of the most momentous transformations in human history: a switch from food gathering for subsistence to producing food for themselves. Substantial numbers of humans began to domesticate animals and raise crops, thereby making possible greater permanence and stability in their settlement patterns. Stable settlements in turn paved the way for further developments we associate specifically with civilization: the emergence of cities, the invention of writing, and the evolution of specialized social roles. A process that takes several thousand years may not seem "revolutionary" to our current sensibilities, but in fact it was. In a relatively short time, people living in a small area of southwestern Asia fundamentally altered patterns of existence that were millions of years old.

The story of this momentous transformation is roughly as follows. By around 11,000 B.C.E. most of the larger game herds had left the ancient Near East. Yet people living in the territories that today comprise Turkey, Syria, Israel, and western Iran were prospering because the warmer, wetter climate created an ideal environment for wild grains to flourish. Throughout this region (known as the Fertile Crescent because of its abundant natural food supply and high agricultural productivity), humans now enjoyed plant resources plentiful enough to sustain seasonal, and sometimes even permanent, settlements. This fact made the shift to a sedentary existence possible.

The emergence of semipermanent and permanent settlements, made possible by a larger and more dependable food supply, had profound effects on human life. Most important was a rapid increase in human numbers, resulting from the fact that women in these sedentary communities bore more children than did

WHAT CHANGES ALLOWED THE TRANSITION FROM HUNTER-GATHERER TO SEDENTARY SOCIETIES?

THE NEOLITHIC REVOLUTION   11

women who lived in hunter-gatherer groups. But this shift to sedentary, grain-dependent communities also entailed risks. The frequency of infectious diseases increased, and people's diets could become overly dependent on carbohydrates, resulting in earlier ages at death than were typical of hunter-gatherer bands. But fertility increases seem to have outweighed these limiting factors, and by about 8000 B.C.E. there is clear evidence that the human population was beginning to exceed the wild food supply. To support their growing numbers, humans had to take steps to increase the food-growing capacity of the land through deliberately managed agriculture.

But the systematic and managed production of plant food required a crucial intermediary step: storage. Even when plentiful, grain is not available for harvesting during the winter. For a grain-dependent community to live permanently at a single site, residents had first to devise ways of preserving and storing grain between harvests. By around 9500 B.C.E., however, the peoples living along the eastern coast of the Mediterranean had learned how to preserve their grain in storage pits. No longer were they forced to move away from their settled communities during periods of the year when no grain was ready to be harvested.

Storage developed as a way to guarantee food supplies in times of natural shortage. But it also allowed Neolithic peoples to store seed they could use to produce even more grain the following year. The importance of this latter discovery cannot be overstated. Once humans began deliberately to sow seed, they could plant crops in a more concentrated fashion, thus producing the higher yields needed to support a higher population. They could also compensate to some extent for disasters (such as flooding or fire) that might inhibit the natural reseeding of the wild grain fields. Even more important, however, intensified seeding and storage provided humans with the stable and predictable surpluses they needed to support domestic animals, which they could now afford to feed year-round.

The earliest archaeological evidence for fully sedentary agriculture comes from several areas in the Fertile Crescent between roughly 8500 and 7000 B.C.E. By 6000 B.C.E., much of the Near East had adopted agriculture as its primary mode of survival, supplemented by the domestication of livestock, now including cattle and pigs as well as sheep and goats. Animal protein was, of course, an ancient feature of human diet. But domestication brought a host of additional benefits, not only guaranteeing a more reliable supply of meat, milk, leather, wool, bone, and horn but also providing animal power to pull carts and plows and to grind grain into flour.

Exactly how the shift to agriculture and domesticated animals became so widespread so quickly is a matter of debate. Similar demographic and environmental conditions around the region may have created a spontaneous shift to agriculture in several places at once. Alternatively, large-scale migrations of populations with knowledge of agricultural methods might have spread the new technology. Some scholars emphasize the role of trade networks in diffusing agricultural knowledge across the region. Others believe that the growth of new agriculturally based communities was the result of deliberate colonization from "mother" settlements, when the higher carrying capacity of the land, improved through agricultural technologies, still proved inadequate to growing populations. As is often the case when dealing with such profound and fundamental change in human history, no single explanation suffices. All these factors must have played some role in the spread of agriculture across the Fertile Crescent to Egypt and even the Balkans by 5000 B.C.E. What remains uncertain is the balance between them.

> Once humans began deliberately to sow seed, they could plant crops in a more concentrated fashion, thus producing the higher yields needed to support a higher population.

THE EMERGENCE OF TOWNS AND VILLAGES

The next step in the Near East's accelerating social evolution was the emergence of towns and villages like Çatalhöyük and the concurrent rise of handicrafts, trade, and warfare—all signs of increasing economic specialization. Hundreds, and probably thousands, of towns and villages grew up in the Near East between 7500 and 3500/3000 B.C.E., when some towns began to evolve into cities. Most settlements were small—a typical village had around 1,000 inhabitants—but populations could vary greatly, and there was not a steady evolution from smaller to larger settlements. At first almost all able-bodied men and women probably engaged in field work, with women taking a leading role in cloth production and child rearing also. But gradually there came to be full-time specialists in handicrafts as well as a few full-time traders.

Among the earliest of these Neolithic villages was Jericho, in the disputed territories that lie between modern Israel and Jordan. Jericho emerged as a seasonal, grain-producing settlement around 9000 B.C.E., probably due to its abundant freshwater springs. Around 8000 B.C.E., however, the inhabitants of Jericho undertook a spectacular building program. Many new dwellings were built on stone foundations, and a massive, skillfully dressed stone wall was constructed around the western edge of the settlement. Built into this perimeter wall was a circular tower whose excavated remains still reach to a height of thirty feet.

We do not know why this wall was built; nor do we know the purpose of the tower. The wall may have guarded the village against flash floods and/or against human marauders. The tower might have been a lookout post, or its ambitious height could have extended toward the heavens for some religious purpose. But whatever

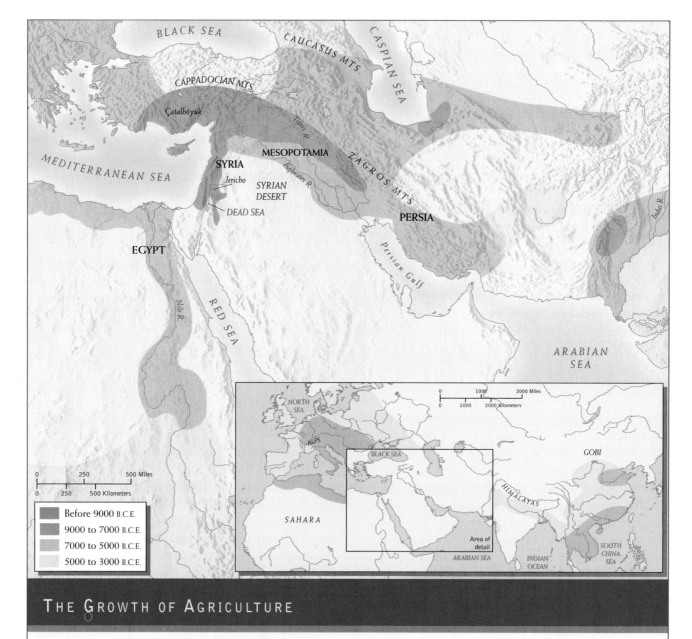

THE GROWTH OF AGRICULTURE

Examine the chronological progression of regions engaging in agriculture. What areas began practicing agriculture first? Consider why agriculture in the Asian Near East did not begin along river valleys but spread there later. Notice the relationship of major rivers to the advance of agriculture. How might rivers have played a crucial role in the spread of farming technologies?

WHAT CHANGES ALLOWED THE TRANSITION FROM HUNTER-GATHERER TO SEDENTARY SOCIETIES?

THE NEOLITHIC REVOLUTION   13

The Jericho Tower. The remains of a stone tower built into the walls of Jericho c. 8500 B.C.E. Even in its present, ruined state, the tower stands thirty feet tall.

their intended functions, the wall and its tower served an impressive population: the early site of Jericho covered at least eight acres and supported a population of 3,000 people. This population was sustained by the intensive cultivation of recently domesticated strains of wheat and barley, irrigated with water from the nearby springs.

Starting in the eighth millenium B.C.E. (8000–7000 B.C.E.), Jericho's inhabitants also produced some of the earliest known pottery. Pottery allowed them to store grain, wine, and oils more effectively than ever before. Its most important benefits, however, were in cooking. For the first time, it now became possible to produce nourishing stews, porridges, and ales. Pottery production quickly became an important industry throughout the Near East, marked by rapidly changing and easily identifiable regional styles. From 6500 B.C.E., pottery fragments (known as shards) are the most common archaeological artifacts we find at human settlement sites. By studying the changing styles of such pottery, archaeologists have been able to construct a reasonably accurate (but still relative and rough) chronology for the period before recorded history.

Jericho and Çatalhöyük also illustrate the impact storable agricultural surpluses were beginning to have

on human social relations. For the first time, significant differences began to arise in the amount of wealth individuals could acquire and stockpile for themselves and their heirs. Dependence on agriculture also made it more difficult for individuals to split off from the community when the consequences of social and economic differentiation became oppresive. The result was the emergence of a much more stratified human society, with more specialization of social roles than ever before.

At both Jericho and Çatalhöyük villagers speculated on the supernatural powers they believed ruled their world and how they might relate to those powers. This too was an immensely important step in the evolution of human culture. Further, the fact that humans believed these forces required special services and gifts in the form of ritual and sacrifice allowed for the emergence over time of a priestly class, individuals uniquely qualified to commune with the supernatural forces that governed the life of the community. Such religious leadership was a natural bridge to more obviously political forms of authority: leading war bands, constructing defenses, and extracting resources from those subject to authority. Through their command of the community's religious, military, and economic resources, village elites were beginning to establish themselves as a self-justifying ruling class.

Trade was another important development in these early Neolithic villages. By 5000 B.C.E. long-distance trade networks were operating across the Near East. Local trade routes were undoubtedly even older but

Early Village Pottery. A shallow bowl from a western Asian village site dating from about 5000 B.C.E.

rarely left any archaeological record by which we can trace them. Exotic goods were frequent objects of long-distance exchange: obsidian was an important commodity at Çatalhöyük, as were marine shells and semiprecious stones such as turquoise, lapis lazuli, and jadeite.

Long-distance trade accelerated the exchange of commodities and ideas throughout the Fertile Crescent. But it also contributed to the increasing social stratification evident within these village communities. Because elite social status was enhanced by special access to high-prestige luxury goods, local elites often sought to monopolize long-distance trade by organizing and controlling the production of marketable goods within their own communities. Control over specialist artisans thus emerged as an important feature of elite social status in these Neolithic village communities.

What underlay all these social and economic changes was the increasing degree of specialization that agricultural surpluses made possible. In hunter-gatherer societies, every member of the community participated in the basic business of food acquisition. In a well-organized agricultural community, however, certain people could devote at least a portion of their labor to pursuits other than agriculture: making pottery or cloth, manufacturing weapons or tools, building houses and fortifications, or facilitating trade. Surpluses and specialization also led to the emergence of social elites who, by organizing and exploiting the labor and production of others, were able to turn ruling itself into another specialist occupation. As villages grew larger and more sophisticated, the amount of specialization increased, until a significant fraction of the population could become full-time nonagriculturalists. This was an essential step in the development of true urban-based civilizations.

CHRONOLOGY

FROM PREHISTORY TO HISTORY

Appearance of figurative artwork	40,000 B.C.E.
End of the Ice Age	11,000 B.C.E.
Beginnings of sedentary agricultural societies	9000 B.C.E.
Emergence of villages	6500–3000 B.C.E.
Development of writing	3300–2500 B.C.E.
Emergence of cities	3100 B.C.E.

THE DEVELOPMENT OF URBAN CIVILIZATION IN MESOPOTAMIA

What were the principal influences behind the early emergence of urban life in Mesopotamia?

It is surprising that the initial shift from village to city and from prehistory to history took place in one of the most inhospitable environments imaginable—the southern desert of Mesopotamia, known to the Greeks as the "Land between the Rivers" but to modern historians as Sumer. Now part of Iraq, Sumer gets only about eight inches (20 cm) of rainfall per year, and summer temperatures there routinely exceed 110°F (44°C). The soils of the region are sandy and infertile unless irrigated. And the two rivers that supply this flat and largely featureless plain with water—the Tigris and Euphrates—are famous for their violence and unpredictability. Both are prone to flooding, and the Tigris in particular was notorious in ancient times for jumping its banks and changing its course from one year to the next. Nevertheless, it was in this uninviting environment that the first true cities emerged.

UBAID CULTURE

The founders of Ubaid culture (so called from its best-known site at al-Ubaid in modern Iraq) appear to have moved into the Sumerian desert around 5900 B.C.E. What attracted them to the unfriendly confines of the Tigris and Euphrates is unclear. In the sixth millenium B.C.E., the headwaters of the Persian Gulf extended at least 100 miles further inland than they do today. As a result, some Ubaid settlements bordered on fertile marshlands as well as arid desert. But whatever it was that induced the Ubaid peoples to move into Sumer, it appears they brought their village culture with them. They were not hunter-gatherers who unluckily stumbled into difficult circumstances.

Almost as soon as we find farming settlements in Sumer, we also find evidence for irrigation systems. Although these began as relatively simple channels and collection pools, Ubaid farmers quickly built more sophisticated canals and pools lined with stone so that they would last from one season to the next. They also constructed dikes and levees to control the seasonal

WHAT WERE THE PRINCIPAL INFLUENCES BEHIND THE EARLY EMERGENCE OF URBAN LIFE IN MESOPOTAMIA?

THE DEVELOPMENT OF URBAN CIVILIZATION IN MESOPOTAMIA   15

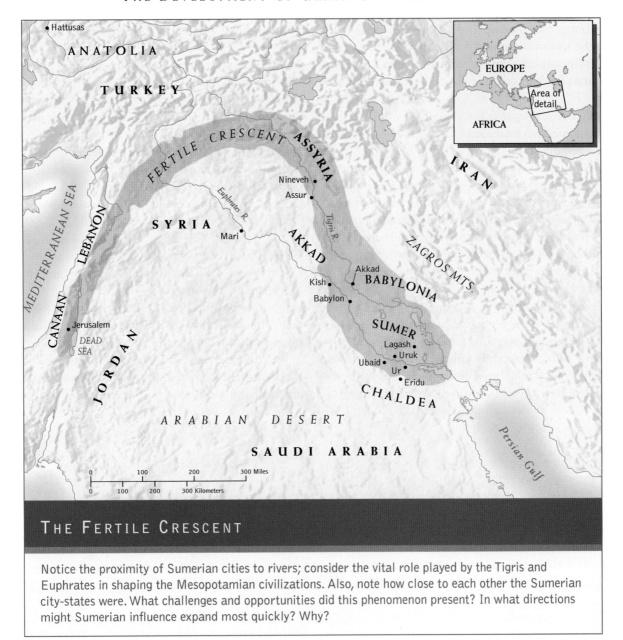

THE FERTILE CRESCENT

Notice the proximity of Sumerian cities to rivers; consider the vital role played by the Tigris and Euphrates in shaping the Mesopotamian civilizations. Also, note how close to each other the Sumerian city-states were. What challenges and opportunities did this phenomenon present? In what directions might Sumerian influence expand most quickly? Why?

flooding of the rivers and to direct the excess water into irrigation canals. Despite the hostility of the environment, Ubaid agricultural communities were soon producing surpluses sufficient to support specialists in weaving, pottery making, metalwork, trade, and construction—the typical attributes of Neolithic village life.

There is also early evidence of central structures that served religious functions. Starting out as simple and fairly humble shrines, these buildings soon evolved into impressive temples built of dried mud brick (the scarcity of stone in the region compelled Ubaid builders to reserve that material for tools). Each larger settlement had such a building, which became progressively larger with successive rebuildings. From these temples, a priestly class acted as both the officiants of religious life and managers of the economic resources of the community, organizing the construction of ever-larger temples and maintaining the complex irrigation systems that made village life possible in the Mesopotamian desert.

URBANISM IN THE URUK PERIOD (4300–2900 B.C.E.)

From about 4300 B.C.E. on, Ubaid settlements began to develop into larger, more prosperous and more highly organized communities. This new period, named after its most impressive site at Uruk (modern Warka), witnessed the transition from the Neolithic Ubaid village to the Sumerian city-state. It marks therefore the true beginning of urban civilization in the Mediterranean world.

Among the principal developments of the Uruk period was a massive increase in the sophistication and scale of temple architecture. The White Temple at Uruk provides a stunning example of this general trend. Sometime between 3500 and 3300 B.C.E., builders constructed a massive sloping platform that towered nearly forty feet above the surrounding flatlands. The platform, oriented with its four corners toward the cardinal points of the compass, was dressed in brick. Atop the platform stood another structure, the shrine or temple proper, also dressed in brick but painted a brilliant white.

Such temples grew up across Sumer, reflecting the central role religion played in civic life. Uruk in particular seems to have owed its rapid urban growth to its importance as a religious center. By 3100 B.C.E., it sprawled across several hundred acres, enclosing a

population of 40,000 people within its massive mud brick walls. But the larger villages of Sumer were also growing rapidly, their teeming economic activity attracting immigrants just as the great cities were doing. To feed this rapidly growing population, grain and cloth production in Sumer increased tenfold during the Uruk Period. Trade routes also expanded dramatically. To manage this increasingly sophisticated and centrally directed economy, the Sumerians also began to develop a new communications technology that moved them fully into the light of history: writing.

THE DEVELOPMENT OF WRITING

Like many of the breakthroughs we have considered in this chapter, the invention of writing did not occur overnight. By 4000 B.C.E., villagers in the Near East were already using clay tokens to keep track of inventories and to facilitate the burgeoning trade of the region. Ultimately, the practice developed of placing all the tokens from a single transaction inside a hollow clay ball and inscribing, on the outside of the ball, the

The White Temple at Uruk, c. 3400 B.C.E. Perhaps dedicated to the sky god, An, the temple may have been designed to provide the gods with a mountaintop home in a part of the world conspicuous in its absence of mountains.

WHAT WERE THE PRINCIPAL INFLUENCES BEHIND THE EARLY EMERGENCE OF URBAN LIFE IN MESOPOTAMIA?

THE DEVELOPMENT OF URBAN CIVILIZATION IN MESOPOTAMIA 17

Cuneiform Writing. Above, a Sumerian clay tablet from about 3000 B.C.E. Here standardized pictures are beginning to represent abstractions. On the right, carvings on limestone from about 2600 B.C.E. The evolution of standardized cuneiform writing is now complete: the inscription proclaims that a king of Ur has built a temple.

shapes of all the tokens it contained. By 3300 B.C.E., the priestly class (or those working for them) realized that they could dispense with the clumsy token-and-ball system altogether and replace it with flat clay tablets on which they could note the desired information by inscribing the appropriate symbols.

In its earliest phases, writing thus evolved as a means of record keeping in connection with economic pursuits. For some time, therefore, writing remained purely pictographic: each symbol marked into the clay resembled the physical object it represented. Over the course of time, however, as the uses of writing evolved, a symbol might come to be used not only to evoke the physical object it represented but also an idea associated with that object. The symbol for a bowl of food, *ninda* (a noun), might thus be used to express a more abstract notion such as bread or sustenance—an idea not otherwise easily represented by a quick sketch into soft clay. In time, such symbols might also come to be associated with a particular phonetic sound. Thus when a Sumerian scribe needed to employ the sound *ninda*, even as part of another word or name, he would use the symbol for a bowl of food. Later, special marks were added to the script so that the reader could discern whether the writer intended the symbol to represent the object itself or the *phonogram* (the sound represented by the symbol).

By 3100 B.C.E. Sumerian scribes had largely abandoned writing with pointed sticks in favor of a more durable reed stylus. Because this stylus left an impression shaped like a wedge (the Latin word for which is *cuneus*),

we refer to this script as *cuneiform* (*kyoo-NEH-form*). Cuneiform symbols could be impressed more quickly into the soft clay and the reeds themselves were less likely to break than were sticks. The clay tablets would then be baked, creating a permanent record. Tens of thousands of these clay tablets still survive. The new stylus did make it more difficult, however, to draw pictograms that accurately reflected the original shape (such as a bowl of food) of the object they were meant to represent. As a result, cuneiform symbols rapidly became more and more abstract, until they barely resembled the original pictograms at all.

Symbols ultimately were invented for every possible vowel–consonant combination in the Sumerian language, reducing the number of symbols necessary to write Sumerian from 1,200 to 600. Nevertheless, it remained very difficult to learn to read and write cuneiform, and only a small minority of the population ever did so. Those who did, however, became important and influential people in Sumerian society. For the entirety of the third millennium, it was largely the sons of the elite who attended the Houses of the Tablet, as the scribal schools were called. But despite the wide variety of symbols and the complicated nature of the script, cuneiform proved remarkably durable. For over 2,000 years it remained the principal writing system of the ancient Near East, even for societies that no longer spoke the Sumerian language. All the masterpieces of ancient Near Eastern literature were written and preserved in cuneiform; examples of the script were still being produced as late as the first century C.E. (Common Era).

THE SUMERIANS ENTER HISTORY

Why did a common religion not create peace among the Sumerians?

After about 2500 B.C.E., the Sumerians used writing for a wide variety of economic, political, literary, and religious purposes. This makes it possible for us to know a great deal more about the Sumerians than we do about any other human society of the time. We can begin to understand their political relationships, their feelings about their gods, and the social and economic structure of their society. The Sumerians are, in this sense, the first historical—as opposed to prehistorical—society.

The great centers of Sumerian culture—such as Uruk, Ur, Lagash, Eridu, and Kish—shared a common culture and a common language. The Sumerian language, however, appears not to be related to any other known language in the world. This has led to bitter scholarly arguments over whether the Sumerians—a label applied to them by their neighbors—moved into southern Mesopotamia from elsewhere or whether their unique culture (language included) developed out of Ubaid culture. The continuity of cult activity supports the latter view, as does the lack of any significant evidence for invasion; but at present, the question cannot be answered with certainty.

Like language, religion was another shared element of Sumerian culture. This common religion did not produce peace among the Sumerian cities, however. Although each Sumerian community recognized all the gods of the Sumerian pantheon (some 1,500 gods), the residents of each individual city-state viewed their city as the property of one particular god, whom they sought to glorify by exalting their own (and the god's)

CHRONOLOGY

ORIGINS OF MESOPOTAMIAN SOCIETY

Ubaid Period	5900–4300 B.C.E.
Uruk Period	4300–2900 B.C.E.
Early Dynastic Period	2900–2500 B.C.E.
Akkadian Period	2350–2160 B.C.E.
Ur Dynasty	2100–2000 B.C.E.

city. The result was intense competition between cities, which frequently escalated into open warfare. Of course there also was an economic dimension to the tension among the Sumerian city-states; water rights as well as access to arable land and to trade routes were often at stake in these conflicts. But the centrality of temple shrines to Sumerian society meant that conflicts over economic resources inevitably also involved a religious dimension. For any city-state to surrender its independence to another city would have been an intolerable offense against the conquered city's god. The Sumerians shared a common culture and a common pantheon; but common government was impossible.

A significant proportion of the cultivable land of each city belonged outright to the temple of the patron god. Much of the economic production of the city therefore passed through the great temple warehouse complexes, where the priests and their officials would redistribute the city's produce to its residents. During the third millennium, these great temples also began to control the production of textiles, creating protofactories that employed thousands of servile women and children. Predictably, temples also played a key role in long-distance trade, both as buyers and sellers of goods.

Each Sumerian city had a ruling aristocracy, from which the priests and important officials of the temples no doubt came; but it was the priests who stood at the top of these highly theocratic societies. In this early period of Sumerian civilization perhaps as much as half the population consisted of commoners, free persons who held a small parcel of land sufficient to sustain themselves and make required payments to the temple complex. The temples also had large numbers of legally free dependents who worked as artisans or as agricultural laborers on temple lands but who owned no land themselves.

There were also many slaves in Sumerian society. In Sumer, as elsewhere in the ancient world, slaves were often prisoners of war. If the slave came originally from another Sumerian city, the master's power over him or her was strictly limited, and he (or she—many slaves were women) had to be released after three years. Non-Sumerians could be held indefinitely, although slaves could sometimes buy their freedom. Despite these safeguards, slaves in Sumer were still the property of their owners. They could be beaten, punished, branded like animals, and bought and sold on their owner's whim. Ancient slavery may not have been quite so horrible as more modern examples (such as that practiced in the New World), but it was still a highly undesirable thing to be a slave.

Why did a common religion not create peace among the Sumerians?

The Sumerians Enter History   19

THE EARLY DYNASTIC PERIOD BEGINS (2900–2500 B.C.E.)

Around 2900 B.C.E. conflicts among the Sumerian city-states became more acute. As the city-states grew larger, competition for scarce resources intensified. Warfare became more frequent and more destructive, leading to the abandonment or destruction of a number of urban centers. During this period of conflict a new type of war leadership began to emerge, which eventually evolved into a much more powerful form of kingship than the Sumerian city-states had known during the Uruk Period. Historians refer to this new phase of Sumerian civilization as the Early Dynastic Period.

As warfare became a regular feature of Sumerian life, successful war leaders began to acquire greater prestige and power, adopting a new title, *lugal* (literally, "big man") to describe their new authority. Unlike the kings of the Uruk Period, Early Dynastic lugals did not conceive of themselves as the humble servants of the city's god or gods. Instead, they saw themselves as the god's representative on earth, whose job it was to lead the god's armies into battle and to exploit the city's wealth for the common glory of the god and the lugal. These developments gave them a new, and sometimes frightening, degree of authority within the city-state.

The most striking indication of the impression this new office made on Sumerian society is the *Epic of Gilgamesh*, the first great literary work in world history, which recounts the legendary exploits of a historical king of Uruk named Gilgamesh. The epic enjoyed tremendous popularity and staying power throughout the Near East, being translated and copied for well over 2,000 years after the original Sumerian version was composed. Scholars have reconstructed a significant proportion of the tale from the various fragments—some lengthy, some meager—discovered over the course of the last century. Although the composite nature of the epic as it exists today means that we may not have a version of the Gilgamesh story exactly like that read in ancient Sumer, most experts agree that the epic as we know it largely reflects Sumerian society and culture during the first half of the third millennium B.C.E.

As he appears in the epic, Gilgamesh was a powerful lugal who had won his reputation through military conquest and general heroism, particularly against nonurbanized barbarians. Through the fame and prestige he acquired, he became so powerful that he could ignore the behavioral constraints that bound the lesser men of his day. We hear at the start of the epic how the people complained about their king, even though they still revered him: he kept their sons away at war for too long; he showed no respect for the nobles, carousing with their wives and daughters as he pleased; he disappointed them by his sacrilegious conduct. His people prayed to the gods for relief, and ultimately the gods fashioned a wild man named Enkidu to challenge Gilgamesh.

The confrontation between Gilgamesh and Enkidu is rich with historically useful information. Gilgamesh is a creature of the city; his challenger was of the wilderness, barely more than a beast himself, until he

A Sumerian Banquet. This fine inlay, made of shell and lapis lazuli, shows animals and foodstuffs (lower two levels) being carried to a banquet (top level), perhaps held to celebrate the military victory illustrated on the opposite side.

THE FLOOD: TWO ACCOUNTS

The Epic of Gilgamesh *preserves a traditional account of a destructive flood sent by the gods to punish humanity. This story probably dates from the first half of the third millennium* B.C.E., *making it at least 1,500 years older than the similar account in the Hebrew Bible. The striking similarities between these two accounts is evidence of the strong cultural influence exerted by older Near Eastern civilizations on the early Hebrews.*

THE EPIC OF GILGAMESH

Utnapishtim spoke to Gilgamesh, saying: "I will reveal to you, Gilgamesh . . . a secret of the gods. . . . The hearts of the Great Gods moved them to inflict the Flood. Their Father Anu uttered the oath (of secrecy). . . . [But the god] Ea . . . repeated their talk [to me, saying]: 'O man of Shuruppak, son of Ubartutu: Tear down the house and build a boat! . . . Spurn possessions and keep alive living beings! Make all living beings go up into the boat. The boat which you are to build, its dimensions must measure equal to each other: its length must correspond to its width. Roof it over like the Apsu.' I understood and spoke to my lord, Ea: 'My lord, thus is the command which you have uttered. I will heed and will do it.' . . . On the fifth day I laid out her exterior. It was a field in area, its walls were each 10 times 12 cubits in height. . . . I provided it with six decks, thus dividing it into seven (levels). . . . Whatever I had I loaded on it. . . . All the living beings that I had I loaded on it. I had all my kith and kin go up into the boat, all the beasts and animals of the field and the draftsmen I had go up.

I watched the appearance of the weather—the weather was frightful to behold! I went into the boat and sealed the entry. . . . All day long the South Wind blew . . . , submerging the mountain in water, overwhelming the people like an attack. . . . Six days and seven nights came the wind and flood, the storm flattening the land. When the seventh day arrived . . .

[t]he sea calmed, fell still, the whirlwind and flood stopped up. . . . When a seventh day arrived, I sent forth a dove and released it. The dove went off, but came back to me; no perch was visible so it circled back to me. I sent forth a swallow and released it. The swallow went off, but came back to me; no perch was visible so it circled back to me. I sent forth a raven and released it. The raven went off, and saw the waters slither back. It eats, it scratches, it bobs, but does not cirlce back to me. Then I sent out everything in all directions and sacrificed (a sheep). I offered incense in front of the mountain-ziggurat. . . .

The gods smelled the savor . . . and collected like flies over a sacrifice. . . . Just then Enlil arrived. He saw the boat and became furious. . . . 'Where did a living being escape? No man was to survive the annihilation!' Ea spoke to Valiant Enlil, saying . . . How, how could you bring about a Flood without consideration? Charge the violation to the violator, charge the offense to the offender, but be compassionate lest (mankind) be cut off, be patient lest they be killed.' Enlil went up inside the boat and, grasping my hand, made me go up. He had my wife go up and kneel by my side. He touched our forehead and, standing between us, he blessed us. . . ."

Maureen Gallery Kovacs, trans., *The Epic of Gilgamesh*, "Tablet XI" (Stanford, Calif., 1985, 1989), pp. 97–103.

BOOK OF GENESIS

The Lord saw that the wickedness of humankind was great in the earth and . . . said "I will blot out from the earth the human beings I have created . . . for I am sorry I have made them." But Noah found favor in the sight of the Lord. . . . God saw that the earth was corrupt and . . . said to Noah, "I have determined to make an end to all flesh. . . . Make yourself an ark of cypress wood; make rooms in the ark, and cover it inside and out with pitch. . . . Make a roof for the ark, and put the door of the ark in its side. . . . For my part I am going to bring a flood on the earth, to destroy from under heaven all flesh. . . . But I will establish a covenant with you; and you shall come into the ark, you, your sons, your wife, and your sons' wives with you. And of every living thing you shall bring two of every kind into the ark, to keep them alive with you. . . . Also take with you every kind of food that is eaten." . . . All the fountains of the great deep burst forth, and the windows of the heavens were opened. . . . The waters gradually receded from the earth. . . . At the end of forty days, Noah opened a window of the ark . . . and sent out the raven, and it went to and fro until the waters were dried up from the earth. Then he sent out the dove from him, to see if the waters had subsided from the face of the ground, but the dove found no place to set its foot,

and it returned. . . . He waited another seven days, and again sent out the dove [which] came back to him . . . and there in its beak was a freshly plucked olive leaf; so Noah knew the waters had subsided from the earth. Then he . . . sent out the dove, and it did not return to him anymore. . . . Noah built an altar to the Lord . . . and offered burnt offerings. And when the Lord smelled the pleasing odor, the Lord said in his heart, "I will never again curse the ground because of humankind . . . nor will I ever again destroy every living creature as I have done.". . . God blessed Noah and his sons.

Genesis 6:5–9:1, *The New Oxford Annotated Bible* (Oxford, 1994).

QUESTIONS FOR ANALYSIS

1. What is the significance of the *Epic of Gilgamesh*? Why was it written? What function did the *Epic of Gilgamesh* serve in ancient Mesopotamia?
2. How did the geography and climate of Mesopotamia influence this epic and Mesopotamians' attitudes toward the gods, kingship, civilization, and the afterlife?
3. How does the account of Noah in the Book of Genesis differ from that of Utnapishtim in the *Epic of Gilgamesh*? Compare both human and divine characters.

was civilized by way of a sexual tryst with a temple prostitute—an urban, specialist profession, to say the least. After his contact with her, Enkidu was unable to return to the simple life, and the animals of the wilderness no longer spoke to him; in Sumerian terms, his urbanization had literally made a man out of him.

This episode reflects the dichotomy the Sumerians perceived between city and wilderness, between what was civilized and what was not. We recognize in Enkidu the hunter-gatherer who was doubtless far more intimate with nature than were the Sumerians after centuries of civic life; but such naturalness was not a quality the Sumerians admired. The epic does not intend to evoke sympathy for Enkidu's loss of innocence. Instead, it is that loss that allows him to fulfill his destiny—to become human so he can first fight and then befriend the king of Uruk. Such disdain on the part of the urbanized and civilized toward those who were uncivilized (and therefore barbarians) is voiced in almost every ancient civilization. Even Aristotle's famous dictum that "man is a political animal" means,

in essence, that humans are creatures who must live in cities; otherwise, they cannot be fully human.

The episode following the friendship forged between Gilgamesh and Enkidu illustrates the hostility and fear Sumerians felt toward the wilderness. The two men set off into the forest to do battle with a terrifying nature demigod named Humbaba, who nearly bests the heroes. In the end, however, they prevail, another triumph of civilized humanity over a natural world that would destroy humanity and its creations if it gained the upper hand.

SUMERIAN RELIGION

In the Uruk Period, the Sumerians identified their gods very closely with the hostile and capricious forces of the natural world in which they lived. By the middle of the Early Dynastic Period, however, the Sumerians had come to see their gods in more and more human terms, as beings who met in councils to deliberate their actions and whose concern for justice made it impossible for them to act with arbitrary cruelty toward their human servants. Like the increasingly powerful lugals who now ruled the Sumerian city-states, the Sumerians' gods desired to live in the finest palaces and temples, to wear the costliest clothing and jewels, and to consume the tastiest foods. Human beings existed to provide such a life for them. This was, indeed, why the gods had created human beings in the first place; for if humanity ever ceased to serve the gods, the gods themselves would starve. There was thus a reciprocal relationship between humanity and divinity. The gods depended on their human servants to honor and sustain them; and in return, the gods were prepared to listen to the petitions of their servants, even when the decrees of the gods initially went against them. The destiny of every human being lay in the hands of the gods, and it was for this reason that the Sumerians tried so hard to determine the future through divination and astrology. But like all rulers, the gods were changeable. A person who could learn his or her fate through divination or the stars might be able to change it through prayer and faithful service to the gods.

> The gods depended on their human servants to honor and sustain them; and in return, the gods were prepared to listen to the petitions of their servants.

Kings bore special responsibilities toward the gods, and as the Early Dynastic Period progressed, the closeness of this relationship was more and more emphasized. Kings ruled by divine sanction and were thus increasingly set apart from all other mortals, including even priests. But like every human being, kings were obliged to serve and honor the gods through offerings, sacrifices, festivals, and massive building projects; and their obligations were greater, just as their power was greater, than that of any other mortal. Kings who neglected these obligations, or who exalted their own power at the expense of the gods, were likely to bring disaster down on themselves and their people. And not even kings could evade death, when the human body returned to clay, and the ghost of the departed individual crossed a man-eating river into the underworld, a gloomy place of silence and blackness from which none ever returned.

Even Gilgamesh, the legendary king of Uruk, could not escape the fate the gods had decreed for all mortals. When his friend Enkidu was killed by the goddess Inanna, whom they had mocked, Gilgamesh's horror at Enkidu's death propelled him on a quest for immortality. His search finally brought him to a deep pool, at the bottom of which grew a plant of eternal life. But when Gilgamesh swam down to retrieve the plant, it was stolen from him as he surfaced by a serpent, who then disappeared into the pool with the plant in his jaws. In the end, the great king of Uruk was left to ponder the futility of all human endeavor. Reflecting on the impermanence of his deeds and even of Uruk's mighty walls, Gilgamesh asked, "Why do I bother working for nothing? Who even notices what I do?"

SCIENCE, TECHNOLOGY, AND TRADE

Sumerian pessimism was deeply rooted, but it was not paralyzing. Their complex relationship with the gods and their adversarial relationship with their environment instead inculcated in the Sumerians a high degree of self-reliance and ingenuity. These qualities helped make them the most technologically inventive people of the ancient world.

The Sumerians became first-rate metallurgists despite the fact that their land had no natural mineral resources. By 6000 B.C.E., a number of cultures throughout the Near East and Europe had learned how to produce copper weapons and tools. Mesopotamia itself had no copper; but by the Uruk Period (4300–2900 B.C.E.), trade routes were bringing raw copper into Sumer, where the Sumerians processed it into weapons and tools. Shortly before 3000 B.C.E., perhaps starting in eastern Anatolia, people discovered that copper could be alloyed with ar-

Sumerian Praying Figures. These statues dating from about 2700 B.C.E. show Sumerians praying to the gods.

WHY DID A COMMON RELIGION NOT CREATE PEACE AMONG THE SUMERIANS?

THE SUMERIANS ENTER HISTORY   23

Sumerian War Chariots. The earliest known representation of the wheel, dating from about 2600 B.C.E., shows how wheels were carpentered together from slabs of wood. (For a later Mesopotamian wheel with spokes, see the illustration on p. 53.)

millennium later, when they learned the technique (probably) from Mesopotamia. In the Western Hemisphere, wheeled transport was unknown (except for Inka children's toys) until the sixteenth century C.E. The Sumerians did not invent the wheel; they probably acquired it from nomadic peoples living on the steppes of southern Russia. But by adapting it to so many different uses, they vastly increased its technological possibilities.

The Sumerians also pioneered the study of mathematics. Their mathematical interests may have been encouraged by the nature of Sumerian agriculture: to construct their elaborate systems of irrigation canals, dikes, and reservoirs, they had to develop sophisticated measuring and surveying techniques as well as the art of map making. Agricultural concerns probably

senic (or later, tin) to produce bronze. Bronze is almost as malleable as copper, but pours more easily into molds and, when cooled, maintains its rigidity and shape better than copper. Because the Sumerians and neighboring cultures engaged in such widespread use of bronze, we refer to a Bronze Age beginning around 3000 B.C.E.

Alongside writing, the invention of the wheel stands at the top of any list of fundamental advances in human technology. The Sumerians were using potter's wheels by the middle of the fourth millennium B.C.E., allowing them to produce high-quality clay vessels in greater quantity than ever before. By around 3200 B.C.E., the Sumerians were also using two-wheeled chariots and four-wheeled carts drawn by donkeys (horses were unknown in western Asia until they were introduced by eastern invaders sometime between 2000 and 1700 B.C.E.). Wheeled chariots were used mainly in warfare; illustrations from about 2600 B.C.E. depict them trampling the enemy. Wheeled carts were an even more important advance, however, because they dramatically increased the productivity of the Sumerian workforce.

The use of the wheel in pottery making may have suggested its application for transport, but such a connection is far from inevitable. The Egyptians were using the potter's wheel by at least 2700 B.C.E., but they did not use the wheel for transport until a

A Sumerian Plow with a Seed Drill. Such plows were developed during the third millennium B.C.E. and were still being used in the seventh century B.C.E., when this black stone tablet was engraved.

also lay behind the lunar calendar they invented, which consisted of twelve months, six lasting 30 days, and six lasting 29 days. Since this produced a year of only 354 days, the Sumerians eventually discovered that they had to add a month to their calendars every few years to predict the recurrence of the seasons with sufficient accuracy. But the Sumerian practice of dividing time into multiples of sixty has lasted to the present day, not only in our notions of the 30-day month (which corresponds approximately with the phases of the moon) but also in our division of the hour into sixty minutes and the minute into sixty seconds. Mathematics also contributed to Sumerian architecture, allowing the Sumerians to build domes and arches thousands of years before the Romans would adopt and spread these architectural forms throughout the Mediterranean world.

The Sumerians' ability to engage in these activities depended on the acquisition of raw materials through trade, for their homeland was almost completely devoid of natural resources. The Sumerians therefore pioneered trade routes up and down the Tigris and Euphrates and into the hilly flanks of Mesopotamia,

following the tributaries of these great rivers. They blazed trails across the deserts toward the west, where they interacted with and influenced the Egyptians. By sea, they traded with the peoples of the Persian Gulf and, directly or indirectly, with the civilizations of the Indus Valley. Like the Neolithic traders who conveyed goods from village to village, the Sumerians carried their ideas with them along with their merchandise, their literature, their art, their use of writing, and the whole cultural complex that arose from their urban way of life. From its Sumerians roots, the idea of civilization thus spread throughout the ancient Near Eastern world.

THE END OF THE EARLY DYNASTIC PERIOD (2500–2350 B.C.E.)

During the period sometimes referred to as Early Dynastic Period III, competition among the Sumerian city-states for prestige, power, and resources reached a fever pitch. Intercity warfare intensified, as did attempts by ambitious lugals to magnify their own stand-

Objects from the Royal Tombs at Ur. On the right, a queen's headdress, made of gold leaf, lapis lazuli, and carnelian. Above, a helmet made of an alloy of gold and silver. Its cloth lining would have been attached through the holes visible around the edges of the helmet.

Why did a common religion not create peace among the Sumerians?

The Sumerians Enter History   25

ing and that of their city. Tensions between temple aristocracy and royal power were lessening, leading to the emergence of a more unified ruling elite, but leaving commoners with even less of a voice than they had had before.

The Royal Tombs of Ur, dating from 2550 B.C.E. to 2450 B.C.E., provide a breathtaking demonstration of the wealth of this Sumerian elite. They also point to a shift in Sumerian ideas about the afterlife. It appears that at least a few elite members of Sumerian society now believed that they would enjoy a different, better kind of afterlife, and that their tombs were stocked specifically for this purpose. Could this have been an idea the Sumerians borrowed from the pharaohs of Egypt? At present, we can only speculate. Such practices do give us some sense, however, of just how lofty the powers of the lugals had become and of the divide that had now opened up between leaders and followers in Sumerian society.

The rich documentary evidence from this period deals mainly with the military exploits of powerful lugals. It tells of a cycle of brutal warfare among the leading city-states, as the lugal of each sought to establish his supremacy over the others by defeating their armies in battle and then forcing the defeated cities to pay him tribute. This was the traditional pattern of Sumerian warfare, which now intensified as the population of Sumer grew and the struggle to control resources and trade routes became more desperate. Inevitably, however, such supremacy was fleeting: conquered cities revolted, and the cycle of warfare began again. No Sumerian lugal ever attempted to create a true and lasting empire by imposing centralized rule over the cities he conquered. As a result, Sumer remained a collection of independent city-states, compelled periodically to acknowledge the supremacy of a particular lugal, but unable to forge any lasting structures of authority larger than an individual city and its patron god. This fact would prove its undoing when Sumer confronted a new style of imperial rulership in the figure of Sargon of Akkad.

The Akkadian Empire (2350–2160 B.C.E.)

The Akkadians were the predominant people of central Mesopotamia, to the north of Sumer. The Sumerians had greatly influenced them. But although they adopted cuneiform script along with much of Sumerian culture, the Akkadians did not adopt the Sumerian language. Instead, they preserved their own Semitic language, a member of the linguistic family that includes Assyrian, Aramaic, Hebrew, Arabic, and Ethiopic. Sumerians tended to regard the Akkadians as barbarians; but in fact, the two peoples were culturally very similar.

As an outsider to Sumerian society, Sargon, the leader of the Akkadians, was not bound by the traditional assumptions and conventions of Sumerian warfare. Instead, he launched a systematic program of conquest, designed to subject all the areas around Sumer to his authority. Only when it was too late did the Sumerians realize that Sargon had their land by the throat. Around 2350 B.C.E., he conquered Sumer, and then moved swiftly to establish direct control over all of Mesopotamia.

From his new capital at Akkad, Sargon installed Akkadian-speaking governors to rule the cities of Sumer, ordering them to pull down fortifications, collect taxes, and do his will. By so doing, Sargon transformed the independent city-states of Sumer and Akkad into a much larger political unit: a kingdom or empire. Sargon supported his empire (arguably the first true empire in human history) by managing and exploiting the network of trade routes crisscrossing the

An Akkadian King. A bronze head, often thought to be of Sargon, but more likely of his grandson Naram-Sin. From the Akkadian Period on, the charismatic leadership of such godlike emperors was an important element in Mesopotamian rulership.

Near East. As a result, his economic influence stretched from Ethiopia to the Indus Valley in India. Sargon's capital became the most splendid city in the world, and he exercised unprecedented power for fifty-six years.

Sargon's imperialism also had a religious aspect. To unite the two halves of his empire, Sargon merged the Akkadian and Sumerian pantheons by identifying Akkadian divinities, such as Ishtar, with their Sumerian counterparts (in this case, the goddess Inanna). He also tried to lessen the hostility between the rival cities of Sumer by appointing a single Akkadian high priest or priestess (often a member of his own family) to preside over the main temples in several Sumerian cities. Perhaps the most successful example of this policy was Sargon's daughter Enheduanna, whom he appointed as high priestess of An, the principal god of Uruk, and Nanna, the chief god of Ur. Enheduanna herself seems to have been particularly devoted to Inanna/Ishtar, her father's patron deity. Enheduanna's hymns to Inanna are the earliest surviving literary works by a named author in world history. Clearly the devotees of An and Nanna did not feel slighted by their high priestess's devotion to Inanna. The precedent she established would continue even after the Sargonid dynasty finally fell; for several centuries thereafter, the kings of Sumer continued to appoint their daughters as high priestesses of both Ur and Uruk.

Sargon was eventually succeeded by his talented grandson Naram-Sin, who reigned, like his grandfather, for over a half century. Naram-Sin extended the Akkadian conquests and consolidated long-distance trade routes. An energetic promoter of culture and a patron of the arts, Naram-Sin encouraged literary and artistic endeavors. Through conquest and the quickened pace of commerce, he also helped stimulate the growth of cities throughout the Near East.

Although the Akkadians' emphasis on political centralization and imperial organization represented a clear break with the Sumerian past, culturally the Sumerians and Akkadians differed little from one another. By 2200 B.C.E. most people in central and southern Mesopotamia would have been able to converse in either language. Although the Akkadians worshiped their own Akkadian deities, they were also careful to respect and revere the gods and practices of the Sumerians. Much of Akkadian literature and art was at its root Sumerian, translated and slightly transformed to appeal to Akkadian tastes. Scholars speak of a Sumero-Akkadian cultural synthesis; and indeed after the reign of Sargon the two civilizations were virtually indistinguishable, except for their different languages. Despite its new imperial trappings, the urban civilization Sargon and Naram-Sin helped promote across the Near East was still essentially the urban model of the Sumerians.

THE DYNASTY OF UR (2100–2000 B.C.E.)

Court intrigue and a series of weak successors followed the long reign of Naram-Sin. After a brief period in which invading hill people from the Iranian Plateau ruled over Sumer and Akkad (2160–2100 B.C.E.), Sumer once again dissolved into a collection of rival, independent city-states. Around 2100 B.C.E., however, a new dynasty from Ur, the so-called Ur Dynasty III, established itself under the rule of its first king, Ur-Nammu, and his son Shulgi. Ur-Nammu was responsible for the construction of the great ziggurat at Ur, which towered seventy feet above the surrounding plain, and for many other architectural marvels. Shulgi continued his father's work, conquering the lands up to the Zagros Mountains and imposing massive tribute payments upon them (one tribute collection site alone accounted for 350,000 sheep per year). Shulgi built state-run textile production facilities to process the wool, staffing them with lower-class women and children. He also promulgated something like a law code, calling for fair weights and measures, the protection of widows and orphans, and limitations on the death penalty for crimes.

Ur-Nammu and Shulgi modeled their kingship on that of Sargon and Naram-Sin, pursuing military conquests, the centralization of Sumerian government, commercial expansion and consolidation, the patronage of art and literature, and an exalted ideology of charismatic imperial rulership. Together, the Akkadian rulers and those of the Ur Dynasty III thus established a pattern of rule that would influence the region for centuries to come.

When Shulgi died, around 2047 B.C.E., he was succeeded by two competent sons who both died young. As a result the throne fell to Shulgi's grandson Ibbi-Sin, a hapless individual most charitably described as in over his head. Something of a mama's boy, he portrayed himself as a beardless youth well into middle age and invariably referred to his mother, even in official records, as Mommy. He surrounded himself with flatterers, and the imperial bureaucracy bloated under his rule.

The records of his reign trace the anatomy of a dying empire. One by one, the royal archives trail off

WHY DID A COMMON RELIGION NOT CREATE PEACE AMONG THE SUMERIANS?

THE SUMERIANS ENTER HISTORY   27

Sumerian Ziggurat. This edifice, built in Ur around 2100 B.C.E., is the best-preserved surviving ziggurat. As can be seen from the diagram of its original form at left, a shrine, reached by climbing four stories and passing through a massive portal, was the goal of the worshiper's ascent and was the most sacred part of the temple.

in the cities under Ur's domination, as Ibbi-Sin gradually lost control of his empire. Finally he turned to his field marshal, a man of Amorite (Semitic) descent named Ishbi-Irra, to rescue him from the consequences of his own inanity. Ishbi-Irra was shrewd and ruthless, time and again allowing affairs to reach an impasse and then intervening at the last possible moment to win more power for himself. Thanks to Ishbi-Irra's military ability, Ibbi-Sin remained on the throne for twenty-four years, until finally an enemy army sacked Ur itself. Only after Ibbi-Sin had been carried off into captivity, however, did Ishbi-Irra spring heroically into action, driving off the remaining invaders and then claiming the kingship of Ur for himself. Ibbi-Sin disappeared; but for the inhabitants of Mesopotamia, his name would resonate for centuries as the epitome of criminal stupidity and hopeless incompetence.

Ishbi-Irra was unable to reassert control over the entire shattered empire of Ur. Many of the cities of the realm had broken free for good and were now under the rule of ambitious and powerful Amorite chiefs much like Ishbi-Irra himself. For the next two centuries, Mesopotamian history would be characterized by incessant warfare among a group of small Amorite kingdoms based on the great urban centers of the Sumero-Akkadian past. Not until the eighteenth century B.C.E. would one of these Amorite-descended

kings, the remarkable Hammurabi of Babylon, create a new imperial unity in the region.

THE SUMERIAN RENAISSANCE AND THE RISE OF THE AMORITES

The rulers of Ur issued their official documents in Sumerian, and consciously reasserted Sumerian culture against the influence of the Semitic-speaking Akkadians. But this backward-looking Sumerian renaissance had little effect on the culture of Mesopotamia, which was by now thoroughly suffused by the influence of the Semitic-speaking peoples who would dominate the region for the next 1,500 years. Three such groups in particular deserve our attention now: the Akkadians, the Amorites, and the Assyrians. We will meet others, including the Phoenicians, the Canaanites, and the Hebrews, in Chapter Two.

The Akkadians were the first Semitic-speaking people to establish themselves in Mesopotamia and became the most thoroughly assimilated into Sumerian civilization. They rapidly adapted to urban life and became important founders of cities elsewhere in the Near Eastern world. The Amorites, by contrast, were nomads, whose military skills made them valuable allies (and eventually masters) of the Sumerian and

Akkadian cities. Like the Akkadians, the Amorites eventually urbanized, but culturally they retained much that reflected their rough-and-tumble roots. Northern Mesopotamia was home to the Assyrians, caravan merchants who pioneered trade routes into Anatolia (modern-day Turkey) soon after 2000 B.C.E. Deeply influenced by Sumero-Akkadian culture, the Assyrians would go on to found an important and long-lasting civilization in their own right. For the time being, however, they had their hands full fending off the advances of their Amorite cousins to the south.

THE OLD BABYLONIAN EMPIRE

How did Hammurabi bind his empire together?

In 1792 B.C.E. a young Amorite ruler named Hammurabi (*hah-muh-RAH-bee*) ascended the throne of Babylon, a weak kingdom in central Mesopotamia based in an insignificant city of the same name. When Hammurabi came to power, Babylon was both fragile and precariously wedged among a number of other, more powerful Amorite kingdoms. Babylon's site on the Tigris and Euphrates had great potential economic and military significance; but it was also dangerous, because Babylon sat perilously amid mighty antagonists who were often tempted to "play through" the city on their way to other conquests.

Hammurabi may have been the first sovereign in world history to understand that power need not be based on brute force. He recognized that the application of intellect, political strategy, and ruthless cunning might accomplish what his army could not. A rich archive of tablets found at the city of Mari (which eventually fell under Hammurabi's rule) testifies to the cleverness and talent of this remarkable king.

Hammurabi used writing as a weapon, but did so with such subtlety that its targets noticed only much too late. He did not try to confront his mightier neighbors directly. Rather, through letters and embassies, double-dealing diplomacy, and general deceit, he induced his stronger counterparts to embroil themselves ever deeper in armed conflict with each other. While the other Amorite kingdoms exhausted themselves in costly and pointless wars, Hammurabi fanned their hatred for one another, skillfully and privately portraying

himself as a friend to all sides. His value as a potential ally caused neighboring rulers to send him resources, in hopes that he might help them. Meanwhile, Hammurabi quietly consolidated his kingdom, augmenting his own strength and, when the time was right, fell on his depleted and weary neighbors. By such policies, he transformed his small Amorite state into what historians describe as the Old Babylonian Empire.

Mesopotamia under Hammurabi's rule achieved an unprecedented degree of political integration. His realm ultimately stretched from the Persian Gulf into Assyria. The southern half of the region, formerly known as Sumer and Akkad, would for the rest of antiquity be known as Babylonia. To help unify these territories, Hammurabi introduced an important innovation by elevating the little-known patron deity of Babylon,

Mesopotamian Royal Head. A diorite head of a Mesopotamian king, conventionally identified as Hammurabi. Such headdresses were worn by the rulers of Mesopotamian cities between roughly 2100 and 1700 B.C.E. Hammurabi is shown wearing such a headdress on p. 29, but there is nothing else to identify this bust with Hammurabi.

Marduk, to be the ruler-god of his entire empire. Although the king was also careful to pay homage to the ancient gods of Sumer and Akkad, Marduk now sat atop the official pantheon. People could continue to worship the ancient patron deities of their cities if they wished; but all now owed allegiance to Marduk.

RELIGION AND LAW

The notion that political rule rested on divine approval was nothing new, of course. Its foundations lay in the practices and beliefs of the Sumerians, and the notion was fully developed by Sargon, Narum-Sin, Ur-Nammu, and Shulgi. Hammurabi's innovation was to use Marduk's supremacy over all other gods to legitimate his own claim to rule, in Marduk's name, over all Mesopotamia because he was king of Marduk's home city of Babylon. Hammurabi thus became the first Near Eastern ruler to launch wars of aggression that he justified specifically by saying he undertook them in the name of his primary god. This precedent would become a characteristic feature of Near Eastern politics thereafter, as we will see in Chapter Two.

In Hammurabi's Babylon, political power and religious practice were thus completely interwoven with each other. At their annual new year celebration, the Babylonians would reenact the victory of Marduk over the Sumerian god of chaos, which had secured for Marduk his place as the chief god of both heaven and earth. Marduk's triumph over chaos in turn made it possible to predict and control the natural environment, the Babylonians believed, and so was intimately connected with the fertility of the land. To guarantee this continuing fertility, during the same new year festivities, as priests chanted the mythological stories recounting Marduk's ascent, the king would retire with a sacred prostitute inside the temple, and the two would have ritual sexual intercourse. Like the pharaohs of Egypt and the emperors of ancient China, the Old Babylonian king was thus an essential link in the chain of relationships that bound human beings to the earth and the heavens.

Hammurabi did not rely solely on religion to bind his empire together. Building on the precedents of centuries and rulers past, he also issued (and had carved in stone) a collection of laws and legal decisions in his own name, which portrayed the king as a fountain of justice and mercy for his entire empire. Preserved on an impressive eight-foot stele discovered in southwestern Iran (and now housed in the Louvre in Paris), the Code of Hammurabi was probably never intended to

Code of Hammurabi. The entire code of Hammurabi survives on an eight-foot column made of basalt. The top quarter of the column depicts the Babylonian king paying homage to the seated god of justice. Directly below one can make out the cuneiform inscriptions that are the law code's text.

be a code of laws in any modern sense. Too many subjects are omitted, including any mention of the punishment for murder; furthermore, the code is never cited or even mentioned in the surviving records of legal cases from Hammurabi's kingdom. Most likely, Hammurabi's code was propaganda, intended to publicize the king's devotion to justice and to urge his officials to show a similar concern in their own legal judgments.

OLD BABYLONIAN SOCIETY

Despite its propagandistic purposes, the Code of Hammurabi tells us a good deal about the structure of Babylonian society. Overall, the more complicated social arrangements of Sumerian civilization had given way to a simpler but more oppressive system. An upper class of nobles—palace officials, temple priests, high-ranking military officers, and rich merchants—controlled large estates and staggering wealth. Beneath this small stratum was an enormous class of legally free individuals

THE CODE OF HAMMURABI

The laws of Hammurabi, published on the authority of the king and set up throughout the Babylonian empire, exhibit the influences both of the urban society on which they were imposed and the rough justice of Amorite tradition. Although Hammurabi built on older, urban legal traditions, he sought to extend the authority of his law into more realms of life and provide sterner punishments for its violation. This sampling of his provisions illustrates the severity of his system for criminals, while providing protections in unusual circumstances.

If a man accuses a man, and charges him with murder, but cannot convict him, the accuser shall be put to death.

If a man steals an ox or sheep, ass or pig, or boat—if it belonged to the god or palace, he shall pay thirty fold; if it belonged to a common man, he shall restore ten fold. If the thief has nothing wherewith to pay, he shall be put to death.

If a fire breaks out in a man's house and a man who goes to extinguish it . . . takes the household property of the owner of the house, that man shall be thrown into the fire.

If a man aids a male or a female slave of the palace, or a male or female slave of a common man, to escape from the city, he shall be put to death.

If a man who is a tenant has paid the full amount of money for his rent for the year to the owner of the house, and he (the owner) says to him before "his days are full," "Vacate," the owner of the house, because he made the tenant move out of the house before "his days were full" shall lose the money which the tenant paid him.

If an agent should be careless and not take a receipt for the money which he has given to the merchant, the money not receipted for shall not be placed to his account.

If the wife of a man be taken in lying with another man, they shall bind them and throw them into the water.

If a woman hates her husband and says, "Thou shalt not have me," her past shall be inquired into for any deficiency of hers; and if she has been careful and without past sin and her husband has been going out and greatly belittling her, that woman has no blame. She shall take her dowry and go to her father's house.

If a man destroys the eye of another man, they shall destroy his eye. If a man knocks out the tooth of a man of his own rank, they shall knock out his tooth . . . if the tooth of a common man, he shall pay one-third mana of silver.

Sara Robbins, ed., *Law: A Treasury of Art and Literature* (New York, 1990), pp. 20–22 (slightly revised).

QUESTIONS FOR ANALYSIS

1. Does the Code of Hammurabi sound harsh, fair, or lenient? Penalties such as exile and mutilation were less severe than death, but was harsh justice necessary in Babylonia? Based on your reading of the code, was Hammurabi an enlightened ruler?
2. In what ways does the Code of Hammurabi exhibit the influences of the urban society from which these laws were imposed? What are the general characteristics of ancient Near Eastern urban society?

who were nonetheless dependents of the palace or the temple or who leased land from the estates of the powerful. These dependents included laborers and artisans, small-scale merchants and farmers, and the minor political and religious officials of the state.

At the bottom of Babylonian society were the slaves. Far more numerous in the Old Babylonian Empire than they had been in the Sumerian Period, slaves were also treated much more harshly. And they were more readily identifiable as a separate group within society. In Babylonia, free men, whether nobles or dependents, wore long hair and beards; male slaves, however, were shaven and branded. Some Babylonian slaves were acquired through trade, another departure from Sumerian practice. Others were captured in war or were free people who had fallen into slavery through debt or as punishment for certain offenses. Slaves could accumulate property and borrow as a means of gaining their freedom, but this was probably not a frequent occurrence.

Old Babylonian society was also highly stratified by class. An offense committed against nobles carried a far more severe penalty than did the same crime committed against a dependent or slave (although nobles were also punished more severely than were commoners for crimes they committed against other nobles). Marriage arrangements and customs also reflected class differences, with bride-price and dowry depending on the status of the parties involved.

Hammurabi's code also provides evidence as to the status and treatment of women in Babylonian society. Women did enjoy certain protections under the law, including the right to divorce abusive, neglectful, or indigent husbands. If a husband divorced a wife "without cause," he was obliged to provide financial support for her and their children. Despite such protections, however, Babylonian law regarded wives as the property of their husbands. A wife who went around her city defaming her spouse was subject to drowning; she would suffer the same fate, along with her lover, if she were caught in adultery. Husbands, by contrast, had a legal right to significant sexual promiscuity not only with temple prostitues but also with slaves and concubines.

HAMMURABI'S LEGACY

Hammurabi died around 1750 B.C.E. Although some contraction of the Old Babylonian Empire followed under his successors, Hammurabi's achievements endured. His administrative reforms, combined with his innovations in religious imperialism, created a durable and important state in Mesopotamia. For another two centuries the Old Babylonian Empire played a significant role in the Near East, until invaders from the north sacked the capital and occupied it. Babylon itself remained the region's most famous city for another thousand years.

Hammurabi's legacy extended well beyond the borders of his own kingdom. His success, and the flair and aplomb with which he achieved it, was instrumental in shaping conceptions of kingship in the ancient Near East. After Hammurabi, unifying state religions would play an increasingly important role in the policies of Near Eastern kings. Hammurabi had also demonstrated the effectiveness of writing as a political tool. Diplo-

Women and Textiles. Women were the predominant producers of textiles throughout the ancient Near Eastern world. Even upper-class women spun thread and wove cloth for their households. Here, a servant fans an elegant lady who is spinning thread with a spindle.

macy, the keeping of extensive archives, international relations—all would characterize subsequent Near Eastern empires. So too would the claim that kings should be the protectors of the weak and the arbiters of justice within their realms. Hammurabi's law code built on the traditions of previous Mesopotamian kings, but it was his greatness that transformed law giving into an imperative for any ambitious ruler of a future Near Eastern kingdom or empire.

THE DEVELOPMENT OF CIVILIZATION IN EGYPT

In what ways did patterns of development in early Egypt differ from those in Sumer?

The other primary civilization of the Mediterranean world arose in Egypt, roughly contemporaneous with Sumer. Unlike the Sumerians, however, the Egyptians did not have to wrest their survival from a hostile and unpredictable environment. Instead, their land was renewed every year by the regular summer flooding of the Nile River. The rich black soil the river left behind made the Nile Valley the richest agricultural region in the entire Mediterranean world. Much of the distinctiveness of Egyptian civilization rests on this fundamental ecological fact.

Ancient Egypt was a narrow, elongated land, snaking north from the First Cataract (a series of rocks and rapids in the river at the ancient city of Elephantine) along both banks of the Nile toward the Mediterranean Sea for a distance of more than 600 miles (1,100 km). Outside this narrow band of territory—which ranged in breadth from a few hundred yards to no more than 14 miles (23 km)—lay an uninhabitable desert, where rain almost never falls. This contrast, between the fertile Black Land along the Nile and the dessicated Red Land beyond, deeply influenced the way the Egyptians viewed their world. Egypt itself they saw as the center of the cosmos. The lands beyond Egypt, however, they regarded as lying utterly beyond the boundaries of civilized life.

As a land, a nation, and a civilization, Egypt has enjoyed remarkable continuity. The roots of Egyptian culture date back to at least 5000 B.C.E., and Egypt would continue to thrive as an independent and distinct culture until its assimilation into the Roman Empire

after 30 B.C.E. From about 3000 B.C.E. on, the defining element in ancient Egyptian culture would be the pervasive influence of a powerful, centralized, bureaucratic state headed by pharaohs whom their people regarded as living gods. No other ancient civilization was ever governed so tightly for so long as was Egypt.

For convenience, historians divide ancient Egyptian history into "kingdoms" and "periods," as shown in the chronology on p. 34. As did ancient Egyptian writers, modern historians generally portray the Old, Middle, and New Kingdoms as times of strength, prosperity, and unity, separated by chaotic interludes when central authority broke down (the First, Second, and Third Intermediate Periods). Although we will follow these traditional divisions, we should note that they do reflect the centralizing (and perhaps therefore distorting) perspective of the ancient Egyptian state itself. As we will see, the First Intermediate Period in particular looks much less chaotic and dismal if viewed from the perspective of local society rather than from the pharaohs' court.

PREDYNASTIC EGYPT (C. 10,000–3100 B.C.E.)

Prehistoric or Predynastic Egypt is the period before the emergence of the pharaohs and their dynasties. Using archaeology to glean information about this age is notoriously difficult. Many predynastic settlements are now buried under innumerable layers of silt or were destroyed long ago by the waters of the Nile. Furthermore, for a long time the abundance of the Nile Valley discouraged the transition to village life that took place elsewhere in the Neolithic Near East. In the Fertile Crescent, population growth forced the Mesopotamians to adopt settled agricultural life during the eighth millennium B.C.E. In Egypt, by contrast, a growing population was able to sustain itself through hunting and gathering until the fifth millennium B.C.E.

Egypt's population rose through a combination of natural increase—itself the product of an abundant food supply—and immigration from elsewhere. Before around 10,000 B.C.E., the region that is now the Sahara supported a rich variety of plant and animal life. With the retreat of the glaciers, however, the area slowly began to turn into a desert, and people and animals looked for better circumstances. Many found their way to the Nile Valley. By the Predynastic Period a multitude of peoples from North Africa, East Africa, and western Asia had settled in Egypt. The remarkable

IN WHAT WAYS DID PATTERNS OF DEVELOPMENT IN EARLY EGYPT DIFFER FROM THOSE IN SUMER?

THE DEVELOPMENT OF CIVILIZATION IN EGYPT 33

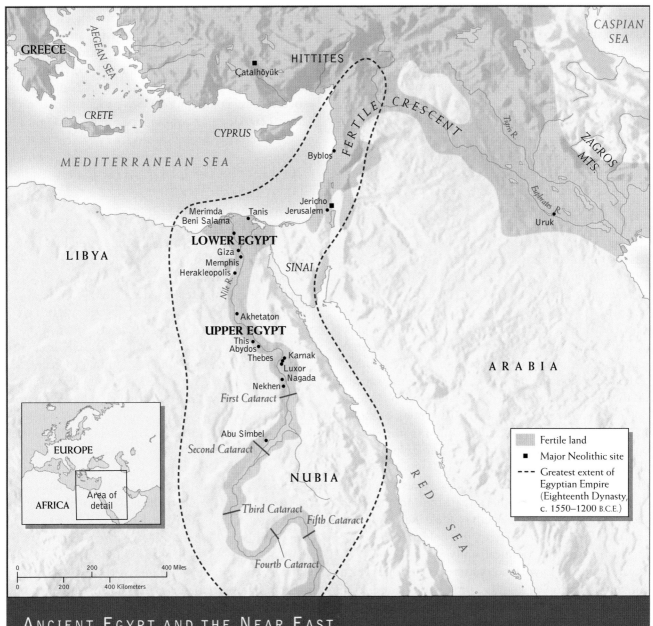

ANCIENT EGYPT AND THE NEAR EAST

Notice the peculiar geography of Egypt and the role played by the Nile. How did the lands on either side of the Nile help isolate Egyptian culture from outside influences? Consider how the Nile helped forge Egypt into a unitary state under a powerful centralized government. How was Egypt's relationship to the Nile as potentially hazardous as it was beneficial?

unity of Egyptian culture thus emerged from extremely heterogeneous roots. It was not the product of any particular ethnic or racial group.

The first known permanent settlement in Egypt dates to approximately 4750 B.C.E., and was situated near the modern town of Merimde Beni Salama, at the southwestern edge of the Nile Delta. It was a thriving farming community that may have numbered as many as 16,000 residents (although this number—being based on burial remains, which are difficult to interpret—is open to contention). Thereafter, the Egyptian economy rapidly became more sophisticated. By around 3500 B.C.E. the residents of Ma'adi, just three miles away from Merimde Beni Salama, had extensive commercial contacts with the Sinai Peninsula; the Near East; and the upper reaches of the Nile, several hundred miles to the south.

Copper was a particularly important import, which allowed the residents to replace stone tools with metal ones. Many other Neolithic farming centers have also been discovered in or near the Nile Delta, where a degree of cultural unity was already developing. In later centuries, this area would be known as Lower Egypt (so called because it was downstream). Comparable developments were also occurring outside the delta. By the end of the Predynastic Period, Egyptian material culture and burial practices were more or less uniform from the southern edge of the delta all the way south to the First Cataract, a vast length of the Nile known as Upper Egypt.

Although towns in Lower Egypt were more numerous, it was in Upper Egypt that the first true Egyptian cities developed. By 3200 B.C.E., important communities such as Nekhen, Naqada, This, and Abydos had all developed high degrees of occupational and social specialization. They had encircled themselves with sophisticated fortifications and had begun to build elaborate temple and shrine complexes to honor the local gods.

This last fact may be key to explaining the growth of these towns into cities. As with Uruk in Mesopotamia, their role as regional cult centers attracted travelers and encouraged the growth of industries. But unlike in Mesopotamia, travel in Upper Egypt was relatively easy. Almost all Egyptians lived within sight of the Nile, enabling the great river to serve as a highway binding the nation together. It was due to the Nile, therefore, that the region south of the delta, despite its enormous geographical length, was able to forge a cultural, and eventually political, unity.

The Nile fed Egypt and united it. The river was a conduit for people, goods, and ideas. Centralizing rulers could project their power quickly and effectively up and down its course. By the close of the Predynastic Period the cities of Upper Egypt had banded together in a confederacy under the leadership of This. The pressure exerted by this confederacy in turn forced the towns of Lower Egypt to adopt their own form of loose political organization. By 3100 B.C.E., the rivalry between these competing regions had given rise to the two nascent kingdoms of Upper and Lower Egypt.

THE UNIFICATION OF EGYPT: THE ARCHAIC PERIOD (3100–C. 2686 B.C.E.)

With the rise of powerful rulers who sought to unify the two Egyptian kingdoms, we enter the dynastic phase of Egyptian history. The numbering system for the pharaonic dynasties was developed (or at least enshrined in writing) by a third-century B.C.E. Egyptian priest named Manetho (*MAHN-uh-thoh*). By and large, Manetho's work has withstood the scrutiny of modern historians and archaeologists, although recent research has led us to recognize a Zero Dynasty, an assortment of early kings instrumental in the initial unification of Egypt whom Manetho did not record. But these rulers, known almost exclusively from archaeological evidence, remain shadowy figures at best. Among their number was an Upper Egyptian strongman known as King Scorpion from a mace head that details—in pictures—his assertion of authority over most of Egypt. Another, King Narmer, appears to have ruled both Upper and Lower Egypt and may be identical with the legendary king Menes or Min whom later Egyptians credited with this feat. These kings probably orginated at Abydos in Upper Egypt, where they were also buried. Their administrative capital, however, was at Memphis, the capital city of Lower Egypt and an important center for trade with the Sinai Peninsula and the Near East.

Following the political unification of Upper and Lower Egypt, the basic features of pharaonic rule took shape along lines that would persist for the next 3,000 years. From a very early date, the pharaoh was identified closely with divinity. By the First and Second Dynasties, he was already regarded as the earthly manifestation of the falcon god, Horus. These early Egyptian rulers thus laid claim to a sacred nature quite different from the early Sumerian lugal, a mortal who merely enjoyed divine favor.

How these early pharaohs established their claims to divinity is a mystery. We do know, however, that legitimating their rule over all Egypt was a difficult

CHRONOLOGY

EGYPTIAN KINGDOMS AND PERIODS

Predynastic Period	c. 10,000–3100 B.C.E.
Archaic Period	3100–c. 2686 B.C.E.
Old Kingdom	c. 2686–2160 B.C.E.
First Intermediate Period	2160–2055 B.C.E.
Middle Kingdom	2055–c. 1650 B.C.E.
Second Intermediate Period	c. 1650–1550 B.C.E.
New Kingdom	1550–1075 B.C.E.

IN WHAT WAYS DID PATTERNS OF DEVELOPMENT IN EARLY EGYPT DIFFER FROM THOSE IN SUMER?

THE DEVELOPMENT OF CIVILIZATION IN EGYPT   35

Narmer Palette, c. 3000 B.C.E. One side shows King Narmer, wearing the white crown of Upper Egypt, striking an enemy with a mace, while Horus, the falcon god, looks on approvingly. The other side shows the king, wearing the red crown of Lower Egypt, viewing the decapitated corpses of his enemies. The long-necked beasts with intertwined necks represent the two kingdoms of Upper and Lower Egypt, united under Narmer.

task. Local civic and religious loyalties remained strong, and for centuries Lower Egyptians would continue to see themselves as distinct in some respects from their cousins to the south. Efforts to create a unified Egyptian identity began very early, however, as we can see from the Narmer palette. It seems probable that the pharaohs' claim to divinity was one approach to solving this problem of political unity. But however precisely the sacralization of Egyptian kingship occurred, it was an astonishing success. By the end of the Second Dynasty the pharaoh was not just the ruler of Egypt; in a sense he *was* Egypt, a personification of the land, the people, and their connection to the divine.

LANGUAGE AND WRITING

Among the many facets of Egyptian culture that have fascinated and mystified later observers is the Egyptian system of pictographic writing. Called *hieroglyphs* (*HI-roh-glifs;* "sacred carvings") by the Greeks, these strange and elaborate symbols remained completely impenetrable and therefore all the more mysterious until the nineteenth century, when a French scholar named Jean François Champollion deciphered them with the help of the Rosetta Stone. This carved stone contains three versions of the same text, written in ancient Greek, demotic (the script of a later version of the Egyptian language), and hieroglyphics. Because he could read the text in Greek, Champollion was able to unravel the demotic and hieroglyphic texts as well. From this beginning,

The Rosetta Stone. This famous stone, carved in 196 B.C.E., preserves the text of a single decree in three different forms of writing: hieroglyphs (top), demotic (middle), and classical Greek (bottom). Nineteenth-century scholars were able to use the classical Greek text (which they could read) to decipher the hieroglyphic and demotic scripts (which had previously been undecipherable).

generations of scholars have added to and refined our knowledge of ancient Egyptian society and language.

The development of hieroglyphic writing in Egypt dates to around 3200 B.C.E. Its pictographic nature may betray an early influence from Mesopotamia; but the two scripts are so unlike each other that they probably developed independently. As in Sumer, writing technology quickly became an important tool for Egyptian government and administration. Unlike Sumerian cuneiform, however, Egyptian hieroglyphics never evolved very far toward a system of phonograms. Instead, the Egyptians developed a simpler, faster, cursive script for representing hieroglyphics called *hieratic*, which they employed for the everyday business of government and commerce. They also developed a shorthand version of hieratic that scribes could use for rapid note taking.

Little early hieratic writing remains, due largely to the perishable nature of the medium on which it was usually written: papyrus. Produced by hammering, drying, and processing river reeds, papyrus was lighter, easier to write on, and more transportable than the clay tablets used by the Sumerians. When sewn together into scrolls, papyrus also made it possible to record and store large quantities of information in a very small space. Production of this versatile writing material remained one of Egypt's most important industries throughout ancient times, and papyrus became a valuable export item. Even in the sandy and arid conditions of Egypt, however, papyrus is fragile and subject to decay. In wetter climates, it almost never survives for archaeologists to unearth. The vast majority of papyrus documents have therefore been lost, a fact that significantly limits our understanding of Old Kingdom Egypt.

The language of the ancient Egyptians has for long been a matter of debate. Early Egyptian exhibits features that tie it both to the Semitic languages of the Near East

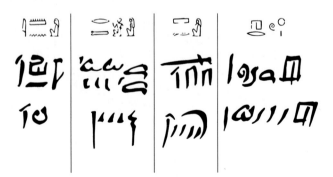

Egyptian Writing. Egyptian scribes used a variety of scripts: hieroglyphs for inscriptions and religious texts, a cursive hieratic script for administrative documents, and a more informal shorthand for note taking. This chart illustrates the relationship between the three forms of writing.

and to a number of African language groups, all of which belong to a linguistic superfamily known as Afro-Asiatic. Some historical linguists have postulated that early Egyptian might represent the survival of a root language from which the other languages of the Afro-Asiatic group evolved. Given the movements of people into, out of, and through the Nile Valley in the prehistoric period, this theory is a distinct possibility. But whatever its origins, the Egyptian language has enjoyed a long history. The language of the Old Kingdom survived and evolved over thousands of years, to become the tongue known as Coptic in classical antiquity. It is still used today in the liturgy of the Coptic Christian church.

THE OLD KINGDOM (C. 2686–2160 B.C.E.)

Because so few of the routine business documents of the Old Kingdom survive, writing a history of this period is a difficult venture. Funerary texts from the tombs of the elite allow us to say something about the achievements of particular individuals and to gain an impression of everyday life, but we know little about the lives of ordinary Egyptians. Further complicating our problem is the attitude of the Old Kingdom Egyptians themselves. Because of their belief in the unchanging, cyclical nature of the universe, history and historical events as we think of them were of little interest to them. It is unlikely, therefore, that we will ever be able to reconstruct their history in any detailed way.

Rich documentation about individuals, practices, and beliefs is nonetheless available to us through the texts and art of this period. One feature that emerges clearly from these sources is the degree to which the pharaohs of the Third Dynasty (c. 2686–2613 B.C.E.) had already built a powerful, centralized administration devoted to the self-glorification of the pharaoh himself. Because the pharaoh *was* Egypt, all the resources of Egypt belonged to him. Long-distance trade was entirely controlled by the pharaoh, and systems for imposing taxation and conscripting labor were already well developed. To administer their kingdom, the pharaohs installed centrally appointed local governors (known to the Greeks as *nomarchs*), many of whom were members of the pharaohs' own family. Old Kingdom pharaohs kept tight control over the nomarchs and their armies of lesser officials, to prevent them from establishing local roots in the territories they administered.

Scribal literacy was widespread in Old Kingdom Egypt, because writing was critical to the management

In what ways did patterns of development in early Egypt differ from those in Sumer?

The Development of Civilization in Egypt   37

and exploitation of Egypt's vast wealth. And because literate bureaucrats were absolutely essential to Egyptian government at both the national and local level, scribal administrators enjoyed power, influence, and status. Even a child just beginning his scribal education was considered worthy of great respect. Training was difficult, but a Middle Kingdom document called "The Satire of the Trades" reminded the scribe in training how much his education would benefit him in the end and how much better off he would be than the practitioners of other trades.

IMHOTEP AND THE STEP PYRAMID

At the dawn of the Old Kingdom, we meet one of the greatest administrative officials in the history of Egypt. Imhotep rose through the ranks of the pharaoh's administration to become a sort of vizier, the right-hand man to Djoser (*ZOH-ser*), an early pharaoh of the Third Dynasty. Imhotep's learning included medicine, astronomy, theology, and mathematics, but above all he was an architect. Earlier pharaohs had already devoted enormous resources to their burial arrangements at Abydos. It was Imhotep, however, who designed the Step Pyramid, the first great monument in world history built entirely of dressed stone. It was not only to be the final resting place of Djoser but a symbol and expression of his transcendent power as pharaoh.

Built west of the administrative capital at Memphis near modern Saqqara, the Step Pyramid towers over the desert to a height of 200 feet. Its design was based on an older form of burial monument, the *mastaba*, a low rectangular building built entirely of brick with a flat top and sloping sides. Imhotep probably began with the *mastaba* pattern in mind, but he radically altered it by stacking one smaller *mastaba* on top of another and constructing each entirely of limestone. Surrounding this impressive monument was a huge temple and mortuary complex, perhaps modeled after Djoser's palace in the capital. These buildings served two purposes. Djoser's *ka* (his spirit after death) would have what it needed to rule in the afterlife, and the design of the buildings, with their immovable doors and labyrinthine passageways, would (it was hoped) frustrate tomb robbers, a chronic problem as pharaonic burials became richer and therefore more tempting to thieves.

Imhotep may have intended his pyramidal design to evoke the descending rays of the life-giving sun; or perhaps the pyramid was meant as the means for the pharaoh's *ka* to ascend into the sky and incorporate itself with the sun on its journey west after death. But whatever the theological import of the design, no one could miss the pharaonic power that lay behind its construction. Imhotep had set a precedent to which pharaohs throughout the Old Kingdom would aspire. Ultimately, the competition to build ever larger and more elaborate pyramids would ruin them.

Old Kingdom Egypt reached its height in the Fourth Dynasty (2613–2494 B.C.E.), the period during which the great pyramids of Giza were built. These were true pyramids, which have become timeless symbols of Egyptian civilization. The Great Pyramid, built for the pharaoh Khufu (*KOO-foo*; or Cheops in Greek), was originally 481 feet high and 756 feet along each side of its base, constructed from more than 2.3 million limestone blocks and enclosing a volume of about 91 million cubic feet. With the exception of a few airways, passages, and burial chambers, the structure is completely solid. In ancient times, the entire pyramid was encased in gleaming white limestone and topped by a massive capstone gilded in gold, as were the two massive but slightly

Step Pyramid of King Djoser, c. 2650 B.C.E.

Pyramids at Giza. The Great Pyramid of Khufu (Cheops) is in the center, c. 2560 B.C.E.

investment of labor and wealth required to build the great pyramids put grave strains on Egyptian society. Natural resources were exploited more intensively than ever before, governmental control over the lives of individual Egyptians increased, and the number of administrative officials employed by the state grew ever larger. So too did the contrast between the splendid cultural achievements of the pharaoh's capital at Memphis and the rest of Egyptian society. The pharaonic cult grew ever more elaborate as these Third- and Fourth-Dynasty rulers began to present themselves not only as manifestations of the falcon god, Horus, but also as the personification of the sun god, Ra. At the same time, however, a gap was opening between the centralizing religious pretensions of the pharaoh and the continuing loyalties of Egyptians to their local gods and their local leaders. These tensions would ultimately spell the end of the Old Kingdom and usher in the important changes of the First Intermediate Period.

SOCIETY IN OLD KINGDOM EGYPT

The social pyramid of Old Kingdom Egypt was extremely steep. At its apex stood the pharaoh and his family. During the Third and Fourth Dynasties their status, prestige, and power were so great as to set them entirely apart from all other Egyptians. There was a class of nobles, but until the Fifth Dynasty they were clearly subordinate, their primary role being to serve as priests and officials of pharaoh's government. Scribes too were usually recruited and trained from among the sons of these noble families. Despite their subordination to pharaoh, however, Egyptian elites lived in considerable luxury. They owned extensive estates with exotic goods and fine furniture. They kept dogs and cats and monkeys as pets and hunted and fished for sport.

Beneath the tiny minority represented by royalty and nobility was everyone else. Most Egyptians were poor, living in crowded conditions in simple mud brick dwellings. During the period of prosperity, however, skilled artisans—jewelers, goldsmiths, and the like—could elevate themselves and enjoy nicer surroundings, though we should not think of them as anything like a middle class. Potters, weavers, masons, bricklayers, brewers, merchants, and schoolteachers also enjoyed some measure of respect and prestige, as well as a higher

smaller pyramids at the site built for Khufu's successors Khafre (*KAH-fray*; Chephren) and Menkaure (*MEHN-kah-ray*; Mycerinus). During the Middle Ages, the builders and rulers of the great Muslim capital of Cairo stripped the casing stones from these pyramids and used them to construct and fortify their new city. The gold capstones had probably disappeared already. But in antiquity these pyramids, with their gleaming limestone facing, would have glistened brilliantly in the bright Egyptian sunshine, making them visible for miles in all directions.

The Greek historian Herodotus (*heh-RAHD-ah-tuhs*), who toured Egypt more than 2,000 years after the pyramids were built, claimed that it took 100,000 laborers 20 years to build the Great Pyramid. This is probably an exaggeration. Then as now, Egyptian guides enjoyed telling visitors tall tales. The impression these monuments made on him, however, may be judged by the fact that Herodotus believed what his Egyptian guides were telling him. Once thought to have been the work of slaves, the pyramids were in fact raised by tens of thousands of peasant workers, who labored most intensively on the pyramids while their fields were under water. Some workers may have been conscripts, but most probably participated willingly in the building projects, which glorifed the living god who ruled them and served as their link to the cosmic order.

The monuments of the Third- and Fourth-Dynasty pharaohs testify to the tremendous power they wielded. There can be little doubt, however, that the massive

IN WHAT WAYS DID PATTERNS OF DEVELOPMENT IN EARLY EGYPT DIFFER FROM THOSE IN SUMER?

THE DEVELOPMENT OF CIVILIZATION IN EGYPT   39

The Pharaoh Menkaure and His Queen, Khamerernebty II. A sculpture from the Fourth Dynasty, c. 2500 B.C.E.—an example of the impassive, stately style.

standard of living than most other Egyptians. The vast majority of Egyptians, however, were peasants: unskilled laborers who provided the brute force necessary for agriculture and construction. Beneath them were slaves, typically captives from foreign wars rather than native Egyptians. But despite the theocratic nature of pharaonic rule and the enormous demands the pharaohs placed on Egypt's wealth, Egyptian society does not appear to have been particularly oppressive. Even slaves had certain legal rights, including the ability to own, dispose of, and bequeath personal property.

WOMEN IN THE OLD KINGDOM

Egyptian women also enjoyed an unusually high degree of legal status and protection by the standards of the ancient world. They were not allowed to undergo scribal training or serve as important officials, but short personal notes between women of social standing

suggest at least some degree of female literacy. In times of crisis, as in the case of Queen Nitocris at the close of the Sixth Dynasty, a woman of the royal family might assume pharaonic authority (although usually she would be careful to represent herself in rather mannish fashion). Egyptian women had standing before the courts as their own persons; they could initiate complaints (including suing for divorce), defend themselves, bear witness, and possess property on their own, without the male guardian or representative who was typically required of women in other ancient societies.

None of this should obscure the fact that Egypt was, at its heart, a rigidly patriarchal society. Aside from the role of priestess, women were barred from state office. While most Egyptians practiced monogamy, important and powerful men could and did keep harems of lesser wives, concubines, and female slaves. Furthermore, any Egyptian man could practice sexual freedom, married or not, with legal impunity; a wife who did so was subject to severe legal punishments. Gender divisions may have been less clearly defined among the peasantry than they were among the elites. Peasant women often worked in the fields during the harvest and carried out a number of menial but vital tasks. As usual in the ancient world, however, we can only glimpse the lives of Egyptian peasants through the eyes of their social superiors.

SCIENCE AND TECHNOLOGY

Their monumental architecture notwithstanding, the Egyptians lagged behind the Sumerians and Akkadians in science and mathematics, as they did in technology generally. Only in the calculation of time did the Egyptians make notable advances. For religious and agricultural reasons, their astronomy was largely devoted to the observation of the sun; the solar calendar they developed was far more accurate and sophisticated than the Mesopotamian lunar calendar. Whereas the Sumerians have bequeathed to us their means of dividing and measuring the day, the Egyptian calendar, adopted for Rome by Julius Caesar, is the direct ancestor of our modern western calendar. Otherwise, education was mostly restricted to reading and writing, making the ingenious polymath Imhotep all the more impressive and unusual. The Egyptians did devise effective irrigation and water-control systems, but they did not adopt such labor-saving devices as the wheel until much later than the Sumerians, perhaps because the available pool of peasant manpower seemed virtually inexhaustible in densely populated Egypt. Nor did the laws and other civil documents produced by the lugals of Mesopotamia have any Old Kingdom parallels. The Egyptians of the Old Kingdom apparently had no need for written law: the law was whatever their pharaoh, a living god, proclaimed it to be.

EGYPTIAN RELIGION AND WORLDVIEW

Old Kingdom Egyptians saw themselves as utterly set apart from all other civilizations. A person was either an Egyptian or a barbarian, and the lines between the two were absolute. Within Egypt, however, what mattered was one's Egyptian-ness; aside from gender, all other distinctions paled in comparison to this fundamental distinction between Egyptians and outsiders. Egyptians' confidence in their own superiority stemmed from their self-conscious awareness of the uniqueness of their country, nurtured by the Nile and guarded by the brutal deserts and vast seas that surrounded it. For Egyptians, it was simply self-evident that their country was the center of the world.

Although the Egyptians constructed a variety of creation myths about the world, they did not concern themselves greatly with how humanity came to exist. Rather, what mattered to the Egyptians was the means by which life itself was created and re-created in an endless cycle of renewal. This cyclical conception gave a certain repetitive, predictable, and ultimately static cast to the way Egyptians perceived the cosmos. They viewed many phenomena as cyclical events, not surprising given the dependence of these people on the annual cycles of the Nile.

> Egyptians' confidence in their own superiority stemmed from their self-conscious awareness of the uniqueness of their country, nurtured by the Nile and guarded by the brutal deserts and vast seas that surrounded it.

At the heart of Egyptian religion lay the myth of the gods Osiris and Isis, brother and sister, husband and wife, and two of the earliest nine gods in Egyptian belief. Osiris was the first to hold kingship on earth, but his brother, Seth, wanted the throne for himself. Seth betrayed and killed Osiris, sealing him in a coffin. Through great effort, Isis retrieved the corpse, but Seth seized it once again, hacked his brother into pieces, and spread his remains throughout Egypt (all Egypt could thus claim Osiris, and shrines to him were prevalent throughout the land). Still undeterred, Isis sought the help of Anubis, the god of mummification, and together they managed to reassemble Osiris. Isis then revived Osiris long enough to conceive a child by him, who became the god Horus. With the help of his mother's magic, Horus withstood the assaults of Seth and his henchmen; Horus and Seth then competed over the vacant throne of Osiris until finally Horus prevailed and avenged his father.

This mythology was extremely important to the Egyptians. The tale of Osiris is a myth about life arising out of death, but it is not a resurrection story: Osiris was revivified only temporarily. The notion the tale embodies, of new life arising from the dead, may have originated in the earliest farming settlements of Egypt, where bodies were already being interred with extensive grave goods and special care. The promise of the continuation of life—rhythmic, cyclical, inevitable—as embodied by Osiris made him an important agricultural deity to the Egyptians.

THE EGYPTIAN DEATH CULT

Osiris was also a central deity in the death cult of the Egyptians. Unlike the Sumerians, the Egyptians did not have a bleak view of death and the underworld. Death was an unpleasant rite of passage, a necessity to be endured on the way to an afterlife that was more or less like one's earthly existence, only better. But the passage was not automatic and was full of dangers. After death, the deceased's *ka*, or otherworldly existence, would have to roam the underworld, the Duat, searching for the House of Judgment. There Osiris and forty-two other judges would decide the *ka's* fate. Demons and evil spirits might try to frustrate the *ka's* quest to reach the House of Judgment, and the journey might take some time. If successful and judged worthy, however, the deceased would then enjoy immortality as an aspect of Osiris. For this reason, the dead were often referred to as "Osiris [name of the deceased]."

Because of their beliefs about death, the Egyptians developed elaborate rituals for dealing with it. It was first of all crucial that the corpse be preserved: this is why the Egyptians developed their sophisticated techniques of embalming and mummification. The body was desiccated, all its vital organs were removed (except for the heart, which played a key role in the final judgment), and then the body was treated with chemicals to preserve it. A funerary portrait mask was also placed on the mummy before burial, so that the corpse would still be recognizable in death despite being wrapped in hundreds of yards of linen. To sustain the deceased on his or her journey through the

In what ways did patterns of development in early Egypt differ from those in Sumer?

THE DEVELOPMENT OF CIVILIZATION IN EGYPT   41

Funerary Papyrus. The scene shows the heart of a princess of the Twenty-First Dynasty being weighed in a balance before the god Osiris. On the other side of the balance are the symbols for life and truth.

underworld, food, clothing, utensils, and other items of vital importance would be placed in the grave along with the body.

"Coffin texts," or books of the dead, also accompanied the corpse. These writings contained much that the deceased would need on his or her journey through the Duat: magic spells, ritual incantations, and the like. This knowledge would help the dead navigate the perils on the way to Osiris; it would also help prepare his or her heart for the final test. On reaching Osiris and the other judges, the deceased would perform a "negative confession," a formulaic denial of a litany of offenses. Then the god Anubis would weigh the heart of the deceased in front of the judges, placing it in the scales with the feather of the goddess Ma'at (*MAH-aht*). Only if the heart and the feather were in perfect balance would the dead person achieve immortality as an aspect of Osiris. In the third millennium this privilege was reserved for the royal family alone, but by the Middle Kingdom participation in these death rituals had become accessible to most Egyptians.

The careful detail with which Egyptians confronted death has often led to the erroneous assumption that theirs was a death culture, completely obsessed with the problem of death. In fact, Egyptian practices and beliefs were mostly life affirming, and the role of Osiris

(also, remember, a god of returning life) and the underworld were viewed not with horror, but with hope. The Egyptians' confidence in the cyclical nature of the cosmos and the resilient power of life is also evidenced by their interpretation of the solar cycle. According to this belief, each morning the sky, personified as the goddess Nut, literally gave birth to the sun (often identified with the god Ra). The sun god then made his way westward across the celestial waters of the sky in his day boat toward the land of death. (Osiris was often called "He Who Rules the West"—that is, the land of the dead.) The sun god's journey in his day boat was observable, a peaceful and orderly course across the sky. His trip in his night boat was full of terrors, including a giant serpent that tried to block the sun on its journey through the underworld. In the deepest part of the night, however, the sun reached the mummified body of Osiris and the two gods became one, giving the sun god the power to continue his journey until his mother, Nut, could once again give birth to him with the dawn. Life always triumphed.

Binding together this endless cycle of life, death, and the return of life was *ma'at*. Like many words in the Egyptian language, it has no exact English equivalent. Our concepts of harmony, order, justice, and truth would all fit comfortably within *ma'at*, though none of

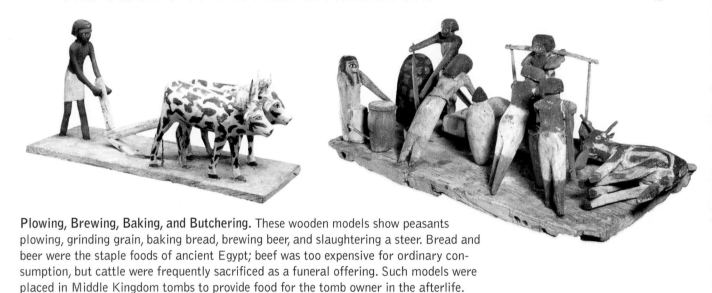

Plowing, Brewing, Baking, and Butchering. These wooden models show peasants plowing, grinding grain, baking bread, brewing beer, and slaughtering a steer. Bread and beer were the staple foods of ancient Egypt; beef was too expensive for ordinary consumption, but cattle were frequently sacrificed as a funeral offering. Such models were placed in Middle Kingdom tombs to provide food for the tomb owner in the afterlife.

these words captures its entire sense. Both the abstract notion and its personification as a female deity named Ma'at were what kept the universe running in its serene, repetitive, predictable fashion. Thus, unlike the Sumerians, the Egyptians of the Archaic Period and the Old Kingdom were a supremely confident and optimistic people. They believed that they lived at the center of the created universe, a paradise where stability and peace were guaranteed by *ma'at* and their connection to it through their pharaoh, who was the earthly manifestation of the gods who ruled them. For most of the third millennium, thanks to a long period of successful Nile floods and Egypt's geographic isolation from the outside world, the Egyptians were able to maintain their belief in this perfectly ordered paradise, in which they perceived that little if anything ever changed.

THE END OF THE OLD KINGDOM

For reasons that are not entirely clear, the Fifth and Sixth Dynasties (2494–2181 B.C.E.) witnessed the slow erosion of pharaonic power. Although pyramid construction continued, the monuments of this period were less impressive in architecture, craftsmanship, and size, mirroring the diminishing prestige of the pharaohs who constructed them. The priesthood of Ra at Nekhen also asserted itself against certain weaker pharaohs, ultimately demoting the pharaoh from being an incarnation of Horus/Ra to being merely the god's son. Most tellingly, however, the nomarchs began to evolve into precisely the type of hereditary local nobility that the vigorous Third and Fourth Dynasty kings had refused to permit. These nobles became so important that one Sixth-Dynasty pharaoh, Pepy I, even

married into their ranks and produced successors by these marriages.

Scholars are uncertain how these local officials and priests wrested power away from the pharaonic center. It may be that the extraordinarily costly building efforts of the Fourth Dynasty had overstrained the economy, leading to resentments and shortages outside the capital city of Memphis. Other evidence points to changing climatic conditions that may have disrupted the regular inundations of the Nile, leading to famine and even starvation in the countryside. One relief sculpture from the late Old Kingdom shows a line of wailing Egyptians, their eyes protruding from their faces and their ribs clearly visible under their skin. These haunting images are evocative of the type of famine and suffering that can ravage northeastern Africa even today. To make matters worse, small states were also beginning to form in Nubia to the south, perhaps in response to Egyptian aggression against their neighbors. With better organization and equipment, the Nubians may have restricted Egyptian access to precious-metal deposits in and around the First Cataract, further crippling the Egyptian economy.

With Egypt suffering these woes, the pharaoh's claim to be a link to *ma'at* diminished accordingly. Instead, local governors and religious authorities began to emerge as the only effective guarantors of stability and order in the countryside. By 2160 B.C.E., when the First Intermediate Period begins, Egypt had effectively ceased to exist as a united country. The central authority of Memphis collapsed, and an ancient pattern of Egyptian history reemerged: a northern center of power based at Herakleopolis opposed by a southern regime headquartered at Thebes, with each dynasty claiming to be the legitimate pharaohs of all Egypt.

THE INSTRUCTION OF PTAH-HOTEP

Egyptian literature often took the form of "instructions" to important personages, offering advice on how they should conduct themselves in office. This document declares itself to be the advice of a high-ranking Fifth Dynasty official to his son and successor. Although the earliest surviving text of this "Instruction" dates from the Middle Kingdom period, the emphasis it places on ma'at *makes it likely that it was composed earlier, perhaps around 2450 B.C.E., during the Egyptian Old Kingdom.*

Be not arrogant because of your knowledge, and be not puffed up because you are a learned man. Take counsel with the ignorant as with the learned, for the limits of art cannot be reached, and no artist is perfect in his skills. Good speech is more hidden than the precious greenstone, and yet it is found among slave girls at the millstones.

. . . If you are a leader commanding the conduct of many seek out every good aim, so that your policy may be without error. A great thing is *ma'at*, enduring and surviving; it has not been upset since the time of Osiris. He who departs from its laws is punished. It is the right path for him who knows nothing. Wrongdoing has never brought its venture safe to port. Evil may win riches, but it is the strength of *ma'at* that endures long, and a man can say, "I learned it from my father.". . . If you wish to prolong friendship in a house which you enter as master, brother or friend, or any place that you enter, beware of approaching the women. No place in which that is done prospers. There is no wisdom in it.

A thousand men are turned aside from their own good because of a little moment, like a dream, by tasting which death is reached. . . . He who lusts after women, no plan of his will succeed. . . . If you are a worthy man sitting in the council of his lord, confine your attention to excellence. Silence is more valuable than chatter. Speak only when you know you can resolve difficulties. He who gives good counsel is an artist, for speech is more difficult than any craft.

Nels M. Bailkey, ed., *Readings in Ancient History: Thought and Experience from Gilgamesh to St. Augustine*, 5th ed. (Boston, 1995), pp. 39–42.

QUESTIONS FOR ANALYSIS

1. Central to the instructions issued by Ptah-Hotep, a sage and adviser, was that the pharaoh was to act in accordance with *ma'at*. What is *ma'at* and why was it so important to Ptah-Hotep? Did the cultures of all ancient civilizations accept the existence of something like *ma'at*?

Beneath the political chaos, however, the First Intermediate Period witnessed some important developments in Egyptian society. Wealth became much more widely and evenly distributed than had been the case during the Old Kingdom. So too did culture, and especially art. Resources that the pharaoh's court at Memphis had once monopolized now remained in the localities, enabling local elites to emerge as both protectors of local society and as patrons for local artists. The result was a rapid diffusion of cultural forms throughout Egyptian society. Many of these forms had been developed originally at the pharaoh's court. Now, however, they became part and parcel of Egyptian society as a whole.

Warfare between the two competing pharaonic dynasties would continue until 2055 B.C.E., when the Theban

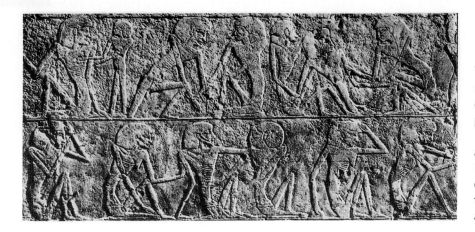

Victims of a Famine. This sculptural relief of famine victims was carved on the causeway leading to the pyramid and mortuary complex of Pharaoh Unas (2375–2345 B.C.E.) at Saqqara. Famine was an increasing problem as the Old Kingdom drew to a close and contributed to the disorder of the First Intermediate Period.

Mentuhotep II conquered the northerners and declared himself the ruler of a united Egypt. His reign marks the beginning of the Middle Kingdom of Egyptian history.

MIDDLE KINGDOM EGYPT (2055–C.1650 B.C.E.)

With the reestablishment of unified government, now centered in the south on Thebes, Egypt entered the period of the Middle Kingdom. Soon after Mentuhotep II's death, a usurper, the vizier Amenemhet (ah-meh-NEHM-het), established himself and his descendants as Egypt's brilliant Twelfth Dynasty. Amenemhet retained Thebes as a center of power but also built a new capital just south of Memphis (whose name, Itj-towy, means "Amenemhet Takes Possession of the Two Lands"). The Twelfth Dynasty remained in power for nearly 200 years, producing a succession of remarkable pharaohs.

Under this dynasty, the Egyptians began to exploit more thoroughly the potential for trade to the south. They mounted expeditions to the land of Punt (probably the coast of Somalia) and secured their border with Nubia. By the middle of the nineteenth century B.C.E., Nubia was firmly under Egypt's control, and the small states and principalities of Palestine and Syria were under heavy Egyptian political and economic influence. But despite Egypt's renewed strength, the Egyptians did not incorporate the lands to the northeast into their realm. Instead, Amenemhet I constructed the Walls of the Prince in Sinai to guard against incursions from Egypt's Near Eastern neighbors.

The huge fortifications built along Egypt's frontiers during the Twelfth Dynasty demonstrate the great resourcefulness of these pharaohs, but they also betray a marked shift in the Egyptian outlook on the world. Long gone was the placid serenity epitomized by *ma'at*. Middle Kingdom Egyptians viewed the world beyond their borders with suspicion and fear. Egypt was not yet an imperial power, because Middle Kingdom pharaohs made no attempt to incorporate their conquests into their kingdom in any meaningful way. But unlike their Old Kingdom counterparts, the Egyptians of the Middle Kingdom were now taking a direct and active interest in events beyond Egypt's borders.

The pharaoh's position had also changed. None of the Middle Kingdom pharaohs portrayed himself with the serene confidence of Old Kingdom depictions. The pharaoh continued to enjoy a special position as god-king, but his authority did not derive from a vaunted, remote position as such. Rather, in the Middle Kingdom pharaohs represented themselves as—and were expected to be—good shepherds, tenders of their Egyptian flock. *Ma'at* could not help them in these duties; only by diligently protecting Egypt from a hostile outside world could pharaohs provide the peace, prosperity, and security desired by their subjects. Portraits of the great pharaohs of the Twelfth Dynasty poignantly reflect the concern and anxiety with which they lived.

Egyptians had lost that vision of the Old Kingdom wherein the land was a perfect and inviolable paradise. The literature of the Middle Kingdom demonstrates the change in attitude. Among the most popular literary forms were "instructions" to various kings, such as the *Instruction of King Merykare* or the *Instruction of Amenemhet*. This literature is characterized by cynicism and resignation. A pharaoh must trust no one: not a brother, not a friend, not intimate companions. He must crush the ambitions of local

> Middle Kingdom Egyptians viewed the world beyond their borders with suspicion and fear.

THE PROPHECIES OF NEFERTY

This text presents itself as a prophecy, pronounced during the Old Kingdom, foretelling the disasters that would strike Egypt during the First Intermediate Period. In fact, it was composed during the Middle Kingdom, shortly after the death of the pharaoh Amenembet I, the founder of the Twelfth Dynasty. By contrasting the disorders that preceded Amenembet's reign with the peace that he established, the document seeks to justify Amenembet's usurpation of the throne and perhaps to legitimize his son's succession, after Amenembet was murdered by his own palace guard.

Arise, oh my heart! Weep for this land wherein you were born! Falsehood is as the flood, and behold, evil is spoken with impunity. . . . The land perishes, and there is no one who cares for it. There is no one who speaks out, no one who makes lament. . . . Perished and gone are those joyful places, the fish ponds where dwell fish-eating birds, ponds alive with fish and fowl. All joy has been driven out, and the land is plunged into anguish by those voracious Asiatics who rove throughout the land. Foes have appeared in the east, Asiatics have entered Egypt. We have no (border) fortress, for foreigners now hold it, and there is no one to heed who the plunderers are. One may expect attack by night; the fortress will be breached and sleep driven from all eyes. . . . The land is destitute, although its rulers are numerous; it is ruined, but its taxes are immense. Sparse is the grain, but great is the measure, for it is distributed as if it were abundant.

But then there shall come a king from the south. His name will be Ameny, justified. He will be the son of a woman of Ta-Sety [Nubia], an offspring of the royal house of Nekhen. He shall receive the White Crown, he shall wear the Red Crown; he shall unite the Two Powers. . . . The people of his time will rejoice, for this son of a man will establish his name for ever and eternity. . . . The Asiatics will fall before his sword, the Libyans will fall before his fire; rebels will fall before his wrath, and enemies will fall through awe of him. . . . Then Ma'at will return to her throne, and Chaos will be driven off. Joyful will he be who will see (these things), he who will serve the king.

William Kelly Simpson, ed., *The Literature of Ancient Egypt: An Anthology of Stories, Instructions, Stelae, Autobiographies, and Poetry,* 3rd ed. (New Haven, Conn., and London, 2003), pp. 214–220.

QUESTIONS FOR ANALYSIS

1. In what ways does the "Prophecies of Neferty" highlight the types of anxieties felt by Middle Kingdom Egyptians? What caused these anxieties?

nobles with ruthless ferocity, and he must always be on the lookout for potential trouble. In return for his exertions on behalf of his people, he should expect neither gratitude nor reward; he should expect only that each new year will bring new dangers and more pressing challenges both at home and abroad. Egyptian chauvinism continued; but their confident isolationism had been shattered.

Although the attitude of Middle Kingdom Egyptians may strike us as overwrought, their feelings of insecurity were justified. Egyptians recognized that they had been drawn, slowly and unwillingly, into a much wider world. But precisely because Egypt remained a highly distinct culture unto itself, this wider world beyond the frontiers of the Two Lands appeared all the more alien, frightening, and potentially dangerous. Middle Kingdom

Sesostris III (1870–1831 B.C.E.). This powerful Twelfth-Dynasty pharaoh led military campaigns into Nubia, constructed massive, garrisoned fortresses along the Nile, and dug new waterways near Aswan. More than 100 portrait busts of Sesostris survive, all with similar features. The overhanging brow, deep-set eyes, and drawn-down mouth are all intended to communicate the enormous burden of responsibility the pharaoh bore as the ruler of all Egypt.

pharaohs were greatly alarmed by the growing power and imperial ambitions of Hammurabi of Babylon. They would soon discover, however, that even greater dangers lay much closer to home.

CONCLUSION

Starting around 11,000 B.C.E., human beings in the eastern Mediterranean world began to make a slow transition from hunter-gatherer societies into settled agricultural and pastoral communities. With the ability to produce and store surpluses, larger villages began to emerge, allowing both a greater degree of functional specialization and a wider differentiation in wealth and status among individuals and families. In Sumer, where the first cities

emerged during the fourth millennium B.C.E., cities were also religious centers with elaborate temple complexes and shrines to the city's gods. By around 2500 B.C.E., a sophisticated form of writing, known as cuneiform, had emerged as an important tool in trade and in the management of these temple complexes.

The third millennium B.C.E. saw the emergence of larger city-states, with more intense warfare between them. The Mesopotamian city-states were now led by kings who claimed divine sanction for their rule and whose power and wealth set them farther and farther apart from their subjects. Around 2350 B.C.E., Sumerian political life was transformed by the Semitic-speaking Akkadians, whose conquests resulted in the creation of the first true empire in world history. This empire would become the model future rulers of Mesopotamia would aspire to emulate.

Despite its political vicissitudes, Mesopotamian civilization remained true to its Sumerian roots for thousands of years. Cuneiform continued as the basic script in which the peoples of the Near East wrote their languages; and although Sumerian itself ceased to be a spoken language around 2000 B.C.E., it remained a language of literature and education for many centuries after it had passed from daily usage. New peoples moved into the region, but by and large they adapted themselves to the patterns of urban life established in Sumer centuries before. They absorbed its heritage and accommodated themselves to its political and religious traditions.

In Egypt, the other major center of Near Eastern civilization during these centuries, political consolidation occurred around 3000 B.C.E., a process assisted by the unique importance of the Nile River system. From that time on, Egypt would be ruled by a powerful, highly centralized bureaucracy, headed by pharaohs whom their people regarded as living gods. But despite the divisions between Upper and Lower Egypt, Egypt in the Old and Middle Kingdoms was never an empire maintained through conquest. It was a highly unified but deeply parochial society, capable of mobilizing resources on a massive scale, but almost always for internal purposes.

Behind these differences in outlook lay fundamental differences in the ecology of these two civilizations. Unlike the Sumerians, the Egyptians did not have to struggle to wrest a precarious living from a forbidding environment. So long as the annual flooding of the Nile occurred, Egyptians could feed themselves easily, with a relative minimum of social tension. This fact lent an air of confidence and ease to Egyptian art that is wholly lacking in Mesopotamia.

In what ways did patterns of development in early Egypt differ from those in Sumer?

SELECTED READINGS   47

These two civilizations have many similarities. During the third millennium, both underwent a process of political consolidation, an elaboration of religious life, and a melding of religious and political leadership. Both engaged in massive building projects; and both mobilized resources on an enormous scale for temples, monuments, and irrigation projects. At the same time, however, each of these civilizations developed an inward focus, verging on parochialism. Although they had some trade relations with each other, and some technology transfers probably took place, there were few significant political or cultural interactions between them. For all intents and purposes, they inhabited separate worlds. This relative isolation was about to change, however. The next millennium would see the emergence of large-scale, land-based empires in the Near Eastern world that would transform life in Mesopotamia, Egypt, and the lands that lay between them. These are the developments we examine in Chapter Two.

KEY TERMS

Sargon	Neolithic	Gilgamesh	Ubaid	Hammurabi
Sumerians	Fertile Crescent	Imhotep	cuneiform	

SELECTED READINGS

Aldred, Cyril. *The Egyptians*. 3d ed. London, 1998. An indispensable, lively overview of Egyptian culture and history by one of the great masters of Egyptology.

Baines, J., and J. Málek. *Atlas of Ancient Egypt*. Rev. ed. New York, 2000. A reliable, well-illustrated survey, with excellent maps.

Bottéro, Jean. *Everyday Life in Ancient Mesopotamia*. Trans. Antonia Nevill. Baltimore, Md., 2001. A wide-ranging, interdisciplinary account by an acknowledged master.

Bottéro, Jean. *Religion in Ancient Mesopotamia*. Chicago, 2001. An accessible, engaging survey.

George, Andrew, trans. *The Epic of Gilgamesh: A New Translation. The Babylonian Epic Poem and Other Texts in Akkadian and Sumerian*. New York and London, 1999. The newest and most reliable translation, which carefully distinguishes the chronological "layers" of this famous text; also includes many related texts.

Hodder, Ian. *The Leopard's Tale: Revealing the Mysteries of Çatalhöyük*. London and New York, 2006. The most up-to-date account of this fascinating archaeological site, written for general readers by the director of the excavation.

Hornung, Erik. *History of Ancient Egypt: An Introduction*. Ithaca, N.Y., 1999. Concise and authoritative.

Kemp, Barry J. *Ancient Egypt: Anatomy of a Civilization*. London, 1989. An imaginative examination of Egyptian social and intellectual history.

Leick, Gwendolyn. *The Babylonians: An Introduction*. London and New York, 2002. A wide-ranging survey of Babylonian civilization across the centuries.

Lichteim, Miriam. *Ancient Egyptian Literature: A Book of Readings*. 3 vols. Berkeley, Calif., 1973–1980. A compilation used by students and scholars alike.

McDowell, A.G. *Village Life in Ancient Egypt: Laundry Lists and Love Songs*. Oxford, 1999. A fascinating collection of translated texts recovered from an Egyptian peasant village, dating from 1539 to 1075 B.C.E.

Mertz, Barbara. *Red Land, Black Land: Daily Life in Ancient Egypt*. Rev. ed. New York, 1990. Emphasizes the role of the Nile and the forbidding natural environment of Egypt.

Pollock, Susan. *Ancient Mesopotamia*. Cambridge, 1999. An advanced textbook that draws on theoretical anthropology to interpret Mesopotamian civilization up to 2100 B.C.E.

Redford, Donald B., ed. *The Oxford Encyclopedia of Ancient Egypt*. 3 vols. New York, 2001. An indispensible reference work, intended for specialists and beginners.

Roaf, Michael. *Cultural Atlas of Mesopotamia and the Ancient Near East*. New York, 1990. An informative, authoritative, and lavishly illustrated guide, with excellent maps.

Robins, Gay. *The Art of Ancient Egypt*. London, 1997. An excellent survey, now the standard account.

Shafer, Byron E., ed. *Religion in Ancient Egypt: Gods, Myths, and Personal Practice*. London, 1991. A scholarly examination of Egyptian belief and ritual, with contributions from leading authorities. Excellent bibliographies.

Shaw, Ian, ed. *The Oxford History of Ancient Egypt*. Oxford, 2000. An outstanding collaborative survey of Egyptian history from the Stone Age to c. 300 C.E., with excellent bibliographical essays.

Snell, Daniel C., ed. *A Companion to the Ancient Near East*. Oxford, 2005. A topical survey of recent scholarly work, particularly strong on society, economy, and culture.

Chapter TWO

GODS AND EMPIRES IN THE ANCIENT NEAR EAST, 1700–500 B.C.E.

I N THE SECOND MILLENNIUM B.C.E., the ancient Near East was transformed by the
arrival of new population groups and by the emergence of extensive, land-based
empires built up through systematic military conquest. These migrations and conquests left a great deal of destruction and upheaval in their wake. But they also led to
widespread cultural assimilation, deepening economic integration, and the emergence
of an international system encompassing most of the eastern Mediterranean world.

The Late Bronze Age (1500–1200 B.C.E.) in particular was a period of intensifying
diplomacy, trade, and internationalism. The two great imperial powers of this age
were New Kingdom Egypt and the Hittite Empire of Anatolia (modern-day Turkey).
Between these two empires, however, a constellation of smaller states emerged along
the eastern Mediterranean coast, fully engaged in the burgeoning trade and cosmopolitan culture of the age. By the thirteenth century, nations from the southern Balkans
to the western fringes of Iran had been drawn into a wide-ranging web of cultural
and economic relationships. By 1250 B.C.E., these early states depended in great
measure on each other for their prosperity.

This international system proved more fragile than its participants had imagined.
Around 1200 B.C.E., a new wave of invasions emanating from the Aegean (ab-JEE-ahn)
Sea brought political and economic collapse from Greece to Egypt and led to the
destruction of nearly every great empire of the Late Bronze Age. Centuries-old centers of political, economic, and military power—not to mention great cultural
achievement—were wiped out. As a result, we enter a new world around the turn of
the first millennium B.C.E., organized along profoundly different lines from the great
empires of the Near Eastern past.

In the new age that was dawning, iron would slowly replace bronze as the primary
component of tools and weapons. New, larger, and more brutal empires would emerge

FOCUS QUESTIONS

• What impact did Indo-European-speaking peoples have on the patterns of Near Eastern life?

• In what ways did New Kingdom Egypt differ
from the Old and Middle Kingdoms?

• What were the principal features of the Late
Bronze Age international system?

• How similar was Mycenaean culture to Minoan
culture?

• Why did Phoenician cities prosper during the
Early Iron Age?

• What were the foundations of Assyrian imperial power?

• In what ways did the Persian Empire differ
from its Near East predecessors? How would
you account for those differences?

• What developments marked the Hebrew transition from polytheism to monotheism?

and new ideas about gods and their relationship to humanity would begin to displace older ones. In the Iron Age Near East, two of the Western world's most enduring religious traditions—Judaism and Zoroastrianism *(zoor-oh-AHS-tree-uh-nihz-uhm)*—were born, fundamentally altering conceptions of religion, politics, ethics, and the relationship between humanity and the natural world. The Iron Age would prove a fateful historical crossroads for Western civilizations, as elements both old and new combined to reconfigure the ancient Near Eastern world.

THE INDO-EUROPEAN MIGRATIONS

What impact did Indo-European-speaking peoples have on the patterns of Near Eastern life?

In 1786 Sir William Jones, a British judge serving in India, made a discovery that transformed knowledge about prehistory and began the formal study of historical linguistics. Turning his spare time toward the study of Sanskrit, the ancient language from which the predominant languages of the South Asian subcontinent derive, Jones discovered that Sanskrit shares features of grammar and vocabulary with Latin and ancient Greek to an extent inexplicable by sheer coincidence. His interest piqued, he then examined the early Germanic tongue called Gothic, the ancient Celtic languages of Europe, and Old Persian and found that they too exhibited marked similarities to Sanskrit. He concluded that all these languages must have evolved from a common but now-extinct linguistic source. Within another generation the ancient language whose existence Jones had hypothesized, and the later languages derived from it, would be labeled Indo-European, reflecting their wide distribution from India to Ireland.

Scholars have done much since Jones to increase our understanding of the Indo-European languages and their speakers. But much remains controversial. Was an original form of the language, Proto-Indo-European (PIE), spoken by a single population at some point in time? If so, when and where? How did Indo-European spread? By conquest? By trade and exchange? By simple migration and slow infiltration? Or by means of a wave-of-advance model, whereby PIE-speaking agriculturalists slowly spread their language(s) as they sought out new land to farm and established new set-

tlements? Can their diffusion be traced archaeologically by the presence of characteristic pottery types and burial practices, or are such things not correlated with linguistic change? At the moment, we have no definitive answers to any of these questions.

It is certain, however, that Indo-European linguistic forms began to appear in the Near East and eastern Mediterranean shortly after 2000 B.C.E., when speakers of early forms of Persian and Sanskrit made their way into and across the Iranian plateau, and the Hittites arrived in their historical homeland in central Anatolia. Around this same time, another group of Indo-European-speaking peoples began to move into the Aegean basin, combining with indigenous linguistic groups to produce an early form of Greek. Other Indo-European speakers went east; some may even have reached western China.

The Indo-Europeans were not the only new peoples moving into the Near East during this period. Semitic-speaking peoples were also entering the region, beginning with the Akkadians and continuing with the Amorites, the Assyrians, the Phoenicians *(feh-NEE-shuhns)*, and the Canaanites. The impact of these migrations was enormous. From the second millennium onward, Western civilizations would be dominated by cultures speaking Semitic or Indo-European languages. But despite the upheavals they caused, these newcomers were not apocalyptic destroyers who wiped the slate clean. However rude they may have been when they first came into contact with the older civilizations of the Near East, they generally accommodated themselves quickly, spreading and developing already established patterns of urban life and organization.

THE RISE OF ANATOLIA

As we saw in Chapter One, urban civilization took shape first in southern and central Mesopotamia, in the regions known as Sumer and Akkad. Farther north, however, the Assyrians also adopted the urban model and played a key role in introducing it into the neighboring region of Anatolia. This mountainous region possessed astonishing natural wealth, but its bountiful resources went largely untapped by the Sumerians and the Akkadians. It was the Assyrians who blazed economic trails into the region and accelerated the pace of urban life and society in Anatolia, especially in the central region known in classical times as Cappadocia. By so doing, the Assyrians laid the foundations for Anatolia's emergence as a major imperial power in later centuries.

By 1900 B.C.E., Assyrian caravan merchants had begun to organize extensive trade networks between

WHAT IMPACT DID INDO-EUROPEAN-SPEAKING PEOPLES HAVE ON THE PATTERNS OF NEAR EASTERN LIFE?

THE INDO-EUROPEAN MIGRATIONS   51

Mesopotamia and Anatolia, as well as within Anatolia itself. But the Assyrians did not seek military gains in the region. Instead, they entered into understandings with the local Cappadocian rulers, who reigned from strongholds not dissimilar to the great villages of the late Neolithic Period. Assyrian merchants relied on the military protection of these local potentates, while they organized the trade that made the rulers of Cappadocia and other parts of Anatolia rich. The great Assyrian families sorted themselves into boards of trade, determining prices, assigning trade routes, and sharing out profits among themselves. Although they usually lived in the outlying districts of the great centers of Anatolian trade, Assyrians nonetheless had a profound impact on Cappadocian culture. Assyrians served as advisers and officeholders to kings and married into important urban families. In the process, they carried Mesopotamian civilization and its trappings into both Anatolia and northern Syria.

HITTITES AND KASSITES

In the wake of this Assyrian-assisted urbanization, new kingdoms and new population groups emerged throughout Anatolia, northern Syria, and Mesopotamia. The Hittites were one of a number of Indo-European-speaking peoples who settled in Anatolia around 2000 B.C.E. Over the course of several centuries, however, the Hittites imposed themselves and their language on the other peoples of the region as a ruling minority class.

Hittite rulers established themselves in the growing cities of central Anatolia, particularly in Cappadocia.

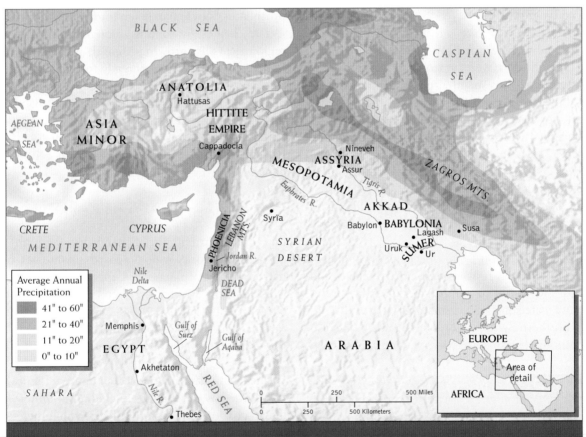

THE BRONZE AGE NEAR EAST

Notice the geographical relationship among the older centers of Sumer and Egypt and among the newer civilizations such as Babylonia, Assyria, Phoenicia, and the Hittite Empire of Anatolia. Which of the emerging cultures were most likely to show the strongest Sumerian influence, and why? Which cultures were more likely to become conduits for trade, and what was their role in spreading the Mesopotamian urban model? Also note where the major civilizations are located, and examine them in relation to the average rainfall displayed in the inset map. What does the comparison demonstrate regarding the relationship between urban activity and environmental factors such as climate?

But they remained politically independent of one another until about 1700 B.C.E., when the ruler of one of these city-states integrated the Hittites into a larger kingdom. About fifty years later, a subsequent ruler of this larger kingdom organized his warrior nobility into a more efficient military machine; expanded the frontiers of the kingdom; and captured Hattusas, a strategic mountain stronghold that dominated the area. To reflect his new capital, the king changed his name to Hattusilis; he was the founder of the Hittite Old Kingdom.

The Hittites fielded some of the greatest armies of the Bronze Age, reflecting their intensely militaristic culture. A great part of any Hittite king's energies was necessarily devoted to warfare and to maintaining control over his fractious and ambitious warrior nobility. Alongside this military tradition, the Hittites adopted enthusiastically the practices of those they conquered, adapting cuneiform to write their own language and using it to record their laws.

Under Hattusilis I, the Hittites extended their power throughout the Anatolian plateau. Like the Assyrians, the Hittites were anxious to control trade routes throughout this wealthy region. Unlike the Assyrians, however, the Hittites also aimed at military conquest. For both reasons, the Hittites were particularly concerned with overland trade routes for copper and arsenic, the latter being one of the metals that can be alloyed with copper to produce bronze, the basic material of tools and weapons in the second millennium B.C.E. Combining plunder with trade, Hattusilis transformed his Hittite kingdom into an economic and military power.

Hattusilis's grandson and successor, Mursilis I (c. 1620–1590 B.C.E.) proved even more dynamic and ambitious. He sought to control the upper Euphrates and to subjugate some of the small but powerful kingdoms of northern Syria. In a brilliant campaign he also drove southeastward into Mesopotamia, collecting

CHRONOLOGY

TRANSFORMATIONS IN THE ANCIENT NEAR EAST

Semitic peoples invade Sumer	2000 B.C.E.
Indo-European peoples arrive in the Near East	2000 B.C.E.
Assyrians organize trade networks	1900 B.C.E.
Rise of Old Babylonian Empire	1800 B.C.E.
Creation of Hittite, Kassite, and Mitanni kingdoms	1800–1400 B.C.E.

booty and tribute until he found himself before the fabled gates of Babylon. Babylon was still the center of an Amorite kingdom, now ruled by a distant descendent of Hammurabi. Mursilis I captured and sacked Babylon in 1595 B.C.E., collecting for himself the accumulated riches of centuries. He then withdrew and abandoned the ruined city to its fate.

What followed was something of a dark age in the history of the Near East, largely because our sources for the period are very poor. The hundred years after the sack of Babylon seem to have been characterized by upheaval. A group known as the Kassites moved into the devastated city and seized control of the Old Babylonian Kingdom. The origins and language of the Kassites are highly debatable; but like many previous invaders of Mesopotamia, the Kassites assimilated themselves speedily to the older civilization they found there. They presided over a largely peaceful and prosperous Babylonian realm for the next 500 years.

The Hittites, by contrast, brought no stability to the region. Mursilis's growing strength alarmed the warrior nobility, who were not yet ready to cede so much prestige and authority to a centralized kingship. Mursilis may have been impelled to abandon Babylon so quickly because of trouble at home; shortly after his arrival back in his capital Hattusas, he fell victim to a palace conspiracy. After his assassination, Hittite power ebbed for the next century or so.

THE KINGDOM OF MITANNI

Like the Hittites, the Mitannians were an Indo-European minority who imposed themselves on the native peoples of the upper Euphrates as a ruling class. This warrior aristocracy then penetrated northern Syria around 1550 B.C.E. Assuming control of territories that Mursilis had already undermined, they knitted the upper Euphrates and northern Syria into a single kingdom, the Kingdom of the Mitanni.

The Mitannians introduced a number of innovations into Near Eastern warfare, including a lighter, horse-drawn chariot with spoked wheels, which they used to carry archers around the field and strike terror into their enemies. They were also masters of horse training and cavalry tactics. For a time, these innovations allowed them to keep the Hittites in check to their west, while to their east they reduced the powerful Assyrians to the status of a vassal kingdom. But when the opponents of the Mitannians began employing chariots themselves and using scale armor to protect both infantry and cavalry, the military balance of power quickly turned against Mitanni.

In what ways did New Kingdom Egypt differ from the Old and Middle Kingdoms?

Egypt in the Second Millennium B.C.E.   53

A Near Eastern War Chariot. Here the chariot is used for lion hunting by the Assyrian king Assurnasirpal II (883–859 B.C.E.).

Weakened by a dynastic dispute in the mid-fourteenth century, Mitanni finally collapsed in the face of renewed Hittite aggression. The Hittites allowed a rump kingdom of Mitanni to survive as a buffer state between themselves and Assyria. But the destruction of the Mitannian kingdom in northern Syria meant that the Egyptians and Hittites now embroiled themselves directly in military conflict with each other, with enormous consequences for both empires. To understand this conflict, however, and the emergence of New Kingdom Egypt as an imperial power, we need to return to Egypt at the end of the Middle Kingdom.

Egypt in the Second Millennium B.C.E.

In what ways did New Kingdom Egypt differ from the Old and Middle Kingdoms?

Egypt too was transformed by the dynamic changes occurring in the early second millennium B.C.E. During the First Intermediate Period, foreigners from western Asia and Nubia penetrated the "center of the cosmos" in large numbers. Some came as immigrants; others were brought to Egypt as mercenaries. This strategy preserved Egypt from large-scale armed invasion. But when the pharaohs of the Middle Kingdom restored central government from Thebes soon after 2000

B.C.E., the confidence Old Kingdom Egyptians had once placed in *ma'at* had been irreparably shattered. Middle Kingdom Egypt was an anxious, uncertain place, uncomfortably aware that it could no longer safely ignore events beyond its borders but not yet committed to being an actively interventionist imperial power in Nubia, Sinai, and the Middle East. Commercial contacts with all these regions were growing, as was Egyptian influence within them. But none of this made Middle Kingdom Egyptians feel secure behind their walls.

Their concerns only deepened after 1700 B.C.E., when Egypt was conquered by a foreign army called the Hyksos (*HIHK-sohs;* a Greek version of the Egyptian *heka khaswt,* or "rulers of foreign lands"). These invaders—whose exact origins are unknown but who may have been Semitic speakers from the Middle East—carved out a kingdom in the eastern delta and projected their authority over most of Lower Egypt. With this conquest, Egyptian central authority once again dissolved, and the country entered into the Second Intermediate Period (c. 1650–1550 B.C.E.)

We know relatively little about the Hyksos, and much of what we do know derives from later, highly propagandistic Egyptian accounts of them. Clearly, however, they took over the machinery of pharaonic government in the north and took steps to legitimize their rule in accordance with Egyptian precedents. Some Hyksos rulers even incorporated the name of Ra into their own names, despite later Egyptian references to them as "those who ruled without Ra." But the Hyksos also retained much of their foreign material culture

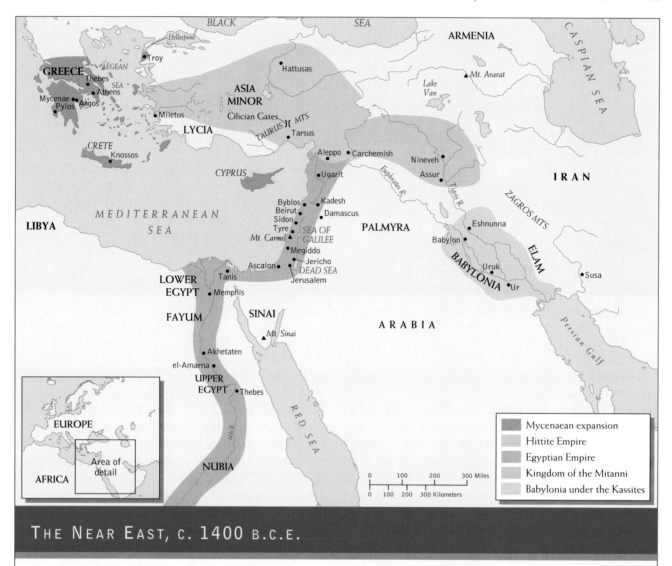

THE NEAR EAST, C. 1400 B.C.E.

How has the spread of the urban model forced us to widen our geographical focus? Notice the proliferation of cities along the eastern shores of the Mediterranean; what does this tell us about the rise of the trade in this region of the Near East? Consider the centrality of this region in relation to the major empires of the time as well as the emerging civilization of the Aegean basin. How crucial is trade becoming to the world of the Late Bronze Age?

while maintaining close economic and diplomatic ties with the Aegean world, Syria, and Palestine. In Upper Egypt, by contrast, Hyksos control was less complete. Here, a native pharaonic regime maintained a tenuous independence at Thebes, although it too sometimes had to acknowledge the suzerainty of the foreigners in the north.

Hyksos domination lasted about a century and later came to be regarded as the great shame of Egyptian national history, despite the fact that, following Mursilis's assassination, the Hyksos established Egypt as the most significant power in the Near East. In the

south, however, the Hyksos conquest did allow the Nubians to break free and found an independent kingdom called Kush. This Nubian kingdom was a much greater threat to the native dynasty at Thebes than to the Hyksos in the north; it therefore provided additional incentive to the southern pharaohs to play on nationalist sentiment by launching wars of liberation against the "hated" Hyksos in the north. Ultimately, this strategy succeeded. By the end of the sixteenth century B.C.E., the southern pharaoh Ahmose had driven out the invaders, establishing the Eighteenth Dynasty and a new era in Egyptian history.

In what ways did New Kingdom Egypt differ from the Old and Middle Kingdoms?

Egypt in the Second Millennium b.c.e.   55

The New Kingdom (1550–1075 b.c.e.)

During the New Kingdom, Egyptian civilization reached the height of its magnificence and power. Although established forms of religious, economic, cultural, and political life continued, the New Kingdom also marked a radical departure in Egyptian history and culture. The dynamism of the New Kingdom—particularly its focus on imperialism and militarism—changed the very fabric of Egyptian life.

Pharaonic Rule in the Eighteenth Dynasty

The Eighteenth Dynasty ruled Egypt for more than two and a half centuries. Striking developments took place during this period. Most important, we witness the rise of a new type of nobility in Egyptian society, an aristocracy of military commanders and leaders whose wealth was acquired through war: not just plunder but also crown lands (and the slaves to work them) received from the pharaoh as rewards for their service.

The Eighteenth Dynasty was forged in battle. Ahmose (AH-mohs) himself won fame as the man who expelled the Hyksos and reunited Egypt. Soon thereafter, Ahmose and his heirs turned their attention south, toward Nubia. By this time, gold had become the standard for Near Eastern commerce and finance. If Egypt was to prosper in this world, it needed to control the rich Nubian gold mines. Under Thutmose I (c. 1504–1492 b.c.e.), the Egyptians also penetrated to the northeast, driving deep into Palestine and Syria. This great pharaoh claimed to rule the land from beyond the Fourth Cataract in the south to the banks of the Euphrates in the north. No previous pharaoh had ever held sway over so much territory. Nor was his success merely fleeting. In the north, the Egyptians would sustain a serious military presence in the Middle and Near East for the next 400 years. In the south, pharaohs undertook massive temple and statuary building projects in the Sudan more than a century after Thutmose's death.

New Kingdom pharaohs pursued an ambitious strategy of defense through offense. The embarrassment of Hyksos domination translated itself into a steely determination to prevent such an episode from occurring ever again, not by preparing for the day when more invaders might arrive but by actively projecting Egyptian strength into regions from which danger might come. The Egyptians also learned something about battle tactics from the Hyksos, employing the horse-drawn battle chariots the Hyksos had used against them to devastating effect against their new enemies.

Queen Hatshepsut and Thutmose III

Military activity peaked during the fifteenth century, in the wake of what could have been a crisis for the Eighteenth Dynasty. In 1479 b.c.e., Thutmose II died young, leaving a youth as his heir, the future Thutmose III. In the past, such incidents often led to instability and even changes of dynasty. On this occasion, however, family politics and a remarkable personality served as a force for cohesion and continuity. It was customary in the New Kingdom for the pharaoh—himself a manifestation of a god—to marry as his official "queen" only someone worthy of such a union. This meant the daughter of the previous pharaoh, and thus a sister or half–sister of the new pharaoh. Such brother–sister unions do not appear to have been the routine way to produce heirs: pharaohs also had a vast harem of subsidiary wives and concubines with whom to procreate. Such was the case with Thutmose II, whose queen was his sister Hatshepsut (baht-SHEHP-soot), but whose son and heir had been borne to him by another wife.

On the death of Thutmose II, Hatshepsut became regent for her stepson/nephew Thutmose III, who was still a small child when his father died. It was common practice during the New Kingdom for a widowed queen to act as regent in such cases, a reflection of the relatively high status that Egyptian women generally enjoyed compared with women in other ancient Near Eastern cultures. What is remarkable in Hatshepsut's case, however, is that within a few years of becoming regent, she declared herself to be pharaoh in her own right and began to portray herself in pictures and statuary with the masculine figure and false beard characteristic of male pharaohs (see illustration on p. 56). She did not pretend to be a man—inscriptions on her statues and portraits almost always indicate her true sex—nor did she usurp the throne from Thutmose III, who continued to be described as her co-ruler. But during the twenty years that she and Thutmose III reigned together, she was clearly the ruling force within the government, and it was her statecraft that proved crucial to the continuing success of the Eighteenth Dynasty and of Egypt. Several successful military campaigns were recorded under her name, and the arts flourished, setting standards that Egyptian craftsmen would emulate for a thousand years. She is best remembered, however, for her spectacular mortuary temple, still one

Hatshepsut as Pharaoh, c. 1460 B.C.E. Notice her masculine figure and ceremonial beard.

own death some thirty years later. In the final decade of his rule, he began to deface Hatshepsut's monuments and to remove her name from inscriptions, to create the impression that he had always ruled alone. But despite his ingratitude, Thutmose III was a great pharaoh. He launched a total of seventeen military campaigns, penetrating deep into Palestine and capturing the strategic town of Megiddo (Armageddon). He followed up that famous victory by seizing vital port towns along the Syrian coast. His son Amenhotep II (c. 1428–1400 B.C.E.) continued his father's Syrian conquests, crossing the Orontes River and extending Egyptian control into the Syrian interior.

These campaigns were intended not only to augment Egyptian strength but also to undermine the economic and military might of the Kingdom of Mitanni. In this they were entirely successful, but to ironic effect. Mitanni was now so weakened that the Hittites were able to reassert themselves and their ambitions in Syria and Mesopotamia. The Assyrians also broke free of their vassalage to Mitanni, and would ultimately prove a far more aggressive foe to Egypt than Mitanni had ever been. At the time, however, the long-term consequences of Mitanni's demise were not apparent, and the Eighteenth Dynasty basked in the glow of its military accomplishments.

In addition to the tremendous power and wealth accrued by Thutmose III and Amenhotep (AH-mehn-HOH-tehp) II, the Eighteenth Dynasty also established a reputation for determination and ruthlessness. Amenhotep III (c. 1390–1352 B.C.E.), known as "The Magnificent," found therefore that he did not have to pursue military conquests equal to his grandfather's or his great-grandfather's. By and large, his task was to administer effectively the territories Egypt had already

of the wonders of ancient Egyptian architecture, where both she and her father, Thutmose I, were ultimately buried. Thereafter, few New Kingdom pharaohs advertised so openly their burial site (see illustration at right). Instead, it became customary for pharaohs to be buried in the famous Valley of the Kings near Thebes—a remote location where, it was hoped, their tombs would remain hidden and thus safe from robbers.

Thutmose III remained in Hatshepsut's shadow until her death in 1458 B.C.E. Thereafter, he ruled alone until his

The Mortuary Temple of Hatshepsut. Unlike the pharaohs of the Old Kingdom, Eighteenth Dynasty pharaohs often chose to be buried in specially built mortuary temples rather than in a separate pyramid or at another gravesite. The innovative architectural style of Hatshepsut's temple, which was built into an excavated hillside and set off by rows of columns, was widely imitated by later pharaohs.

IN WHAT WAYS DID NEW KINGDOM EGYPT DIFFER FROM THE OLD AND MIDDLE KINGDOMS?

EGYPT IN THE SECOND MILLENNIUM B.C.E. 57

acquired and to exploit the economic and diplomatic advantages it had already won. That Amenhotep III did with skill and aplomb. The pharaoh received tribute from far and wide, including a land called Keftiu (usually identified with the biblical Caphtor, and most likely the island of Crete). He concluded treaties with Mitanni and received at least two Mitannian princesses into his harem. So long as Amenhotep III remained vigilant and tended to his diplomatic interests, he had no need to do more than enjoy the benefits of his predecessors' endeavors.

RELIGIOUS CHANGE AND RELIGIOUS CHALLENGE

The great conquests of the Eighteenth Dynasty brought mind-boggling amounts of spoil to Egypt. Much of this wealth went to the personal glorification of the pharaoh through grand temples, tombs, and other monuments and the ubiquitous royal stelae (inscribed stone monuments) that provide us with so much historical information. Another significant portion of the booty went to the military aristocracy that made such conquests possible. But vast quantities of wealth still remained, which went to propitiate the gods with offerings of thanks for Egypt's bountiful success. Temples throughout Egypt enjoyed the profits of conquest, and as the temples became wealthy and powerful, so too did their priests. But no temple complex made out quite so well as that dedicated to Amon in Thebes.

THE TEMPLE OF AMON

Thebes was the capital of the Eighteenth Dynasty; as the city's patron deity, Amon therefore played an important role in the dynasty's own self-image. But Amon was more than just a local god. He had grown in stature and popularity throughout Middle Kingdom Egypt. Increasingly he was identified or incorporated with the sun god, Ra (thus the common New Kingdom formulation Amon-Ra). By 1550 B.C.E., the Amon-Ra godhead had become something like an Egyptian national god, around whom the Thebes-based Eighteenth Dynasty rallied Egypt against the Hyksos. The

dynasty therefore had much reason for gratitude to Amon, whose support had been crucial in their efforts to reunite Egypt.

The favor shown to the priesthood of Amon at Thebes, coupled with the tremendous wealth deposited there, made the priests of Amon a formidable political and economic force. Indeed, by the end of Amenhotep III's reign, the priesthood of Amon enjoyed political clout surpassing even that of the officer class, and the priests themselves had become influential persons at the pharaoh's court. The dynasty's prestige was completely intertwined with that of Amon; but it was starting to be unclear whose was the controlling voice in this relationship.

THE REIGN OF AKHENATEN (1352–1336 B.C.E.)

All these factors came to a fateful intersection in one of history's most intriguing figures. On the death of Amenhotep III, his son succeeded him as Amenhotep IV. Amenhotep IV showed an early inclination toward sun-god worship, as distinct from worship of Amon: Amenhotep's earliest inscriptions exalt Ra, not as an aspect of Amon but as a discrete divinity, visibly manifest in the light of the sun's rays. In his dedications to Ra, Amenhotep laid aside the traditional depiction of a falcon (or a falcon-headed man), replacing it with the *Aten*, the sun

The Temple of Amon at Karnak. This massive temple, just outside Thebes, testifies to the Eighteenth Dynasty's support for the god Amon and his priests.

Akhenaten, His Wife Nefertiti, and Their Children. The Aten is depicted here as a sun disk, raining down power on the royal family.

the *ankh*, the Egyptian hieroglyph for "life." Akhenaten also had himself portrayed in curious fashion, although it is unclear whether the uniqueness of this representation was due to ideology or to features of his own anatomy. In a complete departure from the confident virility of his ancestors, Akhenaten is always shown with an elongated head and limbs, an exaggerated nose, and exceptionally full lips. His eyes are catlike, and the pronounced protrusion of his belly is somewhat reminiscent of female fertility figurines. The overall effect is of a certain androgyny whose significance is unclear. Akhenaten was clearly a family man and had himself pictured as the most human of pharaohs, enjoying the company of his beautiful queen, Nefertiti, as they played with their children. Indeed, a palpable sense of humanity—an almost "common" touch compared with earlier pharaonic art—pervades the Amarna Period.

disk itself, its rays of light reaching toward earth. But soon the new pharaoh went much farther. He changed his name from Amenhotep ("Amon Is Pleased") to Akhenaten (*AH-keh-NAH-ton*; "He Who Is Profitable to the Aten"). As Akhenaten, he built a new capital halfway between Memphis in the north and Thebes in the south, calling it Akhetaten ("The Horizon of the Aten"), the modern site of el-Amarna. The short-lived but quite distinctive culture of Akhenaten's reign is therefore known as the Amarna Period.

Akhenaten introduced a variety of innovations into Egyptian religion and culture. Aten worship was more stringently monotheistic than the evolving view of Amon had been. Whereas Theban Amon theology recognized other gods as aspects of Amon, Akhenaten recognized only the life-giving power of light, embodied by the Aten. Unlike the ancient Egyptian deities, Aten could not be captured or represented in art. The image of the Aten, a dominant feature of Amarna-Period art, is therefore an elaboration of the Egyptian hieroglyph for "light."

Life and its affirmation were central aspects of Akhenaten's religious revolution. The Aten was often depicted with a hand at the end of each ray of light. In each hand was

Great controversy still surrounds Akhenaten's motives for this religious and cultural revolution. Some see him as the world's first revolutionary intellectual, who applied imaginative force and exceptional insight to break the bonds of tradition. Others see him as a reactionary, troubled by the absorption of Ra into Amon and attempting to reassert the traditional worship of the sun. Others see him as a cagey politician, who sought to undermine the influence of Amon's priests by instituting a new religious regime.

These various explanations are not mutually exclusive. Politics and religion were inextricably intertwined in the ancient Near East, as they would be in Greece and Rome also. His own dynasty's particular identification with Amon guaranteed, however, that Akhenaten's religious revolution would also be politically revolutionary, because it would require that the legitimacy of his dynasty be reestablished on new foundations.

But despite the tremendous energy Akhenaten expended in trying to achieve this revolution, most Egyptians did not follow him. Traditional Egyptian religion may seem bewilderingly complex to us, but

Nefertiti. The famous portrait bust executed in Akhenaten's studios at el-Amarna.

AKHENATEN, THE HEBREWS, AND MONOTHEISM

One of the great literary monuments of Akhenaten's religious revolution was his "Hymn to the Aten," extolling the life-affirming virtues of the god he sought to place atop the Egyptian religious system. Although Akhenaten's experiment failed in Egypt, it may have played a significant role in shaping the religious traditions of other societies throughout the Levant, including the ancient Hebrews.

HYMN TO THE ATEN

You appear beautifully on the horizon of the heavens, living Aten, the beginning of life! When you arise on the eastern horizon, you have filled every land with your beauty. You are gracious, great, glistening, and high over every land; your rays encompass the lands to the limit of all that you have made. . . . When you set in the western horizon, the land is in darkness, in the manner of death. They sleep in a room, with heads wrapped up, nor sees one eye the other. All their goods which are under their heads might be stolen, but they would not perceive it. . . .

Creator of seed in women, you who makes fluid into man, who maintains the son in the womb of his mother, who soothes him with that which stills his weeping, you nurse even in the womb, who gives breath to sustain all that he has made! . . . How manifold it is, that which you have made! They are hidden from the face of man. O sole god, like whom there is no other! You created the world according to your desire, while you were alone: all men, cattle, and wild beasts, whatever is on earth, going upon its feet, and what is on high, flying with its wings. . . .

The world came into being by your hand, according to how you have made them. When you have risen they live, when you set they die. You are lifetime itself, for one lives only through you.

James B. Pritchard, ed., *Ancient Near Eastern Texts Relating to the Bible*, 3rd rev. ed. with supplement (based on). (Princeton, N.J., 1969), pp. 370–371

PSALM 104

Bless the Lord, O my soul. . . . You are clothed with honor and majesty, wrapped in light as with a garment. You stretch out the heavens like a tent. . . . You set the earth on its foundations, so that it shall never be shaken. You cover it with the deep as with a garment; the waters stood above the mountains. At your rebuke they flee. . . . You cause the grass to grow for the cattle, and plants for people to use, to bring forth food from the earth, and wine to gladden the human heart. You make darkness, and it is night, when all the animals of the forest come creeping out. The young lions roar for their prey, seeking their food from God.

O Lord, how manifold are your works! In wisdom you have made them all; the earth is full of your creatures. . . . These all look to you to give them food in due season; when you give them to them, they gather it up; when you open your hand, they are filled with good things. When you hide your face, they are dismayed; when you take away your breath they die.

The New Oxford Annotated Bible (Oxford, 1994).

QUESTIONS FOR ANALYSIS

1. How does the "Hymn to the Aten" express monotheism? Why would a pharaoh, already acknowledged as divine, attempt a religious revolution? Why did he fail?
2. The praise of the greatness of God in Psalm 104 suggests an order in Creation. How does this idea of order differ from the *ma'at* of the Egyptians? How does the monotheism of the Hebrews differ from that of Akhenaten? Why did polytheism emerge before monotheism?

Egyptians apparently preferred it to the remote, benevolent but impersonal god their pharaoh was offering them. The powerful priesthood of Amon also put up strenuous resistance to Akhenaten's religious innovations. To make matters worse, Akhenaten seems also to have been largely uninterested in military affairs. His exertions on behalf of his new god may even have encouraged him to neglect Egypt's interests abroad. The revolts that followed cost him the support of his military nobility. Akhenaten's revolution failed.

His failure was the harbinger of the Eighteenth Dynasty's decline. He was ultimately succeeded by Tutankhaten, who changed his name to Tutankhamon (the famous King Tut) to reflect his rejection of Akhenaten's heresies and the restoration of the god Amon and his priesthood. The new capital city of Akhetaten was abandoned and its memory cursed; its neglect thereafter is largely responsible for its high state of preservation today. Akhenaten, meanwhile, was remembered only as "Akhetaten's heretic." His monuments were destroyed throughout the land. But the damage had been done. Egypt's position in the wider world had eroded at an astonishing rate since the outset of Akhenaten's reign, and his heir was a sickly teenager. After the early death of the boy king,

confusion ensued until an important military commander named Horemheb assumed the throne in 1323 B.C.E. Horemheb maintained stability for nearly three decades but had no heir. He passed his position to another general, Rameses I, the founder of the Nineteenth Dynasty, which would restore Egypt to glory in the Near East.

THE INTERNATIONAL SYSTEM OF THE LATE BRONZE AGE

What were the principal features of the Late Bronze Age international system?

The fates of many nations after 1500 B.C.E., including Egypt, are intelligible only within the wider context of international relations. For the next 300 years, the destinies of the various Near Eastern kingdoms became increasingly interwoven as an international system developed throughout the eastern and central Mediterranean.

The Late Bronze Age was an age of superpowers. As we have seen, the great pharaohs of the Eighteenth Dynasty had transformed Egypt into a conquering state, feared and respected throughout the Near East. But the pressure they applied to the Kingdom of Mitanni allowed the emergence of a revived Hittite Empire after 1450 B.C.E. It was the Hittites who dealt Mitanni the most crushing blows, succeeding once again to the mantle of northern power in the region. The Assyrians also revived, and the Kassite kingdom of Babylonia remained a significant force in the economic and military relationships of the age. Between these imperial powers numerous smaller but important states emerged, concentrated along the coasts and river valleys of Syria but extending westward to Cyprus and the Aegean Sea.

INTERNATIONAL DIPLOMACY

Though warfare remained a characteristic feature of international relations, the most powerful states of the Late Bronze Age evolved a balance of power that helped stabilize trade

Throne of "King Tut." Dating from about 1330 B.C.E., this relief in gold and silver is part of the back of the young pharaoh's throne. The relaxed lounging position of the pharaoh's right arm is typical of the stylistic informality of the period.

WHAT WERE THE PRINCIPAL FEATURES OF THE LATE BRONZE AGE INTERNATIONAL SYSTEM?

THE INTERNATIONAL SYSTEM OF THE LATE BRONZE AGE   61

and diplomacy as the period progressed. Internationalism had existed to some degree since the age of Hammurabi. In the fourteenth century, however, an international standard developed, within which many nations and their leaders came to understand that security and stability helped trade flourish, whereas war could prove disruptive and—in the long run—unprofitable for all concerned.

The archives discovered by modern archaeologists at Akhenaten's abandoned capital of el-Amarna provide us with a clear picture of this international diplomatic standard. Flurries of correspondence took place between the leaders of nations, sometimes over great matters but often simply to stay in touch with one another. A language of diplomatic rank developed, in which the most powerful rulers would address one another as "brother," while the princes of lesser states showed their deference and respect to the pharaoh, the Hittite king, and other powerful sovereigns by calling them "father." Breach of this protocol could cause great offense. When a thirteenth-century Assyrian king presumed to address the Hittite ruler Hattusilis III as "brother," he received a stern rebuke: "What is this you keep saying about 'brotherhood'? You and I were born of the same mother? Far from it; even as my father and grandfather were not in the habit of writing about 'brotherhood' to the King of Assyria, so stop writing to me about brotherhood and Great Kingship!"

Rulers of the period exchanged lavish gifts and entered into marriage alliances with each other. Professional envoys journeyed back and forth between the centers of Near Eastern power, conveying valuable gifts and handling politically sensitive missions. In Egypt, such emissaries were often merchants, sent not only to handle matters of diplomacy but also to explore the possibility of trade opportunities for the pharaoh.

INTERNATIONAL TRADE

Trade became an increasingly important aspect of international relations during the Late Bronze Age. Seaborne trade flourished up and down the coast of the eastern Mediterranean, allowing smaller, seaside centers such as Ugarit and Byblos to become powerful merchant city-states. The great coastal cities of the eastern Mediterranean became wealthy entrepôts for the exchange of a bewildering variety of goods. A single merchant vessel's cargo might contain scores of distinct items originating anywhere from the interior of Africa to the Baltic Sea, as is demonstrated by the

breathtaking shipwreck discovered at Ulu Burun. At the same time, the great states of the region continued to exploit their control of overland trade routes, relying more than ever on moving goods to an international market. Trade was rapidly becoming the lifeline of all these Late Bronze Age empires.

Busy and lucrative trade routes also served as a conduit for artistic motifs, literary and religious ideas, architectural forms, and ideas in tool making and weapon smithing. Whereas in the past such influences spread slowly and unevenly, the societies of the Late Bronze Age were now developing a very self-conscious cosmopolitanism. Egyptians delighted in Canaanite glass, Bronze Age Greeks prized Egyptian amulets, and the merchants of Ugarit admired and desired Greek pottery and wool. Examples of such active longing for the products of other cultures could be endlessly multiplied.

A Husband and Wife from New Kingdom Egypt. Marriages had no connection to religious life in Egypt, and divorces were common. But as this carving illustrates, Egyptians expected that spouses would be bound to each other by love and affection and not merely by duty or obligation.

THE MYCENAEANS AND THE NEAR EAST: THE TAWAGALAWAS LETTER

Around 1260 B.C.E., the Hittite king Hattusilis III sent the following missive to the "King of Ahhiyawa," taken by most scholars to be the Hittite equivalent of one early Greek label for themselves, "Akhaiwoi," the Achaeans of Homer. In the letter we see the respect Hattusilis accorded this Greek king as well as the adventures of one Greek warrior upsetting economic and political arrangements in the western Anatolian city of Millawanda (classical Miletus).

I have to complain of the insolent and treacherous conduct of one Tawagalawas. We came into contact in the land of Lukka [Lycia, in western Anatolia], and he offered to become a vassal of the Hittite Empire. I agreed, and sent an officer of most exalted rank to conduct him to my presence: he had the audacity to complain that the officer's rank was not exalted enough; he insulted my ambassador in public, and demanded that he be declared vassal-king there and then without the formality of interview. Very well: I order him, if he desires to become a vassal of mine, to make sure that no troops of his are found in Ijalanda when I arrive there. And what do I find when I arrive in Ijalanda?—the troops of Tawagalawas, fighting on the side of my enemies. I defeat them, take many prisoners . . . scrupulously leaving the fortress of Atrija intact out of respect for my treaty with you. Now a Hittite subject, Pijamaradus by name, steals my 7,000 prisoners, and makes off to your city of Millawanda. I command him to return to me: he disobeys. I write to you: you send a surly message unaccompanied by gift or greeting, to say that you have ordered your representative in Millawanda, a certain Atpas, to deliver Pijamaradus up. Nothing happens, so I go fetch him. I enter your city of Millawanda, for I have something to say to Pijamaradus, and it would be well that your subjects there should hear me say it. But my visit is not a success. I ask for Tawagalawas: he is not at home. I should like to see Pijamaradus: he has gone to sea. You refer me to your representative Atpas: I find that both he and his brother are married to daughters of Pijamaradus; they are not likely to give me satisfaction or to give you an unbiased account of these transactions. . . . Are you aware, and is it with your blessing, that Pijamaradus is going round saying that he intends to leave his wife and family, and incidentally my 7,000 prisoners, under your protection while he makes continual inroads on my dominion? . . . Do not let him use Ahhiyawa as a base for operations against me. You and I are friends. There has been no quarrel between us since we came to terms in the matter of Wilusa [very possibly the Greek Ilios, the territory of Troy]: the trouble there was my fault, and I promise it will not happen again. As for my military occupation of Millawanda, please regard it as a friendly visit. . . . [As for the problems between us], I suggest that the fault may not lie with ourselves but with our messengers; let us bring them to trial, cut off their heads, mutilate their bodies, and live henceforth in perfect friendship.

Denys Page, *History and the Homeric Iliad* (Berkeley, Calif., 1959), pp. 11–12.

QUESTIONS FOR ANALYSIS

1. Why did the Hittite king Hattusilis III have such strong feelings about honor and respect? Why did he write his complaint letter to the king of Ahhiyawa?
2. Are certain standards of behavior expected of civilized nations? Which ancient states adhered to them and which did not? What sanctions or penalties could be imposed on them by the international system?

WHAT WERE THE PRINCIPAL FEATURES OF THE LATE BRONZE AGE INTERNATIONAL SYSTEM?

THE INTERNATIONAL SYSTEM OF THE LATE BRONZE AGE   63

The Temple of Ramses II at Abu-Simbel. Each of these colossal figures stands sixty-six feet high. The smaller figures at Ramses' feet represent his wives and relatives. Ramses II (1279–1213 B.C.E.) lived to be more than ninety years old and fathered at least 100 children.

This cosmopolitanism was particularly marked in large merchants towns. At Ugarit, the swirl of commerce and the multiplicity of languages may have been what impelled its citizens to develop a simpler form of writing than the cuneiform system still current throughout most of the Near East. An Ugaritic alphabet appears at the end of the Bronze Age, consisting of about thirty symbols representing consonants. Vowels had to be inferred, potentially sacrificing some clarity between reader and audience; but the alphabetic system was more easily mastered and more flexible than cuneiform for recording the heady pace of trade in the city's harbors.

The search for markets, resources, and trade routes heightened economic competition but also promoted greater understanding among cultures. After a great battle between Egypt and the Hittites near Kadesh (c. 1275 B.C.E.), the powerful Nineteenth Dynasty pharaoh Ramses II realized that more was to be gained through peaceful relations with his northern neighbors than through endless warfare. The treaty he established with the Hittites served as a pillar of geopolitical stability in the region and allowed further economic integration to develop during the thirteenth century B.C.E. But greater integration also meant greater mutual dependence. If one economy suffered in this international system, the effects of that decline were sure to be felt elsewhere.

> The search for markets, resources, and trade routes heightened economic competition but also promoted greater understanding among cultures.

EXPANSION AND FRAGILITY

Over the course of several centuries, this integrated system of trade and diplomacy grew to encompass the entire eastern Mediterranean world. The farther this system spread, however, the more fragile it became. This fragility was heightened by the fact that many of these new markets involved societies whose own degree of civilization was modest at best. Their rough, warlike spirit made them unreliable partners but even more dangerous adversaries within this integrated, Late Bronze Age world. We turn now to their story.

AEGEAN CIVILIZATION: MINOANS AND MYCENAEANS

How similar was Mycenaean culture to Minoan culture?

The ancient Greeks treasured many legends about their heroic and distant past, when great men mingled with the gods, and powerful kingdoms—larger and stronger than any known to the later world of classical Greece—contended for power and glory. For a long time, however, scholars dismissed any suggestion that there might be a prehistoric component of Greek experience. Tales of the Trojan War, Theseus and the Minotaur, and the great adventures of Odysseus were regarded as myths—products of Greek imagination that reflected no historical truth whatsoever. Greek history therefore began in 776 B.C.E., the date of the first recorded Olympic Games. Bronze Age Greece was thought to be a backwater that played no role in the contemporary Mediterranean world or in the later, glorious history of classical Greece.

Mycenaean Death Mask, c. 1550–1500 B.C.E. When Schliemann discovered this gold mask in the shaft graves at Mycenae, he immediately declared it to be the mask of Agamemnon. Although certainly royal, the mask itself is too early to have been Agamemnon's.

In the late nineteenth century, an amateur archaeologist named Heinrich Schliemann became convinced that these myths were in fact historical accounts. Using the epic poems of Homer as his guide, he found the site of the great city of Troy near the coast of northwest Anatolia. He also discovered a number of once-powerful citadels on the Greek mainland, including the home of the legendary king Agamemnon at Mycenae (*MY-seh-nee*). Soon thereafter, Sir Arthur Evans found a great palace at Knossos on the island of Crete that predated any of the major citadel centers on the Greek mainland. Evans dubbed this wealthy and magnificent culture "Minoan," after King Minos, the powerful ruler who later Greeks believed had once dominated the Aegean Sea from Crete.

Although many of their initial conclusions were erroneous, the discoveries by Schliemann and Evans forced a reevaluation of Greek civilization and its roots. It is now clear that Bronze Age Greece (or, as it is more often termed, Mycenaean Greece, after the mighty kingdom of Greek myth based at Mycenae) was an important and well-integrated part of the Mediterranean world during the second millennium B.C.E. and that the foundations of classical Greek culture were established during this period. Because of the nature of the evidence, much about these cultures remains mysterious. But their importance can no longer be denied.

THE MINOAN THALASSOCRACY

In the fifth century B.C.E. the Athenian historian Thucydides wrote that King Minos had ruled a "thalassocracy"—that is, a sea empire. Until Evans's discoveries at Knossos, Thucydides' claim seemed fanciful. It now appears that he was substantially correct.

Minoan civilization flourished from about 1900 to 1500 B.C.E., making it contemporary with Middle Kingdom Egypt and the Hittite Old Kingdom. But the outlines of a developing civilization on Crete are visible as early as 2500 B.C.E. By 1900 B.C.E. this culture had developed a high degree of material and architectural sophistication; as a result, the period of Minoan civilization from 1900 to 1500 B.C.E. is sometimes referred to as the "Palace Age." Like its Near Eastern counterparts, the Minoan palace sat at the center of a redistributive economy, collecting resources and then parceling them out as the palace bureaucracy saw fit. It was also a production center for textiles, pottery, and metalwork. Several impressive palace complexes from this period have been found on Crete. The brilliant palace at Knossos, with its famous murals and indoor plumbing, covered several acres and comprised hundreds of rooms and winding hallways. It was obvious at once to excavators that these palaces could have inspired the famous story of the Labyrinth, in which the Greek hero Theseus slew the terrible Minotaur.

Minoan success depended on overseas trade. They exchanged a range of exotic goods with Egypt, southwest Anatolia, and Cyprus. Through Cyprus, the Minoans also had contacts with the Levantine coast of modern-day Lebanon and Syria. In addition, artistic influences traveled along these trade routes; among much else, Minoan-style paintings appear regularly from this period in the Nile Delta and in the Levant.

Minoan palaces were not fortified. This fact, coupled with the playful, idyllic scenes depicted in Minoan frescoes (frescoes are paintings executed in fresh plaster), led early-twentieth-century scholars to conclude that the Minoans were a peace-loving people, interested only in the exchange of goods. Evidence of Minoan devotion to a mother goddess, often portrayed with serpents in her hands as she tamed a wild beast at either side, was seen as further proof of the peaceful nature of Minoan life and as evidence for a strong matriarchal element in Minoan culture.

Such romanticism now appears misplaced. Crete's geographical isolation lessened the need for strong land defenses, but the Minoans' extensive trade networks strongly suggest that they possessed a powerful navy, capable of stopping a hostile force before it reached Cretan shores. Evidence for a bull cult—typically associated with patriarchal societies in the Near East—abounds within Minoan civilization. There is also evidence that human sacrifice was a regular part of Minoan religious life. Women were certainly important in Minoan culture, not least as producers of the famous Minoan textiles, one of the island's principal exports. But it now seems unlikely that the Minoans were in any sense either a peaceful or a matriarchal society.

Much about the Minoans remains unknown. They had a written language, which Evans dubbed Linear A to distinguish it from another script, similar but clearly distinct and far better represented, which he discovered and called Linear B. But although we can determine that the language recorded in Linear A is non-Indo-European, we still cannot translate it. Scholars must rely instead on pottery shards and other archaeological objects to determine how and when Minoan culture spread to the other islands and shores of the Aegean Sea.

Cretan Labyrinth Coin. According to legend, King Minos of Crete built a labyrinth to pen in the Minotaur, part man, part bull. This coin from about 300 B.C.E. shows the labyrinth as the emblem of Knossos.

One focus of Minoan commercial activity was clearly the mainland of Greece. The presence of a wide variety of Minoan objects there, including pottery, metalwork, and textiles, suggests the export of Minoan technologies, and perhaps even Minoan craftworkers, from Crete to the mainland. But the exact nature of the relationship between Minoan Crete and Mycenaean Greece remains controversial. Before 1600 B.C.E., the Minoans were clearly much more sophisticated than the mainland Greeks. As a result, they may have been able to dominate the inhabitants of Greece's rocky landscape, at least commercially and perhaps politically. The myth of Theseus and the Labyrinth claims that the hero went to Crete as a hostage, intending to free Athens from the heavy tribute laid on the city by King Minos. Might this story preserve a memory of a time when Crete did so dominate the Greeks of the mainland?

Close contacts between the Minoans and the mainland led to a variety of developments in Mycenaean Greece. The quality of material culture increased, and the mainland was drawn more tightly into the network of international commercial and diplomatic relationships that characterized the Near East during these centuries. The inhabitants of the mainland learned how to build great fortified

Minoan Snake Goddess. A statuette in ivory and gold discovered near the palace of Knossos and dating from 1550 B.C.E.

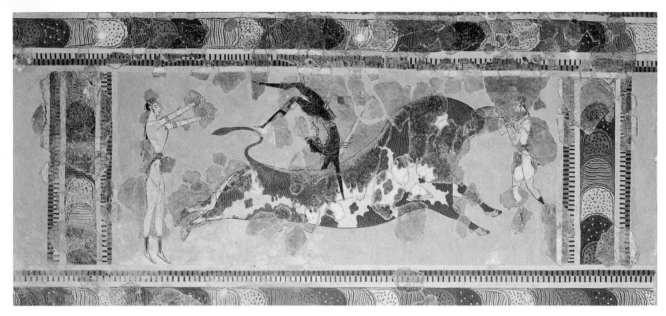

Minoan Mural, c. 1500 B.C.E. Although once thought to depict an actual athletic event, experts now agree that it is impossible to perform a somersault over the back of a charging bull. Some scholars think the mural depicts a constellation; others see it as evidence for a Minoan bull cult.

palaces, hybrids of the Minoan palaces and the imposing strongholds the Hittites favored. The Greeks also learned to write from the Minoans, taking Linear A and modifying it to suit their own language better. The resulting script is the one Evans called Linear B—the earliest written form of Greek.

THE MYCENAEANS

When Linear B was finally deciphered in the 1950s, it turned the world of Greek scholarship decisively toward a reckoning with the Bronze Age past. Until then, scholars could continue to wonder whether the impressive sites unearthed by Schliemann, Evans, and others had anything at all to do with the story of classical Greek civilization. That Linear B represented an ancient but unmistakably Greek dialect proved conclusively that Greek history stretched well back into the Bronze Age. But what role did the Mycenaean Greeks play in that story?

Greek-speaking Indo-Europeans entered Greece in several waves. An early period of immigration may have coincided with the destruction of several important sites in Greece around the turn of the second millennium B.C.E., and with the simultaneous appearance of new styles of architecture and pottery. Another significant displacement of peoples and material goods took place around 1600 B.C.E. These various Greek-speaking groups mingled with each other and with a native, non-Indo-European-speaking people known as the Pelasgians, whom they largely assimilated. But

there was never a single, decisive moment at which Greece became "Greek." As the eminent Mycenaean scholar John Chadwick has suggested, during the Middle and Late Bronze Age the Greeks were always in the process of *becoming* Greek.

Mycenaean civilization represents the culmination of this process. By 1500 B.C.E., powerful citadels dotted the Greek landscape, ruled by warriors who touted their martial prowess on their gravestones and had themselves buried with their implements of war. These early rulers no doubt based their authority on their ability to lead men successfully into battle and to reward their followers with plunder. The most suc-

Linear B Tablet from Knossos.

cessful of them managed to gain control of strategic sites from which they could exploit the major routes through Greece, while never straying too far from the sea, where they engaged in both trade and piracy. The line between trade and piracy was a fine one in the ancient world and would remain so until the nineteenth century of the common era. Like many other maritime peoples, ancient and modern, the Mycenaeans raided where they could and traded where they could not raid.

Over time, and perhaps under the influence of Minoan culture, the Mycenaean palace citadels developed into much more complex societies. Citadels served as both centers of government and warehouses for the storage and redistribution of economic surpluses. By the thirteenth century B.C.E., some rulers had carved out territorial kingdoms with as many as 100,000 inhabitants, dwarfing the typical Greek city-state of the Classical Period.

> Like many other maritime peoples, ancient and modern, the Mycenaeans raided where they could and traded where they could not raid.

These palace centers were an adaptation of a Near Eastern model; but their massive size was not ideally suited to the Greek landscape. In war also, Mycenaean imitation of Near Eastern examples had its limits. Although Mycenaean kings cherished the war chariots used by their Near Eastern contemporaries, such chariots were highly impractical on Greece's rocky terrain.

Despite these and other differences from their neighbors, the Mycenaean Greeks played an important role in the closing stages of the Near Eastern Bronze Age. By about 1400 B.C.E., they had subjugated the island of Crete, taking over Knossos and using it as a Mycenaean center; if the "Keftiu" mentioned by Amenhotep III is indeed Crete, he was probably negotiating with its Mycenaean conquerors. In western Anatolia, at least one Mycenaean king exercised enough influence for a Hittite king to address him as "my brother." The Mycenaeans also enjoyed great prestige

An Artist's Reconstruction of the Great Hall at Pylos. This great Mycenaean hall, with its central hearth, was the focus of life within the palace complex, which would also have included private apartments, storerooms, and meeting rooms.

EUROPE
Area of detail
AFRICA

THRACE

SEA OF MARMORA

CHALCIDICE

SAMOTHRACE

Olympus ▲

LEMNOS

Hellespont

Ilium (Troy) •

PHRYGIA

Ida ▲

MYSIA

ASIA MINOR

CORCYRA

Pelion ▲

LESBOS

ITHACA

Delphi •

EUBOEA

AEGEAN SEA

CHIOS

IONIA

LYDIA

IONIAN SEA

ACHAEA

Gulf of Corinth

Athens •

ATTICA

SAMOS

ARCADIA

Olympia •

Mycenae •

CYCLADES

DELOS

• Miletus

CARIA

PELOPONNESUS

• Sparta

MIRTOAN SEA

Pylos •

MELOS

MEDITERRANEAN

RHODES

SEA OF CRETE

Approximate range of Mycenaean culture

SEA

CRETE

0   50   100 Miles
0   50   100 Kilometers

▲ Idbi   • Knossos

MYCENAEAN GREECE

Note the mountainous landscape of Greece and how the peculiar shape of the region creates thousands of miles of coastline; consider that Greece is almost devoid of major rivers but that few places are far from the sight of the open sea. Notice that a map of "Greece" in antiquity always includes the western coast of Asia Minor as well as the islands of the Aegean. How would this dry, mountainous country surrounded by the sea potentially affect the nature of Greek civilization and its economic interests? Would the Near Eastern model be a good fit for Greece?

in the Near East as warriors and mercenaries. It was their combined activities as traders and raiders that made it possible for the Mycenaeans to support the huge populations of their citadels; by itself, the surrounding hinterland could not begin to sustain such numbers.

The political and commercial foundations of the Mycenaean world—a powerful palace, headed by a king who was also a war leader; a warrior aristocracy; a bureaucracy of local officials; state-regulated land holdings; a redistributive economy; large territorial kingdoms—were more typical of the contemporary Near Eastern world than they were of the Greek Classical Age. Nevertheless, we can trace important features of later Greek civilization back to the Mycenaeans, including of course the Greek language. The Linear B tablets speak of a social group with considerable economic and political rights, the *damos*; this may be the precursor of the *demos*, a popular group that sought full

CHRONOLOGY

CIVILIZATIONS OF THE LATE BRONZE AGE

Minoan civilization	1900–1500 B.C.E.
Mycenaean civilization	1600–1200 B.C.E.
Near Eastern international	
system	1550–1200 B.C.E.
New Kingdom Egypt	1550–1075 B.C.E.

political empowerment in many Greek cities later on. The tablets also preserve the names of several Greek gods familiar from the Classical Period, such as Zeus, Poseidon, Dionysos, and (possibly) Demeter; others, however, are absent or their identities are obscured behind completely different names. Perhaps most important, however, the Classical Greeks themselves believed that they were descended from these legendary Mycenaean forebears, whom they credited with superhuman achievements. In fact, later Greeks knew little about their Mycenaean ancestors; but the impact on the Greek imagination of what they thought they knew about them was considerable.

The Mycenaean world seems to have collapsed under its own weight around the end of the thirteenth century B.C.E. What triggered this collapse is impossible to say: natural disasters, drought, famine, disease, and social unrest have all been posited as causes. None of the theories can be proved or disproved in the current state of our knowledge. But the consequences of the Mycenaean collapse are clearer. Because it was such an integrated part of this international network of commercial, political, and military relationships, the reverberations from the Mycenaean world's collapse were felt across the entire Near East.

THE SEA PEOPLES AND THE END OF THE BRONZE AGE

As the Mycenaean world collapsed, a wave of destruction swept from north to south across the entire Near East. The nature of this devastation is obscure because it was the handiwork of a people so thorough that they obliterated everything in their path until they reached Egypt. Were it not for the narrow victory of Ramses III in about 1176 B.C.E., we might know nothing at all of the invaders who so suddenly unraveled the international system of the Late Bronze Age.

In an inscription and relief set up at Medinet Hebu to commemorate his victory, Ramses III referred to the invaders as the "Sea Peoples." Several of the groups he named as part of this coalition were familiar to the Egyptians, who had employed them as mercenaries or confronted them as mercenaries in the pay of other leaders. From Ramses' depiction of their battle gear and dress, it is also clear that many of the Sea Peoples were Aegean. Most notable of these were the Peleset, who, after their defeat by Egypt, withdrew to populate the coast of the region named after them, Palestine.

The arc of annihilation started in the north and may have helped trigger the final collapse of Mycenaean Greece. Disruption of the northern trade networks must have had a profound effect on the Mycenaean kingdoms, which would suddenly have been faced with an apocalyptic combination of overpopulation, drastic food shortages, and incessant warfare. A wave of desperate refugees must have fled the Aegean basin. The undermining of commerce in the north also devastated the economy of the Hittites, whose kingdom collapsed with astonishing rapidity. We catch only a few glimpses in our sources of a desperate Hittite king fighting to save Hattusas against myriad enemies.

Along the Mediterranean coast we find other clues. The king of Ugarit wrote a letter to his "brother" the king of Alashiya on Cyprus, begging his counterpart for immediate help. Poignantly, however, we have his letter only because the clay tablet on which it was written was baked hard in the fire that destroyed his palace. The letter was never sent. Ugarit was destroyed, and the Sea Peoples moved on.

The eruption of the Sea Peoples destroyed much of civilization as the Mediterranean world had known it. The destruction was not total. Cities did not all disappear, and trade did not vanish. But the Hittite Empire was gone, replaced by a bewildering variety of weak, short-lived principalities. The great cosmopolitan cities of the eastern Mediterranean coast lay in ruins, and new groups—sometimes contingents of the Sea Peoples—populated the seaboard. The citadels of Mycenaean Greece also collapsed. Depopulated by as much as 90 percent over the next century, Greece entered into a dark age of cultural and economic isolation that would last for the next 250 years. The Greeks would have to reinvent urbanism, in forms better suited to their unique environment.

Egypt of course survived the invasions, but with its major trading partners destroyed, it too went into a long decline. Assyria likewise suffered from the effects of the invasions. The next few centuries would see the Assyrians fighting for their very survival, while to the

Naval Battle between the Egyptians and the Sea Peoples from Medinet-Habu. Egyptian ships, on the left and lower right, surround those of the Sea Peoples, who appear to have been taken by surprise. The Egyptians carry rectangular shields and fire bows. The Sea Peoples use round shields, short swords, and long spears, indicative of their Aegean origins. The Philistines are distinguishable from the other Sea Peoples by their feathered headdresses.

south, the peaceful and prosperous rule of the Kassites also collapsed, along with Babylon's economy.

The centuries immediately after the Sea Peoples' invasion witnessed no great empires in the Near East. The international system of the Late Bronze Age, carefully elaborated over half a millennium, had disappeared. In the wake of its destruction, however, new traditions and new cultural experiments began to emerge. New political and religious configurations took shape, and a new metallurgical technology—based on iron—began to supplant the use of bronze. Out of the ashes of the Late Bronze Age, a more enduring, more vibrant cultural world arose, the culture of the Iron Age Near East.

THE SMALL-SCALE STATES OF THE EARLY IRON AGE

Why did Phoenician cities prosper during the Early Iron Age?

With the destruction of the superpower balance of the Late Bronze Age, the geopolitical map of the Near East changed significantly. In Anatolia, a patchwork of small, largely Indo-European realms emerged from the collapse of the Hittite Empire. Similar developments took place in the Levant, the eastern Mediterranean coastal area that today comprises Israel, Lebanon, and

parts of Syria. For centuries, this area had been controlled by either the Egyptians or the Hittites. With the collapse of both these empires, the resulting power vacuum in the region allowed new states to emerge. As political and military powers, the small-scale states of the Early Iron Age were at best second rate. However, they had a profound impact on the intellectual and religious development of Western civilizations.

THE PHOENICIANS

The Phoenicians were Canaanites who spoke a Semitic language closely related to Ugaritic, Hebrew, Amorite, and other West Semitic dialects. Their cultural and political roots lay firmly in the ancient Near East. Phoenician cities were all independent of one another; as in Sumer, a Phoenician's first loyalty was to his or her city, not to any abstract notion of being a Phoenician. In the Levantine homeland, each Phoenician city lived under its own hereditary royal government. In the Phoenicians' overseas colonies, however, a new type of government emerged, in which power was shared among a handful of elite families. This aristocratic form of government would become a model for many other western Mediterranean cities, including Rome.

During the Late Bronze Age, most Phoenician cities had been controlled by Egypt. The erosion of Egyptian imperial power after 1200 B.C.E. gave them the opportunity to capitalize on commercial advantages they had already established. One Phoenician city, Gubla, had been a teeming center of trade under Egyptian rule, particularly as an entrepôt for papyrus, the highly

WHY DID PHOENICIAN CITIES PROSPER DURING THE EARLY IRON AGE?

THE SMALL-SCALE STATES OF THE EARLY IRON AGE   71

prized Egyptian writing material. This connection with the papyrus trade continued during the Iron Age, so much so that the Greek name for the city, Byblos, became the basis for the Greek word *biblion*, meaning "book." The seabeds off the Phoenician coast yielded a valuable purple reddish dye from the murex snail—hence the Greek term *Phoenician*, which essentially means "purple people." Phoenician textiles commanded a high price everywhere their merchants went. So too did timber from the Anti-Lebanon Range (especially cedar) and the famous Canaanite glass. The Phoenicians also became expert metalworkers, ivory carvers, and shipbuilders.

PHOENICIAN CITIES

Tucked along a mountainous coast riven by deep valleys, Phoenician cities oriented themselves toward the sea. Phoenicians became famous as merchants and seafarers. They were also aggressive colonists, confronted by the dual pressures of commercial competition with one another and the limited carrying capacity of their surroundings. Phoenicians planted trading colonies across the Mediterranean. By the end of the tenth century B.C.E., Phoenician merchants were active from one end of the Mediterranean to the other and had probably begun to venture out into the Atlantic Ocean. We have good evidence that Phoenicians ventured as far as Brittany and Cornwall (the latter a good source of tin); the Greek historian Herodotus claims that Phoenician merchant-explorers circumnavigated Africa. At the end of the ninth century B.C.E., colonists from Tyre established Carthage in modern-day Tunisia. Carthage would ultimately become the preeminent power in the western Mediterranean, bringing it into conflict with Rome centuries later.

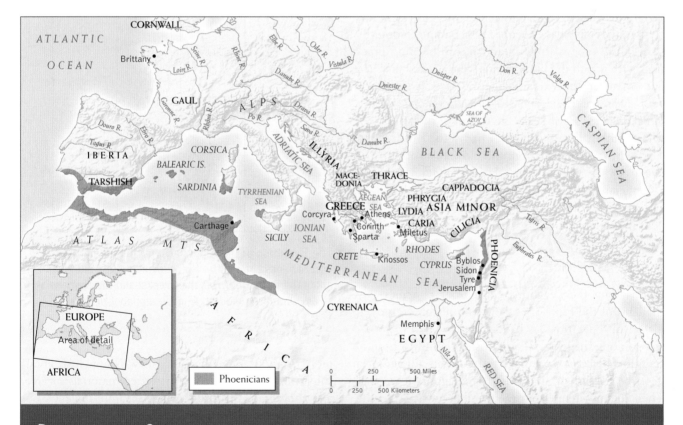

PHOENICIAN COLONIZATION

Examine the map and compare the more detailed one of Palestine on p. 74. Why would overseas colonization be of such crucial importance to Phoenician city-states? Consider in what ways the Phoenicians may have been partly driven by necessity. Notice that Phoenician colonization is concentrated in the western Mediterranean; then consider that the Phoenicians were the most active merchants of the eastern Mediterranean as well. What does their westward colonization imply about the Phoenicians' aims and the level of civilization in the West as compared with the East?

CULTURAL INFLUENCE

The widespread colonial and mercantile efforts of the Phoenicians meant that they influenced cultures across the Mediterranean. Among their early overseas trading partners were the Greeks. Here the Phoenicians may have played an important role in reintroducing urban life into the Greek world after the collapse of the Mycenaean citadels. They also brought with them a number of Near Eastern artistic and literary influences. Without question, however, the most important contribution the Phoenicians made to Greek life was their alphabet.

As we have seen, a thirty-character alphabet had evolved at Ugarit by the end of the Bronze Age. Around 1100 B.C.E., the Phoenicians refined this writing system to twenty-two characters. This simpler, more flexible writing system probably helped facilitate trade and accounting. Why they chose to share their invention with the previously illiterate Greeks is less certain; they may have sought to encourage among the Greeks the type of trading and record-keeping practices with which the Phoenicians were already familiar. But whatever the explanation, the Greeks remained very aware of their debt to the Phoenicians. Later Greek legends ascribed the invention of their alphabet to Cadmus, a Phoenician who had settled in Greece. The debt is also clear from the close relationship between Greek (alpha, beta, gamma, delta . . .) and Phoenician letter names (aleph, bayt, gimel, dalet . . .) and from the obvious similarities in letter shapes evident in the table at right.

THE PHILISTINES

South along the Levantine coast from Phoenicia lay the land of the Philistines. Few cultures have enjoyed historical reputations as bad as theirs. The Philistines were among the great villains of the Hebrew scriptural tradition. *Philistine* continues today as an adjective to describe a boorish, uncultured, and ignorant person. Their infamy stems from their unique position in the Levant at the beginning of the Iron Age, where as descendants of the Peleset—one of the Sea Peoples defeated by Ramses III—they settled, urbanized, and quickly gained the upper hand over their pastoralist neighbors in the region. Among those peoples were the Hebrews, for whom the Philistines were the great national enemy.

The Philistines retained a separate identity from the other peoples of the region for several generations; each new archaeological discovery roots this identity

Phoenician	Hebrew	Classical Greek	Modern Alphabetic
𐤀	א	A	A
𐤁	ב	B	B
𐤂	ג	Γ	G
𐤃	ד	Δ	D
𐤄	ה	E	E
Υ	ו	Y	V
I	ז	Z	Z
𐤇	ח	H	H
⊗	ט	Θ	T
𐤉	י	I	Y
𐤊	כ	K	K
𐤋	ל	Λ	L
𐤌	מ	M	M
𐤍	נ	N	N
‡	ס	Ξ	S
O	ע	O	O
𐤐	פ	Π	P
𐤑	צ		TZ
φ	ק		Q
𐤓	ר	P	R
W	ש	Σ	S
X	ת	T	T

The Evolution of the Alphabet. This table illustrates how letter shapes changed as the Phoenician alphabet was adapted by the Hebrews, the Greeks, and the Romans (from whom the modern English alphabet derives).

more firmly in their Aegean past. We know little about the Philistine language—few written materials survive, and they gradually adopted a Canaanite dialect—but their material culture, behavior, and organization all exhibit close affinities with the Mycenaean world. The Philistines introduced grapevines and olive trees to the Levant from the Aegean basin. With the profits from these industries, they created powerful armies that dominated the region in the twelfth and eleventh centuries B.C.E. They also established a monopoly over metal smithing in the southern Levant, making it virtually impossible for their enemies to forge their own weapons.

WHY DID PHOENICIAN CITIES PROSPER DURING THE EARLY IRON AGE?

THE SMALL-SCALE STATES OF THE EARLY IRON AGE   73

Philistine power was based on five great strongholds, the so-called Pentapolis: Gaza, Ashkelon, and Ashdod on the coast, Ekron and Gath inland. Less cities than citadels, these great Philistine centers are strikingly similar to the fortified palace centers of the Late Mycenaean world and appear to have served many of the same functions. From these heavily fortified citadels, the Philistines sought to dominate the surrounding countryside by organizing agricultural production and controlling major trade routes. An independent lord ruled over each Philistine citadel, and no doubt tensions and rivalries existed among them. But much like the heroes of Greek epic, the Philistines could set aside their differences to confederate for the purpose of waging war.

It is difficult to know the Philistines on their own terms because they have left virtually no written records. We know them primarily through the eyes of their Hebrew enemies, who at first feared them and later held them in contempt. Like other Near Eastern cultures, Hebrew historical tradition slandered its enemies, declaring, for example, that the Moabites and Ammonites were the descendants of Lot's incestuous union with his daughters, and decrying both Philistine and Phoenician cultural practices as "evil in the sight of the Lord." We should not be misled by such invective. The brutish arrogance of Goliath or the sexual treachery of Delilah, the two most infamous Philistines in the Hebrew Bible, offer no basis for sweeping conclusions about the character of Philistine society. Unfortunately, however, we have little else on which to base our evaluations.

The Hebrews had good reason to fear the Philistines. In the Late Bronze Age, these Aegean warriors were highly effective mercenaries; when they established themselves in the Levant, they quickly turned to the conquest and exploitation of their weaker, less well-organized neighbors. Philistine pressure on the central Hebrew hill country was constant, threatening the holy sanctuary at Shiloh, the resting place of the sacred Ark of the Covenant, which contained the original tablets of the law given by the Hebrew god Yahweh to Moses on Mount Sinai. In Hebrew tradition, the desperate tribes of Israel carried the Ark before them against the Philistines, only to lose it in battle and witness the destruction of Shiloh. The Philistines then established garrisons throughout the land of the Hebrews and denied them access to metallurgical technology. Meanwhile, they exacted tribute and, according to the biblical account, engaged in the typical abuses of an occupying people.

THE HEBREWS

We will have occasion at the end of this chapter to discuss the central feature of Hebrew cultural experience, the development of their monotheistic conception of divinity. In this section, we focus our attention on the political development of Hebrew society within the Iron Age Levant. In any discussion of Hebrew society, however, religious conceptions and practices can never be far from the surface. Like all ancient cultures, the Hebrews initially made little distinction between politics and religion. What set them apart, however, was their unusual theology and the effect it had on their development as a people. Were it not for the resilience of their religious tradition and the fundamental influence it has had on the subsequent development of Western civilizations, we would have little reason to discuss the early Hebrews at length. As it is, however, the Hebrews were one of the most important cultures in world history.

ORIGINS

We are blessed as historians with one of the unique achievements of the Hebrews: the Hebrew Bible, known to Christians as the Old Testament. The Bible is an unparalleled historical resource, full of extraordinary detail about cultural practices and historical events, as well as being a guide to the intellectual unfolding of the most important religious tradition of the Western world. It is not, however, a history as modern people would conceive of it. The Bible is a composite work, assembled over many centuries, mostly by unknown authors and compilers. Although it contains some ostensibly historical accounts, it is essentially a story about the relationship between a transcendent creator god and the Hebrews, whom he chose to be

CHRONOLOGY

DEVELOPMENT OF IRON AGE EMPIRES

Phoenicians gain independence from Egypt	1200 B.C.E.
Philistine military dominance	1100–1000 B.C.E.
Consolidation of the Kingdom of Israel	1000–973 B.C.E.
Revival of Assyrian power	883 B.C.E.
Persian defeat and annexation of Babylon	539 B.C.E.

his special people; of the covenant that was forged between them; and of the trials by which that relationship was repeatedly tested and reaffirmed.

The historical accounts contained in the first five books of the Bible are particularly problematic. Aside from the chronological difficulties posed by a series of impossibly long-lived patriarchs (Methusaleh, for example, is said to have lived for more than 900 years), much of this material appears to have been borrowed from other Near Eastern cultures. The Creation and flood stories have Sumerian parallels; the laws and practices of the patriarchs have clear Hurrian antecedents; and the tale of Moses' childhood is virtually a replica of Sargon's legend. Even the story of the exodus from Egypt is fraught with problems from a historical standpoint. Although the Book of Joshua claims that the Hebrews who returned from Egypt conquered and expelled the native Canaanites, archaeological and linguistic evidence suggests that the Hebrews were themselves essentially inland Canaanites, who may have merged with scattered Hebrew refugees from Egypt in the aftermath of the Sea Peoples' invasions but who for the most part had been continuously resident in Canaan for centuries. Important religious and cultural developments clearly occurred among the Hebrews of the second millennium B.C.E., but the first five books of the Bible have the look and feel of retrospective extrapolation and justification, not secure historical record.

Once we move into the so-called historical books of the Bible, the information becomes more credible; but it remains extremely difficult to confirm any of it from archaeological sources. In the Book of Judges, for example, the Hebrews appear as wandering pastoralists who were just beginning to establish permanent settlements around the springs and valleys that provided sustenance in an otherwise arid landscape. The Hebrews were organized into twelve tribes—extended clan units in which families owed mutual aid and protection to one another in times of war, cattle raiding, and judicial dispute. Each tribe was ruled over by a judge, who exercised the typical functions of authority in a clan-based society: war leadership, high priesthood, and dispute settlement. By the middle of the twelfth century B.C.E., these tribes had established some kind of rough territorial turf, those in the south calling themselves Judah, and those in the north Israel.

HEBREWS AND PHILISTINES

These collective labels should not mislead us. In practice, the Hebrew tribes had few effective mechanisms for concerted action, a fact made plain when the

THE HEBREW KINGDOM, C. 900 B.C.E.

Notice the scale of the map and consider the comparatively small size of this world. Why did the Philistines and Phoenicians present such a perceived cultural challenge to the Hebrews? What advantages did the Philistines and Phoenicians possess, geographically and otherwise? What political and religious consequences might have resulted from the division of the kingdom of Israel after the death of King Solomon, especially given the position of Jerusalem and the Temple in the south?

Philistines conquered the Levantine coastal region around 1050 B.C.E. Faced with the threat of extinction, the Hebrews put up desperate resistance from their bases in the hilly interior of the country. To meet the Philistine threat, however, a tighter, "national" form of government was needed. Accordingly, around 1025 B.C.E., Samuel, a tribal judge and holy man, selected a king named Saul to lead Hebrew resistance against the Philistines.

Saul, however, quickly provoked the resentment of Samuel, who withdrew his support from the embattled

WHY DID PHOENICIAN CITIES PROSPER DURING THE EARLY IRON AGE?

THE SMALL-SCALE STATES OF THE EARLY IRON AGE 75

king. Saul also proved an indifferent general. Although he blocked Philistine penetration into the hill country, he could not oust the Philistines from the valleys or coastal plains. So Samuel threw his support behind a young warrior, David, a member of Saul's court who now schemed actively to draw popular support away from Saul. Waging his own independent military campaigns, David achieved one triumph after another over the Philistines. In contrast, the armies of Saul met frequent reverses, which the biblical authors portrayed as divine retribution for Saul's own inadequacies. David, however, was not exactly a national patriot. When Saul finally drove him from his court, David first became an outlaw on the fringes of Hebrew and Philistine society, then a mercenary in Philistine service. It was as a Philistine mercenary that David fought against Saul in the climactic battle in which Saul was killed. Soon thereafter, David himself became king, first over Judah, his home territory, and later over Saul's home kingdom of Israel also.

CONSOLIDATION OF THE HEBREW KINGDOM

With David's ascension to the throne around 1000 B.C.E., the most glorious period in the political history of the ancient Hebrew kingdom began. David took advantage of a number of new developments to strengthen his kingdom. Most important, Egypt went into sharp decline at the very end of the eleventh century, weakening the Philistine economy and disrupting Philistine society. Through cunning, opportunism, and inspired leadership, David reduced the Philistines to an inconsequential strip of coastal land in the south. He also defeated the neighboring Moabites and Ammonites, extending his control east of the river Jordan and the Dead Sea. By David's death in 973 B.C.E., his kingdom stretched from the middle Euphrates in the north to the Gulf of Aqaba in the south, and from the Mediterranean coast in the west into the Syrian deserts beyond the river Jordan. Israel was now a serious force in the politics of the Near East, its status increased by the temporary weakness of its imperial neighbors Egypt and Assyria.

As David's power and prestige grew, he was able to impose on his subjects a highly unpopular system of taxation and forced labor. His goal was to build a glorious political and religious capital at Jerusalem, a Canaanite settlement that he transformed into the central city of his kingdom. It was a shrewd choice. As a newly conquered city, Jerusalem had no previous affiliation with any of Israel's twelve tribes and so stood outside the ancient rivalries among them. Geographically too, Jerusalem lay between the southern tribes of Judah (of which David was a member) and the northern tribes of Israel (from which Saul had come). David also took steps to exalt the city as a religious center by making Jerusalem the resting place of the sacred Ark of the Covenant and reorganizing the priesthood of the Hebrew god Yahweh. By these measures, he sought to forge a new national identity, focused on the House of David and its connections to Yahweh, that would transcend the old divisions between Israel and Judah.

THE REIGN OF KING SOLOMON (973–937 B.C.E.)

Continuing his father's policies but on a much grander scale, David's son King Solomon built a great temple complex at Jerusalem to house the sacred Ark of the Covenant. Such visible support of the Yahweh cult played particularly well with the writers of the Hebrew scripture, who portrayed Solomon's reign as a golden age for the Hebrews.

Despite his proverbial wisdom, however, Solomon was a ruthless and often brutal ruler whose promotion of the Yahweh cult coincided with a program of despotic rule and royal self-aggrandizement. Solomon kept an enormous harem of some 300 wives and 700 hundred concubines, many of them drawn from subject or allied peoples. His palace complex—of which the temple was a part—allowed him to rule in the grand style of ancient Near Eastern potentates. To finance his expensive tastes and programs, Solomon instituted a variety of oppressive taxation and administrative schemes. He imposed customs duties on the lucrative caravan trade that passed through his country. With the help of Hiram, the Phoenician king of Tyre, Solomon also constructed a commercial fleet based at the head of the Gulf of Aqaba. These ships plied the waters of the Red Sea and beyond, trading—among other commodities—the gold and copper mined by

CHRONOLOGY

THE TRANSFORMATION OF HEBREW SOCIETY

Early efforts to form national government	1025 B.C.E.
David crowned king of Israel	1000 B.C.E.
Split between Israel and Judah	924 B.C.E.
Fall of Judah and start of Babylonian Captivity	586 B.C.E.

TWO ACCOUNTS OF SAUL'S ANOINTING

When the judge Samuel anointed Saul as the first king of the Hebrews, he opened a new chapter in the political history of Israel. Saul's kingship was not a success, however, and Samuel ultimately declared against him, throwing his support behind Saul's rival (and son-in-law) David. These two quite different accounts of Saul's elevation by Samuel may reflect the tensions that later arose between the supporters of Saul and of David. The first account also suggests the ambivalence some Hebrew scribes and prophets felt about having a human king at all.

1 SAMUEL 8:4–22, 10:20–25

All the elders of Israel gathered together and [said to Samuel]: "You are old and your sons do not follow in your ways; appoint for us, then, a king to govern us, like other nations." But the thing displeased Samuel [who] prayed to the Lord, and the Lord said to Samuel, "Listen to the voice of the people in all that they say to you; for they have not rejected you, but they have rejected me from being king over them. Just as they have done to me, from the day I brought them up out of Egypt to this day, forsaking me and serving other gods, so they are also doing to you. Now then, listen to their voice; only—you shall solemnly warn them, and show them the ways of the king who shall reign over them." So Samuel reported all the words of the Lord to the people who were asking for a king. "These will be the ways of the king who will reign over you: he will take sons and appoint them to his chariots . . . he will take your daughters to be perfumers and cooks and bakers . . . he will take one-tenth of your grain and your vineyards and give it to his officers and courtiers . . . and one-tenth of your flocks, and you shall be his slaves." But the people refused to listen, and Samuel said to the people, "Each of you return to his home."

Then Samuel brought all the tribes of Israel near, and the tribe of Benjamin was chosen by lot. He brought the tribe of Benjamin near by its families . . . and Saul the son of Kish was chosen by lot. But when they sought him, he could not be found. So they inquired again of the Lord . . . and the Lord said, "See, he has hidden himself among the baggage." Then they ran and brought him from there. When he took his stand among the people, he was head and shoulders taller than any of them. Samuel said, "Do you see the one whom the Lord has chosen? There is no one like him among the people." And the people all shouted, "Long live the king!" Samuel told the people the rights and duties of the kingship; and he wrote them in a book and laid it up before the Lord.

1 SAMUEL 9:1–10:1

There was a man of Benjamin whose name was Kish . . . [who] had a son whose name was Saul, a handsome young man . . . he stood head and shoulders above everyone else. Now the donkeys of Kish had strayed. So Kish said to his son Saul, "Take one of the boys with you; go and look for the donkeys." . . . As they were entering [a] town, they saw Samuel coming out toward them on his way up to the shrine. Now the day before Saul came, the Lord revealed to Samuel, "Tomorrow about this time I will send you a man from the land of Benjamin, and you shall anoint him to be ruler over my people Israel. He shall save my people from the hand of the Philistines; for I have seen the suffering of my people, because their outcry has come to me." . . . Saul approached Samuel inside the gate and said, "Tell me please, where is the house of the seer?" Samuel answered Saul, "I am the seer, go up before me to the shrine. . . . As for your donkeys that were lost three days ago, give no further thought to them, for they have been found. And on whom is all Israel's desire fixed, if not on you and your ancestral house?" Saul answered, "I am only a Benjaminite, from the least of the tribes of Israel, and my family is the humblest of all the families of the tribe of Benjamin. Why then have you spoken of me this way?" . . . As they were going down to the outskirts of town, Samuel said to Saul, "Tell the boy to go on before us . . . that I may make known to you the word of God." Samuel took a vial of oil and poured it on [Saul's] head and kissed him; he said: "The Lord has anointed you ruler over his people Israel. You shall reign over the people of the Lord and you will save them from the hand of their enemies all around."

The New Oxford Annotated Bible (Oxford, 1994) (slightly adapted).

QUESTIONS FOR ANALYSIS

1. According to I Samuel 8:1–4, the sons of the prophet Samuel were dishonest judges, and the elders of Israel asked Samuel to appoint a king, "like [all] other nations have." Was this an expression of popular opinion? Or was it perhaps the view of a promonarchy party? Why were the Israelites unable to govern themselves and unwilling to rely on judges and prophets?
2. How does the brief biblical history of the three kings of united Israel present their personal strengths and weaknesses? How does it explain dangers to the state? Does that history show divine intervention?
3. The writers of Jewish scripture (priests and prophets) judged kings by their observance of the law, their zeal in fighting against competing religious cults, and their support of centralized worship at the temple in Jerusalem. How did this form of theocracy in ancient Israel compare to that in Egypt and Mesopotamia?

Solomon's slaves in the southern Negev. Wealth poured into Israel as never before.

But it was not enough. Solomon maintained a large standing army made up of conscripts from his own people, equipped with chariot and cavalry squadrons and powered by horses purchased abroad. To undertake his ambitious building program, Solomon required many of his subjects, particularly from the agricultural north, to perform forced labor four months out of every year. This level of oppression was too much for many Israelites. The north seethed with rebellion against the royal capital, and after Solomon's death, his son and successor was faced with revolt. Before long the united monarchy had split in two, the House of David ruling the southern Kingdom of Judah with its capital at Jerusalem, the ten northern tribes banding together into the Kingdom of Israel with its capital at Shechem.

THE NORTHERN AND SOUTHERN KINGDOMS

The split not only weakened the Hebrews politically but also had serious religious consequences. The first king of the northern state of Israel, Jeroboam I, hoped to stop the pilgrimages and dedications by the citizens of Israel at the Temple at Jerusalem, which drained resources from the more populous northern kingdom. He therefore revived two ancient sanctuaries at Dan and Bethel and appealed to the popular but theologically taboo symbolism of Canaanite worship. Jeroboam and his successors thus incurred the wrath of the temple-centered, pro-Judean compilers of the Hebrew Bible, who condemned them as idolaters. This, however, is a retrospective view. Both archaeology and the biblical account itself demonstrate that the cult of Yahweh was far from a monopoly in either the north or the south. Foreign ritual and worship, particularly of the Canaanite deities Ba'al and Asherah, remained a prominent feature of Hebrew religious life for several more centuries.

Although the two Hebrew kingdoms would maintain their independence for several centuries—the north until 722 B.C.E., the south until 586 B.C.E.—the changing political situation of the Near East made their divided state increasingly vulnerable. The united Hebrew monarchy created by David and Solomon arose at a time when the traditional imperial powers in the region were temporarily in eclipse. Within a few

Seal of Abdi, Servant of Hosea. An eighth-century B.C.E. Hebrew seal whose owner, Abdi, was a royal official for Hosea (732–722 B.C.E.), the last ruler of the Northern Kingdom of Israel. The winged sun disk on which the figure stands and the figure's strongly Egyptian appearance hint at the religious diversity of the Northern Kingdom in its final centuries.

generations of Solomon's death, however, the Hebrews and the other small states of the Near and Middle East would find themselves menaced by the revived Mesopotamia-based empire of the Assyrians.

THE ASSYRIAN EMPIRE

What were the foundations of Assyrian imperial power?

The Assyrians were a Semitic-speaking people whose homeland lay in northern Mesopotamia. As we saw in Chapter One, by 1900 B.C.E. the Assyrians were already taking advantage of their geographical position to establish trade routes between Mesopotamia and Anatolia. They also played an important role in spreading urban society and organization across the Anatolian Plateau. Thereafter, however, they struggled continuously to protect themselves against a series of aggressive neighbors: first the Old Babylonian Empire of Hammurabi, then the Egyptians, the Mittanians, the Hittites, and finally the Sea Peoples.

This centuries-long fight for existence had a profound effect on the Assyrian worldview. Starting in the ninth century B.C.E., the Assyrians would in turn become the aggressors, extending their power and influence through a terrible, brutal, long-lasting, systematic victimization of their neighbors. Its terrors notwithstanding, their aggression helped shape the religious and political traditions of their neighbors, extending Near Eastern culture to the Aegean basin, synthesizing a new type of imperial organization, and imparting important lessons about what did and did not make for successful governance of a far-flung, international empire.

THE MIDDLE ASSYRIAN PERIOD (1362–859 B.C.E.)

The decline of the kingdom of Mitanni in the fourteenth century gave the Assyrians their first opportunity to establish themselves as a great realm. As Hittite pressure wore down Mitanni from the west, local Assyrian potentates extended their control in the east. Finally one such ruler, the governor of the city of Assur (sometimes spelled Ashur), adopted the name of his city's patron deity and declared himself king of Assyria. Assur-uballit I (1362–1327 B.C.E.) and his successors extended their power over northern Mesopotamia and attacked the Kassite kings of Babylonia, whom they regarded as usurpers. But otherwise, they did little to upset the delicate balance of power in the region.

With the succession of Tukulti-Ninurta I in 1244 B.C.E., however, the restraint was dropped. Tukulti-Ninurta was a conqueror of the first order, remembered in the Hebrew Bible as Nimrud and in Greek tradition as Ninos. Tukulti-Ninurta sacked Babylon, carrying its Kassite king and its patron deity, Marduk, into captivity and claiming the prestigious kingship of Babylon for himself. To maintain his tenuous grip over Babylonia, however, Tukulti-Ninurta had to engage in constant campaigning. This, plus his sacrilegious treatment of the Babylonian god, alienated his own subjects, who murdered him in about 1208 B.C.E.

A century of Assyrian decline followed as its neighbors sought both vengeance and control over the vital trade routes that crisscrossed Assyrian territory. More than once, the Assyrians were almost destroyed; but the constant cycle of desperate fighting forged them into a highly militaristic people. This struggle for survival continued until the close of the Middle Assyrian period, when a brutal but brilliant ruler, Assurnasirpal (*ah-sur-NAH-sur-PAHL*) II (883–859 B.C.E.) revived Assyrian strength and founded the neo-Assyrian Empire. Under his ruthless leadership, the Assyrians conducted aggressive military campaigns on an annual basis. The targets of Assyrian might had to pay tribute or face the full onslaught of the Assyrian war machine, which under Assurnasirpal acquired a deserved reputation for savagery and viciousness. The great Near Eastern scholar A. H. Olmstead referred to Assurnasirpal's policy as one of "calculated frightfulness," a refined name for a strategy of military terror and the extraction of protection money through plunder.

THE NEO-ASSYRIAN EMPIRE (859–627 B.C.E.)

The conquests of Assurnasirpal and his son, Shalmeneser (*SHAHL-meh-NEE-zehr*) III, inspired stiff resistance to Assyrian expansion. The northern Kingdom of Israel, along with several other states in the region of Syria-Palestine, formed an alliance to stop Shalmeneser III (853–827 B.C.E.). Ultimately this coalition fought him to a standstill, forcing him to settle for smaller victories against the Armenians to his northwest and the Medes to his northeast, until a great revolt within Assyria ended his reign and nullified his western gains. The respite proved brief. A usurper who took the name Tiglath-Pileser III seized the Assyrian throne in 744 B.C.E. and immediately prepared a great western campaign. In his first year he demanded tribute from various western kingdoms that had not paid up for generations. Those who refused fell victim to an immediate Assyrian onslaught.

When Tiglath-Pileser III died in 727 B.C.E., many of these recently conquered states rebelled, perhaps hoping that a famiiar pattern of Assyrian dynastic instability would reassert itself on the death of the usurping monarch. But Tiglath-Pileser's son, Shalmeneser V, energetically crushed the rebellions. When he died in battle, he was quickly replaced by one of his military commanders, who took the name Sargon II (722–705 B.C.E.). With typical Assyrian historical consciousness, Sargon II regarded Sargon of Akkad as the "first" Sargon; he was thus claiming to be the direct successor to a Near Eastern empire nearly 1,500 years

in the past. The dynasty that Sargon II founded is called the Sargonid; its century of rule proved the most magnificent in all of Assyrian history.

The Sargonids extended the frontiers of the Assyrian Empire from western Iran to the shores of the Mediterranean. Briefly, they even subjugated parts of Egypt. Sargon himself put an end to the Kingdom of Israel on taking the throne and scared the southern Kingdom of Judah into remaining a loyal and quiet vassal. The ancient Elamite Kingdom in Iran also fell

Assyrian Winged Human-Headed Bull. This relief was found in the palace of King Sargon II (722–705 B.C.E.). It measures sixteen feet wide by sixteen feet high and weighs approximately forty tons.

during the Sargonid period. By the seventh century B.C.E. Assyria was the unrivaled power of the ancient Near East.

GOVERNMENT AND ADMINISTRATION

The neo-Assyrian Empire was an armed state, built on the ability of its army to spread terror and oppress both enemies and subjects alike. At the head of the Assyrian government was the king, a hereditary monarch and the earthly representative of the god Assur. As well as being its military leader, the king was also the empire's chief religious figure; when the army was not in the field the king's time was taken up with elaborate sacrifices and rituals to appease the "great god" Assur. Divination and the consultation of oracles were central features of Assyrian religion. The Assyrian king, as chief priest, had to be able to discern the will of Assur through the portents of nature.

Around the central royal government was an extensive bureaucracy of governors, high priests, and military commanders, professions by no means mutually exclusive in the Assyrian context. These administrators formed the highest class in Assyrian society and exercised local authority on behalf of the king. As a people who ruled principally through military prowess, the Assyrians also understood the importance of transportation and lines of communication. They constructed an extensive network of roads that would serve as the basis for travel and communication across the Near East for centuries. The Assyrians also deployed a system of messengers and spies to report to the royal court on the activities of subjects and provincial governors.

Provincial governors collected tribute, recruited for the army, maintained Assyrian control, and administered the king's law. Not surprising for a people so mindful of tradition, Assyrians modeled their laws on the Code of Hammurabi, though many of their penalties were more severe. The Assyrians reserved the harshest punishments for practices deemed detrimental to reproduction; the penalties for homosexuality and abortion were particularly barbaric and grisly. Assyrian law was also rigidly patriarchal: only husbands had the power of divorce, and they were legally permitted to inflict a variety of penalties on their wives, ranging from corporal punishment to mutilation and even death.

Not surprising for a people so mindful of tradition, Assyrians modeled their laws on the Code of Hammurabi, though many of their penalties were more severe.

THE ASSYRIAN MILITARY-RELIGIOUS ETHOS

Assyrian religious, political, and military ideas took shape in the centuries during which Assyria fought for its survival. As the Assyrians gained the upper hand, however, this ethos became the foundation for their empire's relentless conquests.

The two fundamental characteristics of this Assyrian military-religious ethos were holy war and the exaction of tribute through terror. The Assyrians were convinced that their god Assur demanded that his worship be extended through military conquest. Even more than to the king, therefore, the Assyrian army belonged to Assur; and all who did not accept Assur's supremacy were, by that fact alone, enemies of Assur's people, the Assyrians. Ritual humiliation of a defeated city's gods was therefore a regular feature of Assyrian conquests. Frequently the conquered gods would be carried off to the Assyrian capital, where they would live as hostages at the court of Assur. Meanwhile, an image of Assur himself (usually represented as a sun disk with the head and shoulders of an archer) would be installed in the defeated city, and the conquered people would now be required to worship him. Worship of Assur did not necessarily mean that conquered peoples abandoned their previous gods altogether. But in Assyrian eyes, there was no question that Assur should be the supreme deity for all the peoples of their empire. As time went on, other gods gradually lost their defining characteristics, looking more and more like smaller versions of Assur, who became increasingly remote and aloof, the god of a state religion whom everyone in the Assyrian Empire was expected to serve.

Tribute for the Assyrians initially meant the taking of plunder. But rather than defeat their foes once and impose formal tribute thereafter, the Assyrians raided even their vanquished foes each year, extracting tribute by force. This strategy succeeded in terrifying Assyria's subjects and keeping the Assyrian military machine primed for battle. But it also entailed difficulties. Perpetual reconquests did little to inspire loyalty among subject peoples, who eventually reached a point of desperation at which they had little to lose through rebellion. Moreover, these annual Assyrian invasions sharpened not only the Assyrian army but also the forces of their subjects; and by the end of the ninth century other nations of the region had become accomplished at the Assyrians' own game. It was not

THE SENJIRLI STELE OF KING ESARHADDON

Set up in northern Syria by the Assyrian king Esarhaddon, this inscribed stone monument is one of the most important records of his reign. Accompanying the text (which proclaims his victories over Egypt and the Phoenician coast of Syria) was a depiction of Esarhaddon holding a cup in his right hand and a mace in his left. His left hand also grasped reins fastened to shackles holding a captured prince of Egypt and a Syrian ruler, both of whom begged for mercy. The inscription demonstrates Assyrian kingship's bombastic propaganda, its conscious connection to the Sumero-Akkadian past, and the cruelty that characterized Assyrian conquests. (Assur, Anu, Ba'al, Ea, and Ishtar were all gods or goddesses.)

To Assur, father of the gods, lover of my priesthood, Anu mighty and pre-eminent, who called me by name, Ba'al, the exalted lord, establisher of my dynasty, Ea, the wise, all-knowing . . . Ishtar, lady of battle and combat, who goes at my side . . . all of them who determine my destiny, who grant to the king, their favorite, power and might . . . the king, the offering of whose sacrifices the great gods love . . . their unsparing weapons they have presented him as a royal gift . . . [he] who has brought all the lands in submission at his feet, who has imposed tribute and tax upon them; conqueror of his foes, destroyer of his enemies, the king, who as to his walk is a storm, and as to his deeds, a raging wolf; . . . the onset of his battle is powerful, he is a consuming flame, a fire that does not sink: son of Sennacherib, king of the universe, king of Assyria, grandson of Sargon, king of the universe, king of Assyria, viceroy of Babylon, king of Sumer and Akkad. . . . I am powerful, I am all powerful, I am a hero, I am gigantic, I am colossal, I am honored, I am magnified, I am without an equal among all kings, the chosen one of Assur . . . the great lord [who] in order to show to the peoples the immensity of my mighty deeds, made powerful my kingship over the four regions of the world and made my name great. . . . Of Tirhakah, king of Egypt and Kush, the accursed . . . without cessation I slew multitudes of his men, and him I smote five times with the point of my javelin, with wounds, no recovery. Mem-

phis, his royal city, in half a day . . . I besieged, I captured, I destroyed, I devastated, I burned with fire. . . . The root of Kush I tore up out of Egypt and not one therein escaped to submit to me.

Daniel David Luckenbill, ed., *Ancient Records of Assyria and Babylonia*, Vol. 2 (Chicago, 1926–1927), pp. 224–227.

QUESTIONS FOR ANALYSIS

1. Ancient inscriptions and chronicles often exaggerate when describing royal accomplishments. Can we separate Esarhaddon's actual accomplishments from his boastful propaganda? What function did this inscription serve?

2. The Assyrians have a reputation for arrogance and cruelty toward defeated enemies. What features of this text suggest that reputation may be well deserved?

3. "I slew multitudes of his men," Esarhaddon boasted. Recall that "Saul slew his thousands, and David his ten thousands" (1 Samuel 29:5). Would it surprise you if the harsh Hebrew justice of "an eye for an eye, a tooth for a tooth" (Exodus 21:24; Leviticus 24:20; Deuteronomy 19:21) echoed Assyrian laws? What lasting influence did the Assyrians have on other cultures of the ancient Near East?

until Tiglath-Pileser III that the Assyrians abandoned the policy of collecting tribute by force each year, settling instead for more orthodox forms of payment.

Assyrian warfare was also notoriously savage. Ancient warfare was always brutal: mutilations of prisoners, decapitations, rape, and the mass deportations and/or enslavement of civilian populations were commonplace. The Assyrians, however, relished and celebrated such barbarities as did no other ancient empire. Their artwork and inscriptions revel in the butchering and torture of their enemies. Smiling Assyrian archers are shown shooting fleeing enemies in the back, while remorseless soldiers fling the citizens of a captured Judean town from the walls, impaling them on stakes below.

The army itself had developed by the ninth century into a devastating force. Like many ancient societies, the Assyrians had originally employed a seasonal peasant army of part-time soldiers. But from the reign of Assurnasirpal II (d. 859 B.C.E.) onward, the Assyrians recruited a massive standing army of more than 100,000 soldiers. The Assyrians also mastered large-scale iron-smelting techniques, and by the ninth century could equip their fighting men with high-quality steel weapons that overwhelmed opponents still reliant on bronze.

Assyrian strategy and tactics were the most highly sophisticated the world had yet seen, in great part due to the organization of the army. The core of the Assyrian army was heavily armed and armored shock troops, equipped with a variety of thrusting weapons and bearing tall shields for protection. These Assyrian storm troopers were the main force for crushing enemy infantry in the field and for routing the inhabitants of an enemy city once inside. To harass enemy infantry and break up their formations, the Assyrians deployed light skirmishers with slings and javelins. The Assyrians also combined archery and chariotry as never before. With their swift and efficient two-wheeled design, Assyrian chariots sped about the battlefield, carrying one to two archers and another couple of shield bearers. Thus chariots became highly mobile firing platforms, from which the expert Assyrian archers could wreak havoc. The Assyrians also developed a true cavalry force, with individual warriors mounted on armored steeds wielding bows and arrows or heavy lances.

In the open field the combined arms tactics of Assyrian warfare were too much for their opponents, who tried instead to defend themselves in fortified cities. The Assyrians, however, trained a highly skilled corps of combat engineers to sap walls and to build catapults,

Assyrian Atrocities. These Judean captives are being impaled on stakes after their city has fallen to the Assyrian king Sennacherib (704–681 B.C.E.). This carving comes from the walls of Sennacherib's palace at Nineveh.

siege engines, battering rams, and battle towers. Thus the walls of most cities provided little refuge from Assyrian military onslaught. After a city fell, an especially vicious series of atrocities usually followed: in addition to the usual dismemberments and mutilations, captives might also be burned or skinned alive.

THE END OF ASSYRIA AND ITS LEGACY

The successors of Sargon II continued Assyrian military policies while devoting great energy to what we might broadly consider culture. Sargon's immediate successor Sennacherib (704–681 B.C.E.) rebuilt the ancient Assyrian city of Nineveh, fortifying it with a double wall with a circuit of nine miles. He constructed an enormous palace there, raised on a giant platform decorated with marble, ivory, and exotic woods and ordered the construction of a massive irrigation system, including an aqueduct that carried fresh water to the city from thirty miles away. His son Esarhaddon

(681–669 B.C.E.) rebuilt the conquered city of Babylon and was a famous patron of the arts and sciences.

Esarhaddon's son Assurbanipal (669–627 B.C.E.) was perhaps the greatest of all the Assyrian kings. He maintained a strong military presence throughout the empire and for a time ruled the entire delta region of Egypt. After the Assyrian adventure in Egypt ultimately ended in failure, he turned his attention to a series of internal reforms, seeking ways to govern his empire other than through the traditional weapons of military terror and religious imperialism. Like his father, Assurbanipal was more or less an enlightened Assyrian king, who hoped to transform the empire into something more enduring than an armed camp in a perpetual state of warfare with its subjects and neighbors.

The study of the ancient Near East owes a tremendous debt to Assurbanipal. Like all Assyrian kings, he had a strong sense of the rich traditions of Mesopotamian culture and history and laid claim to this heritage to justify Assyrian rule over the region. Assurbanipal went further, however; at the great Assyrian capital of Nineveh, he ordered the construction of a magnificent library, where all the great works of Mesopotamian literature were to be copied into Assyrian cuneiform and preserved. This library also served as an archive for the correspondence and official acts of the king. Fortunately, this treasure trove of historical documentation survived until the nineteenth century, when it was rediscovered and preserved. All modern editions of the *Epic of Gilgamesh* depend on the Assyrian versions from Nineveh.

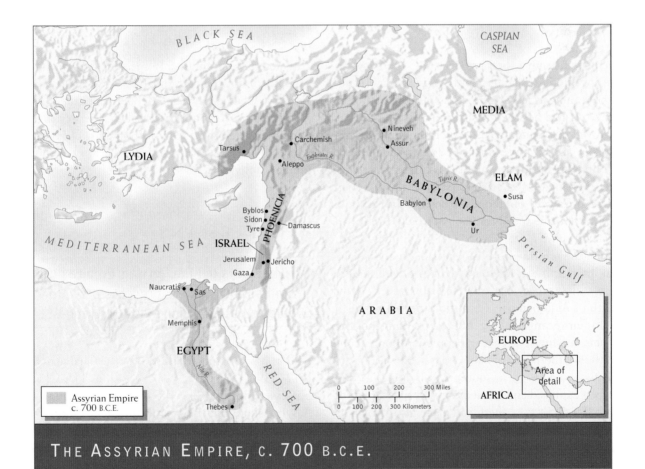

THE ASSYRIAN EMPIRE, C. 700 B.C.E.

What do you find striking about the geography of the Assyrian Empire? Why would the Assyrians concentrate their efforts in the river valleys and along the coast, leaving the Syrian interior largely alone? Notice the location of the Assyrian capitals of Nineveh and Assur; how was their situation in Mesopotamia likely to affect the Assyrians' sense of their own historical identity? Consider the position of Egypt. Why did the Assyrians find it difficult to subjugate Egypt permanently, despite the violence of their conquests?

Assurbanipal Feasting with His Wife in a Garden. The head of his defeated enemy, the king of Elam, can be seen hanging from the pine tree on the left.

When Assurbanipal died in 627 B.C.E., the Assyrian Empire appeared to be at its zenith. Its borders were secure, the realm was largely at peace with its neighbors, and its kings had adorned their capitals with magnificent artwork and hanging gardens. The end of Assyria is therefore all the more dramatic for its suddenness. Within fifteen years of the mighty Assurbanipal's reign, Nineveh lay in ruins; a few years later, the Assyrian state was no more, obliterated from the face of the earth with the same speed and violence by which it had established itself.

Despite the reform efforts of Esarhaddon and Assurbanipal, hatred of the Assyrians remained widespread. Centuries of savagery had not been forgotten. After the death of Assurbanipal, a coalition formed between the Indo-European-speaking Medes of Iran and the Chaldeans, a Semitic-speaking people who once controlled the southern half of Babylonia. In 626 B.C.E., the allies launched a revolt in southern Babylonia. In 612 B.C.E., they captured and burned the Assyrian capital of Nineveh. By 605 B.C.E., the Chaldeans (also known as neo-Babylonians) had destroyed the last remnants of Assyrian power on the upper Euphrates. The Medes retired to the Iranian Plateau to extend their suzerainty there. The Chaldeans succeeded to Assyria's position as the predominant imperial power in Mesopotamia and the Levant.

The Chaldeans proved little better than the hated Assyrians. They quickly earned the enmity of their subjects by exercising the same cruelty that had made the Assyrians infamous, including the mass deportation of

conquered foes from their homelands. The most famous example of this policy came in 587/586 B.C.E., when the ruthless Chaldean king Nebuchadnezzar (*neb-byoo-kuhd-NEHZ-ehr*) captured Jerusalem. He destroyed the Temple and removed tens of thousands of Hebrews to Babylon, an exile known in Jewish history as the Babylonian Captivity.

THE PERSIANS

In what ways did the Persian Empire differ from its Near Eastern predecessors? How would you account for those differences?

Built as it was on plunder and fear, the Chaldean Empire (612–539 B.C.E.) had a very short life. The Chaldeans possessed nothing like the great war machine of the Assyrians, nor did they exhibit the fervor of the Assyrian military-religious ethos. But in the power vacuum that resulted after the fall of Assyria, the Chaldeans went largely unchallenged. The other great powers of the Near East were too distant or otherwise occupied to challenge Chaldean dominance. The Indo-European-speaking Lydians had carved out a wealthy kingdom in western Anatolia, but they tended to orient themselves west toward the Aegean and the Greeks. The Medes, meanwhile, sought to secure dominance over the various, closely related peoples of the Iranian Plateau,

IN WHAT WAYS DID THE PERSIAN EMPIRE DIFFER FROM ITS NEAR EASTERN PREDECESSORS?

THE PERSIANS   85

effectively keeping themselves out of Mesopotamian and Levantine politics. The Persians, rulers of the former Elamite Kingdom, were at this time subject to the Medes. It was the Persians, however, who would emerge to topple the Chaldeans and reunite the ancient Near East.

THE ORIGINS OF THE PERSIAN EMPIRE

Almost nothing is known of the Persians before the middle of the sixth century B.C.E., except that they lived on the eastern shore of the Persian Gulf, spoke an Indo-European language, and were subject to the Medes. The Persians emerged from obscurity suddenly, under an extraordinary prince named Cyrus, who succeeded to the rule of a single Persian tribe in 559 B.C.E. Shortly thereafter Cyrus made himself ruler of all the Persians. Around 549 B.C.E. he threw off the lordship of the Medes, claiming dominion over lands stretching from the Persian Gulf to the Halys River in Asia Minor. Cyrus thus became a neighbor of the kingdom of Lydia. The Lydians had attained great prosperity as producers of gold and silver and as intermediaries for overland commerce between Mesopotamia and the Aegean Sea. They dominated the wealthy Greek cities along the western Anatolian coast and were the first people in the ancient Near East to use a precious-metal coinage as a medium of exchange for goods and services.

When Cyrus reached their border, the reigning king of the Lydians was Croesus (*CREE-subs*), a great ad-

mirer of the culture of the Greeks he ruled and so rich that the expression "rich as Croesus" remains embedded in our language. Distrusting his new neighbor, Croesus decided in 546 B.C.E. to launch a preventive war against the Persians to preserve his own kingdom from conquest. According to Herodotus, Croesus asked the oracle at Delphi in Greece whether he should attack immediately. The oracle replied that if he crossed the Halys he would destroy a great nation. Croesus attacked, but the nation he destroyed was his own. Cyrus defeated his forces and annexed Lydia to the Persian Empire.

Cyrus invaded Mesopotamia in 539 B.C.E., striking so quickly that he took Babylon without a fight. Once he was in Babylon, the entire Chaldean Empire was his. Cyrus allowed the Hebrews captive in Babylon since the time of Nebuchadnezzar to return to Israel and set up a semi-independent vassal state. Cyrus allowed other conquered peoples considerable self-determination as well, especially in terms of cult practices, making Persian rule a welcome change from that of the Assyrians and Chaldeans. Cyrus fell in battle in 530 B.C.E. from wounds he suffered while campaigning near the Aral Sea. He left behind the largest empire the world had yet seen. Persian expansion continued, however, even after his death. In 525 B.C.E., his son and successor Cambyses would conquer Egypt.

THE CONSOLIDATION OF THE PERSIAN EMPIRE

Cambyses was a brilliant general, a worthy successor to his father's military greatness. Difficulties abounded during his reign, however, as both contemporaries and historians have argued over whether the young king was insane. In any event, he died young and without a son, throwing open the question of succession and leaving the Persian Empire a cumbersome and poorly organized collection of rapid conquests.

After a short period of civil war, the aristocratic inner circle that had served both Cyrus and his son settled on a collateral member of the royal family as the new king. Cambyses's successor, Darius I, ruled Persia from 521 to 486 B.C.E. and concentrated on consolidating his predecessors' military gains by improving the administration of the Persian state. Darius divided the empire into provinces called satrapies, each administered by a satrap. The satraps enjoyed extensive powers and considerable

An Early Lydian Coin. Probably struck during the reign of Croesus.

political latitude, but they owed fixed tributes and absolute loyalty to the central government, as did vassal states such as the technically autonomous Hebrew Kingdom.

Adhering to the tolerant policy of Cyrus, Darius allowed the various peoples of the Persian Empire to retain most of their local institutions while enforcing a standardized currency and system of weights and measures. Throughout their empire the Persians required modest tribute payments; but otherwise, they were little interested in imposing onerous taxes, martial law, or their own religious practices on subject peoples. After centuries of Assyrian and Chaldean tyranny, the light hand of Persian rule was welcomed throughout the Near East.

Darius was also a great builder. He erected a new royal residence and ceremonial capital, which the Greeks called Persepolis ("Persia City"). He ordered a canal dug from the Nile to the Red Sea to facilitate trade with the Egyptian interior and installed irrigation systems on the Persian Plateau and on the fringe of the Syrian desert to increase agricultural production. Darius also expanded the Assyrian road system to enhance trade and communications in his far-flung realms. The most famous was the Royal Road, stretching 1,600 miles from Susa near the Persian Gulf to Sardis (the old Lydian capital) near the Aegean. Government couriers along this road were the first postal system, carrying messages and goods in relay stages from one post to another. Each post was a day's horseback ride from the

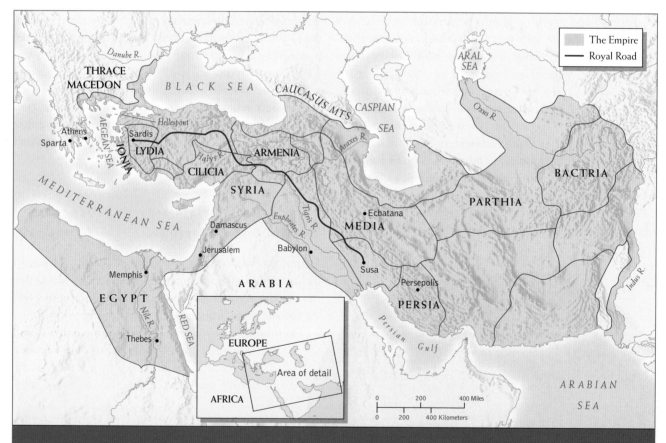

THE PERSIAN EMPIRE UNDER DARIUS I, 521–486 B.C.E.

What accounts for the enormous extent of the Persian Empire in comparison to earlier imperial realms? Why is the Royal Road especially noted on this map? Consider the location of the Persian heartland and the four administrative centers of Persepolis, Susa, Ecbatana, and Sardis. What purpose did such multiple "capitals" serve? Examine the northwest frontiers of the empire. Why would the Persians have an interest in continuing to expand in this direction?

IN WHAT WAYS DID THE PERSIAN EMPIRE DIFFER FROM ITS NEAR EASTERN PREDECESSORS?

THE PERSIANS   87

next: a fresh horse and rider would be ready at each post to carry what had been brought by the "postman" before him. An extensive imperial spy network also used this postal system to inform the crown of developments throughout the massive empire. The "intelligence service" founded by Darius was famed throughout Persian history as "the eyes and ears of the king."

Darius was an extraordinarily gifted administrator. As a military strategist, however, he made an enormous mistake when he attempted to extend Persian hegemony into Greece. Cyrus's conquest of Lydia had made Persia the ruler of the Greek-speaking cities on the western coast of Asia Minor, but these cities disdained Persian rule and yearned for the idealized freedom of other Greek city-states. Consequently, between 499 and 494 B.C.E. the Greeks on the Asian mainland waged a war for independence and briefly gained the support of troops from Athens, who joined the Asian Greeks in burning the important Persian regional administrative center at Sardis. After quelling the uprising in Asia, Darius sent a force across the Aegean to punish Athens and serve notice of his dominion to all European Greeks. At the battle of Marathon in 490, the Athenians dealt Darius the only major setback of his reign. In 480 his son and successor, Xerxes (*ZERK-zees*), attempted to avenge this humiliation by crushing Greece with a tremendous army, but heroic resistance by Athens and Sparta forced him to retreat and abandon his plans a year later. At that point the Persians realized that they had reached the limits of their expansionism. Thereafter, they concentrated on their Asian possessions and used money and diplomacy to keep the Greeks in check.

In fact, from 479 B.C.E. until Alexander the Great's invasion of Asia Minor in 334 B.C.E., the Greeks were usually too embroiled in internal rivalries to pose any challenge to Persia. From the Persian perspective that was fortunate, for during this period the Persian Empire was often beset by governmental instability caused by palace intrigues and provincial rebellions. Nevertheless, the cosmopolitan nature of Persian culture and the general toleration they exhibited served the Persians well in maintaining their enormous empire. Unlike the Assyrians or Chaldeans, the Persians could often count on the loyalty—sometimes even the affection—of their subjects. The Persians established an imperial model based on the accommodation of local institutions and practices, steady and consistent administration through a trained bureaucracy, and rapid communications between center and periphery. Both the Macedonians and the Romans would learn much from this model in later centuries.

ZOROASTRIANISM

Even more enduring than Persia's political legacy was its religious one, embodied in Zoroastrianism. This important world religion, along with Buddhism and Judaism, was one of the three major universal and personal religions known to the world before Christianity and Islam. The religion's founder was Zoroaster (the Greek form of the Persian name Zarathustra). Zoroaster was a Persian who probably lived shortly before 600 B.C.E., although some of the writings attributed to him may be as much as 400 years older than this. Zoroaster sought to reform the traditional customs of the Persian tribes by eradicating polytheism, animal sacrifice, and magic and to redefine worship in ethical rather than ritualistic terms. He was, arguably, the first true theologian in world history, insofar as he attempted to devise a fully developed system of religious belief.

Zoroaster taught that there was one supreme god in the universe, whom he called Ahura-Mazda, the "Wise Lord." Ahura-Mazda embodied the principles of light, truth, and righteousness; there was nothing wrathful or evil about him, and his light shone everywhere, not just on one tribe. Because evil and suffering were inexplicable by reference to Ahura-Mazda, Zoroaster posited the existence of a counterdeity, Ahriman, treacherous and malignant, who presided over the forces of darkness and evil. Zoroaster presented Ahura-Mazda as vastly stronger than Ahriman; but later, the priests of Zoroastrianism, the magi, emphasized the dualistic aspect of the founder's thought by insisting that Ahura-Mazda and Ahriman were evenly matched, engaged in a desperate struggle for supremacy. According to them, only on the last day would light decisively triumph over darkness, when Ahura-Mazda would overpower Ahriman and cast him into the abyss.

Zoroastrianism was a personal religion, making private, spiritual demands as opposed to public, cultic, and ritual ones. Unlike earlier Near Eastern cults, it did not exalt the power of a godlike king. The devotion of the Persian dynasty to Zoroaster's teachings nevertheless made Zoroastrianism important to the conduct of Persian government and helps explain the general eclecticism and tolerance of Persian rule. Unlike the Assyrians, the Chaldeans, or even the Egyptians, all of whom tried to impose their own cultural practices on conquered peoples, the Persian kings saw themselves as presiding over an assemblage of different nations whose customs and religious beliefs they were prepared to tolerate. Whereas Mesopotamian potentates characteristically called themselves "true king," Persian

A Cylindrical Seal of King Darius the Great of Persia (522–486 b.c.e.). The seal shows the king in a chariot, hunting lions with a bow, with the winged representation of the god Ahura Mazda rising above the scene behind him.

rulers took the title "king of kings" or "great king," implying that they recognized the legitimacy of those other kings who ruled under the canopy of Persian overlordship. This same spirit is reflected in Persian architecture, which drew freely and creatively on Mesopotamian, Babylonian, Assyrian, Egyptian, and Greek influences, yet nonetheless created a distinctively Persian style.

Ahura-Mazda patronized neither tribes nor states but only individuals who served his cause of truth and justice. Humans possessed free will and could choose to sin or not to sin. Zoroastrianism urged people not to sin but to be truthful, to love and help one another to the best of their powers, to aid the poor, and to practice generous hospitality. Those who did so would be rewarded in an afterlife, for the religion posited the resurrection of the dead on judgment day and their consignment to a realm either of bliss or flames. In the scriptures of the Zoroastrian faith, known as the Avesta (a work compiled by accretion over the course of many centuries), the rewards for righteousness are explicit.

This recital of Zoroastrianism's tenets reveals numerous similarities to Judaism and Christianity. Zoroastrianism's ethical universalizing resembles the teachings of the Hebrew prophets; its heaven and hell resemble Christian ideas about the afterlife; and its concern with the day of judgment is paralleled in both these other traditions. We should not, however, think

of these similarities as simple borrowings from one faith by another. The religious and intellectual traditions of the ancient Near East took shape in a world characterized by pervasive cross-cultural influences. Rarely if ever is it possible to trace an idea or a religious belief to a single, original source. Zoroastrianism, Judaism, and Christianity all emerged out of the rich cultural soup of the Iron Age Near Eastern world, as of course did the very idea of a universal religion itself.

THE DEVELOPMENT OF HEBREW MONOTHEISM

What developments marked the Hebrew transition from polytheism to monotheism?

Of all the cultural developments that took place in the Iron Age Near East, none was of greater significance to the civilizations of the West than was monotheism—the belief, that is, in but a single god, the creator and ruler of all things. This development is traditionally, and rightly, associated with the Hebrews. But even the Hebrews were not always monotheists. Those who argued for the exclusive worship of Yahweh—a group

WHAT DEVELOPMENTS MARKED THE HEBREW TRANSITION FROM POLYTHEISM TO MONOTHEISM?

THE DEVELOPMENT OF HEBREW MONOTHEISM   89

whom we shall refer to as the Yahwists—were often a minority within Hebrew society, albeit a vocal and assertive one. That the Hebrews came ultimately to recognize Yahweh as the only divine being in the universe, and to root their identity as a people in such an exclusive religious outlook, is a development that can only be explained against the backdrop of the tumultuous and confusing world in which Hebrew society itself arose.

FROM MONOLATRY TO MONOTHEISM

The emergence of Hebrew monotheism took place in a world conditioned by polytheism. For those who later advocated the exclusive worship of Yahweh, the early history of the Hebrews was full of embarrassments. At every turn, the Hebrews of the twelfth through tenth centuries B.C.E. can be found worshiping gods other than Yahweh, especially those of their Canaanite neighbors. Even Yahweh himself, in commanding that his people should "have no other gods before me," seemed implicitly to acknowledge that there were indeed other gods whom his people worshiped. In the Book of Judges, Yahweh is represented as more or less an equal of the Moabite god Chemosh. An older, polytheistic strain is visible also in Hebrew nature sprits such as Azazel and in the popularity of the Canaanite god El, whose name is an important element in many Hebrew word constructions (for example, Bethel). Even Solomon included symbols of Ba'al and altars to Asherah in the temple complex he built for Yahweh at Jerusalem. Later Hebrew kings also continued such toleration of non-Yahwist cult practices, despite the protests of religious purists advocating the exclusive worship of Yahweh.

Despite lingering polytheism, however, by the beginning of the first millennium Hebrew religion had clearly moved into a new stage of national *monolatry*—the exclusive worship of one god, without denying utterly the existence of others. Precisely how this came about is unclear. Although Moses is often credited with beginning the ascendancy of the cult of Yahweh, the promotion of the Yahweh cult probably took place later, under the auspices of the Levites, a tribe whose unique claims to priestly authority made them a religious elite within Hebrew society. Advocating both the ritual and the prophetic elements of Yahweh worship, the Levites sought to enhance their own power and prestige by exalting Yahweh above the other gods traditionally revered in Hebrew and Canaanite society.

The Levites also enjoyed a higher degree of literacy than most of their fellow Hebrews. As a tool for shaping the traditions and consciousness of a society, the power of the written word is formidable. This was especially so in the ancient world, where writing enjoyed a sort of magical aura and the authority surrounding texts was literally awe-inspiring. In an age of constant threats to Hebrew religious and political sovereignty, the literacy of the Levites thus helped preserve and promote Yahweh worship. So too, of course, did the House of David, which by promoting the Yahweh cult and centralizing it in Jerusalem helped link the political and the religious identity of the Hebrews to the worship of Yahweh as the supreme (if not yet the only) god of the universe.

Nevertheless, the worship of other gods persisted. The popularity of Canaanite fertility cults swelled in the eighth and seventh centuries, perhaps in reaction to the austere morality demanded and imposed by the Yahwists. Religious figures as late as Jeremiah (c. 637–587 B.C.E.) continued to rail against "foreign" cults and to warn of the disastrous consequences that would arise if Yahweh's people did not remain faithful to Yahweh alone. Despite his supremacy over all other gods, however, Yahweh remained a somewhat limited god in the eighth and seventh centuries B.C.E., even in the eyes of the Yahwists. He was conceived as possessing a physical body and was sometimes capricious or irascible. Nor was Yahweh omnipotent, for his power was largely limited to the territory occupied by the Hebrews.

Despite these polytheistic holdovers, some of the Hebrews' most important contributions to subsequent Western religious thought had emerged by the middle of the eighth century B.C.E. One was their unique *transcendent theology.* In the eyes of his priests and prophets, Yahweh was not part of nature but entirely outside of it. He could therefore be understood in purely intellectual or abstract terms, entirely apart from the operations of the natural world he had created. Complementing this principle of divine transcendence was the belief that Yahweh had appointed humans to be the rulers of nature by divine mandate. The famous line from Genesis in which Yahweh orders Adam and Eve to "be fruitful and multiply, and replenish the earth and subdue it, and have dominion over . . . every living thing," stands in striking contrast with Babylonian creation accounts, in which humans are created merely to

> The popularity of Canaanite fertility cults swelled in the eighth and seventh centuries, perhaps in reaction to the austere morality demanded and imposed by the Yahwists.

serve the gods, "so that the gods might be at ease." Finally, while not fully developed, universalizing ethical considerations are also present in Hebrew religious thought during this period. According to the Babylonian flood story, a particularly petulant god decided to destroy humans because their noise deprived him of sleep. In Genesis, by contrast, Yahweh sends a flood in response to human wickedness, but saves Noah and his family because "Noah was a just man."

The Hebrews honored Yahweh during the period of monolatry by subscribing to moral precepts, rituals, and taboos. The exact form of the Ten Commandments (as they became known from the seventh century B.C.E. onward, and as they appear in Exodus 20:3–17) may not have existed before the Babylonian Captivity. But the Hebrews certainly observed some set of commandments, including ethical injunctions against murder, adultery, bearing false witness, and "coveting anything that is thy neighbor's." In addition they observed ritualistic demands, such as refraining from labor on the seventh day and not boiling a kid in its mother's milk. But the moral standards enjoined by Yahweh on the Hebrew community were not necessarily binding when the Hebrews dealt with outsiders. Lending at interest, for example, was not acceptable between Hebrews, but was quite acceptable between a Hebrew and a non-Hebrew. Such distinctions applied also to more serious issues, such as the killing of civilians in battle. When the Hebrews conquered territories in Canaan, they took "all the spoil of the cities, and every man they smote with the sword . . . until they had destroyed them, neither left they any to breathe." Rather than having any doubts about such a brutal policy, the Yahwists believed it had been ordered by their Lord himself—indeed, that Yahweh had inspired the Canaanites to resist so that there would be reason to slaughter them: "For it was the Lord's doing to harden their hearts that they should come against Israel in battle, in order that they should be utterly destroyed, and should receive no mercy but be exterminated, as the Lord commanded Moses" (Joshua 11:20).

With the fragmentation of the united Hebrew kingdom after Solomon's death, important regional distinctions also arose within the Yahweh cult. The rulers of the northern kingdom discouraged their citizens from participating in cultic activities at Jerusalem, thereby earning the scorn of the Jerusalem-based Yahwists who shaped the biblical tradition. Disunity and the loss of Hebrew identity was accelerated by the Assyrians, who under Sargon II absorbed the northern kingdom as a province and deported nearly 28,000 Hebrews—the famous Ten Lost Tribes of Israel—to the interior of the Assyrian Empire. The southern Kingdom of Judah survived, but found it expedient to become an Assyrian vassal state. As we have seen, however, political collaboration with the Assyrians also meant acceptance of the Assyrian god Assur.

This Assyrian threat was the whetstone on which the Yahwist prophets sharpened their demands not for monolatry but for an exclusive monotheism. Prophets were political as much as religious figures, and most understood that military resistance to the Assyrians was futile. If the Hebrews were to survive as a people, then they had to exalt the one thing that separated them from everyone else in the region: the worship of Yahweh. The prophets' insistence, during the eighth and seventh centuries B.C.E., that Yahweh alone should be worshiped and that no other gods even existed, was thus an aggressive reaction to the equally aggressive promotion of Assur by the Assyrians. Nor could there be any room for compromise in the Yahwists' demand for a thoroughgoing and exclusive monotheism. Only by worshiping Yahweh alone could the Hebrews combat the insinuating effects of Assyrian religious imperialism.

Although the word *prophet* has come to mean someone who predicts the future, its original meaning is closer to "preacher"—more exactly, someone who has an urgent message to proclaim because he or she believes that the message derives from divine inspiration. The foremost Hebrew prophets were Amos and Hosea, who preached in the Kingdom of Israel before it fell to the Assyrians in 722 B.C.E.; Isaiah and Jeremiah, who prophesied in Judah before its fall in 586 B.C.E.; and Ezekiel and the second Isaiah (the Book of Isaiah was written by at least two, and possibly three, different authors), who prophesied "by the waters of Babylon" during the exile.

Despite some differences in emphasis, the prophets' messages were sufficiently similar to each other to warrant treating them as if they formed a single coherent body of religious thought. Three doctrines made up the core of the prophets' teachings:

> The prophets' insistence, during the eighth and seventh centuries B.C.E., that Yahweh alone should be worshiped and that no other gods even existed, was thus an aggressive reaction to the equally aggressive promotion of Assur by the Assyrians.

The Goddess Asherah. The Canaanite fertility goddess, Asherah, was the wife of the god Ba'al or El, but she also appears occasionally in inscriptions as the wife of the Hebrew god Yahweh. One Hebrew king even placed an image of her in the temple of Yahweh at Jerusalem.

1. They preached absolute monotheism. Yahweh is the ruler of the universe. He even makes use of nations other than the Hebrews to accomplish his purposes. The gods of others are false gods.
2. Yahweh is exclusively a god of righteousness. He wills only the good, and evil in the world comes from humanity, not from him.
3. Because Yahweh is righteous, he demands ethical behavior from his Hebrew people above all else. He cares less for ritual and sacrifice than that his followers should "seek justice, relieve the oppressed, protect the fatherless, and plead for the widow."

The eighth-century B.C.E. prophet Amos summed up "the prophetic revolution" and marked one of the epoch-making moments in human cultural development when he expressed Yahweh's resounding warning in words that have echoed down to our own day:

> I hate, I despise your feasts, and I take no delight in your solemn assemblies.
> Even though you offer me your burnt offerings and cereal offerings,
> I will not accept them, and the peace offerings of your fatted beasts I will not look upon.
> Take away from me the noise of your songs; to the melody of your harps I will not listen.
> But let justice roll down like waters, and righteousness like an ever-flowing stream (Amos 5:21–24).

JUDAISM TAKES SHAPE

Through their insistence that Yahwist monotheism was the cornerstone of the Hebrews' identity as a people, the Yahwists made it possible for the Hebrews to survive under Assyrian domination. As the Assyrian threat receded in the late seventh century B.C.E., the Yahwists triumphed religiously and politically. The new king of Judah, Josiah (621–609 B.C.E.) was a committed monotheist who employed prominent prophets at his court, including Jeremiah. With Assyrian power crumbling, Josiah found himself in a position in which he could pursue a purification of cult practices. His efforts centered on redrafting and revising the "Law of Moses" and expelling corrupt priests and "foreign" practices from holy places of worship. It was probably during his reign that the Book of Deuteronomy was discovered and hailed as another book authored by Moses. As Deuteronomy is by far the most stridently monotheistic book of the Hebrew Bible, it seems likely that it was authored during (or perhaps slightly before) the reign of Josiah to lend the weight and credibility of Moses's great name to the religious and political program Josiah pursued.

To the dismay of the Yahwists, Josiah died in battle at Megiddo while trying to prevent an Egyptian force from aiding the last remnants of Assyrian power. With his death, the monotheists fell hard from power. Jeremiah was placed under house arrest, denied the right to speak in public, and finally carried off into Egypt where he was murdered. All the while, he continued to denounce the corruption of the Hebrews, suggesting that they would fall before the Chaldeans just as they had before the Assyrians, in punishment for their disobedience to Yahweh.

Within a generation of King Josiah's death, Jeremiah's predictions were fulfilled. The Chaldeans under Nebuchadnezzar conquered Jerusalem, destroyed the

Reconstruction of the Ishtar Gate. This is a reconstruction of one of the fifty-foot-high entrance gates built into the walls of Babylon by King Nebuchadnezzar around 575 B.C.E. About half of this reconstruction is original.

Temple, and carried thousands of Hebrews off to Babylon. The Babylonian Captivity brought many challenges for the Hebrews living there, paramount among them being the maintenance of their religious and ethnic identity. The leading voices in defining that identity continued to be the patriotic Yahwists, the same people who would later spearhead the return to Palestine after Cyrus's capture of Babylon. Among the Yahwists, the prophetic tradition thus continued, even in a foreign land. The prophet Ezekiel stressed that salvation could be found only through religious purity, which meant ignoring all foreign gods and acknowledging only Yahweh. States and empires and thrones did not matter in the long run, Ezekiel said. In this he made explicit the passing observations of predecessors such as Nahum and Jeremiah, who had also commented on the transitory nature of human power and existence. What mattered for the Hebrews living in exile was the creature God had made in his image—man—and

> The period of captivity was nevertheless decisive for the emergence of Judaism as a universalizing religion.

the relationship between that creator god, his chosen people, and his creation.

The disassociation of political identity from religious practice that triumphed during the Babylonian Captivity was an intensification of intellectual currents already discernible in the earlier prophetic tradition. The period of captivity was nevertheless decisive for the emergence of Judaism as a universalizing religion. In Babylon, Judaism became something more than simply the national cult of the Hebrews. No longer was Yahweh's worship tied to any particular political entity or dynasty, for after 586 B.C.E., neither a Hebrew state nor a Hebrew ruling dynasty existed. Nor was his worship tied to any specific place. In Babylon and in the Holy Land, Judaism survived the destruction of the Temple and the exile of the Hebrew people from their land. In the ancient world, this was an unparalleled achievement. No other ancient people is known to have survived so long an exile from its central holy place.

After 538 B.C.E., when Cyrus permitted the Hebrews of Babylon to return to the Holy Land and rebuild the Temple, Jerusalem became once again the central holy place of Hebrew religious life. But the new developments that had arisen within Judaism during the captivity would prove lasting, despite the religious conflicts that soon erupted between the returning exiles and the Hebrews who had managed to remain in the Holy Land and so were untouched by the changes that had taken place within Judaism during the exile. These conflicts are a measure of the extent to which Judaism itself had been transformed in Babylon.

Increasingly, Jewish religious teachings would be presented in ethical terms, as obligations owed by all human beings toward their creator, independent of place or political identity. Ritual requirements and religious taboos, by contrast, would remain the exclusive obligation of Jews, for whom they symbolized the special covenant that bound Yahweh to his people; and these would be rigorously reinforced by the late fifth century B.C.E. ruler Nehemiah. But the notion of a creator god who existed outside time, nature, place, and kingship became ever more powerful in Second Temple Judaism and would be taken up later by Christianity and Islam. So too would the Hebrew claim that Yahweh was a jealous god who would not permit his followers to worship any other divinity in any form. In the context of the ancient world, both remained peculiar ideas that would not be fully absorbed for a millennium. But despite their peculiarity, the transcendental monotheism developed by the Hebrews would ultimately become a fundamental feature of the religious outlook of all Western civilizations.

CONCLUSION

The centuries from 1700 to 500 B.C.E. were an age of empires. The two great powers of the second millennium B.C.E. were New Kingdom Egypt and the Hittite Empire of Anatolia. But a host of lesser empires also emerged during this period, including Minoan Crete, Mycenaean Greece, the Kingdom of the Mitanni, and Middle Kingdom Assyria. All these empires were sustained by a sophisticated network of international trade and diplomacy; we can speak even of an international system binding them together by the Late Bronze Age. At the heart of all these Bronze Age empires, however, lay a very old model of social organization: the Mesopotamian city-state as it had developed in Sumer. With

the arguable exception of New Kingdom Egypt, none of these empires came close to being an integrated, territorial state. Instead, they were collections of cities, ruled by kings who claimed some sort of divine sanction for their rule.

Between 1200 and 1000 B.C.E., the devastation wrought by the Sea Peoples brought this international system to an end. Combined with the declining power of Egypt, the invasions cleared the way for a number of new, small groups to establish states in the Near and Middle East, including the Phoenicians, the Philistines, the Hebrews, and the Lydians. Many of the crucial cultural and economic developments of the early Iron Age began in these small states, including alphabetic writing, coinage, exclusive monotheism, and mercantile colonization. But the dominant states of the early Iron Age Mediterranean world continued to be the great land empires centered in western Asia: first the Assyrians, then the Chaldeans, and finally the Persians.

On the surface, it may therefore appear as if nothing very dramatic had changed since the middle of the second millennium B.C.E. But such geographical continuities can be deceiving. The empires of the early Iron Age were quite different from the collections of quasi-independent city-states that had dominated the Near East a thousand years before. These new empires were much more highly unified than earlier empires had been. They had capital cities, centrally managed systems of communication, sophisticated administrative structures, and ideologies that justified their aggressive imperialism as a religious obligation imposed on them by a single, all-powerful god. They commanded armies of unprecedented size, and they demanded from their subjects a degree of obedience impossible for any Bronze Age empire to imagine. They were not, however, all-powerful. As the Assyrian case reveals, a coalition of small states could still sometimes defeat them. But they were larger, stronger, and more thoroughgoing in their claims to political and religious obedience than any previous Western empires.

At the same time that these great land empires were declaring themselves to be the chosen instruments of their god's divine will, we also mark the emergence of more personalized monotheistic traditions in the early Iron Age. Cult and sacrifice were important religious obligations in both Zoroastrianism and Judaism, as they were to all ancient religions. Zoroastrianism in particular proved fully compatible with an imperialist ideology and became the driving spiritual force behind the Persian Empire. Judaism, by contrast, was forged in the struggle to resist the religious imperialism of

Assyria and Chaldean Babylonia. But both Zoroastrianism and Judaism added an important new emphasis on personal ethical conduct as a fundamental element in religious life, and both pioneered the development of authoritative, written scriptures as a foundation for

their religious teachings. These developments would exercise an enormous influence on Western religious life and would provide the models on which Christianity and Islam would ultimately erect their own imperial traditions.

KEY TERMS

Indo-European	Semitic	Minoans	Zoroastrians
Assyrians	Akhenaten	Phoenicians	David
Mycenaeans	Nefertiti	Cyrus	Hittites

SELECTED READINGS

On New Kingdom Egypt, see also the readings listed in Chapter One.

Aubet, Maria Eugenia. *Phoenicia and the West: Politics, Colonies, and Trade.* Trans. Mary Turton. Cambridge, 1993. An intelligent and thought-provoking examination of Phoenician civilization and its influence.

Boardman, John. *Assyrian and Babylonian Empires and Other States of the Near East from the Eighth to the Sixth Centuries B.C.* New York, 1991. Scholarly and authoritative.

Boardman, John. *Persia and the West.* London, 2000. A great book by a distinguished classical scholar, with a particular focus on art and architecture as projections of Persian imperial ideologies.

Boyce, Mary. *Textual Sources for the Study of Zoroastrianism.* Totowa, N.J., 1984. An invaluable collection.

Bryce, Trevor. *The Kingdom of the Hittites.* Oxford, 1998. And *Life and Society in the Hittite World.* Oxford, 2002. An extraordinary new synthesis, now the standard account of Hittite political, military, and daily life.

Curtis, John. *Ancient Persia.* Cambridge, Mass., 1990. Concise, solid, reliable.

Dever, William. *Who Were the Early Israelites and Where Did They Come From?* Grand Rapids, Mich., 2003. A balanced, fairminded account with excellent bibliographical guidance to recent work.

Dickinson, O. T. P. K. *The Aegean Bronze Age.* Cambridge, 1994. An excellent summary of archaeological evidence and scholarly argument concerning Minoan, Mycenaean, and other cultures of the Bronze Age Aegean basin.

Dothan, Trude, and Moshe Dothan. *Peoples of the Sea: The Search for the Philistines.* New York, 1992. The essential starting point for Philistine culture and its links to the Aegean basin.

Drews, Robert. *The End of the Bronze Age: Changes in Warfare and the Catastrophe ca. 1200 B.C.* Princeton, N.J., 1993. A stimulating analysis and survey, with excellent bibliographies.

Finkelstein, Israel, and Nadav Na'aman, eds. *From Nomadism to Monarchy: Archaeological and Historical Aspects of Early Israel.* Jerusalem, 1994. Scholarly articles on the Hebrews' transformation from pastoralists to a sedentary society focused on Yahweh worship.

Fitton, J. Lesley. *Minoans: Peoples of the Past* (British Museum Publications). London, 2002. A careful, reliable debunking of myths about the Minoans, written for nonspecialists.

Kamm, Antony. *The Israelites: An Introduction.* New York, 1999. A short, accessible history of the land and people of Israel up to 135 C.E., aimed at students and general readers.

Kuhrt, Amélie. *The Ancient Near East, c. 3000–330 B.C.* 2 vols. London and New York, 1995. An outstanding survey, written for students, that includes Egypt and Israel as well as Mesopotamia, Babylonia, Assyria, and Persia. Excellent bibliographies.

Luckenbill, Daniel David, ed. and trans. *Ancient Records of Assyria and Babylonia.* 2 vols. Chicago, 1926–1927. Still one of the best and most readily accessible collections of primary sources on Assyrian attitudes and policies in war, religion, and politics.

Metzger, Bruce M., and Michael D. Coogan, eds. *The Oxford Companion to the Bible.* New York, 1993. An outstanding reference work, with contributions by leading authorities.

Niditch, Susan. *Ancient Israelite Religion.* New York, 1997. A short, suggestive introduction designed for students, emphasizing the diversity of Hebrew religious practice.

Redford, Donald B. *Egypt, Canaan, and Israel in Ancient Times.* Princeton, N.J., 1992. An overview of the interactions between these peoples from about 1200 B.C.E. to the beginning of the Common Era.

Renfrew, Colin. *Archaeology and Language: The Puzzle of Indo-European Origins*. Cambridge, 1987. A masterful but controversial work by one of the most creative archaeologists of the twentieth century.

Saggs, H. W. F. *The Might That Was Assyria*. London, 1984. A lively narrative history of the Assyrian Empire, with analysis of the institutions that underlay its strength.

Sandars, Nancy K. *The Sea Peoples: Warriors of the Ancient Mediterranean*. Rev. ed. London, 1985. An introductory account aimed at students and scholars.

Tubb, Jonathan N., and Rupert L. Chapman. *Archaeology and the Bible*. London, 1990. A good starting point for students that illustrates clearly the difficulties in linking archeological evidence to biblical accounts of early Hebrew history and society.

Wood, Michael. *In Search of the Trojan War*. New York, 1985. Aimed at a general audience, this carefully researched and engagingly written book is an excellent introduction to the late Bronze Age context of the Trojan War.

PART II

THE GREEK AND ROMAN WORLDS

THE CLASSICAL CIVILIZATIONS of Greece and Rome dominated the Mediterranean world from the sixth century B.C.E. until the sixth century C.E. Both drew heavily on the traditions and achievements of the ancient Near East, but each represented a distinct departure from this earlier world. Together, however, Greece and Rome constituted the seedbed out of which all subsequent Western civilizations would develop.

Beginning in the eighth century B.C.E., Greek civilization took shape in the warring, particularistic, and fiercely independent city-states that grew up around the Aegean and the Adriatic seas. But it was not until the end of the fourth century B.C.E., when the conquests of Alexander the Great created an empire that stretched from Greece through Persia to India and Egypt, that Greek civilization became the common cultural currency of the Mediterranean and Near Eastern worlds.

In central Italy, the city of Rome was slowly extending its dominion over the Italian peninsula. In the last two centuries B.C.E., Rome expanded its rule throughout the entire Mediterranean world and into western Europe. By the end of the first century C.E., Rome had built an empire larger even than Alexander's. In an extraordinary triumph of organization, discipline, and cultural adaptability, the Romans maintained that empire, substantially intact, for the next 400 years.

	POLITICS	SOCIETY AND CULTURE	ECONOMY	INTERNATIONAL RELATIONS
B.C.E. 1150		The Dark Age of Greece (1150–800 B.C.E.)	Greek trade increases in Aegean Sea (1000–800 B.C.E.)	
	Birth of the Greek polis (800 B.C.E.)	Introduction of Phoenician alphabet into Greece (900 B.C.E.)		Carthage founded (800 B.C.E.)
		Archaic Greece (800–480 B.C.E.)		
		Homer's *Iliad* and *Odyssey* are written down (800 B.C.E.)		
		First Greek colonies appear (800–600 B.C.E.)		
		First Olympic games (776 B.C.E.)		Rome founded (753 B.C.E.)
	Spartans enslave Messenians (700–680 B.C.E.)			
	Kylon sent into exile for tyranny (632 B.C.E.)			
600	Hoplite tactics become military standard (600 B.C.E.)		Solon encourages cash-crop farming and urban industries (600–550 B.C.E.)	Miletus becomes colonial power (600–400 B.C.E.)
	Tarquin the Proud gains kingship over Rome (543 B.C.E.)			
500	Roman Republic (500–27 B.C.E.)		Athens becomes principal exporter of olive oil, wine, and pottery (500 B.C.E.)	
	Xerxes succeeds Darius the Great (486 B.C.E.)	Sophocles, author of *Oedipus*, (496–406 B.C.E.)		The Ionian Revolution (499–494 B.C.E.)
	Plebian rebellion leads to Law of the Twelve Tables (480 B.C.E.)	Emergence of Greek sculpture (490–480 B.C.E.)		Persians sack Eritrea (490 B.C.E.)
		Golden age of Greek civilization (480–323 B.C.E.)		Hellenic League formed (480 B.C.E.)
		Socrates (469–399 B.C.E.)		Persian army defeated at battle of Salamis (480 B.C.E.)
	Pericles elected strategos of Athens (462–461 B.C.E.)	Thucydides (460–400 B.C.E.)		
		Sophists emerge (450 B.C.E.)		Athens gains control of Delian League (450s B.C.E.)
		Parthenon built in Athens (447–438 B.C.E.)		Peloponnesian War (431–404 B.C.E.)
		Plato, author of the *Republic* (429–349 B.C.E.)		
		Aristotle, author of *Nicomachean Ethics* (384–322 B.C.E.)		Corinthian War (394–387 B.C.E.)
	Reign of Philip II (359–336 B.C.E.)	Greek migrations into western Asia (325–225 B.C.E.)	Alexander's conquests open commercial routes between Greece and Asia (323 B.C.E.)	Philip II defeats Greek alliance and forms League of Corinth (338 B.C.E.)
	Reign of Alexander III, the Great (336–323 B.C.E.)	Euclid, *Elements of Geometry* (300 B.C.E.)		Reign of Alexander the Great (336–323 B.C.E.)
300				Ptolemy establishes dynasty in Egypt (332 B.C.E.)
				Alexander defeats the Persian army (331 B.C.E.)
				Seleucus establishes dynasty in Persia (281 B.C.E.)
			First standard coinage in Rome (269 B.C.E.)	Punic Wars (264–146 B.C.E.)
	Roman slave revolts (146–130 B.C.E.)			Carthage razed (146 B.C.E.)
100		Cicero (106–43 B.C.E.)	Roman commerce relies on 1 million slaves (100 B.C.E.)	
	Spartacus's revolt (73–71 B.C.E.)	Virgil, author of the *Aeneid* (70–19 B.C.E.)		
		Horace (65–8 B.C.E.)		
	Caesar defeats Pompey (48 B.C.E.)	Livy, author of *History of Rome* (59 B.C.E.–17 C.E.)		
	Octavian becomes emperor (27 B.C.E.)	Ovid, author of *Metamorphoses* (43 B.C.E.–17 C.E.)		
	The Principate or early Roman Empire (27 B.C.E.–180 C.E.)			

POLITICS	SOCIETY AND CULTURE	ECONOMY	INTERNATIONAL RELATIONS	
				C.E. 10
	Jesus (c. 4 B.C.E.–c. 30 C.E.) Saul of Tarsus, or Paul the Apostle (10–67 C.E.) Christians begin arriving in Rome (40 C.E.)		Claudius enters Britain (48 C.E.) Romans destroy the Temple of Jerusalem (70 C.E.)	
Pax Romana (96–180 C.E.)	Gospel of Mark is written (70 C.E.)	Romans excel in engineering aqueducts and roads and develop new tax system under Trajan (98–117 C.E.)	Romans destroy the city of Jerusalem (135 C.E.)	100
The Third-Century Crisis in Roman Empire (180–284 C.E.)	Neoplatonism (200–300 C.E.) Growth of monasticism (300s C.E.)	Roman Empire loses one third of population due to disease, low birth rate, and war (180–284 C.E.)	Goths defeat Romans and cross the Danube (251 C.E.)	
The Dominate or later Roman Empire (284–610 C.E.) Diocletian, soldier-emperor (284–305 C.E.)		Currency is stabilized and new coinage introduced under Diocletian (284–305 C.E.)		
	The Great Persecution of Christians (303–313 C.E.)			300
Reign of Constantine over Western Roman Empire (312–324 C.E.) Reign of Constantine over Roman Empire from Constantinople (324–337 C.E.)	Conversion of Constantine to Christianity (312 C.E.) Saint Jerome (c. 340–420) Saint Ambrose (c. 340–397) Saint Augustine, author of *Confessions* and *On the City of God* (354–430) Christianity becomes official Roman religion (c. 392)		Council of Nicea condemns Arianism (325 C.E.) Visigoths defeat Romans (378 C.E.) Visigoths sack Rome (410 C.E.)	400
	Saint Benedict (480–547)		Vandals sack Rome from the sea (455 C.E.)	
Justinian rules as emperor in East (r. 527–565 C.E.) Corpus Juris Civilis (534 C.E.)			Justinian recaptures Italy from Ostrogoths (536 C.E.) The Lombards seize northern parts of Italy (568 C.E.)	
Tenure of Pope Gregory I (Saint Gregory the Great) (590–604 C.E.)	Papacy of Saint Gregory the Great (590–604)			

Chapter THREE

THE GREEK
EXPERIMENT

THE image that comes most often to mind when Americans or Europeans think of the ancient world is the Acropolis of Athens, its gleaming temples and shrines still impressive despite their age and ruined condition. The rationality, harmony, and repose of this symbol of Greek culture seem to many to bespeak something quintessentially "Western": the triumph of reason and freedom over the "superstition" and "despotism" of "Eastern" cultures such as Assyria or Persia.

Such easy and self-congratulatory contrasts tell us more about ourselves than they do about the ancient Greeks and ancient Near East cultures. In fact, Greek civilization has been deeply influenced by its Near East neighbors from the Mycenaean Period until the present day. The achievements of classical Greek civilization would have been impossible without the debt Greece owed to Phoenician, Assyrian, and Egyptian examples.

The flowering of Greek civilization during the first millennium B.C.E. is nonetheless a watershed in the development of Western civilizations. Building on their historical experiences after the Bronze Age collapse, the Greeks of the Iron Age came to cherish assumptions and values that differed greatly from those of their Near Eastern neighbors. Human dignity, individual liberty, participatory government, artistic innovation, scientific investigation, constitutional experimentation, confidence in the creative powers of the human mind—the Greeks espoused all of these values, although, as ever in human affairs, practice often fell short of their ideals.

What we mean by such terms as *democracy, equality, justice,* and *freedom* differs from what the Greeks meant by them. Nonetheless, the modern West can find an intelligibility in the institutions and beliefs of this tenacious, quarrelsome, and energetic people, whose small-scale societies started a cultural revolution and created a civilization distinctly different from any before it. The democracies of the modern Western world are not the only heirs of this Greek experiment but are unimaginable without it.

FOCUS QUESTIONS

• What cultural changes marked the end of the Dark Age of Greece?

• How did the emergence of hoplite tactics affect Greek political norms?

• How and why did the Athenian, Spartan, and Milesian poleis differ from each other?

 • How were the Greek armies able to defeat the much larger Persian forces?

• To what exent was the culture of Athens in the golden age the product of Athenian democracy?

• How did the Peloponnesian War influence Greek philosophy?

THE DARK AGE OF GREECE (1150–800 B.C.E.)

What cultural changes marked the end of the Dark Age of Greece?

By the end of the twelfth century, the last remnants of Mycenaean civilization had vanished, and Greece entered an undocumented Dark Age. Mainland Greece witnessed depopulation of up to 90 percent in the century or so following 1200 B.C.E. Except at Athens, the great citadels were destroyed in the conflagrations at the end of the Bronze Age; and even at Athens, the population steadily declined. Many inhabitants fled to the highlands of southern Greece or across the sea to Cyprus and the coast of Anatolia. In Greek historical tradition, their flight was precipitated by the arrival of a new group of Greeks from the north, the Dorians. Although scholars now doubt the veracity of this tradition, tensions between speakers of the Doric dialect (such as the Spartans and Corinthians) and the "older," Ionian-Attic-speakers (such as the Athenians, the

Aegean islanders, and the residents of the Anatolian coast) continued until the end of the classical period of Greek history.

The depopulation at the beginning of the Dark Age had severe effects on the social organization, economy, and material culture in Greece. Settlements shrank in size and moved inland, away from vulnerable locations near the sea. Pottery and burial remains suggest a world that remained static and backward, cut off from the centers of Near Eastern civilization. Even nearby Greek communities had little economic contact with each other. Some villages may have had chiefs, but a chief's home and material possessions differed little from those of his neighbors. This Dark Age background, with its presumptions of the political and economic equality of self-sufficient households, had a profound effect on the later political assumptions of the classical Greeks.

Religion and ritual were woven into the fabric of Greek society, but the Greeks were suspicious of their gods and did not see them as necessarily positive forces. The gods were capricious, possessing all the failings of human beings while wielding superhuman power and delighting in interfering in human affairs. For the Greeks, the gods were to be appeased and propitiated,

The Parthenon. The largest and most famous of Athenian temples, the Parthenon is considered the classic example of Doric architecture. Its columns were made more graceful by tapering them in a slight curve toward the top. Its friezes and pediments were decorated with lifelike sculptures of prancing horses, fighting giants, and confident deities.

WHAT CULTURAL CHANGES MARKED THE END OF THE DARK AGE OF GREECE?

THE DARK AGE OF GREECE (1150–800 B.C.E.)   103

but never trusted fully. Although Greeks relied far more on the power of the individual human spirit than on divine intervention, they did also develop the idea of *hubris* (excessive pride) to discourage men from becoming too proud of their own accomplishments. Hubris attracted the attention of the gods and threatened them; the gods would punish such a man with relish.

HOMER AND THE HEROIC TRADITION

By the year 1000 B.C.E., the complete isolation of Greece was ending, and Greek society was becoming gradually more complex. Pottery also became more sophisticated, reflecting an upswing in the material culture and prosperity of the Greek mainland, and providing Greek traders with a valuable commodity to exchange for luxury goods from abroad.

As trade became an increasingly important feature of the Dark Age Greek economy, wealth increased and social stratification became more pronounced. A small group of aristocrats began to emerge, who justified their preeminence as a reflection of their own superior qualities as the "best men." Their wealth derived from a shifting combination of trade, plunder, and piracy. But in Dark Age Greece, wealth alone was not sufficient to establish one's aristocratic standing. A great man had also to be a singer of songs, a doer of deeds, a winner of battles, and above all favored by the gods. In short, he had to be a hero.

Most of what we know about the heroic ideal of late Dark Age Greece derives from the *Iliad* and the *Odyssey*, epic poems ascribed to the authorship of Homer. Though these astonishing epics—among the finest examples of literature in the Western tradition—were not written down until after 800 B.C.E., they were rooted in a much older oral tradition. For historians, this fact makes them complex and difficult sources to analyze. Homer's poems are set at the end of the Bronze Age; but over centuries of retelling, the social and political relationships portrayed in the poems changed to reflect the assumptions of later ages. As a result, although the great events and many of the material objects described in the Homerics epic are from the Bronze Age, the society the epics reveal to us is by and large the society of late Dark Age Greece.

Homer depicts a world in which competition and status are of paramount concern to the warrior elite. Through the exchange of expensive gifts and hospitality, aristocrats might create important ties of guest friendship with one another. In some ways, indeed, aristocrats had more in common with each other than

they did with the local societies they dominated. But this did not lessen the rivalries among them.

Competition among aristocratic households frequently led to violence, as it did during the Trojan War. But it could also take religious form in the creation of hero cults. Such cults might begin when an important family claimed an impressive nearby Mycenaean tomb as that of their own famous ancestor and then practiced dutiful sacrifice and other observances at the tomb. This devotion could extend to their followers and dependents; sometimes an entire community would identify itself with such a famous local hero. The heroic ideal thus became a deeply ingrained feature of Greek society, which Homer's epics would preserve and propagate throughout the classical period and beyond.

FOREIGN CONTACTS AND THE RISE OF THE POLIS

The ninth century B.C.E. saw dramatic changes throughout the Aegean basin. Contacts between Greeks and Phoenicians intensified. Most crucial, the Greeks adopted the Phoenician alphabet, improving it by converting unneeded consonantal symbols to represent vowels. The rolling melody and power of Homeric epic could now not only be heard but also recorded and read. The Phoenicians also introduced many artistic and literary traditions of the Near East into Greece, which the Greeks incorporated and reshaped to their own purposes.

The Phoenicians also pointed the way to a new activity among the Greeks—seafaring. Until the tenth century B.C.E., most Greeks traders waited at home for the Phoenicians to come to them. By the end of the

CHRONOLOGY

GREECE EMERGES FROM THE DARK AGE

Adoption and refinement of Phoenician alphabet	900–800 B.C.E.
Increase in commercial shipping throughout Aegean	900–800 B.C.E.
Sharp increase in Greek population	900–700 B.C.E.
Rise of the polis as major political unit	800 B.C.E.

GREEK GUEST FRIENDSHIP
AND HEROIC IDEALS

Before the reemergence of true state mechanisms in Greece, relations among communities depended largely on the personal and heritable connections made between the leading families of different villages and peoples. Often founded on the exchange of gifts or hospitality, the bonds of guest friendship imposed serious obligations on those involved in such relationships. Honoring them was part and parcel of the heroic ideal, as this encounter in Homer's Iliad *between the Greek hero Diomedes and the Lycian Glaukos, fighting for Troy, illustrates. Hospitality remained an important value of Greek society throughout its ancient history.*

Now Glaukos, sprung of Hippolochos, and the son of Tydeus came together in the space between the two armies, battle bent. . . . First to speak was Diomedes of the great war cry: "Who among mortal men are you, good friend? Since never before have I seen you in the fighting where men win glory, yet now you have come striding far out in front of all others . . . unhappy are those whose sons match warcraft against me. . . ."

Then in turn the shining son of Hippolochos answered: "High-hearted son of Tydeus, why ask of my generation? . . . Yet if you wish to learn . . . of my genealogy, there are plenty of men who know it. . . . Bellerophontes went to Lykia . . . and the lord of wide Lykia tendered him full-hearted honour. . . . Then when the king [of Lykia] knew him for the powerful stock of the god, he . . . offered him the hand of his daughter. . . . His bride bore three children to valiant Bellerophontes: Isandros, and Hippolochos and Laodameia. . . . Hippolochos begot me, and I claim [am proud?] that he is my father; he sent me to Troy, and urged me . . . to be always among the bravest. . . . Such is my generation and the blood I claim to be born from."

He spoke, and Diomedes of the great war cry was gladdened. He drove his spear deep into the prospering earth, and in winning words of friendliness he spoke. . . . "See now, you are my guest friend from far in the time of our fathers. Brilliant Oineus once was host to Bellerophontes the blameless, in his halls . . . and these two gave to each other fine gifts in token of friendship. . . . Therefore I am your friend and host in the heart of Argos; you are mine in Lykia, when I come to your country. Let us avoid each other's spears. . . . There are plenty of Trojans . . . for me to kill . . . [and] many Achaians for you to slaughter, if you can do it. . . ."

So they spoke, and both springing down from behind their horses gripped each other's hands and exchanged the promise of friendship.

Homer, *Iliad*, trans. Richard Lattimore (Chicago, 1951), pp. 156–159.

QUESTIONS FOR ANALYSIS

1. What is heroic about the meeting of Glaukos and Diomedes recounted in the *Iliad*? How do the participants identify themselves?

2. Instead of fighting one another, Glaukos and Diomedes resolve to be friends and "keep clear of each other's spears." Can soldiers on opposing sides be friends and continue to kill others? Does warfare create brotherhood, or fraternity, among fighters? Can the spirit of fraternity be created among college students? Is it desirable in all contexts?

WHAT CULTURAL CHANGES MARKED THE END OF THE DARK AGE OF GREECE?

THE DARK AGE OF GREECE (1150–800 B.C.E.)   105

Dark Age, however, Greeks had copied Phoenician designs for merchant vessels, allowing them to set out on trading ventures of their own and also to engage in piracy. As commercial activity increased, significant numbers of Greeks began to move among the homeland, the islands, and Anatolia, foreshadowing the colonial explosion that would issue from the Aegean in the eighth and seventh centuries B.C.E.

These economic and cultural developments were accompanied by dramatic growth in the Greek popu-lation. Around Athens, the population may have quadrupled during the ninth and early eighth centuries. Such rapid population growth placed heavy demands on the resources of Greece, a mountainous country with limited agricultural land. As smaller villages grew into towns, inhabitants of these rival communities came into more frequent contact with each other. Some degree of economic, political, and social cooperation among the inhabitants of these towns soon became necessary. But the heroic values of Dark Age

THE ATTIC PENINSULA

This map highlights the numerous city-states, or poleis, that dotted the Attic peninsula. It also shows the surrounding territories of Euboea, Boeotia, and Megaris. Where were the natural boundaries between these territories? Why were citizens of the other Attic poleis regarded as citizens of Athens also, even though they did not live in Athens?

Greek society did not make such cooperation easy. Each local community treasured its traditional autonomy and independence, celebrated its own religious cults, and honored its own aristocratic luminaries. On what basis, then, could such communities unite?

The Greek solution to this challenge was the *polis*. The Greek polis was a unique blend of institutional and informal structures of organization. Although *polis* is the root from which we derive the word *political*, many Greeks thought of the polis less as a state than as a social collectivity. Ancient sources refer to "the Athenians," "the Spartans," and "the Thebans" more often than to *poleis* (the plural of *polis*). And even when Greeks did speak about the polis as such, they frequently spoke as if all its residents were members of a single extended family that was divided in turn into smaller, kin-based groups such as tribes, clans, and households.

Poleis differed widely in size and organization. Structurally, however, most poleis were organized around a political and social center known as the *asty*, where markets and important meetings were held and where the basic business of the polis was conducted in the open air. Surrounding the urbanized asty was the *khora*, the "land." The khora of a larger polis might support several other towns besides the asty, as well as numerous villages; for example, all the residents of the entire territory of Attica were considered to be citizens of Athens. The vast majority of Athenian citizens were thus farmers, who might come to the asty to participate in the affairs of their polis but who did not reside in the urban center.

Synoikismos (the "bringing together of dwellings") was how Greeks described the process of early polis formation. Synoikismos—or synoecism—could come about through conquest or absorption and/or through the slow process of neighboring communities working together and accommodating one another. What spurred synoecism is a matter of debate. Some poleis took shape around defensible hilltops such as the Acropolis in Athens. Greeks may also have borrowed a Near Eastern (and particularly Phoenician) practice of orienting an urban center around a temple precinct. In Greece, however, the central temple site of a polis was not always located within the city's walls; at Argos, for example, the massive temple to Hera was located several miles away from any sizable settlement. In many Greek cities, moreover, temple building may have been a consequence of polis formation rather than its cause, as elites competed with one another to exalt their polis and bring glory on themselves. As was typical of Greek life generally, there was probably no standard pattern by which the early Greek poleis took shape.

ARCHAIC GREECE (800–480 B.C.E.)

How did the emergence of hoplite tactics affect Greek political norms?

With the emergence of the polis and the return of writing and literacy, the Archaic Age begins. After languishing in obscurity for nearly four centuries during the Dark Age, Greek civilization now burst forth with breathtaking dynamism and energy. Archaic Greece is remarkable not only for its achievements but also for its willingness to explore new avenues in religion, society, and politics. Aptly, this period has also been called the Age of Experiment.

COLONIZATION AND PANHELLENISM

In the eighth and seventh centuries, smaller-scale Greek trading ventures and migrations throughout the Aegean developed into a full-fledged colonization effort. Each colony was an independent foundation, with emotional and sentimental ties to its mother city, but no political obligations. By the end of the sixth century B.C.E., Greeks had founded several hundred new colonies from the Black Sea to the western Mediterranean, permanently altering the cultural geography of the Mediterranean world. The western shores of Anatolia would remain a stronghold of Greek culture until the end of the Middle Ages; so many Greeks settled in southern Italy and Sicily that the Romans called the region Magna Graecia, "Greater Greece." By the fourth century B.C.E., more Greeks lived in Magna Graecia than in Greece itself. Greek colonies could also be found farther westward, along the southern coasts of France and Spain.

Motives for colonization varied. Some poleis, such as Corinth, were blessed by geography but cursed by the agricultural poverty of their land. Trade therefore became their lifeblood. The ruling aristocratic clan of eighth-century Corinth undertook an ambitious colonization scheme, planting colonies up the coast of the Adriatic and in Sicily as a way to promote trade. Other poleis, confronted by population pressures and political turmoil, used colonization as an outlet for excess population and/or troublemakers.

Colonial expansion intensified Greek contacts with other cultures, especially Egypt and Phoenicia. Phoenician pottery brought new artistic motifs and mythological

HOW DID THE EMERGENCE OF HOPLITE TACTICS AFFECT GREEK POLITICAL NORMS?

ARCHAIC GREECE (800–480 B.C.E.)   107

figures into Greece; Egypt profoundly influenced early Greek sculptural representations of the human form (see illustration on p. 124). At the same time, however, intensified contact with other cultures sharpened Greeks' awareness of their own common identity and peculiarity as Hellenes (the Greeks' name for themselves). Such self-conscious Hellenism did not necessarily lead to greater political cooperation among the fiercely independent poleis. Like the Sumerians, the Greeks were particularists who had little use for permanent political associations larger than the individual polis. They were also divided by linguistic distinctions between Ionian- and Dorian-speakers. But nonetheless the Hellenes had an emerging sense of a common culture and outlook, despite their political fractiousness.

Hellenism also encouraged the growth of Panhellenic ("all-Greeks") cult sites such as the Oracle of Delphi, and of Panhellenic festivals such as the Olympic Games. At Delphi, people from all over the Greek world came to seek advice from the priestess of Apollo as she sat over a vent in the earth, munching eucalyptus leaves. Her unintelligible answers, delivered while she was in a trancelike state, would then be translated by the attending priests into perfect verse. These answers were sufficiently vague that the oracle could rarely be proven wrong, even in hindsight. At the Olympic Games, Greeks honored the king of the gods, Zeus, near the giant temple to him at Olympia. The Greeks took great pride in these athletic competitions; Greek historians even dated events by Olympiads, four-year periods that began with the sup-

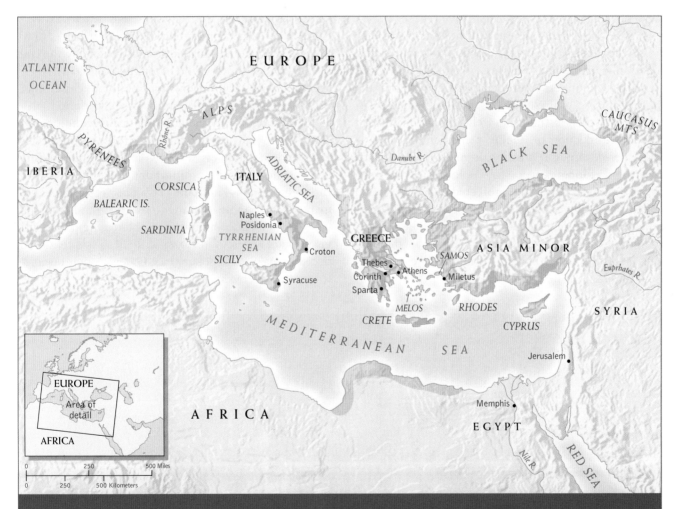

GREECE AND ITS SETTLEMENTS, C. 550 B.C.E.

Compare this map with the one on p. 71. How would you explain the different areas colonized by Greeks and Phoenicians? Were Greek colonies likely to compete with Phoenician colonies? Where were such conflicts most likely to erupt?

posed date of the first games in 776 B.C.E. Only Greeks were permitted to participate in the games, and all wars among Greeks were to cease while they took place. A victory in the games brought great prestige to the victor, who could be catapulted into a position of social and even political power within his polis. Predictably, such competitions did little to stop contentiousness and rivalry among the poleis; but they did strengthen the Greeks' sense that they shared a common culture, despite their political and linguistic differences.

HOPLITE WARFARE

During the Dark Age, the military power of a Greek community rested with the elite, who had the time, resources, and training to become Homeric warrior heroes. Common foot soldiers played a secondary role as followers and supporters of the aristocratic warriors who dueled in single combat. This aristocratic monopoly on military prowess gave the aristocracy tremendous political and social leverage within the nascent poleis. As a result, aristocrats dominated political offices and priesthoods as well as economic life.

The introduction of hoplite tactics during the Archaic Period brought aristocratic military dominance to an end. Hoplites were foot soldiers, armed with spears or short swords, and protected by a large round shield (a *hoplon*), a breastplate, a helmet, and sometimes wrist and leg guards. In battle, hoplites stood shoulder to shoulder in a close formation called a phalanx, several rows across and several lines deep, with each hoplite carrying his shield on the left arm to pro-

tect the unshielded right side of the man standing next to him. In his right hand each hoplite carried a thrusting weapon such as a spear or short sword, so that an approaching phalanx presented a nearly impenetrable wall of armor and weaponry to its opponents. If a man in the front rank fell, the one behind him stepped up to take his place; indeed, the weight of the entire phalanx was literally behind the front line, each soldier aiding the assault by leaning with his shield into the man in front of him. The tight formation and heavy armor (as much as seventy pounds including the shield) required but one skill: the ability to stay together. As long as the phalanx remained intact, it was a nearly unbeatable formation.

Where, when, and how hoplite tactics first came to Greece remains a mystery. The Greeks may have learned them from the Assyrians. But wherever they came from, once hoplite tactics were introduced into Greece, all the poleis rushed to adopt them. By the end of the seventh century B.C.E., hoplite tactics (with their accompanying requirements for training in close-order drill) were a standard element in Greek warfare.

The result was a social and political revolution. Because every polis needed a hoplite force to protect its independence, farmers who could afford the requisite armor soon became a political and social force within the archaic polis—a hoplite class. But the sacrifices demanded by hoplite warfare were great, and the men who had now become indispensable to the polis's survival quickly grew restless without a share in its decision making. Scholars once believed their disquiet was sufficient by itself to force concessions from the

Hoplite Infantry Advancing into Combat. This Corinthian vase, dating to around 650 B.C.E., is the earliest known depiction of hoplites fighting in a phalanx formation.

How did the emergence of hoplite tactics affect Greek political norms?

Archaic Greece (800–480 b.c.e.)   109

aristocrats, including access to political decision making and the writing down of laws to guarantee "equal" justice. But the real impetus toward political change may in fact have come from disgruntled aristocrats.

ARISTOCRATIC CULTURE AND THE RISE OF TYRANNY

For the better part of the seventh and sixth centuries B.C.E., aristocrats continued to dominate the Greek poleis. Struggles for influence among competing aristocratic families were commonplace. Aristocratic families sought to checkmate their rivals by using new laws and the dispatching of colonial expeditions as weapons. Despite their quarrels with each other, however, aristocrats held all the official power within the polis, not least because they were the only members of society who could afford to hold these unsalaried but time-consuming political offices.

The aristocrats of the Archaic Age pursued not only wealth, power, and glory but also a distinct culture and defining lifestyle. Holding office and participating in politics was part of this lifestyle; but so too was the symposium, an intimate gathering at which elite men would enjoy wine (sometimes in prodigious quantities), poetry (ranging from epics to bawdy drinking songs),

A Bearded Greek Male and His Young Lover. This illustration is from a red-figure cup, c. 480 B.C.E.

dancing competitions, and female courtesans who provided both musical and sexual services. Respectable women were excluded from such meetings, as they were from all other aspects of social and political life. So too were nonaristocratic men. The symposium was thus far more than a social occasion. It was an essential feature of aristocratic male life within the polis.

Homosexuality was another important aspect of aristocratic culture in the Archaic Period. Appropriate aristocratic homosexual behavior was regulated by social custom. Typically, a man in his late twenties to late thirties and on the rise in political life would take as his lover and protégé an aristocratic youth in his early to mid-teens. The two would form a close and intimate bond of friendship, in which sexual intercourse played an important role. This intimate bond between man and boy was believed to benefit the younger partner, as he learned the workings of government and society and through his older lover made important political and social connections that would benefit him later in life. Plato, indeed, would argue that true love could only exist between two such male lovers, because only within such a relationship could a man find a partner worthy of his affections.

A whole complex of values, ideas, practices, and assumptions thus informed aristocratic identity in the Archaic Period. As a result, it was impossible for those outside this elite world to participate fully in the public life of the polis. By the middle of the Archaic Age, however, the circle of the aristocratic elite was narrow-

Scene from a Symposium. This scene, from a red-figure drinking cup made around 480 B.C.E., shows an aristocratic young man reclining on a couch, holding two flutes, while a slave girl (identifiable by her short hair) dances before him.

THRASYBOULOS ON HOW TO BE A TYRANT

The fifth-century historian Herodotus relates how Periander, tyrant of Corinth from 627 to 587 B.C.E., sought advice from his older contemporary Thrasyboulos of Miletus on how best to secure tyrannical power. This excerpt describes Thrasyboulos's response to Periander's emissary and the Corinthian's response to his strange reply. Although Herodotus's negative attitude toward tyranny is typical of later classical thought, Periander and his father before him had in fact been instrumental in breaking a narrow aristocratic regime and increasing Corinth's commercial prosperity.

At the beginning Periander was gentler than his father [Cypselus] had been. But afterwards, when he had dealt with Thrasyboulos, prince of Miletus, he became yet bloodier than Cypselus. . . . Thrasyboulos had led out Periander's messenger, outside the city, and with him entered a sown field; then he walked through the corn, questioning, and again questioning the herald, about his coming from Corinth. And ever and again as he saw one of the ears growing above the rest he would strike it down, and what he struck down he threw away, until by this means he had destroyed all the fairest and strongest of the corn. So he passed through the whole place and, having added no suggestions, sent the herald away. When the herald came back to Corinth, Periander was anxious to know what suggestion Thrasyboulos had made. But the man said that Thrasyboulos had made no suggestion at all, and indeed he wondered what sort of man this was he had been sent to, a madman and a destroyer of his own property. . . . But Periander understood the act of Thrasyboulos and grasped in his mind that what he was telling him was that he should murder the most eminent of the citizens. And so from this time forth he displayed every form of wickedness toward his fellow countrymen. Whatever Cypselus had spared of death and banishment, Periander completed.

Herodotus, v. 92, trans. David Grene (Chicago and London, 1987), pp. 397–398 (somewhat revised).

QUESTIONS FOR ANALYSIS

1. Tyrants in Greece sometimes ruled by terror and other times by popular consent. Can you suggest positive aspects of tyrant rule in the Greek states? Was Thrasyboulos simply a bad example, an unheroic character lacking in aristocratic virtue?

---

ing even further. A small number of aristocrats now dominated the higher offices of the polis, putting themselves in a position to control a wide swath of civic life at the expense of their rivals. Many aristocrats were left on the outside of their own culture, looking in. For these men, a remedy to their problem lay close at hand—the hoplites, who had complaints of their own about their exclusion from political power.

As the circles of political power narrowed during the seventh century, violence between aristocratic groups increased, ultimately giving rise to the emergence of tyranny as an alternative form of government. The word *tyrannos* was not originally Greek, but borrowed from Lydia, signifying someone who seized power and ruled outside the traditional constitutional framework. A tyrant in Archaic Greece was thus not necessarily an

How and why did the Athenian, Spartan, and Milesian poleis differ from each other?

The Archaic Polis in Action   111

abusive ruler. Classical Greek thinkers were fascinated and horrified by the unrestrained power of archaic tyrants, and Aristotle would condemn tyranny as a perversion of the pure form of monarchy: hereditary kingship. In the Archaic Period, however, tyranny often led the way to wider political enfranchisement.

A Greek tyrant was usually an aristocrat who had tired of his exclusion from the elite or had become frustrated with the petty rows of aristocratic factions within the polis. Would-be tyrants appealed instead to the hoplite class, whose armed might could propel them to a position of sole power. In return, tyrants would then extend rights of political participation to the hoplites, or at least offer them new economic and judicial guarantees, while striving to retain the reins of power in their own hands. This was an inherently unstable state of affairs, because after the original tyrant had fulfilled the wishes of the hoplites, the continuance of tyranny became an obstacle to even greater power for the people, the *demos*. For this reason, tyrannies rarely lasted for more than two generations. Tyranny more often served as a way station on the road from aristocracy to more broadly participatory forms of government, such as democracy.

Lyric Poetry

Characteristic of archaic Greek culture is lyric poetry, a new departure in literature that originated in the seventh century B.C.E. and continued thereafter. The first monuments of Greek literature are the imposing epics of Homer, magnificent in scope and brimming with the heroic themes of Dark Age Greek society. Homer's successor, Hesiod (c. 700 B.C.E.), composed shorter epic poems imbued with traditional outlooks. His *Theogony* (thee-AW-guh-nee) describes the origins of the gods and the created cosmos; his *Works and Days* is a personal diatribe against his scheming brother and the elite of his hometown that also addresses such topics as the rewards of hard work, the place of justice in the polis, and the importance of treating one's neighbors well.

The next generations of poets were less ambitious in scope, but their work often has a greater appeal because of its highly personal nature. Often, they named themselves within the lines of their poems. Lyric poets avoided conventional tropes to concentrate on themes of more interest to themselves. Some flouted typical mores and values quite explicitly. Archilochus of Paros (c. 680–640 B.C.E.), for example, commemorated his service as a mercenary by writing, "Some barbarian waves my shield, as I had to abandon it / . . . but I es-

caped, so it matters not / . . . I can get another just as good." So much for heroism and standing firm in battle! Archilochus happily threw away his equipment and fled to save himself. He also gave vent to his personal anger with a faithless lover and the best friend she ran off with, comparing her to a fig tree that feeds every raven and wishing that his friend would be taken as a slave to the wild country of Thrace.

Among the most famous and accomplished of the lyric poets was Sappho (SAF-foh; c. 620–550 B.C.E.), who lived in the polis of Mytilene on the island of Lesbos. Sappho wrote beautiful and poignant poetry on romantic longing and sexual desire, sometimes about men, but more often and more passionately about other women. In one famous poem she wrote, "Like the very gods in my sight is he who / sits where he can look in your eyes, who listens / close to you, to hear the soft voice, its sweetness murmur in love and / laughter, all for him. . . . Let me only glance where you are, the voice dies, I can say nothing, / but my lips are stricken to silence, under / neath my skin the tenuous flame suffuses." Another poem opens with the following lines: "Some there are who say that the fairest thing seen / on the black earth is an array of horsemen; / some, men marching; some would say ships; but I say she whom one loves best is the loveliest."

Although some lyric poets did extol martial virtues and praise heroism, the intimacy of lyric reveals to us something quite new in the history of the West: the individual who expresses his or her feelings, even when these are at odds with the dominant culture of the time.

The Archaic Polis in Action

How and why did the Athenian, Spartan, and Milesian poleis differ from each other?

The Archaic poleis developed in very different ways. To illustrate this diversity, we examine three particularly well-documented examples: Athens, Sparta, and Miletus. None, however, is typical of the historical development of the Greek poleis as a whole. There were approximately 1,000 such poleis in Greece. About most of them we know almost nothing. It seems unlikely, however, that amid such diversity we will ever be able to describe a typical polis.

ATHENS

The Athenians believed that they and their city had existed continuously since the Bronze Age; this claim was integral to their identity and their sense of self-importance within the larger Greek world. But although Attica was among the most populous and prosperous regions in Dark Age Greece, Athens itself was of no great significance at this early date. Even in the early Archaic Period, Corinth was the leading commercial city of Greece; Sparta was the preeminent military power; and the Aegean islands, along with the central coast of Anatolia, were the leading cultural centers.

Athens emerged from the Dark Age with a distinctly agricultural economy. Whatever gains its aristocrats acquired through trade they had reinvested in land. By the early Archaic Age, the Athenian elite regarded commerce as a disreputable means of earning a living. Their city's orientation toward the Aegean, together with the excellent harbors along the Attic coast, would eventually make Athens famous as a mercantile and seafaring polis. But until the sixth century B.C.E., the aristocracy of Athens remained firmly entrenched on the land.

Aristocratic dominance over Athens rested on the elected magistracies, which they monopolized, and the council of state, which was composed of former magistrates. By the early seventh century B.C.E., aristocratic officials called archons wielded executive power in Athens; ultimately nine archons in all presided over the civil, military, judicial, and religious functions of the polis. The archons served a term of one year, after which they became lifetime members of the Areopagus (*ahr-ee-OP-ah-guhs*) Council. The council was where the real power in Athens resided. The Areopagus elected the archons, thus controlling its own future membership. It also served as a kind of high court, with tremendous influence over the judicial procedures of Athens.

Deep economic and social divisions developed in Athenian society during the seventh century, as a significant proportion of the population fell into debt slavery (the practice of securing a loan with one's person as collateral and, when unable to pay up, becoming indentured to the creditor). Rivalries between aristocratic political factions also destabilized the polis. In 632 B.C.E. a prominent aristocrat named Kylon attempted to establish a tyranny, only to surrender under a pledge of safe conduct. Kylon's political rivals violated

their promise of immunity, however, slaughtering his supporters and driving Kylon himself into exile. Hard feelings would endure for a generation.

The endless cycle of revenge killing that followed Kylon's failed coup inspired the first attempt at written law in Athens. In 621 B.C.E., an aristocrat named Drakon was charged with "setting the laws"; in particular, he sought to control homicide through harsh ("draconian") punishments. His attempt at stabilizing Athens failed, however, and the city soon found itself on the brink of civil war. Hoping to avoid this, in 594 B.C.E. aristocrats and hoplites alike agreed to make Solon the sole archon for one year and to give him sweeping powers to reorganize Athenian government. Solon was an aristocrat who had made his name and fortune as a merchant; this led everyone in Athenian society to trust Solon, because he was not beholden to any single interest.

Solon's political and economic reforms laid the foundations for the later development of Athenian democracy. He forbade the practice of debt slavery and set up a fund to buy back Athenian debt slaves sold abroad. He encouraged the Athenians to cultivate olives and grapes, thus spurring cash-crop farming and the urban industries (such as pottery, oil production, and shipbuilding) necessary to make Athens a commercial power. He also broadened rights of political participation. Solon set up courts in which a broader range of citizens served as jurors and to which any Athenian might appeal if he disliked a decision of the Areopagus. He based eligibility for political office on property qualifications, thus making it possible for someone not born an aristocrat to gain access to power through the accumulation of wealth. He also gave the Athenian citizen assembly (known as the *ekklesia*) the right to elect the archons. This was a significant step, since all free-born Athenian men over the age of eighteen could participate in the assembly.

Solon's reforms did not succeed. The aristocracy thought them too radical; the demos, not nearly radical enough. In the resulting turmoil, an aristocrat named Peisistratos (*pi-SIS-trah-tohs*) finally succeeded in establishing himself as tyrant in 546 B.C.E. Peisistratos allowed the organs of government to function as Solon intended and launched a massive campaign of public-works projects. Behind the apparent mildness of his rule, however, lay the quiet but persistent intimidation that Peisistratos practiced through the hiring of

> Solon's political and economic reforms laid the foundations for the later development of Athenian democracy.

How and why did the Athenian, Spartan, and Milesian poleis differ from each other?

The Archaic Polis in Action   113

Harvesting Olives, c. 520 B.C.E. Olive oil became one of Athens' most important exports in the sixth and fifth centuries B.C.E.

foreign mercenaries and the ruthlessness with which he crushed any dissent from his regime. By enforcing Solon's reforms, Peisistratos strengthened the demos and encouraged the taste for self-government. He remained a popular ruler until his death. His sons, on the other hand, proved much less popular; and after one son was murdered in an aristocratic feud, the other was quickly overthrown with the help of the Spartans.

In the aftermath of the Peisistratid overthrow, in 510 B.C.E., came a brief aristocratic counterrevolutionary regime, supported by the Spartans. However, two generations of increasing access to power left the Athenian demos with no interest in returning to an elite oligarchy. For the first time in history, the populace at large spontaneously rose up and overthrew the government. They rallied behind Cleisthenes (*CLIS-the-nees*), also an aristocrat but a man who had served the Peisistratid government ably and who had championed the

cause of the demos after the fall of tyranny. Once voted in as archon in 508/7 B.C.E., Cleisthenes quickly took steps to limit aristocratic power. By reorganizing the Athenian population into ten voting "tribes" he suppressed regional identities within Attica; these had been an important source of aristocratic influence. He further strengthened the Athenian citizen assembly and extended the machinery of democratic government to the local level throughout Attica. He also introduced the practice of ostracism, whereby the Athenians could decide each year whether they wanted to banish some-

Harmodius and Aristogiton. The two were lovers who slew Peisistratos' son Hipparchus and so helped bring the Peisistratid tyranny over Athens to an end. Athenians celebrated them as liberators. This statue is a Roman copy of an original carved around 500 B.C.E.

Ostracism. The system took its name from the pot shards (in Greek, *ostraka*) on which the names of unpopular citizens were scratched. Many of the ballots have survived. Here we see Aristeides, Kimon, and Themistokles.

one for ten years and, if so, whom. Cleisthenes believed that with this power, the demos could prevent the return of a tyrant and quell factional strife if civil war seemed imminent.

By 500 B.C.E., Athens had become the principal exporter of olive oils, wines, and pottery in the Greek world. The political struggles of the sixth century had also given it a far more democratic temper than any other Greek polis possessed, simultaneously strengthening its institutions of central government. Athens was poised to assume the role it would claim for itself during the fifth century, as the exemplar of Greek culture and the proponent of its own style of participatory democracy.

CHRONOLOGY

THE CHANGING LANDSCAPE OF ARCHAIC GREECE

Panhellenic colonial expansion by Greek poleis	800–400 B.C.E.
Hoplite tactics become standard in Greek warfare	725–650 B.C.E.
Emergence of tyrannical governments	700–600 B.C.E.
Militarization of Sparta	600 B.C.E.
Solon's reforms	594 B.C.E.
Cleisthenes' reforms	508 B.C.E.

SPARTA

Located in the southern part of the Peloponnesus (*pel-oh-poh-NEE-subs;* the large peninsula that forms southern Greece), the Spartans represented everything that Athens was not. Athens was cultured, sophisticated, cosmopolitan; Sparta was basic, earthy, and traditional. Depending on one's point of view, either set of adjectives might serve as admiration or criticism.

Sparta took shape when four villages (and ultimately a fifth) combined to form the polis of Sparta. Perhaps as a relic of the unification process, Sparta retained a dual monarchy throughout its history, with two royal families and two lines of succession. Although seniority or capacity usually determined which of the two ruling kings had more influence, neither was technically superior to the other, a situation that led to political intrigue within Sparta.

The Spartan system depended on its conquest of Messenia, an agriculturally wealthy region west of Sparta. Around 720 B.C.E., the Spartans subjugated the region and enslaved the population. These *helots* (as the enslaved Messenians were now called) remained to work the land, which was now parceled out among the Spartiates. Around 650 B.C.E., however, the helots revolted, gaining support from several neighboring cities and briefly threatening Sparta with annihilation. Eventually, Sparta triumphed; but the shock of this rebellion brought about a permanent transformation in Spartan society.

Determined to prevent another uprising, Sparta became the most militarized polis in Greece. By 600 B.C.E., everything in Sparta was oriented to the maintenance of its hoplite army, a force so superior that the Spartans confidently left their city unfortified. The Spartan system made every full citizen, called a Spartiate (or, alternatively, an Equal), a professional soldier of the phalanx. At a time when Athenian society was becoming more democratic, in Sparta the citizenry was "aristocratized," making every citizen-soldier into a warrior-champion of the hoplite phalanx.

Sparta became a society organized for war. At birth, every child was examined by Spartan officials who determined whether it was healthy enough to raise (if not, the infant was abandoned in the mountains). If deemed worthy of upbringing, a child was placed at age seven in the state-run Spartan educational system. Boys and girls trained together until age twelve, participating in exercise, gymnastics, and other physical drills and competitions. Boys then went to live in the barracks, where their military training would commence in earnest.

How and why did the Athenian, Spartan, and Milesian poleis differ from each other?

The Archaic Polis in Action 115

Girls continued an education in letters until they married, usually around the age of eighteen.

Barracks training was rigorous, designed to accustom the young Spartan male to physical hardships. At age eighteen, the young man would try to gain membership in a *syssition*, a communal mess tent as well as a kind of fighting brotherhood. Failure meant that the young man could not become a full Spartiate and would lose his rights as a citizen. If accepted into a syssition, however, men remained in the barracks until they were thirty years of age. Although they were required to marry between the ages of twenty and thirty, men living in the barracks were permitted to meet their

wives only surreptitiously—a fact that may account in part for the notably low birthrate among Spartiate couples. After age thirty, a Spartiate male could live with his family. He remained on active military duty, however, until he was sixty, although he was unlikely to participate in phalanx combat beyond the age of forty-five.

All Spartiate males aged thirty and over were members of the citizen assembly, the *apella*, which voted yes or no, without debate, on matters proposed to it by a council consisting of twenty-eight elders (the *gerousia*) plus the two kings. The gerousia (*gher-OO-see-ah*) was the main policymaking body of the polis and also its

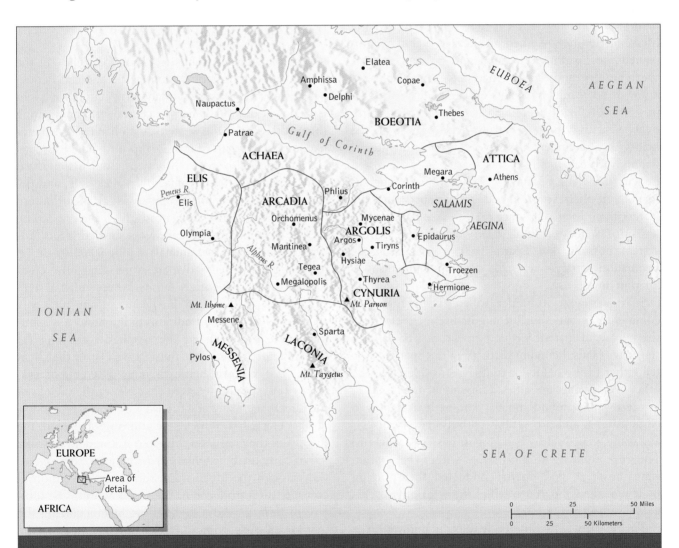

THE PELOPONNESUS

Located on the Peloponnesian peninsula, the highly militarized society of Sparta dominated the southern region known as Laconia. How might Sparta's geographical position have influenced its outlook on foreign affairs? Did geography make conflict between Athens and Sparta inevitable?

primary court. Its members were elected by the apella for life but had to be over the age of sixty before they could stand for election. Five ephors, elected annually by the apella, supervised the educational system and acted as guardians of Spartan traditions. In the latter role, an ephor could even depose an errant king from command of the army while on campaign. The ephors also supervised the Spartan secret service, the *krypteia*, recruiting agents from among the most promising young Spartiates. Agents spied on citizens, but their main job was to infiltrate the helot population, identify potential troublemakers, and kill them.

Spartan policy often hinged on the precarious relationship between the helots and the Spartiates. The helots outnumbered the Spartiates ten to one, and Messenia routinely seethed with revolt. Helots accompanied the Spartans on campaign as shield bearers, spear bearers, and baggage handlers; remarkably, we know of no revolts by helots on campaign. At home, however, the helots were a constant security concern. Every year the Spartans ritually declared war on the helots, as a reminder that they would not tolerate attempts to break free. But the Spartiates never rested easy in their beds; Spartans were notoriously reluctant to commit their army abroad, in part because they feared its prolonged absence might encourage a helot uprising at home. Helot slavery made the Spartan system possible, but Sparta's reliance on a hostile population of slaves was also a serious limitation on Spartan power.

Spartiates were forbidden to engage in trades or commerce, because wealth might distract them from the pursuit of martial virtue. Nor did Spartiates farm their own lands. Economic activity in the Spartan state fell either to the helots or to the free residents of the other Peloponnesian cities (known as the *perioikoi*, "those dwelling round about"). The perioikoi enjoyed certain rights and protections within Spartan society, and some grew wealthy handling its business concerns. They exercised no political rights within the Spartan state, however, and Sparta conducted their foreign policy for them. Spartiates who lost their rights as citizens also became perioikoi.

The Spartans self-consciously rejected innovation or change. They styled themselves the protectors of the "traditional constitutions" of Greece, by which they meant older, aristocratic regimes. In this role, Sparta tried to prevent the establishment of tyrannies in neighboring states and tried to overthrow them when they arose. Sparta's stern defense of tradition made it an object of admiration throughout the Greek world,

even though few Greeks had any desire to live as the Spartans did.

The fatal flaw in the Spartan system was demographic. There were many ways to fall from the status of Spartiate, including criminal behavior and cowardice. The only way to become a Spartiate, however, was by birth—and the Spartan birthrate simply could not keep pace with the demand for Spartiates. As a result, the number of full Spartiates declined from perhaps as many as 10,000 in the Archaic Period to only about 1,000 by the middle of the fourth century B.C.E.

MILETUS AND THE IONIAN REVOLUTION IN THOUGHT

Across the Aegean from the Greek mainland lay the Greek cities of Anatolia. During the Archaic Period, Miletus was the foremost commercial, cultural, and military power of Ionia, a narrow coastal strip dominating the central part of the western Anatolian coast. Miletus had long been a part of the Greek world, but Near Eastern influences also shaped Milesian culture in important ways. Ionia was the birthplace of Greek epic, and debate continues over the extent to which Near Eastern models might have influenced the Homeric epics. Certainly other creative endeavors showed Near Eastern influence. Fantastic animals, a long-standing theme of Near Eastern decorative art, were frequently represented on Milesian pottery during the seventh and sixth centuries B.C.E. Milesian intellectuals were also well aware of Near Eastern traditions of literature and learning. Some even echoed the bombastic openings of Persian imperial decrees ("thus speaks Darius the Great King. . . .") to make their own, quite different observations ("thus speaks Hecataeus of Miletus: the sayings of the Greeks are many and foolish").

The close but difficult relationship between the Ionians of the coast and the interior kingdom of Lydia led to particularly extensive cross-cultural exchange. It was through the Ionians that the Lydian invention of coinage was introduced to the Greek world. The Ionians, in turn, played a crucial role in Hellenizing the interior of Asia Minor. Under the pressure of the Lydians—who sought the excellent ports of the Anatolian coast for themselves—the major cities of Ionia ultimately banded together to form the Ionian League, a political and religious confederation of independent poleis pledged to support each other in time of need. This was the first such organization known in the Greek world.

The Milesians founded many colonies, especially in and around the Black Sea. They were also active in Egypt, where the main Greek trading outposts were Milesian foundations. Their colonial efforts, combined with their advantageous position for trade with the rest of Asia Minor, brought Miletus great wealth. Miletus reached the peak of its power in the early sixth century, when its tyrant Thrasyboulos successfully warded off Lydian aggression and (probably) constructed a fleet to protect Milesian shipping interests. After his death, however, continuing Lydian pressure, combined with competition from the Ionian island of Samos, led to Miletus's slow decline over the course of the sixth century.

> Miletus also became a center for Greek speculative thinking and philosophy.

Miletus also became a center for Greek speculative thinking and philosophy. Beginning in the sixth century B.C.E., a series of thinkers known as the pre-Socratics (because they came before the great philosopher Socrates; *SAH-kruh-tees*) raised serious questions about the relationship between the natural world (the *kosmos*), the gods, and men. Oftentimes, their explanations moved divine agency to the margins or removed it altogether—and for that, everyday Greeks looked on them with suspicion. The

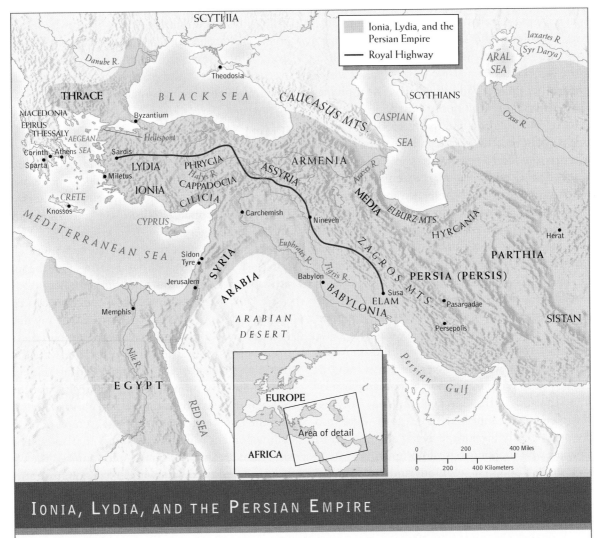

IONIA, LYDIA, AND THE PERSIAN EMPIRE

During the seventh and sixth centuries B.C.E., the Greek cities of the Ionian coast were the cultural and commercial leaders of Greece. During the fifth century B.C.E., however, they lost this position to Athens. How does Ionia's geographical position help explain this change in its fortunes? And how might this change have influenced Ionian attitudes toward the Persian Empire?

so-called Milesian School consisted of three successive thinkers: Thales, Anaximander, and Anaximenes. All three built on older traditions of Near Eastern learning, such as Babylonian astronomy; but in typically Greek fashion, they turned those ideas on their heads. Calculating and observing the movements of the heavens, the thinkers of the Milesian School sought physical explanations for what they saw, refusing to presume that the heavenly bodies were gods. By making the observations of men, not the will of the gods, the starting point for their thinking, the Milesian School began to formulate rational theories to explain the physical universe they observed.

Stimulated by the cosmopolitanism of their city, Milesian philosophers also began to rethink their place in the human world, inaugurating what has sometimes been called "the Ionian revolution in thought." Hecataeus of Miletus, the first Greek to draw a map of the known world, wrote his remark about the foolishness of the Greeks after extensive travels during which he studied other cultures and their gods. Xenophanes (*zee-NAHF-uh-nees*) of Colophon observed that the Thracians (a barbarian people living to the north of the Greeks) believed the gods had blue eyes and red hair, whereas the Ethiopians portrayed their gods as dark skinned and curly haired. He concluded that human beings made gods in their own image, not the other way around. If oxen could speak and make objects, Xenophanes declared, they would pray and fashion idols to gods who looked like oxen. Such relativism was new, but it would become a distinctive strand in later Greek philosophy.

This widening fissure between religious belief and philosophical speculation was a crucial development in the history of Western thought. It was less complete, however, than is often imagined. Philosophy was a game for a few, not for the average Greek; and as philosophers turned their attention to humanity's relationship to the gods, citizens in even the most progressive of poleis were unnerved. The gods were too central a part of daily life for the average Greek not to feel threatened by such impious philosophizing.

The struggle between religion and philosophy would ultimately be fought out not in Miletus but in Athens more than a hundred years after Xenophanes' bold proclamation. The Ionian revolution in thought slowed after 546 B.C.E., when the Persians conquered Lydia and acquired Lydia's suzerainty over the Greek city-states of Asia Minor, including Miletus. Ultimately, Milesian resistance to Persian rule would trigger the greatest clash the Greek world had yet known—war with the mighty Persian Empire.

THE PERSIAN WARS

How were the Greek armies able to defeat the much larger Persian forces?

The Archaic Period of Greek history closed with dramatic struggles against Persia. When hostilities began, Persia was the mightiest state the world had ever seen, capable of mustering over a million armed men. The Greeks, in contrast, remained a collection of poleis, fiercely suspicious of one another and competitive to the bitter end. An exceptionally large polis, such as Athens or Sparta, might put 10,000 hoplites in the field; but the vast majority of Greek states could provide only a few hundred each. For two decades the threat of Persian conquest loomed on the Greek horizon. When finally the immediate danger to Greek freedom receded, the experience of war had changed the Greek world immeasurably.

THE IONIAN REVOLT (499–494 B.C.E.)

Our main source for the Persian Wars is Herodotus, the Father of History. His account reflects many of the intellectual currents of mid-fifth-century Athens, where he lived and worked. Reflecting a kind of geographical and cultural determinism, he ascribed the war between Persia and Greece to an ancient hatred between Europe and Asia. But his own narrative shows that the immediate cause of the war was a political conflict in Miletus.

By 501 B.C.E., Aristagoras—the Persians' puppet tyrant of Miletus—grew concerned that his days as a favorite of Darius the Great were numbered. Turning from puppet to patriot, he roused the Milesians and the rest of Ionia to revolt against Persian rule. He also sought military support from the Greek mainland. The Spartans refused to send their army abroad, but Athens and the city of Eretria on Euboea, sympathetic to their fellow Ionians, agreed to send a total of twenty-five ships and crews. This small force captured the old Lydian capital of Sardis (now a Persian administrative center) and burned it to the ground. But the Athenians and Eretrians then sailed home, leaving the Ionians to their own devices. After five years of brave struggle, the rebels were finally overwhelmed by the vastly superior might of Persia in 494 B.C.E.

Darius realized, however, that so long as his Greek subjects in Asia Minor could cast a hopeful eye to their cousins across the Aegean, they would long for freedom. Darius therefore set out on a punitive expedition

How were the Greek armies able to defeat the much larger Persian forces?

THE PERSIAN WARS   119

CHRONOLOGY

THE PERSIAN WARS

Croesus, king of Lydia, conquers Greek cities of Anatolia	c. 560 B.C.E.
Cyrus, king of Persia, conquers Lydia and controls Greek cities	546 B.C.E.
Ionian Revolt	499–494 B.C.E.
Battle of Marathon	490 B.C.E.
Xerxes invades Greece	480 B.C.E.
Battles of Thermopylae and Salamis	480 B.C.E.
Battle of Plataea	479 B.C.E.
Formation of the Delian League, led by Athens	478–477 B.C.E.

to teach Athens and Eretria a lesson. The king sent 20,000 soldiers under two of his finest generals on an island-hopping campaign across the Aegean. Landing on Euboea in the summer of 490, Persian forces sacked and burned Eretria and sent its population into captivity in Persia. They then crossed the narrow strait to Attica, landing in the plain of Marathon.

MARATHON AND ITS AFTERMATH

Recognizing the danger they now faced, the Athenians sought help from the Spartans, who responded that they were unable to assist due to an ongoing religious festival. Only the small, nearby polis of Plataea offered the Athenians aid. The Athenian phalanx would have to engage the mighty Persians on its own.

Heavily outnumbered and without effective cavalry to counter the Persians, the Athenian phalanx took a position between two hills blocking the main road to the asty. After a standoff of several days, the Athenian general Miltiades received word that the Persians were watering their horses, and that the Persian infantry (numerically superior but poorly equipped compared with the 10,000 Athenian hoplites) was vulnerable. Miltiades led a charge that smashed the Persian force and resulted in catastrophic losses for the Persians. Herodotus records that 6,400 Persians fell, compared with only 192 Athenians. The Persians withdrew.

The Athenians had defeated the world's greatest empire, and they had done it without Spartan help. It was a tremendous boost to Athenian confidence, and many exulted in their victory, a victory of the demos. The Athenian politician Themistocles (the-MIS-tah-

klees) believed, however, that Greece had not seen the last of the Persians, who would inevitably return in much greater force. In 483 B.C.E., the Athenians discovered a rich silver vein in the Attic countryside. Themistocles persuaded them not to divide the windfall among themselves (the customary practice) but to use it to build a fleet of 200 triremes, state-of-the-art warships. Athens thereby transformed itself into the preeminent naval power of the Greek world just in time to confront a new Persian onslaught.

XERXES' INVASION

Darius died in 486 B.C.E. and was succeeded by his son Xerxes, who began preparing a massive overland invasion of Greece designed to conquer the entire country. Supported by a fleet of 600 ships, Xerxes' grand army (which numbered at least 150,000 men and may have been as large as 300,000) set out from Sardis in

Bust of Themistocles. His leadership enabled Athens to defeat Persia and become the primary naval power in the Aegean Sea.

THE PERSIAN WARS WITH GREECE

Imagine you are Xerxes, planning the conquest of Greece in 480 B.C.E. To what extent would geographical considerations dictate your military strategy? Xerxes' attempt at conquest failed. What would you have done differently? Could any Persian expedition have succeeded in conquering Greece?

480 B.C.E., crossing the narrow strait separating Europe from Asia on pontoon bridges. Unlike his father, who had dispatched talented generals against Athens, Xerxes led this campaign himself.

Many Greek cities capitulated immediately. Athens, Sparta, Corinth, and some thirty others refused to bow, however, and formed the Hellenic League to defeat the Persian menace. Under the military leadership of Sparta, the outnumbered Greek allies confronted Xerxes at the pass of Thermopylae (*ther-MO-pih-lee*) in August of 480. For three days the Greeks held off the Persian multitude, while the Greek fleet engaged a

Persian flotilla at nearby Artemisium. The Spartan-led defense at Thermopylae failed, but their sacrifice allowed the fleet, under Themistocles' guidance, to inflict heavy losses on the Persians and then withdraw safely to the south.

Realizing they could no longer defend their city, Themistocles persuaded his fellow Athenians to abandon Athens for the island of Salamis off the coast of Attica. In early September, the Athenians watched the Persians put Athens to the torch. Time, however, was on Themistocles' side. Xerxes' massive army depended on his fleet for supplies. Bad weather made sailing the

To what extent was the culture of Athens in the golden age the product of Athenian democracy?

THE GOLDEN AGE OF CLASSICAL GREECE   121

Aegean in autumn a risky business; the Persians were now desperate to force a decisive battle before the season turned against them.

In late September, the numerically superior Persian fleet, believing the Greeks were about to flee Salamis, sailed into the Bay of Eleusis, only to find that Themistocles had the Greek fleet ready for combat. The Greeks smashed the Persian fleet while Xerxes watched the disaster from a throne above the bay. The following year, a Greek army prevailed on land at the battle of Plataea, driving the Persians completely from mainland Greece. Against all odds, the small, fractious, outnumbered Greek poleis had defeated the mightiest empire of the Mediterranean world. It was a turning point in the history of Greece, ushering in the Classical (or golden) Age.

THE GOLDEN AGE OF CLASSICAL GREECE

To what extent was the culture of Athens in the golden age the product of Athenian democracy?

In the half century after the battle of Salamis, Athens enjoyed a meteoric rise in power and prestige, becoming the premier naval power of the eastern Mediterranean and a military rival even of Sparta. Athens also emerged as the leader of the Delian League, a group of poleis pledged to continue the war against Persia. As the leader of the league, Athens controlled its funds and resources. This fact allowed the Athenians to make their polis—in the words of their brilliant political leader Pericles (*PEHR-eh-klees*)—the "school of Hellas." The fifth century B.C.E. witnessed the greatest achievements of Greek culture and the flowering of Athenian democracy. Both were fueled, however, by the increasingly awkward relationship Athens enjoyed with its allies, who by the 430s had begun to look more like Athenian subjects than free poleis.

PERICLEAN ATHENS

The reforms of Cleisthenes encouraged further experiments in Greek democracy, including the selection of major officeholders by lot. Only one key position was now filled by traditional voting: the office of *strategos*, or general. Because a man could be elected strategos year after year, this office became the focus for Athens'

Greek Forces Defeat Persians. This detail from a fifth-century B.C.E. Attic bowl depicts an Athenian soldier standing over a defeated Persian soldier of Xerxes' army. Notice the differences in their military equipment.

most talented and ambitious public figures. Themistocles had been strategos, as was Cimon (*Ki-mahn*), who led the Delian League to stunning victories over Persia in the 470s and 460s. But Cimon also turned the league against members who tried to opt out, suppressing their revolts by force of arms and turning the league more and more into an instrument of Athenian policy.

Cimon's military successes made him the most powerful politician in Athens. By the 460s, however, the political mood in Athens was changing. New voices were demanding a greater role in government, especially the *thetes*, the lowest of the four classes established by Solon. As rowers, these men were the backbone of the all-important Athenian fleet; as citizens, however, they played little role in the government of their polis.

An unlikely champion emerged for their cause, an aristocrat from one of Athens' most prestigious noble families—Pericles. A political rival of Cimon's, Pericles used a platform of greater enfranchisement of the thetes and an anti-Spartan foreign policy to defeat Cimon. Pericles was elected strategos for 462–461 and secured the ostracism of Cimon from Athens. He then pushed through reforms to make Athens more fully democratic. He gave every Athenian citizen the right to propose and amend legislation, not just to vote yes or no in the citizen assembly. He also made it easier for poorer citizens to participate in the assembly and the

Bust of Pericles. A Roman copy, in marble, of a Greek original, made in bronze during Pericles' own lifetime. Like the tyrant Peisistratos, Pericles is said to have had a deformed head. Pericles wore a helmet to conceal this potentially provocative resemblance.

great appeals courts of Athens by paying an average day's wage for attendance. Through these and other measures, the thetes became a dominant force in politics, loyal to the man who had made that dominance possible.

Pericles glorified Athens' democracy with an ambitious scheme of public building and lavish festivals to the gods, especially Athena. He was also a generous patron of the arts, sciences, and literature, attracting the greatest minds of the day to Athens. His populist political stance, combined with his ability to inspire a sense of Athenian superiority, ensured his reelection as strategos for the next three decades. During these years, Athenian culture flourished as never before. Pericles would prove to be a disastrous political leader; but Periclean Athens represents a dramatic and brilliant moment in the history of Western civilizations.

LITERATURE AND DRAMA

Periclean Athens was not the only city to produce great works of literature during the golden age, but our knowledge of classical Greek literature is dominated by the poetry and drama (both tragic and comedic)

produced there. Epic and lyric poetry were already well-established Greek literary forms when the fifth century began. Drama, however, appears to have been an innovation that developed in Athens out of the poetic odes chanted by choruses to the god Dionysius at the great spring festival devoted to him. It was probably the tyrant Peisistratos who first organized the Great Dionysia and Cleisthenes who converted it into a festival at which tragic dramas were presented. From the beginning, therefore, Athenian drama was closely connected to the political and religious life of the state that sponsored it. Credit for transforming the Dionysian odes into a genuine drama with characters and a chorus belongs, however, to the great tragedian Aeschylus (*AH-skihl-uhs*; 525–456 B.C.E.), who by introducing a second (and later a third) character into the performance, made it possible to present conversation, and hence human conflict, on the stage for the first time. Staging remained very simple, but the emotional impact of tragic drama could be overwhelming.

Aristotle declared that the purpose of tragedy was to inspire pity and fear in the audience and so to purge these emotions through a catharsis. Although enormously influential, this formulation is probably too limiting to be helpful in trying to understand Greek tragedy. Tragedy's fundamental themes—justice, law, and the conflicting demands of piety and obligation that drove a heroic man or woman to destruction—were derived from Homer. Most tragedies told well-known tales from a legendary past: Agemmemnon's sacrifice of his daughter; his murder by his wife, Clytemnestra; and the vengeance taken by his son Orestes; or the Oedipus (*ED-ih-pus*) story about a king who unwittingly slays his father and marries his mother. But tragedy could also have a decidedly contemporary aspect. In his *Persians*, Aeschylus retold the great Athenian victory at Salamis (in which Aeschylus may have participated) through the eyes of the Persian king Xerxes, who thus became its tragic hero. Sophocles' (496–406 B.C.E.) great masterpiece, *Oedipus at Colonus*, was presented in the midst of Athens' disastrous war with Sparta. Euripides' (485–406 B.C.E.) *Trojan Women* was presented in 415, the year of the expedition to Syracuse and the turning point in the Athenians' march toward defeat in the Peloponnesian War (discussed later in this chapter). Tragedy dealt in absolutes, most memorably perhaps in Sophocles' *Antigone*, the story of a clash between justice and law and the competing obligations of familial piety and civic necessity; but its context was inevitably the history of Athens in the period of its own greatest achievements and failures.

To what extent was the culture of Athens in the golden age the product of Athenian democracy?

THE GOLDEN AGE OF CLASSICAL GREECE   123

Comedy was even more directly a genre of direct political commentary. Comedy was crude, parodic, and outspoken, full of slapstick, absurdity, and vulgarity. Its themes were (in the scholar Peter Levi's words) "sex, life on the farm, the good old days, the nightmare of politics, the oddities of religion, the strange manners of the town." Aristophanes (*EHR-ib-STAHF-ah-nees;* c. 448–382 B.C.E.), the greatest of the Athenian comedic playwrights, ridiculed everything that offended or amused him: the philosophy of Socrates, the tragedies of Euripides, and especially the imperialistic warmongering of contemporary politicians such as Cleon. But above all else, Aristophanes was a social critic who routinely savaged the powerful political figures whom he believed (with justice) were leading Athens to its doom. He was repeatedly dragged into court to defend himself against the politicians whom he had attacked. But despite their anger, the politicians

never dared to shut down the comedic theater for long. It was too much a part of the spirit of democratic Athens.

Periclean Athens was also fertile ground for the development of Greek prose. During the sixth century, Greeks typically expressed ideas through poetry; the Milesian thinkers and Xenophanes enshrined their ideas in verse, and Solon likewise used poetry to justify his political reforms. In the fifth century, however, perhaps reflecting the increasing functional literacy of the Athenians, prose emerged as a distinct literary form. Herodotus found a ready market for his "inquiries" (*historiai*) in Athens. His younger contemporary Thucydides (*thu-SID-ib-dees;* c. 460 – c. 400 B.C.E.) wrote a masterful history of the great war between Athens and Sparta. Between them, these two historians developed a new approach to history, emphasizing the reliability of their sources and looking for human explanations for historical events. The development of prose would make possible in the fourth century even further literary achievements, such as the great philosophical treatises of Plato and Aristotle and the stirring political and legal speeches of the great Attic orators we will meet in the next chapter.

ART AND ARCHITECTURE

The Greeks of the golden age revealed the same range of genius in the visual arts as they did in their drama. Their comic gift—exuberance, cheerful sensuality, and coarse wit—can be seen especially in their black figure vases and jugs, whose characters often look like

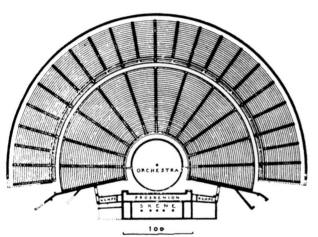

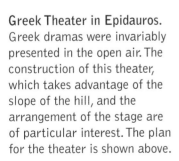

Greek Theater in Epidauros. Greek dramas were invariably presented in the open air. The construction of this theater, which takes advantage of the slope of the hill, and the arrangement of the stage are of particular interest. The plan for the theater is shown above.

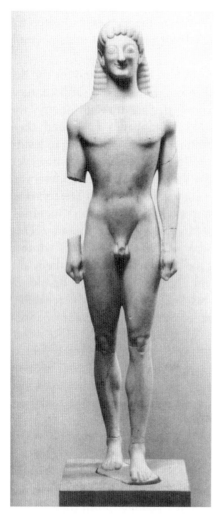  

Apollo of Tenea, Apollo of Piombino, and the Critian Boy. These three statues, dating from about 560, 500, and 480 B.C.E., respectively, display the progressive "unfreezing" of Greek statuary art. The first stiff and symmetrical statue is imitative of Egyptian sculpture (see statue of the pharaoh Menkaure, p. 39). Roughly half a century later it is succeeded by a figure that begins to display motion, as if awakening from a sleep of centuries in a fairy tale. The last figure introduces genuine naturalism in its delicate twists and depiction of the subject's weight resting on one leg.

glinting rascals up to some sort of mischief, usually sexual. More dignified were the marble statues and sculptured reliefs the Greeks made for temples and public places. Athenian sculptors in particular took human greatness as their theme, depicting the beauty of the human form in statuary that was simultaneously naturalistic and idealizing.

Perhaps the most striking development in fifth-century Greek sculpture was the relatively sudden appearance of the well-proportioned, naturalistic nude. This happened first in Athens in the years around 490 to 480 B.C.E. Nothing like it had ever been seen before, and it is difficult not to conclude that the triumph of Greek ideals of human dignity and freedom in the Persian War had something to do with it. Convinced that

all Persians bowed down to their rulers like slaves, whereas they themselves enjoyed political and social equality, the Greeks expressed their ideal of human greatness by commemorating the dignity of the un-adorned human body in stone.

The Athenians also made exceptional contributions to architecture. All Greek temples sought to create an impression of harmony and repose, but the Parthenon of Athens, built between 447 and 438 B.C.E., is generally considered the finest example of its genre. Construction of this stunning, expensive, and difficult building was urged on the Athenians by Pericles, who saw it as a symbol of devotion to their patron goddess, Athena, and a triumphant celebration of their own power and confidence.

To what extent was the culture of Athens in the Golden Age the product of Athenian democracy?

THE GOLDEN AGE OF CLASSICAL GREECE   125

The Shrine of Athena in the Parthenon. This is a replica of the statue of Athena that once stood inside the Parthenon. Made of gold and ivory by the great Athenian sculptor Phidias, the statue stood forty feet high; its image would have been reflected in a shallow pool of water located in front of the statue.

WOMEN AND MEN IN THE DAILY LIFE OF ATHENS

Toward the end of his famous Funeral Oration, Pericles urged the married women of Athens to do three things: rear more children for the sake of Athens, show no more weakness than was "natural to their sex," and avoid gossip. His remarks reveal widely held male attitudes toward women in classical Greece, but especially in Athens.

Rather than leading to greater equality among the sexes, the growth of democracy had the opposite result. In the Dark Age, aristocratic women were sometimes portrayed as possessing extraordinary traits of beauty, wisdom, or courage. These women gave shrewd advice on political and military matters and played an active role in the world around them. But as aristocratic ideals gave way to more democratic ones, life in the shadows increasingly became women's lot. An emphasis on the hoplite infantry and its spirit of equality encouraged men to train together and develop close relationships, sometimes of a homosexual nature. That same spirit of equality also discouraged displays of wealth, especially by women. Instead, the rearing of children to supply the infantry became a female imperative. Public spaces were restricted to male activities such as athletics and political gatherings, while domestic, private spaces were reserved for female activities such as child rearing and weaving. By the fifth century B.C.E., respectable

Women Processing in the Panathenaea, c. 447–438 B.C.E. This image shows a portion of a sculptural frieze from the Parthenon in Athens. Every four years, this annual religious procession in honor of Athena was celebrated in a particularly elaborate manner. This procession was one of the few public occasions on which respectable Athenian women were permitted to appear in public.

Women and Weaving. Wool-working and weaving were highly gendered activities in ancient Greece, in which women of all social ranks were expected to participate. On this red-figure vase, dating from 460–450 B.C.E., we see the woman on the left carding wool, and the two women on the right spinning it into wool threads which could then be woven into cloth.

women lived in seclusion, rarely if ever venturing forth from their houses.

In Athens, girls could be married at age fourteen—as soon as they were biologically capable of childbearing—to husbands more than twice their age. (Younger men were supposed to devote themselves to war.) A girl's father arranged her marriage without concern for her preferences and provided a dowry that her husband could use for her support. Legally, however, wives became the property of their husbands. Shortly after a wife entered her new home, a regular schedule of childbearing would usually begin. Typically the interval between births was between two and four years, meaning that the average young wife would bear between four and six children before she died, usually around the age of thirty-five.

Women seldom went out of doors, as it was thought immodest for them to be seen by other men. Slaves did whatever shopping or marketing the household required. Even at home, women were expected to withdraw into private rooms if visitors arrived. Because the ideology of democratic Athens opposed excessive displays of wealth or leisure, women were not supposed to sit around idly; their main occupation was probably cloth weaving. But since women's work was basically menial, men looked down on women for engaging in it. Available evidence suggests that husbands customarily had little emotional attachment to their wives, regarding them as natural inferiors. In a revealing passage Herodotus says of a certain Lydian king, "[T]his Candaules fell in love with his own wife, a fancy that had strange consequences." An Athenian orator remarked, "[P]rostitutes we have for pleasure,

concubines for daily physical attendance, wives to bear us legitimate children and be our faithful housekeepers."

Athenian society was as dependent on its slaves as the Spartans were on the helots. Without slavery, none of the extraordinary Athenian accomplishments in politics, thought, or art would have been possible. The Athenian ideal of dividing and rotating governmental duties among all free men depended on slaves who worked in fields, businesses, and homes while free men engaged in politics. In fact, the Athenian democratic system began to function fully only with the expansion of Athenian mining and commerce around 500 B.C.E., which enabled the Athenians to buy slaves from the north and east in vastly larger numbers. Freedom and slavery were inescapably linked.

Although widespread, Athenian slavery was small in scale. Slaves did not ordinarily work in large teams or in factories. The only exceptions were the state-owned silver mines, where large numbers of slaves toiled in miserable conditions. But most slaves were owned in small numbers by a wide range of Athenian families, includ-

Flute Player. An Athenian marble relief dating from about 470 B.C.E. The relaxed pose (reclining position, crossed legs) and naturalistic representation of the naked female form were unprecedented in human art before the classical age of the Greeks.

ing the relatively poor. As domestic servants and farm laborers, slaves were seldom treated with complete barbarity, although their masters were free to beat them and to abuse them sexually. But slaves were not regarded as being entirely human either—a notion that made it easier for Athenian free men to assume that nature had chosen some for servile labor and others, like themselves, for political life.

For free men, however, daily life in Periclean Athens had numerous attractions. Male citizens enjoyed considerable social and economic equality. Small-scale farming and commerce were the norms, and what little industry existed—mostly pottery and armaments manufacture—was carried on in shops owned by individual artisans who produced their own wares. Factories employing large numbers of workers were rare but on the rise: one of the largest in fifth-century Athens, a shield factory, was staffed by 120 workers and owned by a resident alien. Some citizens were of course richer than others, but the richest were required to donate some of their wealth to support public festivals or equip the navy. Athens in the fifth century was an exciting, bustling, cosmopolitan center of commerce and culture—a city of which the Athenians themselves were inordinately proud.

League Building and the Peloponnesian War

How did the Peloponnesian War influence Greek philosophy?

Athenians saw themselves as the freest of men, but their freedom rested on the servitude of others. Slaves performed much of the labor at home, while Athens' allies in the Delian League provided the resources that underlay Athenian greatness. Without the surplus wealth flowing into Athens from the league, none of the projects Pericles undertook—pay for political participation, massive building projects (also, incidentally, an employment program for poorer citizens), the patronage of Athenian drama—would have been possible. These projects kept Athens powerful, its democracy vibrant, and Pericles popular and in power. But Athens' democratic achievements rested on its control over an alliance it had transformed into an empire.

Since the 470s, Athens had faced attempts by its allies to break away, and it had crushed those efforts

ruthlessly. Through the 450s, such revolts were rare. But in the early 440s, Pericles determined on a more aggressive policy toward Sparta, by then Athens' only real rival for supremacy in the Greek world. To give himself a freer hand, he concluded a formal peace with Persia. After this peace, the purpose of the Delian League evaporated, and Athens had no justification for compelling its allies to remain within it. Many remained loyal nonetheless, paying their contributions and enjoying the economic benefits of warm relations with Athens. Others, however, did not, and Athens found itself increasingly forcing its allies back into line, often installing Athenian garrisons and planting Athenian colonists—who retained their Athenian citizenship—to ensure future loyalty.

In the context of Greek culture, such behavior was disturbing. The Delian League had been established to preserve Greek independence against the Persians. Now many Greeks accused Athens of having become a tyrannical empire itself. Foremost among the accusers were the Corinthians, whose own economic standing was seriously threatened by Athenian dominance of the Aegean. The Corinthians were close allies of the Spartans, the dominant power in what historians call the Peloponnesian League. (The Greeks called it simply the "Spartans and their allies.") When war finally erupted between Athens and Sparta, the great historian Thucydides ascribed it to the growing power of Athens and the fear and envy this inspired in Sparta. No modern historian has improved on Thucydides' formulation. For the Athenian democracy and its leader, there could be no question of relinquishing the empire, the cornerstone of Athens' cultural and political ascendancy. By the 430s, however, Athens could not preserve that empire without threatening the interests of Sparta and its allies.

The Peloponnesian War Erupts

After a series of provocations, the Athenians and Spartans found themselves at war with one another in 431 B.C.E. Athens could not defeat Sparta on land; but neither Sparta nor its allies had a fleet capable of facing the Athenians on the seas. Pericles therefore developed a bold strategy: he would pull the entire population of Attica within the walls of Athens and its harbor, abandoning the countryside to Sparta, while the superior Athenian fleet supplied Athens from the sea and ravaged the coasts of Spartan territory. As in many of history's pivotal contests, both sides believed a conclusion would come quickly. Instead, the war dragged on for twenty-seven years.

The Spartans plundered the farms and pastures of Attica, frustrated that the Athenians would not send their hoplites out for a decisive battle. Meanwhile, the Athenians inflicted significant destruction on Spartan territory in a series of lightning raids and successfully encouraged revolt among the helots. Time appeared to be on Athens' side, but in 429 B.C.E. the crowded conditions of the besieged city gave rise to a typhus epidemic that killed over a third of the Athenian population, including Pericles. Pericles' death showed that he was the only man capable of managing the democratic political forces he had unleashed. His successors were mostly demagogues, ambitious men who played to the worst instincts of the demos to gain power for themselves. The most successful of these was a warmonger named Cleon, a particular target of Aristophanes' invective, who refused a Spartan offer of peace in 425 B.C.E. and continued the war until his own death in battle four years later.

A short-lived truce then ensued, authored by an able Athenian leader named Nicias. But the Athenian demos was in no mood for a long peace and soon fell under the spell of a charming, flamboyant, but unscrupulous aristocrat named Alcibiades, who convinced the Athenians in 415 B.C.E. to reopen hostilities with an ill-advised attack on the distant city of Syracuse in Sicily. The expedition failed, with thousands of Athenians killed or enslaved in Sicily.

News of the Syracusan disaster shattered the Athenian demos. Recriminations began immediately. Many political leaders were driven from the polis, and in 411 B.C.E. the demos suffered a momentary but monumental lack of self-confidence. While the rowers in the fleet were away from the city, the Athenians essentially voted the democracy out of existence, replacing it with an oligarchy of 400 citizens. The Athenian fleet, stationed in Samos, responded by declaring a democratic government in exile under the leadership of none other than Alcibiades. The oligarchy proved to be brief, and democracy was restored to Athens by 409. But the fact that the war could force such desperation did not bode well for the future.

THE END OF THE WAR

The Spartans too despaired of bringing the war to an end. Despite Athens' problems, its fleet was still invincible. Finally, Sparta turned to the Persians, who agreed to supply the gold and the naval expertise necessary to create an effective Spartan fleet. By 407, a talented and ambitious Spartan commander, Lysander, was successfully harrying the Athenians throughout the Aegean Sea.

Perhaps the most disturbing development of the closing years of the war was the self-destructive passion with which the Athenians now began to turn against each other. To take but one example: in 406, the Athenians won a key naval victory at Arginusae (ar-geh-NOO-si). After the engagement, however, a sudden storm came up, preventing the Athenian commanders from rescuing the sailors whose ships had been wrecked in the battle. The sailors drowned, and a firestorm of protest erupted in Athens, fanned by demagogues who secured through show trials the execution of those generals foolish enough to return to Athens. One of those executed was Pericles, the son of Pericles, who thus became a victim of the democracy his father had brought into being. Through such measures, the Athenians killed or exiled many of their most experienced and able commanders.

The result should have been predictable. Lysander destroyed the poorly led Athenian fleet in 404 B.C.E.

A Modern Replica of an Athenian Trireme. These versatile warships were powered by both oars and sail.

Without their fleet the Athenians could neither feed themselves nor defend their city. Lysander sailed around the Aegean unopposed, installing pro-Spartan oligarchies among the former allies of Athens. Finally, he besieged Athens itself. Facing the inevitable, the Athenians surrendered. Corinth and Thebes called for Athens' destruction. The Spartans refused to allow this but imposed harsh terms: the dismantling of Athens' walls, the scrapping of its fleet, and the acceptance of an oligarchic government of thirty Athenians.

The war's postscript was grim. At Athens, the so-called Thirty Tyrants confiscated property and mur-dered over 1,500 of their political opponents in the eighteen months of their rule. Their excesses drove committed democrats to desperate resistance; a blood-bath was averted only through the reasoned interven-tion of the Spartan king Pausanias. By the end of 401, Athens was once again a democracy and more moder-ate in its behavior than during the war—although, as we will see, it still had one last act of brutality and shortsightedness to perform.

With its victory, Sparta succeeded Athens as the ar-biter of the Greek world. This was a thankless job, made worse by the losses Sparta itself had suffered during

THE PELOPONNESIAN WAR

Consider the balance of power between Athens and Sparta at the outbreak of the Peloponnesian War. Which side had the geographical advantage? Which neutral powers might have been able to tip the balance by entering the war on one side or the other? What strategic and military choices did geography impose on the two combatants and their allies?

the war and by the fact that the Spartans were even more ham fisted in their control of the Aegean than the Athenians had been. The Spartans now found themselves in a position they had avoided throughout their history, as their far-flung imperial interests sapped their manpower and undermined their control over the helots. They also faced a reinvigorated Persian Empire, which had used the Greeks' fratricidal struggles to increase its own influence over the Aegean world. Within a decade of the Peloponnesian War's end, Sparta found itself opposed by four poleis whose ancient hatreds for each other were legendary—Athens, Argos, Thebes, and Corinth. Their cooperation speaks volumes about how unpopular Spartan preeminence had become in just a few short years.

For the Greeks, the Peloponnesian War was a disaster. From the long perspective of historical distance, we may view it as demonstrating the limitations of the polis system. The competitive ethos that characterized the Greek poleis proved to be their tragic flaw. To the Greeks themselves, however, the war offered no such clear lessons. Instead, it brought demoralization and a questioning of all the old certainties. Democracies had collapsed, empires had crumbled, and oligarchies like Sparta had proven incapable of rising to the challenges they now confronted. Even the gods seemed to be in disarray. These were the circumstances in which the great Athenian philosopher Socrates (469–399 B.C.E.) attempted to refound ethical and political life on new and more certain principles. To understand his accomplishments, however, we must trace briefly the history of philosophical speculation in the half century before his birth.

THE PYTHAGOREANS AND THE SOPHISTS

After the Persian conquest of Asia Minor, many of the Milesian philosophers fled to Sicily and southern Italy. Philosophical speculation thus continued in the Greek "far west," but it was now tinged with a pessimism and religious coloration that reflected the Greeks' distress over the loss of their freedom. Typifying this reaction was Pythagoras, a thinker who migrated around 530 B.C.E. from the island of Samos to southern Italy, where he founded a sect—half philosophical, half mystical—in the city of Croton. Pythagoras and his followers regarded the speculative life as the highest good, but they believed that to pursue it, one must be purified of desires of the flesh. They believed that the essence of things was not matter but number, and so they concen-

trated on the study of mathematics and musical theory, discovering harmonies and dividing numbers into categories such as odd and even. Pythagoreans also proved an old Babylonian assumption, known today as the Pythagorean theorem—that the square of the hypotenuse of any right-angled triangle is equal to the sum of the squares of the other two sides. Thus, even though the Pythagoreans turned away from the material world, they still exhibited the characteristic Greek quest for regularity and predictability in that world.

Victory in the Persian War enabled the Greeks to overcome the failure of nerve exemplified by the Pythagoreans. Above all in Athens, the increasing power of the individual citizen inspired philosophical inquiry into how such individuals might best act in the here and now. To fulfill the demand to cultivate such worldly wisdom, a new group of teachers emerged, known as Sophists, a term simply meaning "those who are wise." Unlike the Milesians or the Pythagoreans, the Sophists were professional teachers who made a living from selling their knowledge.

The Sophists were not a coherent philosophical school. Their work did display some common threads, however, that are best exemplified by Protagoras, who was active in Athens from about 445 to 420 B.C.E. His famous dictum, "man is the measure of all things," meant that goodness, truth, and justice are relative to the needs and interests of human beings. In religious matters Protagoras was agnostic, declaring that he did not know whether the gods existed or what they did, "for there are many hindrances to such knowledge— the obscurity of the subject and the brevity of life." Since he knew nothing of the gods, he concluded that there could be no absolute truths or eternal standards of right and wrong. If sense perception was the only source of knowledge, there could be only particular truths valid for the individual knower.

Such teachings struck many Athenians as dangerous. By encouraging people to examine each new situation

C H R O N O L O G Y

EVOLUTION OF GREEK PHILOSOPHY	
Emergence of the Milesian School (pre-Socratics)	600–500 B.C.E.
Pythagoreans emerge in southern Italy	530 B.C.E.
Rise of the Sophists	450 B.C.E.
Death of Socrates	399 B.C.E.

on its own terms and merits, Sophists for the first time made everyday life a subject for philosophical discussion. But the relativism of such Sophists as Protagoras could easily degenerate into the doctrine that the wise man is the one who knows best how to manipulate others and gratify his own desires and so could be used to rationalize monstrous acts of brutality. To some critics, such ideas were antidemocratic; to others, they smacked of atheism and anarchy. If there were no final truth, and if goodness and justice were merely relative to the whims of the individual, then religion, morality, the state, and society itself could not be maintained. This conviction led to the growth of a new philosophical movement grounded on the theory that truth is real and that absolute standards do exist. The initiator of this new trend was Socrates.

> Sophists for the first time made everyday life a subject for philosophical discussion.

THE LIFE AND THOUGHT OF SOCRATES

Socrates was wealthy enough that he never had to teach for a living. Having twice fought as part of the Athenian infantry, he was an ardent patriot who believed Athens was being corrupted by the shameful doctrines of the Sophists. But he was not an unthinking patriot who cherished slogans. Rather, he wished to submit every presumed truth to rigorous examination, to reconstruct Athenian life on a firm foundation of ethical certainty. It is bitterly ironic that such a dedicated idealist should have been put to death by his own countrymen. Shortly after the end of the Peloponnesian War, in 399 B.C.E., when Athens was reeling from the shock of defeat and violent internal upheavals, a democratic faction decided that Socrates was a threat to the state. A democratic court agreed, condemning him to death for impiety and "corrupting the youth." Although his friends made arrangements for him to flee, Socrates decided to accept the popular judgment and abide by the laws of his polis. He died by calmly drinking a cup of poison.

Because Socrates wrote nothing himself, it is difficult to determine exactly what he taught. Contemporary reports, however—especially by his student Plato—make a few points clear. First, Socrates subjected all inherited assumptions to rigorous criticism. Styling himself a gadfly, he continually engaged his contemporaries in "Socratic" questioning, seeking to show them that all their supposed certainties were merely unexamined prejudices resting on false assumptions. According to Plato, an oracle once said that Socrates was the wisest person in the world and Socrates agreed: everyone else thought he knew something, but he was wiser because he knew he knew nothing. Second, he sought to base his philosophical speculations on sound definitions of words. Third, he focused his attention on ethics rather than on studying the physical world. He shunned the traditional discussions of Milesian philosophers about why things exist, why they grow, and why they perish. Instead, Socrates urged people to reflect on principles of proper conduct, both for their own sake and for that of society. One should consider the meaning of one's life and actions at all times, for according to one of his most memorable sayings, "the unexamined life is not worth living."

All this might make Socrates sound rather like a Sophist; indeed, he felt compelled at his trial to insist that he was not. Like the Sophists, he was a "philosopher of the marketplace" who held tradition and cliché up to doubt in order to help people improve their lives. But the overwhelming difference between Socrates and the Sophists lay in his belief in certainties—even if he avoided saying what they were—and in the standard of absolute good rather than expediency he applied to

Socrates. According to Plato, Socrates looked like a goatman but spoke like a god.

TWO VIEWS OF SOPHISM

SOCRATES AS A SOPHIST

The image of Socrates held by most people is of the sage thinker who challenged the prevailing prejudices of his day and opposed the Sophists. During his own time, however, he was not so universally admired. In his comedy The Clouds, *Aristophanes' protagonist Strepsiades—ruined by the wastefulness of his son—goes to Socrates and his "Thought Shop" so that Socrates can make him and his son, Pheidippides, orators capable of winning lawsuits and thus enriching himself. Aristophanes implies throughout that Socrates is essentially just another Sophist, a man who teaches word games and logic tricks for hire.*

STREPSIADES: See that he [Pheidippides] learns your two Arguments, whatever you call them—oh yes, Right and Wrong—the one that takes a bad case and defeats Right with it. If he can't manage both, then at least Wrong—that will do—but that he must have.

SOCRATES: Well, I'll go and send the Arguments here in person, and they'll teach him themselves.

STREPSIADES: Don't forget, he's got to be able to argue against any kind of justified claim at all.

RIGHT: This way, Let the audience see you. . . .

WRONG: Sure, go wherever you like. The more of an audience we have, the more soundly I'll trounce you.

RIGHT: What sort of trick will you use?

WRONG: Oh, just a few new ideas.

RIGHT: Yes, they're in fashion now, aren't they, [to the audience] thanks to you idiots. . . . [to Pheiddipides] You don't want to be the sort of chap who's always in the agora telling stories about other people's sex lives, or in the courts arguing about some petty, filthy, little dispute. . . .

WRONG: People here at the Thought Shop call me Wrong, because I was the one who invented ways of proving anything wrong, laws, prosecutors, anything.

Isn't that worth millions—to have a really bad case and yet win? . . . Suppose you fall in love with a married woman—have a bit of fun—and get caught in the act. As you are now, without a tongue in your head, you're done for. But if you come and learn from me, then you can do whatever you like and get away with it . . . and supposing you do get caught with someone's wife, you can say to him. . . . "What have I done wrong? Look at Zeus; wasn't he always a slave of his sexual passions? And do you expect a mere mortal like me to do any better than a god?" . . .

STREPSIADES [to Socrates]: I wonder if you'd accept a token of my appreciation? But my son, has he learned that Argument we were listening to a moment ago?

SOCRATES: Yes, he has.

STREPSIADES: Holy Fraud, how wonderful!

SOCRATES: Yes, you'll now be able to win any case at all.

STREPSIADES: Even if the witnesses were actually there when I was borrowing the money?

SOCRATES: Even if there were a thousand of them.

Aristophanes, *The Clouds*, trans. Alan H. Sommerstein (New York, 1973), pp. 148–150, 154, 159–160 (slightly revised).

SOPHISTRY IN ACTION: THE MELIAN DIALOGUE

During the truce authored by the Athenian statesman Nicias in 421 B.C.E., both Athens and Sparta continued to pursue a "dirty war," living by the letter of their agreement but not its spirit, while preparing for the inevitable reopening of the conflict. The Aegean island of Melos—originally a Spartan colony—had so far maintained a policy of neutrality between Athens and Sparta. In 416, however, the Athenians insisted on their submission, and the Athenian envoys justified their position with a chillingly logical argument that might makes right.

ATHENIANS: For ourselves, we will not trouble you with specious pretenses—either of how we have a right to our empire because we overthrew the Mede, or are now attacking you because of wrong that you have done us—and make a long speech which would not be believed; and in return we hope that you, instead of thinking to influence us by saying that you did not join the Spartans, although their colonists, or that you have done us no wrong, will aim at what is feasible, holding in view the real sentiments of us both; since you know as well as we do that right, as the world goes, is only in question between equals in power, while the strong do what they can and the weak suffer what they must. . . . We would desire to exercise empire over you without trouble, and see you preserved for the good of us both.

MELIANS: And how, pray, could it turn out as good for us to serve as for you to rule?

ATHENIANS: Because you would have the advantage of submitting before suffering the worst, and we should gain by not destroying you.

MELIANS: So you would not consent to our being neutral, friends instead of enemies, but allies of neither side?

ATHENIANS: No; for your hostility cannot so much hurt us as your friendship will be an argument to our subjects of our weakness, and your enmity of our power.

MELIANS: Is that your subjects' idea of equity, to put those who have nothing to do with you in the same category with peoples that are most of them your own colonists, and some conquered rebels?

ATHENIANS: As far as right goes they think one has as much of it as the other, and that if they maintain their independence it is because they are strong, and that if we do not molest them it is because we are afraid; so that besides extending our empire we should gain in security by your subjection. . . .

MELIANS: What is this but to make greater the enemies that you have already, and to force others to become so who would otherwise have never thought of it? . . . we know that the fortune of war is sometimes more impartial than the disproportion of numbers might lead one to suppose; to submit is to give ourselves over to despair, while action still preserves for us a hope that we may stand. . . .

ATHENIANS: Hope . . . may be indulged in by those who have abundant resources, if not without loss, at all events without ruin; but its nature is to be extravagant, and those who go so far as to stake their all upon the venture see it in its true colors only when they are ruined. . . . Let not this be the case with you, who are weak and hang on a single turn of the scale; nor be like the vulgar, who, when abandoning such security as human means may still afford, when visible hopes fail them in extremity, turn to the invisible, to prophecies and oracles, and other such inventions that delude men with hopes to their destruction. . . . When we come to your notion about the Spartans, which leads you to believe that shame will make them help you, here we bless your simplicity but do not envy your folly. . . . You do not adopt the view that expediency goes with security, while justice and honor cannot be followed without danger; and danger the Spartans generally court as little as possible. . . . Is it likely that while we are masters of the sea they will cross over to an island?

MELIANS: Should the Spartans miscarry in this, they would fall upon your land, and upon those left of your allies . . . and instead of places which are not yours, you will have to fight for your own country and your own confederacy.

ATHENIANS: Some diversion of the kind you speak of you may one day experience, only to learn, as others have done, that the Athenians never once yet withdrew from a siege for fear of any. . . . Think over the matter, therefore, and reflect once and again that it is for your country that you are consulting, and that upon this one deliberation depends its prosperity or ruin.

Thucydides, Book 5. *The Landmark Thucydides*, ed. Robert Strassler (New York, 1995), pp. 352–356.

QUESTIONS FOR ANALYSIS

1. Socrates reportedly denied being a sophist and refused to teach the art of "making the weaker argument defeat the stronger"—a mark of sophism. In *The Clouds*, Aristophanes shows him teaching Right and Wrong how "to win any case at all." From your reading of the text, was Socrates really a sophist? What is the true meaning of *sophisticated*?

2. Rhetoric and the philosophy of persuasion became more important in classical Greece than in earlier cultures. How was this related to politics and government in the polis?

Socrates Gaining Wisdom from the Wise Woman Diotima. In Plato's *Symposium,* Socrates learns the philosophical meaning of love from Diotima, an ethereal female being, wiser than he. In this sculptural representation of the scene the winged figure between Diotima and Socrates is probably a personification of love itself.

the Athenians took slavery for granted. Women throughout the Greek world were exploited by what today would be called a patriarchy—a repressive system managed by fathers and husbands. Greek statecraft was characterized by imperialism and aggressive war. The Greeks made no great advances in economic enterprise, and they scorned commerce. Finally, not even the Athenians could be described as tolerant. Socrates was not the only man put to death merely for expressing his opinions.

And yet the profound significance of the Greek experiment for the history of Western civilizations is undeniable. This significance can be seen with particular clarity if we compare Greek cultural traits with those of Mesopotamia and ancient Egypt. Mesopotamian and Egyptian civilizations were dominated by autocracy, supernaturalism, and the subjection of the individual to the group. The typical political regime of the ancient Near Eastern world was that of an absolute monarch supported by a powerful priesthood. Culture was mainly an instrument to enhance the prestige of rulers, and economic life was controlled by palaces and temples.

all aspects of life. Socrates' death made clear, however, that to reestablish the polis, it would be necessary to go farther than Socrates himself had, by constructing a system that revealed a positive framework of truth and reality. This was the task Socrates' most brilliant student, Plato, would undertake in the wake of the disasters of the Peloponnesian War. In so doing, he would lay the groundwork for all subsequent Western philosophical thinking up to the present day.

CONCLUSION

Ever since the Renaissance, Europeans have liked to think of themselves as the heirs of the classical Greeks and to imagine the Greeks as mirror images of themselves. Such uncritical admiration is misleading, both about the Greeks and ourselves. Despite the religious skepticism of a few intellectuals, the Greeks were neither secularists nor rationalists. Although they invented the concept of democracy, only a small percentage even of the male population of Athens was ever permitted to play a role in political affairs. The Spartans kept the mass of their population in serflike subjection, and

In contrast, the civilization of Greece, notably in its Athenian form, was founded on ideals of freedom, competition, individual achievement, and human glory. The Greek word for freedom—*eleutheria*—cannot be translated into any ancient Near Eastern language, not even Hebrew. The culture of the Greeks was the first in the West to be based on the primacy of the human intellect; there was no subject they feared to investigate. As Herodotus has a Greek (in this case a Spartan) say to a Persian, "You understand how to be a slave, but you know nothing of freedom. . . . If you had but tasted it you would counsel us to fight for it not only with spears but with axes."

Another way of appreciating the enduring importance of Greek civilization to the Western world is to recall some of the words that come to us from this civilization: politics, democracy, philosophy, metaphysics, history, tragedy. These are all ways of thinking and acting that have enriched human life immeasurably but that had hardly been known before the Greeks invented them. To a startling degree the Western concept of *humanity* itself—the exalted role within nature of the human race in general and the individual human being in particular—comes to us from the Greeks. For the Greeks, the aim of existence was the fullest development of one's human potential: the work of becoming a person, called in Greek *paideia*, meant that every free man was supposed to be the sculptor of his own statue.

When the Romans took up this ideal from the Greeks, they called it *humanitas*, from which we derive the English word *humanity*. The Romans admitted their indebtedness when they remarked that "Greece was where humanity was invented." It is hard to doubt that they were right.

KEY TERMS

hero cults
polis
oracle at Delphi

hoplite
Sappho
Solon

Spartiate
pre-Socratics
Pericles

Peloponnesian War
Sophists
Socrates

SELECTED READINGS

Penguin Classics and the Loeb Classical Library both offer reliable translations of Greek literary, philosophical, and historical texts.

Boardman, John, Jaspar Griffin, and Oswyn Murray, eds. *Greece and the Hellenistic World*. Oxford, 1988. A reprint of the Greek and Hellenistic chapters from *The Oxford History of the Classical World*, originally published in 1986. Excellent, stimulating surveys, accessible to a general audience but provocative to specialists.

Brunschwig, Jacques, and Geoffrey E. R. Lloyd. *Greek Thought: A Guide to Classical Knowledge*. Translated by Catherine Porter. Cambridge, Mass., 2000. An outstanding, up-to-date work of reference.

Buckley, Terry, ed. *Aspects of Greek History, 750–323 B.C.: A Source-Based Approach*. London, 1999. An outstanding collection of source materials.

Cartledge, Paul A. *The Spartans: An Epic History*. New York, 2003. A lively and authoritative history of Sparta from its origins to the Roman conquest.

Dover, Kenneth J. *Greek Homosexuality*. Cambridge, Mass., 1978. The standard account of an important subject.

Fantham, Elaine, Helene Foley, Natalie Kampen, Sarah B. Pomeroy, and H. A. Shapiro. *Women in the Classical World: Image and Text*. Oxford, 1994. Wide-ranging analysis drawing on both visual and written sources, covering both the Greek and the Roman periods.

Fornara, Charles W., and Loren J. Samons II. *Athens from Cleisthenes to Pericles*. Berkeley, 1991. An excellent narrative history of Athenian politics during the first half of the fifth century B.C.E.

Freeman, Charles. *The Greek Achievement: The Foundation of the Western World*. New York, 1999. An admiring survey written for a general audience.

Garlan, Yvon. *Slavery in Ancient Greece*. Ithaca, N.Y., 1988. Now the standard account.

Hanson, Victor Davis. *The Other Greeks: The Family Farm and the Agrarian Roots of Western Civilization*. New York, 1995. Occasionally polemical and idiosyncratic but convincing in its emphasis on small-holding farmers as the backbone of Greek urban society.

Jones, Nicholas F. *Ancient Greece: State and Society*. Upper Saddle River, N.J., 1997. A concise survey from the Minoans up to the end of the Classical Period that emphasizes the connections between the social order and politics.

Lefkowitz, Mary, and Maureen Fant. *Women's Life in Greece and Rome: A Source Book in Translation*. 3rd ed. Baltimore, Md., 2005. A remarkably wide-ranging collection, topically arranged, invaluable to scholars and to students.

Levi, Peter. *Atlas of the Greek World*. New York, 1984. Excellent maps and illustrations supplement an outstanding text.

Morris, Ian, and Barry Powell, eds. *A New Companion to Homer*. Leiden, 1997. A collection of thirty specialist but accessible scholarly articles, encompassing the most recent research on Homer and Dark Age Greece.

Pomeroy, Sarah B., Stanley M. Burstein, Walter Donlan, and Jennifer Tolbert Roberts. *Ancient Greece: A Political, Social, and Cultural History*. Oxford, 1999. An outstanding new textbook: clear, lively, and up to date, with good bibliographies.

Price, Simon. *Religions of the Ancient Greeks*. Cambridge, 1999. Concise and authoritative, this survey extends from the Archaic Period up to the fifth century C.E.

Strassler, Robert B., ed. *The Landmark Thucydides*. New York, 1996. Reprints the classic Richard Crawley translation with maps, commentary, notes, and appendices by leading scholars.

Thomas, Carol G., and Craig Conant. *Citadel to City-State: The Transformation of Greece, 1200–700 B.C.E.* Bloomington, Ind., 1999. A lucid and accessible study that examines developments at a number of different Dark Age sites.

CHAPTER FOUR

THE EXPANSION
OF GREECE

THE SUPREME TRAGEDY OF THE GREEKS was their failure to solve the problem of internecine political conflict. The fifth century in Greece had ended with a debilitating and destructive war of attrition between Athens and Sparta. The fourth century continued along much the same path, as the major poleis—Sparta, then Thebes, then Athens again—jockeyed for dominance within the Greek world. But the independent temper of Greek political life could not suffer such dominance for long; and so as each great polis appeared on the brink of realizing its goals, a coalition of age-old enemies would form to defeat it. Despite mounting calls for the Greeks to set aside their local differences and unite in a common cause, they could not escape their heritage of particularism.

Social and economic difficulties were also mounting. These problems stemmed from ideologically driven civil wars within the poleis as well as from the endemic warfare among them. Faith in the old ideals of equality decayed as a vast gulf opened up between the rich and the poor. Increasingly, the wealthy withdrew from politics altogether; meanwhile, the number of free citizens declined as poverty-stricken freemen and freewomen descended into slavery. The result was despair and cynicism.

The age did not lack for creative energy. Philosophy, science, and literature blossomed in the fourth century, as men of talent shunned the vagaries of public life and turned their attention instead to the life of the mind. As the polis system decayed, serious thinkers debated what the polis was, how and why it functioned, and how it might be improved. But even the greatest of these thinkers remained enclosed within the parochial world of the polis.

The unhappy equilibrium of the Greek world was shattered in the last half of the fourth century by the sudden emergence of the kingdom of Macedonia. The extraordinary conquests of Philip of Macedon unified Greece. Those of his son Alexander

FOCUS QUESTIONS

• What conditions led to the growing number of mercenaries in the fourth century B.C.E.?

• Why did Plato's ideal polis differ from Aristotle's?

• What accounts for the remarkable success of the Macedonian conquests?

• What characteristics defined and distinguished the three major Hellenistic kingdoms?

• Why was prosperity so unevenly distributed in the Hellenistic economy?

• What was the relationship between Epicureanism and Stoicism?

• What were the principal themes of Hellenistic architecture and sculpture?

• Why did science and medicine flourish in this period?

• What changes occurred during the Hellenistic period to the polis-based culture of classical Greece?

the Great extended Greek culture by force of arms from Egypt to Persia to the frontiers of India. Alexander's empire did not last. But the cosmopolitan, Greek-like (hence *Hellenistic*, as opposed to *Hellenic*) culture to which it gave rise became the most powerful and pervasive cultural influence the Near Eastern world would know until the rise of Islam almost a thousand years later.

FAILURES OF THE FOURTH-CENTURY POLIS

What conditions led to the growing number of mercenaries in the fourth century B.C.E.?

There is little in the early fourth century B.C.E. to suggest that the greatest age of Greek cultural influence still lay ahead. The Peloponnesian War had left Sparta as the preeminent power in the Greek world, but the Spartans showed little talent for the position their unexpected victory had thrust on them. At home, Spartan politicians remained deeply divided over the wisdom of committing Spartan forces beyond their frontiers; while abroad, the Spartans showed even less restraint than had the Athenians in strong-arming their subject-allies. In 395, a significant portion of Greece—including such traditional enemies as Athens, Argos, Corinth, and Thebes—aligned itself against Sparta in the so-called Corinthian War (395–387 B.C.E.). The Spartans, for their part, could bring matters to a resolution only by forcing a peace on their fellow Greeks brokered from the outside—essentially composed and guaranteed by the Persians. This pattern was repeated time and again over the next fifty years, during which the advantage shifted steadily toward Persia.

THE STRUGGLE FOR HEGEMONY

After the Corinthian War, the Spartans placed a garrison in Thebes for four years. This was a grave affront to the freedom of another great polis. After the Thebans regained their autonomy, they elected Epaminondas their leader, a fierce patriot and a military genius. For decades, Greeks had been experimenting with the basic form of the hoplite phalanx, adding light skirmishers and archers to enhance its effectiveness. Epaminondas now went further. In imitation of the Spartan system, he formed an elite hoplite unit known as the Theban Sacred Band, made up of 150 homosexual couples. Epaminondas also developed lighter-armed troops. By the early 370s he was ready for another trial of strength with the Spartans.

Theban and Spartan armies met at Leuctra in 371. Epaminondas eschewed convention, placing his best troops (the Sacred Band) not on the right-hand side of his formation, but on the left. He stacked the left-hand side of his phalanx fifty rows deep, a surprise he disguised with a flurry of arrow and javelin attacks. When the two sides met, the weight of the Theban left smashed the Spartan right, and with its best troops overrun, the Spartan phalanx collapsed. Epaminondas followed his victory by marching through Messenia and freeing the helots. Spartan power—and in a sense Spartan society—was at an end. Overnight, Epaminondas had reduced Sparta to a merely local power.

As Theban power grew, so did the animosity of the other Greek poleis toward it. In 371 Athens had supported Thebes against Sparta; but when the Thebans and Spartans squared off again in 362, the Athenians allied themselves with the Spartans. Although the Theban army again carried the day, Epaminondas fell in battle. Theban hegemony died with him. Athens attempted to fill the vacuum by establishing a naval confederacy, organized more equitably than the Delian League. But the Athenians quickly reverted to abusing their allies, and the naval confederacy dissolved in rebellions. Greece thus remained a constellation of petty warring states, all greatly weakened by their struggles with each other.

> Greece thus remained a constellation of petty warring states, all greatly weakened by their struggles with each other.

The poleis were also beset by internal turmoil. Athens was spared the political revolutions many other cities suffered, mostly because the Thirty Tyrants had discredited the cause of oligarchy there; but elsewhere in the Greek world, strife between democrats and oligarchs worsened. An abortive coup attempt was even uncovered at Sparta, plotted by a disenfranchised Spartiate who hoped to rally the disaffected elements of Spartan society.

SOCIAL AND ECONOMIC CRISES

The incessant warfare, combined with internal political struggles, profoundly affected society and economy throughout the Greek world. Even wealthy cities such as Athens and Sparta had exhausted their resources through war. Many personal fortunes had been lost, and many ordinary people had been driven from their homes or reduced to slavery. Country towns had been ravaged, some repeatedly, as had farmlands throughout Greece. The destruction of orchards and vineyards was particularly devastating, because of the long time it takes to nourish olive trees and grapevines to a productive state; but even arable land was now less productive than it had been earlier. As a result, standards of living declined significantly during the fourth century. Although prices rose in general around 50 percent (and some staples tripled and quadrupled in cost), wages remained more or less the same. Taxes increased, and in Athens the wealthy were required to employ their personal wealth to underwrite the construction of public theaters and buildings, the maintenance of warships, and the presentation of festivals. Even so, state treasuries were never again as flush as they had been in the fifth century, and the kind of ambitious public spending undertaken by the tyrants or by Pericles was unknown in the fourth-century polis.

Unemployment was widespread, especially among the growing population of the cities. During wartime, men might find employment as rowers or soldiers in the service of their city. When their city was at peace, many turned instead to mercenary service. The Greek states of Sicily and Italy hired mercenaries from the mainland, as did Sparta to supplement its own campaigns in Asia Minor. A pretender to the Persian throne even hired a mostly Greek mercenary army in an attempt to overthrow his older brother, the reigning king. These Greeks fought their way into the heart of the Persian Empire, and when the pretender fell in battle, the 10,000 Greek mercenaries fought their way back out. It was a stunning demonstration of what even a smallish Greek army might accomplish on Persian soil.

CHRONOLOGY

DECLINE OF THE GREEK POLIS

Sparta becomes leading Greek polis	404 B.C.E.
Prices rise by 50 percent throughout Greece	400–350 B.C.E.
Corinthian War	395–387 B.C.E.
Epaminondas defeats Spartans at Leuctra	371 B.C.E.

The Cultural and Intellectual Response

Why did Plato's ideal polis differ from Aristotle's?

The breakdown of polis society during the fourth century had a profound impact on philosophy, the arts, and political thought. Scholars have sometimes presented fourth-century culture as if it represented a decline from the great artistic and intellectual achievements of the fifth century B.C.E. But such a sweeping verdict on fourth-century B.C.E. culture is unjustified. It underestimates not only the continuities between fifth- and fourth-century Greek culture but also the originality and creativity of these new developments.

ART AND LITERATURE

Sculptors were already attempting to achieve a heightened sense of realism, especially in portraiture, when the fourth century B.C.E. began. Realism had been a hallmark of classical art as well; but in the fourth century, artists tried increasingly to render objects as they actually looked, rather than portraying them in an idealized, dignified form. Fourth-century artists also paid more attention to life and movement, a trend that would culminate in the breathtaking works of the Hellenistic period.

Drama, by contrast, changed profoundly. No fourth-century authors emerged to match the great tragedians of the Athenian golden age. Audiences seem to have preferred the tragedies of Sophocles, Aeschylus, and Euripedes to the works of their own fourth-century contemporaries. Nor did the comic genius of Aristophanes have any true fourth-century successors. Even in his own lifetime, however, Aristophanes' biting, satirical style was beginning to give way to a milder, less provocative drama that bears some resemblance to modern television comedies. It was this new style that laid the groundwork for the New Comedy of the fourth and third centuries B.C.E.

Perhaps the most striking development in fourth-century drama is the flight from social and political commentary. Fourth-century audiences looked to drama for diversion and escape; they no longer cared for the scathing indictments of society and of prominent individuals that Aristophanes had pioneered. Comedic humor was now based on mistaken identities, tangled familial relationships, comic misunderstandings, and breaches of etiquette. Similar trends are apparent in novels, a new literary genre that emerged during the fourth century. Here, too, lovers face extraordinary obstacles, but their affairs almost always end happily, with the lovers reunited after perilous adventures and a long separation.

The most famous comic dramatist of the age was Menander (342 B.C.E.?–292 B.C.E.). Most of his work survives only in fragments. To some modern critics, his comedies can seem contrived and artificial. To his contemporaries, however, and also to the Romans (who based their own comedic tradition on the works of Menander and his contemporaries), these frothy, light-hearted comedies of daily life had great appeal.

PHILOSOPHY AND POLITICAL THOUGHT IN THE AGE OF PLATO AND ARISTOTLE

The intellectual shift begun by Socrates was carried on brilliantly by his most talented student, Plato. Born in Athens to an aristocratic family around 429 B.C.E., Plato joined Socrates' circle as a young man and soon saw his mentor condemned to death. This experience made such an indelible impression on Plato that from then until his own death around 349 B.C.E. he shunned direct political involvement, seeking instead to vindicate Socrates by constructing a philosophical system based on Socratic precepts. Plato taught this system in Athens in an informal school (no buildings, tuition, or set curriculum) called the Academy, and also by writing a series of *dialogues* (treatises expressed in dramatic form) in which Socrates was the main speaker. The Platonic dialogues, among which some of the most important are the *Phaedo*, the *Symposium*, and the *Republic*, are enduring works of literature as well as the earliest surviving complete works of philosophy.

Plato was influenced by the two worlds in which he lived. As a young man, he had watched his teacher engage the relativism of the Sophists; as an adult, he lived in a rapidly changing world that had lost confidence in absolute truths. Plato understood that to combat skepticism and refute the Sophists he needed to provide a secure foundation for ethics. This he did by means of his doctrine of Ideas. He conceded that relativity and change are characteristics of the world we perceive with our senses, but he denied that this world of appearances was an appropriate foundation for philosophy. A higher, spiritual realm exists, com-

Plato.

posed of eternal forms or Ideas that only the mind can grasp. These unchanging Ideas are not mere abstractions but have a real existence. Each is the pattern of some class of objects, or relationship between objects, on earth. Thus there are Ideas of chair, tree, shape, color, proportion, beauty, and justice. Highest is the Idea of the Good, the cause and guiding principle of the universe. The things we perceive through our senses are merely imperfect copies of the supreme realities, the Ideas, and relate to them as shadows relate to material objects. By understanding and contemplating the Good, one might achieve the ultimate goal of fulfillment through virtue.

Understanding that a virtuous life would be difficult to attain in a society full of turbulence, Plato addressed himself to politics in his most famous dialogue, the *Republic*, the first systematic treatment of political philosophy ever written. Because Plato sought social harmony and order rather than liberty or equality, he argued for an elitist state in which most of the people—the farmers, artisans, and traders—would be governed by an intellectually superior group of "guardians." Guardians would be chosen for their naturally superior attributes of intelligence and character. All guardians would serve first as soldiers, living together without private property; those found to be the wisest would then receive more education and ultimately become "philosopher-kings." These enlightened rulers would see to it that every aspect of life was subordinated to the Idea of the Good and would in turn choose only the wisest to succeed them. Later commentators have often found this ideal of rule by the wisest to be seductive, but they ask of Plato, "Who will guard the guardians?" Plato's system presumed that properly educated rulers would never be corrupted by power or wealth—a proposition that has yet to be sustained in practice.

ARISTOTELIAN THOUGHT

Such practical considerations were more typical of the thought of Plato's own greatest student, Aristotle (384–322 B.C.E.). Aristotle was the son of a physician, who learned from his father the importance of carefully observing natural phenomena. He accepted Plato's assumption that there are some things only the mind can grasp, but his own philosophical system was based on his confidence that the human mind could understand the universe through the rational ordering of sense experience. In contrast to Plato, who taught that everything we see and touch is but an untrustworthy reflection of some intangible truth, Aristotle believed in the objective reality of material objects and taught that systematic investigation of tangible things, combined with rational inquiry into how they function, could yield full comprehension of the natural order and of human beings' place within it.

Aristotle surveyed a wide variety of subjects in separate but interrelated treatises on logic, metaphysics, ethics, poetics, and politics. He was the first formal logician known to human history, and probably the greatest. He established rules for the syllogism, a form of reasoning in which certain premises inevitably lead to a valid conclusion, and he established precise categories underpinning all philosophical and scientific analysis, such as substance, quantity, relation, and place. Aristotle's central belief was that all things in the universe consist of the imprint of form on matter. This was a compromise between Platonism, which tended to ignore matter, and the purest materialism, which saw no patterns in the universe other than the accidents of matter impinging on matter. For Aristotle, forms are the purposeful forces that shape the world of matter; thus the presence of the form of humanity molds and directs the human embryo until it ultimately becomes a human being. Since everything has a purposeful form, the universe for Aristotle is teleological—that is, every item and every class of items is inherently aiming toward its own particular end. Aristotle's universe is

therefore in a constant state of motion, as everything within it moves toward its ultimate perfected form (known in Greek as its *telos*).

Aristotle's moral philosophy was expressed most fully in his *Nicomachean (NEE-ko-MAH-kee-an) Ethics*, although important aspects of his ideas are also contained in his *Politics*. Aristotle taught that the highest good consists in the harmonious functioning of the individual human mind and body. Humans differ from the animals by virtue of their rational capacities, and so they find happiness by exercising these appropriately. For most people this will mean exercising reason in practical affairs. Good conduct is virtuous conduct, and virtue resides in aiming for the golden mean: courage rather than rashness or cowardice, temperance rather than excessive indulgence or ascetic denial. Better than the practical life, however, is the contemplative life, for such a life allows those few men equipped for it by nature to exercise their rational capacities to the utmost. Aristotle believed therefore that philosophers were the happiest of men, but he understood that even they could not engage in contemplation without interruption. As a practical person, moreover, he deemed it necessary for them to intersperse their speculative activities with practical life in the real world.

Aristotle.

Whereas Plato conceived of politics as a means to an end, the orderly pursuit of the supernatural Good, Aristotle thought of politics as an end in itself, the collective exercise of the good life. But Aristotle also took it for granted that some people—barbarians—were not fully human and so were meant by nature to be slaves. He also excluded women from the life of the polis, and so from a full measure of humanity, because they could not share in the life of the state in which human rational faculties enjoyed their fullest exercise. All male citizens, on the other hand, were meant to share in it, for, as Aristotle proposed, "man is by nature a political animal" (or, to be more faithful to the Greek, "a creature of the polis"). This view did not mean that the best form of government was democracy, however; like Plato, Aristotle saw that as a "debased" form of government. What he preferred was the polity, in which monarchical, aristocratic, and democratic elements were combined by means of checks and balances. Such a government would allow free men to realize their rational potential, showing themselves to be located in nature's hierarchy above the animals and right below the gods.

For all of their brilliance and originality, Plato and Aristotle offered few prescriptions for reforming their own societies. Both imagined the perfect society as one made up of a few thousand households, largely engaged in agriculture and living in a face-to-face, participatory society. Although Greek civilization had begun in such a world, the realities of fourth-century political life were very different. The fact that Plato and Aristotle considered the problem at all is testament to their recognition that something was wrong with the polis; but for both men, the answer was a reorganization of the existing polity, not something new in its place.

XENOPHON AND ISOCRATES

Another product of the Socratic intellectual tradition was Xenophon (*ZEH-noh-fohn*), a contemporary of Plato. Xenophon had served in the mercenary army that fought its way out of Persia and also fought for the Spartan king Agesilaus in Asia Minor. Disillusioned with what his fellow Athenians had done to his teacher, Socrates, Xenophon lived most of his life as a comfortable exile in Spartan territory. There, Xenophon composed histories (including the tale of the 10,000 Greeks who fought their way out of Persia);

biographies; memories of Socrates; and treatises on ideal kingship, the Spartan constitution, household management (the *Oikonomikos*, the root of our word *economics*), and the raising of hunting dogs. Like most Greeks, Xenophon assumed that good government was to be sought through exemplars and moral paragons. This led him to embellish or omit facts that did not contribute toward moral uplift. Still, he was aware that the world had changed for the worse, a point driven home to him as he watched Epaminondas cripple the state Xenophon so admired, Sparta. So contemptuous was he of the Theban leader that in his "continuation" of Thucydides' history, Xenophon refused to record Epaminondas' name.

The Athenian orator Isocrates (436–338 B.C.E.) was also well aware that something had gone horribly awry. Again, his solution was not an overhaul of the Greek polis or the creation of more inclusive forms of political organization. What he proposed was a great invasion of Persia led by a man of vision and ability, someone who could unite the Greek world behind his cause. Isocrates cast about most of his life for such a man, favoring at one point Agesilaus of Sparta, at other times powerful tyrants from other parts of the Greek world. Toward the end of his life, he began to think the man for the job was a man whom most Athenians considered no Greek at all: Philip II, the king of Macedon. Isocrates issued an open letter to Philip, detailing the ills of the Greek world and declaring that masterful action was needed to rescue Greece from its endless cycle of self-destruction.

Isocrates issued an open letter to Philip, detailing the ills of the Greek world and declaring that masterful action was needed to rescue Greece from its endless cycle of self-destruction.

THE RISE OF MACEDON AND THE CONQUESTS OF ALEXANDER

What accounts for the remarkable success of the Macedonian conquests?

By the middle of the fourth century, the Greeks had become so embroiled in political and socioeconomic turmoil that they at first barely noticed the growing power of Macedon, a kingdom on the northern fringes of the

WHAT ACCOUNTS FOR THE REMARKABLE SUCCESS OF THE MACEDONIAN CONQUESTS?

THE RISE OF MACEDON AND THE CONQUESTS OF ALEXANDER   143

Greek world. They had little reason to do so; until the fourth century, Macedon had been a weak kingdom, ruled by a royal house barely strong enough to control its own nobility, and beset by intrigue and murderous ambition from within. As recently as the 360s, Macedon had teetered on collapse, surrounded by barbarian neighbors who nearly overran the kingdom. Most Greeks viewed the Macedonians themselves as barbarians, despite the efforts of a few Macedonian kings to add a bit of Hellenic culture to their court. (One late-fifth-century king had successfully invited Euripides and Sophocles to Macedon; Socrates had refused a similar request.) Therefore, when a young and energetic Macedonian king named Philip II consolidated the southern Balkans under his rule, many Greek patriots saw it as a development no less troubling than the approach of the Persian barbarians in the fifth century.

THE REIGN OF PHILIP II (359–336 B.C.E.)

Philip came to the throne of Macedon after his older brother died fighting a barbarian invasion, leaving as his heir a small boy. Philip had himself made regent for the boy, but soon dispensed with that fiction and took the throne himself. By 356, he certainly considered himself king. That same year a son was born to him; Philip named the child Alexander and marked him out as his successor.

Philip's first problem was to stabilize his northern borders. Through a combination of warfare and diplomacy, he subdued the tribes of the southern Balkans and incorporated their territory into Macedonia. Philip's success had much to do with his reorganization of the Macedonian army. As a young boy, Philip had been a hostage at the court of Epaminondas; the observant youth may have learned something from watching the Theban general. In any event, Philip turned the Macedonian phalanx from an ill-organized peasant army into a highly drilled, well-armed fighting machine. The mineral resources Philip captured early in his reign made him wealthy enough to establish what was in essence a professional army—just one of his gold mines produced as much in one year as the Delian League collected annually at its height. Philip also organized an elite cavalry squad—the Companions—who fought with and beside the king. These elite horsemen were drawn from the nobility; Philip hoped to inspire a greater esprit de corps among them as well as a deeper loyalty to the royal house. Philip recruited future Companions (and gained valuable hostages) by

bringing the most promising sons of the nobility to his capital at Pella, where they trained as pages with the crown prince Alexander. Through a series of dynastic marriages, Philip also managed to gain the good will and alliance of many neighboring kingdoms.

The growing power of Macedon alarmed some in the Greek world, most notably an Athenian orator named Demosthenes. Whereas some Greeks, like Isocrates, saw in Philip a potential answer to Greece's woes, Demosthenes and others believed that Philip was a treacherous barbarian whose ultimate aim was to end the independence of the poleis and subject Greece to his rule.

There is no doubt of the threat that Philip now posed; but Demosthenes and other Athenians misunderstood Philip's true goals. Philip's expansion in the north was not aimed at Athens; instead, it was designed to secure his frontiers and the resources necessary to support an invasion of Persia. From 348 on, he was keen to conciliate the major Greek poleis, especially Athens. At one point, he even asked for an alliance whereby the Athenians would provide the war fleet for his proposed invasion of the Persian Empire; in return he would support their claim to hegemony over Greece. The Athenians took Demosthenes' advice, and refused to cooperate with Philip. This miscalculation would prove disastrous for Athens.

Iron and Gold Chest Armor of Philip II. Found in the excavation of his tomb at Vergina.

Philip II of Macedon. This tiny ivory head was discovered in the tomb of Philip of Macedon. The damaged right eye strongly suggests that it is a portrait of Philip himself, whose eye was damaged by a catapult bolt.

Philip's inability to reach any understanding with Athens, despite his strenuous diplomatic efforts, ultimately led to war between the Macedonians on one side and Athens, Thebes, and a number of smaller poleis on the other (Sparta remained aloof). At the battle of Chaeronea in 338 B.C.E., the Macedonians won a narrow victory over the Athenians and their allies. In the aftermath, Philip called delegates from around mainland Greece to Corinth, where he established a new league. By and large, he left the independence of the major Greek poleis unaffected. The main purpose of the League of Corinth was to provide forces for the invasion of Persia by electing Philip as their military commander. But the league also played some role in maintaining peace among the rival Greek poleis.

Philip never realized his dream of invading Persian territory. At a festival in Macedon in 336 B.C.E., a disgruntled lover charged into the arena and assassinated him. The kingship now fell to the twenty-year-old young man who had led his father's cavalry at Chaeronea, Alexander III. To the Greeks he would be known as Alexander Poliorcetes, the Sacker of Cities. To the Romans, far more impressed by conquerors than were the Greeks, he was Alexander the Great.

THE CONQUESTS AND REIGN OF ALEXANDER (336–323 B.C.E.)

Alexander is a difficult figure for historians to understand, not least because in his own lifetime romantic legend had already built up around him and his achievements. Scholars have seen in Alexander a visionary, a genius, and a butcher; what he did was nothing less than transform the world, translating Greek culture from its parochial, small-scale homeland into a world culture, spreading it as far as the modern states of Afghanistan and Pakistan.

Alexander's military victories are well known. After first quelling revolts in Greece that erupted immediately on his father's death, by 334 he was ready to invade the Persian Empire, then under the rule of Darius III. Persia had experienced internal weakness for over a decade. Darius III had been placed on the throne by a scheming vizier who sought to control the young nobleman, only to find that his puppet had designs of his own. Darius killed the vizier and then ruled capably during the few years of peace he enjoyed until Alexander's appearance in Asia.

The Macedonian king won a series of startling victories, starting in northwest Asia Minor. At one point,

Macedonian Phalanx. Philip of Macedon's infantry—and Alexander the Great's thereafter—was armed with two-handed pikes and massed in squares sixteen rows deep and wide. Members of the phalanx were trained to wheel in step in any direction or to double their front by filing off in rows of eight.

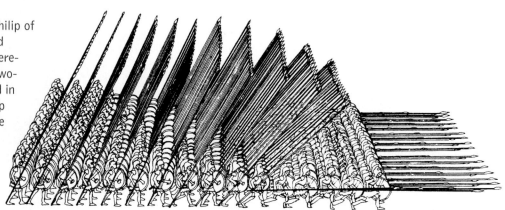

TWO VIEWS OF PHILIP

Philip II of Macedon provoked strong reactions among the Athenians, through whose eyes we must evaluate him due to the nature of our sources. As these passages illustrate, we could interpret his actions very differently, depending on whether we see in him a savior of Greece or a barbarian would-be conqueror.

ISOCRATES, TO PHILIP

As I kept going over these questions [of war and peace] in my own thoughts, I found that . . . the greatest states of Hellas should resolve to put an end to their mutual quarrels and carry the war beyond our borders into Asia. . . . I am going to advise you to champion the cause of concord among the Hellenes and of a campaign against the barbarian. . . . I affirm that, without neglecting any of your own interests you ought to reconcile Argos and Lacedaemon [Sparta] and Thebes and Athens; for if you can bring these cities together, you will not find it hard to unite the others as well. . . . If you can persuade four cities only to take a sane view of things, you will deliver the others also from many evils. . . . No quarrel should ever have arisen between you and any one of them. But unfortunately we are all prone by nature to do wrong more often than right. . . . For the future you must be on your guard to prevent a like occurrence, and must consider what service you can render them which will make it manifest that you have acted in a manner worthy both of yourself and what these cities have done. . . . It is a good thing to have the appearance of conferring benefits upon the greatest states of Hellas and at the same time to profit yourself no less than them. . . . You see how utterly wretched these states have become because of their warfare . . . and now perhaps someone will venture to object to what I have proposed, saying that I am trying to persuade you to set yourself to an impossible task. . . . While I grant that no one else in the world could reconcile these cities, yet nothing of the sort is difficult for you; for I see that you have carried through to a successful end many undertakings which the rest of the world looked upon as hopeless and unthinkable.

Isocrates, vol. 1, trans. George Norlin (Cambridge, Mass., 1928), pp. 251, 255, 263–271.

DEMOSTHENES, SECOND AND THIRD OLYNTHIACS

I do not choose, Athenians, to enumerate the resources of Philip and by such arguments to call on you to rise to the occasion. Because it seems to me that any dissertation on that topic is a tribute to his enterprise, but a record of our failure. For the higher he has raised himself above his proper level, the more he wins the admiration of the world; but the more you have failed to improve your opportunities, the greater is the discredit you have incurred. . . . Now to call a man perjured and faithless, without drawing attention to his acts, might justly be termed mere abuse. . . . I have two reasons for thinking the whole story worth telling: Philip shall appear as worthless as he really is, and those who stand against his apparent invincibility shall see that he has exhausted all the acts of chicanery on which his greatness was founded at the first, and that his career has now reached the extreme limit. . . . He has hoodwinked everyone that has had any dealings with him; he has played upon the folly of each party in turn and exploited their ignorance of his own character. This is how he has gained his power. . . . Never was there a crisis that demanded more careful handling than the present. . . . Quite apart from the disgrace that we should incur if we shirk our responsibilities [to our threatened allies], I see not a little danger . . . if there is nothing to hinder Philip, when he has crushed his present foe, from turning his arms against Attica.

Demosthenes, vol. 1, ed. and trans. J. H. Vince (Cambridge, Mass., 1930), pp. 23–27, 43, 47.

QUESTIONS FOR ANALYSIS

1. Isocrates, in his advice to Philip, seems to have had in mind an ideal union of the Greek states and various imperfect copies. Why had previous attempts at national unity come to grief? How did Isocrates think Philip could succeed?
2. Philip II of Macedon had many other concerns besides unifying quarreling Greeks. How would unification have helped him achieve his grand design? Was his campaign morally justified?
3. Rather than praising Philip for his leadership, Demosthenes denounced the Greeks for their failures. What specifically had they done and left undone?

Darius offered to cede his western possessions to Alexander in exchange for his family (whom Alexander had captured in battle) and a peace treaty. Alexander's field marshal, Parmenio, advised "I would accept it, if I were you." Alexander replied, "And I would too, if I were Parmenio." Within three years of his initial invasion, Alexander had subdued Anatolia and the Syria–Palestine coast and had detached Egypt from the Persian Empire. During his time in Egypt, Alexander appears to have reflected on what he had already

achieved and to have become increasingly convinced of his own superhuman qualities. Indeed, to many Alexander had already achieved more than one might have expected out of the squabbling, petty gods of Mount Olympus, who seemed to grow smaller by comparison as Alexander and his talented staff of officers achieved ever more.

In September of 331 B.C.E., Darius mustered the remaining strength of his empire to face Alexander's Greco-Macedonian army in what is today northern

Alexander Defeats King Darius of Persia at the Battle of Issus (333 B.C.E.). This Roman mural, discovered at Pompeii, shows Darius fleeing from the battlefield in his chariot, pursued by Alexander, who is the mounted figure on the left.

WHAT ACCOUNTS FOR THE REMARKABLE SUCCESS OF THE MACEDONIAN CONQUESTS?

THE RISE OF MACEDON AND THE CONQUESTS OF ALEXANDER   147

CHRONOLOGY

MACEDONIAN CONQUEST

Philip II crowns himself king of Macedon	356 B.C.E.
Defeat of Athens and formation of the League of Corinth	338 B.C.E.
Alexander defeats the Persian army	331 B.C.E.
Death of Alexander	323 B.C.E.

Iraq. At the battle of Gaugamela, Alexander destroyed the Persian army. Darius himself fled to the hills, where he was captured and slain by a chieftain hoping to ingratiate himself to Alexander. But as the new king of Persia, Alexander executed the chieftain for having

killed his predecessor. The next spring, Alexander destroyed the Persian capital of Persepolis, lest it serve as a rallying point for Persian resistance.

Over the next few years, Alexander campaigned in the mountains of Bactria (modern Afghanistan), the hardest fighting of the campaign. He ultimately succeeded in conquering much of the region, but his grasp there was tenuous. Among the Bactrians he found the woman he would take as his queen, Roxane. From there he moved down the Indus Valley, meeting stiff resistance. At the mouth of the Indus, his soldiers mutinied and refused to press on. Alexander reluctantly led them back toward Babylon, arriving there by the end of 324 B.C.E.

What Alexander planned to do with his new empire is difficult to say. Some scholars see him merely as a pirate, bent on conquest and plunder in a self-serving quest for glory worthy of the Homeric heroes from

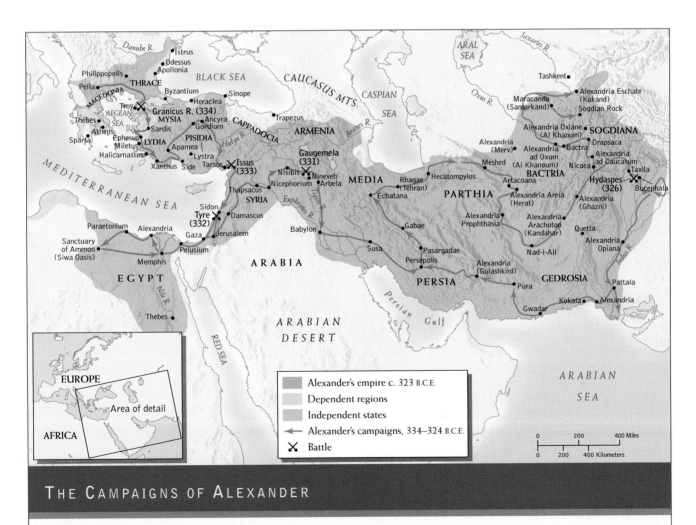

THE CAMPAIGNS OF ALEXANDER

The conquests of Alexander the Great brought Greek culture to the vast area of the former Persian Empire as far east as the Indus River. Notice the number of cities named after Alexander. Why did Alexander and his followers establish so many new cities, particularly in regions that were already highly urbanized?

whom he claimed descent. Others counter by pointing to his systematic foundation of Greek-style cities along his campaign route. These new cities served not only as garrisons to control the local populations but also as foci of Greek culture. There is also the bizarre mass marriage he forced on his officers, compelling them to put aside their wives and take Persian noblewomen as brides. Once seen as a reflection of Alexander's supposed visionary desire to eliminate ethnic distinctions within his empire, this act is now viewed as an attempt to breed a new nobility, loyal not to Macedonian or Persian concerns but to him and his successors alone. Alexander took no realistic steps to create an administration for his new realm, although he did move various officers and groups of veterans about in an attempt to reshuffle certain responsibilities. Our sources hint at plans for further conquests, perhaps Arabia, perhaps toward Italy and Sicily in the west. Given what we know about Alexander, it is hard to imagine him ever being satisfied with what he had.

We will never know for certain. In late May 323, Alexander fell ill with malarial symptoms and, ignoring the advice of his doctors, continued to play the part of the Homeric king, drinking mightily and exerting himself incautiously. Alexander had often been wounded in battle during the course of his career, and no doubt his body was the worse for wear. His condition declined, until on June 10, 323 B.C.E., Alexander died, not yet thirty-three years old. His friends and officers had gathered around his deathbed and asked to whom he wished to leave his empire. One source states that, just as he went unconscious, a wry smile adorned Alexander's face as he whispered "To the strongest." This might mean any of several talented and ambitious generals around him, who were second only to Alexander himself in prestige and martial skill.

THE HELLENISTIC KINGDOMS

What characteristics defined and distinguished the three major Hellenistic kingdoms?

After Alexander's death, epic struggles unfolded among the men and women who wanted to keep the realm together, those who wished to mark out their own kingdoms, and—among the latter—those who wanted the biggest possible share. The wars and intrigues that took place in the two generations after the death of the great conqueror are too involved to describe in detail. By 275 B.C.E., however, three separate axes of military and political power had emerged, each with a distinctive outlook despite their common background and their Greco-Macedonian ruling class. One of the striking features of the period is the renewal of ancient political patterns, especially in the Near East and Egypt, where the successors of Alexander the Great established sprawling cities and revived the concept of the god-king.

PTOLEMAIC EGYPT

After Alexander's death in Babylon, his inner circle met to decide the fate of his empire. For the moment, the empire remained united, but Ptolemy (*TAHL-uh-mee*) asked to be made governor of Egypt. The rest of Alexander's generals seem to have been glad to let Ptolemy have the hot, sweltering land of Egypt, but Ptolemy himself recognized the country's vast potential and its virtual invulnerability to attack. As soon as he arrived, Ptolemy set about making Egypt an independent kingdom under his rule. The dynasty he established would rule Egypt for the next 300 years. The

Marble Head of Alexander. Alexander the Great was reputed to have been very handsome, but all surviving representations doubtless make him more handsome still. This one dates from about 180 B.C.E. and is typical in showing Alexander with lion's-mane hair.

WHAT CHARACTERISTICS DEFINED AND DISTINGUISHED THE THREE MAJOR HELLENISTIC KINGDOMS?

THE HELLENISTIC KINGDOMS   149

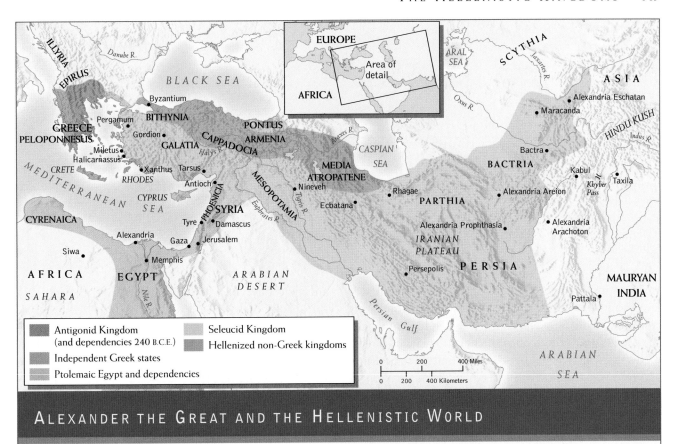

ALEXANDER THE GREAT AND THE HELLENISTIC WORLD

Note the position of the three successor kingdoms to Alexander's empire; notice how each was based on one of the three major axes of civilization we have studied so far: Egyptian, ancient Near Eastern, and Aegean. What might the division of Alexander's empire along such traditional lines suggest about the durability of his empire even if he had lived to rule it?

male heirs of the line all took the name Ptolemy, hence Ptolemaic Egypt.

Ruling from Alexandria, the great coastal city founded by Alexander, the Ptolemies acted as Macedonian kings toward their Greek and Macedonian subjects living in the thriving capital. Outside of Alexandria, however, they played the role of pharaohs, surrounding themselves with the trappings and symbols of Egypt's pharaonic heritage. The Ptolemies were by no means a political failure. The third century in particular was a time of prosperity and internal peace for Ptolemaic Egypt. But even in antiquity, people recognized the divide between the Macedonian kings and the ancient land they ruled. Geographers described Alexandria as "by" Egypt, not "of" it. No matter how well they aped the Egyptian rulers of the past, the Macedonian ruling class largely disdained their subjects. Until the last Ptolemaic ruler, Cleopatra VII, no Ptolemaic ruler even bothered to learn Egyptian.

For the Ptolemies as for the ancient pharaohs, all of Egypt was basically crown land, to be exploited for the benefit of the royal house. Supporting this Egyptian tradition, however, was the Macedonian idea that conquered land—land won by the spear—was plunder, to be used for personal enrichment and glorification. The Ptolemies attempted to squeeze every last drop of wealth from the Egyptian countryside. Most of this wealth ended up in Alexandria. There was little interest in improving the lot of the Egyptian peasantry; in the ancient world it was often assumed that what kept the poor complacent and dutiful was their desperate poverty. The Ptolemies, however, overdid it, and from the end of the third century they faced regular and dangerous revolts from the native peasantry.

Nevertheless, Ptolemaic Egypt proved the most durable of the Hellenistic kingdoms. The dynasty used the wealth of the country to patronize science and the arts. Early in the dynasty the museum and library of Alexandria were established, and the city became a center of scholarship that attracted the greatest minds of the Hellenistic world, displacing even Athens, which had retained some importance as a sort of university

Two Portraits of Ptolemy I of Egypt. The Ptolemies presented themselves as Greeks to their Macedonian and Greek subjects (shown here on a gold coin) but as pharaohs to their Egyptian subjects.

town. Many breakthroughs in astronomy, applied sciences, and physics took place in Alexandria; and the study of medicine advanced greatly under Ptolemaic rule. Freed from the taboos of their homeland, Greek medical researchers in Egypt were permitted to perform autopsies on the bodies of dead criminals, making it possible for anatomy to become a scientific discipline in its own right. The Ptolemies were not selfless patrons. They were largely interested in the glory and prestige their patronage brought them, rather than the practical benefits that might arise from the research they sponsored. But whatever its motives, Alexandrine scholarship left a permanent mark on the Mediterranean world.

SELEUCID ASIA

The vast Asian possessions of Alexander the Great eventually fell to another Macedonian, Seleucus (*seh-LOO-kubs*), by 281 B.C.E. Seleucus had not been a senior officer during Alexander's lifetime, but he had navigated the turmoil after Alexander's death successfully, exploiting the fears and suspicions among Alexander's more prominent successors.

Ruling such an expansive realm proved as much curse as blessing. The Persian dynasty founded by Seleucus, the Seleucids, struggled with the problem of secession throughout its history. Their hold on the easternmost provinces was especially tenuous—even during Alexander's lifetime that had been the case—as Seleucus recognized. He therefore ceded much of the Indus Valley to the great Indian warrior-king Chandragupta in exchange for peace and a squad of war elephants. By the middle of the third century, the Seleucids had also lost control of Bactria, where a series of Indo-Greek states were emerging with a unique cultural complex of their own. (One Bactrian Greek king, Menander, is remembered in Buddhist tradition

and may have had Buddhist sympathies himself.) By the 260s, they had also lost control of the western half of Asia Minor. The Seleucid heartland now became Syria–Palestine, Mesopotamia, and the western half of Persia: still a great, wealthy kingdom, but far less than what Alexander had left.

Like the Ptolemies, the Seleucids offered two faces to their subjects, one rooted in ancient Near Eastern tradition for their Persian and Mesopotamian subjects, another decidedly more Greek for the heavily Hellenized populations of the coast. Seleucus' son, Antiochus I, proclaimed in terms reminiscent of a Sargon or a Hammurabi, "I am Antiochus, the Great King, the legitimate king . . . king of Babylon, king of all countries." Throughout their empire, the Seleucids encouraged the recognition of their divine status and the divine honors owed to them. In the great urban centers of Seleucid Asia, shrines and temples were built for the cult of the living ruler.

Seleucid rulers continued the tradition of Alexander, planting new cities throughout their empire, cities that were fundamentally Greek in their assumptions but in many cases grew to be thriving commercial and industrial cities, such as Antioch. These cities attracted a great deal of professional and mercantile talent eastward, encouraging trade and manufactures on which the Seleucids imposed a wide variety of taxes, tariffs, and levies. Although their bureaucracy was less organized than that of the Ptolemies, in an empire of as many as 30 million inhabitants even haphazard tax collection could reap huge rewards. Like their Persian predecessors, however, the Seleucids did not reinvest their gains into what we would call capital improvements. Instead, they hoarded their wealth in great state treasuries. All the same, they had more than enough cash to provide for the smooth operation of their government and to defend their borders through

WHY WAS PROSPERITY SO UNEVENLY DISTRIBUTED IN THE HELLENISTIC ECONOMY?

THE GROWTH OF TRADE AND URBANIZATION   151

the third century, a period of regular warfare with the Ptolemies. It was not until the second century, when Antiochus III lost a costly war with the Romans, that he had to plunder temples and private wealth to pay off his war indemnity.

ANTIGONID MACEDON AND GREECE

The Macedonian homeland did not possess the vast wealth of the new kingdoms carved from Alexander's conquests. It also remained highly unstable from the time of Alexander's death until 276 B.C.E., when a general named Antigonus was finally able to establish his rule over the area. Macedon drew its strength from considerable natural resources and from its influence over Aegean trade, as well as its de facto overlordship of the Greek homeland. Furthermore, the Macedonians could still field the finest army of any of the successor states, and the Antigonid kings of Macedon held what many of the monarchs of the Hellenistic world desired, the kingship of the land once held by Philip and Alexander.

Antigonus was influenced by the Stoic outlook (discussed later in this chapter) and viewed kingship as something of a noble servitude, an office to be endured rather than enjoyed. This outlook, combined with his modest resources, convinced him not to compete with the Seleucids and Ptolemies for dominance. Instead, Antigonid policy was to keep these other two powers at war and away from the Macedonian sphere of influence. Antigonus and his successors thus pursued a policy more reminiscent of Philip than of Alexander. They secured the northern frontiers, maintained a strong, standing military, and kept the fractious Greeks to the south at heel.

The Greeks, however, were restive under the Antigonids, and two emergent forces within the Greek world served as rallying points for cries of freedom and war against the barbarian. These two forces, the Aetolian League and the Achaean League, were a departure in Greek political organization. Unlike the defensive alliances of the classical period, these two leagues represented a real political unification, with some centralization of governmental functions. Citizens of the member poleis participated in councils of state that dealt with foreign policy and military affairs, trials for treason, and the annual election of a league general (also the chief executive officer) and his second in command. New members were

admitted on an equal footing with existing members, and all citizens of the various poleis enjoyed joint citizenship throughout the league. The same laws, weights and measures, coinage, and judicial procedures also applied throughout this federal system. So impressive was the degree of cooperation and unification that James Madison, John Jay, and Alexander Hamilton employed the Achaean League as one of their models in advocating federalism in the United States.

THE GROWTH OF TRADE AND URBANIZATION

Why was prosperity so unevenly distributed in the Hellenistic economy?

The Hellenistic world was generally prosperous, owing to the growth of long-distance trade, finance, and cities. Alexander's conquests opened up a vast trading area stretching from Egypt to the Persian Gulf, dominated by Greek-speaking rulers and newly established merchant communities. These conquests also stimulated the mercantile economy by putting into circulation hoards of Persian gold and silver coins, jewelry, and utensils acquired through plunder. Industries also benefited, because manufacturing was encouraged by autocratic rulers as a means of increasing their revenues through trade.

New trading ventures were particularly vigorous and lucrative in Ptolemaic Egypt and the area of western Asia ruled over by the Seleucid monarchs, the heartland of which was Syria. Every facility was provided by the Ptolemies and the Seleucids for the encouragement of trade. Harbors were improved, warships were sent out to police the seas, and roads and canals were built. The Ptolemies even employed geographers to discover new routes to distant lands and thereby open up valuable markets. As a result of such methods Egypt developed a flourishing commerce in the widest variety of products. Into the port of Alexandria came spices from Arabia, gold from Ethiopia and India, tin from Britain, elephants and ivory from Nubia, silver from Spain, fine carpets from Asia Minor, and even silk from China. Profits for the government

So impressive was the degree of cooperation and unification that James Madison, John Jay, and Alexander Hamilton employed the Achaean League as one of their models in advocating federalism in the United States.

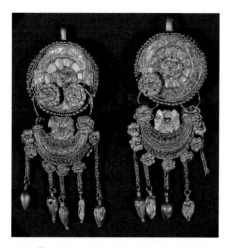

Hellenistic Earrings. These exquisite pieces of jewelry illustrate the enormous wealth and extraordinary craftsmanship available to the upper classes of the Hellenistic world.

and for some of the merchants were often as high as 20 or 30 percent.

Cities grew enormously during the Hellenistic Age, for both political and economic reasons. Entirely aside from economic motives, Greek rulers imported Greek officials and especially Greek soldiers to maintain their control over non-Greek populations. Many such settlements were new foundations. Alexander the Great himself had founded some 70 cities as outposts of Greek domination, and in the next two centuries his successors founded about 200 more. But urbanization also increased because of the expansion of commerce and industry and the proliferation of governmental bureaus.

Population growth in some urban centers was explosive. At Antioch in Syria, the population quadrupled during a single century. Seleucia on the Tigris grew from nothing to a metropolis of several hundred thousand in less than two centuries. Alexandria in Egypt, the largest and most famous of all the Hellenistic cities, had half a million inhabitants. Before imperial Rome, no other city in ancient times surpassed it in size or in magnificence. Its streets were well paved and laid out in regular order. It had splendid public buildings and parks, a museum, and a library of half a million scrolls.

Despite the overall growth of the Hellenistic economy, by no means did everyone enjoy prosperity. Agriculture remained the major occupation and primary source of wealth in the Hellenistic world, and small farmers in particular suffered severely from the exploitative tax policies of Hellenistic mon-

archs. Although industrial production increased, industry continued to be based on manual labor by individual artisans, most of whom lived in poverty. Among the teeming populations of Hellenistic cities, unemployment was a constant concern. Those who could not find work were forced to beg, steal, or prostitute themselves to survive.

Even those who prospered in the new economy were often subject to drastic fluctuations in their fortunes, owing to the natural precariousness of mercantile endeavors. A trader who did very well selling a luxury cloth might invest heavily in it, only to find that tastes had changed or that a ship he had dispatched to convey his wares had sunk. Merchants were also particularly exposed to the boom-and-bust syndrome. A merchant, thinking he would make a fortune during an upward price spiral, might go into debt to take advantage of the upward trend, only to find that supply in the commodity he traded suddenly exceeded demand, leaving him nothing with which to pay back his creditors.

All told, therefore, it seems clear that the economic landscape of the Hellenistic world was one of contrasting extremes, an image worth remembering as we move to a consideration of Hellenistic thought and culture.

HELLENISTIC CULTURE: PHILOSOPHY AND RELIGION

What was the relationship between Epicureanism and Stoicism?

Hellenistic philosophy exhibited two trends that ran almost parallel throughout the civilization. The major trend, exemplified by Epicureanism and Stoicism, saw reason as the key to resolving the anxieties of human life.

The philosophers and religious enthusiasts of the Hellenistic Age generally agreed on one thing: the necessity of finding some release from the trials of human existence.

This trend was a manifestation of Greek influence, although philosophy and science, as combined by Aristotle, had now come to a parting of the ways. The minor trend, exemplified by the Skeptics and various cults, tended to reject reason, to deny the possibility of attaining truth, and in some cases to turn toward mysticism and reliance on faith. Despite the differences in their teachings, the philosophers and religious enthusiasts of the Hellenistic Age generally agreed on one thing: the necessity of finding some release from the trials of human existence, for with the decline of free civic life as a means for the expression of human idealism, alternatives needed to be found to make life seem meaningful, or at least endurable.

EPICUREANISM AND STOICISM

Epicureanism and Stoicism both originated about 300 B.C.E. The founders were, respectively, Epicurus (c. 342–270 B.C.E.) and Zeno (fl. after 300 B.C.E.), both residents of Athens. The two philosophies had several features in common. Both were individualistic, concerned not with the welfare of society but with the good of the individual. Both were materialistic, denying the existence of any spiritual substances; even divine beings and the soul were declared to be formed of matter. Stoicism and Epicureanism also contained elements of universalism. Both taught that people are the same the world over and recognized no distinctions between Greeks and non-Greeks.

But in most ways the two systems were quite different. The Stoics believed that the cosmos is an ordered whole in which all contradictions are resolved for ultimate good. Evil is therefore relative; the particular misfortunes that befall human beings are but necessary incidents to the final perfection of the universe. Everything that happens is rigidly determined in accordance with rational purpose. No individual is master of his or her fate; people are free only in the sense that they can accept their fate or rebel against it. But whether they accept or rebel, they cannot overcome it. Their supreme duty is to submit to the order of the universe in the knowledge that this order is good. Through such an act of resignation the highest happiness will be attained, which consists of tranquillity of mind. Those who are most truly happy are thus the ones who by the assertion of their rational natures have accomplished a perfect adjustment of their lives to the cosmic purpose and purged their souls of all bitterness and protest against evil turns of fortune.

The Stoics' ethical and social theory grew from their general philosophy. Believing that the highest good is serenity of mind, they emphasized duty and self-discipline as cardinal virtues. Recognizing the prevalence of particular evils, they taught tolerance for and forgiveness of each other. They also urged participation in public affairs as a duty for those of rational mind. They condemned slavery and war, although they took no real actions against these evils since they believed that the results that might arise from violent measures of social change would be worse than the diseases they were meant to cure. With appropriate qualifications, the Stoic philosophy was one of the noblest products of the Hellenistic Age in teaching egalitarianism, pacifism, and humanitarianism.

The Epicureans based their philosophy on the materialistic "atomism" of an earlier Greek thinker named Democritus, who lived in the latter part of the fifth century B.C.E. According to this theory the ultimate constituents of the universe are atoms, infinite in number, indestructible, and indivisible. Every individual object or organism in the universe is the product of a fortuitous combination of atoms. Epicurus and his followers concluded, therefore, that because there is no ultimate purpose in the universe, the highest good is pleasure—the moderate satisfaction of bodily appetites; the mental pleasure of contemplating excellence and satisfactions previously enjoyed; and above all, serenity of soul in the face of death. An individual who understands that the soul is material and therefore cannot survive the body, that the universe operates of itself, and that no gods intervene in human affairs will have no fear of death or any other supernatural phenomena. The Epicureans thus came by a different route to the same general conclusion as the Stoics—nothing is better than tranquillity of mind.

The Epicureans thus came by a different route to the same general conclusion as the Stoics—nothing is better than tranquillity of mind.

The practical moral teachings and the politics of the Epicureans rested on utilitarianism. In contrast to the Stoics, they did not insist on virtue as an end in itself but taught that the only reason one should be good is to increase one's own happiness. In like manner, they denied that there is any such thing as absolute justice: laws and institutions are just only insofar as they contribute to the welfare of the individual. Certain rules have been found necessary in every society for the maintenance of order. These rules should be obeyed solely because it is to each individual's advantage to do so. Epicurus considered the state as a mere convenience and taught that the wise man should take no active part in politics. Because the evils in the world cannot be eradicated by human effort, the wise individual will withdraw to study philosophy and enjoy the fellowship of a few congenial friends.

SKEPTICISM

A more radically defeatist philosophy was that propounded by the Skeptics. Skepticism reached the zenith of its popularity about 200 B.C.E. under the influence of Carneades. The chief source of its inspiration was the teaching that all knowledge is derived from sense perception and therefore must be limited and relative. From this the Skeptics deduced that people cannot prove anything. Because the impressions of our senses deceive us, no truth can be certain. All we can say is that things appear to be such and such; we do not know what they really are. We have no definite knowledge of the supernatural, of the meaning of life, or even of right and wrong. It follows that the sensible course to pursue is suspension of judgment; this alone can lead to happiness. If we will abandon the fruitless quest for absolute truth and cease worrying about good and evil, we will attain peace of mind, which is the highest satisfaction that life affords. The Skeptics were even less concerned than the Epicureans with political and social problems. Their ideal was one of escape from a world neither reformable nor understandable.

RELIGION

Hellenistic religion similarly tended to offer vehicles of escape from collective political commitments. Greek religion in the age of the city-states had emphasized the worship of the gods who protected the polis. This sense of connection between a locality and its gods continued during the Hellenistic period. Nevertheless, for some people such civic-oriented worship was losing its vitality in the rootless, cosmopolitan world of the second and third centuries B. C. E. In its place, some elite members of society gravitated toward the ethical philosophies of Stoicism, Epicureanism, and Skepticism. Ordinary people, on the other hand, were beginning to embrace emotional personal religions offering elaborate ritual in this world and salvation in the next.

In Greek-speaking communities especially, cults that stressed extreme ascetic atonement for sin, ecstatic mystical union with divinity, and otherworldly salvation attracted many followers. Among these mystery cults, so called because their membership was secret and their rites held in private, one of the most popular was the Dionysiac cult, based on the myth of the death and resurrection of the god Dionysius. The Egyptian cult of Isis sounded these same themes of death and rebirth; so too did Zoroastrianism, which became increasingly dualistic, with Zoroastrian magi insisting that everything material was evil and demanding that believers practice austerities to ready their immaterial souls for ethereal joy in the afterlife.

Like the peoples of the Hellenistic world, the gods migrated to new lands. Temples to Greek gods and goddesses were dedicated throughout the Near East and Egypt; temples to Near Eastern divinities were also constructed in the cities of the Greek homeland. Alexandria in Egypt was a particularly important place where Egyptian and Near Eastern myths were recorded and reformulated for Greek-speaking audiences. Here, as elsewhere in the Hellenistic world, Greek and non-Greek cults combined to create a dizzying variety of religious possibilities.

Even where such assimilationist impulses met with resistance, as they did for example among the Jews of Palestine, Hellenistic culture struck deep roots, especially among the upper classes. Greek influence was even more pronounced among the Jewish communities living outside Palestine, which by the end of the second century B.C.E. outnumbered the Palestinian Jewish population by a considerable margin. To meet the religious needs of these Greek-speaking Jewish communities, a Greek-language version of the Hebrew Bible (known as the Septuagint) was produced, which quickly became an authoritative text in its own right. Legend had it that seventy scribes, each working independently, produced a translation from Hebrew into Greek that was identical in every respect, thus proving that the Septuagint (so called from the Greek word for "seventy") was the product of divine inspiration.

HELLENISTIC CULTURE: LITERATURE AND ART

What were the principal themes of Hellenistic architecture and sculpture?

Both the literature and the art of the Hellenistic age were characterized by a tendency to take aspects of earlier Greek accomplishments to extremes, as writers and artists strove to demonstrate their purely formal skills to impress their autocratic patrons. The greater uncertainties of existence in Hellenistic times may also have led consumers of art to seek gratification from more dramatic and less subtle forms of artistic expression. Whatever the explanation, rather than being an integral expression of civic life, art during this period became more of a commodity. Artistic works became more numerous and more widely available: we know the names of at least 1,100 Hellenistic authors. Many of these works are mediocre, but some are enduring masterpieces of art and literature

THE GREEK INFLUENCE ON ISRAEL

Greek culture was a powerfully intoxicating force throughout the Hellenistic world, even in a comparative cultural backwater like Israel. In the second century B.C.E., the Hellenized ways of the Jewish upper classes in Jerusalem finally occasioned a revolt by a native Hebrew dynasty known as the Maccabees, who decried the "debaucheries" Greek culture had introduced into Jewish life. In the passage that follows, note that even the high priest of the Temple bears the Greek name Jason.

In those days [the reign of Antiochus IV Epiphanes, 175–164 B.C.E.] certain renegades came out from Israel and misled many, saying, "Let us go and make a covenant with the Gentiles [Greeks] around us, for since we separated from them many disasters have come upon us." . . . Some of the people went to the king, who authorized them to observe the ordinances of the Gentiles. So they built a gymnasium in Jerusalem, according to Gentile custom, and removed the marks of circumcision, and abandoned the holy covenant. They joined with the Gentiles and sold themselves to do evil. . . . When Antiochus succeeded to the kingdom, Jason the brother of Onias obtained the high priesthood by corruption. . . . He at once shifted his compatriots over to the Greek way of life. . . . Despising the sanctuary and neglecting the sacrifices, they hurried to take part in the unlawful proceedings in the wrestling arena after the signal for the discus-throwing, disdaining the honors prized by their ancestors and putting the highest value upon Greek forms of prestige. . . . When the quadrennial games were being held at Tyre and the king was present, Jason sent envoys . . . to carry three hundred silver drachmas for the sacrifice to Heracles. . . . Harsh and utterly grievous was the onslaught of evil. For the Temple was filled with debauchery and reveling by the Gentiles, who dallied with prostitutes and had intercourse with women within the sacred precincts. . . . The altar was covered with abominable offerings that were forbidden by the laws.

1 Maccabees 2; 2 Maccabees 4–6. *The New Oxford Annotated Bible.* (Oxford, 1994).

QUESTIONS FOR ANALYSIS

1. The Jews had disobeyed their religious leaders many times before they encountered Hellenistic culture. Why did Hebrew priests and prophets think the Greeks were so dangerous? What did they personally have to fear from corruption?

2. Why was the building of a gymnasium, or "Greek secondary school," in Jerusalem particularly symbolic and offensive to Jews? Could anyone have stopped the project? By their insistence on maintaining separatism, were the Jews resisting or demanding special privileges from the rulers of the Hellenistic successor kingdoms?

ESCAPE TO THE COUNTRYSIDE

The bewildering urban centers and social upheaval wrought by the Hellenistic age encouraged some people to retreat into an imaginary world of simple country pleasures expressed in poetry and prose. Theocritus (born around 300 B.C.E. in Syracuse) was one of the poets who crafted such fantasies of the simple life for an anxious urban audience.

I finished my song, and with an ingenious laugh he gave me the (shepherd's) crook, a token of what we had shared. Then taking the road to the left which leads to Pyxa he parted from us. Eucritus and I turned off, with young Amyntas, for Phrasidemus's farm. There, happy in our welcome, we flung ourselves down on couches of fragrant reeds and freshcut vineleaves. Above our heads a grove of elms and poplars stirred gently. We could hear the noise of water, a lively stream running from the cave of the Nymphs. Sunburnt cicadas, perched in the shadowy thickets, kept up their rasping chatter; a distant tree-frog muttered harshly as it picked its way among thorns; larks and linnets were singing, a dove made moan, and brown bees loitered, flitting about the springs. The tall air smelt of summer, it smelt of ripeness. We lay stretched out in plenty, pears at our feet, apples at our sides and plumtrees reaching down, branches pulled earthward by the weight of the fruit. The seal broken from the wine jars was four years old. Nymphs of Castalia, haunters of steep Parnassus, tell me, was Heracles given such wine to drink by ancient Chiron in Pholus's rocky cave? . . . May I set the winnowing fan in another year's heaped grain while the laughing goddess clutches her poppies and sheaves.

The Idylls of Theocritus, trans. Robert Wells (Manchester and New York, 1988), pp. 86–87.

QUESTIONS FOR ANALYSIS

1. Theocritus depicted the countryside as idyllic, but did his poetry have more fantasy in it than reality? Who is doing the farm labor while the well-fed urbanites frolic and pretend to be shepherds?

PASTORAL LITERATURE

The most prominent Hellenistic verse form was the pastoral, a new genre depicting a make-believe world of shepherds and wood nymphs. The inventor of the genre was a Greek named Theocritus, who wrote around 270 B.C.E. in the big-city environment of Alexandria. Theocritus was a merchant of escapism. In the midst of urban bustle, faced with despotic rulers, and within sight of overcrowded, slumlike conditions, he celebrated the charms of hazy country values and idealized the simple pleasures of rustic folk. One of his pastorals might start like this: "Begin my country song, sweet muses, begin, I am Thrysis from Etna, this is Thrysis's lovely voice." To many the falseness of such verse is alienating; how could shepherds talk this way? But other readers enjoy the poetic lushness. In creating the pastoral Theocritus founded an enduring tradition that outlasted the Hellenistic world to be taken up by such masters as Virgil and Milton and that provided a wealth of themes for the visual arts. Even composers of modern concert music, such as Claude Debussy in his

WHAT WERE THE PRINCIPAL THEMES OF HELLENISTIC ARCHITECTURE AND SCULPTURE?

HELLENISTIC CULTURE: LITERATURE AND ART   157

Prelude to "The Afternoon of a Faun," owe a debt to the escapist poet from Alexandria.

PROSE

Hellenistic prose literature was dominated by historians and biographers. By far the most profound of the writers of history was the mainland Greek Polybius, who lived during the second century B.C.E. According to Polybius, historical development proceeds in cycles, nations passing so inevitably through stages of growth and decay that it is possible to predict exactly where a nation is heading if one knows what has happened to it in the past. From the standpoint of historical method, Polybius deserves to be ranked second only to Thucydides among all the historians of ancient times, and he even surpassed Thucydides in his grasp of the importance of social and economic forces. Although most biographies of the time were light and gossipy, their popularity bears eloquent testimony to the literary tastes of the Hellenistic period.

ARCHITECTURE

Consonant with the despotic style of rule, the main traits of Hellenistic architecture were grandeur and ornamentation. In place of the balance and restraint that had characterized Greek architecture of the fifth and early fourth centuries B.C.E., Hellenistic public building drew on Greek elements but moved toward standards

Persian Gold Drinking Cup. Persian fondness for lions probably derived from the art of the Assyrians.

set by Persian monarchs and Egyptian pharaohs. Two examples (both of which unfortunately no longer survive) are the great lighthouse of Alexandria, which rose to a height of nearly 400 feet with three diminishing stories and eight columns to support the light at the top, and the citadel of Alexandria, built of stone covered with blue-tinted plaster, and said by a contemporary to

The Marble Streets of Ephesus. Taken from the Persians by Alexander in 334 B.C.E., this cosmopolitan city on the west coast of Asia Minor was noted for its splendor.

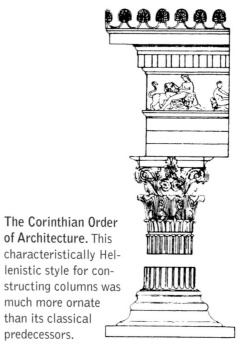

The Corinthian Order of Architecture. This characteristically Hellenistic style for constructing columns was much more ornate than its classical predecessors.

have "risen into mid-air." In Pergamon in Asia Minor an enormous altar to Zeus (transported in modern times to Berlin) and a huge open-air theater looked out over a high hill. In Ephesus, not far away, the streets were paved with marble. The signature of Hellenistic architecture of whatever dimension was the Corinthian column, a form of column more ornate than the simple and dignified Doric and Ionic alternatives that had predominated in earlier Greek building.

SCULPTURE

In the final analysis, probably the most influential of all products of Hellenistic culture were works of sculpture. Whereas earlier Greek sculpture had sought to idealize humanity and to express Greek ideals of modesty by understated restraint, Hellenistic sculpture emphasized extreme naturalism and unashamed extravagance. Sculptors now went to great lengths to re-create facial furrows, muscular distensions, and complex folds of drapery. Awkward human postures were considered to offer the greatest challenges to the artist in stone, to the degree that sculptors might prefer to show people stretching themselves or balancing themselves on one leg in ways that hardly ever occur in real life. Because most Hellenistic sculpture was executed for wealthy private patrons, it is clear that the goal was to create something unique in terms of its conception and craftsmanship—something a collector could show off as the only one of its type. It is not surprising, therefore, that complexity came to be admired for its own sake, and extreme naturalism sometimes teetered on the brink of distorted stylization. Yet when moderns see such works they frequently experience a shock of recognition, for the bizarre and exaggerated postures of Hellenistic sculptures exerted an enormous influence on Michelangelo and his followers and later inspired some of the most modern sculptors of the

Old Market Woman, Second Century B.C.E. Sculptures of this period often showed ordinary people engaged in ordinary activities. This realistic marble sculpture is of an old, tired woman who is carrying a basket of fruits and vegetables and chickens to market.

nineteenth and twentieth centuries. Three of the most famous examples of Hellenistic sculpture, which reveal different aspects of Hellenistic aesthetic ideals, may be cited here: the *Dying Gaul*, done in Pergamon around 220 B.C.E., shows consummate skill in portraying a twisted human

Dying Gaul. A famous example of Hellenistic realism and pathos, this statue was executed around 220 B.C.E. in the court of Pergamon in Asia Minor. (The original is lost; shown here is a Roman copy.) The sculptor clearly wished to exhibit skill in depicting an unusual human posture and succeeded remarkably in evoking the thin line that separates human dignity from unappeasable loneliness and physical suffering.

The Winged Victory of Samothrace. In this figure, done around 200 B.C.E., a Hellenistic sculptor preserved some of the calmness and devotion to grace and proportion characteristic of Hellenic art in the golden age.

Laocoön. In sharp contrast to the serenity of the *Winged Victory* is this famous sculpture group from the first century B.C.E., depicting the death of Laocoön. According to legend, Laocoön warned the Trojans not to touch the wooden horse sent by the Greeks and was punished by Poseidon, who sent two serpents to kill him and his sons. The intense emotionalism of this work was to have a great influence on western European art from Michelangelo onward.

body; the *Winged Victory of Samothrace* of about 200 B.C.E. displays flowing drapery as if it were not stone but real cloth; and the *Laocoön* group, of the first century B.C.E., offers one of the most intensely emotional and complex compositions known in the entire history of sculptural art.

SCIENCE AND MEDICINE

Why did science and medicine flourish in this period?

The Hellenistic period was the most brilliant age in the history of science before the seventeenth century C.E. There are two major reasons for this. One was the enormous stimulus given to intellectual inquiry by the fusion of Mesopotamian and Egyptian science with the learning and the curiosity of the Greeks. The other was that many Hellenistic rulers were generous patrons of scientific research, subsidizing scientists who belonged to their retinues just as they subsidized sculptors.

It was once thought that the motives for such patronage were practical—that rulers believed the progress of science would enhance the growth of industry in their territories and would also improve their own material comforts. Yet students of Hellenistic civilization now doubt that any ruler was hoping for an industrial revolution in the sense of applying technology to save human labor, for labor was cheap and autocratic princes were completely indifferent to the sufferings of the laboring classes. As for the supposed connection beween science and the enhancement of material comfort, Hellenistic rulers had adequate numbers of slaves to fan them and were not inclined to introduce mechanical devices that would have lessened the public grandeur of being tended by deferential subordinates.

To be sure, practical aims motivated the patronage of science in some areas, above all in medicine and anything that might relate to military technology. But the rulers who financed scientific endeavors did so primarily for motives of prestige: rulers could show off a scientific gadget to visitors just as they would show off their sculptures. Even purely theoretical achievements were so much admired among the Greek-speaking leisure classes that a Hellenistic prince who subsidized such a breakthrough would share the prestige for it in the way the mayor of an American city might bask in prestige today if his or her city's football team were to win the Super Bowl.

ASTRONOMY, MATHEMATICS, AND GEOGRAPHY

The prinicipal Hellenistic sciences were astronomy, mathematics, geography, medicine, and physics. The most renowned of the earlier Hellenistic astronomers was Aristarchus of Samos (310–230 B.C.E.), sometimes called the Hellenistic Copernicus. His primary accomplishment was his deduction that the earth and the other planets revolve around the sun. This view was not accepted by his successors because it conflicted with the teachings of Aristotle and with the conviction of the Greeks that humanity, and therefore the earth, must be at the center of the universe. Later the fame of Aristarchus was overshadowed by that of Ptolemy of Alexandria (second century C.E.). Although Ptolemy made few original discoveries, he systematized the

work of others. His principal writing, the *Almagest*—based on the view that all heavenly bodies revolve around the earth—was handed down to medieval Europe as the classic summary of ancient astronomy.

Closely allied with astronomy were mathematics and geography. The most influential Hellenistic mathematician was Euclid, the master of geometry. Until the middle of the nineteenth century his *Elements of Geometry* (written around 300 B.C.E. as a synthesis of the work of others) remained the accepted basis for the study of that branch of mathematics. The most original of the Hellenistic mathematicians was probably Hipparchus (second century B.C.E.), who laid the foundations of both plane and spherical trigonometry. Hellenistic geography owed most of its development to Eratosthenes (c. 276–c. 196 B.C.E.), an astronomer and librarian of Alexandria. By means of sundials placed some hundreds of miles apart, he calculated the circumference of the earth with an error of less than 200 miles. Eratosthenes was also the first to suggest the possibility of reaching eastern Asia by sailing west. One of his successors divided the earth into the five climatic zones that are still recognized and explained the ebb and flow of the tides as due to the influence of the moon.

MEDICINE

Other Hellenistic advances in science were in the field of medicine. Especially significant was the work of the Alexandrian scholar Herophilus of Chalcedon (c. 335–c. 280 B.C.E.). Herophilus was the greatest

Roman Instruments. Instruments like these were used for surgical procedures by both Hellenistic and Roman doctors, but they also had a variety of non-medical uses. Shown here are a grinding stone, spoons, probes, depressors, and tongs. The large, flat-headed tool may have been used for cauterizing wounds. The inscription visible on the stone in the upper left-hand corner was probably a recipe for eye medicine.

What changes occurred during the Hellenistic period to the polis-based culture of classical Greece?

The Transformation of the Polis   161

anatomist of antiquity and probably the first to practice human dissection. Among his achievements were a detailed description of the brain, with an insistence (against Aristotle) that the brain is the seat of human intelligence; the discovery of the significance of the pulse and its use in diagnosing illness; and the discovery that the arteries contain blood alone (not a mixture of blood and air as Aristotle had taught) and that their function is to carry blood from the heart to all parts of the body. About the middle of the third century, Erasistratus of Alexandria gained much of his knowledge of bodily functions from vivisection. He discovered the valves of the heart and distinguished between motor and sensory nerves. In addition, he rejected Hippocrates' theory that the body consists of four "humors" and consequently criticized excessive bloodletting as a method of cure. Unfortunately the humoral theory and an emphasis on bloodletting were revived by Galen, the great encyclopedist of medicine who lived in the Roman Empire in the second century C.E. Galen's baleful influence lasted until the eighteenth century C.E.

PHYSICS

Before the third century B.C.E., physics had been a branch of philosophy. It was made a separate, experimental science by Archimedes of Syracuse (c. 287–212 B.C.E.), who discovered the law of floating bodies, or specific gravity, and formulated with scientific exactness the principles of the lever, the pulley, and the screw. Among his memorable inventions were the compound pulley and the screw propeller for ships. Although he has been considered the greatest technical genius of antiquity, in fact he placed no emphasis on his mechanical contraptions and preferred to devote his

time to pure scientific research. Tradition relates that he discovered "Archimedes' principle" (specific gravity) while pondering possible theories in his bath: when he reached his stunning insight he dashed out naked into the street crying "Eureka" ("I have found it").

THE TRANSFORMATION OF THE POLIS

What changes occurred during the Hellenistic period to the polis-based culture of classical Greece?

The Hellenistic period saw the creation of great kingdoms in Egypt and Asia Minor and the rise of new forms of political organization in the Greek world such as the Achaean League. What, however, became of the polis, the foundation of classical Greek culture?

The apparent eclipse of the poleis is to some extent the result of a misleading impression. Some poleis continued to thrive as centers of trade. It is also important to remember that the great Hellenistic kingdoms remained, in many respects, collections of cities and that, for the most part, their Greco-Macedonian rulers continued to carry with them the cultural and political baggage of the polis world.

Nevertheless, the Hellenistic polis—even when it had not become a sprawling megalopolis such as Alexandria or Antioch—was in many ways a fundamentally different place from its classical precursor. As we have seen, the changes afoot in the fourth century were already disrupting the traditional bonds of Greek social and political life. What Alexander's conquests provided was a chance for many Greeks to escape the constraints of their fourth-century homeland. Alexander had created, perhaps unwittingly, a cosmopolitan world full of economic opportunity for a Greek speaker. By 300 B.C.E., a common Greek-based culture encompassed the eastern Mediterranean and western Asia, transcending political and geographical boundaries. Into this vast, exciting world, Greeks poured en masse, reducing the population of the Greek mainland by as much as one half in the century between 325 and 225 B.C.E. Hundreds of thousands of Greeks left Greece to seek their fortunes in a Mediterranean world of massive empires and cosmopolitan cities whose scale dwarfed anything imaginable even in Periclean Athens.

CHRONOLOGY	
SCIENTIFIC LUMINARIES OF THE HELLENISTIC WORLD	
Herophilus of Chalcedon	c. 335–c. 280 B.C.E.
Euclid	330?–270? B.C.E.
Aristarchus of Samos	310–230 B.C.E.
Archimedes of Syracuse	c. 287–212 B.C.E.
Eratosthenes	c. 276–c. 196 B.C.E.

Such a transformation had serious effects on Greek culture and the polis. The small-scale Dark Age communities and archaic poleis from which classical Greek culture grew were societies in which everybody knew virtually everyone else; innumerable social and political ties bound the citizens. Greek traditions of participation in government had led to a greater share in the franchise than any other culture had achieved in antiquity. Every citizen of the Greek world, to a lesser or greater extent, had some share, some stake in his society, its institutions, its gods, its army, and its cultural life.

If we transport this ingrained outlook into the swirling cosmopolitanism of the Hellenistic city, we can perhaps appreciate the magnitude of the change. All of those things that defined one's life as a person and a citizen were by and large gone. The intimate connection with the political life of the state, often even at the local level, had vanished. In place of the nexus of social and familial relationships prevalent in the Greek mainland, an average Greek in one of the Hellenistic kingdoms might have only his immediate family to rely on, if even that. What resulted was a traumatic separation between the traditional values and assumptions of Greek life and the social and political realities of the day.

> What resulted was a traumatic separation between the traditional values and assumptions of Greek life and the social and political realities of the day.

CONCLUSION

Judged from the vantage of classical Greece, Hellenistic civilization may at first seem no more than a degenerate phase of Greek civilization. The autocratic governments of the Hellenistic age appear repugnant in contrast to Athenian democracy, and the Hellenistic penchant for extravagance may appear debased in contrast to earlier Greek taste. Even the best Hellenistic literary works lack the inspired majesty of the great Greek tragedies, and none of the Hellenistic philosophers matched the profundity of Plato and Aristotle. Yet Hellenistic civilization had its own achievements that the classical age could not match. Most Hellenistic cities offered a greater range of public facilities, such as museums and libraries, than earlier Greek cities did, and the numerous Hellenistic thinkers, writers, and artists left to posterity important new ideas, impressive new genres, and imaginative new styles. Scientific advances also demonstrate the intellectual creativity that marked the Hellenistic world.

Probably the most important contribution of the Hellenistic era to subsequent historical development was the role it played as intermediary between Greece and Rome. In some cases the Hellenistic contribution was simply that of preservation. Most of what the ancient Romans would know of classical Greek thought came to them through copies of Greek philosophical and literary texts preserved in Hellenistic libraries. In other areas, however, transfer involved transmutation. Hellenistic art, for example, evolved from earlier Greek art into something related but quite different, and it was this "Greek-like" art that exerted the greatest influence on the tastes and artistic accomplishments of the Romans. A similar case might be made for drama.

In conclusion, two particularly remarkable aspects of Hellenistic culture deserve special comment—Hellenistic cosmopolitanism and Hellenistic modernity. The word *cosmopolitan* itself comes from a Greek word meaning "universal city," and it was the Greeks of the Hellenistic period who came the closest among Westerners to turning this ideal of cosmopolitanism into reality. Around 250 B.C.E. a leisure-class Greek could have traveled from Sicily to the borders of India, always meeting people who spoke his language, both literally and in terms of shared ideals. Nor would this same Greek have been a nationalist in the sense of professing any exclusive loyalty to a city-state or kingdom. He would more likely have considered himself a citizen of the world.

Hellenistic cosmopolitanism was partly a product of the cosmopolitanism of Persia and helped, in turn, create the cosmopolitanism of Rome; but in contrast to both it was not imperial—that is, it was entirely divorced from constraints imposed by a supranational state, even though it was achieved by exploiting subject peoples. Other aspects of Hellenistic civilization will seem even more familiar to observers today. Authoritarian governments, ruler cults, economic instability, extreme skepticism existing side by side with intense religiosity, rational science existing side by side with irrational superstition, flamboyant art and ostentatious art collecting: all these aspects of the Hellenistic age might make the thoughtful student of history regard it as one of the most relevant in the entire human record for comparison with our own.

KEY TERMS

Plato's *Republic*	Alexander	Menander	Euclid
Nicomachean ethics	Ptolemy	Epicureanism	
Philip II	Seleucus	Stoicism	

SELECTED READINGS

Penguin Classics and the Loeb Classical Library both offer reliable translations of scores of literary and historical texts from this period. Particularly important are historical works by Arrian (*Anabasis of Alexander*) and Plutarch (*Lives*).

Adcock, F. E. *The Greek and Macedonian Art of War.* Berkeley, 1957. Still a valuable introduction to the guiding principles and assumptions of Greek and Macedonian warfare.

Austin, M. M. *The Hellenistic World from Alexander to the Roman Conquest: A Selection of Ancient Sources in Translation.* Cambridge, 1981.

Bagnall, R. S., and P. Derow. *Greek Historical Documents: The Hellenistic Period.* Chico, Calif., 1981.

Borza, Eugene N. *In the Shadow of Olympus: The Emergence of Macedon.* Princeton, N. J., 1990. The standard account of the rise of Macedon up to the accession of Philip II.

Bosworth, A. B. *Conquest and Empire: The Reign of Alexander the Great.* Cambridge, 1988. A political and military analysis of Alexander's career that successfully strips away the romance, maintaining a clear vision of the ruthlessness and human cost of his conquests.

Bosworth, A. B. *The Legacy of Alexander: Politics, Warfare, and Propaganda under the Successors.* Oxford, 2002. The most recent survey of the half century following Alexander's death and of the people who created the Hellenistic kingdoms of Egypt, Persia, and Macedon.

Burstein, Stanley M., ed. and trans. *The Hellenistic Age from the Battle of Ipsos to the Death of Kleopatria VII.* Cambridge, 1985. An excellent collection, with sources not found elsewhere.

Cartledge, Paul A. *Agesilaus and the Crisis of Sparta.* Baltimore, Md., 1987. A thorough but readable analysis of the social and political challenges besetting Sparta in the fourth century B.C.E.

Green, Peter. *Alexander to Actium: The Historical Evolution of the Hellenistic Age.* Berkeley, Calif. 1990. An outstanding, comprehensive, and wide-ranging history of the period; balanced and sensible.

Green, Peter. *Alexander of Macedon, 356–323 B.C.* Berkeley, Calif., 1991. Revised edition of the author's 1972 biography; entertainingly written, and rich in detail and insight.

Hammond, Nicholas G. L. *The Genius of Alexander the Great.* Chapel Hill, N. C., 1998. A clear, authoritative, admiring account, distilling a lifetime of research on the subject.

Hansen, Mogens H. *The Athenian Democracy in the Age of Demosthenes.* Oxford, 1991. An intelligent examination of the political institutions of Athens in the fourth century B.C.E.

Lloyd, Geoffrey, and Nathan Sivin. *The Way and the Word: Science and Medicine in early China and Greece.* New Haven, Conn., 2002. An extraordinary comparative study of scientific thinking between 400 B.C.E. and 200 C.E. in the Hellenistic world and in China.

Ober, Josiah. *Mass and Elite in Democratic Athens: Rhetoric, Ideology, and the Power of the People.* Princeton, N. J., 1989. An excellent study of the ideology of democracy in Athens in the fourth century B.C.E. that borrows intelligently from modern social scientific insights.

Pollitt, Jerome J. *Art in the Hellenistic Age.* New York, 1986. The standard account, written from the perspective of cultural history as well as art history.

Sherwin-White, Susan, and Amélie Kuhrt. *From Samarkhand to Sardis: A New Approach to the Seleucid Empire.* London, 1993. A stimulating examination of the relationship between rulers and ruled in the vast expanses of the Seleucid empire.

Shipley, Graham. *The Greek World after Alexander, 323–30 B.C.* New York and London, 2000. A recent study of the social, intellectual, and artistic changes in the Hellenistic era, more accessible for students than Green, but with extensive bibliography.

Thomas, Carol G. *Alexander the Great in His World.* Oxford and Malden, Mass., 2007. A study of the contexts—familial, political, and social—that shaped Alexander's career.

Tritle, Lawrence A. ed. *The Greek World in the Fourth Century: From the Fall of the Athenian Empire to the Successors of Alexander.* New York, 1997. A wide-ranging collection of scholarly essays.

Worthington, Ian. *Alexander the Great: A Reader.* London and New York, 2002. A collection of influential interpretations of Alexander by modern historians.

Chapter FIVE

Roman Civilization

WHILE THE GREEKS STRUGGLED against the Persians and then each other, a new civilization was emerging on the banks of the Tiber River in central Italy. By the end of the fourth century B.C.E., Rome was already the dominant power on the Italian peninsula. For five centuries thereafter Rome's power steadily increased. By the first century C.E., it ruled most of the Hellenistic world as well as most of western Europe. Rome's conquests united the Mediterranean world for the first time, and made the Mediterranean itself a "Roman lake." Rome's empire brought Greek institutions and ideas not only to the western half of the Mediterranean world but also to Britain, France, Spain, and Romania. Rome was thus the builder of a great historical bridge that connected Europe to the cultural and political heritage of the ancient Near East. Without Rome, European civilization as we know it would not exist.

Rome was deeply influenced by Greek culture, but it was also a distinctive civilization in its own right. The Romans were much more attached to their traditional values than were the Greeks. Rome revered its old agricultural traditions, its household gods, and its sternly military values. But as their empire grew, Romans also came to see themselves as having a divinely ordained mission to civilize the world by teaching it the arts of law and government that were Rome's own peculiar genius. Virgil (70–19 B.C.E.), the great epic poet of Rome, expressed this self-conscious sense of Rome's historical mission in the *Aeneid*, which tells one of the several competing legends Romans treasured about the founding of their city. Here, Anchises of Troy speaks prophetically to his son Aeneas, who (in Virgil's account) would go on to become one of the founders of the city of Rome. Speaking about the Romans, Anchises tells his son of his people's future:

FOCUS QUESTIONS

• How did the Etruscans and Greeks influence early Roman society?

• How democratic was the early Roman Republic?

• What were the consequences of Roman territorial expansion during the third and second centuries B.C.E.?

• What impact did Rome's expanding empire have on Roman society and culture?

• What issues caused the social struggles of the late republic?

• Why did the Augustan system succeed?

• Why did so many critics of Roman life during the Principate focus their criticisms on the behavior of women?

• What factors brought the Roman Empire to the brink of ruin?

• Did Roman civilization come to an end in the third century C.E.?

Others will cast more tenderly in bronze
Their breathing figures, I can well believe,
And bring more lifelike portraits out of marble;
Argue more eloquently, use the pointer
To trace the paths of heaven accurately
And accurately foretell the rising stars.
Roman, remember by your strength to rule
Earth's peoples—for your arts are to be these:
To pacify, to impose the rule of law,
To spare the conquered, battle down the proud.

Virgil, *Aeneid*, Book VI, lines 848–857, trans. Robert Fitzgerald
(New York, 1982) p. 190.

Not all the peoples whom Rome conquered welcomed the experience. But all were transformed by it.

EARLY ITALY AND THE ROMAN MONARCHY

How did the Etruscans and Greeks influence early Roman society?

The geography of the Italian peninsula had a decisive influence on Rome's development. Ancient Italy had sizable forests and much more fertile land than did Greece. But it was never a land of ease. Italy has few mineral resources, aside from excellent supplies of marble and small quantities of lead, tin, copper, iron (on the island of Elba), and silver. Its extensive coastline has only a few good harbors, and most of these are on the western coast, facing away from Greece and the Near East. Nor does the land have any secure natural defenses. The Alps posed no effective barrier to the influx of peoples from Europe, and the low-lying Italian coastline invited conquest by sea. In short, Italy was rich enough to be attractive, but not rich enough to make it easy to defend. The Romans were a sternly military society almost from the moment they settled on Italian soil, because they were continually forced to defend their own conquests against other invaders.

THE ETRUSCANS

The dominant early settlers on the Italian peninsula were a non–Indo-European-speaking people known as the Etruscans. Our knowledge of the Etruscans is severely limited by the fact that their language, although written in a Greek alphabet, has not yet been fully deciphered. It

appears, however, that Etruscan settlements go back to the late Bronze Age, and that they were in early and frequent contact with both Greece and Assyria. By the sixth century B.C.E., the Etruscans had established a confederation of independent city-states in north-central Italy. They were skilled metalworkers, artists, and architects, from whom the later Romans took their knowledge of the arch and the vault, among much else. In addition to their alphabet, the Etruscans also shared with the Greeks a religion based on the worship of gods in human (rather than animal or meteorological) form.

In contrast with Greek practice, Etruscan women enjoyed a comparatively elevated place in society. Etruscan women participated in public life and sporting events,

An Etruscan Married Couple. On this mid-fourth-century B.C.E. sarcophagus lid, the deceased couple lie together naked, emphasizing by their embrace the closeness of their marital bond.

How did the Etruscans and Greeks influence early Roman society?

Early Italy and the Roman Monarchy   167

they attended dramatic performances and athletic competitions (both forbidden to Greek women), and they danced in ways that shocked both Greeks and Romans. Etruscan wives ate meals with their husbands, reclining together on the same couch even at formal banquets; and after death, they were buried together in the same mortuary vaults. Some Etruscan families even traced their descent through the female line. Roman women were probably less sequestered than were Greek women in the fifth and fourth centuries B.C.E., but they were nowhere near as free as were Etruscan women.

In other respects, however, early Roman society was deeply influenced by Etruscan example. Not only the Roman arch and vault but also the cruel sport of gladiatorial combat and the practice of foretelling the future by studying the entrails of animals or the flight of birds went back to Etruscan beginnings. The Roman practice of centering urban life around massive stone temples with their attendant cults probably also derived from an Etruscan example. Even the two most famous myths the Romans told about the founding of Rome itself they probably drew from the Etruscans: that involving Aeneas of Troy (noted earlier in connection with Virgil's *Aeneid*) and that involving the infant twins Romulus and Remus, who were raised by a female wolf after being abandoned by their parents.

The Romans also borrowed heavily from the Greek settlers of Italy. Colonists from mainland Greece began to arrive in southern Italy and Sicily in large numbers during the eighth century B.C.E. By the end of the seventh century B.C.E., Greek civilization in Italy was as advanced as it was in Greece itself. Such famous Greeks as Pythagoras, Archimedes, and even Plato for a time lived in Greek Italy, which became a key battleground in the Peloponnesian War between Athens and Sparta. From the Greeks, the Romans derived their alphabet, many of their religious concepts (it is difficult to disentangle Etruscan from Greek influence here), and much of their art and mythology. The high culture of Rome was thoroughly and pervasively Greek in inspiration and imitation.

THE RISE OF ROME

The Romans were descended from a cluster of Indo-European–speaking peoples who crossed the Alps into Italy during the second millennium B.C.E. Recent archaeological research has pushed the origins of the

Romulus and Remus. A sixth-century B.C.E. Etruscan bronze statue known as the *Capitoline Wolf*. Although the statues of the twins were added during the fifteenth century C.E., there were probably comparable figures of Romulus and Remus in the same basic posture in the original statue.

city back to at least the tenth century B.C.E., several centuries earlier than the traditional date of 753 B.C.E., which the Romans themselves considered their city's foundation year. Rome's strategic location along the Tiber brought it many advantages. Trading ships—but not large war fleets—could navigate the Tiber as far as Rome, but no farther; the city could thus serve as a port without being threatened by attack from the sea. Rome's famous hills increased the defensibility of the site. Rome also sat astride the first good ford across the Tiber River, making it a major land and river crossroads. Its location on the frontier between Latium (the territory of the Latins, i.e., the Romans) and Etruria (the Etruscan homeland) also contributed to its commercial and strategic importance.

The topography of Latium—a broad, flat plain with few natural obstacles—also influenced the way Rome dealt with neighboring communities. At an early date, the Romans established with the other Latin communities a series of common rights, including *commercium* (all contracts between Latins were enforceable throughout Latium), *connubium* (Latins could intermarry with legal recognition in the community of both husband and wife), and *migratio* (a Latin of one town could migrate to another and, if he remained there for a year, transfer his citizenship). These privileges, known as the Latin Right, stand in sharp contrast to the rigid particularism and jealous suspicion that divided the cities of Sumer or Greece. Roman willingness to extend the Latin Right even beyond Latium was a key factor in the success of their later expansion within Italy.

According to legend, Roman government was initially a monarchy in which a patriarchal king exercised jurisdiction over his subjects comparable to what a male family head would exercise over the members of his household. A senate, or council of elders (*senex* is Latin for "old man"), was composed of the heads of the various clans that formed the community, but its function in this early period is unclear. It was probably an advisory body to Rome's kings.

The monarchy, however, did not last. Legend has it that in 534 B.C.E. an Etruscan tyrant, Tarquin the Proud, gained control of the kingship in Rome. Etruscan overlordship helped transform Rome from a prosperous village into a true urban center, as Tarquin used Rome's strategic location to dominate Latium and the agriculturally wealthy district of Campania to the south. But Tarquin lorded it over the Romans with extreme cruelty. The final indignity came in 510 B.C.E., when Tarquin's son raped a virtuous Roman wife, Lucretia. When Lucretia committed suicide rather than living on "in dishonor," the Romans rose up in revolt, overthrowing not only the Etruscan tyranny but the entire form of monarchical government itself.

The story of Lucretia is probably patriotic myth, but there was a change in government in Rome around 500 B.C.E. (whether gradual or sudden is unknown) that ended the kingship and replaced it with a republic. Thereafter, the Romans would hold kingship in the same fear and contempt with which Greeks ultimately held the name *tyrant*. Whatever the truth of Lucretia's story, it does tell us something important about early Roman attitudes toward government and the family.

THE EARLY REPUBLIC

How democratic was the early Roman Republic?

The early Roman Republic was marked by almost constant warfare. The Romans were initially on the defensive; but as time went on they steadily gained ground, conquering first the other Latin territories, then Etruria and the Greek cities of southern Italy. The Romans did not usually impose heavy burdens on the cities they conquered. More often, they demanded that their defeated foes contribute soldiers to the Roman army. Rome also extended the Latin Right to many of the cities it conquered, giving them a further stake in Rome's continued political and military success. Thus Rome gained for itself nearly inexhaustible reserves of fighting men. By the middle of the third century B.C.E., Rome's army may have numbered as many as 300,000 men—a huge force by the standards of the ancient or the medieval worlds.

This long series of conflicts reinforced both the agrarian and the military character of the Roman nation. The acquisition of new lands made it possible for needy Roman citizens to maintain themselves as farmers in the new Roman colonies. By accommodating its increasing population in this way, Rome was thus able to remain a staunchly agricultural civilization for a surprisingly long time. As a result, it developed an interest in shipping and commerce fairly late, compared with the Greeks or Phoenicians. Continual warfare also confirmed among the Romans a steely military ideal. Many of the most familiar Roman legends of martial heroism date from the early republican period, including the story of Horatius, who held a key bridge against an entire army, and the retired soldier and statesman Cincinnatus (with whom George Washington would be frequently compared) who left his farm at a moment's notice to fight for Rome on the battlefield.

THE GOVERNMENT OF THE EARLY REPUBLIC

Meanwhile, Rome underwent a slow political evolution. Even the replacement of the monarchy was highly conservative: its chief effects were to substitute for the king two elected officials called *consuls* and to exalt the position of the Senate by granting it control over the public funds. Although the consuls were chosen by the *comitia centuriata* (the Roman "people in arms"), this body differed from the citizen assembly of ancient Athens because it met in groups. Each group in the Roman assembly had one vote, and since groups consisting of the wealthiest citizens voted first, a majority could be reached even before the votes of the poorer groups were cast. Consequently the consuls, who each served a one-year term, were inevitably senators who acted as the agents of aristocratic interests. Each consul exercised the full executive and judicial authority that the king had previously wielded, limited by the right each possessed to veto the action of the other. If a conflict arose between them, the Senate might be called on to decide; or in time of grave emergency, a dictator might be appointed for a term not longer than six months.

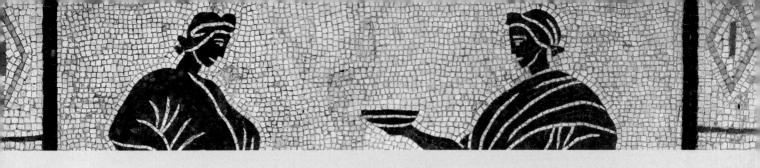

THE RAPE OF LUCRETIA

The Roman historian Livy compiled his history of Rome in the last half of the first century B.C.E., and most of what survives of his treatise involves the early history of Rome. The events he described surrounding Rome's beginnings are of dubious authenticity in historical terms, but nevertheless help illustrate the archetypes and values that Romans had long held paramount in their society. The tale of Lucretia, her violation by an Etruscan prince, and the resulting revolution (traditionally dated to 509 B.C.E.) provides one such example.

The young princes spent most of their leisure enjoying themselves in entertainments on the most lavish scale. They were drinking one day in the quarters of Sextus Tarquinius—Collatinus was also present—when someone chanced to mention the subject of wives. Each of them extravagantly praised his own, until Collatinus cried, "Stop! What need is there of words, when in a few hours we can prove beyond doubt the incomparable superiority of my Lucretia? We are all young and strong: why shouldn't we ride to Rome and see with our own eyes what kind of women our wives are?". . .

They reached the city as dusk was falling; and there the wives of the royal princes were found enjoying themselves with a group of young friends at a dinner-party, in the greatest luxury. The riders then went on to Collatia, where they found Lucretia very differently employed: it was already late at night, but there, in the hall of her house, surrounded by her busy maidservants, she was still hard at work by lamplight upon her spinning. Which wife had won the contest in womanly virtue was no longer in doubt. . . .

A few days later Sextus, without Collatinus's knowledge, returned where he was hospitably welcomed in Lucretia's house. . . . He waited till the house was asleep, and then, when all was quiet, he drew his sword and made his way to Lucretia's room. . . . Sextus urged his love, threatened . . . but not even the fear of death could bend her will. "If death will not move you," Sextus cried, "dishonor shall. I will kill you first, then cut the throat of a slave and lay his naked body by your side." . . . Even the most resolute chastity could not have stood against this dreadful threat. Lucretia yielded. Sextus enjoyed her and rode away, proud of his success.

[After Lucretia told her father and husband what had happened], she said, "What is due to [Sextus] is for you to decide. As for me I am innocent of fault, but I will take my punishment. Never shall Lucretia provide a precedent for unchaste women to escape what they deserve." With these words she drew a knife from under her robe, drove it into her heart and fell forward, dead.

Her father and husband were overwhelmed with grief. While they stood weeping helplessly, Brutus [a family associate] drew the bloody knife from Lucretia's body, and holding it before him cried: "By this girl's blood—none more chaste till a tyrant wronged her—and by the gods, I swear that with sword and fire, and whatever else can lend strength to my arm, I will pursue Lucius Tarquinius the Proud, his wicked wife, and all his children, and never again will I let them or any other man be King in Rome!"

Livy, i.57–59, based on *Livy: The Early History of Rome*, trans. A. de Selincourt (New York, 1960), pp. 97–99.

QUESTIONS FOR ANALYSIS

1. Livy believed that moral decline was responsible for the destruction of the Roman Republic. What historical and political functions did his anecdotes serve? Would it make any difference to him and his readers if the stories were mythical rather than factual?

2. If the rape of Lucretia is a myth—a vivid portrayal of a deep truth, not a factual report of what happened—consider its symbolic significance. Lucretia's assailant, Sextus, was a playboy prince, son of King Tarquin the Proud. In response to the attack, Brutus vowed vengeance not merely against Sextus but also against the tyrant king and his entire family. How was the Etruscan King Tarquin's reign equivalent to rape of the motherland of Rome, the "virtuous" country?

After the establishment of the republic the political dominance of the early aristocracy, known as the *patricians*, began to be challenged by the *plebeians*, who made up nearly 98 percent of the citizen population but who initially had no access to political power. The 200-year struggle between them is sometimes known

ROMAN EXPANSION TO 265 B.C.E.
- Controlled by Rome in 485 B.C.E.
- To 387 B.C.E.
- To 334 B.C.E.
- To 300 B.C.E.
- To 290 B.C.E.
- To 265 B.C.E.

ROMAN EXPANSION IN ITALY, 485–265 B.C.E.

This map illustrates the pattern of early Roman expansion in central and southern Italy. What does this pattern of expansion suggest about the threats Rome faced? Why did the Romans wait so long to conquer Etruria, even though it was so close to Rome? By transforming itself into the dominant power on the Italian peninsula, whose interests would Rome threaten after 265 B.C.E.?

as the Struggle of the Orders. The plebeians were a diverse group. Some had grown wealthy through trade or agriculture, but most were small-holding farmers, merchants, or the urban poor. The grievances of the plebeians were numerous. Forced to serve in the army in time of war, they were nevertheless excluded from holding office. They frequently felt themselves the victims of discriminatory decisions in judicial trials. They did not even know what legal rights they were supposed to enjoy, for the laws were unwritten, and the patricians alone had the power to interpret them. Worst was the oppression that could stem from debt because a debtor could be sold into slavery outside Rome by his creditor.

These grievances prompted a plebeian rebellion in the early fifth century B.C.E. that forced the patricians to agree to the election of new officers known as *tribunes* who could protect the plebeians by vetoing unlawful patrician acts. This victory was followed by a successful demand for codification of the laws. The result was the issuance, in about 450 B.C.E., of the famous Law of the Twelve Tables, so called because it was written on tablets ("tables") of wood. Although this law was later revered by the Romans as a kind of charter of the people's liberties, it was really nothing of the sort; it mostly perpetuated ancient custom without even abolishing enslavement for debt. Nevertheless, at least there was now a clear definition of what the law was. Roughly a generation later the plebeians won eligibility to positions as lesser magistrates, and about 367 B.C.E. the first plebeian consul was elected. Gradually, plebians also gained access to the Senate. The final plebeian victory came in 287 B.C.E. with the passage of a law stipulating that measures enacted by the *concilium plebis* (a more democratically organized assembly composed only of plebeians) would be binding on the Roman government whether the Senate approved them or not. It is from the decisions of this citizen assembly that English derives its modern word *plebiscite.*

These reforms had several important consequences, although they took a very long time to manifest themselves, owing to the conservative outlook of the Romans and the constitutional safeguards of the republic. Because successful plebeians could now work their way into the upper reaches of Roman society and government, the Roman aristocracy gradually shifted (at least to some degree) from one of birth to one of wealth. In an attempt to prevent wealth from becoming too much of a factor in Roman political life, laws were passed barring senators from engaging directly in commerce. But this restriction only fueled the rise of the important equestrian order: men who had the wealth and influence of senators but who chose a life of business rather than one in politics. But the equestrians and the senators were never wholly distinct from each other. Often, some members of important families would stay aloof from politics by becoming equestrians while underwriting the political careers of their brothers and cousins, who served as silent partners in the family's business concerns. Meanwhile, those few families who managed to win election generation after generation became increasingly prestigious and disproportionately influential. As a result, by the first century B.C.E. even powerful and aristocratic Romans were coming to feel excluded from real political influence within their city, tempting some to pursue their private political agendas by styling themselves the champions of a downtrodden public interest.

Scholars continue to debate how democratic Rome was in the fourth, third, and second centuries B.C.E. A republic differs from a monarchy insofar as supreme power resides in a body of citizens and is exercised by officers in some way responsible to those citizens. But a republic is not necessarily democratic, for it can devise systems for reserving power to an oligarchy or privileged group. The Roman constitution ensured oligarchical rule by the balance it struck between competing governmental institutions: the assembly, the Senate, and officeholders such as consuls, tribunes, judges, and administrators. In this system no single individual or family clique could become overwhelmingly strong, nor could direct expressions of the popular will unduly affect Roman policy. For the Greek historian Polybius, the Roman constitution was thus an ideal balance of monarchical, oligarchic, and democratic principles. It was, in his view, a perfect Aristotelian polity.

CHRONOLOGY

THE RISE OF ROME, 753–THIRD CENTURY B.C.E.

Legendary founding of the city of Rome	753 B.C.E.
Establishment of the Latin Right	493 B.C.E.
Roman Republic established	c. 500 B.C.E.
Struggle of the Orders	c. 450–287 B.C.E.
Law of the Twelve Tables	c. 450 B.C.E.
Concilium plebis gains power	287 B.C.E.
Equestrian order established	Third century B.C.E.

A Roman Noble of the First Century B.C.E. Here the man is holding the busts of two of his ancestors. Honoring one's ancestors was an important part of Roman social and religious life, especially among the aristocracy.

CULTURE, RELIGION, AND MORALITY

Political changes in early republican Rome moved glacially. So too did intellectual and cultural ones. Although writing had been adopted as early as the sixth century B.C.E., the Romans made little use of it except for laws, treaties, and funerary inscriptions. Education was largely limited to instruction imparted by fathers to sons in manly sports, practical arts, and military virtues; as a result, literary culture long remained a minor part of Roman life, even among the aristocracy. War and agriculture continued to be the chief occupations for the bulk of the population. A few artisans could be found in the cities, and a minor development of trade had occurred. But the fact that the Republic had no standard system of coinage until 289 B.C.E. reflects the comparative insignificance of Roman commerce at this time.

During the period of the early Republic, religion assumed the character it retained through the greater part of Roman history. In several ways this religion resembled that of the Greeks—not surprising, since it was directly influenced by Roman knowledge of Greek beliefs. Thus major Roman deities performed the same functions as their Greek equivalents: Jupiter corresponded to Zeus as god of the skies, Neptune to Poseidon as god of the waves, Venus to Aphrodite as goddess of love. Like the Greeks, the Romans had no dogmas or sacraments, nor did they place great emphasis on rewards and punishments after death. But there were also significant differences between the two religions. One was that Romans literally revered their ancestors; their household gods included deceased members of a lineage who were worshiped to ensure a family's continued prosperity. Another difference was the extent to which Roman religion was tied up with political life. Religion and politics were always closely integrated in the ancient world. But because Romans conceived of their state as if it were a giant household, they believed that their state, like their households, could flourish only if the gods of Rome lent it their continuing and active support. The Roman state therefore appointed committees of priests virtually as branches of government to tend to the worship of the city's gods, preside over public rites, and serve as guardians of sacred traditions. These priests were not full-time professionals, but rather prominent aristocrats who rotated in and out of priestly offices while also serving as leaders of the Roman state. Their dual role as priests and politicians made Roman religion an even more integral part of the fabric of public and political life than it had been in Greece.

WHAT WERE THE CONSEQUENCES OF ROMAN TERRITORIAL EXPANSION DURING THE THIRD AND SECOND CENTURIES B.C.E.?

THE FATEFUL WARS WITH CARTHAGE   173

An Early Roman Coin. This coin, minted around 270 B.C.E., is one of the first to be issued by the Romans. On its front, we see a depiction of Hercules; on the back, Romulus and Remus being nursed by a wolf, with the word *Roman* beneath them. The excellent condition of this coin suggests that it may never have circulated.

The Romans looked to their gods to bestow on their households and their city the blessings of prosperity, victory, and fertility. Roman morality emphasized patriotism, duty, masculine self-control, and respect for authority and tradition. Its chief virtues were bravery, honor, self-discipline, and loyalty to country and family. A Roman's primary duty was to honor his ancestors by his conduct, but the greatest honor attached to those who sacrificed themselves for Rome. For the good of the Republic, therefore, citizens had to be ready to sacrifice not only their own lives but, if necessary, those of their family and friends. The cold-bloodedness of certain consuls who put their sons to death for breaches of military discipline was to the Romans a matter of deep admiration bordering on awe.

> Roman morality emphasized patriotism, duty, masculine self-control, and respect for authority and tradition.

THE FATEFUL WARS WITH CARTHAGE

What were the consequences of Roman territorial expansion during the third and second centuries B.C.E.?

By 265 B.C.E. the Romans controlled most of the Italian peninsula, freeing them to engage in overseas ventures. Scholars disagree as to whether the Romans continually extended their rule as a matter of deliberate policy, or whether their conquests grew more accidentally, by a series of reactions to changes in the status quo that seemed to threaten Rome's security. Probably the truth lies between these extremes. Whatever the case, beginning in 264 B.C.E., a year after its final victory over the Etruscans, Rome became embroiled in a series of wars with overseas nations that decidedly altered the course of its history.

THE PUNIC WARS

By far the most crucial was the struggle with Carthage, a great maritime empire that stretched along the northern coast of Africa from modern-day Tunisia to the Strait of Gibraltar and included parts of Spain, Sicily, Sardinia, and Corsica. Carthage had been founded about 800 B.C.E. as a Phoenician colony, but it developed into a rich and powerful independent state. In naval might, commercial prowess, and control of crucial material resources, Carthage in the third century B.C.E. was far superior to Rome.

The protracted struggles between Rome and Carthage are known collectively as the Punic Wars because the Romans called the Carthaginians Poeni—that is, Phoenicians. The First Punic War began in 264 B.C.E., apparently because of Rome's genuine fear that the Carthaginians might gain control of Messina, a Sicilian port directly across from the Italian mainland. Twenty-three years of bitter fighting ensued. Finally, by a peace agreement in 241, Carthage was forced to cede all of Sicily to Rome and to pay a large indemnity. Sicily thus became Rome's first overseas province. Shortly after the war, a faction of Roman senators sought to renegotiate the terms, seizing Corsica and Sardinia in the process; hard feelings on the Carthaginian side understandably ran deep.

Because the Romans had fought so hard to defeat Carthage, they were determined not to let their enemy extend its control to other Mediterranean areas. Accordingly, in 218 the Romans interpreted Carthage's

A Hannibal Coin. This coin was issued by Hannibal's family in Spain around 230 B.C.E. Its front shows the Carthaginian god Melqart in the guise of Hercules (notice the club over his shoulder). The other side of the coin shows a war elephant with a mounted rider, like the ones that would be used by Hannibal against Rome a generation later.

attempt to expand its rule in Spain as a threat to Roman interests and responded with a declaration of war. The renewed struggle, known as the Second Punic War, raged for sixteen years. At first Rome was entirely thrown off guard by the brilliant exploits of the famous Carthaginian commander Hannibal, who brought a Spanish army, including war elephants, through southern France and then over the Alps into Italy. With Carthaginian troops on Italian soil, Rome escaped defeat by the narrowest of margins. Only delaying tactics ultimately saved the day, for time was on the side of those who could keep an invader short of supplies and worn down by harassment. Equally decisive, however, was Hannibal's failure to win the support of Rome's Latin allies. Generous treatment had made them unshakable supporters of Rome.

Deep reserves of Roman manpower and the discipline of Rome and its closest allies ultimately overcame Hannibal's military genius. From 212 B.C.E. on, the Romans increasingly put the Carthaginians on the defensive in Italy, Sicily, and even Spain. The architect of the Spanish offensive, Publius Cornelius Scipio, then invaded North Africa and defeated Hannibal at Zama, near Carthage, in 201 B.C.E. His victory ended the Second Punic War, and Scipio was honored with the additional name "Africanus," the conqueror of Africa.

Carthage was now compelled to abandon all its possessions except the city of Carthage itself and its surrounding territory in Africa, and to pay an indemnity three times greater than that paid at the end of the First Punic War. Yet Roman suspicion of Carthage remained obsessive. By the mid-second century B.C.E. Carthage had recovered some of its former prosperity—and this was enough to provoke the displeasure of the Romans. Nothing short of the total demolition of the Carthaginian state would now satisfy influential Roman senators such as Cato the Censor, who ended every speech he made in the Senate with the same words: "Carthage must be destroyed." The Senate agreed, and in 149 B.C.E. seized on a minor pretext to demand that the Carthaginians abandon their city and settle at least ten miles from the coast. Because this demand amounted to a death sentence for a nation dependent on commerce, it was refused—as the Romans probably realized it would be. The result was the Third Punic War, fought between 149 and 146 B.C.E. When the Romans finally breached the walls of Carthage, frightful butchery took place. As the victorious Roman general—Scipio Aemilianus, the grandson of Africanus—watched the flames devour Carthage, he said, "It is a glorious moment, but I have a strange feeling that some day the same fate will befall my own homeland." The 55,000 Carthaginians who survived the massacre were sold into slavery, and their once magnificent city was razed to the ground. (The legend of the Romans sowing the land with salt was clearly an exaggeration, because a generation later a Roman politician proposed founding a Roman colony on the site.)

TERRITORIAL EXPANSION

The wars with Carthage brought an enormous increase in Roman territory, leading to the creation of new overseas provinces in Sicily, North Africa, and Spain. This

CHRONOLOGY

THE WARS WITH CARTHAGE

First Punic War	264–241 B.C.E.
Second Punic War	218–201 B.C.E.
Third Punic War	149–146 B.C.E.
City of Carthage destroyed	146 B.C.E.

WHAT WERE THE CONSEQUENCES OF ROMAN TERRITORIAL EXPANSION DURING THE THIRD AND SECOND CENTURIES B.C.E.?

THE FATEFUL WARS WITH CARTHAGE   175

not only brought Rome great new wealth—above all Sicilian and African grain and Spanish silver—but was the beginning of a policy of westward expansion that proved to be one of the great formative influences on the history of Europe.

Rome's expanding overseas commitments also brought it into conflict with eastern Mediterranean powers, paving the way for further conquests. During the Second Punic War, Philip V of Macedon entered into an alliance with Carthage; soon afterward, he moved aggressively into Greece and was rumored to have designs on Egypt. Rome sent an army to eject Philip from Greece; a decade or so later, another Roman army thwarted similar plans by the Seleucid monarch Antiochus III. In neither campaign did Rome set out to conquer Greece militarily; by 146 B.C.E., however, both Greece and Macedon had become Roman provinces, Seleucid Asia had been deprived of most of its territories, and Ptolemaic Egypt was largely a pawn of Roman commercial and naval interests.

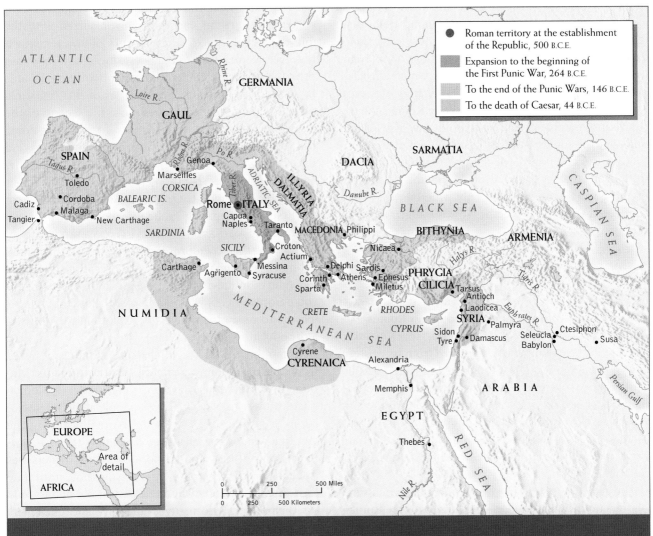

THE EXPANSION OF ROME, 264–44 B.C.E.

By the death of Julius Caesar in 44 B.C.E., the Roman world had become an empire that united the eastern and the western Mediterranean regions. How did these two parts of the empire differ from one another? What impacts were these differences likely to have on the way Rome ruled its empire? What particular problems did Julius Caesar create by extending Roman rule into Gaul, well away from Rome's Mediterranean roots?

SOCIETY AND CULTURE IN THE LATE REPUBLIC

What impact did Rome's expanding empire have on Roman society and culture?

Rome's inadvertent conquest of Greece and Asia Minor transformed the economic, social, and intellectual life of the later republic. Vast new wealth poured into Rome, increasing the social and economic inequalities within Roman society and undermining traditional Roman values of austerity and self-sacrifice. Small farmers left the land for the cities, unable to compete with the huge agricultural estates (known as *latifundia*) owned by aristocrats and worked by gangs of slaves. Slaves also played an increasing role in Roman society as artisans, merchants, and household servants. Roman rule over the Hellenistic East also had a pervasive impact on the cultural life of the late republic; so much so, indeed, that by the end of the republican period, Romans were wondering openly whether they had conquered Greece, or whether it was Greece that had conquered Rome.

ECONOMIC AND SOCIAL CHANGE

Like nearly all the peoples of the ancient world, Romans took slavery for granted. Nothing in Rome's earlier experience prepared it, however, for the huge increase in slave numbers that resulted from its western and eastern conquests. As noted, in 146 B.C.E., 55,000 Carthaginians were enslaved after the destruction of their city; not long before, 150,000 Greek prisoners of war had met the same fate. By the end of the second century B.C.E., there were a million slaves in Italy alone, making Roman Italy one of the most slave-based economies known to history.

The majority of these slaves worked as agricultural laborers on the vast (and growing) estates of the Roman aristocracy. Some of these estates were the result of earlier Roman conquests within Italy itself. But others were constructed by aristocrats buying up the land holdings of thousands of small farmers who found themselves unable to compete with the great *latifundia* in producing grain for the market. Soldiers in particular—who might now be required to serve for years at a time on campaigns in Spain or the Greek East—often found it impossible to maintain their family farms. In-

stead, they moved to the city, selling their farms (often at a very good price) to aristocrats eager to invest in land the huge profits they had made from war and empire. In the cities, however, there was often little work to be had. Rome never made a transition to industrialism. With slaves to do all the hard work, a great disincentive existed for the technological initiative that might have led to industrialism; but without large-scale manufacturing, the urban population remained underemployed and politically volatile. By the first century B.C.E., almost a third of Rome's 1 million inhabitants were receiving free grain from the state, partly to keep them alive and partly to keep them quiet.

As we have seen, the Roman economy remained fundamentally agrarian and noncommercialized until the mid-third century B.C.E. During the following century, however, Rome's eastern conquests brought it fully into the sophisticated commercial economy of the Hellenistic world. The principal beneficiaries of this economic transformation were the equestrians, the second of the four orders into which the society of republican Rome was divided (senatorial aristocrats, commoners, and slaves being the other three). As overseas merchants, the equestrians profited handsomely from Rome's voracious appetite for foreign luxury goods. As representatives of the Roman government in the provinces, they operated mines, built roads, and collected taxes, always with an eye toward their own profit. They were also the principal moneylenders to the Roman state and to distressed individuals. Interest rates were high, and when the state could not pay its bills, it would often allow the moneylenders to repay themselves by exploiting the defenseless population of the provinces.

Commoners who lost their lands certainly suffered from these economic changes; but the principal victims of Rome's transformation were its slaves. Roman slaves were scarcely considered people at all but instruments of production like cattle. Notwithstanding the fact that some were cultivated foreigners taken as prisoners of war, the standard policy of their owners was to get as much work out of them as possible until they died of exhaustion or were released in old age to fend for themselves. The ready availability and cheapness of slaves, a consequence of Rome's conquests, made Roman slavery a far more impersonal and brutal institution than it had been in other ancient civilizations. Although domestic slaves were sometimes treated decently, and some slave artisans in the city of Rome were permitted to run their own businesses, the general lot of the slave was horrendous.

Slaves grew much of Rome's food supply and did much of the work in urban shops as well. Slaves were

WHAT IMPACT DID ROME'S EXPANDING EMPIRE HAVE ON ROMAN SOCIETY AND CULTURE?

SOCIETY AND CULTURE IN THE LATE REPUBLIC 177

also employed in numerous nonproductive activities. Some businessmen owned slaves whom they trained as gladiators, to be slaughtered by wild animals or by other gladiators for amusement. The growth of luxury also required the employment of thousands of slaves in domestic service. Wealthy families insisted on having doorkeepers, litter bearers, couriers, valets, and tutors for their children. Some great households had special servants with no other duties than to rub the master down after his bath or to care for his sandals. All such servants would have been slaves.

This extreme reliance on slave labor, combined with the relative cheapness of slaves, encouraged a mindset wherein the Romans had little use for the application of mechanical science and labor-saving inventions. Water mills and a crude steam engine, among many potential industrial innovations, were known to the Romans dur-

ing the course of their history, but they showed little interest in them. They had little need for such devices when cheap human labor seemed inexhaustible.

FAMILY LIFE AND THE STATUS OF WOMEN

Another change that accompanied the acquisition of new territories was a change in the nature of family life and the status of women. In earlier times the Roman family was based on the husband's nearly absolute powers over his household. During the second century B.C.E., however, two legal innovations greatly altered this pattern of patriarchal control. One was the introduction of free marriage, whereby the wife's share of her father's property remained her own instead of pass-

Roman Mystery Rites. The Villa of the Mysteries in Pompeii preserves an astonishing cycle of wall paintings done around 50 B.C.E. The exact meaning is debatable, but the most persuasive interpretation is that it shows a succession of cult rites. Here a young woman is being whipped, probably an initiation ceremony, while a cult member performs a solemn dance in the nude.

ing to her husband and then reverted to her father or her father's heirs on her death. Together with free marriage came new rules for divorce, whereby either side, instead of just the man, could initiate proceedings.

These changes were intended to prevent the transfer of property from one family to another, which would diminish the size of the large estates created with the influx of slaves. But they also gave wives greater legal independence. The slave system also gave wealthy women greater practical independence, for slaves could now take over women's traditional tasks of child rearing and household maintenance. Upper-class Roman women now spent more time away from the home and began to engage in a range of social, intellectual, and artistic activities.

> The slave system also gave wealthy women greater practical independence, for slaves could now take over women's traditional tasks of child rearing and household maintenance.

The conquest of the Hellenistic East also brought the wide-scale adoption of Greek ideas and customs into upper-class Roman life. In earlier centuries, Romans had taken pride in the simplicity of their cultural lives. Now, however, upper-class Romans began to see Greek culture as a mark of refinement, which they had the wealth to pursue. Bilingualism in Latin and Greek became increasingly common, and Greek literature became a standard against which Roman authors measured themselves. Roman children were given Greek educations, and theater and literature became fashionable. The creature comforts that Hellenistic Greeks enjoyed in Syria and Egypt were also quickly adopted by the Roman conquerors of the Mediterranean world. Some Romans viewed such changes with repugnance. For them the "good old Roman ways" of paternal authority and stern military discipline were giving way to the debilitating allure of soft living. Their protests struck a chord, but they did little to stem the tide of change. Rome was being irreversibly transformed from a republic of farmers into a complex society with vast gaps between rich and poor and new habits of personal autonomy for both men and women.

EPICUREANISM AND STOICISM

The late republic was also deeply influenced by Greek philosophical ideas. The most renowned of the Roman exponents of Epicureanism was Lucretius (98–55 B.C.E.), the author of a book-length philosophical poem, *On the Nature of Things*. In writing this work Lucretius wished to explain the universe in such a way as to remove fear of the supernatural, which he regarded as the chief obstacle to peace of mind. Though he admitted the existence of the gods, he conceived of them as living in eternal peace, neither creating nor governing the universe. Everything that exists on earth, including the human mind, is the result of fortuitous combinations of atoms. Since mind is indissolubly linked with matter, death means utter extinction; consequently, no part of the human personality can survive to be rewarded or punished in an afterlife. Lucretius's conception of the good life was simple: what one needs, he asserted, is not enjoyment but "peace and a pure heart." Lucretius's philosophical ideas were not original, but his musical cadences, sustained majesty of expression, and infectious enthusiasm make him one of the greatest poets who ever lived.

Stoicism was introduced into Rome about 140 B.C.E. and soon numbered among its converts many influential leaders of public life. The greatest of these was Cicero

A Young Worshiper of Isis. Temples to Isis were erected throughout the Roman world. Outside Egypt, one of the largest was dedicated by Julius Caesar in Rome, where this statue was made about 200 years later. The long locks of hair above this boy's right ear mark him out as a follower of Isis. At puberty, these would be shaved off and offered to the goddess.

THE INFLUENCE OF GREEK LUXURY

Lucius Licinius Lucullus (106?–57 B.C.E.) was a partisan of the dictator Sulla and a member of Rome's highest aristocracy. He commanded Roman forces admirably in the East, but his demands for discipline from the army and his intolerance of corruption among the equestrians and senatorial governors made him powerful enemies. His conquests made him quite wealthy; and once he tired of trying to preserve his political career against his foes, he retired from public life. This passage from Plutarch's biography of him demonstrates the effects Eastern luxury could have on the Roman elite, the staggering wealth they could acquire, and their enjoyment of it especially once they abandoned the public career for one of private pleasure.

And indeed, Lucullus' life, like the Old Comedy, presents us at the commencement with acts of policy and of war, at the end offering nothing but good eating and drinking, feastings, and revelings, and mere play. For I give no higher name to his sumptuous buildings, porticos, and baths, still less to his paintings and sculptures, and all his industry about these curiosities, which he collected with vast expense, lavishly bestowing all the wealth and treasure he got in the war upon them, insomuch that even now, with all the advance of luxury, the Lucullean gardens are counted the noblest the emperor has. Tubero the Stoic, when he saw his buildings at Naples, where he suspended the hills upon vast tunnels, brought in the sea for moats and fish-ponds round his house, and built pleasure-houses in the waters, called him Xerxes in a toga. He had also fine seats in Tusculum, belvederes, and large open balconies for men's apartments, and porticos to walk in, where Pompey, coming to see him, blamed him for making a house which would be pleasant in summer, but uninhabitable in winter; whom Lucullus answered with a smile, "You think me, then, less provident than cranes and storks, not to change my home with the season." . . . Lucullus's daily entertainments were ostentatiously extravagant, not only with purple coverlets, and plate adorned with precious stones, and dancings, and interludes, but with the greatest diversity of dishes and the most elaborate cookery, for the vulgar to admire and envy. . . . Cato [the Younger] was his friend and connection, but, nevertheless, so hated his life and habits that when a young man made a long and tedious speech in praise of frugality and temperance, Cato got up and said, "How long do you mean to go on making money like Crassus, living like Lucullus, and talking like Cato?"

Plutarch, *Life of Lucullus,* based on *Plutarch's Lives,* trans. John Dryden (New York, 1992), pp. 621–622.

QUESTIONS FOR ANALYSIS

1. Why does Plutarch recount the life of Lucius Licinius Lucullus, who went from high commands in the army and offices in the state to a buffoon-like private life? What can we learn from this gossipy account?
2. Despite having left office, Lucullus had powerful friends, such as Sulla, Pompey, and Cato, which implied that he was still politically influential. How might his wealth and entertainments corrupt Roman politics just as much as military intervention did?

(106–43 B.C.E.), the Father of Roman Eloquence. Although Cicero adopted doctrines from a number of philosophers, including Plato and Aristotle, he derived more of his ideas from the Stoics than from any other source. Cicero's ethical philosophy was based on the Stoic premises that virtue is sufficient for happiness, and tranquillity of mind is the highest good. He conceived of the ideal human being as one who has been guided by reason to an indifference toward sorrow and pain. Cicero diverged from the Greek Stoics in his greater approval of the active, political life. To this degree he still spoke for the older Roman tradition of service to the state. Cicero never claimed to be an original philosopher; his goal was to bring the best of Greek philosophy to the West. In this he was remarkably successful, for he wrote in a rich and elegant Latin prose style that has never been surpassed. Cicero's prose immediately became a standard for Latin composition and has remained so until the present century. Thus even though not a truly great thinker, Cicero was the most influential Latin transmitter of ancient thought to medieval and modern Europe.

Lucretius and Cicero were not the only fine writers of the later Roman Republic. It now became the fashion among the upper classes to learn Greek and to strive to reproduce in Latin some of the more popular forms of Greek literature. Some results of enduring literary merit were the ribald comedies of Plautus (257?–184 B.C.E.), the passionate love poems of Catullus (84?–54? B.C.E.), and the crisp military memoirs of Julius Caesar.

RELIGION

The religious beliefs of the Romans also altered in various ways in the last two centuries of the republic—again mainly because of Rome's interaction with the Hellenistic world. Most pronounced was the spread of Eastern mystery cults, which satisfied the craving for a more emotional religion than traditional Roman worship and offered the reward of immortality to the wretched of the earth. From Egypt came the cults of Isis and Osiris (or Serapis, as the god was now more commonly called), while from Asia Minor was introduced the worship of the Great Mother, with her eunuch priests and ritualistic orgies. But despite the attractions of these new cults, most Romans continued to honor the traditional gods of their household and their city. Roman polytheism was not an exclusive system. So long as the traditional gods were paid the reverence due them, newer gods could be added and honored.

THE SOCIAL STRUGGLES OF THE LATE REPUBLIC

What issues caused the social struggles of the late republic?

The period from the end of the Third Punic War in 146 to about 30 B.C.E. was one of enormous turbulence. Social conflicts, assassinations, struggles between rival dictators, wars, and insurrections were the common occurrences of the time. Slave uprisings were also part of the general disorder. Some 70,000 slaves defeated a Roman army in Sicily in 134 B.C.E. before this revolt was put down by Roman reinforcements. Slaves ravaged Sicily again in 104 B.C.E. But the most threatening slave revolt of all was led by a slave named Spartacus. Spartacus, who was being trained to become a gladiator (which meant certain death in the arena), escaped with a band of fugitives to Mount Vesuvius near Naples, there attracting a huge host of other fugitive slaves. From 73 to 71 B.C.E. the escapees under his leadership held off Roman armies and overran much of southern Italy until they were finally defeated and Spartacus was slain in battle. About 6,000 of those captured were left crucified along the length of a road from Capua to Rome (about 150 miles) to provide a terrible warning.

THE GRACCHI

Meanwhile, an extended conflict among elements of the Roman governing class began in 133 B.C.E. with the attempts at social and economic reform instituted by the two Gracchus brothers. Though of aristocratic lineage themselves, they proposed to alleviate social and economic stress by granting government lands to the landless. They and their senatorial allies stood to gain from the electoral loyalty of the many clients who would have received this land, but Tiberius Gracchus also seems to have been motivated by genuine concern for the welfare of Rome's farmers and the attendant manpower shortage in the army. A man had to meet certain property qualifications to serve in the Roman army, and at a time when Rome's military commitments were expanding, the available pool of citizen soldiers was contracting. In 133 B.C.E. Tiberius Gracchus, as tribune, proposed a law that restricted the current renters or holders of state lands to a maximum of 300 acres per citizen plus 150 acres for each child in

WHAT ISSUES CAUSED THE SOCIAL STRUGGLES OF THE LATE REPUBLIC?

THE SOCIAL STRUGGLES OF THE LATE REPUBLIC   181

the family. The excess was to be given to the poor in small plots. Conservative aristocrats bitterly opposed this proposal and engineered its veto by Octavius, Tiberius's fellow tribune. Tiberius then removed Octavius from office, a highly irregular action, and when his own term expired attempted to stand for reelection. Both of these moves seemed to threaten a dictatorship and offered the conservative senators an excuse for resistance. Armed with clubs, they went on a rampage during the elections and murdered Tiberius and many of his followers.

Nine years later, Tiberius's younger brother, Gaius Gracchus, renewed the struggle. Though Tiberius's land law had finally been enacted by the Senate, Gaius believed that the campaign had to go further. Elected tribune in 123 B.C.E., and reelected in 122, he enacted several laws for the benefit of the less privileged. One stabilized the price of grain in Rome by building public granaries along the Tiber. Another imposed controls on governors suspected of exploiting the provinces for their own advantage and gave the equestrian order a judicial role in checking the administrative abuses of the senatorial class. In an attempt to gain further support, Gaius also proposed to extend full Roman citizenship to vast numbers of Italian allies, a move that would have completely altered the political landscape of Rome. These and similar measures provoked so much anger among the vested interests that they resolved to eliminate their enemy. The Roman Senate proclaimed Gaius Gracchus an outlaw and authorized the consuls to take all necessary steps for the defense of the republic. In the ensuing conflict Gaius was killed, and about 3,000 of his followers lost their lives in vengeful purges.

ARISTOCRATIC REACTION

After the downfall of the Gracchi, two military leaders who had won fame in foreign wars successively made themselves rulers of the state. The first was Marius, who was elevated to the consulship by the plebeian party in 107 B.C.E. and reelected six times. Marius, however, was no statesman and accomplished little for his followers beyond demonstrating how easily a general with an army behind him could override opposition. Partly for political motives and partly to meet the shortfall in manpower, Marius scrapped the property qualification for the army altogether. Thereafter, Rome's soldiers would come increasingly from the ranks of the urban poor and the landless country dwellers. The result was that gradually, Roman armies became more loyal to the individual interests of their commanders than they were to the republic itself, because the political success of their generals could best guarantee rewards for the impoverished soldiers of the army.

Following Marius's death in 86 B.C.E., conservatives took a turn at governing through the army. Their champion was Sulla, another victorious commander. Appointed dictator in 82 B.C.E. for an unlimited term, Sulla ruthlessly proceeded to exterminate his opponents. He extended the powers of the Senate (whose ranks, depleted by civil war, he packed with men loyal to himself) and curtailed the authority of the tribunes. After three years of rule Sulla decided his job was done and retired to a life of luxury on his country estate.

POMPEY AND JULIUS CAESAR

The effect of Sulla's decrees was to give control to a selfish aristocracy. Soon, however, new leaders emerged to espouse the cause of the people. The most prominent were Pompey (Gnaeus Pompeius Magnus, 106–48 B.C.E.) and Julius Caesar (100–44 B.C.E.). For a time they cooperated in a plot to gain control of the government, but later they became rivals and sought to outdo each other in bidding for popular support. Both were men who, despite their successes, failed to gain complete acceptance from the established elite, but who in any event would have found the rules too much of an obstacle to their personal talents and ambitions. Pompey won fame as the conqueror of Syria and Palestine, and Caesar devoted his energies to a series of campaigns against the Gauls. These added to the Roman state the territory of

CHRONOLOGY

STRUGGLES OF THE LATE REPUBLIC, 146–27 B.C.E.

Third Punic War	149–146 B.C.E.
Slave revolts in Sicily	134–104 B.C.E.
Gracchian reforms	133–122 B.C.E.
Rule of Marius	107–100, 86 B.C.E.
Sulla becomes dictator	82 B.C.E.
Spartacus leads slave revolt	73–71 B.C.E.
Pompey becomes sole consul	52 B.C.E.
Caesar becomes sole consul	48 B.C.E.
Caesar becomes dictator	46 B.C.E.
Caesar assassinated	44 B.C.E.
Rule of Octavian, Mark Antony, and Lepidus	42–31 B.C.E.
Octavian becomes sole consul	31 B.C.E.
Octavian becomes emperor	27 B.C.E.

modern Belgium, Germany west of the Rhine, and France, greatly increasing Caesar's reputation and cementing the loyalty of his army. They came at a high price to the Gauls, however; perhaps a million Gauls were killed in these campaigns and another million were enslaved.

In 52 B.C.E., after protracted mob disorders in Rome, the Senate turned to Pompey and engineered his election as sole consul. Caesar, stationed in Gaul, was branded an enemy of the state, and Pompey conspired with the Senate to deprive him of political power. The result was a deadly war between the two men. In 49 B.C.E. Caesar crossed the Rubicon River into Italy (ever since an image for a fateful decision) and marched on Rome. Pompey fled to the East in the hope of gathering an army large enough to regain control of Italy. In 48 B.C.E. the forces of the rivals met at Pharsalus in Greece. Pompey was defeated and soon afterward murdered by supporters of Caesar.

Caesar then intervened in Egyptian politics at the court of Cleopatra (whom he left pregnant). Then he conducted another military campaign in Asia Minor in which victory was so swift that he could report, "I came, I saw, I conquered" (*Veni, vidi, vici*). After that Caesar

Ides of March Coin. This coin celebrates the assassination of Julius Caesar by Marcus Junius Brutus. Brutus is shown on the front; on the back, a liberty cap (customarily given to freed slaves) is shown between two daggers. Below is *Eid Mar,* the Latin abbreviation for "the Ides of March."

returned to Rome. No one now dared challenge his power. With the aid of his veterans he cowed the Senate into granting his every desire. In 46 B.C.E. he was named dictator for ten years; and two years later, for life. In addition, he assumed nearly every other title that could augment his power. He obtained from the Senate full authority to make war and peace and to control the revenues of the state. For all practical purposes he was above the law, and rumors spread that he intended to make himself king. Such fears led to his assassination on the Ides of March (the 15th) in 44 B.C.E. by a group of conspirators under the leadership of Brutus and Cassius, who hoped to return Rome to republican government.

Although Caesar was once revered by historians as a superhuman hero, he is now often dismissed as insignificant. Both extremes of interpretation should be avoided. Certainly he did not save Rome, nor was he

Julius Caesar.

the greatest statesman of all time. He treated the republic with contempt and made the problem of governing more difficult for those who came after him. Yet some of the measures he took as dictator did have lasting effects. With the aid of a Greek astronomer he revised the calendar so as to make a 365-day year (with an extra day added every fourth year). This Julian calendar—adjusted by Pope Gregory XIII in 1582—is still with us. Appropriately, the seventh month is named after Julius as "July." By conferring citizenship on thousands of Spaniards and Gauls, Caesar took an important step toward eliminating the distinction between Italians and provincials. He also helped relieve economic inequities by settling many of his veterans and some of the urban poor on unused lands. Vastly more important than these reforms, however, was Caesar's farsighted resolve, made before he seized power, to invest his efforts in the West. Whereas Pompey, and before him Alexander, went to the East to gain fame and fortune, Caesar was the first Roman leader to recognize the potential significance of northwestern Europe. By incorporating Gaul into the Roman world he brought Rome great agricultural wealth and helped bring urban life and culture to what was then the wild West. Western European civilization, later to be anchored in just those regions that Caesar conquered, might not have been the same without him.

THE PRINCIPATE OR EARLY EMPIRE (27 B.C.E.–180 C.E.)

Why did the Augustan system succeed?

In his will, Julius Caesar had adopted as his primary heir his grandnephew Octavian (63 B.C.E.–14 C.E.), then a young man of eighteen acting in his uncle's service in Illyria across the Adriatic Sea. On learning of Caesar's death, Octavian hastened to Rome to try to claim his inheritance. He soon found that he had to join forces with two of Caesar's powerful friends, Mark Antony and Lepidus. The following year the three formed an alliance to crush the political faction responsible for Caesar's murder. The methods employed were not to the new leaders' credit. Prominent members of the opposition were hunted down and slain and their property confiscated. The most notable of the victims was Cicero, brutally slain by Mark Antony's thugs; though he had taken no part in the conspiracy against Caesar's life,

Cicero had actively sought to undermine Antony during his term as consul and have him branded a public enemy. Caesar's real murderers, Brutus and Cassius, escaped and organized an army, but they were defeated by Antony and Octavian near Philippi in 42 B.C.E.

With the "republican" opposition effectively crushed, tensions mounted between the members of the alliance, inspired primarily by Antony's jealousy of Octavian. The subsequent struggle became a contest between East and West. Antony went to the East and made an

Octavian. When Octavian gained sole rule he became known as Augustus. Many statues of him survive, all of them idealized.

alliance with Cleopatra, hoping to use the resources of the Egyptian kingdom in the power struggle with Octavian. Octavian, as the junior partner, established himself in Italy and the West. It was a risky move. Octavian had to deal with the problems of resettling veterans while maintaining his position in the roiling political environment in Rome. But Italy provided him with manpower and the opportunity to style himself as the protector of Rome and its heritage against Antony, whom he skillfully portrayed as being in the clutches of a foreign, female potentate who intended to become queen over Rome. As in the earlier contest between Caesar and Pompey, the victory went to the West. In the naval battle of Actium (31 B.C.E.) Octavian's forces defeated those of Antony and Cleopatra, both of whom soon afterward committed suicide. Egypt's independent existence came to an end, and Rome reigned supreme throughout the Mediterranean world.

THE AUGUSTAN SYSTEM OF GOVERNMENT

The victory at Actium ushered in a new period in Roman history, the most glorious and the most prosperous that Rome ever experienced. When Octavian returned to Rome he announced the restoration of complete peace. This was a great relief to the people of Italy, who had suffered grievously from a decade of civil war. For four years he ruled as consul, until he accepted from the Senate the honorific titles of *imperator* (emperor) and *augustus*, a step that historians count as the beginning of the Roman Empire. This periodization is somewhat arbitrary because Octavian was as strong before his title change as after; moreover, *imperator* at the time meant only "victorious general"; *augustus* signified "venerable" or "worthy of honor." But gradually, after his successors took the title of emperor as well, it became the primary designation for the ruler of the Roman state. The title Octavian himself preferred was the more modest *princeps*, or "first citizen." For this reason the period of his rule and that of his successors is properly called the Principate (or, alternatively, the early empire), to distinguish it from the periods of the republic (c. 500–27 B.C.E.), the Third-Century Crisis (180 C.E.–284 C.E.), and the later empire or Dominate (284–610 C.E.).

Octavian, or Augustus as he was now called, was determined not to appear to be a dictator. He therefore left most republican institutions in place, even though they now exercised little independent power.

In theory the Senate and the citizens remained the supreme authorities; but in practice, Augustus himself controlled the army and determined governmental policy. Fortunately he was an able ruler. He instituted a new coinage system throughout the empire; he introduced a range of public services in the city of Rome, including police and fire fighting; he reorganized the army; and he allowed cities and provinces more substantial rights of self-government than they had enjoyed before. He also abolished the old, corrupt system of collecting taxes. Previously tax collectors were remunerated by being allowed to keep a portion of the taxes they collected, a system that led inevitably to graft and extortion. Now Augustus appointed his own representatives as tax collectors, paid them regular salaries, and kept them under strict supervision. Augustus also built new colonies in the provinces. These shifted the excess free population out of Italy, thereby removing a major source of social and political tension and promoting the integration of the Roman heartland with its far-flung empire.

Augustus presented himself as a stern defender of traditional Roman morality. He rebuilt temples and prohibited Romans from worshiping foreign gods. In an attempt to increase the Roman birthrate, he penalized citizens who failed to marry and required widows to remarry within two years of their husbands' deaths. He also introduced laws punishing adultery and making divorces more difficult to obtain. To hammer the message home, Augustan propaganda portrayed the imperial family as a model of domestic virtue and sexual propriety. These portrayals were only moderately successful. The emperor's own extramarital affairs were well known; and the sexual promiscuity of his daughter Julia finally led Augustus to exile her to a distant island.

From the time of Augustus until that of Trajan (98–117 C.E.), the Roman Empire continued to expand. Augustus gained more land for Rome than did any other Roman ruler. His generals advanced into central Europe, conquering the modern-day territories of Switzerland, Austria, and Bulgaria. Only in what is today central Germany did Roman troops meet defeat, a setback that convinced Augustus to hold the Roman borders at the Rhine and Danube. Subsequently, in 43 C.E., the emperor Claudius began the conquest of Britain, and at the beginning of the next century Trajan pushed beyond the Danube to add Dacia (now Romania) to the empire's realms. Trajan also conquered territories in Mesopotamia but in so doing aroused the enmity of the Parthian rulers of Persia. His successor, Hadrian, halted the conquests and embarked on a defensive policy epitomized by the construction of Hadrian's Wall in northern Britain. The Roman Empire had now reached its territorial limits; in the third century these limits would begin to recede.

When Augustus died in 14 C.E. after four decades of rule, his remarkable experiments in statesmanship might have died with him. His system was so ingenious, however, that Rome enjoyed nearly two centuries of peace, prosperity, and stability as a result of his reforms. Aside from one brief period of civil war in 68 C.E., the transition of power between emperors was generally peaceful, and the growing imperial bureaucracy managed affairs competently even when individual emperors proved to be vicious. Nevertheless, the fact that Rome had become an autocratic empire became harder and harder to conceal. Several talented men succeeded Augustus, but few of them had his panache for disguising the true power of the princeps. Many of his successors had difficult relationships with the Senate; be-

The Forum. The civic center of imperial Rome consisted of avenues, public squares, triumphal arches, temples, and government buildings. The arch of Titus, erected to celebrate Rome's final victory over Hebrew rebels, is in the background at the far right. Roman streets and buildings were arranged in rectilinear patterns to emphasize a sense of order and to facilitate triumphal processions.

cause members of the senatorial elite were almost invariably the historians of the time, several imperial reputations have suffered unfairly. Tiberius (14–37 C.E.) and Claudius (41–54 C.E.) were both skilled administrators, but tensions with the Senate led them at times to extreme measures that angered the elite. Nero (54–68 C.E.) and Domitian (81–96 C.E.) were both reviled by the senatorial aristocracy but were popular among the masses at Rome and in the provinces; indeed, Domitian's reforms of provincial government and his murderous disregard for senatorial privilege account for both the aristocracy's hostility and his subjects' adoration.

The height of the Augustan system came between 96 and 180 C.E., under the so-called Five Good Emperors: Nerva (96–98 C.E.), Trajan (98–117 C.E.), Hadrian (117–138 C.E.), Antoninus Pius (138–161 C.E.), and Marcus Aurelius (161–180 C.E.). All were capable administrators, and all proved worthy successors of Augustus, respecting the Senate and preserving republican forms while running an essentially autocratic

government. Until 180, none had a son who survived him, and so each adopted a man worthy to succeed him. They thus avoided the difficulties of dynastic politics, one of the great horrors of first-century imperial life in the eyes of senatorial historians.

Rome's successful governance of such a vast empire from the time of Augustus to that of Marcus Aurelius was certainly one of its greatest accomplishments. During these two centuries, Rome had few external enemies. The Mediterranean was now under the control of a single military power; on land, Roman officials ruled from the borders of Scotland to those of Persia. A contemporary orator justly boasted that "the whole civilized world lays down the arms which were its ancient burden, as if on holiday . . . [A]ll places are full of gymnasia, fountains, monumental approaches, temples, workshops, schools; one can say that the civilized world, which had been sick from the beginning . . . has been brought by right knowledge to a state of health."

TWO VIEWS OF AUGUSTUS'S RULE

AUGUSTUS SPEAKS FOR HIMSELF

The emperor Augustus was a master propagandist with an unrivaled capacity for presenting his own actions in the best possible light. This document was written by Augustus himself and was to be carved on two bronze pillars set up before his tomb, to tell the world what Augustus wanted remembered about his deeds.

Below is a copy of the accomplishments of the deified Augustus by which he brought the whole world under the empire of the Roman people, and of the moneys expended by him on the state and the Roman people. . . .

1. At the age of nineteen, on my own initiative and at my own expense, I raised an army by means of which I liberated the Republic, which was oppressed by the tyranny of a faction.

2. Those who assassinated my father I drove into exile, avenging their crime by due process of law.

3. I waged many wars throughout the whole world by land and by sea, both civil and foreign, . . .

5. The dictatorship offered to me . . . by the people and by the senate . . . I refused to accept. . . . The consulship, too, which was offered to me . . . as an annual office for life, I refused to accept.

6. [T]hough the Roman senate and people together agreed that I should be elected sole guardian of the laws and morals with supreme authority, I refused to accept any office offered me which was contrary to the traditions of our ancestors.

7. I have been ranking senator for forty years, . . . I have been *pontifex maximus*, augur, member of the college of fifteen for performing sacrifices, member of the college of seven for conducting religious banquets, member of the Arval Brotherhood, one of the

Titii sodales, and a fetial [all priestly offices under the Republic].

9. The senate decreed that vows for my health should be offered up every fifth year by the consuls and priests. . . . [T]he whole citizen body, with one accord, . . . prayed continuously for my health at all the shrines.

17. Four times I came to the assistance of the treasury with my own money. . . . providing bonuses for soldiers who had completed twenty or more years of service.

20. I repaired the Capitol and the theater of Pompey with enormous expenditures on both works, without having my name inscribed on them. I repaired . . . the aqueducts which were falling into ruin in many places . . . I repaired eighty-two temples . . . I reconstructed the Flaminian Way. . . .

34. [H]aving attained supreme power by universal consent, I transferred the state from my own power to the control of the Roman senate and people. . . . After that time I excelled all in authority, but I possessed no more power than the others who were my colleagues in each magistracy.

35. At the time I wrote this document I was in my seventy-sixth year.

"Res Gestae Divi Augusti," in *Roman Civilization, Sourcebook II: The Empire*, ed. Naphtali Lewis and Meyer Reinhold (New York, 1966), pp. 9–19.

THE HISTORIAN TACITUS
WEIGHS UP AUGUSTUS'S REIGN

Writing in the first decades of the second century C.E., the senatorial historian Tacitus began his chronicle of imperial rule, the Annals, with the death of Augustus in 14 C.E. Tacitus placed the two contrasting evaluations that follow in the mouths of Augustus's contemporaries. Tacitus used this literary device often; but despite the appearance of even-handedness he thus creates, Tacitus's own views are rarely in doubt.

Intelligent people praised or criticized Augustus in varying terms. One opinion was as follows. Filial duty and a national emergency, in which there was no place for law-abiding conduct, had driven him to civil war—and this can be neither initiated nor maintained by decent methods. He had made many concessions to Antony and to Lepidus for the sake of vengeance on his father's murderers. When Lepidus grew old and lazy, and Antony's self-indulgence got the better of him, the only possible cure for the distracted country had been government by one man. However, Augustus had put the State in order not by making himself king or dictator but by creating the Principate. The empire's frontiers were on the ocean, or on distant rivers. Armies, provinces, fleets, the whole system was interrelated. Roman citizens were protected by the law. Provincials were decently treated. Rome itself had been lavishly beautified. Force had been sparingly used—merely to preserve peace for the majority.

The opposite view went like this. Filial duty and national crisis had been merely pretexts. In actual fact, the motive of Octavian, the future Augustus, was lust for power. Inspired by that, he had mobilized ex-army settlers by gifts of money, raised an army—while he was only a half-grown boy without any official status—won over a consul's brigade by bribery, pretended to support Sextus Pompeius [the son of Pompey], and by senatorial decree usurped the status and rank of a praetor. Soon both consuls . . . had met their deaths—by enemy action; or perhaps in the one case by the deliberate poisoning of his wound, and in the other at the hand of his own troops, instigated by Octavian. In any case, it was he who took over both their armies. Then he had forced the reluctant Senate to make him consul. But the forces given him to deal with Antony he used against the State. His judicial murders and land distributions were distasteful even to those who carried them out. True, Cassius and Brutus died because he had inherited a feud against them; nevertheless, personal enmities ought to be sacrificed to the public interest.

Next he had cheated Sextus Pompeius by a spurious peace treaty, Lepidus by spurious friendship. Then Antony, enticed by treaties and his marriage with Octavian's sister, had paid the penalty of that delusive relationship with his life. After that, there had certainly been peace, but it was a bloodstained peace. . . . And gossip did not spare his personal affairs—how he had abducted [Livia] the wife of Tiberius Claudius Nero, and asked the priests the farcical question whether it was in order for her to marry while pregnant. Then there was the debauchery of his friend Publius Vedius Pollio. But Livia was a real catastrophe, to the nation, as a mother and to the house of the Caesars as a stepmother.

Tacitus, *Annals* i.9–10. Based on Michael Grant, trans. *Tacitus: The Annals of Imperial Rome* (New York, 1989), pp. 37–39.

QUESTIONS FOR ANALYSIS

1. "The emperor Augustus was a master propagandist." The list of deeds that he thought most important begins with "the deified Augustus" recalling his campaigns as a young man seeking to liberate the republic, avenge the death of Julius Caesar, and remain true to accepted legal forms. Like traditional Roman heroes, Augustus repeatedly refuses honors and takes power only with great reluctance. Who would believe such inscriptions? Who was Augustus trying to impress?
2. Was Tacitus a moralist historian like Livy? What is his overall evaluation of Augustus?

THE ROMAN EMPIRE AT ITS GREATEST EXTENT, 97–117 C.E.

By the second century C.E., Roman expansion had pushed well beyond the Mediterranean basin and into northern and central Europe. This expansion largely followed the courses of the major European river systems. Why do you suppose this was so?

ROMANIZATION AND ASSIMILATION

This Roman Peace (*Pax Romana*) was not universal. In Britain, the Roman army massacred tens of thousands of Britons in the aftermath of Queen Boudicca's revolt. In Judea, perhaps the most restive of all the Roman provinces, a Roman army destroyed the Temple at Jerusalem in 70 C.E. in the wake of one rebellion and in 135 C.E. destroyed the entire city of Jerusalem in the wake of another, massacring its inhabitants and scattering the survivors throughout the empire. Upwards of half a million people may have been killed in Judea during these years, and an equal number enslaved. Jerusalem, meanwhile, was refounded by the emperor Hadrian as a pagan capital named Aelia Capitolina. For the next 500 years, Jews would be forbidden to live there.

Such rebellions were not the norm, however, even in Judea. Although the Roman Empire rested on the backs of its armies, the empire was not really a military occupation. Rome controlled its far-flung territories by assimilating their residents into the common cultural and political life of Rome itself. Local gods became Roman gods and were adopted into the Roman pantheon of divinities. Cities were constructed, and the amenities of urban life introduced: baths, temples, amphitheaters, aqueducts, and paved roads. Rights of citizenship were extended, and able provincials could rise far in Roman service. Some, like Trajan and Hadrian, even rose to become emperors.

Even the frontier areas of the empire need to be understood in this light. Although for convenience's sake historians speak of the empire's borders, in fact these borders were highly fluid and permeable. We

WHY DID SO MANY CRITICS OF ROMAN LIFE DURING THE PRINCIPATE FOCUS THEIR CRITICISMS ON THE BEHAVIOR OF WOMEN?

CULTURE AND LIFE IN THE PERIOD OF THE PRINCIPATE   189

ought, more properly, to speak not of "borders" but of "frontiers," and to see these frontiers as zones of particularly intensive cultural interaction between provincial Romans and the non-Roman peoples who lived beyond them. Roman influence thus reached far beyond the frontier areas, across the Rhine and the Danube into the heartland of Germany and the Gothic lands to the east. When, in the third century, frontier garrisons were withdrawn to take part in civil wars within the empire itself, many of these Romanized Germans and Goths moved into the empire, sometimes as plunderers but often as settlers and aspiring Romans.

CULTURE AND LIFE IN THE PERIOD OF THE PRINCIPATE

Why did so many critics of Roman life during the Principate focus their criticisms on the behavior of women?

The cultural and intellectual changes that began in Rome during the late republican period came to fruition during the Principate. Three eminent exponents of Stoicism lived in Rome during this period: Seneca (4 B.C.E.–65 C.E.), wealthy adviser for a time to Nero; the slave Epictetus (60?–120 C.E.); and the emperor Marcus Aurelius (121–180 C.E.). All of them agreed that inner serenity is the ultimate human goal and that true happiness can be found only in surrender to the benevolent order of the universe. They preached the ideal of virtue for virtue's sake, deplored the sinfulness of human nature, and urged obedience to conscience. Seneca and Epictetus both expressed deep mystical yearnings as part of their philosophy, making it almost a religion. They worshiped the cosmos as divine, governed by an all-powerful Providence that ordained all that happened for ultimate good. The last of the Roman Stoics, Marcus Aurelius, was more fatalistic and less hopeful. Although he did not reject the concept of an ordered and rational universe, he was inclined to think of humans as creatures buffeted by evil fortune for which no distant perfection of the whole could fully compensate. He urged, nevertheless, that people should continue to live nobly, that they should not abandon themselves to gross indulgence or angry protest, but that they should derive what contentment they could from dignified resignation to suffering and tranquil submission to death.

Marcus Aurelius. This equestrian statue is one of the few surviving from the ancient world: the Christians destroyed most Roman equestrian statues because they found them idolatrous, but they spared this one because they mistakenly believed that it represented Constantine, the first Christian Roman emperor. The statue stood outdoors in Rome from the second century until 1980, when it was taken into storage to protect it from air pollution.

LITERATURE OF THE GOLDEN AND SILVER AGES

Roman literature of the Principate is conventionally divided into two periods: works of the Golden Age, written during the reign of Augustus, and works of the Silver Age, written during the first and early second centuries C.E. Most of the literature of the Golden Age was vigorous, affirmative, and uplifting, and—it should be noted—much of it served the propagandistic purposes of Augustus's government. The poetry of the greatest of all Roman poets, Virgil (70–19 B.C.E.), was prototypic. In a set of pastoral poems, the *Eclogues*, Virgil expressed an idealized vision of human life led in harmony with nature, while implicitly extolling Augustus as the bringer of such peace and abundance. Virgil's masterpiece, the *Aeneid* (*ib-NEE-ibd*), is an epic poem about a Trojan hero, Aeneas (whom the family of Caesar and Augustus claimed as an ancestor), who was reputed to have played a role in the formation of the Roman people (see p. 165). Written in elevated, yet sinewy and stirring metrical verse ("Arms and the man, I sing. . . ."), the *Aeneid* tells of the founding of a great state through warfare and toil and foretells Rome's glorious future.

Other major Golden Age writers were Horace (65–8 B.C.E.), Livy (59 B.C.E.–17 C.E.), and Ovid (43 B.C.E.–17 C.E.). Of these, Horace was the most philosophical. His *Odes* combined Epicurean justification of pleasure with Stoic fortitude in the face of suffering. Livy's *History of Rome* is often factually unreliable but is filled with dramatic stories designed to appeal to patriotic emotions. Ovid was the least typical of the Latin Golden Age writers insofar as his outlook tended to be more satiric than heroically affirmative. His main poetic accomplishment was a highly sophisticated retelling of Greek myths in a long poem of fifteen books, the *Metamorphoses*, full of wit and eroticism. Augustus delighted in the *Aeneid* but found the mocking and dissolute tone of Ovid's verses so abhorrent that he banished Ovid from Rome. Augustus was trying to present himself as a stern moralist, whereas Ovid's verses treated such subjects as how to attract women at the race track and his adulterous (although perhaps imaginary) affair with the wife of a Roman senator.

The literature of the Silver Age was typically less calm and balanced than that of the Golden Age. Its effects derived more often from self-conscious artifice. The tales of Petronius and Apuleius describe the more exotic and sometimes sordid aspects of Roman life. The aim of the authors is less to instruct or uplift than to tell an entertaining story or turn a witty phrase. But

an entirely different viewpoint is presented by two other important writers of this age. The satirist Juvenal (60?–140 C.E.) wrote with savage indignation about the moral degeneracy he saw in his contemporaries. His taste for bitingly compressed rhetorical phrases has made him a favorite source for quotation. A similar attitude toward Roman society characterized the writings of Tacitus (55?–117? C.E.), a senatorial historian, who described the events of his age not with a view to dispassionate analysis but largely for the purpose of moral indictment. His *Annals* offer a subtle but devastating portrait of the political system constructed by Augustus and ruled by his heirs; his *Germania* contrasts the manly virtues of the German barbarians with the effeminate vices of the decadent Romans. Like Juvenal, Tacitus was a master of ironic wit and brilliant aphorism. Referring to Roman conquests, he makes a barbarian chieftain say, "They create a wilderness and call it peace."

ART AND ARCHITECTURE

Roman art first assumed its distinctive character during the Principate. Before this time what passed for an art of Rome was really an importation from the Hellenistic East. Conquering armies brought back to Italy wagonloads of statues, reliefs, and marble columns as part of

A Roman Floor Mosaic. This fine mosaic from Roman London shows Bacchus, the god of wine, mounted on a tiger, a reference to the myth that the god had visited India.

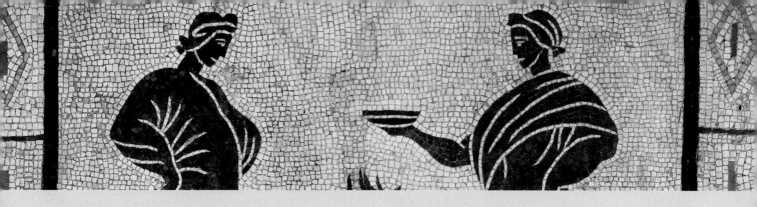

A SCATHING CRITIQUE OF ROMAN SOCIETY

Roman society, even at its height under the Five Good Emperors, was not without its critics. Among the most famous and resonant indictments were those of Juvenal, whose Satires *attacked everything from the general erosion of public morality to the effete tastes of the elite. His language is often bitter, and he did not shy away from lacing his elegant verses with a vulgarity still shocking across the centuries. Like those of Aristophanes, many of his references are highly topical, and their exact meaning is lost to us. No doubt his audience understood the allusions, making his public excoriations all the more personal and pointed. Contrast this portrayal of contemporary women with the model of the virtuous Lucretia.*

What conscience has Venus drunk? Our inebriated beauties can't tell head from tail at those midnight oyster suppers when the best wine's laced with perfume, and tossed down neat from a foaming conch-shell, while the dizzy ceiling spins round, and the tables dance, and each light shows double. Why, you may ask yourself, does the notorious Maura sniff at the air in that knowing, derisive way as she and her dear friend Tullia pass by the ancient altar of Chastity? And what is Tullia whispering to her? Here, at night, they stagger out of their litters and relieve themselves, pissing in long hard bursts all over the goddess's statue. Then, while the Moon looks down on their motions, they take turns to ride each other, and finally go home. So you, next morning, on your way to some great house, will splash through your wife's piddle. Notorious, too, are the ritual mysteries of the Good Goddess, when flute-music stirs the loins, and frenzied women, devotees of Priapus, sweep along in procession, howling, tossing their hair, wine-flown, horn-crazy, burning with the desire to get themselves laid. . . . So the ladies, with a display of talent to match their birth, win all the prizes. No make-believe here, no pretense, each act is performed in earnest, and guaranteed to warm the age-chilled balls of a Nestor or a Priam.

Juvenal, *Sixth Satire* 301–326; based on *Juvenal: The Sixteen Satires*, trans. Peter Green (New York, 1974), pp. 138–139.

---

the plunder from Greece and Asia Minor. These became the property of the wealthy and were used to embellish their sumptuous mansions. As demand for such works increased, hundreds of copies were made by Roman artisans. None, however, represents a truly indigenous Roman artistic style.

Encouraged by the patronage of Augustus himself, the Principate witnessed the development of a more distinctively Roman art. This art was more varied than is often assumed, running from the most magnificent public architecture to the most intimate wall paintings. Roman architecture was often grandiose, its massive proportions made possible by the expertise Roman engineers had developed in working with concrete. Among the largest such public buildings were the Pantheon, with its 142-foot-diameter dome, and the Colosseum, which could accommodate 50,000 spectators at gladiatorial combats. Except on public monuments, Roman sculpture was less bombastic. Relief sculpture was particularly notable during this period for its delicacy and naturalism. Even on their coins, emperors were portrayed very much as they looked in real life; and since the images on coins were recut annually, we can trace on successive issues a ruler's receding

The Pantheon in Rome. Built by the emperor Hadrian, it boasted the largest dome without interior supports of the ancient world. The dome forms a perfect sphere, exactly as high as it is wide.

Roman Aqueduct at Segovia, Spain. Aqueducts conveyed water from mountains to the larger cities.

WHY DID SO MANY CRITICS OF ROMAN LIFE DURING THE PRINCIPATE FOCUS THEIR CRITICISMS ON THE BEHAVIOR OF WOMEN?

CULTURE AND LIFE IN THE PERIOD OF THE PRINCIPATE   193

The Colosseum. Built by the Roman emperors between 75 and 80 C.E. as a place of entertainment, it was the scene of gladiatorial combats. The most common form of Greek secular architecture was the theater (see p. 123), but the most common Roman form was the amphitheater.

hairline or his advancing double chin. Painting, however, was the Romans' most original and most intimate art. Romans loved intense colors; those who could afford to do so surrounded themselves with brilliant wall paintings and mosaics (pictures produced by fitting together small pieces of colored glass or stone). These created a gamut of effects from fantastic seascapes to dreamy landscapes to introspective portraiture.

Closely related to their achievements in architecture were Roman triumphs in engineering. The imperial Romans built marvelous roads and bridges, many of which still survive. Under Trajan, eleven aqueducts brought water into Rome from the nearby hills and provided the city with 300 million gallons daily for drinking and bathing and for flushing a well-designed sewage system. Water was cleverly funneled into the homes of the rich for their private gardens, fountains, and pools. The Emperor Nero built a famous Golden House in the center of Rome with pipes fitted for sprinkling his guests with perfume, baths supplied with medicinal waters, and a pond "like a sea." In addition, a spherical ceiling in the banquet hall revolved day and night like the heavens, all contributing to Nero's

deserved reputation as a voluptuary. (Supposedly, when Nero moved in he was heard to say, "At last I can live like a human being.")

ARISTOCRATIC WOMEN UNDER THE PRINCIPATE

One of the most striking aspects of Roman society under the Principate was the important role played by upper-class women. As we have seen, the wealthy women of late-republican Rome were much less confined to domesticity than were their counterparts in Classical Athens. This trait became even more pronounced during the Principate. It is true that Roman women were often assigned the names of their fathers with feminine endings—for example, Julia from Julius, Claudia from Claudius, Marcia from Marcius. At the same time, however, Roman women had a status quite independent from that of their husbands. They did not ordinarily adopt their husband's name when they married. Despite laws that kept them formally under the legal supervision of a male guardian, in practice wealthy

Female Gladiators. Like men, enslaved women also fought as gladiators. This marble relief commemorates the freeing of two such fighters, "Amazon" and "Achilia," presumably as a reward for their successes in the arena.

A Gladiator's Helmet. This bronze helmet was found at Pompeii. It was buried by volcanic ash when Mount Vesuvius erupted and destroyed the city in 79 C.E.

women could own property, invest in commercial ventures, and make public benefactions of their own volition. They could not hold political office, but they could act as priestesses and civic patrons. Both roles gave them considerable influence in public affairs. With numerous slaves to take care of their households and wealth of their own on which to draw, upper-class Roman women were free to engage in intellectual and artistic pursuits. Some wrote poetry, others studied philosophy, and others presided over literary salons. They also exercised a degree of sexual freedom unknown elsewhere in the ancient world and profoundly shocking to conservative male critics. Aristocratic Roman women often had their portraits painted or chiseled in stone. Several emperors' wives or daughters even appeared on Roman coinage, partly because the emperors wished to proclaim the greatness of their families, and partly because some of these women really did play an influential role (albeit an informal one) in affairs of state.

The lives of lower-class women are far less well known. Most were probably married at some point in their lives, and the wives of shopkeepers in particular played an important role in the businesses that sustained their families. Married women who survived the dangers of childbirth could probably expect to give birth to three or four children, not all of whom would live to adulthood. But death rates were high, especially for women. In Rome, the median recorded age at death for women was 34; for men, between 40 and 46. If enslaved women were more fully represented in these figures, they would likely be even lower.

GLADIATORIAL COMBATS

To most modern sensibilities, the most repellant aspect of Roman culture during the Principate was its spectacular cruelty. Gladiatorial contests were not new, but they were now presented in ampitheaters built to hold thousands of spectators. Commoners, aristocrats, and even emperors attended these events, which became steadily bloodier and more brutal. Individual gladiators fought to the death with swords, tridents, or simply fists wrapped with leather thongs loaded with iron or lead; when a fighter went down with a disabling wound, the crowd would be asked to decide whether his life should be spared or whether his opponent should kill him on the spot. Between gladiatorial contests, condemned prisoners might be released into the arena to be torn apart and eaten by wild animals. If the arena floor became too sodden with blood, a fresh layer of sand would be spread so that the performance could continue.

Most gladiators were condemned criminals or slaves, but some were volunteers from the respectable classes. Even Commodus, the erratic and violent son of the emperor Marcus Aurelius, competed several times as a gladiator, reveling in the plaudits of the mob and fancying himself a modern-day Hercules.

ROMAN LAW

One of the most important legacies the Romans left to succeeding cultures was their system of law. The Roman legal system's gradual evolution began with the

WHY DID SO MANY CRITICS OF ROMAN LIFE DURING THE PRINCIPATE FOCUS THEIR CRITICISMS ON THE BEHAVIOR OF WOMEN?

CULTURE AND LIFE IN THE PERIOD OF THE PRINCIPATE   195

publication of the Twelve Tables around 450 B.C.E. Over several centuries, this primitive legal code was transformed by new precedents and principles reflecting changes in customs; new philosophical ideas, especially Stoicism; the decisions of judges; and the edicts of the *praetors* (*pree-TAWRS*), who had the authority to define and interpret the law in a particular case and to issue instructions to judges.

The most sweeping changes, however, occurred during the Principate. This was partly because, with the growth of the Roman Empire, Roman law now extended over a much wider field of jurisdiction, embracing the far-flung provinces as well as the citizens of Italy. But the major reason for the rapid development of Roman legal thinking during these years was the fact that Augustus and his successors appointed a small number of eminent jurists to deliver opinions on the legal issues raised by cases under trial in the courts. The most prominent of these jurists were Gaius, Ulpian, Papinian, and Paulus. Although most of them held high judicial office, they gained their reputations primarily as lawyers and writers on legal subjects. Their legal opinions came to embody a systematic philosophy of law unlike anything that had gone before, and became the foundation for all subsequent Roman jurisprudence.

Roman law as it was developed by the jurists comprised three great branches or divisions: the civil law, the law of peoples, and the natural law. The civil law was the law of Rome and its citizens, both written and unwritten. It included the statutes of the Senate, the decrees of the emperor, the edicts of magistrates, and ancient customs that had the force of law. The law of peoples was the law held to be common to all people regardless of nationality, a sort of rudimentary international law. This law authorized slavery and private ownership of property and defined the principles of purchase and sale, partnership, and contract. It was not superior to the civil law but supplemented it, especially with respect to the alien inhabitants of the empire.

The most interesting and in many ways the most important branch of Roman law was the natural law, a product not of judicial practice but of philosophy. The Stoics had developed the idea of a rational order of nature that is the embodiment of justice and right. They had affirmed that all men are by nature equal, and that they are entitled to certain basic rights that governments have no authority to transgress. The father of the law of nature as a legal principle, however, was not

one of the Hellenistic Stoics, but Cicero. "True law," he declared, "is right reason consonant with nature, diffused among all men, constant, eternal. To make enactments infringing this law, religion forbids, neither may it be repealed even in part, nor have we power through Senate or people to free ourselves from it." This law came before the state itself, and any ruler who defied it automatically became a tyrant.

Most of the great jurists subscribed to conceptions of the law of nature very similar to those of the philosophers. Although the jurists did not regard this law as an automatic limitation on the civil law, they thought of it as an ideal to which the statutes and decrees of men ought to conform. The practical law applied in local Roman courts often bore little resemblance to the laws of nature. Nonetheless, the development of a concept of abstract justice as a legal principle was one of the noblest achievements of Roman civilization.

The development of a concept of abstract justice as a legal principle was one of the noblest achievements of Roman civilization.

THE ECONOMY OF ITALY DURING THE PRINCIPATE

Manufacturing increased, and the mass production of pottery, textiles, metal, and glasswork brought even the poor a level of material abundance and domestic comfort unmatched by any previous Mediterranean society. Merchants carried these specialized, mass-produced goods throughout the empire, so successfully and in such quantities that in Rome, there is still a mountain 150 feet high, made up entirely of broken pottery vessels (*amphorae*) from the second and third centuries C.E. These amphorae were used to transport olive oil from southwestern Spain for consumption in Rome. Historians have calculated that the mountain consists of some 53 million amphorae, which would once have contained approximately 1.5 billion American gallons of oil.

But there were also signs of strain in this sophisticated, complex, but fragile economic world. The upper classes lived in spectacular luxury in their city and country houses. In the countryside, however, the diminishing number of slaves captured in war was beginning to result in labor shortages on the great aristocratic *latifundia*. These shortages were only partially made up by the declining social and economic position of small farmers, many of whom wound up as semiservile agricultural workers (*coloni*) tied to the great estates. The western empire in general, and Italy in particular, also had a decidedly unfavorable balance of trade with the eastern provinces. Western bulk goods, particularly wine, grain, oil, and pottery, traveled eastward in massive quantities, but it was still not enough to balance the cost of luxury goods imported from the eastern provinces, India, and China. So long as imperial revenues continued to flow from east to west to support the army and the imperial administration, the economic system of the later Principate was relatively stable. Should that flow of cash dry up, however, or should the trade routes between east and west be disrupted, the economy of the western empire risked being thrown quickly into crisis.

THE CRISIS OF THE THIRD CENTURY (180–284 C.E.)

What factors brought the Roman Empire to the brink of ruin?

With the death of Marcus Aurelius in 180 C.E. the period of beneficent imperial rule came to an end. One reason for the success of the Five Good Emperors was that the first four designated particularly promising young men, rather than sons or close relatives, for the succession. But Marcus Aurelius broke this pattern with unfortunate results. Although he was one of the most philosophic and thoughtful rulers who ever reigned, he was not wise enough to recognize that his son, Commodus, was a self-indulgent adolescent who lacked the discipline or the capacity to rule effectively. To some degree, Marcus Aurelius had his hands tied; it is likely that any attempt to make someone other than his natural son his heir would have met with stiff resistance from the army. Commodus, however, promptly alienated the army by withdrawing from the costly wars in which his father had been engaged. This was an eminently sensible step but one that made him unpopular with both the army and the Senate. Thereafter, he vacillated between accommodating the senators and bullying them into submission. If neither approach worked, Commodus would try to placate them by executing one or more of his advisers; understandably, this made talented people reluctant to work for him. He also scorned the traditional expectations for aristocratic conduct, indulging his taste for public and private perversities and even appearing as a gladiator in the Colosseum. His erratic and frequently violent behavior resulted in a conspiracy originating inside his own palace: his wrestling coach finally strangled him in 192 C.E. Matters there-

after became worse. With no obvious successor to Commodus, the armies of the provinces raised their own candidates and civil war ensued. A provincial general, Septimius Severus (193–211 C.E.), emerged victorious, making it clear that provincial armies could now interfere in imperial politics at will.

THE SEVERAN DYNASTY

Severus and his successors aggravated the problem by eliminating even the theoretical rights of the Senate and ruling as military dictators. On his deathbed, Severus advised his two sons, "Enrich the soldiers, boys, and ignore the rest." His son Caracalla was little more than a thug who murdered his brother and co-emperor Geta. So desperate was Caracalla to raise revenues and pay bonuses to his increasingly covetous

The Emperor Septimius Severus. This statue, carved during the emperor's lifetime, emphasizes his career as a military commander and his North African ancestry.

Coin Depicting Emperor's Wife. This Roman coin, dating from about 200 C.E., bears the image of Julia Domna, wife of the emperor Septimius Severus.

armies (especially to appease them after his assassination of his more popular brother), that he made everyone in the empire a Roman citizen. This was hardly an act of enlightenment but rather was aimed at increasing the tax base of the Roman state. In the process, he cheapened Roman citizenship, once the prized glue that held the vast empire together. His successors in the Severan Dynasty proved no better. Elagabalus tried to introduce an eastern sun cult as the official religion of Rome, and he flouted sexual and moral convention on the very floor of the Senate.

If not for a series of remarkable imperial women fighting to keep the dynasty and empire together, the results might have been disastrous. First Julia Domna, the wife of Septimius Severus, helped manage the empire for her son Caracalla and seems to have acted as the one restraint on his vicious personality; she took her own life when he fell victim to an assassin in 217 C.E. Her sister Julia Maesa was the grandmother of both Elagabalus and his successor, Severus Alexander. Her political influence was considerable, and she proved instrumental in Elagabalus's downfall when his abuses endangered the state. Finally, her daughter Julia Mamaea, the mother of Severus Alexander, enjoyed unusual prominence and popularity during the reign of her young son (222–235 C.E.), and exercised an almost regentlike authority within his government. But they could not stem the tide started by the dynasty's founder, Septimius. The growing prominence of the army made it increasingly uncontrollable. Once the role of brute force was openly revealed, any aspiring general could try his luck at seizing power. Severus Alexander and Julia Mamaea were murdered in 235 C.E. when the army turned against them. Fifty years of endemic civil war followed. From 235 to 284 C.E. there were no fewer than twenty-six "barracks emperors," of whom only one managed to escape a violent death.

THE HEIGHT OF THE THIRD-CENTURY CRISIS

In the half century between 235 and 284 C.E., political chaos combined with other factors to bring the empire to the brink of ruin. Civil wars undermined the economy, not only by interfering with agriculture and trade but also by encouraging aspiring emperors to enrich their soldiers by debasing the coinage and imposing exorbitant taxation on civilians in their provinces. The result was inflation. Landlords, small farmers, and artisans suffered the most. Many were driven to the most abject destitution. In the wake of war and hunger, disease also ran rampant. In the reign of Marcus Aurelius a terrible plague, probably smallpox, swept through the empire, decimating the army and the population at large. In the middle of the third century the pestilence returned and struck at the population again.

The resulting decline in population came at a time when Rome could least afford it, for still another threat to the empire in the middle of the third century was the advance of Rome's external enemies. With Roman ranks thinned by disease and Roman armies fighting each other, Germans in the west and Persians in the east broke through the old Roman defense lines. In 251 C.E. the Goths defeated and slew the emperor Decius, crossed the Danube, and marauded at will in the Balkans. An even more humiliating disaster came in 260 C.E. when the emperor Valerian was captured in battle by the Persians and made to kneel as a footstool for their ruler. When he died his body was stuffed and hung on exhibition. For a time, the western provinces broke free as an independent empire in their own right, despairing of Rome's ability to protect them. Clearly the days of Augustus were far in the past.

NEOPLATONISM

Understandably, the culture of the third century was marked by pervasive anxiety. One can see the worry even in surviving statuary, as in the bust of the emperor Philip (244–249 C.E.), who appears almost to realize that he will soon be killed in battle. As despair spread, new philosophical systems emerged that encouraged believers to withdraw from the world around them. One such system was Neoplatonism ("New Platonism"). Although Neoplatonism was loosely based on spiritualist tendencies in Plato's thought, its real founder was Plotinus (204–270 C.E.), an Egyptian who came to Rome and won many followers among the Roman upper classes.

Neoplatonism explained the evils of the world by a set of beliefs about creation. Plotinus taught that everything that exists proceeds from the divine in a continuing stream of emanations. The initial stage in the process is the emanation of the world-soul. From this come the divine Ideas, or spiritual patterns, and then the souls of particular things. The final emanation is matter. But matter has no form or quality of its own; it is simply the residue that is left after the spiritual rays from the divine have burned themselves out. The material world is thus entirely cut off from the realm of the divine.

Plotinus's second major doctrine was mysticism. The human soul was originally a part of God, but through its union with matter it became separated from its divine source. The highest goal of life should be mystic reunion with the divine, which can be accomplished through contemplation and through emancipation of the soul from its bondage to matter. Human beings should be ashamed of the fact that they possess a physical body and should seek to subjugate it in every way possible. Asceticism was therefore the third main teaching of his philosophy.

Plotinus's successors diluted his philosophical ideas with more and more bizarre superstitions. But despite its antirational viewpoint and its utter indifference to the state, Neoplatonism became so popular in Rome in the third and fourth centuries C.E. that it almost completely supplanted Stoicism. It also came to have a considerable influence on Christianity, as we will see in Chapter Six. It is hard to imagine a philosophy more completely at odds with the traditional values and commitments of

The Emperor Philip the Arab. An artistic legacy of the Roman age of anxiety.

Roman society than Neoplatonism. Its popularity is therefore eloquent testimony to the changes brought about in Roman society and government by the crises of the third century.

ROMAN RULE IN THE WEST: A BALANCE SHEET

Did Roman civilization come to an end in the third century C.E.?

As Rome was not built in a day, so it was not lost in one. As we will see in the next chapter, strong rule returned in 284 C.E. Thereafter the Roman Empire endured in the west for 200 years more and in the east for a millennium. But the restored Roman state differed greatly from the old one—so much so that it is proper to end the story of characteristically Roman civilization here and to review the reasons for Rome's transformation into a distinctly different type of society, one that we examine in detail in the next chapter.

EXPLAINING THE DECLINE AND FALL OF ROME

More has been written on the decline and fall of Rome than on the death of any other civilization. The theories offered to account for the decline have been many and varied. Perhaps the strangest recent one is that Rome fell from the effects of lead ingested from cooking utensils, but if this were true we would have to ask why Rome did so well for so long. Moralists have found the explanation for Rome's decline in the descriptions of lechery and gluttony presented by such authors as Juvenal and Petronius. But such an approach overlooks the facts that much of this evidence is patently overdrawn and that nearly all of it comes from the period of the early Principate. In later centuries, when the empire was more obviously collapsing, morality became more austere through the influence of ascetic religions. One of the simplest explanations is that Rome fell because of the severity of German attacks. But German barbarians had always stood ready to attack Rome: German invasions succeeded only when Rome was already weakened internally. Indeed, from the fourth century C.E. onward, increasing numbers of Germanic tribes were less interested in destroying Rome than in becoming a

Did Roman civilization come to an end in the third century c.e.?

Roman Rule in the West: A Balance Sheet   199

part of it. Many of the Germanic tribes who would overrun the western empire during the fifth century C.E. were in fact Roman allies, provoked to invade the empire by Roman bigotry, maladministration, and abuse.

POLITICAL FAILURES

It is best then to concentrate on Rome's most serious internal problems. Some of these were political. The most obvious failing of the Roman constitution under the Principate was the lack of a clear law of succession. Especially when a ruler died suddenly, there was no certainty about who was to follow him. In modern America the death of a president might shock the nation, but people at least knew what would happen next; in imperial Rome no one knew, and civil war increasingly became the result. For all of Augustus's achievements, this was his system's greatest failure. Indeed, because the reality of autocratic rule was disguised behind republican forms, there was little any emperor could do to provide for an orderly succession to an imperial position that did not officially exist. So long as respect for the institutions of republican Rome remained, transitions might be effected more or less smoothly. But from 235 to 284 C.E. warfare and instability fed on each other. Civil war was also nurtured by the lack of constitutional means for reform. If regimes became unpopular, as most did after 180 C.E., the only means to alter them was to overthrow them. But resorting to violence always bred more violence, especially as the soldiery became the arbiter of the success or failure of an imperial regime.

ECONOMIC CRISIS

The Roman Empire also had its share of economic problems, though the lessons to be drawn from this remain unclear. Rome's worst economic problems derived from its slave system and from labor shortages. Roman civilization was based on cities, and Roman cities existed largely by virtue of an agricultural surplus produced by slaves. Slaves were worked so hard that they did not normally reproduce to fill their own ranks. Until the time of Trajan (98–117 C.E.), Roman conquests provided fresh supplies of slaves to keep the system going, but thereafter the economy began to run out of human fuel. Landlords could no longer be so profligate with human life, barracks slavery came to an end, and the countryside produced less of a surplus to feed the towns. The fact that no technological advance took up the slack may also be attributed to slavery. Later in Western history, agricultural surpluses were produced by technological revolutions, but Roman landlords were indifferent to technology because interest in it was thought to be demeaning. As long as slaves were available to do the work, Romans had no interest in labor-saving devices, and attention to any sort of machinery was deemed a sign of slavishness. Landlords proved their nobility by their interest in higher things, but while they were contemplating these heights their agricultural surpluses were beginning to disappear.

Labor shortages also aggravated Rome's economic problems, especially in the west. With the end of foreign conquests and the decline of slavery there was a pressing need for people to stay on the farm, but barbarian pressures meant that there was also a steady need for men to serve in the army. The plagues of the second and third centuries sharply reduced the population just at the worst time. It has been estimated that between the reign of Marcus Aurelius and the restoration of strong rule in 284 C.E., disease, warfare, and a declining birthrate combined to reduce the population of the Roman Empire by one third. The result was that there were neither sufficient farmers to work the land nor enough soldiers to fight Rome's enemies.

Despite all of this, it is important to remember that Rome was scarcely poverty-stricken. Wealth still poured into Roman society from the east, but in the western provinces especially it tended to be concentrated in the hands of a very few families. These families gradually accrued to themselves such extensive privileges that they rarely contributed anything to the coffers of the Roman state. The burden for the upkeep of cities thus fell increasingly on a local elite that could not shoulder it; as these men were reduced to poverty or fled the cities altogether, the urban basis of classical Roman civilization and its shared civic ideals were further undermined. Regional differences were also growing more pronounced, leading to a series of secessionist movements among the western provinces. Enormous dedication and exertion on the part of its citizenry might just possibly have saved the empire, but too few citizens were now willing to work hard for the public good. Ultimately, the decline of Rome was marked by a lack of interest among its citizens in preserving it. As a result, the Roman world came to an end not so much with a bang as with a whimper.

ROMAN ACHIEVEMENTS

Attention to the dynamics of Rome's decline in the west should not cause us to overlook the many ways in which Roman society was a towering success. No state has ever encompassed so much territory, with such a large percentage of the world's population under its dominion, for so long a span of time. Roman rule maintained its vitality in the west from the first century B.C.E. until the fifth century C.E. In the east, the Roman empire survived until 1453. Part of that success resulted from the Roman government's ability to create and maintain systems of communication, trade, and travel as no other state had done before and as none would do again until modern times. Underlying these successes was the fundamental strength of the Roman economy. Although much is made of the collapse of the Roman economy in the third century C.E. and its runaway inflation, the Romans had maintained a relatively stable currency and a prosperous international trade for four previous centuries without any of the mechanisms or safeguards of a modern market economy. This too remains an unparalleled achievement.

Most fundamental, however, the Roman Empire's survival was a political achievement. The Roman political system was inclusive to a degree no modern empire has ever matched. Through their willingness to extend the franchise to non-Romans, to allow even provincials to become senators and ultimately emperors, Rome gave a share of power to its population that no Near Eastern or Greek empire could have ever imagined. Although the Persians were tolerant of foreign cultic practice and the Athenians were generous with political rights among their own citizenry, extending real political power to outsiders was out of the question. For the Romans, extension of the franchise was key to their success, from the Latin Right in early Italy to the granting of citizenship to all the inhabitants of the empire under Caracalla. As a prominent historian of Rome once remarked, if the British Empire had been as willing to extend its franchise as the Romans were to extend theirs, the American Revolution might never have occurred.

CONCLUSION

It is tempting to believe that we today have many similarities to the Romans: first of all, because Rome is nearer to us in time than the other civilizations of antiquity; and second, because Rome seems to bear such a close kinship to the modern temper. The resemblances between Roman history and the history of Great Britain or the United States in the nineteenth and twentieth centuries have often been noted. Like America's, the Roman economy evolved from a simple agrarianism to a complex urban system with problems of unemployment, gross disparities of wealth, and financial crises. Like the British Empire, the Roman Empire was founded on con-

quest. And like both the British and the American empires, the Roman Empire justified itself by celebrating the peace its conquests allegedly brought to the world.

Ultimately, however, such parallels are superficial. Rome was an ancient, not a modern, society that differed profoundly from any of the societies of the modern Western world. As noted already, the Romans disdained industrial activities. Neither did they have any idea of the modern national state; their empire was more like a collection of cities than an integrated territorial body politic. The Romans never developed an adequate representative government, and they never solved the problem of succession to imperial power. Nor were Roman social relations in any way comparable with those of more recent centuries. The Roman economy rested on slavery to a degree unmatched in any modern society. Technology was primitive, social stratification was extreme, and gender relations were profoundly unequal. Roman religion rested on the assumption that religious practice and political life were inseparable from one another, and Roman emperors were worshiped (especially in the east) as living gods.

Nevertheless, the civilization of Rome exerted a great influence on later cultures. Roman architectural forms survive to this day in the design of many of our government buildings, and Roman styles of dress continue to be worn by the clergy of the various Christian churches. Through the sixth-century code of the emperor Justinian (see Chapter 6), Roman law was handed down to the Middle Ages and on into modern times. American judges still cite legal maxims coined by Gaius or Ulpian; and third-century legal precedents continue to be valid in the legal systems of nearly all continental European countries and the American state of Louisiana. Roman sculpture provided the model on which virtually all modern sculpture rests, and Roman authors set the standards for prose composition in Europe and America until the twentieth century. Even the organization of the Catholic Church was adapted from the structure of the Roman state; today the pope bears the title of supreme pontiff (*pontifex maximus*), once borne by the emperor in his role as head of the Roman civic religion.

But perhaps the most important of all Rome's contributions to the future was its role in transmitting Greek civilization throughout the length and breadth of its empire. When, finally, the united Roman Empire did collapse, three different successor civilizations would emerge to occupy Rome's former territories: Byzantium, Islam, and western Europe. Each of these civilizations would be characterized by a distinctive religious tradition, and each would adopt and adapt different aspects of its Roman inheritance. What these three Western civilizations shared, however, was a common cultural inheritance derived from Greece by way of Rome—an inheritance of urbanism, cosmopolitanism, imperialism, and learning that would forever mark the West as a unique experiment in human history.

This cultural inheritance would be Rome's epitaph; and in the mid-third century C.E., it must have seemed that an epitaph was the only thing needed to bring the Roman Empire to an end. But in fact, the Roman Empire did not collapse. It went on to enjoy another several centuries of life. Rome did not fall in the third century, or the fourth century, or even the fifth. But it was transformed, and in this transformed state the Roman inheritance would pass to the Western civilizations of the Middle Ages. It is to those transformations that we now turn.

KEY TERMS

Etruscans	plebians	Cicero	Virgil	Gaul
patricians	Carthage	Augustus	aqueducts	Plotinus

SELECTED READINGS

Translations of Roman authors are available in the Penguin Classics series and in the Loeb Classical Library.

Barker, Graeme, and Tom Rasmussen. *The Etruscans.* Oxford and Malden, Mass., 1998. A fine survey, from the Blackwell *Peoples of Europe* series.

Beard, Mary, John North, and Simon Price. *Religions of Rome,* vol. 1: *A History.* Cambridge, 1998. An authoritative account, full of new ideas.

Beard, Mary, John North, and Simon Price. *Religions of Rome,* vol. 2: *A Sourcebook.* Cambridge, 1998. A definitive source collection that supplements vol. 1.

Boardman, John, Jasper Griffin, and Oswyn Murray. *The Oxford History of the Roman World.* Oxford, 1990. Reprint of relevant portions of the excellent *Oxford History of the Classical World* (1986). Stimulating, accessible topical chapters by British specialists.

Cornell, T. J. *The Beginnings of Rome: Italy and Rome from the Bronze Age to the Punic Wars (c. 1000–264 B.C.).* London, 1995. An expert, ambitious survey of the archaeological and historical evidence for early Rome.

Crawford, Michael. *The Roman Republic.* 2d ed. Cambridge, Mass., 1993. A lively, fast-paced survey of republican Rome. An excellent place to start.

Fantham, Elaine, Helene Peet Foley, Natalie Boymel Kampen, Sarah B. Pomeroy, and H. Alan Shapiro. *Women in the Classical World.* Oxford, 1994. A lively, expert survey of both Greece and Rome.

Garnsey, Peter, and Richard Saller. *The Roman Empire: Economy, Society, and Culture.* Berkeley, Calif., 1987. A straightforward short survey.

Gruen, Erich S. *The Hellenistic World and the Coming of Rome.* 2 vols. Berkeley, Calif., 1984. A massive survey, focused on the unpredictable rise of Rome to a position of dominance within the Mediterranean world.

Harris, William V. *War and Imperialism in Republican Rome, 327–70 B.C.* Oxford, 1979. A challenging study arguing that Rome's need for military conquest and imperial expansion was deeply embedded in the political and social fabric of Roman life.

Lancel, Serge. *Carthage: A History.* Trans. Antonia Nevill. Oxford, 1995. An up-to-date account of Rome's great rival for control of the Mediterranean world.

Lewis, Naphtali, and M. Reinhold. *Roman Civilization: Selected Readings.* 2 vols. New York, 1951–1955. The standard collection, especially for political and economic subjects. Vol. 1 covers the republic; vol. 2, the empire.

Millar, Fergus G. B. *The Emperor in the Roman World, 31 B.C.–A.D. 337.* London, 1977. A classic work that showed (among much else) the importance of emperor worship to the religious outlook of the Roman Empire.

Millar, Fegus G. B. *The Crowd in Rome in the Late Republic.* Ann Arbor, Mich., 1999. A revisionist account that emphasizes the reality of Roman democracy in the late republic, against those who would see the period's politics as entirely under the control of aristocratic families.

Ward, Allen M., Fritz Heichelheim, and Cedric A. Yeo. *A History of the Roman People,* 3d ed. Upper Saddle River, N.J., 1999. An informative, well-organized textbook covering Roman history from its beginnings to the end of the sixth century C.E.

Wells, Colin. *The Roman Empire,* 2d ed. Cambridge, Mass., 1992. An easily readable survey from the reign of Augustus to the mid-third century C.E., particularly useful for its treatment of the relationship between the Roman central government and its Italian provinces.

Chapter SIX

CHAPTER CONTENTS

CHRISTIANITY
AND THE
TRANSFORMATION
OF THE
ROMAN WORLD

The Roman Empire declined after 180 C.E., but it did not collapse. In 284 C.E. the vigorous soldier-emperor Diocletian began a reorganization of the empire that gave it a new lease on life. Throughout the fourth century the Roman state continued to encompass the entire Mediterranean world. During the fifth century the western half of the empire fell under the political control of German-speaking invaders; but many Roman institutions continued to function in these new Germanic kingdoms, and in the sixth century the emperor Justinian reconquered much of the western Mediterranean shoreline. Only in the seventh century did it become clear that the divisions between the eastern and western halves of the Roman Empire would be permanent and that the two regions would thereafter develop in fundamentally different ways. With this transition, the world of classical antiquity came to an end.

Historians used to underestimate the longevity of Roman institutions and would begin their discussions of medieval history in the third, fourth, or fifth century C.E. Because historical periodization is always approximate and depends largely on which aspects of development a historian chooses to emphasize, this approach cannot be dismissed. Certainly the transition from the ancient to the medieval world was gradual, with some "medieval" ways emerging in the West as early as the third century C.E. But it is now more customary to conceive of ancient history as continuing after 284 C.E. and lasting until the Roman Empire lost control over the Mediterranean in the seventh century. The period from 284 to about 610 C.E., although transitional (as, of course, all ages are), has certain themes of its own and is best described as neither Roman nor medieval but as the age of late antiquity.

Three major cultural trends characterized the world of late antiquity. The first was the spread and triumph of Christianity throughout the Roman world. At first Christianity was just one of many otherworldly religions that appealed to increasing numbers of people during the later empire. But in the fourth century it was adopted

FOCUS QUESTIONS

• What were the principles by which Diocletian reformed the Roman Empire?

• How did Christianity become the majority religion within the Roman Empire?

• What major changes did Christianity undergo during the fourth century?

• Why did the Germanic invasions succeed?

• What distinctive themes of western Christian thought were emerging during the fourth and fifth centuries?

• How was classical culture Christianized?

• Why did Justinian's plan to reunite the Roman Empire fail?

as the Roman state religion and thereafter became one of the greatest shaping forces in the development of Western civilizations.

The gradual extension of Christianity, first from city to city and then from city to countryside, was one element in a larger process of cultural assimilation that characterized the entire late-antique world. New cultural developments were more widely diffused than ever before, and a wider range of people participated in them. As Roman culture became more uniform and more widespread, however, it also became less sophisticated and distinctive. The result was a watering down of the high culture of the classical era—a process we shall call *vulgarization*.

Cultural influences from outside the Mediterranean world were also having an increasing impact, especially on the western parts of the empire. The Romans called this process *barbarization*, from the Greek word *barbaros*, meaning "foreigner." Barbarian culture was not necessarily primitive, but it was nonurban and non-Greek—and in the eyes of Mediterranean elites, these facts alone were enough to stigmatize it. But barbarian influence grew steadily nonetheless, first within the army and then throughout society. None of these processes was cataclysmic; but by the end of the sixth century C.E., Christianization, vulgarization, and barbarization had combined to bring the ancient Mediterranean world to an end.

THE REORGANIZED EMPIRE

What were the principles by which Diocletian reformed the Roman Empire?

The chaos of the mid–third century C.E. might well have destroyed the Roman Empire. That it did not is largely due to the efforts of a remarkable soldier named Diocletian, who ruled as emperor from 284 to 305 C.E. Diocletian imposed a number of fundamental political and economic reforms on the empire. Most important, however, he restored the majesty and prestige of the emperorship itself. By so doing, Diocletian laid the foundations on which all subsequent Roman and Byzantine emperors would base their authority.

THE REIGN OF DIOCLETIAN

Like Augustus, Diocletian was acutely aware of the dignity of his imperial office and of the importance of political symbolism in maintaining it. But unlike Augustus,

who tried to cloak the reality of his power in the trappings of republicanism, Diocletian presented himself to his subjects as an undisguised autocrat. His title was not *princeps* ("first citizen"), but *dominus* ("lord"). He wore a diadem and a purple gown of silk interwoven with gold and introduced Persian-style ceremonial deference at his court. His officials bore elaborate titles indicating their rank; a supplicant could judge his own importance by the rank (higher or lower) of the administrators whom he was permitted to see. Diocletian himself remained apart from the ordinary business of his court, physically removed behind a maze of doorways, rooms, and curtains. Those lucky enough to gain an audience with him had to prostrate themselves before him; a privileged few would be allowed to kiss his robe. For the barracks emperors of the earlier third century, too much familiarity with their soldiers and courtiers had bred contempt. As a soldier-emperor himself, Diocletian was determined to avoid their mistake.

In another breach with Augustan tradition, Diocletian also took steps to define formal rules of imperial

The Tetrarchy: Diocletian and His Colleagues in Rule. Every effort is made to make the two senior rulers and their two junior colleagues look identical. Note also the impassive, symmetrical faces and the emphasis on military strength.

WHAT WERE THE PRINCIPLES BY WHICH DIOCLETIAN REFORMED THE ROMAN EMPIRE?

THE REORGANIZED EMPIRE   205

succession. Realizing that the empire had now become too large for a single, all-powerful ruler to control it effectively, Diocletian divided the empire in half, entrusting the western part to a reliable junior colleague named Maximian while retaining the wealthier, eastern half for himself. The two "augusti" (as Diocletian and Maximian called themselves) then each chose a lieutenant, called a caesar, to govern a subsection of their respective territories. When the two augusti retired, the caesars would step into their place and appoint new caesars in turn to assist them. This system (known as the *tetrarchy*, the "rule of four") was intended to provide more effective governance over the empire by permitting a degree of decentralization. But it was also designed to end the succession disputes that had proven to be the fatal weakness of the Augustan political

system and that had brought the third-century empire to its knees.

Diocletian was also an energetic administrative reformer. Although he retained close personal control over the army, he took steps to separate military from civilian chains of command. Never again would Roman armies make and unmake emperors as they had done in the third century. To control the devastatingly high rates of inflation that were undermining the economy of the empire, Diocletian stabilized the currency and attempted (without much success) to fix prices and wages by legislative fiat. He reformed the tax system, adjusting tax assessments and appointing a small army of new (and immensely unpopular) tax collectors. He also moved the administrative capital of the empire itself from Italy to Nicomedia in modern-day Turkey.

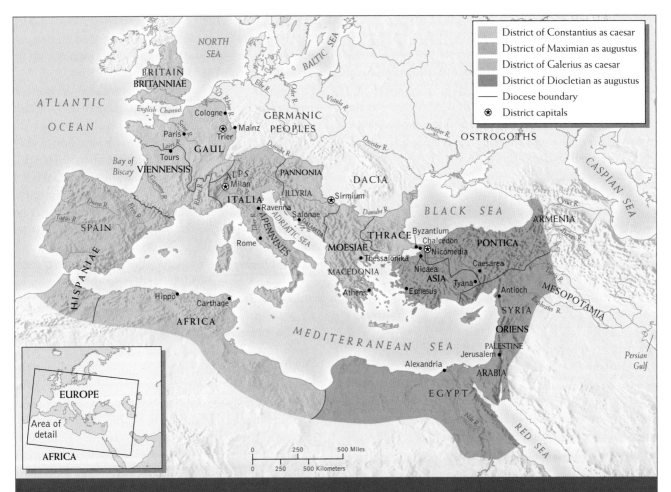

DIOCLETIAN'S DIVISION OF THE EMPIRE, C. 304 C.E.

In a desperate bid to save the Roman Empire from collapse, Diocletian divided it in half. He would control the eastern portion, and Maximian would have the west. Each emperor then chose a lieutenant, thus creating what was called the *tetrarchy* ("the rule of four"). To what extent do the divisions shown on this map mirror those that would characterize the later history of the Mediterranean and European worlds?

Diocletian's Palace in Split. An artist's reconstruction, based on the surviving remains. Its layout was modeled on a Roman army camp.

Rome remained the spiritual and symbolic capital of the empire, not least because the Senate continued to meet there. But Diocletian had little need for the Senate's advice, and the growing disparities of wealth between the eastern and western regions made Nicomedia a more appropriate capital than Rome for an empire that now rested on the backs of its bureaucrats.

THE REIGN OF CONSTANTINE

In 305 C.E. Diocletian built a palace for himself at Split (Croatia) and retired there to raise cabbages—an unprecedented move for a late Roman ruler. At the same time he obliged his colleague Maximian to retire also, and their two caesars moved peacefully up the ladder of succession. But the concord did not last. Civil war broke out among Diocletian's successors and continued until Constantine, the son of one of the original caesars, emerged victorious. From 312 until 324 Constantine ruled as augustus over the western empire, while a junior augustus ruled in the east. In 324 Constantine did away with this arrangement and ruled the reunited empire singlehandedly until his death in 337.

Except for the fact that he favored Christianity (an epoch-making decision to be examined in the next section), Constantine's government followed the precedents laid down by Diocletian. Both men ruled by decree, and both relied on an extensive network of spies and informants to control their empire. In an at-tempt to ensure adequate numbers of troops, Diocletian had already declared army service hereditary. Constantine extended this policy, also binding farmers and craftsmen to their fathers' occupations. These restrictions cannot have been widely enforced, but they are powerful evidence of the social and political regimentation that both Diocletian and Constantine aspired to impose on the empire.

Art and architecture also reflected this new spirit of conformity. Diocletian's palace at Split was laid out like an army camp. The baths he built at Rome covered thirty acres, making up in size what they lacked in grace. Fourth-century imperial portrait busts became impersonal, impassive, and almost interchangeable in their features—a marked change from the strikingly naturalistic and individualized busts of the third century. They also became increasingly bombastic and propagandistic. One of Constantine's statues, located near the forum in Rome, showed the seated emperor at seven times life size, the enlarged eyes emphasizing his spiritual discernment.

In keeping with Constantine's grandiose conception of himself, he built a new capital starting in 324 C.E. and named it Constantinople. Founded on the site of the ancient city of Byzantium, this new capital epitomized the continuing shift in the weight of Roman civilization toward the east. Situated at the mouth of the Black Sea on the border between Europe and Asia, Constantinople had commanding advantages as a center for communications, trade, and defense. Surrounded on three sides by water and protected on land by walls, it would remain the political and economic center of the Roman Empire until 1453, when the city was finally conquered by the Ottoman Turks.

> Situated at the mouth of the Black Sea on the border between Europe and Asia, Constantinople had commanding advantages as a center for communications, trade, and defense.

In one crucial respect, however, Constantine abandoned the precedents established by Diocletian. By making succession to the imperial throne hereditary within his own family, Constantine brought Rome back to the principle of dynastic monarchy it had thrown off 800 years earlier. To make matters worse, Constantine divided the empire among his three sons on his death. Civil war was the predictable result, made worse by differences in the type of Christianity each son espoused.

Dynastic conflicts among Constantine's descendants would continue for most of the fourth century, interrupted periodically by challenges from usurpers aspiring to the imperial throne. But these conflicts were never so serious as the civil wars of the third century,

How did Christianity become the majority religion within the Roman Empire?

The Emergence and Triumph of Christianity   207

Colossal Head of Constantine. This enormous statue of the seated emperor was located just outside the Forum in Rome. It stood forty feet high; the head alone weighed nine tons. The enlarged eyes emphasize the emperor's spiritual vision.

and from time to time a contestant would still be able to reunite the empire. The last to do so was Theodosius I (379–395 C.E.), who butchered thousands of innocent citizens of Thessalonica in retribution for the death of one of his officers but whose efforts to protect the empire against invasions still gave him some claim to his title "the Great." Before Theodosius died, however, he too divided the empire between his two sons: this time with disastrous results, as we shall see in a moment.

Behind these quarrels over the imperial throne we can also discern some larger developments in the history of the fourth-century empire. Most fundamental, divisions between the eastern and the western halves of the empire were becoming steadily more pro-

nounced. As the Greek-speaking east grew more populous, more prosperous, and more central to imperial policy, the Latin-speaking west was becoming poorer and more peripheral to the political, economic, and cultural life of the empire. Many western cities now relied on transfers of funds from the east to keep them going; when these funds dried up or military units were transferred away, these cities declined. Even Rome was becoming something of a backwater in its own empire. When emperors did reside in the west, they found it more convenient to live at Milan, or Ravenna, or on the Rhine frontier at Trier. After the early fourth century, no emperors lived in Rome, and only twice thereafter did an emperor even visit the city.

Nor were the divisions between east and west the only fault lines within an increasingly fractious empire. Secessionist movements cropped up repeatedly among the residents of Britain, Gaul, Spain, and Germany, who were beginning to think of themselves as citizens of a separate, Gaulish empire. Egyptians were particularly hard hit by high levels of taxation on their agricultural lands. North Africans felt ignored by emperors who were concerned primarily with defending their eastern frontiers against the Persians, the Goths, and the Huns. Beneath the surface of imperial autocracy, the fourth-century empire was slowly dissolving into its constituent parts.

THE EMERGENCE AND TRIUMPH OF CHRISTIANITY

How did Christianity become the majority religion within the Roman Empire?

Between the first and fifth centuries C.E., Christianity grew from obscure beginnings in Judea to become the official state religion of the Roman world. Thereafter, it became a dominant (perhaps even the dominant) force in shaping the civilizations of the Western world up to the present day. For Christians, their religion's extraordinary growth and impact is testimony to its truth. For historians, however, it poses an enormous interpretive problem: how can we explain the appeal of early Christianity without making its eventual success seem predictable or even inevitable?

In attempting to do this, it may be useful to recognize at the outset that Christianity appealed to differing groups of people at different stages in its early history

CHRONOLOGY	
THE FOURTH-CENTURY EMPERORS	
Diocletian	284–305 C.E.
Galerius	305–311 C.E.
Constantine	312–337 C.E.
Julian, the Apostate	360–363 C.E.
Theodosius I, the Great	379–395 C.E.

and that each of these groups understood its appeal in rather different ways. Christianity began with the teachings of Jesus, delivered to the Jews of Judea and Galilee around the year 30 C.E. It took firm root, however, largely among the Greek-speaking town dwellers of the eastern Mediterranean during the second and third centuries C.E. Then, starting with Constantine, it became the favored religion of the imperial family and, ultimately, the official religion of the Roman Empire. We will examine these stages in order, starting with the career of Jesus himself.

THE CAREER OF JESUS

There is no doubt that Jesus was a historical figure; he is in fact one of the better-attested figures of the ancient world. But it remains extremely difficult to know very much about him. No strictly contemporary sources mention him, although we do have references to some of his opponents, including the Roman governor Pontius Pilate and the high priest Caiaphas. The earliest written sources that mention Jesus are the letters of one of his followers, the apostle Paul, written during the 50s and 60s C.E.; and the four gospel accounts of Jesus' life plus the Acts of the Apostles, all written between c. 70 and 100 C.E. All these works, together with a number of later sources, are contained in the New Testament, a collection of Christian writings added to the text of the Hebrew Bible during the first three centuries C.E. Other sources also circulated during those years, including a now-lost compilation of Jesus' sayings from which the gospel writers drew some material. It is possible, therefore, that even fairly late, nonbiblical sources such as the second-century Gospel of Thomas may preserve some authentic record of Jesus' teachings. Most historians, however, prefer to rely on the first-century sources in trying to interpret his career.

Jesus was born to a Galilean Jewish family sometime shortly before the beginning of the Common (or Christian) era. He was not born precisely in the year one—we owe this mistake in our dating system to a sixth-century monk. When Jesus was around thirty years old, he was acclaimed by a preacher of moral reform, John the Baptist, as one "mightier than I, whose shoes I am not worthy to untie." Thereafter, Jesus' career was a continuous course of preaching, healing, and teaching, mostly in the rural areas of Galilee and Judea. Around the year 30 C.E., however, he staged an openly messianic entry into Jerusalem during Passover, a religious holiday that brought large and excitable crowds of Jews into the city. Three of the gospel accounts say that he compounded this offence by

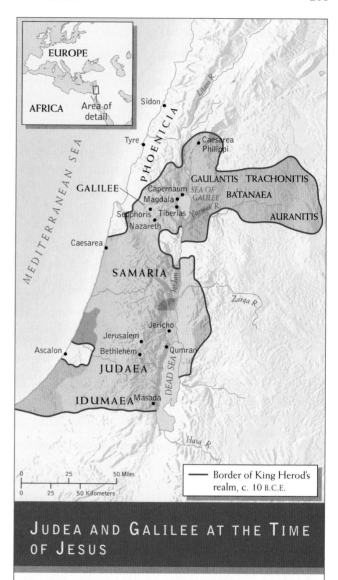

JUDEA AND GALILEE AT THE TIME OF JESUS

Note some of the names of the cities in first-century C.E. Judaea. What was the effect of the Roman occupation on political and everyday life? Why did some Jews resist Roman rule? How did Roman rule affect people's reaction to the Jesus movement? Where were the Dead Sea Scrolls discovered? What did they reveal about life in Ancient Judea?

physically attacking merchants and moneychangers associated with the Temple sacrifices. The city's religious leaders quickly arrested him and turned him over to Pontius Pilate, the Roman governor, for sentencing. Pilate's main concern was to preserve peace during a volatile religious festival; he was also no doubt anxious to maintain good relations with the religious authorities in Jerusalem. He chose to make an example of Jesus by condemning him to death by crucifixion, a standard Roman criminal penalty for those judged guilty of sedition against Rome.

How did Christianity become the majority religion within the Roman Empire?

The Emergence and Triumph of Christianity 209

This might have been the end of the story. But soon after Jesus' execution, rumors began to spread that Jesus was alive and had been seen by some of his followers. He had risen from the dead, his followers now proclaimed, and after forty days had ascended into heaven, promising to return again at the end of time. In life Jesus had been a religious teacher and healer; in death, however, he had been revealed as something more. His entire career now had to be rethought and reinterpreted by his followers. The evidence of this reinterpretation has come down to us in the letters of Paul and in the gospel narratives of Matthew, Mark, Luke, and John.

JESUS AND SECOND TEMPLE JUDAISM

In 1947, a Bedouin boy discovered an extraordinary cache of Jewish religious texts that had been hidden in a cave near Qumran at some point during the first century C.E. Only since the mid-1980s, however, has the bulk of this material, known collectively as the Dead Sea Scrolls, been made widely available to scholars. These scrolls have revolutionized our understanding of Jewish religious practice and belief around the time of Jesus. Most of all they emphasize its extraordinary diversity.

When Jesus was born, the Roman conquest of Judea was less than a generation old. Banditry, sometimes tinged with nationalism, was commonplace in the countryside; in the cities and villages, there was talk of rebellion and hope for a messiah who would restore Jewish rule over the holy land of Israel. Most extreme of those who sought hope in politics were the Zealots, who sought to expel the Romans by force of arms. Their activities eventually led to two disastrous revolts. The first, between 66 and 70 C.E., brought about the destruction of the Jewish Temple at Jerusalem by the avenging Romans. The second, in 132–135 C.E., caused the destruction of the city of Jerusalem and the expulsion of its entire Jewish population.

This political context is important to understanding Pilate's decision to execute Jesus; but it tells us little about what Jesus actually taught or how his teachings might have been understood by his fellow Jews. To this purpose, the religious divisions within contemporary Judaism are much more important.

In the centuries after the Jews' return from Babylon and the rebuilding of the Temple, Judaism became an uncompromisingly monotheistic religion, built on the covenantal relationship between Yahweh and his chosen people. By the first century B.C.E., however, important differences had emerged in how Jews understood what that covenant required of them. Jesus' teachings need to be seen in the context of these debates.

The guardians of the written traditions enshrined in the Torah (the first five books of the Hebrew Bible) were the hereditary Temple priesthood and their aristocratic allies, a group known as the Sadducees. As one would expect in the ancient world, the alliance between religious and political authorities in Judea was close. Before the Roman conquest, the high priest of the Temple at Jerusalem had been appointed by the Hasmonean Jewish monarchs, who had secured their independence from the Seleucid rulers of Syria during the second century B.C.E. After the Roman conquest, however, the high priest was appointed by Rome. As a result, the Sadducees were inevitably tainted by suspicions of

> In the centuries after the Jews' return from Babylon and the rebuilding of the Temple, Judaism became an uncompromisingly monotheistic religion, built on the covenantal relationship between Yahweh and his chosen people.

Jesus. This depiction of Jesus with long hair and a beard from a third-century C.E. stone inlay is strikingly different from the Roman style.

collaborationism, despite the central role they played in the religious observances of the Temple cult.

Their main rivals for the religious allegiance of the people were the Pharisees, a group of teachers and preachers of religious law who were in some ways the heirs to the prophetic tradition of the First Temple period. In contrast to the Sadducees, who considered most of the requirements of religious law to pertain only to the priesthood, the Pharisees insisted that all 613 of Yahweh's commandments were binding on all Jews. As interpreters of religious law, they rested their authority on their claim that at Sinai, Yahweh had given Moses both a written and an oral Torah. The written Torah was contained in the Bible; but the oral Torah, which explained how the written Torah should be interpreted and applied to daily life, had been handed down by the spoken word, from teachers to students, down the generations from Moses to the present day.

The Pharisees urged rigorous devotion to religious law, but they were also quite flexible in applying it to daily life. For example, to allow neighbors to dine together on the Sabbath day of rest (when Jews were forbidden to work, even by carrying food outside their homes), the Pharisees were quite prepared to regard an entire neighborhood as constituting a single home for the purposes of Sabbath observance. They also believed in a life after death characterized by individual rewards and punishments. They actively sought out converts through preaching and looked forward to the imminent arrival of the messiah whom God had promised to his people. In all these respects they differed from the more traditional Sadducees. Even more radical, however, were various splinter groups such as the Essenes, a quasi-monastic group that hoped for spiritual deliverance through asceticism, repentance, and strict sectarian separation from their fellow Jews.

Although some scholars see Essene influence behind the career of Jesus, his Jewish contemporaries probably saw Jesus as some sort of radical Pharisee. Jesus' emphasis on the ethical requirements of the law (love of God and neighbor; the obligation to do good even to those who harm you and to forgive those who wrong you), his apparent belief in life after death and in the imminent coming of "the kingdom of God," and his exhortations to obey the spirit rather than the letter of religious law all fitted well within a Pharisaic framework. Nevertheless, he seems to have carried these

principles considerably further than did most Pharisees. When, for example, his followers broke the laws of the Sabbath by gathering grain to eat, Jesus justified them by declaring, "The Sabbath was made for man, not man for the Sabbath." By extending Pharisaic reasoning to such a degree, Jesus' teachings threatened to undermine completely the obligatory nature of Jewish law as the Pharisees understood it.

None of these groups was monolithic; even the Essenes, the most sectarian of them all, included a variety of different beliefs and practices within their order. And the vast majority of Jews would not have identified themselves with any of these groups. Even the Sadducees are best regarded as a sect within the larger Temple priesthood. For most Jews at the time of Jesus, Judaism consisted of going up to the Temple at Jerusalem a few times a year on holy days; paying the annual Temple tax; reciting the morning and evening prayers; and observing certain fundamental religious laws, such as circumcision (for men), ritual purity (especially for women), and prohibitions on Sabbath work and on the consumption of such forbidden foods as pork, blood, and shellfish.

Jesus may have stretched such observances, but there is no evidence he sought to abrogate them. Rather, what made him controversial within the larger Jewish community was his followers' claim that he was the messiah promised by God to deliver Israel from its enemies. After his death and alleged resurrection, such claims grew louder and more assertive, but they never persuaded more than a small minority of Jesus' fellow Jews. As his followers began to preach to non-Jewish audiences, however, they began to reinterpret Jesus' role as messiah in terms that drew on Greek theological ideas. Jesus, his followers now proclaimed, was not merely a messiah for the Jews. He was the *Christ* (from the Greek for "anointed one"), the divine Son of God sent to earth to suffer and die for the sins of all humanity, who had risen from the dead and ascended into heaven, and who would return to judge all the world's inhabitants at the end of time.

> In contrast to the Sadducees, who considered most of the requirements of religious law to pertain only to the priesthood, the Pharisees insisted that all 613 of Yahweh's commandments were binding on all Jews.

THE GROWTH OF CHRISTIANITY IN THE HELLENISTIC WORLD

The key figure in developing this new theological understanding of Jesus' messiahship was Saul of Tarsus (c. 10–c. 67 C.E.). Saul was a Jew born in southeast Asia

HOW DID CHRISTIANITY BECOME THE MAJORITY RELIGION WITHIN THE ROMAN EMPIRE?

THE EMERGENCE AND TRIUMPH OF CHRISTIANITY   211

Saint Paul. This early Christian mosaic depicts the self-declared apostle to the gentiles, formerly known as Saul of Tarsus, who was a key figure in developing the theological understanding of Jesus' messiahship.

communities had already begun to reinterpret Jewish religious ideas within a Greek intellectual and cultural context. As Paul's own example suggests, to some of these Hellenized Jews the new Christian teachings must have been attractive. Even more so, however, Christianity probably appealed to the groups of non-Jews (known as "God-fearers") who tended to gather around these Greek-speaking Jewish communities. God-fearers did not follow all the precepts of Jewish law (most Greeks and Romans regarded circumcision with particular horror); but they admired Jews for their monotheism and for their uncompromising moral and ethical standards and modeled their own lives after Jewish example. But Christianity must also have made inroads among ordinary Greeks, many of whom would already have been familiar with other, superficially similar cults (such as Mithraism and the cult of Serapis) that also stressed elaborate initiation ceremonies (for Christians, baptism) and the importance of special religious knowledge for salvation.

Certain differences between Christianity and these other mystery religions do stand out. Unlike other contemporary sects that also stressed individual transformation through personal conversion, Christianity had a strongly communal aspect. Organizational structures evolved very early; by the middle of the second century, the Christian church at Rome already had a bishop who presided over a small army of lesser office-holders, including priests, deacons, confessors, and exorcists. Women were also notably prominent in these

Minor. A staunch Pharisee, Saul was initially a persecutor of Jesus' followers; but after a blinding conversion experience, he joined the Jesus movement, changed his name to Paul, and devoted his limitless energy to interpreting and preaching the new faith to the Greek-speaking, mainly non-Jewish communities of Greece and Asia Minor. Declaring himself to be the apostle to the gentiles (non-Jews), Paul rejected the binding nature of Jewish religious law, declaring it to be irrelevant to salvation for Jesus' followers. This stance initially caused offense among the Jewish Christians of Jerusalem, a group led by Jesus' brother, James; but after a wrenching debate, Paul's position triumphed. Some Christians would continue to obey Jewish religious law, but the movement's future now lay clearly with the non-Jewish converts it was making outside Judea and Galilee.

It is not entirely clear who the majority of these new converts were. By the first century C.E., sizable Jewish communities existed in most major cities of the eastern Mediterranean world, including Rome itself. These

Mithras Slaying the Bull. The bull's blood brought about the rebirth of light at midwinter and so the revival of life. Mithras's Phrygian cap and leggings emphasize his eastern origins.

early Christian communities, not only as patrons and benefactors (a role upper-class Roman women had often played in new religious cults) but also as office-holders (although we know of no female bishops or priests, female deacons are well attested). This relatively high status of women was quite unusual and distinguished Christianity markedly from Mithraism, which excluded women even from membership in the cult, much less from holding any office within it. Christians were also well known for supporting their poorer members through charity. Christianity drew its adherents from a broad range of social classes, but it may have had a special appeal to people (such as urban artisans) whose livelihoods could disappear with a shift of the economic winds.

All these factors help explain the appeal of the new religion, especially to the Greek-speaking urban dwellers who made up the vast majority of Christian converts during the second and third centuries C.E. Nevertheless, why people chose to become Christians remains an impossible question for historians to answer with certainty. It is often suggested that Christianity's promise of salvation was a powerful inducement to conversion, especially in the chaotic world of the third century C.E. This may be so; but the claim rests simply on the facts that Christianity was growing during the third century and that Christians believed in life after death. We have no real way to prove that the second fact led to the first. All we can say for certain is that a growing number of people in the second- and third-

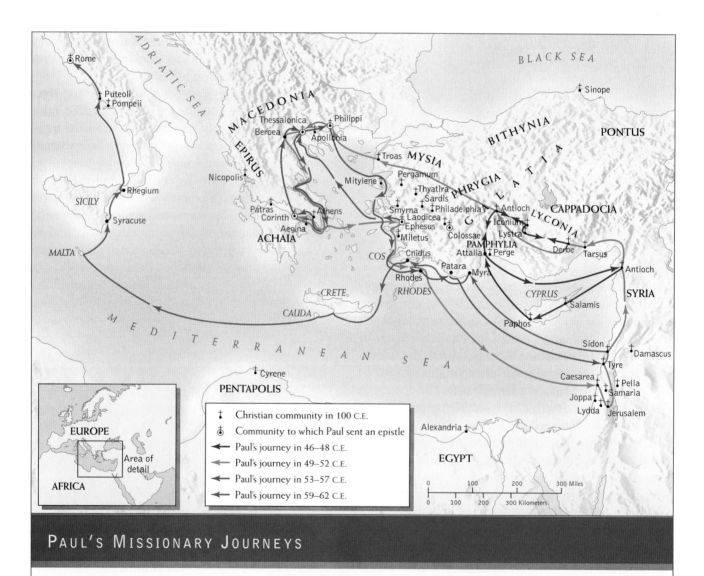

PAUL'S MISSIONARY JOURNEYS

Why did the message of Paul and the Jesus movement appeal to the non-Jews of the Mediterranean world? What was the main issue that divided Paul and the Christian Jews of Jerusalem? What were the consequences of Paul's travels throughout the Greek world?

How did Christianity become the majority religion within the Roman Empire?

The Emergence and Triumph of Christianity   213

century Mediterranean world believed Christian teachings to be true and that they were prepared to accept these teachings despite the disapproval they generated within Greco-Roman and Jewish society.

One final consequence of Christianity's growth within these Greek-speaking communities needs to be mentioned: the developing hostility between Christianity and Judaism. Both religions were redefining themselves during the second and third centuries: Christianity as it accommodated itself to its new Greek cultural milieu, and Judaism as it adapted itself to the destruction of the Temple and the mass exile of Jews from the Holy Land. By and large, the Jewish scholars who reshaped Judaism's understanding of religious law during these years ignored Christianity. It simply did not matter to them, any more than did Mithraism or the cult of Serapis. Christians, however, could not ignore Judaism. Their religion rested on the belief that Jesus was the savior promised by God to Israel in the Hebrew Bible. That so few Jews accepted this claim was therefore seen by Christians as a standing rebuke to their faith, one that undermined (at least potentially) the credibility of the entire Christian message.

Christians might have responded as did Marcion, a second-century Christian scholar who declared the Hebrew Bible irrelevant to Christianity. Most Christians, however, refused to abandon their religion's Jewish roots. Instead, they reinterpreted the messianic prophecies and the covenantal relationship between God and Israel. Christians, they now argued, were the true Israel; when Jews rejected Jesus as messiah, God rejected the Jews and made Christians his new chosen people. At the end of time, Judaism would disappear; until then, its only reason for existing was to testify, through its own messianic prophecies and its people's tragedies, that Christians were right about Jesus and that Jews were wrong.

Christianity and the Roman Empire

So long as Christianity remained a minority religion within the Roman Empire, such attitudes had no effect on the position of Jews under the Roman state. Throughout the second and third centuries C.E., Judaism remained a legally recognized religion within the Roman Empire. Whatever their attitudes toward Jewish belief and practice, Romans respected the fact that Jews were at least maintaining the religious customs of their ancestors.

Christianity, in contrast, was an innovation; and in the eyes of traditional Romans, novelty in religion was not a good thing. Nevertheless, the official attitude of the Roman state toward Christianity was usually one of indifference. During the first and second centuries C.E., Christians were tolerated by Roman authorities except when local magistrates chose to prosecute them for refusing to worship the official state gods. During the third century there were some concerted, centrally organized persecutions; the last of these took place toward the end of Diocletian's reign and the beginning of the reign of his successor Galerius. But these were too intermittent and short lived to do irreparable damage; and by the early fourth century, the religion had gained too many adherents to be wiped out by persecution, a fact Galerius finally recognized by issuing an edict of toleration just before his death in 311 C.E.

Still, however, the number of Christians was not large. No reliable statistics exist, but most scholars now believe that in the year 300 only 1 to 5 percent of the total population of the empire was Christian. Even in the relatively more Christianized eastern parts of the empire, no more than 10 percent of the population was Christian, and this estimate is probably generous. Christian numbers were growing and might have continued to grow. But it seems unlikely Christianity would ever have become the majority religion in the empire without the help of the emperor Constantine.

Constantine's Christian Symbol. This mosaic, from a fourth-century Roman villa in southern England, shows the chi–rho symbol Constantine saw in the sky shortly before his victory at the Milvian Bridge. Chi and rho are the first two letters in the Greek word for "Christ." Flanking this monogram are the first and last letters of the Greek alphabet, alpha and omega, which were also used to refer to Jesus (Revelation 1:8).

PROSECUTING CHRISTIANS

THE LETTERS OF PLINY THE YOUNGER
AND THE EMPEROR TRAJAN

Until the third century, the Roman imperial government rarely initiated the persecution of Christians. Local administrators, such as the younger Pliny, were anxious to follow proper legal procedures in dealing with the new sect, which they regarded as absurd but not particularly dangerous. But neither Pliny nor the emperor Trajan (98–117 C.E.) wanted to see the Roman state actively seek out Christians for punishment.

LETTER 97: PLINY TO TRAJAN

It is a rule, Sir, which I inviolably observe, to refer myself to you in all my doubts; for who is more capable of removing my scruples, or informing my ignorance? Having never been present at any trials concerning those who profess Christianity, I am unacquainted not only with the nature of their crimes, or the measure of their punishment, but how far it is proper to enter into an examination concerning them. . . .

The method I have observed towards those who have been brought before me as Christians, is this: I interrogated them whether they were Christians; if they confessed I repeated the question twice again, adding threats at the same time; when, if they still persevered, I ordered them to be immediately punished: for I was persuaded, whatever the nature of their opinions might be, a contumacious and inflexible obstinacy certainly deserved correction. . . .

But this crime spreading (as is usually the case) while it was actually under prosecution, several instances of the same nature occurred. An information was presented to me without any name subscribed, containing a charge against several persons, who upon examination denied they were Christians, or had ever been so.

They repeated after me an invocation to the gods, and offered religious rites with wine and frankincense before your statue (which for the purpose I had ordered to be brought together with those of the gods); and even reviled the name of Christ: whereas there is no forcing, it is said, those who are really Christians, into a compliance with any of these articles: I thought proper therefore to discharge them. . . .

I judged it . . . necessary to endeavor to extort the real truth [about Christian rites and beliefs] by putting two female slaves to the torture, who were said to administer in their religious functions: but I could discover nothing more than an absurd and excessive superstition. I thought proper therefore to adjourn all further proceedings in this affair, in order to consult with you. . . . For this contagious superstition is not confined to the cities only, but has spread its infection among the country villages. Nevertheless, it still seems possible to remedy this evil and restrain its progress. The temples, at least, which were once almost deserted, begin now to be frequented; and the sacred solemnities, after a long intermission, are again revived. . . . From hence it is easy to imagine, what numbers might be reclaimed from this error, if a pardon were granted to those who shall repent.

LETTER 98: TRAJAN TO PLINY

The method you have pursued, my dear Pliny, in the proceedings against those Christians which were brought before you, is extremely proper; as it is not possible to lay down any fixed plan by which to act in all cases of this nature. But I would not have you officiously enter into any enquiries concerning them. If indeed they should be brought before you, and the crime is proved, they must be punished; with the restriction, however, that where the party denies himself to be a Christian, and shall make it evident that he is not, by invoking our gods, let him (notwithstanding any former suspicion) be pardoned upon his repentence. Information without the accuser's name subscribed ought not to be received in prosecutions of any sort, as it is introducing a very dangerous precedent, and by no means agreeable to the equity of my government.

W. Melmoth, trans. *The Letters of Pliny the Consul,* vol. 2 (London, 1770), pp. 671–677. Reprinted in Brian Tierney and Joan Scott, eds., *Western Societies: A Documentary History,* vol. 1 (New York, 1984), pp. 166–168.

QUESTIONS FOR ANALYSIS

1. Pliny and Trajan were friends, but Pliny was careful to get the emperor's approval of his legal procedures. He was unsure whether simply being a Christian was a crime, but he knew that lying about church membership constituted perjury and refusing to perform ritual honors to the emperor was equal to rebellion and treason, all crimes that should be punished. What does this say about official Roman ideas of honor, propriety, and justice?

2. During judicial examinations, subjects were routinely tortured to extort more information from them. Yet when Pliny tortured two deaconesses, he found only "absurd and excessive superstition." What did he conclude from this? What seemed the best way to fight this superstition?

Constantine's decision to become a Christian continues to puzzle historians. He must have had some contact with Christianity as a young man; he may even have been a nominal Christian at the time he launched his bid for the imperial throne. His real commitment to the faith came later, however, after he saw a Christian symbol in the sky while preparing for battle at the Milvian Bridge (312 C.E.) and heard a heavenly voice declaring, "In this sign, conquer." Constantine ordered his soldiers to paint the symbol on their shields; the victory they won that day propelled him to the imperial throne.

As emperor, Constantine showered favors on the Christian clergy and patronized the construction of churches throughout the empire. By the end of his reign, his support for Christianity was costing him more than his entire civil service. But Constantine did not make Christianity the official religion of the empire, nor did he prohibit pagan worship. He did, however, make Christianity the favored religion of the imperial family, transforming Christianity, almost overnight, into a prestigious and potentially profitable religion for the ruling classes of the empire to adopt. Gradually, the rest of the citizens of the empire followed suit. By the end of the fourth century C.E., a clear majority of the empire was Christian, and bishops had emerged as dominating influences in the political life of their cities.

Constantine himself retained both pagan and Christian officials around his court and was careful in his public pronouncements to speak in terms that would be acceptable to a non-Christian audience. His successors, however, became more and more uncompromisingly Christian in their orientation and less and less inclined to tolerate competing faiths. A brief exception was the reign of Julian "the Apostate" (360–363 C.E.), who abandoned Christianity and attempted to revive traditional Roman paganism. But Julian was killed in battle with the Persians, his pro-pagan edicts were revoked, and the Christian officials around the imperial court became more insistent that imperial power be used to suppress competing cults. Finally, Theodosius the Great (379–395 C.E.) did so, prohibiting pagan worship of any sort within the empire and removing the altar of the goddess Victory from the Senate house in Rome. Fifteen years later, Rome fell to the Visigoths. Pagan spokesmen noted the connection.

> As emperor, Constantine showered favors on the Christian clergy and patronized the construction of churches throughout the empire. By the end of his reign, his support for Christianity was costing him more than his entire civil service.

THE NEW CONTOURS OF FOURTH-CENTURY CHRISTIANITY

What major changes did Christianity undergo during the fourth century?

As Christianity became politically influential and socially prestigious, it underwent major changes in doctrine, organization, and outlook. As a result, Christianity at the end of the fourth century was in many respects a quite different religion from the one persecuted by Diocletian and Galerius only a century before.

DOCTRINAL QUARRELS

One consequence of Christianity's new prominence was the flaring up of bitter doctrinal disputes. Christians had of course disagreed about doctrinal matters before; but as long as Christianity remained the religion of an unimportant minority, these disagreements were of little political or social consequence. With Constantine's accession to the imperial throne, however, such disagreements now had the potential to ignite political quarrels (even rioting) among bishops and their opponents and to undermine imperial support for the church itself. It was imperative, therefore, that such doctrinal disputes be resolved, if necessary through the active intervention of the Christian emperor himself.

The most fundamental doctrinal dispute to erupt was between the Arians and Athanasians over the nature of the Trinity. The Arians—not to be confused with Aryans (a racial term)—were followers of a priest named Arius. Influenced by Greek philosophy, they rejected the idea that Jesus, as the Christ, could be equal with God. Instead they maintained that as the Son of God, Jesus was created by the Father in time and therefore was not coeternal with him or formed of the same substance. The followers of Saint Athanasius argued the opposite: even though Christ was the Son he was also fully God; and so Father, Son, and Holy Ghost (the Trinity) were all absolutely equal and composed of an identical substance. After protracted struggles, the Athanasian doctrine became the orthodox Christian position, and Arianism was declared a heresy. But Arianism continued to attract followers for the next 200 years.

This new emphasis on the importance of orthodoxy (Greek for "correct teaching") was one of the most important developments within fourth-century Christianity. It would color the entire subsequent history of the church. From its earliest days, Christianity had insisted on the importance of correct belief to salvation. But the beliefs on which it insisted were initially fairly simple: there was one God; Jesus was the Christ; to be saved, his followers must renounce sin and be baptized into the church. By the fourth century, Christian theology had already become considerably more complex. Now, however, Christian intellectuals had to show that their beliefs could withstand the most intense philosophical scrutiny. To present Christianity as true philosophy, Christian theology had to be made compatible with Greek and Roman philosophical presumptions. But just as there were many different schools of Greek and Roman thought, so there arose many different interpretations of Christian doctrine.

Resolving such disputes was intensely difficult. Often they involved not only doctrinal differences but regional and political differences as well. They also raised difficult questions of authority. In the second and third centuries C.E., doctrinal disputes had been resolved by discussions among bishops at local or regional councils. But if the losing party refused to accept the verdict, such councils had no coercive authority by which to enforce their decisions. Now, however, the stakes were higher. In the fourth century, doctrinal disputes often had political consequences; and the emperor himself was also involved. As a result, the Roman state became increasingly enmeshed in the governance of the church, especially in the eastern half of the empire. Constantine himself began this process in 325 C.E., when he summoned and presided over the Council of Nicea, which condemned Arianism. His successors carried it much further. Gradually, these Christian emperors began to claim that in presiding over such councils, they were assuming a role as Christ's representative on earth which entitled them to decide what Christian doctrine was and should be. Some even dispatched troops to suppress Christian groups who refused to accept the emperor's decisions on orthodoxy. Those who rejected such decisions were labeled heretics and could suffer both legal and ecclesiastical penalties.

Ever since Augustus, Roman emperors had acted as the presiding religious authorities for the civic observances of Roman paganism. Constantine and the Christian emperors who succeeded him were now showing how this traditional imperial role could be adapted to fit the new realities of a Christianizing Roman Empire.

WHAT MAJOR CHANGES DID CHRISTIANITY UNDERGO DURING THE FOURTH CENTURY?

THE NEW CONTOURS OF FOURTH-CENTURY CHRISTIANITY   217

GROWTH OF ECCLESIASTICAL ORGANIZATION

This fourth-century consolidation of religion with imperial authority was reflected also in the church's own internal organization. As we have seen, church offices had existed since at least the second century C.E. During the fourth century, however, the church became a much more clearly defined hierarchical organization, as urban-centered bishops (often from powerful local families) began to assert closer control over the priests and deacons of their surrounding areas. Distinctions of rank among the bishops themselves also began to emerge. Bishops who ruled from the larger cities came to be called metropolitans (today known in the West as archbishops), with authority over the clergy of an entire province. In the fourth century the still higher rank of patriarch was established to designate bishops who ruled over the oldest and largest Christian communities, such as Rome, Jerusalem, Constantinople, Antioch, and Alexandria. By 400 C.E., the Christian clergy was thus made up of a definite hierarchy of patriarchs, metropolitans, bishops, priests, and deacons —from which women were now firmly and completely excluded.

The climax of this development was the primacy of the bishop of Rome, or the rise of the papacy. The bishop of Rome's claim to preeminence over the other patriarchs of the church rested on several foundations. Rome itself was venerated by the faithful as the place where the apostles Peter and Paul had been martyred. Peter was widely regarded as having been the first bishop of Rome; and the New Testament said (Matthew 16:18–19) that Jesus himself had commissioned Peter as his representative on earth, with the power to admit or deny the entrance of any Christian to the kingdom of heaven. As Peter's successors, subsequent bishops of Rome claimed to exercise the same powers Jesus had given to Peter.

The bishops of Rome also enjoyed some more prosaic advantages over the other bishops within the church. Unlike the eastern bishops, the Roman bishop after 330 C.E. rarely had an emperor on his doorstep. As a result, he could act with considerably more

Early Christian Mosaic from the Mausoleum of Galla Placidia, Fifth Century C.E. This mosaic depicting Jesus as the good shepherd was built in a church honoring Galla Placidia, the devout Christian daughter of Emperor Theodosius I, half-sister of Emperors Honorius and Arcadius, wife of Emperor Constantius, and mother of Emperor Valentinian III.

independence than could the patriarch of Constantinople. At the same time, however, it was often convenient for eastern emperors to support papal claims to authority over the western bishops as a way of maintaining some semblance of imperial control over the western empire. This was probably what lay behind the decree in 445 C.E. by the eastern emperor Valentinian III commanding all western bishops to submit to the jurisdiction of the pope. Centuries later, this decree would be cited to justify the dominance the papacy had by then achieved over the western church. At the time, however, it was ignored by everyone except the pope himself. Most eastern bishops regarded the pope's claims to primacy over the entire church as brazen effrontery, and even many western bishops paid no attention to him. The prestige of the bishops of Rome was nonetheless growing during the fourth and fifth centuries; and although the popes were not yet the monarchical rulers they would eventually become, the roots of their primacy lie here.

The increasing effectiveness of ecclesiastical organization and administration during the fourth century helped the church both conquer the Roman world and minister to the needs of the faithful. The existence of an episcopal ("bishop-centered") administrative structure was particularly important in the west, as the Roman Empire decayed and eventually collapsed during the fifth century. In the deepening chaos, western bishops took over many of the functions of urban government and preserved the vestiges of Roman rule. As a result, when barbarian armies arrived it was usually with the local bishop whom they negotiated.

THE SPREAD OF MONASTICISM

To most Christians, the increasing administrative responsibilities of the church seemed natural: religion and politics had always been closely connected throughout the history of the Roman Empire. To some Christians, however, the new world seemed a far cry indeed from the simple faith of Jesus and his apostles. Monasticism was one outgrowth of such disillusionment. Today we tend to think of monks as groups of priests who live communally and dedicate themselves to contemplation and prayer. In their origins, however, monks were not priests but laymen, who almost always lived alone and who sought extremes of self-denial rather than ordered lives of corporate prayer and service.

Monasticism began to emerge in the third century as a response to the anxieties of that age, but it became a dominant movement within Christianity only in the

CHRONOLOGY

THE GROWTH OF CHRISTIANITY, FIRST–FIFTH CENTURIES C.E.

Life of Jesus	c. 4 B.C.E.–c. 30 C.E.
Paul's missionary journeys	46–62 C.E.
Destruction of the Temple at Jerusalem	69–70 C.E.
Expulsion of the Jews from Jerusalem	132–135 C.E.
Constantine becomes the first Christian emperor	312 C.E.
Council of Nicea	325 C.E.
Christianity becomes official religion of the Roman Empire	c. 392 C.E.
Era of doctrinal quarrels	fourth–fifth centuries C.E.

fourth century. There were two main reasons for monasticism's appeal. As persecution of Christians ended, extreme asceticism sometimes functioned as a substitute for martyrdom. More obviously, however, the growth of monasticism was a response to the increasing worldliness of the fourth-century church. Christians seeking to avoid earthly temptations fled to the deserts and woods to practice an ascetic lifestyle altogether different from the lives led by the well-to-do men and women who were now flocking to join the religion of their emperor. In a church filled with such social Christians, monasticism seemed to some purists the only certain road to salvation.

Monasticism first emerged in the east, where it spread rapidly during the fourth century. Early monks lived mostly as hermits and practiced extraordinary feats of self-denial and self-abasement. Some grazed in the fields like cows, others penned themselves into small cages, while others hung heavy weights around their necks. A monk named Cyriacus stood for hours on one leg like a crane until he could bear it no more. Another, Saint Simeon Stylites, lived on top of a high pillar for thirty-seven years, where he performed self-punishing exercises while crowds gathered below to worship "the worms that dropped from his body."

Soon, however, monastic leaders began to realize that the movement would benefit from a more organized and disciplined approach. In the east, the most important architect of this new, more communal form of monastic life was Saint Basil (c. 330–379). Basil's

WHAT MAJOR CHANGES DID CHRISTIANITY UNDERGO DURING THE FOURTH CENTURY?

THE NEW CONTOURS OF FOURTH-CENTURY CHRISTIANITY   219

guidelines prohibited monks from engaging in prolonged fasts or lacerating their flesh; instead he encouraged monks to discipline themselves by useful labor. He also urged them to embrace the virtues of poverty and humility and to spend many hours each day in silent religious meditation. He continued, however, to urge them to live as far away from the world as they could; as a result, Basilian monasticism ultimately had less effect on the world outside the cloister than did the Benedictine monastic tradition in western Europe.

Monasticism did not initially spread as quickly in the west as it did in the east. Only in the sixth century, when Saint Benedict of Nursia (c. 480–c. 547) drafted his famous Latin Rule, did monasticism begin to grow rapidly in western Europe; and even then it took many forms, of which Benedictine monasticism was but one. Only in the eighth century did the monastic tradition established by Benedict become the predominant pattern for western monasticism; and from the thirteenth century on, Benedictine monasticism once again had many rivals. Its impact, however, was enormous, especially during the Middle Ages. We shall consider only its origins here; we will discuss its influence in several subsequent chapters.

Benedict copied much of his Rule from an earlier and much harsher Latin text known as the Rule of the Master. Benedict, however, produced a very different document: a "simple rule for beginners" as he called it, notable for its brevity, flexibility, and moderation. The rule established a carefully defined cycle of daily prayers, lessons, and communal worship. It laid down guidelines for how monks ought to live together; what they should eat (a sufficiency of simple food; a small amount of wine; meat only for the sick or on special occasions), and how the work of the monastery should be performed. Physical labor was encouraged —idleness, Benedict declared, was "an enemy of the soul"—but he also reserved time for private study and contemplation. In all such matters, however, Benedict left much to the discretion of the abbot, the leader of the monastery, whom all the monks were expected to obey without hesitation.

Those who sought entrance to a Benedictine monastery had to fulfill a lengthy probationary period. Only at the end of this period could they take their final, lifelong vows as a monk. Scholars have sometimes summarized the Benedictine vows as requiring "poverty, chastity, and obedience." This, however, is misleading. Certainly these were important virtues, but they were not the essence of the Rule to which a Benedictine monk committed himself. Rather, the chief virtues of Benedictine life were stability, perseverance, and commitment to the monastic life itself. The goal of the Rule, as of monastic life generally, was to enable the monks who lived by it to transform their lives in accordance with the will of God. The Rule itself was the means by which this transformation could be accomplished.

Saint Simeon Stylites on His Pillar. The devil is shown as a huge snake. Admirers who wished to speak to the saint would climb the ladder shown on the left. This gold plaque dates from the sixth century.

CHANGING ATTITUDES TOWARD WOMEN, MARRIAGE, AND THE BODY

The sweeping changes in Christian attitudes and institutions that occurred during the fourth century had a particular impact on the position of women. As we have seen, women exercised an unusual degree of influence within the early church. Saint Paul had relied heavily on the support of prominent women in his missionary journeys. He declared in his letter to the Galatians (3:28) that among Christians there should be no spiritual distinctions, either between slaves and freemen or between men and women: all were equal in the eyes of God. Upper-class women were also important patrons of the early church at Rome and elsewhere. Women were prominent among the martyrs of the early church, and in some churches women also served as teachers, prophets, and officers of the local congregation. Women's roles were clearly controversial in the early church; but the diversity of opinions reflected in the New Testament shows clearly that the early church was not a uniformly patriarchal institution.

An Early Christian Woman. This fresco of a woman praying in the orans position (with her hands stretched out) is from the catacomb of Giordani in Rome.

With the growth of asceticism as a spiritual ideal during the third and fourth centuries, denigration of women as dangerously "fleshly" creatures became more pronounced. Monks, of course, shunned women completely—one reason they fled to deserts and forests. But the Christian clergy were also swept up by the increasingly puritanical sexual and social attitudes that characterized the late antique world. Several of Jesus' apostles had been married, and in the early church it was commonly accepted that priests and bishops would be married men. Indeed, marriage was so important a marker of social respectability in the Roman world that an unmarried man would often be greeted with suspicion. Only philosophers were customarily exempted from expectations of marriage. During the fourth century, however, the idea developed that, like philosophers, priests and bishops also ought not to marry; or, if they were already married, that they should live in sexually chaste relationships with their wives.

Virginity for both men and women thus came to be accepted as the highest spiritual standard within the church. Marriage remained acceptable for the laity, but it was very much a second-best option for those who lacked the willpower to be sexually abstinent. Saint Jerome expressed this view most earthily when he declared virginity to be wheat, marriage barley, and sexual relations outside marriage to be cow dung. Since people should not eat cow dung, God permitted them barley; but wheat was by far the preferable food. The purpose of marriage was to prevent fornication and to produce children; Jerome, however, praised marriage principally because it brought more virgins into the world.

Because women were regarded as more innately lustful than men, this denigration of sexuality had a disproportionately negative effect on male attitudes toward women. But by rejecting marriage (or at least presenting it as an undesirable alternative to virginity) and exalting monastic withdrawal from the world, fourth-century Christianity also made a decisive break with earlier Roman attitudes toward the human body and the state. Traditionally, Romans had regarded citizens' bodies as being at the service of the state: men as soldiers and fathers, women as mothers and wives. Now, however, Christians were asserting that their bodies belonged not to the state but to God and that to serve God fully meant that they would no longer serve the state by bearing children. This was a revolutionary shift in attitudes, one more sign of the way the ancient world was slowly passing away during late antiquity.

CHANGING ATTITUDES TOWARD THE CELIBACY OF BISHOPS

Bishops, priests, and deacons had emerged as key figures in the organization of the early Christian church by the mid-second century C.E. Until the fourth century, Christians presumed that such officials would be married, as we see from the Didascalia, an early third-century church manual. In the fourth century, however, efforts were made, especially in the west, to require these officials to be celibate. This shift reflects an increasing admiration for asceticism as a mark of holiness that characterized both Christians and non-Christians during the fourth century.

THE DIDASCALIA

The shepherd who is appointed bishop and head among the presbyterate [that is, the priesthood] in the church in every congregation: "It is required of him that he shall be blameless, in nothing reproachable" [1 Timothy 3:2; Titus 1:7], one remote from all evil, a man not less than fifty years of age, who is now removed from the conduct of youth and from the lusts of the adversary, and from the slander and blasphemy of false brethren. . . . But if it is possible, let him be instructed and able to teach; but if he does not know letters, he shall be capable and skilful in the word; and let him be advanced in years.

And let him be vigilant and chaste and stable and orderly; and let him not be violent, and let him not be one who exceeds in wine; and let him not be malicious; but let him be quiet and not be contentious; and let him not be money-loving. And let him not be youthful in mind, lest he be lifted up and fall into the judgment of Satan, for everyone that exalts himself is humbled.

But it is required that the bishop shall be "a man that has taken one wife, and who has managed his house well" [1 Timothy 3:2, 4]. And thus let him be proved when he receives the imposition of hands to sit in the position of the episcopacy: whether he is chaste, and whether his wife also is a believer and chaste; and whether he has brought up his children in the fear of God, and admonished and taught them; and whether his household fear and reverence him and all of them obey him. For if his household in the flesh stands against him and does not obey him, how shall they who are without his house become his, and be subject to him?

Didascalia Apostolorum Corpus Scriptorum Christianorum Orientalium, ed. Arthur Vööbus (Louvain, 1979). Reprinted in Bart D. Ehrman, ed., *After the New Testament: A Reader in Early Christianity* (Oxford and New York, 1999), pp. 333–334.

LETTER OF POPE DAMASUS I (366–384 C.E.)
ON PRIESTLY CELIBACY

This is what has been decided, about bishops in the first place, but also about priests and deacons, whose duty it is to take part in the divine sacrifice [of the Eucharist] and whose hands confer the grace of baptism and make present the body of Christ. It is not only us but divine Scripture that binds them to be perfectly chaste. . . . How could a bishop or priest dare to preach continence to a widow or virgin, or urge anyone to keep his bed pure, if he himself were more concerned to have children for this world than for God? Why did Paul say, "You are not in the flesh but in the spirit" and "Let those who have wives live as though they had none"? Would he, who so exhorted the people, complaisantly allow carnal activity to priests? — he who also said, "Make no provision for the flesh, to gratify its desires" and "I wish that all were as I myself am." One who is in the service of Christ, who sits in the chair of the master, can he not observe the rule of service. . . . Even idolaters, in order to celebrate their impious cult and sacrifice to demons, imposed continence on themselves as regards women and abstained from certain foods so as to remain pure. And you ask me if the priest of the living God, who is to offer spiritual sacrifices, should live always in a state of purity or if, wholly involved in the flesh he should give himself to the cares of the flesh. . . . Intercourse is defilement. . . . that is why the mystery of God may not be entrusted to men of that sort, defiled and faithless. . . . They doubtless know that "flesh and blood cannot inherit the kingdom of God, nor does the corrupt inherit the incorruptible"; shall a priest or deacon dare then to lower himself to act as the animals do?

Brian Tierney and Joan Scott, eds., *Western Societies: A Documentary History*, vol. 1 (New York: Knopf, 1984), p. 174.

QUESTIONS FOR ANALYSIS

1. According to the two documents, why should leaders of the Christian church possess a balance of worldly and spiritual qualities? Isn't good moral character enough? Why must the bishop be old ("not less than fifty years of age") and married once, at least?

2. Early Christians held mixed views on marriage. Some believed that Jesus would return in their lifetimes; if the world was coming to an end, they saw no need for marriage on earth or in heaven. The New Testament reports that Jesus attended a wedding and performed his first miracle, changing water into wine there, but Jesus and Paul also praised celibacy. Paul saw marriage as a moral compromise for weak individuals who could not remain celibate: "It is better to marry than to burn with lust." What is the Didascalia's view of marriage?

THE GERMANIC INVASIONS AND THE FALL OF THE WESTERN ROMAN EMPIRE

Why did the Germanic invasions succeed?

While Christianity was transforming the Roman Empire from within, the empire was also coming under renewed pressure from beyond its frontiers. During the third and fourth centuries C.E., the growing power of Persia forced the Roman Empire to maintain a large and expensive military presence along its eastern frontiers. To sustain this large army in the east, the empire was forced to reduce the number of troops it could station in the west. Partly as a result of this reduction in troops, the western Roman Empire suffered a devastating series of attacks by Germanic tribes during the mid-third century C.E. During the fourth century, however, relations between Romans and Germans were generally peaceful, and the empire remained agriculturally and commercially prosperous. But starting in the early fifth century, a new series of German-led invasions overwhelmed the western half of the empire with startling rapidity. Out of this collapse a group of new Germanic kingdoms emerged in western Europe and North Africa that would permanently alter the region's history and culture.

GERMAN–ROMAN RELATIONS

The Germans were barbarians in Roman eyes because they did not live in cities and were illiterate; but in no sense were the Germans savages. They were settled agriculturalists and sophisticated metalworkers who had enjoyed trading relationships with the Roman world for centuries. German soldiers were familiar figures in Roman armies; one German, a man named Stilicho, was in fact the military leader of the western Roman Empire in the early fifth century when the Germanic invasions of the western empire began. In some frontier areas, entire tribes of Germans had been settled inside Roman borders as *foederati*, to reinforce depleted or withdrawn Roman garrisons. By the end of the fourth century, many German tribes had also adopted Christianity, albeit of the heretical, Arian variety. All these interactions made the barbarians very familiar with Roman civilization and substantially favorable to it.

The sequence of events that led to the collapse of the western empire began in central Asia during the mid-fourth century, when a warlike group of people known as the Huns began to migrate westward into the region north and east of the Black Sea. This invasion forced a number of other peoples, most important of which were the Goths, to migrate south and west in great distress toward the Roman frontier along the Danube River. Although the Goths had never been conquered by the Romans, they had been clients of the Roman state for several centuries. In 376, they were also too numerous and too desperate to easily disperse by force. The Romans therefore permitted them to cross the Danube and settle within the empire. In return for food and supplies, the Goths were to guard the region against incursions by other barbarians who might try to follow them into the empire.

The Romans, however, failed to supply the food and supplies they had promised. Instead, Roman local officials forced the starving Goths to sell themselves and their children into slavery in return for food. In 378, the Goths revolted. The Roman army sent to suppress them was defeated at the battle of Adrianople, and the emperor Valens (who led the expedition) was killed.

The new emperor, Theodosius the Great (379–395), quickly restored peace by accomodating the Goths' demands for supplies and farmland and by enrolling them in the Roman army under their own military leaders. For the time being, it appeared that the Gothic problem had been solved.

Before Theodosius died, however, he divided the empire between his two young sons, whose advisers quickly set about trying to undermine each other. In these promising circumstances, the Goths, now united under the leadership of Alaric, rebelled again. The eastern emperor bought them off, encouraging them instead to attack his imperial rival in the west. Gothic invasions of Italy quickly followed. Meanwhile, the Huns were continuing to move westward into modern-day Hungary, forcing several other groups of Germanic-speaking peoples westward toward the Rhine frontier of the Roman Empire.

On New Year's Eve 406/7, the gathering storm broke. A group of allied Germanic tribes led by the Vandals crossed the frozen Rhine and invaded Gaul. To repulse them, the leader of the western imperial armies, Stilicho, made an alliance with Alaric and his Goths. But after Stilicho was deposed in a palace coup just a few months later, the Goths too joined in the invasion of the western empire. In 410, the Christian Goths captured and sacked the city of Rome itself. Rome, however, had little to offer in the way of either food or land. The Goths therefore moved on, eventually settling in southern Gaul and Spain where they established what came to be known as the Visigothic ("West Gothic") kingdom. The Vandals too set out for Spain but ultimately crossed the Strait of Gibraltar to settle in the rich agricultural regions of North Africa. In 455, they launched a seaborne attack on Rome. Further Germanic tribes, including the Franks, the Burgundians, and the Alamans, quickly followed the Vandals across the Rhine into Gaul, where they set about erecting kingdoms of their own. By the mid-fifth century, even the Huns had joined the invasions, under the leadership of their famous warlord Attila.

In 476, the last Roman emperor in the west, an ineffectual usurper derisively known as Romulus Augustulus ("Little Augustus"), was toppled by Odovacer, a Hun in charge of a mixed army of Germans, Huns, and disgruntled Romans. This event conventionally marks the ending date of the western Roman Empire. In the east, however, a Roman emperor continued to rule and continued to claim authority over the western half of the empire. By 476, however, the eastern emperor could affect events in the west only by encouraging

CHRONOLOGY

GERMANIC INVASIONS OF THE ROMAN EMPIRE, FIFTH CENTURY C.E.

Gothic victory at the battle of Adrianople	378
Vandals cross Rhine to invade Gaul, Spain, and North Africa	406–407
Visigoths sack Rome	410
Vandals sack Rome	455
Odovacer deposes Romulus Augustulus	476
Theodoric the Ostrogoth rules Italy	493–526

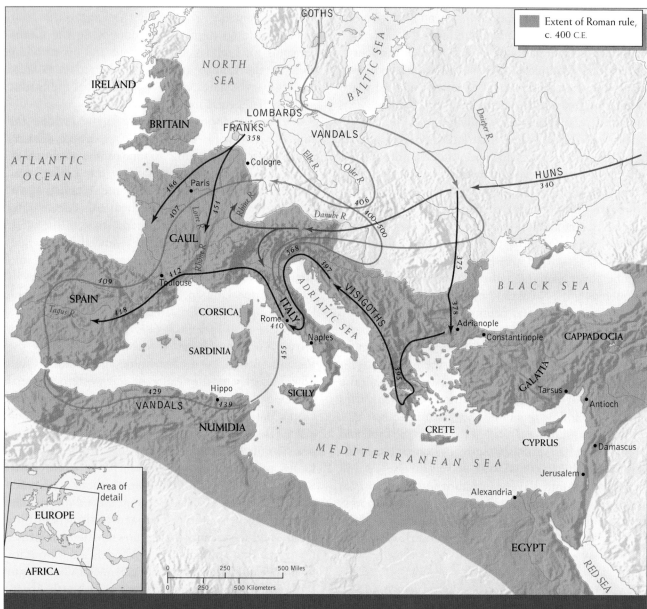

THE BARBARIAN INVASIONS OF THE ROMAN EMPIRE

What do the invasion routes followed by these different barbarian-led armies suggest about the invaders' identity and motives? Why did so many different armies attack the city of Rome, even though the city was no longer the capital even of the western Roman Empire?

one barbarian king to depose another. To assert his own control over Italy, the emperor Zeno therefore commissioned Theodoric to lead his Ostrogoth ("East Goths") army from the Balkans to Rome to get rid of Odovacer. In a decade of fierce fighting, the Goths completely eliminated the Huns from Italy. Theodoric thereupon established an Ostrogothic kingdom in Italy, which he ruled with imperial support until shortly before his death in 526.

THE SUCCESS AND IMPACT OF THE GERMANIC INVASIONS

The collapse of the fifth-century western empire is in many ways surprising. The armies that invaded the empire were small, probably no more than 100,000 fighting men in total, and they were divided between a number of competing warlords. Once the invasions had begun, these armies probably grew on the march as they were joined by disgruntled Romans and Germanic *foederati* already settled within the empire; but the numbers involved were still very low. Nor was the western Roman Empire already in a state of collapse. Recent archaeological work has shown that the population of the western empire was stable, that the rural economy was buoyant, and that local and long-distance trading networks were still active in the year 400. By the year 500, however, the economic and political world of the western Roman Empire had disappeared. How then can we explain this sudden and sweeping collapse?

The western empire's inability to defend itself was, first and foremost, a military failure. Behind this failure lay a number of related problems. Many Roman armies in the west were already in a poor state when the fifth century began. The best of them had already been withdrawn to protect the richer, eastern half of the empire; those that remained were undermanned and underfunded. Efforts to make the army more self-supporting had already produced a force that was more and more "civilized." By 400, many soldiers were married and some army units grew their own food, making it difficult to move troops even in an emergency. Nor could the resources to support the army be easily increased. Tax levels were already high; any attempt to increase them further risked sparking a revolt by disgruntled taxpayers. Civilian morale was also low. The bureaucratic regime of the fourth-century empire inspired little loyalty, even among aristocrats. The Germans, meanwhile, were seldom regarded with horror, having become a familiar element in Roman society over several centuries. As a result, relatively few pitched battles were fought between Romans and Germans during the fifth century invasions. Often, invading armies triumphed by default, because the residents of the empire simply did not care enough to defend themselves. And when battles were fought, they generally featured mixed armies of Romans, Germans, and Huns on both sides, with each side fighting in the name of its own warlords.

Morale may have been higher in the eastern empire; but the primary reason that the eastern Roman Empire survived the fifth-century invasions while the western empire did not is that the east was simply richer and so could better afford to maintain its military forces. By the fifth century, many western cities had shrunk to a fraction of their former size; often they were little more than administrative or military centers. In the east, by contrast, cities remained teeming centers of industry and trade. Because the eastern part of the empire had greater wealth to tax, it could sustain the burdens of the imperial bureaucracy more easily than could the west. Its borders were shorter, and its armies better supplied; it could also afford to buy off invaders willing to have their attentions redirected toward the west. For all these reasons, the eastern empire stayed afloat and even prospered during the fifth century, while the western empire floundered and sank.

As we have seen, this difference in wealth between east and west had existed for several centuries. It was made much worse, however, by the effects of the fifth-century invasions themselves. Every territory plundered or captured by the invaders represented tax revenues lost to the western empire. The scale of these losses was enormous. Ten years after the Goths sacked Rome in 410, the area was still producing only about 15 percent of its presiege tax revenues. Similar reductions in tax revenues resulted from the initial German attacks on Gaul and Spain. After 420 or so, as the invaders began to set up their own kingdoms, these areas ceased to pay any tax at all to the Roman imperial authorities. By 439, when the Vandals captured North Africa, the richest of all Rome's western provinces, the imperial government's revenues were reduced to whatever sums it could collect from those parts of Italy that it still controlled.

The economic consequences of this collapse were profound. In the year 400, the economy of the western Roman Empire was still characterized by the mass production of low-cost, high-quality consumer goods that were transported in massive quantities throughout the empire. By the year 500, this world was gone. Although regional and local systems of exchange continued, long-distance trade in bulk goods continued

Mass-Produced Roman Pottery. The Roman Empire produced millions of high-quality, low-cost ceramics, which were shipped and sold throughout the empire. In the early fifth century, however, the last factories that produced this pottery in western Europe disappeared.

only in the eastern half of the empire. Standards of craftsmanship, especially in pottery making and ceramics, also declined dramatically. So too did standards of living and (probably) the overall population of the western empire. It seems probable, indeed, that the population of western Europe as a whole did not return to its fourth-century levels for a thousand years.

Other aspects of Roman life in the western empire changed much more gradually. Roman tax systems often survived, even though their proceeds now went into the purses of the new barbarian rulers. So too did Roman legal and administrative systems. On the land, Roman agricultural patterns continued in most areas, often under the same landlords. Roman aristocrats continued to dominate civic life, and Roman cities continued to dominate their surrounding regions, especially in southern Gaul and Spain. Nor did the invasions bring an end to Roman culture or to the influence of Roman example on the new immigrants. As Theodoric, the Ostrogothic conqueror of Italy, was fond of remarking: "An able Goth wishes to be like a Roman; but only a poor Roman would want to be like a Goth."

THE SHAPING OF WESTERN CHRISTIAN THOUGHT

What distinctive themes of western Christian thought were emerging during the fourth and fifth centuries?

As the western Roman Empire declined during the fourth and fifth centuries, a small group of western Christian thinkers formulated a theological outlook on the world that would guide western thought for the next 800 years. This concurrence of political decline and theological advance was not coincidental. As the western empire collapsed, it seemed clearer than ever to thinking Christians that the classical inheritance was passing away and that God had not intended the world to be anything more than a transitory testing place. How, then, should Christians live? What did God require of them?

Answers to these questions were worked out by the four great Fathers of the western church: Saint Jerome (c. 340–420), Saint Ambrose (c. 340–397), Saint Augustine (354–430), and Pope Saint Gregory the Great (540–604). Jerome, Ambrose, and Augustine were contemporaries who knew and influenced one another.

We will deal with their work here. Pope Gregory's contributions will be discussed in Chapter Seven.

SAINT JEROME AND SAINT AMBROSE

Jerome's greatest single contribution was his translation of the Bible from Hebrew and Greek into Latin. His translation, known as the Vulgate (or "common" version), was not the first attempt to produce a Latin Bible; but it quickly became the standard one and would remain so until the sixteenth century. Jerome's translation was vigorous, colloquial, and clear; its powerful prose and poetry would influence all subsequent Latin authors for a thousand years. Jerome was also an influential commentator on how the Bible ought to be interpreted; it is largely to him that we owe the western tradition of interpreting biblical passages allegorically and symbolically as well as literally and historically.

Jerome was a rigorous ascetic himself and a fervent supporter of monasticism. Although he had respectful relationships with a number of contemporary women, his views on women as a group were intensely misogynistic. He was not a notably original thinker, but he exercised great influence by his eloquent formulations of the ideas of others. He was also an extremely important influence in arguing that classical learning could and should be studied by Christians, so long as it was thoroughly subordinated to Christian aims. Jerome himself was not certain, however, that he had succeeded in subordinating his love for the classics to his love for God. When, in a dream, he imagined himself arriving at the gates of heaven, God reproved him for being more of a follower of Cicero than of Christ.

Jerome was primarily a scholar. Saint Ambrose, in contrast, was principally a man of the world. As archbishop of Milan, the aristocratic Ambrose fearlessly rebuked even the Christian emperor Theodosius the Great for massacring innocent civilians at Thessalonica. Theodosius of course remained emperor; but until he did penance as a Christian for his sin, Ambrose refused to admit him into the church, declaring that on matters of faith, "The emperor is within the church, not above the church." Eventually, Theodosius capitulated and did penance before Ambrose in his cathedral at Milan. This famous incident reflects the western church's developing sense of autonomy on religious matters, even when faced with the power of an emperor.

Like Jerome, Ambrose was an admirer of Cicero and wrote an ethical work, *On the Duties of Ministers*, that drew heavily on Cicero's tract *On Duties*. Unlike Cicero, however, Ambrose argued that the beginning and end of human conduct should be reverence for God

ROMANIZED BARBARIANS AND BARBARIANIZED ROMANS

These two letters from Sidonius Apollinaris (c. 430–c. 480) illustrate the ways in which cultural assimilation in the late-fifth-century western empire was rapidly blurring the boundaries between "Roman" and "barbarian." Sidonius himself was the descendant of an illustrious Roman provincial family in Gaul. He was one of the admired Latin stylists of his day, in both poetry and prose. Although he eventually became a bishop and was regarded locally as a saint after his death, his letter collection (from which these extracts are taken) tells us much more about the late Roman literary culture of Visigothic southern Gaul than it does about his Christianity. Arbogastes was the Frankish governor of Treves; Syagrius was from an ancient Gaulish Roman family.

LETTER 4:17: SIDONIUS TO HIS FRIEND ARBOGASTES

My honored Lord, your friend Eminentius has handed me a letter written by your own hand, a really literary letter, replete with the grace of a three-fold charm. The first of its merits is certainly the affection which prompted such condescension to my lowly condition, for if not a stranger I am in these days a man who courts obscurity; the second virtue is your modesty. . . . In the third place comes your urbanity which leads you to make a most amusing profession of clumsiness when as a matter of fact you have drunk deep from the spring of Roman eloquence and, dwelling by the Moselle, you speak the true Latin of the Tiber: you are intimate with the barbarians but are innocent of barbarisms, and are equal in tongue, as also in strength of arm, to the leaders of old, I mean those who were wont to handle the pen no less than the sword.

Thus the splendor of the Roman speech, if it still exists anywhere, has survived in you, though it has long been wiped out from the Belgian and Rhenic lands: with you and your eloquence surviving, even though Roman law has ceased at our border, the Roman speech does not falter. For this reason . . . I rejoice greatly that at any rate in your illustrious breast there have remained traces of our vanishing culture. If you extend these by constant reading you will discover for yourself as each day passes that the educated are no less superior to the unlettered than men are to beasts.

LETTER 5:5 SIDONIUS TO HIS FRIEND SYAGRIUS

You are the great-grandson of a consul, and in the male line too—although that has little to do with the case before us; I say, then, you are descended from a poet, to whom his literary glory would have brought statues had not his magisterial glories done so . . . and the culture of his successors has not declined one whit from his standard, particularly in this respect. I am therefore inexpressibly amazed that you have quickly acquired a knowledge of the German tongue with such ease.

And yet I remember that your boyhood had a good schooling in liberal studies and I know for certain that you often declaimed with spirit and eloquence before your professor of oratory. This being so, I should like you to tell me how you managed to absorb so swiftly into your inner being the exact sounds of an alien race, so that now after reading Virgil under the schoolmaster's cane and toiling and working the rich fluency of [Cicero] . . . you burst forth before my eyes like a young falcon from an old nest.

You have no idea what amusement it gives me, and others too, when I hear that in your presence the barbarian is afraid to perpetrate a barbarism in his own language. The bent elders of the Germans are astounded at you when you translate letters, and they adopt you as umpire and aribitrator in their mutual dealings. . . . And although these people are stiff and uncouth in body and mind alike, they welcome in you, and learn from you, their native speech combined with Roman wisdom.

Only one thing remains, most clever of men: continue with undiminished zeal, even in your hours of ease, to devote some attention to reading; and, like the man of refinement that you are, observe a just balance between the two languages: retain your grasp of Latin,

lest you be laughed at, and practice the other, in order to have the laugh of them. Farewell.

W. B. Anderson, ed., *Sidonius, Poems and Letters*, vol. 2 (Cambridge, Mass., 1980), pp. 127–129, 181–183.

QUESTIONS FOR ANALYSIS

1. What is the topic of the letter from Sidonius Apollinaris to Arbogastes?
2. In his letter to Syagrius, Sidonius says that he is amazed that Syagrius has "quickly acquired a knowledge of the German tongue." He remembers that Syagrius had "a good schooling in liberal studies." How does that help Syagrius in his official duties? Why is it amusing to Sidonius that barbarians fear to make mistakes in their own language when they appear before Syagrius? Why does Sidonius advise him to continue reading and to maintain his knowledge of both Latin and German?

rather than social or political advancement. Even more fundamental, however, Ambrose argued that although God assists all Christians by sharing with them the power of divine grace, God nonetheless gives more grace to some Christians than to others. Ambrose's emphasis on the necessity and mystery of grace (Why does God give more grace to some than to others?) would be refined and greatly amplified by his disciple, Saint Augustine of Hippo.

THE LIFE AND THOUGHT OF SAINT AUGUSTINE

Augustine was the greatest of all the Latin fathers; indeed he was one of the most powerful Christian thinkers of all time. Augustine's influence on medieval thought was incalculable, but his theology also had a profound influence on the development of Protestantism. Even in the twentieth century many leading Christian thinkers would describe themselves as neo-Augustinians.

Augustine's Christianity may have been so searching because he began his career by searching for it. Although his mother was a Christian, he hesitated until the age of thirty-three to be baptized, passing from one philosophical system to another without finding

intellectual or spiritual satisfaction in any. Only his increasing doubts about all other alternatives, the appeal of Saint Ambrose's teachings on grace, and a mystical experience movingly described in his autobiographical *Confessions* led Augustine to embrace the faith wholeheartedly in 387. Thereafter he advanced rapidly in ecclesiastical positions, becoming bishop of the North African city of Hippo in 395. Although he led an extremely active life as bishop (he died in 430 while defending Hippo against the Vandals), he still found time to write more than a hundred profound, complex, and powerful treatises analyzing the most fundamental problems of Christian belief.

Augustine's theology revolved around a single, fundamental question: How could humanity be so profoundly sinful, if human beings were created by an omnipotent God whose nature is entirely good? Augustine was in no doubt about the full extent of human depravity. One of his most vivid illustrations of this appears in the *Confessions*, when he tells how he and some other boys once stole pears from a neighbor's garden, not because they were hungry or because the pears were beautiful, but simply for the sake of the evil itself. Any suggestion that humans acted badly because they did not know any better was unacceptable to Augustine. The human inclination toward evil was much more deeply rooted than a failure of knowledge.

WHAT DISTINCTIVE THEMES OF WESTERN CHRISTIAN THOUGHT WERE EMERGING DURING THE FOURTH AND FIFTH CENTURIES?

THE SHAPING OF WESTERN CHRISTIAN THOUGHT   229

Augustine's answer to the question of evil went back to the Garden of Eden, where God had given Adam and Eve, the first human couple, the freedom either to follow his will or to follow their own. By eating the one fruit that God had forbidden them to eat, Adam and Eve chose to follow their own wills rather than God's will. Thereafter, says Augustine, God simply left Adam and Eve's descendants to their own devices, by withdrawing from human beings the divine power (grace) by which they might overcome their own wills to follow his. All the evils that plague the world are thus ultimately the result of the innate human propensity to place our own desires ahead of God's.

God would be justified if he condemned all human beings to hell; but because he is also merciful he chose instead to save some human beings through the sacrifice of his son, Jesus. No one, however, has by nature the grace necessary to become a Christian, much less to deserve salvation. God alone makes this choice; by granting grace to some and not to others, he predestines a portion of the human race to salvation and sentences the rest to be damned. If this seems unfair, Augustine's answer is, first, that strict fairness would condemn everyone to hell and, second, that the basis for God's choice is a mystery shrouded in his omnipotence —far beyond the realm of human comprehension.

Even though it might seem to us that the practical consequences of this rigorous doctrine of predestination would be lethargy and fatalism, neither Augustine nor his later followers saw it that way at all. Those who are "chosen" will of course do good; but since no one knows who is chosen and who is not, all should try to do good insofar as God makes it possible for them to do so. For Augustine the central guide to doing good was the doctrine of charity, which meant leading a life devoted to loving God and loving one's neighbor for the sake of God, rather than a life of cupidity, of loving earthly things for their own sake.

To respond to those who blamed Christianity for the fall of Rome in 410, Augustine wrote one of his most famous works, *On the City of God*. In this work, he developed his ideas about predestination into an inter-

The City of Man. A late-medieval illustration for Augustine's *On the City of God* showing Cain slaying his brother, Abel, and Romulus slaying his brother, Remus. Its message is that all earthly government is a product of sin.

pretation of all human history. Augustine argued that the entire human race from the creation until the last judgment was and will be composed of two opposing societies, those who "live according to man" and love themselves, and those who "live according to God." The former belong to the "City of Man"; their rewards are the riches, fame, and power they may garner on earth. The City of Man is not useless; earthly rulers bring peace and order and therefore deserve the obedience of Christians. But only those predestined to salvation, and who are thus members of the "City of God," will on Judgment Day put on the garment of immortality. Christians should therefore behave on earth as if they were travelers or pilgrims, never forgetting that their true home lies in heaven. As for the time when the last judgment would come, Augustine argued vehemently that no human could know its exact date; nonetheless because the judgment might come at any time, all mortals should devote their utmost efforts to preparing for it by leading lives of righteousness.

Although Saint Augustine formulated major new aspects of Christian theology, he believed that he was doing no more than drawing out truths found in the Bible. Indeed, he was convinced that the Bible alone contained all the wisdom worth knowing. But he also believed that much of the Bible was expressed obscurely and that a certain amount of education was needed to understand it thoroughly. As a consequence Augustine approved of some Christians' acquiring an education in the liberal arts (as he himself had done), so long as they directed their education toward its proper end: the study of the Bible. Along with Jerome, Augustine thus laid the groundwork for western Christians to preserve the literary and educational traditions of the classical past. But Augustine intended liberal education only for an elite; most Christians simply needed to be catechized, or drilled, in the faith. He also thought it was far worse to study classical thought for its own sake than for someone to know nothing at all about Latin and Greek learning. The true wisdom of mortals, he insisted, was piety.

BOETHIUS LINKS CLASSICAL AND MEDIEVAL THOUGHT

One of Augustine's most interesting and influential followers was Boethius (bob-EE-thee-US), a Roman aristocrat who lived from about 480 to 524. Because Boethius was interested in ancient philosophy; wrote in a polished, almost Ciceronian style; and came from a noble Roman family, he has often been described as the "last of the Romans." But in fact he intended the classics to serve Christian purposes, just as Augustine had prescribed, and his own teachings were basically Augustinian.

Because Boethius lived a century after Augustine he could see far more clearly that the ancient world was coming to an end. His goal, therefore, was to preserve as much of the best ancient learning as possible by composing a series of handbooks, translations, and commentaries. He wrote handbooks on two of the seven liberal arts (arithmetic and music; the other liberal arts are grammar, rhetoric, logic, astronomy, and geometry), summarizing what a Christian should know about each subject. He devoted most of his attention to logic, however, translating from Greek into Latin several of Aristotle's logical treatises along with an introductory work on logic by Porphyry (another ancient philosopher). He also wrote his own explanatory commentaries on these works to help beginners. Because Roman writers had never been much interested in logic, Boethius's translations and commentaries established a crucial link between the thought of the

Greeks and that of the Middle Ages. They also endowed the Latin language with a logical vocabulary; when interest in logic was revived in the twelfth-century West it rested first on a Boethian basis.

Although Boethius was an exponent of Aristotle's logic, his worldview was not Aristotelian but Augustinian. This can be seen both in his treatises on Christian theology and in his masterpiece, *The Consolation of Philosophy*. Boethius wrote the *Consolation* at the end of his life, after he had been condemned to death for treason by Theodoric the Ostrogoth, whom he had served as an official. (Historians are unsure about the justice of the charges.) In it Boethius asks the age-old question of what is human happiness and concludes that it is not found in earthly rewards such as riches or fame but only in the "highest good," which is God. Human life, then, should be spent in pursuit of God. Since Boethius speaks in the *Consolation* as a philosopher rather than a theologian, he does not refer to Christian revelation or to the role of divine grace in salvation. But his basically Augustinian message is unmistakable. *The Consolation of Philosophy* became one of the most popular books of the Middle Ages because it was extremely well written,

Boethius. This ivory diptych (a two-paneled image) shows the famous philosopher dressed as a Roman aristocrat.

CHRONOLOGY

SHAPING OF WESTERN CHRISTIAN THOUGHT, FOURTH–SIXTH CENTURIES

Saint Jerome	
Translates Bible from Hebrew and Greek into Latin	c. 340–420
Saint Ambrose	
Furthers the church's autonomy on religious matters	c. 340–397
Saint Augustine	
Writes *Confessions*, *On the City of God*	354–430
Boethius	
Provides link between classical and medieval thought	480–524
Cassiodorus	
Justifies monks' studying and copying classical literature	c. 490–c. 583

because it appropriated and subordinated classical ideas within a clearly Christian framework, and most of all because it seemed to offer a real meaning to life. In times when earthly things seemed crude or fleeting, it was genuinely consoling to be told eloquently and philosophically that life has purpose if led for the sake of God.

THE CHRISTIANIZATION OF CLASSICAL CULTURE IN THE WEST

How was classical culture Christianized?

As we have seen, none of the Christian intellectuals of late antiquity was prepared to throw out altogether the classical traditions of learning he had inherited. For all of them, however, this tradition posed severe challenges. It was, in the first place, thoroughly pagan, and paganism remained a significant threat to Christianity even after the empire became formally Christian. Classical learning was also associated with syncretism—that is, with the easy acceptance of both Christian and pagan beliefs

simultaneously, which had been so marked a feature of aristocratic culture during the fourth century. There was no denying the seductive lure of classical literature and philosophy, however. Jerome worried that on Judgment Day, God would find him less a follower of Christ than of Cicero; and Augustine spent years fighting to free himself from the attractions of pagan philosophical systems such as Manicheanism, which explained why there was evil in the world by positing the existence of two competing gods, one good, the other evil.

Christian thinkers were also working within a world that still celebrated philosophers as purveyors of wisdom about the good life. Christian intellectuals—indeed, the Christian clergy generally—wanted desperately to be regarded as philosophers so they could replace the doctrines of pagan philosophy with the doctrine of Christ. To do this, however, they needed a way of Christianizing the classical inheritance and conveying it to the Christian masses in an intellectually satisfying way. The political collapse of the western empire and the growing barbarization of western Roman culture further emphasized the urgency of the task. It was, therefore, to the preservation and reinterpretation of classical Latin culture for a mixed audience of vulgar Romans and aspiring barbarians that the Christian intellectuals of the fourth, fifth, and sixth centuries devoted themselves.

This process took two forms. The first was a gradual winnowing out of the classical texts produced in Greece and Rome between the fifth century B.C.E. and the second century C.E. Much of this winnowing had been accomplished already. By and large, Roman readers of the third and fourth centuries C.E. had little taste for the scientific and mathematical works of the classical Greeks. They preferred bestiaries, with their entertaining tales of hyenas that changed their sex yearly and of weasels who conceived through the ear. Nor did they have much interest in the philosophical works of Plato and Aristotle or the literary works of the classical Greek dramatists. They preferred Neoplatonism (see Chapter Five), a quasi-mystical set of doctrines that posited a divine principle of some sort as lying behind the created world and that saw creation and existence as part of a continuing process by which the material world emanated from this divinity and gradually returned to it. In literature, later Roman tastes ran toward comedies and novels, of which Petronius's *Satyricon* is a ribald, but not atypical, example.

The second challenge was to arrive at an understanding of the purposes of classical culture for a Christian audience. Tertullian had raised this question around 200 C.E. by asking, "What has Athens [the symbol of classical learning] to do with Jerusalem [the symbol of Christian salvation]?" Tertullian's answer had been "Nothing"; but this answer did not suit the changed circumstances of the Christian church from the fourth century on. Jerome and Augustine were more hopeful about Christianizing the classical tradition; but on the whole, the early monastic movement sided with Tertullian. Despite the role Benedictine monasteries would later play in copying and preserving Latin literary texts, Saint Benedict himself was no admirer of classical culture. Quite to the contrary, he wanted his monks to serve only Christ—not literature or philosophy. But unlike some of his monastic contemporaries, he did believe that monks should be able to read well enough to study the Bible. To guarantee this, some schooling within the monastery would be necessary, especially for boys given over from birth to the monastic profession. For Benedict, however, preserving classical learning was no part of a monastery's proper duties.

> Despite the role Benedictine monasteries would later play in copying and preserving Latin literary texts, Saint Benedict himself was no admirer of classical culture. Quite to the contrary, he wanted his monks to serve only Christ—not literature or philosophy.

CASSIODORUS AND THE BENEDICTINE TRADITION OF LEARNING

The impetus behind the development of Benedictine monasticism's tradition of learning came not from Benedict himself, but from Cassiodorus (c. 490–c. 583), another official at Theodoric's court. Early in his career, Cassiodorus wrote a *History of the Goths* for his barbarian overlord, which showed the Goths to themselves in a Roman mirror, as a people whose history was a part of the history of Rome. He also composed (and eventually published) several volumes of his official correspondence, reflecting his training in the classical rhetorical tradition. During the last forty years of his life, however, Cassiodorus turned his attention toward religion, composing commentaries on the Psalms and founding an important monastery at Vivarium in southern Italy.

It was for his monks that Cassiodorus composed his most influential work, the *Institutes*. Inspired by Saint Augustine, Cassiodorus believed that study of classical literature was the essential preliminary to a proper understanding of the Bible and the Church Fathers. His *Institutes* were basically a reading list, comprising first the essential works of classical, pagan literature a monk should know before he moved on to the more difficult and demanding study of theology and the Bible. Through the *Institutes*, Cassiodorus thus defined a clas-

sical literary canon that would influence Christian educational practice until the end of the Middle Ages.

To provide these books, Cassiodorus also encouraged his monks to copy manuscripts, arguing that such copying was in itself manual labor of the sort that Saint Benedict had demanded and that it might even be more appropriate work for monks than laboring in the fields. As Benedictines began to subscribe to these ideas, Benedictine monasteries emerged as the most important centers for the preservation and study of classical literature in the Latin-speaking West. Hardly any of the works of classical Latin literature, including such "licentious" writings as the poems of Catullus and Ovid, would survive today had they not been copied and pre-

Cassiodorus. This frontispiece from a Bible, drawn in an English Benedictine monastery around 700, depicts Cassiodorus as a copyist and preserver of books. Because books were expensive and rare until the invention of printing in the fifteenth century, they customarily were stored in cupboards, lying flat, as we see them here.

served during the early Middle Ages by Benedictine monks following the example of Cassiodorus.

Others too were active in trying to preserve and Christianize what remained of the classical literary tradition. At the request of Pope Symmachus (498–514), Priscian (c. 500) composed what would become the standard treatise of the Middle Ages on Latin grammar. At the request of another pope, the sixth-century scholar Dionysius Exiguus undertook to collect and codify the laws of the Roman church; yet another pope, Agapetus (535–536), assembled the greatest Christian library in Rome—a library from which his relative, Pope Gregory the Great (590–604), would draw most of his knowledge of Saint Augustine. To some degree, of course, all such efforts were aimed at an educated, aristocratic elite that was fast disappearing from the sixth-century Latin West. But this fact should not obscure the extent to which this Christianized classical culture was slowly becoming the common possession not only of aristocratic Christian bishops but also of their barbarian overlords.

Boethius and Cassiodorus both worked at the court of Theodoric the Ostrogoth, the most thoroughly Romanized ruler in the sixth-century barbarian world. Yet all their efforts to extend, preserve, and Christianize the classical cultural tradition testify to their awareness that this world was passing away. Theodoric ruled Italy as the designated representative of the emperor at Constantinople. A great admirer of Roman civilization, he fostered agriculture and commerce, repaired public buildings and roads, patronized learning, and maintained a policy of religious toleration. In short, he provided Italy with a more enlightened government than it had known for several centuries. But none of this was sufficient to erase the corrosive distrust that in Theodoric's final years tore his kingdom apart. The problem was that for all their *romanitas* ("Romanness"), Theodoric and the Goths were Arian heretics, whereas the local bishops and landowners of Italy were orthodox Trinitarian Christians—and this fact made the Italian aristocrats the faithful subjects not of Theodoric, but of his imperial sponsor in Constantinople. When, in 523, the emperor pronounced an edict, valid also in Italy, forbidding Jews, pagans, and heretics (by whom he probably meant Arians) from holding public office, the storm broke. Although Cassiodorus remained loyal to Theodoric, Boethius was imprisoned, accused of conspiring to return Italy to direct imperial rule. Theodoric's last years were marked by his continuing persecution of Trinitarian Christians. When he died in 526, he left no son to succeed him, while religious tensions continued to tear his kingdom apart. Ten years

Theodoric the Ostrogoth. The barbarian ruler is shown here in Roman dress, with an ornate Roman hairstyle and a Roman symbol of victory in his hand. The inscription reads *Rex Theodericvs pivs princis,* Latin for "King Theodoric, pious prince."

later, Theodoric's fears would be confirmed when a new emperor, Justinian, attempted to reconstitute the Roman Empire of Augustus by reconquering Italy from the Ostrogoths.

EASTERN ROME AND THE WESTERN EMPIRE

Why did Justinian's plan to reunite the Roman Empire fail?

Boethius's execution by Theodoric in 524 was in many ways an important historical turning point. Boethius was the last noteworthy philosopher and the last writer of cultivated Latin prose the West was to have for many hundreds of years. Boethius was also a layman; for hundreds of years afterward almost all western European writers would be priests or monks. Boethius's execution was also a harbinger of the political collapse of the Ostrogothic kingdom in Italy, because it showed that Arian and Catholic Christians could not live in harmony anywhere in the barbarianized western empire. Soon afterward, the Ostrogoths were overthrown by the eastern Roman Empire. That event in turn was to be a major factor in the ultimate divorce between East and West and the consequent final disintegration of the old Roman world.

JUSTINIAN'S REVIVAL OF THE ROMAN EMPIRE

The conquest of the Ostrogoths was part of a larger plan to revive the Roman Empire conceived and directed by the eastern emperor Justinian (527–565). The eastern empire, with its capital at Constantinople, had faced many external and internal pressures since the time of Theodosius (d. 395). But it had managed to weather these assaults and divisions and had preserved its economic and political unity. Although the eastern empire—which then encompassed the modern-day territories of Greece, Turkey, most of the Middle East, and Egypt—was largely Greek- and Syriac-speaking, Justinian himself came from a western province (modern-day Serbia) and spoke Latin. A student of history, he saw himself as the heir of imperial Rome, whose ancient power and western territories he aspired to restore. Aided by his astute and determined wife, Theodora, who played an influential role in his reign, Justinian worked strenuously to recover the West and restore the empire. Although his efforts ultimately failed, they had a lasting influence on the entire Mediterranean world.

THE CODIFICATION OF ROMAN LAW

One of Justinian's most impressive and lasting accomplishments was his codification of Roman law. This project was part of his attempt to emphasize continuities with earlier imperial Rome and was also meant to enhance his own prestige and absolute power. Codification of the law was necessary because between the third and sixth centuries the volume of statutes had continued to grow, with the result that the vast body of enactments contained many contradictory or obsolete elements. Moreover, conditions had changed so radically that many of the old legal principles could no longer be applied. When Justinian came to the throne in 527, he immediately decided to revise and systematize existing law to bring it into harmony with new conditions and to establish it as an authoritative basis for his rule.

To carry out this work he appointed a commission of lawyers under the supervision of his minister Tribonian. Within two years the commission published the first result of its labors. This was the Code, a systematic compilation of all the imperial statutes that had been issued from the reign of Hadrian to Justinian's own. The Code was later supplemented by the Novels, which contained the legislation of Justinian and his immediate successors. By 532 the commission had also completed the Digest, a summary of the writings of the great jurists. The commission's final product was the Institutes, a textbook of the legal principles reflected in the Digest and the Code. All four volumes together constitute the *Corpus Juris Civilis,* or the "body of civil law."

Justinian's *Corpus* was a brilliant achievement: the Digest alone has been justly called "the most remarkable and important lawbook that the world has ever seen." In the East, the *Corpus* immediately became the foundation on which all subsequent legal developments would rest. In the West, by contrast, the *Corpus* was initially little known; most early medieval law codes drew instead on the fifth-century compilation of the emperor Theodosius II (408–450). From the twelfth century on, however, Justinian's *Corpus* would be intensively studied in the West as well, influencing both the conduct of government and the developing legal systems of late medieval and early modern Europe. Even the nineteenth-century Napoleonic Code (still current in France, Spain, much of Latin America, and the American state of Louisiana) is fundamentally the Institutes of Justinian in modern dress.

The *Corpus* also had a profoundly important influence on Western political thought. Starting from the maxim that "what pleases the prince has the force of law," the *Corpus* granted unlimited powers to the emperor and therefore was adopted by late medieval and early modern European rulers as a foundation for absolutism. But the *Corpus* also provided some theoretical support for constitutionalism because it maintained that the sovereign's powers were delegated to him by the people: since government came from the people it could in theory be given back to them. Equally important and influential was its view of the state as an abstract entity much like a modern corporation. In the Middle Ages the state was often viewed either as the private property of the ruler or as a supernatural creation meant to control sin. The modern conception of the state as a public entity with its own interests and purposes gained strength toward the end of the Middle Ages largely because of the revival of assumptions found in Justinian's legal compilation.

> Starting from the maxim that "what pleases the prince has the force of law," the *Corpus* granted unlimited powers to the emperor and therefore was adopted by late medieval and early modern European rulers as a foundation for absolutism.

Justinian and Theodora. Sixth-century mosaics from the Church of San Vitale, Ravenna. The emperor and empress are presented here as holy figures (notice the halos around their heads) who exercise priestly responsibilities. As they advance toward the altar, they carry the communion dish and the chalice, symbols of the body and blood of Christ. On the hem of Theodora's gown we see the three wise kings from the East who visited the infant Jesus. Just as these three magi once had supernatural knowledge of Christ, so now do their counterparts, Justinian and Theodora.

JUSTINIAN'S MILITARY CONQUESTS

Justinian's initial attempts to reconquer the western Roman Empire succeeded easily. In 533 his brilliant general Belisarius conquered the Vandal kingdom in northwest Africa; by 536 Belisarius appeared to have conquered Italy, where he was welcomed by the Catholic subjects of the Ostrogoths. But the early victories of the Italian campaign were illusory; the war would drag on for decades until the exhausted imperial forces finally reduced the last Gothic outposts in 563. Because Justinian had already recaptured northwest Africa and the coastal parts of Spain, the Mediterranean was once again a Roman lake when he died in 565. But the costs of this endeavor had been enormous and would soon call into question the very existence of the eastern Roman Empire.

Justinian's western campaigns were ill-advised for two reasons. One was their enormous cost. Belisarius seldom had enough troops to do the job properly: he began his Italian campaign with only 8,000 men. To provide the troops his generals needed, Justinian imposed oppressive taxation, which undermined support for the empire in such vitally important regions as Egypt and Syria. Even the Trinitarian Christians of Italy and North Africa resented the costs their liberation imposed on them. Justinian's western campaigns also distracted attention from dangers closer to home: in particular, the developing strength of Persia. To respond to the Persian threat, Justinian's successors were forced to withdraw their troops from Italy and North Africa; this left both regions dangerously exposed to further barbarian invasions and was still not sufficient to guarantee the safety of the eastern empire. Only a heroic reorganization of the eastern empire after 610 saved Constantinople from falling to the Persians; but as we will see, this reorganization also marks the final end to Justinian's dream of reuniting the eastern and the western Mediterranean worlds.

THE IMPACT OF JUSTINIAN'S RECONQUEST ON THE WESTERN EMPIRE

Justinian's wars caused tremendous devastation throughout northern and central Italy. Around Rome, aqueducts were cut, and parts of the countryside returned to marshes; some would not be drained again until the twentieth century. In 568, another, much more primitive Germanic tribe, the Lombards, took advantage of the

chaos to conquer the northern third of the peninsula. Thereafter, Italy would be divided between Lombard territories in the north, east Roman territories in the south, and papal territories located precariously between them. The actors would shift, but this division among northern, central, and southern Italy would continue to characterize Italian political life until the nineteenth century.

Eastern Roman control over North Africa lasted only a few generations longer than it did in Italy. Weakened by religious dissension and heavy taxation, this area fell during the seventh century to the invading armies of Islam, along with Egypt and the rest of Roman Africa. When it did, Christianity in North Africa largely disappeared.

Farther north, the Visigothic kingdom of Spain continued to control the interior portions of the country, despite Justinian's conquest of the Mediterranean coast. After the imperial armies departed, the Visigoths resumed such control as they had ever exercised over these coastal regions. But tensions between the Arian Visigoths and their Catholic subjects continued even after 587, when the Visigothic king Reccared finally converted to orthodox Christianity. Hostility among the Visigothic kings, their Catholic bishops, and the Romanized population of the Mediterranean coast would last until the end of the Visigothic kingdom. Despite the Visigothic kings' efforts to pattern their

CHRONOLOGY

THE ROMAN REVIVAL OF JUSTINIAN, 527–568

Reign of Justinian	527–565
Publication of the *Corpus Juris Civilis*	529–534
Justinian conquers the Vandal kingdom of northwest Africa	533
Justinian reconquers Italian peninsula	536
Justinian defeats last Gothic outposts	563
Justinian rules over Mediterranean world	563–565
Death of Justinian	565
Germanic Lombards conquer northern Italy	568

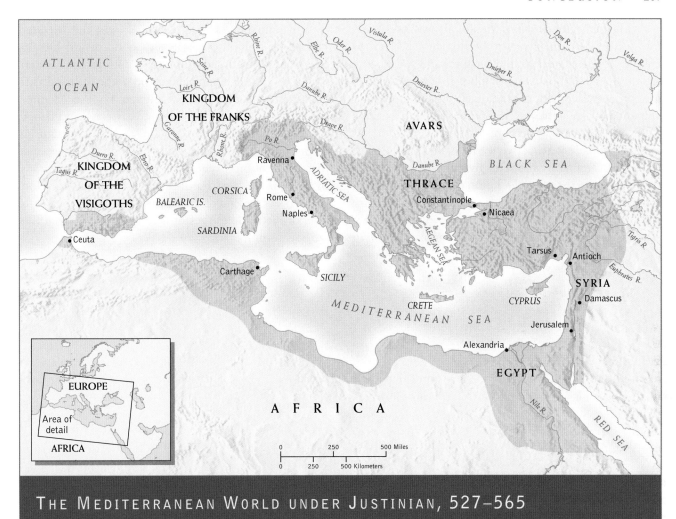

THE MEDITERRANEAN WORLD UNDER JUSTINIAN, 527–565

Compare this map with the one on p. 224. Which areas of the former Roman Empire did Justinian not attempt to reconquer? Is there any strategic logic to Justinian's reconquests? What would have been necessary to hold this newly reconstituted Roman Empire together after Justinian's death?

rule on Byzantine example, their kingdom quickly collapsed in the early eighth century when Muslim armies crossed the Strait of Gibraltar. By the end of the century, Christian rulers controlled only the northernmost parts of the Iberian peninsula and the area around Barcelona. For the next 300 years, Spain would be an important part of the Muslim world.

CONCLUSION

From its earliest days, Rome had been characterized by its remarkable capacity to assimilate the disparate cultures of the lands Rome conquered. In this process, both Rome and its empire were steadily transformed. The pace of these transformations accelerated markedly, however, from the mid-third century on—so much so that historians now commonly refer to the period from the mid-third century to the early seventh century as "late antiquity" to distinguish it from the classical Roman world that preceded it. During these centuries, larger numbers of immigrants entered the Roman Empire than ever before, drawn by a combination of land hunger, opportunity, and the desire to participate in the material and cultural benefits of Roman life. In the western empire especially, the number of these new immigrants became so large during the late fourth and fifth centuries that the frontier areas of the empire ceased to be distinguishable from the more Romanized areas of the interior.

At the same time, internal cultural processes were transforming what it meant to be Roman. The learned culture of the Greek and Roman world was being steadily extended to larger numbers of people; but in the process, learned culture itself was increasingly vulgarized. And finally, the empire itself became Christian, first by persuasion, as Constantine and his successors made it attractive for individuals to convert to the new religion, and later by coercion, as Christianity became the official religion of the entire Roman Empire. As a result, a new fusion of Christian culture and late Roman governance began to evolve, not only around the imperial court at Constantinople but also in the provinces.

What did not change, however, was the Mediterranean focus of this evolving late-antique world. Despite the emergence of new political units in the western Roman Empire, Roman civilization in the fifth and sixth centuries remained firmly centered on the Mediterranean Sea. That too, however, was soon to change. The seventh century would witness the final fracturing of this unified Mediterranean world and the emergence in its place of three quite different Western civilizations: Byzantium, western Europe, and Islam. This development marks the end of the classical world and the beginning of the Middle Ages. It is to this development that we now turn.

KEY TERMS

tetrarchy	Arians	Cassiodorus
Constantinople	Saint Benedict of Nursia	Justinian
Pharisees	Visigoths	
Paul	Saint Augustine	

SELECTED READINGS

Saint Augustine. *The City of God*. Trans. Henry Bettenson. Baltimore, Md., 1972.

Saint Augustine. *Confessions*. Trans. Henry M. Chadwick. Oxford, 1991.

Saint Augustine. *The Enchiridion on Faith, Hope and Love*. Trans. H. Paolucci. Chicago, 1961.

Saint Augustine. *On Christian Doctrine*. Trans. D. W. Robertson Jr. New York, 1958.

Boethius. *The Consolation of Philosophy*. Trans. R. Green. Indianapolis, Ind., 1962.

Bowersock, G. W., Peter Brown, and Oleg Grabar. *Late Antiquity: A Guide to the Postclassical World*. Cambridge, Mass., 1999. An authoritative compilation. The first half is devoted to essays on the cultural features of the period; the second half is organized as an encyclopedia.

Brown, Peter. *Augustine of Hippo*. Berkeley, Calif., 1967. A great biography, by the greatest living scholar of late antiquity.

Brown, Peter. *The Body and Society: Men, Women and Sexual Renunciation in Early Christianity*. New York, 1988. A revealing study of one of the fundamental transformations Christianity brought to the late antique world.

Brown, Peter. *Power and Persuasion in Late Antiquity: Toward a Christian Empire*. Madison, Wis., 1992. An important revisionist account of the effect of Christianization on the political culture of the later Roman Empire.

Brown, Peter. *The Rise of Western Christendom: Triumph and Diversity, 200–1000*, 2d ed. Oxford, 2002. Evocatively written picture of the diverse forms Christianity took as it spread east and north from the Mediterranean world.

Brown, Peter. *The World of Late Antiquity*. New York, 1971. Still the best short survey of the period, with excellent illustrations.

Cameron, Averil. *The Later Roman Empire, A.D. 284–430*. London, 1993. Now the standard account of its period, with an emphasis on imperial politics.

Cameron, Averil. *The Mediterranean World in Late Antiquity, A.D. 395–600*. London, 1993. Masterful, with excellent, succinct bibliographical essays.

Cassiodorus. *An Introduction to Divine and Human Readings*. Trans. L. W. Jones. New York, 1946.

Chadwick, Henry M. *Augustine*. Oxford, 1986. The best short introduction to Augustine's thought.

Chadwick, Henry M. *Boethius*. Oxford, 1981. The best intellectual biography of this important thinker.

Clark, Gillian. *Christianity and Roman Society*. Cambridge, 2004. A short, stimulating survey that places early Christianity firmly in its Roman social context.

Clark, Gillian. *Women in Late Antiquity*. Oxford, 1993. A clear, compact account of an important subject.

Coogan, Michael, ed. *The Oxford History of the Biblical World*. Oxford, 1998. A reliable but rather traditional account of the historical events recounted in the Hebrew Bible and the New Testament.

Eusebius. *The History of the Church*. Trans. G. A. Williamson. Baltimore, Md., 1965. An indispensible narrative account of Constantine's reign, written by one of his courtier-bishops.

Eusebius. *Eusebius' Life of Constantine*. Trans., Averil Cameron and Stuart Hall. Oxford, 1999. An admiring life that reflects Constantine's own vision of his religious authority.

Heather, Peter. *The Fall of the Roman Empire. A New History of Rome and the Barbarians*. Oxford, 2006. A lively narrative account of the events that resulted in the collapse of the western Roman Empire.

Lane Fox, Robin. *Pagans and Christians*. New York, 1987. A subtle, perceptive, lengthy, but highly readable exploration of the pagan world within which Christianity grew up.

Lawrence, Clifford Hugh. *Medieval Monasticism*, 3d ed. London, 2000. Concise, intelligent, perceptive survey of monasticism from its beginnings to the end of the Middle Ages.

Markus, R. A. *The End of Ancient Christianity*. New York, 1990. An expert synthetic study of Christianity in the western Roman Empire between 350 and 600 C.E.

Moorhead, John. *Justinian*. New York, 1994. A readable survey of the emperor and his times.

Pelikan, Jaroslav. *The Christian Tradition*. Volume I: *The Emergence of the Catholic Tradition*. Chicago, 1971. A history of Christian doctrine that is one of the tours de force of twentieth-century scholarship. Synthetic, clear, and objective.

Potter, David. *The Roman Empire at Bay*, A.D. *180–395*. London and New York, 2004. The most up-to-date and accessible synthetic account of the empire's decline.

Procopius. *The Secret History*. Trans. G. A. Williamson. Baltimore, Md., 1966. All the gossip from Justinian's court, much of it salacious.

Sanders, E. P. *The Historical Figure of Jesus*. London and New York, 1993. The best of the recent studies of Jesus in his first-century Jewish context.

Shanks, Hershel, ed. *Christianity and Rabbinic Judaism: A Parallel History of Their Origins and Early Development*. Washington, D.C., 1992. Accessible chapters written by top authorities, describing both Jewish and Christian developments from the first to the sixth centuries C.E.

Wallace-Hadrill, John Michael. *The Barbarian West*, 3d ed. London, 1966. Still the most interesting and suggestive analysis of the Romano-Germanic world created by the invasions of the fifth century C.E.

Whittaker, C. R. *Frontiers of the Roman Empire: A Social and Economic Study*. Baltimore, Md., 1994. A convincing picture of the frontiers of the Roman Empire as zones of intensive cultural interaction.

Williams, Stephen. *Diocletian and the Roman Recovery*. New York, 1997. Thorough and authoritative.

PART III

THE MIDDLE AGES

THE TERM *MIDDLE AGES* was coined by Europeans in the seventeenth century to express their view that a long and dismal period of interruption extended between the glorious accomplishments of Greece and Rome and their own "modern age." Because the term became so widespread, it is now an ineradicable part of our historical vocabulary; but no serious scholar today uses it with the sense of contempt it once invoked. To the contrary, most scholars would now argue that it was during the Middle Ages—roughly the years between 600 and 1500—that the cultural, political, and religious foundations of all three Western civilizations were established. Whether we speak of Byzantium, the Islamic world, or Europe, the Middle Ages were a formative and creative period in the history of Western civilizations.

Only with respect to Europe, however, do the years between 600 and 1500 constitute a true "middle age." For the Islamic world, these centuries witnessed the birth, expansion, and maturation of a new civilization that drew heavily on its classical past but fused that past with a sweeping new religious vision. For Byzantium, the so-called Middle Ages ended in 1453 with the conquest of the Byzantine Empire by the Ottoman Turks. Even for Europe, the metaphor of a middle age is to some extent misleading. Like Islamic civilization, European civilization began to take shape from the seventh century on, but it was not until the twelfth century that a truly distinctive European tradition with respect to politics, religion, and art emerged.

	POLITICS	SOCIETY AND CULTURE	ECONOMY	INTERNATIONAL RELATIONS
570	Muhammad, founder of Islam, born (570)			
	Pope Gregory I (Saint Gregory the Great) (590–604)	Growth of monasteries (600–700)		
	Ascension of Byzantine emperor Heraclius (610)			
		The Hijrah (622)		
				Arabs, under Abu-Bakr, rout Byzantine army in Syria (636)
				Arabs take Antioch, Damascus, and Jerusalem (636)
			Economic unity of Mediterranean world ends (650)	
	Shiite-Sunni Schism (661)			
	Umayyad family governs Islamic world (661–750)			Attempts by Muslims to take Constantinople (677, 717)
700			Agricultural revolution (700–1300)	
	The Carolingians share power with the Merovingian kings (717–751)	Iconoclast Controversy begins (717)		Arabs take Visigothic Spain (711–717)
	Abbasid family governs Islamic world (750–1258)			
	Pepin becomes king of the Franks (751)			
800	Charlemagne crowned Holy Roman emperor (800)			
	Charlemagne dies (814)			
				Rus sack Constantinople (860)
900		Cluniac reform of monasteries (900–1050)	Invention of iron horseshoe (900)	
		Islamic civilization's middle period (900–1250)	Rus establish principality near Kiev (900s)	
		Rise of Romanesque architecture (900–1150)		
		Avicenna, author of *Canon of Medicine* (980–1037)		Otto I defeats Hungarians at Lechfield (955)
1000	Capetian dynasty (987–1328)	European population triples (1000–1300)		
		Song of Roland (1050)	Invention of tandem harness for plowing (1050)	
	Split between Roman and Byzantine churches (1054)	Number of monks increases tenfold (1066–1200)	Water mill becomes widely used in Europe (1050)	
				Battle of Hastings, England falls to the Normans (1066)
				Battle of Manzikert, Turks take Anatolia (1071)
	Saxon civil war begins (1073)			
	Investiture Conflict (1075–1122)	Peter Abelard (1079–1142)		
		Cistercian order flourishes (1090–1153)		First Crusade (1095–1099)
		Hildegard of Bingen (1098–1179)		

POLITICS	SOCIETY AND CULTURE	ECONOMY	INTERNATIONAL RELATIONS	
	Rise of Gothic architecture (1100–1300)	Manorial lords begin trading serfs' freedom for cash (1100s)		1100
Concordat of Worms distinguishes temporal power of kings from spiritual power of clergy (1122)				
	Umar Khayyam, author of the *Rubiyat* (d. 1123)			
	Averroës, Spanish philosopher, theologian, and physician (1126–1198)			
	Catharism in southern France (1150–1300)			
	Rise of chivalry (1150)			
	Troubadour poets travel Europe (1150–1300)			
Reign of Frederick I, Barbarossa, as Holy Roman emperor (1152–1190)				
	Chretien de Troyes, author of Arthurian legends (1165–1190)			
	Saint Dominic (1170–1221)	Proliferation of windmills (1170s)		
	Rome decrees all cathedrals must support one schoolteacher (1179)			
	Saint Francis of Assisi (1182–1226)			
			Muslim leader, Saladin, recaptures Jerusalem (1187)	
	Theater appears outside of church (1200)			1200
	The Cid and Norse sagas are written down (1200s)			
			Crusaders sack Constantinople (1204)	
			England ousted from Normandy, Anjou, and Brittany (1204)	
Magna Carta (1215)	Saint Thomas Aquinas, author of *Summa Theologica* (1225–1274)		Mongols conquer eastern Slavic region (1200s)	
Fourth Lateran Council (1215)			Mongols take Kiev (1240)	
	Dante Alighieri, author of *The Divine Comedy* (1265–1321)		Mongols dispose of Abbasid caliphate (1258)	
	Giotto of Florence, painter (1267–1337)			
Emergence of English Parliament (1272–1307)				
Formation of French Estates General (1285–1314)	William of Ockham, founder of nominalism (1285–1349)			
French King, Philip IV (1285–1314)			Jews expelled from southern Italy, England, and France (1288–1306)	

CHAPTER SEVEN

ROME'S THREE HEIRS: THE BYZANTINE, ISLAMIC, AND EARLY MEDIEVAL WORLDS

A NEW PERIOD in the history of Western civilizations began in the seventh century. In the year 600, it was still possible for the rulers of the Roman Empire living in Constantinople to imagine their empire as uniting the entire Mediterranean world. By the end of the seventh century, however, three different successor civilizations to the Greco-Roman world of antiquity had emerged: the Byzantine, the Islamic, and the western European, each with its own language and distinctive ways of life. The history of Western civilizations from the seventh to the eleventh centuries is largely a story of the rivalries and interactions among these three emerging worlds, each of which preserved and extended different aspects of the late-antique inheritance they shared.

Like the provinces of the eastern Roman Empire over which it ruled, Byzantine civilization after 610 was Greek-speaking. It combined the bureaucratic and imperial traditions of late Roman governance with an intense pursuit of the Christian faith. This fusion had been pioneered in the fourth century by Constantine and his successors and was continuously elaborated in the eastern Roman Empire thereafter. Islamic civilization, in contrast, was Arabic-speaking. It was the most cosmopolitan and wide ranging (both geographically and culturally) of the three successor civilizations. The Islamic world was the heir both to the Roman vision of an expansive empire itself and to Roman ideals of cultural and religious assimilation as essential attributes of imperial rule. By combining the philosophical and scientific interests of the Hellenistic world with the literary and artistic culture of Persia, Islam created the most dynamic cultural amalgam of the early Middle Ages.

Western Christian civilization in the early Middle Ages was rooted in Latin but with important cultural influences from Germanic, Celtic, and Latin-derived vernacular languages. In contrast to Byzantium and Islam, it owed relatively little to Roman ideals of empire, except briefly under the Carolingians. It was, however, profoundly influenced by Roman ideals of law and local government, which carried with them a continuing influence from the republican traditions of ancient Rome. For western Europe in the early Middle Ages, law and Latin Christianity were

FOCUS QUESTIONS

- How did the Byzantine state survive for nearly a millennium?

- How was Islam able to spread so rapidly?

- What forces combined to undermine the political unity of the Islamic world?

- What caused economic and social change in seventh-century western Europe?

- How did Charlemagne redefine the relationship between Christianity and kingship?

the pinnacles of Roman cultural achievement. They were, indeed, the very essence of what it meant to be Roman; and to be Roman remained an almost universal aspiration in early medieval Europe. If we measure civilizations by their highest philosophical and literary accomplishments, western Europe in the early Middle Ages was a laggard in comparison with Byzantium and the Islamic world. It was also the least economically advanced of these three successor states and faced the greatest organizational weaknesses in both government and religion. By the twelfth century, however, Latin Christian civilization was no longer on the defensive against its rivals in military, economic, or religious terms. Rather, it stood at the beginning of an extraordinary period of expansion and conquest that would bring it ultimately to a dominant position in world affairs during the early modern and modern eras.

THE BYZANTINE EMPIRE AND ITS CULTURE

How did the Byzantine state survive for nearly a millennium?

It is impossible to date the beginning of Byzantine history with any precision because the Byzantine Empire was the uninterrupted successor of the Roman state. For this reason, different historians prefer different beginnings. Some argue that Byzantine characteristics had already emerged in Roman history under Diocletian; others assert that Byzantine history began when Constantine moved his capital from Rome to Constantinople, the city that subsequently became the center of the Byzantine world. Diocletian and Constantine, however, continued to rule a united Roman Empire. As we have seen, as late as the sixth century, after the western part of the empire had fallen to the Germans, the eastern Roman emperor Justinian thought of himself as an heir to Augustus and fought hard to win back the West. Justinian's reign was clearly an important turning point in the direction of Byzantine civilization because it saw the crystallization of new forms of thought and art that can be considered more Byzantine than Roman. But this still remains a matter of subjective emphasis: some scholars emphasize these newer forms, whereas others respond that Justinian continued to speak Latin and dreamed of restoring old Rome. Only after 610 did a new dynasty emerge that came

from the East, spoke Greek, and maintained a fully eastern or Byzantine orientation. Hence, although good arguments can be made for beginning Byzantine history with Diocletian, Constantine, or Justinian, we will begin here with the accession in 610 of the emperor Heraclius.

It is also convenient to begin in 610 because from then until 1071 the main lines of Byzantine military and political history were determined by resistance against successive waves of invasion from the east. When Heraclius came to the throne, the very existence of the Byzantine Empire was being challenged by the Persians, who had conquered almost all of the empire's Asian territories. As a symbol of their triumph the Persians in 614 even carried off from Jerusalem the relic believed to be part of the original cross on which Jesus had been crucified. This relic had become a potent symbol of the Christian legitimacy of the eastern Roman emperors. By enormous effort Heraclius rallied Byzantine strength and turned the tide, routing the Persians, recapturing Jerusalem, and retrieving the cross in 627. But soon thereafter new armies began to invade Byzantine territory, swarming out of hitherto placid Arabia. Inspired by the new religion of Islam and profiting from Byzantine exhaustion after the struggle with Persia, the Arabs made astonishingly rapid gains. By 650 they had taken most of the Byzantine territories that the Persians had occupied in the early seventh century, including Jerusalem, which became a holy site for Muslims no less than for Christians and Jews. Arab armies also conquered Persia itself, and rapidly made their way westward across North Africa, where Byzantine control had long been resented. Having become a Mediterranean power, the Arabs also took to

CHRONOLOGY

THE BYZANTINE EMPIRE, 610–1100

Ascension of the emperor Heraclius	610
Arabs seize most of Byzantine territory	c. 650
Constantinople nearly falls to the Arabs	717
Byzantines reconquer most of Asia Minor	717–750
Stalemate between Arabs and Byzantines	750–950
Byzantines reconquer most of Syria	c. 950–1000
Seljuk Turks overrun eastern Byzantine provinces	1071
First Crusade	1095–1099

HOW DID THE BYZANTINE STATE SURVIVE FOR NEARLY A MILLENNIUM?

THE BYZANTINE EMPIRE AND ITS CULTURE   247

the sea. In 677 they tried to conquer Constantinople with a fleet. Failing that, they attempted to take the city again in 717 by means of a concerted land and sea operation.

The Arab threat to Constantinople in 717 marked a new low in Byzantine fortunes, but the threat was countered by the emperor Leo the Isaurian (717–741) with the same resolution Heraclius had shown against the Persians a century before. With the help of a secret incendiary mixture known as "Greek fire" and great military ability, Leo was able to defeat the Arab forces on sea and land. Leo's defense of Constantinople in 717 was one of the most significant battles in European history. Had the Islamic armies taken Constantinople there would have been little to stop them from sweeping through the rest of Europe. Over the next few decades, however, the Byzantines reconquered most of Asia Minor, which became the heartland of their empire for the next 300 years. In the eleventh century, however, a new Islamic power, the Seljuk (sehl-JOOK) Turks, reversed the Byzantine gains. In 1071 the Seljuks annihilated a Byzantine army at Manzikert in Asia Minor, a stunning victory that allowed them to overrun Byzantium's eastern provinces. Constantinople was now thrown back on itself more or less as it had been in the days of Heraclius and Leo. By and large, it would remain on the defensive for the next 400 years. The last remnants of the Byzantine Empire fell to the Ottoman Turks in 1453. Turks continue to rule in Constantinople—which they renamed Istanbul —to the present day.

SOURCES OF STABILITY

That Constantinople was finally taken was no surprise. What is a cause for wonder is that the Byzantine state survived for so many centuries in the face of so many different hostile forces. This wonder becomes all the greater when we recognize that the internal political history of the empire was exceedingly tumultuous. Because Byzantine power was so completely focused on the imperial court at Constantinople and because rulers followed their late Roman predecessors in claim-

Byzantine Soldiers Clashing with Arab Soldiers. This illustration from the Scylitzes chronicle dates back to the eleventh century, when the Seljuk Turks started to reverse the Byzantine gains in Asia in an offensive that would ultimately end the Byzantine Empire in the fifteenth century.

ing the powers of divinely appointed absolute monarchs, there was no way of opposing them other than by intrigue and violence. Hence Byzantine history was marked by repeated palace revolts involving mutilations, murders, and blindings. Byzantine political life became so famous for its behind-the-scenes complexity that we still use the word *byzantine* to refer to highly complex and devious backstage machinations. Fortunately for the empire, some very able rulers did emerge from time to time to wield their unrestrained powers effectively. Even more fortunately, an efficient bureaucracy continued to function even during times of palace upheaval.

Efficient bureaucratic government was one of the major reasons for Byzantine success and longevity. Literate Byzantine bureaucrats supervised education and religion and presided over all forms of economic endeavor. Imperial officials in Constantinople regulated prices and wages, maintained systems of licensing, controlled exports, and enforced the observance of the Sabbath. Even chariot racing fell under strict governmental supervision, with the populace of Constantinople being assigned by governmental command to root for particular teams. Bureaucratic methods also regulated the army and navy, the courts, and the diplomatic service, endowing these agencies with organizational strengths incomparable for their time.

Another explanation for Byzantine endurance was the comparatively sound economic base of the state, at least until the eleventh century. Commerce and cities continued to flourish in the Byzantine east, as they had done in the late-antique period. Constantinople in the ninth and tenth centuries was a vital trade emporium for Far Eastern luxury goods and western raw materials. The empire also nurtured and protected its own industries, most notably silk making, and it was renowned until the eleventh century for its stable gold and silver coinage. Nor was Constantinople (which at times may have had a population of close to a million) its only great urban center. During certain periods Antioch and, up until the end of Byzantine history, the bustling cities of Thessalonica and Trebizond were also large and prosperous.

> The Iconoclasts wished to prohibit the veneration of icons—that is, images of Christ and the saints. Honoring such images seemed to the Iconoclasts to smack of idolatry and paganism.

Historians emphasize Byzantine trade and industry because these were so advanced for the time and provided most of the surplus wealth that supported the state. But agriculture lay at the heart of the Byzantine economy. Byzantine agricultural history was marked by the struggles of independent peasant farmers to stay free of the encroachments of large estates owned by wealthy aristocrats and monasteries. Until the eleventh century the free peasantry managed to maintain its position with the help of state legislation. After 1025, however, the aristocracy gained power in the government and began to transform the peasants into impoverished tenants. This had many unfortunate results, not least that peasants became less interested in resisting the enemy. The defeat at Manzikert in 1071 was in part the result of the government's short-sighted acquiescence to aristocratic ambitions.

BYZANTINE RELIGION

So far we have spoken about military campaigns, government, and economics as if they were the keys to Byzantine survival. Seen from hindsight they were, but what the Byzantines themselves cared about most was the religious orthodoxy of their empire. Byzantines fought and died over the proper wording of religioius creeds. This intense preoccupation with questions of doctrine could cause great harm during periods of religious dissension, but it also endowed the Byzantine state with a powerful sense of confidence and mission.

Byzantine doctrinal disputes were greatly complicated by the fact that the emperors took an active role

in them. Emperors exercised great power in the life of the church; some even determined the outcome of religious debates. Nonetheless, especially in the face of provincial separatism, rulers could never force all their subjects to believe the same doctrines they themselves did. Even Byzantine governmental authority did not stretch that far. Only after the loss of many eastern provinces and the refinement of doctrinal formulae did religious peace seem near in the eighth century. But then it was shattered for still another century by what is known as the Iconoclastic Controversy.

The Iconoclasts wished to prohibit the veneration of icons— that is, images of Christ and the saints. Honoring such images seemed to the Iconoclasts to smack of idolatry and paganism. They argued that nothing made by human beings should be worshiped by them, that Christ was so divine that he could not be represented artistically in any fashion, and that the prohibition of

King Roger II of Sicily (1095–1154) Being Crowned by Christ. Byzantine rulers used imagery such as this mosaic to show that their powers came to them supernaturally.

How did the Byzantine state survive for nearly a millennium?

The Byzantine Empire and Its Culture   249

worshiping graven images in the Ten Commandments (Exodus 20:4) put the matter beyond dispute. Traditionalists responded that it was not the images themselves that were being worshiped but the heavenly reality that lay beyond them. Like Byzantine art generally, icons were intended to act as windows through which a glimpse of heaven might be granted to human beings on earth.

The Iconoclastic movement was initiated by Emperor Leo the Isaurian and subsequently directed with even greater energy by his son Constantine V (740–775). Their motives remain a subject of dispute among historians. Because Leo the Isaurian was the emperor who saved Constantinople from Muslim attack in 717, and since Muslims opposed all religious images as "the work of Satan" (Qur'ān, V. 92), iconoclasm may have been an attempt to answer one of Islam's greatest criticisms of Christianity as well as to ensure that the Christian empire was worshiping God correctly. There may also have been political and financial considerations behind the campaign. By proclaiming a radical new religious movement, the emperors may have intended to reassert their control over the church and combat the growing strength of monasteries. As events turned out, the monasteries did rally behind the cause of images; and as a result, they were bitterly persecuted by Constantine V, who took the opportunity to confiscate much monastic wealth.

The Iconoclastic Controversy was resolved in the ninth century by a return to the status quo—namely, the veneration of images—but the century of turmoil over the issue had some lasting results. One was the destruction by imperial order of a large amount of religious art. Pre-eighth-century Byzantine religious art that survives today comes mostly from places such as Italy or Palestine, which were beyond the reach of the Iconoclastic emperors. A second consequence of the controversy was the opening of a serious religious breach between the Greek east and the Latin west. The pope, who until the eighth century had usually been a close ally of the Byzantine emperors, strongly opposed Iconoclasm, not least because Iconoclasm tended to question the cult of saints, and the claims of papal primacy were based on the pope's role as Saint Peter's successor. Papal opposition to Iconoclasm during the eighth century led to worsening relations between east and west that culminated with the crowning of the Frankish leader Charlemagne as the new Roman emperor in the west on Christmas Day 800.

The ultimate defeat of Iconoclasm led to the reassertion of some major traits of Byzantine religiosity, which from the ninth century until the end of Byzantine history remained predominant. One of these traits was a renewed emphasis on the traditional, orthodox faith of the empire as the key to its political unity and military success. Religious tradition became the touchstone of doctrinal correctness and political legitimacy. As one opponent of Iconoclasm said, "If an angel or an emperor announces to you a gospel other than the one you have received, close your ears." This emphasis on tradition lessened religious conflicts, and helped orthodoxy gain new adherents in the ninth and tenth centuries. But it also reinforced the hegemony of Constantinople's own religious traditions within the empire, thus marginalizing even further the rival religious traditions of Syrian and Armenian Christianity. Fear of heresy also tended to inhibit free speculation, not just in religion but also in related intellectual matters. Although the Byzantine emperors founded and supported a university in Constantinople, they never permitted it to exercise any significant degree of intellectual freedom, in marked contrast with the freewheeling intellectual atmosphere of the growing universities of twelfth- and thirteenth-century western Europe.

Byzantine Culture

Religion dominated Byzantine life; but commitment to Christianity by no means inhibited the Byzantines from preserving and revering their ancient Greek heritage. Byzantine schools based their instruction on classical Greek literature, and especially Homer, to an astonishing degree. Educated people around the Byzantine court could quote but a single line of Homer and expect that their audience would know immediately the entire passage from which it came. In the English-speaking world, only the King James Bible has ever achieved a degree of cultural saturation comparable with Homer in Byzantium. Like the seventeenth-century Bible, Homer for the Byzantines was simultaneously a literary model, an instructional textbook, and a guide to personal morality and wisdom.

Byzantine scholars also studied intensively the philosophy of Plato and the historical prose of Thucydides. Aristotle's works were also known but were regarded with less interest. By and large, the Greek scientific and mathematical tradition was neglected by the Byzantines, and even philosophy was considerably restricted. Justinian, for example, shut down the Athenian philosophical academies that had existed since Plato's day, declaring that everything worth knowing was already known; the emperor Alexius Comnenus (d. 1118) similarly put a stop to the teaching of Aristotelian logic. The inventive rejuvenation of tradition was prized in

BYZANTINE CLASSICISM

This poem, by an eleventh-century Byzantine scholar, illustrates the sense of continuity learned Byzantines felt between their own Christian world and the world of the ancient Greek philosophers and authors.

May Christ Save Plato and Plutarch from Eternal Damnation

If perchance you wish to exempt certain pagans from punishment, my Christ,
May you spare for my sake Plato and Plutarch,
For both were very close to your laws in both teaching and way of life.
Even if they were unaware that you as God reign over all,
In this matter only your charity is needed,
Through which you are willing to save all men while asking nothing in return.

Deno John Geanokoplos, ed. and trans., *Byzantium: Church, Society, and Civilization Seen through Contemporary Eyes.* (Chicago, 1984), p. 395.

QUESTIONS FOR ANALYSIS

1. The poetic prayer by an eleventh-century Byzantine scholar expresses a pious hope not only for Plato and Plutarch but also for the author, who wanted to hold on to both pagan classics and Christianity. From a Christian point of view, what problems arise from this position?

2. What would have to be changed in Plato's works (e.g., The Republic) to make them acceptable to orthodox Christians? Do the Platonic dialogues assist Christianity in any way? Would Christianity be something very different without Plato?

Byzantine culture, but originality was not the goal toward which Byzantine intellectual life was directed. Preservation rather than innovation was the hallmark of Byzantine classicism. Nevertheless, such dedicated classicism enriched Byzantine intellectual and literary life and helped preserve the Greek classics for later ages. The bulk of classical Greek literature that we have today survives only because it was copied by Byzantine scribes.

Byzantine classicism was a product of an educational system for the laity that extended to women as well as to men. Given attitudes and practices in the contemporary Christian West and in Islam, Byzantine commitment to female education was truly unusual. Girls from aristocratic or prosperous families did not go to schools but were educated at home by private tutors. In the Byzantine world of the ninth through eleventh centuries, learned women were praised for being able to discourse like Plato or Pythagoras. The most famous of these Byzantine female intellectuals was the princess Anna Comnena, who described the deeds of her father, Alexius, in an urbane biography in which she copiously cited Homer and Euripides. But in addition to such literary figures there were also female physicians in the Byzantine Empire, a fact of note given their scarcity in other Western societies until recent times.

Byzantine achievements in the realms of architecture and art are more familiar. The finest example of Byzantine architecture was the church of Santa Sophia (Holy Wisdom) in Constantinople, constructed at enormous cost by the emperor Justinian in the sixth century. Although built before the date taken here as the begin-

How did the Byzantine state survive for nearly a millennium?

The Byzantine Empire and Its Culture 251

ning of Byzantine history, it quickly came to define a characteristically Byzantine architectural style. Its purpose was not to express pride in human accomplishment but rather to symbolize the inward and spiritual character of the Christian religion. For this reason the architects gave little attention to the external appearance of the building. Nothing but plain brick covered with plaster was used for the exterior walls; there were no marble facings, graceful columns, or sculptured friezes. The interior, however, was decorated with richly colored mosaics, gold leaf, colored marble columns, and bits of tinted glass set on edge to refract the rays of sunlight like sparkling gems. To emphasize a sense of the miraculous, the building was constructed in such a way that light appeared not to come from the outside at all, but to be generated within.

The structural design of Santa Sophia was something altogether new in the history of architecture. The church was designed in the form of a cross with a magnificent dome over its central square. The main problem was how to fit the circumference of the dome to the square area it was supposed to cover. The solution was to have four great arches spring from pillars at the four corners of the square. The rim of the dome was then made to rest on the keystones of the arches, with the curved triangular spaces between the arches filled in with masonry. The result was an architectural framework of marvelous strength, which at the same time made possible a style of imposing grandeur and delicacy. The great dome of Santa Sophia has a diameter of 107 feet and rises to a height of nearly 180 feet from the floor. So many windows are placed around its rim that the dome appears to have no support at all but to be suspended in midair.

BYZANTIUM AND THE WESTERN CHRISTIAN WORLD

After the conflicts of the Iconoclastic period, relations between eastern and western Christians remained tense, partly because Constantinople resented Western claims (initiated by Charlemagne in 800) to rule a rival Roman Empire but most of all because religious differences between the two continued to grow. From the Byzantine point of view westerners were uncouth and ignorant, unable to understand the Greek language in which all serious theologians worked; whereas to western European eyes, the Byzantines were arrogant, effeminate, and prone to heresy. In 1054, papal claims to primacy over the eastern church provoked a religious schism that has never healed. Soon thereafter the Crusades drove home the dividing wedge.

After the sack of Constantinople in 1204 by crusaders, Byzantine hatred of westerners became intense. "Between us and them," one Byzantine wrote, "there is now a deep chasm: we do not have a single thought in common." Westerners called easterners "the dregs of the dregs . . . unworthy of the sun's light." Easterners called westerners the children of darkness, alluding to the fact that the sun sets in the west. The beneficiaries of this hatred were the Turks, who conquered Constantinople in 1453 and soon thereafter conquered most of southeastern Europe.

Santa Sophia. The greatest monument of Byzantine architecture. The four minarets were added after the fall of the Byzantine Empire, when the Turks turned the church into a mosque.

In view of this long history of hostility (which we will discuss more fully in the next chapter), it is best to end our treatment of Byzantine civilization here by recalling how much the western European world owes to it. The Byzantine Empire acted as a bulwark against Islam from the seventh to the eleventh centuries, thus helping preserve an independent and Christian West. Western Europeans also owe an enormous cultural debt to Byzantine scholars, who preserved much of the classical Greek literary tradition during centuries when these texts were entirely unknown in western Europe. Byzantine art has also exerted a profound influence on the art of western Europe. Saint Mark's Basilica in Venice reflects this influence; so too does the art of such great Western painters as Giotto and El Greco. Modern travelers who view Byzantine mosaics in such cities as Ravenna and Palermo are awestruck; those who make their way to Istanbul still find Santa Sophia breathtaking. In such jeweled beauty, the light from the Byzantine Empire continues to glow.

> Indeed, more than Judaism or Christianity, Islam has been a great experiment in trying to build a worldwide society based on the fullest harmony between religious requirements and precepts for everyday existence.

Interior of Santa Sophia Showing the Cupola. The revolutionary dome structure, shown here, made it appear as if the dome floated on light. After 1453, Santa Sophia became a mosque. It is now a museum.

THE GROWTH OF ISLAM

How was Islam able to spread so rapidly?

In contrast to Byzantine history, which has no clearly datable beginning but a definite end in 1453, the history of Islamic civilization has a clear point of origin, beginning with the career of Muhammad in the seventh century, but no end. Believers in Islam, known as Muslims, currently make up about one-seventh of the global population: in their greatest concentrations they extend from Africa through the Middle East and the states of the former Soviet Union to South Asia and Indonesia. All Muslims subscribe to both a common religion and a common way of life, for Islam has always demanded from its followers not just adherence to common forms of worship but also adherence to certain social and cultural norms. Indeed, more than Judaism or Christianity, Islam has been a great experiment in trying to build a worldwide society based on the fullest harmony between religious requirements and precepts for everyday existence. In this section we will trace the early history of Islam, with primary emphasis on its westward expansion. Nonetheless we must remember that Islam expanded in many directions and that it ultimately had as much influence on the history of Africa and South Asia as it did on that of Europe or western Asia.

THE RISE OF ISLAM

Islam was born in Arabia, a desert land so backward before the founding of Islam that the two dominant neighboring empires, the Roman and the Persian, had not even bothered to conquer it. Most Arabs were Bedouins (*BEHD-oo-ihns*), wandering camel herders who lived off the milk of their animals and the produce of desert oases. In the second half of the sixth century Arabia saw a quickening of economic life owing to a shift in long-distance trade routes. The protracted wars between the Byzantine and Persian Empires made Arabia a safer transit route than other alternatives for caravans passing between Africa and Asia. Some towns grew to direct and take advantage of this growth of trade. The most prominent of these was Mecca, which not only lay on the junction of major trade routes but also had long been a local religious center. In Mecca was located the Kabah, a pilgrimage shrine containing the Black Stone, a meteorite worshiped as a miraculous relic by adherents of many different divinities. The men who controlled this shrine and also directed the economic life of the Meccan area belonged to the tribe of Quraish *(kur-RAYSH)*, an aristocracy of traders and entrepreneurs who provided the area with what little government it knew.

Muhammad, the founder of Islam, was born in Mecca to a family of Quraish about 570. Orphaned early in life, he entered the service of a rich widow whom he later married, thereby attaining financial security. Until middle age he lived as a prosperous trader little different from his fellow townsmen, but around 610 he underwent a religious experience that changed the course of his life and ultimately that of a good part of the world. Although most Arabs until then had been polytheists who recognized at most the vague superiority of a more powerful god they called Allah, Muhammad in 610 heard a voice from heaven tell him that there was no god but Allah alone. In other words, as the result of a conversion experience he became an uncompromising monotheist. Thereafter he received further messages that became the basis for a new religion and that commanded him to accept the calling of "Prophet" to proclaim the new monotheistic faith to the Quraish. At first he was not very successful in gaining converts beyond a limited circle, perhaps because the leading Quraish tribesmen believed that establishment of a new religion would deprive the Kabah, and therewith Mecca, of its central place in local worship, with its attendant economic benefits. The town of Yathrib to the north, however, had no such concerns, and its representatives invited Muhammad to emigrate there so that he could serve as a neutral arbiter of local rivalries. In 622 Muhammad and his followers accepted the invitation. Because their migration—called in Arabic the Hijrah *(HIJ-ruh;* or Hegira)—saw the beginning of an advance in Muhammad's fortunes, Muslims regard it as marking the beginning of their era: as Christians begin their era with the birth of Christ, so Muslims begin their dating system with the Hijrah of 622.

Muhammad changed the name of Yathrib to Medina ("city of the Prophet") and quickly established himself as ruler of the town. In the course of doing this he consciously began to organize his converts into a political as well as a religious community. But he still needed to find some means of support for his original Meccan followers, and he also wanted to consolidate his political and prophetic authority among the Quraish. Accordingly, he started leading his followers in raids on Quraish caravans traveling beyond

The Kabah. It contains the Black Stone, which was supposed to have been miraculously sent down from heaven and rests in the courtyard of the great mosque in Mecca.

Mecca. The Quraish tried to defend themselves, but after a few years Muhammad's band, fired by religious enthusiasm, succeeded in defeating them. In 630, after several desert battles, Muhammad entered Mecca in triumph. The Quraish thereupon submitted to the new faith, and the Kabah was not only preserved but made the main shrine of Islam, as it remains today. After the capture of Mecca other tribes throughout Arabia in turn accepted the new faith. Thus, although Muhammad died in 632, he lived long enough to see the religion he had founded become a success.

THE RELIGIOUS TEACHINGS OF ISLAM

The word *islam* means "submission," and the faith of Islam calls for absolute submission to Allah, the Creator, God Almighty—the same omnipotent deity worshiped by Christians and Jews. Instead of saying, then, that Muslims believe "there is no god but Allah," it is more correct to say they believe that "there is no divinity but God." In keeping with this strict monotheism, Muslims believe that Muhammad himself was God's last and greatest prophet but not that he was God himself.

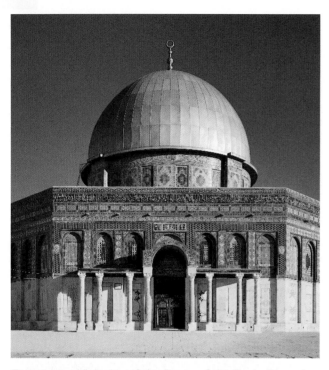

Exterior and Interior of the Dome of the Rock, Jerusalem. According to Muslim tradition, Muhammad made a miraculous journey to Jerusalem before his death and left a footprint in a rock. The mosque that was erected over the site in the seventh century is one of Islam's holiest shrines.

Men and women must surrender themselves entirely to God because divine judgment is imminent. Mortals must make a fundamental choice about whether to begin a new life of divine service: if they decide in favor of this, God will guide them to blessedness; but if they do not, God will turn away from them, and they will become irredeemably wicked. On Judgment Day the pious will be granted eternal life in a paradise of delights, but the damned will be sent to a realm of eternal fire and torture. The practical steps the believer can take are found in the Qur'an (Kuh-RAHN), the compilation of the revelations sent by God to Muhammad and hence the definitive Islamic scripture. These steps include thorough dedication to moral rectitude and compassion, and fidelity to set religious observances—a regimen of prayers and fasts, pilgrimage to Mecca, and frequent recitation of parts of the Qur'an.

The fact that much in the religion of Islam resembles Judaism and Christianity is not coincidental; Muhammad was definitely influenced by the two earlier religions. (There were many Jews in Mecca and Medina; Christian thought was also known to Muhammad, although more indirectly.) Islam most resembles Judaism and Christianity in its strict monotheism; its emphasis on personal morality and compassion; and its reliance on written, revealed scripture. Muhammad proclaimed the Qur'an as the ultimate source of religious authority but accepted both the Hebrew Bible and the Christian New Testament as divinely inspired. From Christianity Muhammad may also have derived his doctrines of the Last Judgment, the resurrection of the body with after death rewards and punishments, and his belief in angels (he reported that God's first message to him had been sent by the angel Gabriel). But although Muhammad accepted Jesus Christ as one of the greatest of a long line of prophets, he did not believe in Christ's divinity. Nor did Muhammad claim to have performed any miracles himself beyond his role in transmitting the Qur'an from heaven to earth.

Islam is a religion without sacraments or priests. Every Muslim believer has direct responsibility for living the life of the faith without intermediaries; instead of priests there are only religious scholars who comment on problems of Islamic faith and law and who act as judges in disputes. Muslims are expected to pray together in mosques, but there is no such thing as a Muslim liturgy. The absence of clergy makes Islam more like Judaism, a similarity that is enhanced by Islamic stress on the inextricable connection among the religious, social, and political life of the divinely inspired community.

Unlike Judaism, however, Islam has historically aspired to unite the world into a single community of believers under the rule of Allah.

THE ISLAMIC CONQUESTS

This move toward worldwide influence began immediately on Muhammad's death. Because he had made no provision for a successor, it was unclear whether Muhammad's community would survive at all. But his closest followers—led by his father-in-law, Abu-Bakr (ab-BOO-BAK-uhr), and a zealous early convert named Umar—quickly took the initiative by naming Abu-Bakr *caliph*, meaning "deputy of the Prophet" and so the supreme religious and political leader of all Muslims. Immediately after becoming caliph, Abu-Bakr began a military campaign to subdue various Arab tribes that had followed Muhammad but were not willing to accept his successor's authority. In the course of this successful military action Abu-Bakr's forces began to spill northward beyond the borders of Arabia, where they met only minimal resistance from Byzantine and Persian forces.

Abu-Bakr died two years after his accession but was succeeded as caliph by Umar, who continued to direct his armies against Byzantium and Persia. In the following years Arab triumphs were virtually uninterrupted. In 636 the Arabs routed a Byzantine army in Syria and then quickly swept over the entire area, occupying the leading cities of Antioch, Damascus, and Jerusalem. In 637 they destroyed the main army of the Persians and marched into the Persian capital of Ctesiphon. Once the Persian administrative center was taken, the highly centralized Persian Empire offered little resistance. By 651 the Arabian conquest of the entire Persian realm was complete. The Islamic forces now turned west toward North Africa, capturing Byzantine Egypt by 646 and extending their control throughout the rest of North Africa during the following decades. Attempts in 677 and 717 to capture Constantinople failed; but in 711 the Arabs crossed from North Africa into Visigothic Spain and quickly took almost all of that area too. Thus within less than a century the forces of Islam had conquered all of ancient Persia and much of the late Roman Mediterranean world.

How can we explain this prodigious expansion? The best approach is to see first what impelled the conquerors and then to see what circumstances helped ease their way. Contrary to widespread belief, the early spread of Islam was not achieved through a religious crusade. At first the Arabs were not interested in converting other peoples; instead, they hoped that conquered populations would not convert so that they could maintain their own identity as a community of rulers and tax gatherers. But although their motives for expansion were not religious, religious enthusiasm played a crucial role in making the hitherto unruly Arabs take orders from the caliph and in instilling a sense that they were carrying out the will of God. What really moved the Arabs out of the desert was the search for richer territory and booty; what kept them advancing was the ease of acquiring new wealth as they progressed.

The Arabs' inspiration by Islam also coincided with a period of weakness in their principal enemies. The Byzantines and Persians had become so exhausted by their long wars with each other and with the barbarians that they could hardly rally for a new effort. Moreover, many of the local populations of Egypt, North Africa, and Asia Minor were already fed up with the financial demands made by their bureaucratic rulers. To them, Islamic conquest brought deliverance, not only from oppressive taxation but also from the persecuting religious authorities of Constantinople, who had sought to suppress heretical Christian groups in all these areas. Because the Arabs did not demand that Jews or Christians convert to Islam and because they exacted fewer taxes than the Byzantines and the Persians, they were often preferred to the old rulers. One Christian writer in Syria went so far as to say, "the God of vengeance delivered us out of the hands of the Romans [that is, the Byzantine Empire] by means of the Arabs." For all these reasons Islam quickly spread over the territory between Egypt and Iran, and has been rooted there ever since.

THE SHIITE–SUNNI SCHISM

Despite the success of the Arab conquests, succession disputes soon began to divide Muslims against one another. In 644, when the caliph Umar died, he was replaced by Uthman, a weak ruler who belonged to the Umayyad family (oo-MY-yad), a wealthy clan from Mecca whose members had initally resisted Muhammad's call. Uthman's opponents rallied around the Prophet's cousin and son-in-law, Ali, whose warrior spirit and family ties to Muhammad made him seem a more appropriate choice to be caliph. When Uthman

> Thus within less than a century the forces of Islam had conquered all of ancient Persia and much of the late Roman Mediterranean world.

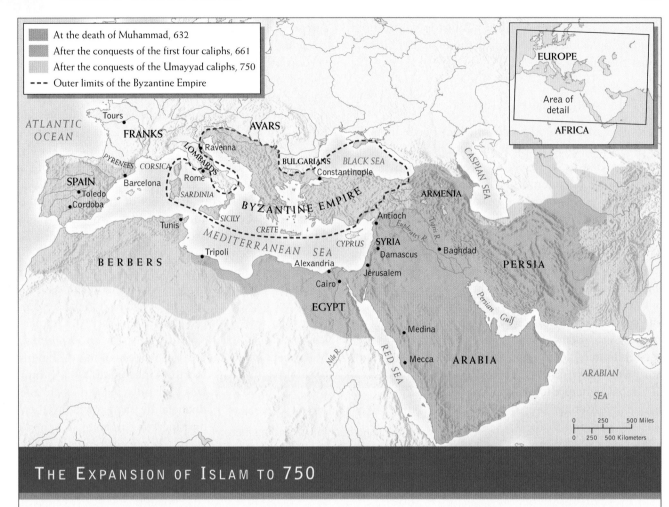

	At the death of Muhammad, 632
	After the conquests of the first four caliphs, 661
	After the conquests of the Umayyad caliphs, 750
- - -	Outer limits of the Byzantine Empire

THE EXPANSION OF ISLAM TO 750

This map shows the steady advance of Islam from the time of Muhammad to the middle of the eighth century. Note the rapid expansion in the generation after Muhammad's death. Which aspects of Islam's organization and fervor helped contribute to the spread of Muslim armies? What does the rapid advance suggest about the preparedness of their initial foes, such as Byzantium and Persia? Why were these foes not better able to resist? Why was the capture of Constantinople so crucial to successive Muslim rulers even after Islam had spread well beyond the eastern Mediterranean?

was murdered in 656 by mutineers, Ali's supporters declared him to be the new caliph. But Uthman's powerful family refused to accept Ali. Soon thereafter, Ali was murdered and Uthman's party emerged triumphant. In 661 another member of the Umayyad family took over as caliph, and that house ruled the Islamic world from its capital at Damascus until 750.

Ali's followers, however, did not accept defeat. As time went on they hardened into a minority religious party known as Shiites (*shi'a* is Arabic for "party" or "faction"). The Shiites insisted that only descendants of Ali and his wife, Fatimah (the daughter of the Prophet), could legitimately rule the Muslim community (the *umma*). Nor did the Shiites accept as binding the customary religious practices (*sunna*) that had

developed under the first two caliphs, Abu-Bakr and Umar. The Shiites' opponents did regard these customs as binding and thus were called Sunnis. This division between Shiites and Sunnis, which crystalized during the tenth century, has lasted until the present day. Often persecuted by the Sunni majority as heretics, Shiites developed a powerful commitment to martyrdom and a deep sense of themselves as being the only true exponents of Islam. During the middle ages, Shiites sometimes held political power in Egypt and North Africa, but the largest number of Shiites lived farther east. Today, Shiites rule Iran and are the largest single Muslim group in Iraq, but they make up only about one tenth of the worldwide population of Islam.

MUSLIMS, JEWS, AND CHRISTIANS UNDER ISLAMIC RULE

THE PACT OF UMAR

When the caliph Umar (d. 644) conquered the city of Jerusalem, he issued a charter of protection to the people of the city, defining the relationship that should exist in the future between the Muslim conquerors and their Christian subjects. In its surviving form, the "Pact of Umar" contains provisions that were probably not in Umar's original document. Nonetheless, the pact does describe accurately the rules that governed Christians and Jews living under Muslin rule during the early Middle Ages.

This letter is addressed to Allah's servant Umar, the Commander of the Faithful, by the Christians of such-and-such city. When you advanced against us, we asked you for a guarantee of protection for our persons, our offspring, our property, and the people of our sect, and we have taken upon ourselves the following obligations toward you, namely:

We shall not build in our cities or in the vicinity any new monasteries, churches, hermitages, or monks' cells. We shall not restore . . . any of them that have fallen into ruin or which are located in the Muslims' quarters.

We shall keep our gates wide open for passersby and travelers. We shall provide three days' food and lodging to any Muslims who pass our way. . . .

We shall not teach our children the Koran.

We shall not hold public religious ceremonies. We shall not seek to proselytize anyone. We shall not prevent any of our kin from embracing Islam if they so desire.

We shall show deference to the Muslims and shall rise from our seats when they wish to sit down.

We shall not attempt to resemble the Muslims in any way. . . .

We shall not ride on saddles.

We shall not wear swords or bear weapons of any kind, or ever carry them with us. . . .

We shall not display our crosses or our books anywhere in the Muslims' thoroughfares or in their marketplaces. We shall only beat our clappers in our churches very quietly. We shall not raise our voices when reciting the service in our churches, nor when in the presence of Muslims. Neither shall we raise our voices in our funeral processions. . . .

We shall not build our homes higher than theirs. . . .

Norman A. Stillman, ed. and trans., *The Jews of Arab Lands: A History and Source Book.* (Philadelphia, 1979), pp. 157–158.

PASSAGES FROM THE QUR'AN ON JEWS AND CHRISTIANS

Like the Hebrew and Christian Bibles, the Qur'an is a complex compilation of materials of varying dates and differing perspectives. The selections here reflect the range of views to be found in the Qur'an on the way Muslims should deal with Jews and Christians.

Wretchedness and baseness were stamped upon [the Jews], and they were visited with wrath from Allah. That was because they disbelieved in Allah's revelations and slew the prophets wrongfully. That was for their disobedience and transgression. (Sura 2:61).

There is to be no compulsion in religion. Rectitude has been clearly distinguished from error. So whoever disbelieves in idols and believes in Allah has taken hold of the firmest handle. It cannot split. Allah is All-hearing and All-knowing. (Sura 2:256).

Have you not seen those who have received a portion of the Scripture? They purchase error, and they want you to go astray from the path. But Allah knows best who your enemies are, and it is sufficient to have Allah as a friend. It is sufficient to have Allah as a helper. Some of the Jews pervert words from their meanings . . . twisting with their tongues and slandering religion. . . . But Allah has cursed them for their disbelief, so they believe not, except for a few. (Sura 4:44–46)

Indeed, you will find that the most vehement of men in enmity to those who believe are the Jews and the polytheists. But you will also surely find that the closest of them in love to those who believe are those who say, "We are Christians." That is because there are among them priests and monks, and because they are not arrogant. (Sura 5:82).

The Jews say, "Ezra is the son of Allah," and the Christians say, "The Messiah is the son of Allah." Those are the words of their mouths, conforming to the words of the unbelievers before them. Allah attack them! How perverse they are! They have taken their rabbis and their monks as lords besides Allah, and so too the Messiah son of Mary, though they were commanded to serve but one God. There is no God but He. Allah is exalted above that which they deify beside Him. (Sura 9:30–31).

Norman A. Stillman, ed and trans., *The Jews of Arab Lands: A History and Source Book* (Philadelphia, 1979), pp. 150–151.

QUESTIONS FOR ANALYSIS

1. Why did the Muslims tolerate other religions? If they believed all other religions were false, why didn't they stamp them out? Was early Christianity a religion of tolerance?
2. The Pact of Umar contains a long list of Christian promises to the ruler. What would the effect on the Christian community have been in the short or long term, if all these promises had been observed? Was it a good deal for them?
3. According to the Qur'an, how should Muslims deal with Jews and Christians?

UMAYYADS AND ABBASIDS

The triumph of the Umayyads in 661 began a more settled period in the history of the caliphate that would last until the tenth century. During these centuries there were two major governing orientations: the westward-looking one represented by the Umayyads and the eastward-looking orientation of their successors, the Abbasids. The Umayyad capital was Damascus in the old Byzantine territory of Syria, and in many ways the Umayyad caliphate functioned as a Byzantine successor state, continuing even to employ formerly Byzantine bureaucrats. The Umayyads concentrated their energies on dominating the Mediterranean and conquering Con-

stantinople. When their massive attack on the Byzantine capital failed in 717, Umayyad strength was seriously weakened; it was only a matter of time before a new orientation would develop.

This new perspective came with the takeover of the caliphate by a new family, the Abbasids, in 750. Their rule stressed Persian more than Byzantine elements. Characteristic of this change was a shift in capitals from Damascus to Baghdad in Iraq, where the second Abbasid caliph, al-Mansur (754–775) built a new capital city near the ruins of the old Persian city. The Abbasids also modeled both their administration and their absolutist style of rule on Persian example, imposing heavy taxation to support a large professional army and presid-

Exterior and Interior of the Great Umayyad Mosque at Damascus. This mosque was built by Caliph al-Walid between 705 and 715 on the former site of a pagan Roman temple; it incorporates a shrine to St. John the Baptist. Byzantine influence is apparent in its arched colonnades, its mosaics (the ones over the main door indicate that the worshiper is entering paradise), and its series of domes. Its horseshoe arches and interior striping influenced much subsequent Islamic architecture; see, for example, the Great Mosque of Cordoba on p. 261.

ing over an extravagantly luxurious and elaborate court. This is the world described in the *Arabian Nights,* a collection of stories written in Baghdad under the Abbasids. The dominating presence in these stories, Harun al-Rashid, ruled as caliph from 786 to 809. His lavish but brutal reign marked the height of Abbasid power.

After 750, the Umayyad Dynasty continued to rule only in Spain. Relations between the Spanish Umayyads and the Persian Abbasids were cold, with each dynasty claiming to be the only legitimate successors of the Prophet. But because their capitals were so far apart, the hostility between them rarely erupted in war. Instead, the two courts competed for preeminence through literary and cultural patronage. Philosophers, artists, and especially poets flocked to both courts, which became important cultural and intellectual centers. The *Arabian Nights* was but one product of this rivalry. At Cordoba, the caliph Al-Hakem II (961–976) amassed a library of more than 400,000 volumes at a time when, in western Europe, a monastery with 100 books qualified as a center of learning. Nothing remotely comparable had been seen in the Mediterranean world since the heady days of imperial Rome.

For the Christians of Byzantium and western Europe, the Abbasid caliphate was significant not only for its cultural achievements but also because its eastern orientation took a certain amount of military pressure off the

Mediterranean West. The Byzantine state, accordingly, was able to recover somewhat after a century of military pressure from the Umayyads. Farther west, the Franks of Gaul also benefited from the advent of the Abbasids. Because an Umayyad Dynasty continued to

CHRONOLOGY

The Spread of Islam, 622–750

Expulsion of Muhammad from Mecca (Hijrah)	622
Muhammad returns to Mecca	630
Muhammad dies	632
Abu-Bakr becomes caliph	632
Umar becomes caliph	634
Arabs occupy Antioch, Damascus, and Jerusalem	636
Arabs occupy Persian capital	637
Arabs invade Egypt	646
Arabs conquer Persian Empire	651
Shiite–Sunni schism	661
Arabs conquer North Africa	646–711
Umayyad Dynasty	661–750
Arabs invade Spain	711
Beginning of Abbasid Dynasty	750

control Spain, the great Frankish ruler Charlemagne (*SHAHR-leh-mayn,* 768–814) maintained diplomatic and trade relations with the Abbasid caliphate of Harun al-Rashid against their common Umayyad enemy. The most famous symbol of this connection was the elephant that Harun al-Rashid sent to Charlemagne. More important, however, was the flow of silver that found its way from the Abbasid Empire north through Russia and the Baltic and into the Rhineland in exchange for Frankish exports of furs, slaves, wax, honey, and leather. Jewels, silks, spices, and other luxury goods from India and the Far East also flowed north and west into the Frankish world through the Abbasid Empire. These trading links with the Abbasid world helped fund the extraordinary cultural achievements of the Carolingian Renaissance, which we describe in the next section of this chapter.

THE CHANGING ISLAMIC WORLD

What forces combined to undermine the political unity of the Islamic world?

During the ninth and tenth centuries the power of the Abbasid Dynasty rapidly declined. An extended period of decentralization followed that was mirrored during the eleventh century in Umayyad Spain. A major cause of the Abbasid collapse was the gradual impoverishment of their economic base—the agricultural wealth of the Tigris-Euphrates basin—resulting from ecological crises and a devastating revolt by the enslaved African workforce that farmed the southern Iraqi marshlands. Tax revenues from the Abbasid Empire were also declining, as provincial rulers in North Africa, Egypt, and Syria retained larger and larger portions of those revenues for themselves. As their revenues declined, the Abbasids found themselves unable to support either their large civil service or the new-style mercenary army they had built up. This new army was manned largely by slaves whose loyalties lay not with the caliphate itself but with the individual caliphs who employed them. To defend its interests, the army soon became a dominant force in making and murdering caliphs. Massively expensive

building projects, including the refoundation of the Abbasid capital of Baghdad, further exacerbated the fiscal, military, and political crisis.

Behind the Abbasid crisis lay two fundamental developments of great significance for the future of the Islamic world: the growth of regionalism and the sharpening religious divisions between Sunnis and Shiites and among the Shiites themselves. In 909 regional and religious hostilities came together when a local Shiite dynasty known as the Fatimids seized control of the Abbasid province of North Africa. In 969, the Fatimids succeeded in conquering Egypt also. Meanwhile, another Shiite group, rivals of both the Fatimids and the Abbasids, attacked Baghdad in 927 and Mecca in 930, seizing the Kabah. Thereafter, the effective power of the Abbasids over their empire collapsed entirely. Although an Abbasid caliphate continued to exist in Baghdad until 1258, when invading Mongol armies finally disposed of it, in practice the Abbasid Empire had disappeared by the 930s. In its place a new order began to emerge in the eastern Muslim world centered around an independent Egyptian kingdom and a new Muslim state based in Persia.

In Spain, Umayyad weakness was more directly a consequence of political failures and succession disputes than of economic collapse. Muslim Spain in the ninth and tenth centuries was an enormously wealthy agricultural and commercial region. But from the mid-ninth century on, renewed military pressure from the reviving Christian kingdoms of northern and eastern Spain increased the internal political difficulties of the Umayyad caliphate. In the opening years of the eleventh century, the united Umayyad caliphate in Spain finally dissolved, to be replaced by a host of local, small-scale *taifa* kingdoms, some of which were now paying tribute to the Christian rulers of the north.

In 1085, the great city of Toledo fell to the Christian king Alfonso of León. Alarmed, a new group of North African Islamic purists known as the Almoravids invaded Muslim Spain, checking the Christian advance and joining Islamic Spain with their North African empire. Another such group, the Almohads, repeated this pattern during the twelfth century. But neither the Almoravids nor the Almohads succeeded in reuniting the warring petty kingdoms of Islamic Spain. One by one, these local kingdoms gradually fell victim to the advancing forces of the Christian kings of Spain. Although the last Muslim kingdom, the principality of Granada, would not fall to the Christians until 1492,

> Behind the Abbasid crisis lay two fundamental developments of great significance for the future of the Islamic world: the growth of regionalism and the sharpening religious divisions between Sunnis and Shiites and among the Shiites themselves.

WHAT FORCES COMBINED TO UNDERMINE THE POLITICAL UNITY OF THE ISLAMIC WORLD?

THE CHANGING ISLAMIC WORLD   261

The Great Mosque of Cordoba, Spain. Built in stages between 784 and 990, the building features striped horseshoe-shaped arches, characteristic features of Islamic architecture at this time. A Christian cathedral was later constructed within a small portion of this enormous structure.

the Christian reconquest of Spain was essentially complete by the middle of the thirteenth century.

Extravagance and incompetence by the Muslim rulers of eleventh-century Spain certainly played a role in the Umayyad caliphate's collapse. But there were larger factors at work in breaking up the unity of the Islamic world that transcended the failures of particular caliphs. Although Islamic society was religiously tolerant, at least with respect to Jews and Christians (who, as *dhimmis*, "peoples of the book," were permitted to retain their religions by paying a special tax to their Muslim rulers; pagans, however, were forced to convert to Islam), ethnic tensions within the Islamic world were rampant and grew more divisive as the early idealism of the initial conquests faded with time. These ethnic tensions among Arabs, Turks, Berbers, sub-Saharan Africans, and Persians also complicated the deep regional divisions that had characterized this area of the world for centuries before the Islamic conquests began. Adding further to the political instability of the Muslim world was the uncompromising monotheism and religious egalitarianism of Islam itself. Muslim

rulers (such as some of the Abbasids) who took on Persian styles of semidivine rulership were frequently murdered as blasphemers. Tensions between the universality of Islamic belief and the realities of regional particularism, ethnic hostility, and religious conflict between Sunnis and Shiites thus combined to undermine the political unity of the Islamic Empire.

MUSLIM SOCIETY AND CULTURE, 900–1250

The political decentralization of the Muslim world did not automatically bring cultural decay, however. In fact, Islamic civilization prospered greatly in the middle period, above all from about 900 to about 1250. During these centuries Islamic rule expanded into modern-day Turkey and India despite the collapse of the caliphates. Islamic history is certainly not a story of steady decline from the time of Harun al-Rashid. On the contrary, Islam's most creative cultural period was only beginning as the ninth century came to an end.

Islamic culture and society were extraordinarily cosmopolitan and dynamic from their earliest days. Muhammad himself was not a desert Arab but a town-dwelling trader imbued with advanced ideals. Subsequently, Muslim culture became highly cosmopolitan for several reasons: it inherited the sophistication of Byzantium and Persia; it remained centered at the crossroads of long-distance trade between the Far East and West; and the prosperous town life in most Muslim territories counterbalanced agriculture. The importance of trade meant much geographical mobility. Muhammad's teachings furthermore encouraged social mobility because the Qur'an stressed the equality of all Muslims. The result was that at the courts of Baghdad and Córdoba, and later at those of the Muslim states that succeeded them, careers were open to men with talent. Because literacy was remarkably widespread—a rough estimate for around the year 1000 is that 20 percent of all Muslim males could read the Arabic of the Qur'an—many could rise through education. Offices were seldom regarded as hereditary, and "new men" could arrive at the top by enterprise and skill.

There was one major exception to this rule of Muslim egalitarianism: the treatment of women. Perhaps because social status was so fluid, successful men were extremely anxious to preserve and enhance their positions and their honor. They could accomplish this by maintaining or expanding their worldly possessions, which included women. For a man's females to be most valuable to his status, their inviolability had to be ensured. The Qur'an allowed a man to marry four wives, so women were at a premium, and married women were segregated from other men. A wealthy man would also have a number of female servants and concubines, whom he kept in a part of his residence called the harem, where they were guarded by eunuchs—that is, castrated men. Within these enclaves women vied with each other for preeminence and engaged in intrigues to advance the fortunes of their children. Although large harems could be kept only by the wealthy, the system was imitated as far as possible by all classes. Based on the principle that women were chattel property, these practices did much to debase women and to emphasize attitudes of domination in sexual life. Although male homosexual relations were tolerated in upper-class society, these relationships too were based on patterns of domination, usually of a powerful adult over an adolescent boy, much as they had been in the ancient Greek world.

Two major avenues were open to men wishing to devote themselves to Islamic religious life. One was that of the *ulama*, learned men whose job was to study and offer advice on all aspects of religion and religious law. These men usually stood for tradition and rigorous maintenance of the faith; often they exerted great influence on the conduct of public life. Complementary to them were the *Sufis*, religious mystics who might be equated with Christian monks were it not for the fact that they were not committed to celibacy and seldom withdrew from the life of the community. Sufis stressed contemplation and ecstasy as the ulama stressed religious law; they had no common program and in practice behaved very differently. Some Sufis were "whirling dervishes," so known in the West because of their dances; others were *faqirs*, associated in the West with snake charming in marketplaces; and others were quiet, meditative men who practiced no exotic rites. Sufis were usually organized into brotherhoods that did much to convert outlying areas such as Africa and India. Throughout the Islamic world Sufism provided a channel for the most intense religious impulses. The ability of the ulama and the Sufis to coexist is testimony to the cultural pluralism of the Islamic world. But the absence of any avenues for religious women comparable with the convents of the Christian world is a reminder of the limits imposed by gender on that pluralism.

MUSLIM PHILOSOPHY, SCIENCE, AND MEDICINE

Islamic philosophy in the Middle Ages was firmly rooted in the Greek philosophical tradition. Even before the rise of Islam, a number of Greek philosophical texts had been translated into Syriac, a Semitic dialect. Translations into Arabic soon followed, many sponsored by the Abbasid court at Baghdad, which established a special school for this purpose known as the House of Wisdom. By the end of the tenth century, Arabic translations of Aristotle, Porphyry, Plotinus, and Plato were widely available and intensively studied throughout the Muslim world. Even in the remote Persian city of Bukhara, the great Muslim philosopher Avicenna (Ibn Sīnā, 980–1037) was able to read all of Aristotle's works before he reached the age of eighteen.

The two greatest influences on medieval Islamic philosophy were Aristotelianism and Neoplatonism. Muslim philosophers strove to reconcile these two quite different philosophical traditions with each other and with the tenets of Islamic theology. Reconciling Aristotelianism and Neoplatonism was in some ways the easier task. Many of the Aristotelian translations and commentaries from which Muslim philosophers worked were already deeply imbued with Neoplatonism. Aris-

WHAT FORCES COMBINED TO UNDERMINE THE POLITICAL UNITY OF THE ISLAMIC WORLD?

THE CHANGING ISLAMIC WORLD   263

totle and the Neoplatonists also shared a number of common assumptions, including the eternity of the world; the rationality (perhaps even the rational necessity) of the world's existence; and the freedom of individual human beings to choose between good and evil.

Reconciling Greek philosophy with Islamic theology was more difficult. Like Judaism and Christianity, Islam holds firmly to the view that a single omnipotent God created the world in time as an act of pure will and that the world will continue to exist only for so long as God wills it to do so. Islamic theology also believes in the immortality of the individual human soul, another doctrine flatly in conflict with Aristotelian and Neoplatonic thought. There were also conflicts over predestination and free will. Although medieval Muslim theologians strongly emphasized the individual responsibility of believers to choose between good and evil, virtually all Muslims agreed that nothing good could occur unless God actively willed it. At times, such convictions could rise to a kind of fatalism wholly at odds with Greek philosophical presumptions.

Islamic philosophers took many different positions in response to these challenges. Al-Farabi (d. 950) used Aristotelian logic to support the conclusions of Muslim theology, but his Neoplatonic ideas about the created world emanating from and returning to God led him into mystical positions at odds with mainstream theology. Avicenna, perhaps the most original of all these great thinkers, offered famous proofs for the reality of human consciousness and for the existence of God. But Neoplatonism led him also toward potentially heretical positions on the eternity of the world and the world's relationship to God. Al-Ghazzali (1058–1111), in contrast, was a much more thoroughgoing Aristotelian, who attacked both Al-Farabi and Avicenna for their religious heterodoxy. Al-Ghazzali himself, however, was able to resolve the conflicts between Aristotelian philosophy and Islamic theology only through a mystical conversion experience that led him finally to Sufism. His advice to all sides to moderate their views had little effect; and his own philosophical mysticism was too idiosyncratic to gain wide acceptance.

Al-Ghazzali's successor, the Spaniard Averroës (ah-VER-oh-eez; Ibn Rušd, 1126–1198), turned his back on the mysticism that had characterized both Avicenna's and al-Ghazzali's thought. A consummate rationalist and the greatest Aristotelian scholar of his day, Averroës wrote a series of commentaries on the works of Aristotle that sought to purge them of all Neoplatonic influences. Translated from Arabic into Latin, these commentaries influenced the way all thirteenth-century Christian scholars, including Aquinas and Dante, read and understood Aristotle. Like Avicenna, Averroës was a physician as well as an expert in Muslim law and theology. Unlike Avicenna, however, Averroës thoroughly subordinated theology to philosophy. Averroës considered both theology and philosophy to be true, but in different ways. Philosophical assertions were true in their literal meaning; theological statements, however, were often true only when interpreted allegorically or symbolically—and only philosophers were capable of determining which theological statements were literally true because philosophers alone were the experts on literal meaning.

Such views did not sit well with the fundamentalist Almohad rulers of Spain. After burning several of Averroës' works, they exiled him to Morocco, where he died in 1198. His death marks a turning point in Islamic philosophy. Thereafter, philosophy tended either to blend into Sufistic mysticism, the direction taken by Al-Ghazzali, or became too constrained by the demands of Islamic orthodoxy to lead an independent existence. But in its heyday between 900 and 1200,

Aristotle Teaching Arab Astronomers, Early Thirteenth-Century Manuscript. Greek philosophers, particularly Aristotle, greatly influenced Islamic philosophy and science.

Islamic philosophy was far more advanced and sophisticated than anything found in Byzantium or western Europe.

Islamic philosophers were often distinguished physicians and scientists also. Philosophy brought few rewards in the Muslim world; but successful physicians and astrologers might rise to positions of wealth and power, especially if they had connections with rulers and their courts. Both astrology and medicine were applied sciences that relied on careful, accurate observation of natural phenomena. Muslim observations of the heavens were so accurate indeed that some astronomers concluded that the earth must rotate on its axis and revolve around the sun, rather than remaining stationary with the sun and planets revolving around it. Because such theories conflicted with ancient Greek assumptions, they were not generally accepted. They may, nonetheless, have had some influence on Copernicus, the sixteenth-century European astronomer who is generally credited as the first to suggest that the earth orbited the sun.

Islamic accomplishments in medicine were equally remarkable. Avicenna discovered the contagious nature of tuberculosis, described pleurisy and several varieties of nervous ailments, and noted that diseases could spread through contaminated water and soil. His *Canon of Medicine* would remain an authoritative textbook in the Islamic world and in western Europe until the seventeenth century. Rhazes (865–925) discovered through

Bloodletting Scene Painted on a Ceramic Bowl, Thirteenth-Century Iraq. Muslim physicians were pioneers in organizing hospitals and regulating the practice of medicine. Even leeches used for bloodletting were inspected regularly.

his clinical work the difference between measles and smallpox. Later Islamic physicians would learn the value of cauterization and of styptic agents, diagnose cancer of the stomach, prescribe antidotes in cases of poisoning, and make notable progress in treating eye diseases. They also recognized the infectious character of bubonic plague, pointing out that it could be transmitted by clothing. Muslim physicians were also pioneers in organizing hospitals and licensing medical practitioners. At least thirty-four great hospitals were located in the principal cities of Persia, Syria, and Egypt, each with separate wards for particular illnesses, a dispensary for giving out medicine, and a library. Chief physicians and surgeons lectured to students and graduates, examined them, and issued licenses to practice medicine. Even the owners of leeches (used for bloodletting, a standard medical practice of the day) had to submit the worms for inspection at regular intervals.

Islamic scientists also made important advances in optics, chemistry, and mathematics. Islamic physicists studied the theory of magnifying lenses and the velocity, transmission, and refraction of light. Islamic chemistry was an outgrowth of alchemy, a Hellenistic Greek system based on the principle that all metals were the same in essence, so base metals could be transmuted into gold if the right techniques were employed. Muslim alchemists produced no gold, but they did discover a number of new substances and compounds, including carbonate of soda, alum, borax, nitrate of silver, saltpeter, and nitric and sulfuric acids. They were also the first to describe the chemical processes of distillation, filtration, and sublimation.

Islamic mathematicians united the geometry of the Greeks with the number science of the Hindus. Using what Westerners know as Arabic numerals (but which are in fact Hindu in origin), Muslim mathematicians developed a decimal arithmetic based on place values (the zero was critical to this). They also made fundamental advances in algebra and algorithms (both Arabic words). Building on Greek geometry with reference to heavenly motion, they also made great progress in spherical trigonometry. Muslim mathematicians thus brought together and pushed forward all the areas of mathematical knowledge that would be adopted and developed in western Europe from the sixteenth century on.

LITERATURE AND ART

Poetry was a highly developed literary form in the Arab world even before the conversion to Islam. Thereafter, it quickly became a route to advancement at the Umayyad and Abbasid courts. Not all of this poetry

A HEBREW POEM IN PRAISE OF WINE, BY SAMUEL THE NAGID

In the courts of tenth- and eleventh-century Muslim Spain, Jewish poets and courtiers began to write a new style of Hebrew verse closely modeled on contemporary Arabic examples. Samuel the Nagid was perhaps the most remarkable of this group of poets. He became the military leader of the Muslim kingdom of Granada as well as the head of the Jewish community there. In addition to his three volumes of poetry, he also wrote treatises on Hebrew grammar and on Jewish religious law.

Your debt to God is righteously to live,
  And His to you, your recompense to give.
Do not wear out your days in serving God;
  Some time devote to Him, some to yourself.
To Him give half your day, to work the rest;
  But give the jug no rest throughout the night.
Put out your lamps! Use crystal cups for light.
  Away with singers! Bottles are better than lutes.
No song, nor wine, nor friend beneath the sward—
  These three, O fools, are all of life's reward.

Raymond P. Scheindlin, ed. and trans., *Wine, Women, and Death: Medieval Hebrew Poems on the Good Life* (Philadelphia, 1986), p. 47.

QUESTIONS FOR ANALYSIS

1. Is this poem consistent with Jewish religious laws and traditions? Why or why not?
2. What does the career of Samuel the Nagid—poet, general, and lawyer—suggest about relations between Jewish and Muslim communities in medieval Spain?

was written in Arabic; particularly around the Abbasid court, poets writing in Persian enjoyed great renown. The best known of these poets to western European audiences is Umar Khayyam (d. 1123), whose *Rubiyat* was turned into a popular English poem by the Victorian Edward Fitzgerald. Although Fitzgerald's translation distorts much, the hedonism of Umar's poem ("a jug of wine, a loaf of bread—and thou") faithfully reflects a theme common to much Muslim poetry of the period. Lyric poetry was particularly uninhibited. One poet wrote of his lover, "such was my kissing, such my sucking of his mouth / that he was almost made toothless." As these lines will suggest, much of this poetry was frankly homosexual, a fact that occasioned no concern within the elite court circles for which it was composed and performed.

Jews too participated in this elite literary world, especially in Spain, where they wrote sensuous, playful poems in both Hebrew and Arabic, praising wine, sexuality, and song. Muslim Spain also saw a great flowering of Jewish religious culture. The greatest Jewish scholar of the period was Moses Maimonides (*my-MAHN-eh-dees;* 1135–1204), whose systematic exposition of Jewish law in his famous *Mishneh Torah* earned him the title "the second Moses." Scores of other Jewish scholars—grammarians, biblical commentators, and legal authorities—preceded Maimonides. But few followed him, at least in Spain. Maimonides himself was driven into exile by the Almohads, first to North Africa and then to Egypt, where he became court physician to the Muslim ruler of Cairo. His story is a reminder of the reactionary religious winds blowing through the Islamic world during the twelfth century that would ultimately bring this Islamic cultural efflorescence to an end, first in Spain but ultimately throughout the Mediterranean world.

Like Muslim philosophy and literature, Muslim art was highly eclectic. Its main influences came from Byzantium and Persia. Architecture was perhaps the most distinctive of the Islamic arts. Its characteristic elements (the dome, the column, and the arch) came initially from Byzantium but were modified over time into a distinctive architectural style featuring bulbous domes, horseshoe arches, minarets, stone tracery, twisted columns, mosaics, and alternating strips of color. From Persia, Muslim artists drew the intricate, nonnaturalistic designs they used as decorative elements in all the arts, along with a taste (shared also by the Byzantines) for rich and sensuous color. Because Muslim theology regarded any artistic representation of Allah as idolatrous, a general prejudice developed against any portrayal of the human form in art. This tended to inhibit the development of both painting and sculpture. Muslim artists did, however, produce gorgeous pile carpets and rugs, magnificent leather tooling, brocaded silks and tapestries, inlaid metalwork, enameled glassware, and painted pottery, all decorated with Arabic script, interlacing geometric designs, plants, fruits, flowers, and fantastic animal figures (another Persian influence). These complex designs can often seem strikingly modern, precisely because they are nonrepresentational and abstract.

> Many of the characteristic features of Islamic civilization—bureaucratic record keeping, high levels of literacy and book production (especially copies of the Qur'an), even the standard form of cursive Arabic script known as Kufic—would have been impossible without the widespread availability of paper.

TRADE AND INDUSTRY

Although the economy of seventh-century Arabia was relatively primitive, many of the territories conquered by Muhammad's followers were wealthy and highly urbanized. Syria, Egypt, and Persia in particular lay at the crossroads of the Mediterranean world, linking the major trade routes between Africa, Europe, India, and China. Conversion to Islam did not diminish their economic importance; if anything, it increased it, as their trading contacts grew in tandem with the growth of the Islamic world. By the tenth century, Muslim merchants had penetrated into southern Russia and equatorial Africa and had become masters of the caravan routes that led eastward to India and China. Ships from the Muslim world established new trade routes across the Indian Ocean, the Persian Gulf, and the Caspian Sea, and for a time dominated the Mediterranean world also. During the tenth and eleventh centuries, however, Western Christian merchants gradually took control over the Mediterranean Sea routes; in the sixteenth century, they would

extend that control into the Indian Ocean. Both these developments were serious blows to the economy of the Muslim world.

The growth of Muslim commerce in the early Middle Ages reflects the development of a number of important industries. Mosul, in Iraq, was a center for the manufacture of cotton cloth; Baghdad specialized in glassware, jewelry, pottery, and silks; Damascus was famous for its fine steel and for its woven-figured silk known as "damask"; Morocco and Spain were both noted for leatherworking; Toledo produced excellent swords. Drugs, perfumes, carpets, tapestries, brocades, woolens, satins, metal goods, and a host of other products turned out by Muslim artisans were carried throughout the Mediterranean world by Muslim merchants.

One product in particular deserves special mention, however, and that is paper. Muslims learned papermaking from the Chinese but quickly became masters of the art. By the end of the eighth century, Baghdad alone had more than a hundred shops where blank paper and books written on paper were sold. Paper was cheaper to produce, easier to store, and far easier to write on than papyrus or parchment. As a result, by the early eleventh century, paper had replaced

Arabic Calligraphy. Muslim artists experimented with the art form of calligraphy to make complex, sometimes almost abstract designs. This ink-on-paper drawing of a bird from the seventh century also represents the Muslim mastery of papermaking.

What caused economic and social change in seventh-century western Europe?

Western Christian Civilization in the Early Middle Ages   267

papyrus even in Egypt, the heartland of papyrus production for almost 4,000 years.

The ready availability of paper brought about a revolution in the Islamic world. Many of the characteristic features of Islamic civilization—bureaucratic record keeping, high levels of literacy and book production (especially copies of the Qur'ān), even the standard form of cursive Arabic script known as Kufic—would have been impossible without the widespread availability of paper. Only in the thirteenth century would western Europeans master papermaking; when they did, however, they quickly began to undercut the market for Islamic paper. By the end of the fifteenth century, the Muslim world was importing almost all of its paper from western Europe, despite the fact that the watermarks on European papers often contained Christian symbols offensive to Islam.

The Effect of Early Islamic Civilization on Europe

Until the twelfth century, the cultural, economic, intellectual, and political achievements of Islamic civilization completely overshadowed those of Latin Christian Europe. And when Latin Europe did move forward, it relied heavily on what it had learned from the Islamic world. The commercial influence of the Muslim world on Europe is reflected in a large number of common English words of Arabic and Persian origin: *traffic, tariff, magazine, alcohol, muslin, orange, lemon, alfalfa, saffron, sugar, syrup,* and *musk,* to name just a few. Europeans also adopted a good deal of Muslim technology, including irrigation systems, papermaking, and the distillation of alcohol. The word *admiral* also comes from Arabic —in this case from the Arabic title *emir.*

Latin Europe was equally indebted to the Muslim world in intellectual and scientific life. Here too, borrowed words tell some of the story: *alchemy, algebra, algorithm, alkali, almanac, amalgam, cipher, soda,* and *zero*—not to mention the names of stars such as Aldebaran and Betelgeuse—all derive from Arabic originals. Islamic civilization preserved and extended Greek philosophical and scientific knowledge throughout the early Middle Ages at a time when such knowledge was almost entirely forgotten in the Latin-speaking world. Most of the important Greek scientific works surviving today were translated into Arabic and from the twelfth century on were translated from Arabic into Latin through the combined efforts of Muslim, Jewish, and Latin Christian scholars. Above all, the preservation and interpretation of the works of Aristotle was one of

Islam's most enduring contributions to western European culture. Between roughly 1150 and 1250, approximately two thirds of Aristotle's surviving works became available to European Christian scholars for the first time through Latin translations of Arabic texts. Aristotle's ideas were then studied by Christian scholars with the aid of Muslim interpreters, especially Averroës, whose prestige was so great that Latin-speaking philosophers called him simply "The Commentator," as if there were no others. Arabic numerals, adopted from India by Muslim mathematicians, are another crucially important intellectual legacy from the Islamic world, as anyone will discover by trying to balance a checkbook with Roman numerals.

The Islamic world also had an enormous influence on the imagination and the self-perception of Christian Europe. Byzantine civilization was at once too closely linked to Christian Europe and, from the eleventh century on, too weak to compel European Christians to take account of it. Western Christians in the high and late Middle Ages usually looked down on the Byzantine Greeks, but they respected and feared the Muslims. And they were right to do so, for Islamic civilization at its zenith (to use another Arabic word) was surely one of the world's greatest. Though loosely organized, Islam brought Arabs, Persians, Turks, Egyptians, Africans, and Indians together into a common cultural and religious world, creating a diverse society and a splendid legacy of original discoveries and accomplishments that continue to shape the world today.

Western Christian Civilization in the Early Middle Ages

What caused economic and social change in seventh-century western Europe?

In western Europe also, the seventh century marked the transition between the late antique and the early medieval worlds. At the end of the sixth century, the Frankish chronicler Gregory of Tours still saw himself as living in a discernibly Roman world of cities, trade, taxation, and local administration. Gregory was proud of his family's status as Roman senators and took it for granted that he and his male relatives should be bishops who ruled, by right of birth and status, over their episcopal

Charlemagne. A silver penny struck between 804 and 814 in Mainz (as indicated by the letter *M* at the bottom) showing Charlemagne in a highly stylized fashion as emperor with Roman military cloak and laurel wreath. The inscription reads Karolus Imp Avg (Charles, Emperor, Augustus). Charlemagne's portrait is closely modeled on the imperial portraits seen on Hellenistic and Roman coins.

cities and the surrounding countryside. Like others of his class, Gregory still spoke and wrote Latin—a quite different Latin from the polished prose of Cicero 600 years before, but a Latin that was nonetheless the same language and that had certainly changed less since Cicero's day than English has changed since the time of Chaucer. Gregory was of course aware that the western Roman Empire was now in the hands of Frankish, Visigothic, and Lombard kings. But he saw those kings as Romans nonetheless, because they ruled in accordance with Roman models and, in the case of the Franks, because they ruled with the approval of the Roman emperor in Constantinople. It was also a source of satisfaction to Gregory that in recent years, all these barbarian kings had converted to orthodox Catholic Christianity. This too, for Gregory, reinforced their *romanitas* ("Roman-ness") and thus lent legitimacy, both earthly and heavenly, to their rule.

Two hundred years later, however, when Charlemagne, the greatest of all the Frankish rulers, was crowned as the new Roman emperor in the West, the sense of direct continuity that Gregory of Tours had had with the Roman world was gone. When Charlemagne set out to reform the cultural, religious, and political life of his empire, his goal was to revive a

> Charlemagne sought a *renovatio Romanorum imperii*—a renewal of the empire of the Romans—thus conceding in his very motto that he sought to revive an empire that had fallen.

Roman Empire from which he and his contemporaries now saw themselves as estranged. Charlemagne sought a *renovatio Romanorum imperii*—a renewal of the empire of the Romans—thus conceding in his very motto that he sought to revive an empire that had fallen. Somewhere between Gregory of Tours and Charlemagne a rupture occurred in western Europeans' relationship to their Roman past. Cultured Europeans ceased to see themselves as living in a continuing Roman Empire and began instead to dream of reconstructing that empire. This awareness of a break with the Roman past developed during the seventh century. It was the consequence of profound economic, religious, and cultural changes; and it marks the beginning of a new era in the history of western European civilization.

ECONOMIC DISINTEGRATION AND POLITICAL INSTABILITY

As we have seen, the economy of the western Roman Empire was becoming increasingly regionalized from the third century C.E. onward. The Mediterranean world, however, remained a reasonably well-integrated economic unit until the late sixth century. In the year 550, a gold coinage still circulated in both the eastern and the western Roman Empire; a luxury trade in silks, spices, swords, and jewelry continued to move west; and slaves, wine, grain, and leatherwork still moved east from North Africa, Gaul, and Spain toward Constantinople, Egypt, and Syria. By 650, however, the economic unity of the Mediterranean world had broken down. This breakdown resulted partly from the destructiveness of Justinian's efforts to reconquer the western empire. Partly it was a consequence of ruinous Byzantine taxation of agricultural land, especially in Egypt and North Africa, where the resentments of overtaxed peasant farmers prepared the way for the Islamic conquests. Piracy by Muslim raiders also played a role in undermining the economy of the seventh-century Mediterranean world —although Muslims quickly became important maritime traders, and in the long run Muslim conquests did more to reconstruct than to destroy the patterns of Mediterranean commerce.

For western Europe, however, the most important causes of these seventh-century economic changes were internal. The cities of Italy, Gaul, and Spain continued

WHAT CAUSED ECONOMIC AND SOCIAL CHANGE IN SEVENTH-CENTURY WESTERN EUROPE?

WESTERN CHRISTIAN CIVILIZATION IN THE EARLY MIDDLE AGES   269

to decline. Although bishops still ruled from cities, and so continued to provide a market for certain kinds of luxury goods, the kings and nobles of western Europe were moving to the countryside during the seventh century, living as much as possible from the produce of their own estates rather than purchasing their supplies in the marketplace. At the same time, agricultural land was passing out of cultivation, especially on the larger estates, whose owners were finding it difficult to control an increasingly independent peasantry. As trade declined, so too did the revenues lords took from tolls. The late Roman system of land taxes was also collapsing, not least because free-born Franks and Goths were claiming exemptions from it, leaving only the Roman population and the peasantry to pay these taxes. The coinage systems of western Europe were also breaking down. From the 630s on, the Islamic conquests seriously reduced the supply of gold available in western Europe; but gold coins were already too valuable to be useful in local marketing anyway. From the 660s on, western European rulers shifted from a gold to a silver coinage. Europe would remain a silver-based economy for the next 1,000 years.

> During the seventh century, western Europe thus became a basically two-tier economy. Gold, silver, and luxury goods circulated among the wealthy, but the peasantry relied mainly on barter and various currency substitutes to facilitate their transactions.

During the seventh century, western Europe thus became a basically two-tier economy. Gold, silver, and luxury goods circulated among the wealthy, but the peasantry relied mainly on barter and various currency substitutes to facilitate their transactions. Lords collected rents from their peasants in foodstuffs but found it difficult to convert these payments of grain, wine, and meat into the weapons, jewelry, and silks that brought prestige in seventh-century aristocratic society. In a world in which the power of lords depended on their ability to give such high-prestige gifts to their military followers, the inability to convert peasant rents into cash was a serious handicap. It meant that for great men to give weapons and jewelry to their followers, they first had to acquire these items either through traders and artisans, or else through plunder and tribute. Either way, the processes by which such gifts were acquired were likely to be destabilizing.

The successful rulers of the seventh, eighth, and ninth centuries tended to be those whose territories adjoined wealthy but poorly defended territories that could be easily and profitably attacked. Such "soft frontiers" provided rulers with land and wealth they could distribute

Treasures from the Seventh-Century Anglo-Saxon Burial Mound at Sutton Hoo, Essex. These high-status objects were buried with their owner inside a ship, which was then heaped over with dirt. The helmet is modeled on those worn by fourth- and fifth-century Roman cavalry officers. The belt buckles, made of gold and garnet, are also of a style popular with both Romans and Germans from the fourth century on. Ownership of such luxury items was an important aspect of early medieval rulership in western Europe.

to their followers. Successes of this sort would bring more followers to a lord's service; so long as more conquests then followed, the process of amassing power and wealth would continue. But power acquired through plunder and conquest was inherently unstable. A few defeats might speedily reverse the entire process.

Another factor contributing to the instability of power in this world was the difficulty all the royal dynasties of the early Middle Ages experienced in trying to regulate the succession to their thrones. The kings who established themselves during the invasion period of the fifth and sixth centuries did not come from the traditional royal families of their peoples. Moreover, the barbarian armies who took over the western Roman Empire during these years were rarely if ever composed of a single people anyway. They were usually made up of many different peoples, including a sizable number of disaffected Romans. Such unity as they possessed was largely the creation of the charismatic warrior-kings who led them, and this charisma was not easily passed on by inheritance.

Of all the barbarian groups that set up kingdoms in the western empire during the fifth and sixth centuries, only the Franks succeeded in establishing a single royal dynasty from which the future kings of the Franks would be drawn for the next 250 years. This dynasty was established by Clovis (d. 511), the great warrior-king of the Franks, who by converting to orthodox Catholic Christianity also established an alliance between his dynasty and the powerful Roman bishops of Gaul. But the dynasty itself came to be known as the Merovingians, after Clovis's legendary grandfather Merovech, who was a sea dragon. We need not take this claim seriously; but it does suggest that no one was quite sure who Clovis's grandfather actually was.

Even in Gaul, however, the Merovingians were not the only noble family with a plausible claim to be kings; and in Visigothic Spain, Anglo-Saxon England, and Lombard Italy, the numbers of such rival royal families were even greater. Nor was the right of succession limited to the eldest male claimant of each competing royal family. Early medieval Europe was a world in which all the sons of a king (and frequently all his cousins and nephews too) could stake a plausible claim to the throne. In Visigothic Spain, the bloody succession disputes that resulted when a reigning king died so horrified the resident Roman population that they spoke of this inability to regulate the succession as a kind of a sickness: the *morbus Gothorum*, the "sickness of the Goths." In Gaul, the Franks were more successful in restricting claims to kingship to descendants of the Merovingian dynasty; but the Merovingians' custom of dividing the kingdom up into its constituent, regional parts, and installing a different king over each part, guaranteed plenty of civil strife in Merovingian Gaul as well.

MEROVINGIAN GAUL

The brutal conflicts between these rival Merovingian kings, together with the blackening of their reputations by their Carolingian rivals and successors, can easily obscure the real strength and sophistication of Merovingian governance. Many elements of late Roman local administration survived throughout the Merovingian period. Literacy remained an important element in Merovingian administration, providing a foundation on which the Carolingians would build. Even the cultural renaissance associated with the reign of Charlemagne really began in the late seventh century, with the production of deluxe biblical and other manuscripts at Merovingian monasteries such as Luxeuil.

Monasteries grew remarkably under the Merovingians, especially during the seventh century, reflecting the great wealth of the country. Of the approximately 550

Book Cover. The cover of the Lindau Gospels, gilt silver encrusted with jewels and ivory cameos, was presented by Pope Gregory the Great to a Lombard queen around the year 600.

WHAT CAUSED ECONOMIC AND SOCIAL CHANGE IN SEVENTH-CENTURY WESTERN EUROPE?

WESTERN CHRISTIAN CIVILIZATION IN THE EARLY MIDDLE AGES   271

monasteries that existed in Gaul by the year 700, more than 300 had been established in the preceding century. The Frankish bishoprics also prospered under the Merovingians, amassing approximately three quarters of their total landed possessions by the end of the seventh century. This massive redistribution of wealth reflected a fundamental shift in the economic gravity of the Frankish kingdom. In the year 600, the wealth of Gaul was still concentrated in the south, where it had been throughout the late Roman period. By the year 750, however, the economic center of the kingdom lay north of the Loire, in the territories that extended from the Rhineland westward to the North Sea. It was here that most of the new monastic foundations of seventh-century Gaul were established.

Behind this shift in wealth from south to north lay a long and successful effort to bring under cultivation the rich, heavy soils of northern France. This effort was assisted by the development of heavy-wheeled plows capable of cutting and turning grassland sod and heavy clay and by increasingly efficient devices for harnessing animals (particularly oxen, but sometimes horses) to pull these plows. Gradually warming weather improved the fertility of these wet, northern soils, lengthening the growing season and so making possible more efficient crop-rotation systems. The population began to expand as food became more plentiful. Northern France remained a land of scattered settlements separated by heavy forest, but it was a much more densely populated region by 750 than it had been in 600. All these developments would continue during the Carolingian period and beyond. But although the Carolingians would enjoy the fruits of this gradually increasing northern agricultural prosperity, the developments that made it possible began during the seventh century under their Merovingian predecessors.

MONASTICISM AND CONVERSION

Momentous developments also took place in religious life during the seventh century, especially in the monasteries. Throughout Christian Europe, the seventh century witnessed a rapid increase in the foundation of monastic houses. Monasteries had existed in Gaul, Italy, and Spain since the fourth century, but most were located in the highly Romanized cities of

southern Spain, Gaul, and northern Italy. In Gaul, where the Merovingian kings were Catholic, kings had begun to forge ties with monasteries during the sixth century. In Spain, Italy, and England, whose rulers had previously been Arian heretics (Spain and Italy) or pagans (England), ties between monasticism and monarchy arose only in the seventh century, after the royal dynasties of these areas had converted to Catholic Christianity. Even in Gaul, however, relations between the Merovingian kings and the Frankish monasteries became markedly closer from the late sixth century on, as the royal dynasty and the principal noble families embarked on a massive campaign of new monastic foundations that permanently altered the spiritual geography of western Europe.

Most of the new monastic foundations of the seventh century were deliberately located in rural areas, where they played an important role in the continuing struggle to Christianize the countryside. Often they were granted special privileges known as immunities, which by freeing them from the control of local bishops cemented their dependence on their founders. Frequently these new foundations were either double monasteries (in which a house of religious men was joined to a house of religious women), or convents, established for women only. Either way, they were usually ruled over by abbesses drawn from among the women of the royal family: dowager queens, royal princesses, or sometimes even a reigning queen herself.

Monastic life had great appeal to the royal and noble women of the early Middle Ages. It provided them with a socially sanctioned arena within which they could exercise a degree of power over their lives denied them outside the cloister. It gave them an honorable position in society from which they could influence the affairs of their families and which protected them from abduction, rape, or forced marriages arranged to promote their families' diplomatic or dynastic interests. And it also guaranteed them salvation, at a time when salvation outside the cloister seemed a perilously uncertain prospect. But convents and double monasteries served the interests of the male members of these royal dynasties also—one reason, of course, that they founded and supported them. Convents provided a dignified place of retirement for inconvenient but potentially powerful women, such as dowager queens. The prayers of holy

> Monastic life had great appeal to the royal and noble women of the early Middle Ages. It provided them with a socially sanctioned arena within which they could exercise a degree of power over their lives denied them outside the cloister.

women were regarded as particularly effective in securing divine support for the kingdom. And by limiting the number of royal women who could reproduce, convents also helped reduce the number of potential claimants to the throne. Establishing royal women in convents was thus an important way of controlling the succession disputes that so regularly tore these early medieval kingdoms apart.

Many of these new monastic establishments also played an important role in the new round of missionary activity that characterized the seventh-century world. The most famous example of such monastic missionary activity is the conversion of Anglo-Saxon England. In northern England, the work of Christianization began in the late sixth century, led by missionary monks from Ireland. The decisive moment came in 597, however, when a group of forty Benedictine monks, sent by Pope Gregory I (590–604) and led by Saint Augustine of Canterbury (not to be confused with Saint Augustine of Hippo), brought the traditions of Roman Christianity to the kingdom of Kent in southeastern England. Despite some initial setbacks, by the end of the seventh century all of England had been brought firmly within the boundaries of the Roman Christian world, and English monks had begun their own missionary campaigns in Frisia and Saxony. Frankish missionaries were also active in these areas, as they were in the Low Countries and the Basque lands of the southwest also. But it was the particular loyalty the English monks felt toward the papacy that was to have the most momentous consequences, not only for the papacy but also for Gaul.

THE REIGN OF POPE GREGORY I

The architect of this new alliance between the Roman papacy and Benedictine monasticism was Pope Gregory I, known as Saint Gregory the Great. Until his time the Roman popes were generally subordinate to the emperors in Constantinople and to the greater religious prestige of the Christian East. Byzantine power in Italy was declining, however, and although Gregory worked hard to prevent a breach with Constantinople, he also sought to create a more autonomous, Western-oriented Latin Church. As a theologian—the fourth great Latin Father of the church—he built on the work of Saint Jerome, Saint Ambrose, and especially Saint Augustine of Hippo, in articulating a theology with distinctively Western elements. Among these were an emphasis on the necessity of penance for the forgiveness of sins and the concept of purgatory as a place where the soul was purified before it was admitted into

heaven. (Western belief in purgatory was thereafter to become one of the major differences in the teachings of the eastern and western churches.) Gregory emphasized the importance of pastoral care by bishops toward the laity, writing an influential book on the subject in a deliberately simplified Latin prose style that made it one of the most accessible and influential books of the early Middle Ages. A powerful liturgical chant with unaccompanied vocal music in Latin has become known as "Gregorian chant," although Gregory's role in creating this music is conjectural and debatable. All these innovations helped make the Christian West religiously and culturally more independent of the Greek-speaking East than it had ever been before.

Gregory was also a statesman and ruler in the model of his Roman forebears. Within Italy he ensured the survival of the papacy against the barbarian Lombards by clever diplomacy and expert management of the papacy's estates and revenues. He maintained good relations with Byzantium while asserting his authority as pope over the other bishops of the Western church.

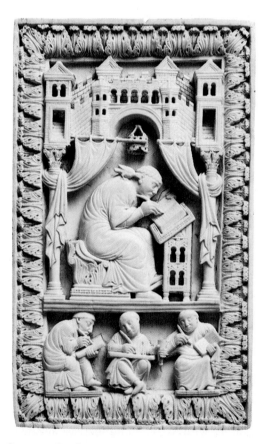

Pope Gregory the Great. In this tenth-century German ivory panel the pope is receiving inspiration from the Holy Spirit in the form of a dove.

HOW DID CHARLEMAGNE REDEFINE THE RELATIONSHIP BETWEEN CHRISTIANITY AND KINGSHIP?

THE RISE OF THE CAROLINGIANS   273

Above all, he patronized the order of Benedictine monks. Gregory's patronage helped the Rule of Saint Benedict become the predominant monastic rule in the West; through his encouragement, Benedictine monks emerged as the most important missionary group in early medieval western Europe. Among these Benedictine missionaries, Englishmen such as Saint Boniface and Saint Willibrord deserve pride of place. Their missionary work in Frisia and Germany brought both regions into the western Catholic Church and laid the groundwork for an alliance between the papacy and the Frankish monarchy that would transform early medieval Europe. Gregory did not live to see this alliance, but his policy of invigorating the western church contributed greatly to bringing it about.

THE RISE OF THE CAROLINGIANS

How did Charlemagne redefine the relationship between Christianity and kingship?

In Gaul, the weaknesses of the Merovingian dynasty were becoming steadily more apparent as the seventh century drew to a close. Tensions between noble families in the Merovingian heartland of Neustria and those in the border region of Austrasia were increasing. The Austrasian nobles had profited from their steady push into the soft frontier areas east of the Rhine, acquiring wealth and military power in the process. The Merovingians, based in Neustria, had no such easy conquests at their disposal. Moreover, a considerable portion of the land they did hold had been given to the church in the course of the seventh century. A succession of short-lived Merovingian kings complicated matters further, producing a series of civil wars between Austrasians and Neustrians. Briefly, in 687, the leader of the Austrasian nobility, Pepin of Heristal, succeeded in forcing his way into office as "mayor of the palace," seeking thereby to control both Austrasia and Neustria. But not until 717, when Pepin's illegitimate son Charles Martel ("the Hammer") finally triumphed over his opponents in both territories, was Pepin's family secure in its control over the Merovingian court. Thereafter, however, the Merovingian kings were largely figureheads in a kingdom ruled by Charles Martel and his sons.

Charles Martel is sometimes considered the second founder (after Clovis) of the Frankish state. His claim to this title is twofold. First, in 733 or 734 (the traditional date of 732 is erroneous), he turned back a Muslim force from Spain at the battle of Tours (not Poitiers), some 150 miles from the Merovingian capital of Paris. Although the Muslim contingent was a raiding party rather than a full-scale army, the incursion was nonetheless the high-water mark of Umayyad progress toward northwestern Europe, and Charles's victory won him great prestige. Equally important, Charles began to develop an alliance with the English Benedictine missionaries who were attempting to convert Frisia and central Germany to Christianity. Charles's family had long been active in the drive to conquer and settle these areas, and he understood clearly how missionary work and Frankish expansion could go hand in hand. Charles readily assisted Saint Boniface and his followers in their conversion efforts. In return, the English Benedictines brought Martel and his descendants into contact with the papacy and assisted him in his efforts to reform (and so control) the Frankish church.

Charles Martel died in 741. Although Charles never sought to become king himself, during the last years of his life he was so clearly the effective ruler of Gaul that he did not even bother to arrange for a new king to be selected when, in 737, the reigning Merovingian king died. In 743, however, Martel's sons, Carloman and Pepin, bowed to the forces of legitimism, and a new Merovingian king took the throne. By 750, however, Carloman had withdrawn from public life to a monastery, and Pepin had decided to seize the throne for himself. To effect such a change in dynasties, Pepin needed the support of the Frankish church. It was highly unlikely, however, that the bishops of Merovingian Gaul would support such a usurpation without papal approval. This did not deter Pepin. Through his family's support for Saint Boniface, Pepin was already well regarded in Rome. And the papacy, locked in a bitter fight with the Byzantine emperors over Iconoclasm and with the Lombard kings for control over central Italy, proved only too happy to cooperate in Pepin's elevation, hoping that a powerful new Frankish ruler would take over from the Byzantines the responsibility for protecting papal interests in Italy against the Lombards.

In 751 Saint Boniface, acting as papal emissary, anointed Pepin as king of the Franks. The idea of anointing a newly created king with holy oil was borrowed from the Bible, in which the Hebrew prophet

Samuel had anointed Saul as the first king of Israel. The power of these Old Testament associations would grow under Pepin's son Charlemagne (who thus became David) and his grandson Louis the Pious (who became Solomon). In 751, however, they mainly underscored the novelty and uncertainty of the process by which the last Merovingian king was deposed and sent to a monastery, and a new king, who had not a drop of Merovingian blood, was raised to the Frankish throne for the first time in almost three centuries. In 756, Pepin repaid his debt to the pope by launching a military expedition against the Lombards in Italy; but when the expedition went badly, Pepin abandoned it and returned home. Pepin's coronation symbolized the integration of the new Frankish monarchy into the papal–Benedictine orbit. For the moment, however, Pepin had his hands full simply trying to control his new kingdom.

THE REIGN OF CHARLEMAGNE

The real consolidation of this new pattern of papal–Frankish–Benedictine relations took place during the reign of Pepin's son, Charlemagne, from whom the new dynasty takes its name of Carolingian (from "Carolus," the Latin form of "Charles"). When Charlemagne came to the throne in 768, it seemed possible that the Frankish kingdom would break up into its hostile regional parts of Austrasia, Neustria, and Aquitaine. But in an astonishing series of military campaigns, Charlemagne united the Franks by leading them on a series of conquests that annexed the Lombard kingdom of Italy, the greater part of Germany including Saxony, portions of central Europe, and Catalunya. These conquests set a seal of divine approval on the new Carolingian dynasty. They also provided the plunder, booty, and new lands that enabled Charlemagne to promote his Frankish followers to dizzying heights of wealth and grandeur. Many of the peoples whom Charlemagne conquered were already Christians. In Saxony, however, Charlemagne's armies campaigned for twenty years before finally subduing the pagan Saxons and forcing their conversion to Christianity. Germany was thus forcibly integrated into the Frankish realm. Equally momentous was the connection Charlemagne's conquest of Saxony forged between conquest and conversion, which would characterize western Christian thinking for the next 1,000 years.

Pepin and Charlemagne Giving Edicts to a Clerk.
Cementing the papal–Frankish–Benedictine commitment, Charlemagne's reign outshone that of this father, Pepin.

Charlemagne also created a new coinage system, based on a division of the silver pound into 240 pennies, which would last in France until the French Revolution and in Great Britain until the 1970s, when it was finally replaced by a decimal-based currency.

To rule the vast empire he had conquered, Charlemagne appointed Frankish aristocrats called counts (in Latin, *comites*, meaning "followers") to supervise local administration within their territories. Among the counts' many duties were the administration of justice and the raising of armies. Charlemagne also established a network of other local administrators to supervise courts, collect tolls, administer crown lands, and extract taxation. Charlemagne also created a new coinage system, based on a division of the silver pound into 240 pennies, which would last in France until the French Revolution and in Great Britain until the 1970s, when it was finally replaced by a decimal-based currency. As we have seen, much of the silver for this new coinage originated in the Abbasid Empire. Scandinavian traders carried it north through

How did Charlemagne redefine the relationship between Christianity and kingship?

The Rise of the Carolingians   275

Russia and the Baltic Sea and then into the Rhineland, where they exchanged it for furs, cloth, and slaves captured in Charlemagne's wars against the Saxons, which they then transported to Baghdad.

Like Carolingian administration generally, this new monetary system depended on the regular use of written records and instructions. But Charlemagne did not rely on the written word alone to make his will felt. Periodically he sent special representatives from his court (known as *missi*) on tours through the countryside to relay his instructions personally and check up on local administrators. Charlemagne's governmental system was far from perfect. Local officials abused their positions; nobles sought to turn free peasants into unfree serfs; justice in local courts was more often denied than done. But Charlemagne's system produced nonetheless the best government Europe had seen since the Romans, and it became the model on which Western rulers would base their own administrations for the next 300 years.

CHRISTIANITY AND KINGSHIP

Throughout his reign, Charlemagne took seriously his responsibilities as a Christian king. As his empire expanded, however, he came to see himself not only as the ruler of the Franks but as the leader of a unified Christian society, Christendom, which he was obliged

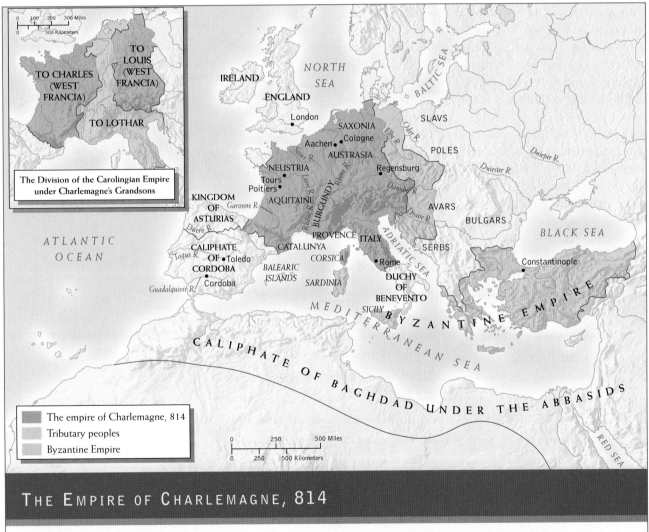

THE EMPIRE OF CHARLEMAGNE, 814

By 814, Charlemagne had created an empire that embraced most of the territory of the former western Roman Empire. Could he legitimately claim to be renewing the Roman Empire? How did his possession of Rome strengthen such a claim? How might it complicate his family's traditional alliance with the papacy? Note the inset in the upper left. What forces led to the division of Charlemagne's empire along these particular borders?

to defend both militarily and spiritually against its enemies. The Carolingian world did not make the distinctions between the religious and the political realms that would characterize European life from the twelfth century on, any more than did Byzantium or Islam. Especially among churchmen, kingship in early medieval Europe was regarded as a sacred office created by God to protect the church, defend the Christian people, and promote their salvation. Religious reforms were therefore no less central to proper kingship than were justice and defense. In some ways, indeed, a king's responsibilities for his kingdom's religious life were even more important than his other responsibilities: for surely no kingdom could prosper if the lives of its subjects were displeasing to God.

These ideas about the spiritual responsibilities of kingship were not new in the late eighth century, but they took on a new importance as a result of the extraordinary power Charlemagne wielded over his empire. Like other early medieval kings, Charlemagne appointed and deposed bishops and abbots, just as he did his counts and other officials. But he also changed the liturgy of the Frankish church, reformed rules of worship in Frankish monasteries, declared changes in basic statements of Christian belief, prohibited pagan observances, enforced tithes on the Frankish peasantry (a tithe was a tenth of a peasant's produce, owed to the church), and imposed basic Christian observances, in-

cluding baptism, on the conquered peoples of Saxony. To Charlemagne, such measures were clearly required if God's new Israel, the Franks, were to avoid the fate that befell biblical Israel whenever its people turned away from their obedience to God.

As the dominant political power in central Italy, Charlemagne was also the protector of the papacy. Although carefully acknowledging the pope's role as the spiritual leader of western Christianity, Charlemagne dealt with the pope much as he did with the other bishops of the Frankish Empire. He supervised and approved papal elections, while protecting the pope against his enemies. In 796, just after the election of Pope Leo III, Charlemagne explained the relationship between his authority and that of the pope in the following words: "It is for us," wrote Charlemagne to Leo,

> in accordance with the help of divine goodness, outwardly to defend by force of arms the Holy Church of Christ in all places from the incursions of pagans and the ravages of infidels, and inwardly to fortify her with our confession of the Catholic faith. It is for you, most holy father . . . to aid our armies, to the end that with you as intercessor and with God as guide and giver, our Christian people may in all places have the victory over the enemies of its holy name, and that the name of Our Lord Jesus Christ may be renowned throughout all the world.

Carolingian Handwriting. Even the untrained reader has little difficulty in reading this excerpt from a Carolingian manuscript. For example, the first two words in the heading read "Incipit Liber," and the two words below them "Haec Hannibal."

How did Charlemagne redefine the relationship between Christianity and kingship?

The Rise of the Carolingians   277

The Carolingian Renaissance

Similar ideals lay behind the Carolingian Renaissance, a cultural and intellectual flowering that took place around the Carolingian royal court. Like their biblical exemplars, the Hebrew kings David and Solomon, Charlemagne and his son Louis the Pious took seriously their role as patrons of poetry and learning. In so doing, they created an ideal of the court as an intellectual and cultural center that would profoundly influence western European cultural life until the end of the nineteenth century. What lay behind the Carolingians' support for scholarship, however, was their conviction that classical learning was the foundation on which Christian wisdom rested and that such wisdom was essential to the salvation of God's people. Supporting scholarship was therefore a paramount obligation for a Christian king.

To promote classical learning and Christian wisdom, Charlemagne recruited scholars from throughout Europe to his court, including the English Benedictine monk Alcuin, whose command of classical Latin grammar established him as the intellectual leader of Charlemagne's court school. Carolingian scholars produced a good deal of original Latin poetry and an impressive number of theological and pastoral tracts. Under Alcuin, however, their primary efforts were devoted to collating, correcting, and recopying classical Latin texts, including, most important, the text of the Latin Bible, which had become corrupted by generations of copyists' mistakes. To detect and correct these errors, Alcuin and his associates gathered as many different versions of the biblical text as they could find and compared them word by word. After determining the correct version among all the variants, they made a new, corrected copy and destroyed the other versions. They also developed a new style of handwriting, with simplified letter forms and spaces inserted between words, that further reduced the likelihood that subsequent copyists would misread the corrected texts. Although modified again by Italian Renaissance scholars in the fifteenth century, this new style of handwriting, known as Carolingian miniscule, is the foundation for the typefaces in which almost all European books, including this one, are still printed.

Charlemagne and the Revival of the Western Roman Empire

The climax of Charlemagne's career came in Rome on Christmas Day 800, when he was crowned as the new Roman emperor in the west by Pope Leo III. Centuries

CHRONOLOGY	
The Rise of the Carolingian Empire, 717–814	
Charles Martel becomes mayor of the palace	717
The Carolingians (Charles, Pepin, and Carloman) share power with the Merovingian kings	717–751
Pepin becomes king of the Franks	751
Charlemagne succeeds Pepin	768
Charlemagne is crowned Holy Roman emperor	800
Louis the Pious becomes emperor	813
Charlemagne dies	814

later, popes would cite their role in this event as precedent for the political superiority they claimed over the Holy Roman emperor (a title that became common only in the twelfth century but that can be used for convenience to designate the western emperors from Charlemagne on). In the year 800, however, Pope Leo was entirely under Charlemagne's thumb. Although Charlemagne said later that he would never have gone to church that day had he known Leo's plans to crown him, it is highly unlikely Pope Leo would have mounted such a coronation ceremony without Charlemagne's knowledge or consent, not least because it was certain to anger the Byzantines, with whom Charlemagne already had strained relations. Nor did the imperial title add much to Charlemagne's position as king of the Franks. Why, then, did he accept it, and in 813 transfer it to his son Louis the Pious?

Historians do not know. What is clear, however, is the symbolic significance of the action. Until 800 only the Roman emperor who ruled in Constantinople could lay claim to being the direct heir of Caesar Augustus. Although the Byzantines had lost most of their influence in the West, they continued to regard it vaguely as an outlying province of their empire. Charlemagne's assumption of the imperial title was a clear slap in the face to the Byzantines, who were already suspicious of Charlemagne's relationship with Byzantium's enemy Harun al-Rashid, the Abbasid caliph in Baghdad. In the west, however, it was a declaration of self-confidence and independence that was never forgotten. With only occasional interruptions, western

CHARLEMAGNE ON THE IMPORTANCE OF MONKS' STUDYING CLASSICAL LITERATURE

To Charlemagne and his contemporaries, a Christian king bore total responsibility for the salvation of his people. To this end, Charlemagne believed it essential to encourage the study of both classical and Christian literature within his kingdom. Copies of this letter were probably sent to most of the monasteries in the Frankish kingdom.

We, Charles, by the grace of God king of the Franks and Lombards and patrician of the Romans, to Abbot Baugulf and all your congregation. . . . Be it known to your devotion . . . that we, along with our faithful advisers, have deemed it useful that the bishoprics and monasteries, which through the favor of Christ have been entrusted to us to govern should, in addition to the way of life prescribed by their rule and their practice of holy religion, devote their efforts to the study of literature and to the teaching of it . . . so . . . that those who seek to please God by living aright may not fail to please him also by rightness in their speaking. . . . For . . . letters have often been sent to us in these last years from certain monasteries . . . and we found that in most of these writings their sentiments were sound but their speech uncouth. . . . And so . . . we began to fear that their lack of knowledge of writing might be matched by a more serious lack of wisdom in the understanding of holy scripture. We all know well that, dangerous as are the errors of words, yet much more dangerous are the errors of doctrine. Wherefore we urge you, not merely to avoid the neglect of the study of literature, but . . . to strive to learn it, so that you may be able more easily and more rightly to penetrate the mysteries of the holy scriptures. For since there are figures of speech, metaphors and the like to be found on the sacred pages, there can be no doubt that each man who reads them will understand their spiritual meaning more quickly if he is first of all given full instruction in the study of literature. . . . For we want you, as befits the soldiers of the Church, to be inwardly devout and outwardly learned, pure in good living and scholarly in speech; so that whoever comes to see you in the name of God and for the inspiration of your holy converse, just as he is strengthened by the sight of you, so he may be instructed also by your wisdom, both in reading and chanting, and return rejoicing, giving thanks to Almighty God.

H. R. Loyn and J. Percival, eds., *The Reign of Charlemagne.* Documents of Medieval History 2 (London, 1975), pp. 63–64.

QUESTIONS FOR ANALYSIS

1. Compare the attitudes in this official letter by Charlemagne with the Byzantine prayer for Plato and Plutarch. Why did Charlemagne think the study of pagan classics was necessary?

2. According to Charlemagne's letter, before one can understand the Scriptures, solid grounding in classical literataure is required. Problems in reading the "figures of speech, metaphors and the like" of the Scriptures could lead to grave errors in understanding. What did this mean in Charlemagne's time?

How did Charlemagne redefine the relationship between Christianity and kingship?

The Rise of the Carolingians   279

Europeans would continue to crown Roman emperors until the nineteenth century. Whatever his specific motives may have been, Charlemagne's revival of the western Roman Empire thus proved to be a major step in the developing self-consciousness of western European civilization.

The Collapse of the Carolingian Empire

When Charlemagne died in 814, his empire descended intact to his only surviving son, Louis the Pious. Under Louis, however, the empire rapidly began to disintegrate. When Louis died in 843, the empire was divided between his three sons. Western Francia, which became France, went to Charles the Bald; Eastern Francia, which became Germany, went to Louis the German; and the so-called Middle Kingdom, stretching from the Rhineland to Rome, went to Lothair, along with the imperial title. When Lothair's line died out in 856, a civil war erupted between the East Franks and the West Franks for control over Lothair's former territories and the imperial mantle. These territories, known as Lotharingia (or, in French, Alsace-Lorraine), would remain a flashpoint for hostilities between France and Germany until the end of World War II.

The collapse of the Carolingian Empire is often blamed on Louis the Pious's incapacity as a ruler, but this is much too simple. Louis was not an incompetent ruler, but he faced an almost impossible task in trying to hold together the empire his father had created. Charlemagne's empire had been built on successful conquest. By 814, however, Charlemagne had pushed the borders of his empire as far as they could reasonably go. To the west, he now faced the Umayyad rulers of Spain; to the north, the Vikings; and in the east, his armies were too preoccupied with settling the German territories they had already conquered to push far into the Slavic lands that lay beyond them. The pressures that had driven the Frankish conquests, however—the need for booty, land, and plunder with which to reward and promote one's followers—had become even more pronounced as a result of Charlemagne's successes. Under Charlemagne, the number of counts in the Frankish Empire had tripled, from approximately 100 to 300. Louis the Pious could not possibly turn 300 counts into 900. The resources to do so simply did not exist.

Frustrated by their emperor's inability to reward them, Frankish nobles turned on each other. Civil wars erupted among Louis's quarrelsome and difficult sons; regional hostilities between Austrasians, Neustrians,

and Aquitanians flared up again. As central imperial authority broke down, free peasants, a critical group in the eighth-century Carolingian world, found themselves increasingly under the thumb of powerful local nobles who treated them as if they were unfree serfs, bound to the soil and forbidden to leave it. At the same time, internal troubles in the Abbasid Empire caused a breakdown in the foreign trade routes through which Viking traders brought Abbasid silver into Carolingian domains. The Vikings then turned to destructive raiding along the coasts and up the river systems. Under these combined pressures the Carolingian Empire fell apart completely, and a new political map of Europe began to emerge.

The Vikings

Scandinavian traders were already familiar figures in the North Sea and Baltic ports of Europe when the Carolingian era began. They had also begun to establish trading settlements in northern Russia, from which they opened trade routes down the Russian river system to Byzantium (through the Black Sea) and the Abbasid calphate (through the Caspian Sea). Starting in the 790s, however, Scandinavian raiders (known to their enemies as Vikings, a word meaning "robbers") began to attack the coastal ports of northern Europe.

A Hoard of Viking Silver, c. 905. This collection of silver coins and jewelry, weighing almost 90 pounds, was found buried in a lead-lined chest in northwestern England in 1840. Although the coins are English, the jewelry is mainly Irish, suggesting that the Vikings who buried it may have come from Dublin. More than 8,500 silver objects are contained in the hoard, representing the savings of hundreds, and perhaps thousands, of families.

Initially, these raids were driven by the desire for profit through plunder, ransom, tribute collection, and slaving. By the mid-ninth century, however, some Viking attacks involved organized armies with thousands of men, whose aim was to conquer and settle independent principalities in England, Scotland, Ireland, and northern France. By the early eleventh century, Vikings had established settlements in Iceland, Greenland, and Newfoundland; Viking leaders ruled principalities in Scotland, Ireland, Normandy ("the land of the Northmen," i.e., the Vikings), and Russia; and a Viking army had just placed King Cnut of Denmark on the throne of England. Thereafter, however, the threat of Viking attacks lessened. In Scandinavia, conversion to Christianity proceeded rapidly from the late tenth century on; while in France, Scotland, Ireland and England, Viking rulers and settlers were fairly rapidly assimilated into the cultural and political world of northwestern Europe. In 1066, an army of Norman Vikings conquered England at the Battle of Hastings; but to the conquered English (many of whom were themselves the descendants of Viking invaders), their Norman conquerors in 1066 were perceived as Frenchmen rather than Vikings.

The effect of the Vikings on Europe continues to be controversial. What seems clear, however, is that no simple verdict of the good Vikings/bad Vikings sort is either possible or helpful. Although the destructiveness of Viking raids is undeniable, the Vikings were not the only source of disorder in the ninth and tenth centuries. Civil wars in Carolingian France, Muslim attacks in southern Italy and Provence, Hungarian attacks in southeastern Germany, and local political rivalries nearly everywhere contributed mightily to the chaos of the post-Carolingian world. Nor were the Vikings solely a source of disorder. In Ireland and eastern England, Vikings founded a series of new towns, initiating the mass manufacture of high-quality pottery in these areas for the first time since the Roman period. As long-distance traders, Vikings transported large quantities of silver into western Europe, first in the early ninth century and then in the first half of the tenth century, fueling the European economy. And as we shall see in a moment, in those areas of Europe where rulers did succeed in fending off Viking attacks, the prestige resulting from their victories enabled them to construct much more powerful kingdoms and principalities than

had existed before. By focusing so many of their raids on monasteries, the Vikings destroyed much of the intellectual and cultural work of the Carolingian renaissance. At the same time, however, the wide geographical range of their influence, combined with their conversion to Latin Christianity, helped tighten the cultural and political links that bound the European world together.

THE LEGACY OF THE CAROLINGIANS

The Carolingians' vision of a united, Christian Europe collapsed in the chaos of the ninth and tenth centuries. In its place, however, new political divisions within Europe began to emerge that would have decisive consequences for the future. England, which had never been part of Charlemagne's empire and which hitherto had been divided into at least half a dozen small kingdoms at war with each other, emerged as a unified kingdom for the first time under King Alfred the Great (871–899) and his successors. Alfred and his heirs reorganized the army, infused new vigor into local government, founded new towns, and codified English laws. In addition, Alfred established a court school and fostered an interest in Anglo-Saxon writing and other elements of a national culture. In all these respects, Alfred modeled himself closely on Carolingian example. His success in defending his own West Saxon kingdom from Viking attacks, combined with the destruction of every other competing Anglo-Saxon royal dynasty by the Vikings, allowed Alfred and his successors to claim for themselves the mantle of a single, united English monarchy. The increasing prosperity of the country, largely a product of the wool trade, also brought increasing power to the monarchy. By the year 1000, Anglo-Saxon England had become the most administratively sophisticated state in western Christian Europe.

On the Continent, the most powerful monarchs of the tenth century were the dukes of Saxony, who became kings of Germany (East Francia) in 917 after the Carolingian line of kings expired. Like the West Saxon kings of England, the Saxon kings of Germany modeled their kingship closely on Carolingian example. They drew, however, on different aspects of their common Carolingian inheritance. Tenth-century England became a highly effective administrative monarchy, with a centralized monetary and judicial system and

> The increasing prosperity of the country, largely a product of the wool trade, also brought increasing power to the monarchy. By the year 1000, Anglo-Saxon England had become the most administratively sophisticated state in western Christian Europe.

How did Charlemagne redefine the relationship between Christianity and kingship?

The Rise of the Carolingians   281

extensive control over towns and trade. In Germany, by contrast, royal power in the tenth century rested much more on the profits of successful conquest than it did on the profits of trade and administration. In the eighth century, the Carolingians had built their power on successful conquests in Saxony. In the tenth century, the Ottonian kings of Germany, based in Saxony, built their authority on successful conquests into the Slavic lands that lay on their soft eastern frontier. They were also careful to nurture their image as Christian kings on the Carolingian model. In 955, Otto I defeated the pagan Hungarians in a decisive battle while carrying a sacred lance that had once belonged to Charlemagne. This victory established Otto as the dominant power in central Europe and as a man worthy to inherit Charlemagne's imperial throne. In 962 Otto went to Rome to be crowned western emperor by the pope, a thoroughly dissolute young man named John XII, who hoped to use Otto in his own factional squabbles in Rome. Otto, however, refused to go home when Pope John had no further use for him. Scandalized by John's behavior as pope, Otto instead deposed John and selected a new pope to replace him.

The Crown of the Tenth-Century Holy Roman Emperors.

By becoming emperor, Otto hoped to strengthen his control over the church in Germany and to claim a variety of dormant but potentially lucrative imperial rights in northern Italy and Burgundy, parts of the Middle Kingdom once held by the emperor Lothair. Protecting the papacy was, of course, Otto's responsibility as a Carolingian-style emperor, but Otto also needed papal support to achieve these other, more concrete objectives. In Italy, however, Otto quickly discovered that unless he was prepared to remain in Rome full time, he could not even control the papacy, much less the rapidly growing and highly independent towns of northern Italy. If he remained in Italy too long, however, his authority in Saxony would break down, as local lords began to lead and profit from the continuing conquests in the Slavic east. Balancing their local concerns in Saxony with their imperial concerns in Italy presented a dilemma neither Otto I nor his son (Otto II, 973–983) nor his grandson (Otto III, 983–1002) was able to solve. The result was a gradually increasing alienation of the Saxon nobility from their emperor. This alienation accelerated dramatically

after 1024, when the German throne passed to a new dynasty, the Salians, centered not in Saxony but in Franconia. It was not until the 1070s that the Salian king Henry IV finally attempted to reassert his control over the formerly royal lands in Saxony and the Slavic east. When he did so, he touched off a civil war between himself and the Saxon nobility that was to have momentous repercussions not only for Germany but for the entirety of western Europe. The consequences of this great Saxon war are discussed more fully in Chapter Nine.

Aspects of the Carolingian inheritance also survived in the tenth-century Mediterranean world. In Catalunya, counts descended from Carolingian appointees continued to administer public, territorial law in public courts throughout the tenth century. Free peasants prospered as they settled new lands. Classical and Christian learning flourished in reformed Benedictine abbeys and cathedrals. The counts drew their revenues from public fiscal lands and from tolls on a rapidly expanding trade; and the city of Barcelona grew rapidly as both a long-distance and a regional market under the protection of the Catalunyan counts. In Aquitaine also, the counts of Poitiers and Toulouse continued to

EUROPE IN THE ELEVENTH CENTURY

This map shows the alignment of geopolitical power that had emerged by 1050. Based on this map, which political entities would you expect to dominate the twelfth-century European world? Why? Consider the geographical position of Kievan Russia. What influences pulled it toward the West? In what respects was it isolated from the West?

rest their authority on Carolingian foundations until the eleventh century, when in both Aquitaine and Catalunya these Carolingian traditions of public authority finally collapsed.

The tenth century also witnessed a remarkable growth of towns and cities in western Europe, particularly in areas where rulers patterned themselves on Carolingian example. In Anglo-Saxon England, the West Saxon kings established new towns and encouraged existing ones. They tightly regulated coinage and encouraged the growth of marketing, not least by insisting that the taxation they collected be paid in coin. By 1066, when England fell to the invading Normans, at least 10 percent of the English population lived in towns, making it the most highly urbanized country in eleventh-century Europe. Cities also

grew rapidly in the Low Countries and the Rhineland, fueled by long-distance trade (especially in wool and wool cloth) and by the discovery of silver deposits in the mountains of Saxony. In Catalunya, the growth of Barcelona was beginning to transform the political and social life of the country; while in Aquitaine, both Poitiers and Toulouse prospered from their location along the overland trade route that connected Mediterranean with Atlantic Europe.

In tenth- and eleventh-century Italy, urban growth occurred in the absence of an effective Carolingian-style ruler. Instead, the prosperity of tenth-century Italian cities depended on the success of the Byzantine emperors in suppressing Muslim piracy in the eastern Mediterranean. The most prosperous cities in tenth-century Italy lay in the Byzantine-controlled areas of the peninsula: Venice in the north, Amalfi, Naples, and Palermo in the south. Their prosperity rested on their role in the carrying trade that brought silks, spices, and other luxury goods from the Byzantine and Muslim worlds into western Europe. In the eleventh century, however, Norman invasions of southern Italy disrupted this trade, as Turkish invasions of Asia Minor turned Byzantine attentions eastward. By the end of the eleventh century, it would be the north Italian cities whose navies controlled the eastern Mediterranean and that would profit from their role as middlemen in the lucrative traffic among Byzantium, the Muslim world, and western Europe.

In the Carolingian heartland, however, these developments had little influence. Here, Carolingian-style kingship disintegrated during the tenth century under the combined weight of Viking raids, economic collapse, and the growing power of local lords. In some areas, a few Carolingian institutions, such as public courts and a centrally minted coinage, survived in the hands of counts and dukes who used them in building up new, essentially autonomous territorial principalities such as Anjou, Normandy, Flanders, and Aquitaine. Elsewhere in France, even this modicum of continuity with the Carolingian world disappeared. France still had a king who continued to be recognized as the ruler of the western part of Charlemagne's former territories. After 987, however, the kings of France were no longer Carolingians. Instead, a new dynasty, the Capetians, had taken the throne, after having established their reputation as counts of Paris by defending that city against the Vikings. But it would be another century before the Capetian kings of France could reverse the trends that had destroyed their predecessors and begin again to rebuild monarchical power in France on new foundations.

CONCLUSION

This spectacle of Carolingian collapse may suggest that little had changed in western Europe between 750 and 1000. Any such impression would, however, be seriously misleading. It is certainly true that compared with Byzantium or the Muslim world, western Europe remained an intellectual and cultural backwater, more so perhaps by the year 1000 than it had been two centuries before. Politically, no western European ruler in the year 1000 could approach the power of the Byzantine emperor or the Umayyad caliph of Córdoba. Economically also, western Europe was a dependency of Byzantium and Islam, importing finished and luxury goods and exporting furs, leather, and slaves. Beneath the surface, however, western European society was becoming steadily more formidable. Urbanization was proceeding rapidly on the margins of the collapsing Carolingian world. Long-distance trade was also growing. Italian traders were active in Constantinople, and Muslim traders were common in the south Italian ports. Anglo-Saxon merchants were regular visitors to Italy, the Low Countries, and the Rhineland. Jewish merchants in the Rhineland were carrying on an active trade with the Jewish communities of Muslim Egypt, while Viking traders had reopened the trade routes from the Baltic through Russia to the Black Sea and were busily founding cities from Novgorod to Dublin.

Western Europe's borders were also expanding. By the year 1000, its boundaries extended from the Baltic to the Mediterranean Sea, and from the Pyrenees to Poland. Within this vast territory, moreover, every ruler was, or would soon be, Christian. The Latin Christian church was as yet highly localized, but the emergence of new confederations of reformed Benedictine monasteries under papal protection (to be discussed in more detail in Chapter Nine) was beginning to point the way toward a more unified and centralized church. Political omens were less promising. But out of the chaos of tenth-century western Europe, effective territorial principalities and kingdoms were beginning to emerge. During the early Middle Ages, Europe had become a society mobilized for war to a degree unmatched in either Byzantium or the Islamic world. This was, to be sure, a mixed blessing. In the centuries to come, however, the militarization of western European society was to prove a decisive factor in the steadily shifting balance of power among Europe, Byzantium, and the Muslim world.

KEY TERMS

Santa Sophia   Shiites   Charlemagne
Muhammad   Sunnis   Holy Roman Empire
Mecca   Moses Maimonides
Qur'an   Pope Gregory I

SELECTED READINGS

Bede. *A History of the English Church and People.* Trans. Leo Sherley-Price. Baltimore, Md., 1955. The fundamental source for early Anglo-Saxon history, written by the greatest historian of eighth-century Europe.

Bloom, Jonathan M. *Paper before Print: The Impact and History of Paper in the Islamic World.* New Haven, Conn., 2001. A fascinating account, with beautiful illustrations.

Saint Boniface. *Letters of Saint Boniface.* Trans. Ephraim Emerton. New York, 1972.

Campbell, James, ed. *The Anglo-Saxons.* Oxford, 1982. The best and most interesting treatment of its subject, splendidly illustrated.

Collins, Roger. *Early Medieval Europe, 300–1000.* 2d ed. New York, 1999. Dry and detailed, but a useful textbook nonetheless.

Donner, Fred. *The Early Islamic Conquests.* Princeton, N.J., 1981. A scholarly but readable narrative and analysis.

Einhard and Notker the Stammerer. *Two Lives of Charlemagne.* Trans. Lewis Thorpe. Baltimore, 1969. Lively and entertaining.

Fletcher, Richard A. *The Barbarian Conversion: From Paganism to Christianity.* Berkeley, Calif., 1999. Slow paced but informative, perceptive, and enjoyable to read.

Fletcher, Richard A. *Moorish Spain.* Berkeley, Calif., 1993. The best short survey in English.

Geanakoplos, Deno John, ed. *Byzantium: Church, Society and Civilization Seen through Contemporary Eyes.* Chicago, 1984. An outstanding source book, with a great deal of fresh material.

Geary, Patrick J. *Before France and Germany: The Origins and Transformation of the Merovingian World.* New York, 1988. Accessible introduction to recent scholarship, much of it otherwise unavailable in English.

Gregory of Tours. *History of the Franks.* Trans. Lewis Thorpe. Baltimore, Md., 1974. Difficult to follow, but by far the most revealing single source on Merovingian kingship.

Gregory, Timothy E. *A History of Byzantium.* Malden, Mass., and Oxford, 2005. The most accessible of the recent textbooks on Byzantium. An excellent place to start.

Herrin, Judith. *The Formation of Christendom.* Princeton, N.J.,1987. A synthetic history of the Christian civilizations of Byzantium and western Europe from 500 to 800, written by a prominent Byzantinist.

Hodges, Richard, and David Whitehouse. *Mohammed, Charlemagne and the Origins of Europe.* London, 1983. An analysis and recasting of the "Pirenne thesis," which claimed (wrongly, as this book shows) that the advent of Islam disrupted the economic unity of the Mediterranean world.

Hourani, Albert. *A History of the Arab Peoples.* New York, 1992. A sympathetic, clear, and intelligent survey written for non-specialists.

Kazhdan, Alexander P., ed. *The Oxford Dictionary of Byzantium.* 3 vols. Oxford, 1991. An authoritative reference work.

Kennedy, Hugh. *The Prophet and the Age of the Caliphates.* 2d ed., Harlow, UK, 2004. A lucid introduction to the political history of the Islamic world from the sixth through the eleventh centuries.

Krautheimer, Richard. *Early Christian and Byzantine Architecture.* 4th ed. New York, 1986. A classic work by one of the greatest Byzantine art historians of the twentieth century.

Leyser, Karl. *Rule and Conflict in an Early Medieval Society: Ottonian Saxony.* Oxford, 1979. A concise, challenging, brilliant account of the dynamics of rule in tenth-century Saxony, which pays special attention to the importance of royal women.

Loyn, Henry R., and John Percival, eds. and trans. *The Reign of Charlemagne.* London, 1975. An excellent collection of sources; not easy to find, but worth the trouble.

Mango, Cyril, ed. *The Oxford History of Byzantium.* Oxford and New York, 2002. Full of sharp judgments and attractively illustrated.

McKitterick, Rosamond. *The Frankish Kingdoms under the Carolingians, 751–987.* New York, 1983. An authoritative account of politics and intellectual developments.

McKitterick, Rosamond, ed. *The Uses of Literacy in Early Medieval Europe.* New York, 1990. A superb collection of essays representing some of the freshest recent thinking on this subject.

McNamara, Jo Ann, and John E. Halborg, eds. *Sainted Women of the Dark Ages.* Durham., N.C., 1992. Translated saints' lives from Merovingian and Carolingian Europe.

Pelikan, Jaroslav. *The Christian Tradition,* Volume II: *The Spirit of Eastern Christendom.* Chicago, 1974. An outstanding synthetic treatment of the doctrines of Byzantine Christianity.

Peters, F. E. *Aristotle and the Arabs.* New York, 1968. Well written and engaging.

Reuter, Timothy. *Germany in the Early Middle Ages, 800–1056.* New York, 1991. The best and most up-to-date survey in English.

Sawyer, Peter, ed. *The Oxford Illustrated History of the Vikings.* Oxford, 1997. The best one-volume account, lavishly illustrated.

Stillman, Norman A. *The Jews of Arab Lands: A History and Source Book.* Philadelphia, Pa., 1979. An essential resource.

Todd, Malcolm. *The Early Germans.* Oxford, 1992. A reliable survey, particularly strong in its use of archaeological evidence.

Treadgold, Warren. *A History of the Byzantine State and Society.* Stanford, Calf., 1997. A massive, encyclopedic narrative of the political, economic, and military history of Byzantium from 284 until 1461.

Wallace-Hadrill, John Michael. *Early Germanic Kingship in England and on the Continent.* Oxford, 1971. A remarkably interesting analysis of changing ideas about the nature and responsibilities of kingship in early medieval Europe, emphasizing the links between Anglo-Saxon and Carolingian theories of kingship.

Wallace-Hadrill, John Michael. *The Frankish Church.* Oxford, 1983. A masterful account that links together the Merovingian and the Carolingian churches.

Watt, W. Montgomery. *Islamic Philosophy and Theology,* 2d ed. Edinburgh, UK, 1985. The standard English account.

Wemple, Suzanne Fonay. *Women in Frankish Society: Marriage and the Cloister, 500–900.* Philadelphia, Pa., 1981. An influential account of changing attitudes toward marriage among the early Franks.

Whittow, Mark. *The Making of Orthodox Byzantium, 600–1025.* London, 1996. Emphasizes the centrality of orthodoxy in shaping Byzantine history. Particularly good on Byzantine relations with the peoples outside the empire.

Wood, Ian. *The Merovingian Kingdoms, 450–751.* New York, 1994. Full of the latest thinking, but detailed and difficult for beginners.

CHAPTER EIGHT

THE EXPANSION OF EUROPE: ECONOMY, SOCIETY, AND POLITICS IN THE HIGH MIDDLE AGES, 1000–1300

BETWEEN 1000 AND 1300, the balance of power among western Europe, Byzantium, and the Islamic world shifted profoundly. In the year 1000, Europe remained politically fractured and militarily threatened by Viking, Hungarian, and Muslim attacks. Although towns in western Europe were beginning to grow, none could compare in size or sophistication with the ancient Mediterranean cities of Byzantium and the Islamic world. Economically, western Europe continued to depend on Byzantine and Islamic traders for its cotton, silk, spices, and gold. With respect to literature and learning, the imbalances were even greater. Europeans had access to only a small portion of the cultural and intellectual riches Byzantium and Islam had inherited from the classical world. Outside Sicily, Venice, and the Muslim-controlled areas of Spain, western Europeans knew no Arabic and virtually no Greek. Even Latin, the language of western learning for more than a thousand years, was increasingly a foreign tongue. King Alfred (871–899) complained that in his day hardly anyone in England knew enough Latin to conduct correctly the services of the Christian church. A century later, Latin learning in England and Germany was somewhat better. In France and Italy it was probably worse.

By the year 1300, however, Europe was the dominant military, economic, and political power among the three western successor civilizations to Greece and Rome. Hungary, Poland, Scandinavia, and Bohemia were now thoroughly integrated parts of a Catholic, European world. Combining conquest with conversion, European Christians had forcefully pushed their borders eastward into Prussia, Lithuania, Livonia, and the Balkans. They had conquered Spain from the Muslims and Constantinople from the Byzantines. They had also established (and in 1300, just lost) a Latin kingdom in the Middle East, with its capital at Jerusalem. European navies

FOCUS QUESTIONS

• What impact did the medieval agricultural revolution have on the lives of Europeans?

• What were the major causes of urban growth during the High Middle Ages?

• How did the First Crusade alter the balance of power between Europe and Byzantium?

• What was the relationship between chivalry and the cult of courtly love?

• How did government and politics change during the High Middle Ages?

• What was the relationship between feudalism and the rise of national monarchies?

controlled the Mediterranean Sea and had outposts on the Black Sea and the Caspian Sea, allowing European traders to dominate the long-distance trade routes that brought eastern luxury goods into western Europe. European missionaries and traders were beginning to follow these trade routes back through Central Asia, opening up connections with Mongolia and China. To the west, Italian merchants had initiated a seaborne trade route through the Strait of Gibraltar, thus connecting the Mediterranean and the north Atlantic world.

This expansion of European commerce, both local and long distance, was accompanied by significant urbanization. By 1300, Europe could claim at least a dozen cities with populations between 50,000 and 100,000 people, with hundreds of smaller towns and cities scattered across the landscape. The growth of cities mirrored the general growth in the European population which, on a rough estimate, tripled between 1000 and 1300. The economy grew even more rapidly, however, leading to increased per capita wealth and a rising standard of living. By no means, however, were these economic gains distributed equally among the entire population. Governments grew more powerful, and social stratification increased. New wealth increased the demand for luxury goods among social elites and freed up huge sums of money for investment in agriculture, commerce, and construction. It also fueled remarkable new religious, cultural, and intellectual developments, which will be discussed in the next chapter.

Not all of this growth proved sustainable. By 1300, living standards for many Europeans were falling as western Europe began to approach the demographic limits of its natural resources. More powerful governments kept better internal peace, but they also claimed a larger proportion of their subjects' wealth, which they used to support bigger armies and grander campaigns of conquest and domination. In the fourteenth century, famine, war, and plague reduced the European population by at least a third, fundamentally transforming the economic, political, and social order of the High Middle Ages. Despite these setbacks, however, the predominance western Europe established over Byzantium and the Islamic world during the High Middle Ages would endure, providing the foundation on which the European world empires of the early modern era would be built.

> In western Europe, however, the agricultural changes that took place between 700 and 1300 were so sweeping and their consequences so profound that comparisons with the more famous agricultural revolution of the early eighteenth century seem justified.

THE MEDIEVAL AGRICULTURAL REVOLUTION

What impact did the medieval agricultural revolution have on the lives of Europeans?

Like all premodern economies, the western European economy in the Middle Ages rested on agriculture. Change in agricultural practices tends to be slow; even so, it may seem absurd to speak of agricultural changes that took place across 600 years as constituting a "revolution." In western Europe, however, the agricultural changes that took place between 700 and 1300 were so sweeping and their consequences so profound that comparisons with the more famous agricultural revolution of the early eighteenth century seem justified. Technological innovations, combined with a warming climate; new crop-rotation systems; and increased investment in tools, livestock, and mills, increased the productivity of European agriculture dramatically. As agricultural productivity increased, so too did the marketing of agricultural surpluses, leading to increased specialization of production with resulting efficiencies of scale. Without these changes, western Europe could never have supported the tripling of its overall population, or the massive investments in buildings, ships, books, armies, and art that shaped the high medieval world.

TECHNOLOGICAL ADVANCES

The basic technological advances that made possible the increasing productivity of high medieval agriculture were developed in the early Middle Ages. The heavy-wheeled plow, fitted with an iron-tipped coulter and dragged by a team of oxen or horses, could cut and turn the rich, wet soil of northern Europe to a depth impossible for the Mediterranean scratch plow to reach, thus aerating the soil and providing excellent drainage for water-logged territories. The new plow also saved labor, allowing more frequent plowing and better control of weeds. Related improvements in collars and harnesses increased the efficiency of plow oxen and made it possible for the first time for horses to pull heavy loads without choking themselves. Oxen remained the

WHAT IMPACT DID THE MEDIEVAL AGRICULTURAL REVOLUTION HAVE ON THE LIVES OF EUROPEANS?

THE MEDIEVAL AGRICULTURAL REVOLUTION   289

most commonly used plow animals in Europe until at least the fourteenth century. They were cheaper, more powerful, and less prone to disease than were horses, and when they died they could be eaten. Horses, however, were faster and more efficient cart animals, especially after the development of iron horseshoes (around 900) and tandem harnessing (around 1050), which allowed horses to pull behind each other. As marketing of agricultural produce increased during the twelfth and thirteenth centuries, so too, therefore, did the prevalence of horses in the European countryside.

Other labor-saving devices further increased the productivity of high medieval agriculture. Despite the advent of the heavy-wheeled plow, most of the work of raising crops continued to be done by individual peasant farmers using hand tools. As iron became more common during the High Middle Ages, the quality of these hand tools steadily improved. Iron-tipped hoes,

forks, and shovels were much more effective than the wooden implements with which most eighth-century farmers had had to make do; the increasing number of iron sickles and scythes made it easier to harvest hay and grain, especially by women, whose field labor was critically important, particularly during harvesttime. Wheelbarrows were another homely but important technological innovation. So too was the harrow, a tool drawn over the field after the plow to level the earth and mix in the seed. Technology also had an impact on cooking techniques and hence on nutrition. Iron pots allowed food to be boiled rather than just warmed, reducing the chances of contamination; communal ovens preserved a larger share of the nutrients in food than did boiling.

Mills represented another major technological innovation in food processing. The Romans had known about water mills but relied mainly on human- and animal-powered wheels to grind grain into flour. Starting around 1050, however, there was a veritable craze in northern Europe for building water mills of steadily increasing efficiency. One French area saw a growth from 14 water mills in the eleventh century to 60 in the twelfth; in another part of France about 40 mills were built between 850 and 1080, 40 more between 1080 and 1125, and 245

Light Plow and Heavy Plow. Note that the peasant using the light plow (top) had to press his foot on it to give it added weight. The major innovation of the heavy plow (often wheeled; bottom) was the long moldboard, which turned over the ground after the plowshare cut into it. The bottom picture depicts a second crucial medieval invention as well—the padded horse collar, which allowed horses to throw their full weight into pulling.

between 1126 and 1175. Once Europeans had mastered the complex technology of building water mills, they turned their attention to windmills, which proliferated rapidly from the 1170s on, especially in flat lands such as Holland that had no swiftly flowing streams. Although the major use of mills was to grind grain, they could be adapted to drive saws, process cloth, press oil, provide power for iron forges, and crush pulp for manufacturing paper. The importance of such mills cannot be overstated. They would remain the world's only source of mechanical power for manufacturing until the eighteenth-century invention of the steam engine.

Peasants Harvesting Grain. This illustration, drawn around 1340, shows two women harvesting grain with sickles, while a third woman stretches out her back and a man bundles up the sheaves.

A Medieval Harrow. By covering the seed with dirt, harrows increased the percentage of seed that germinated, and decreased losses to birds, such as the crows shown here.

An Early Fourteenth-Century Watermill. This mill was constructed so that its wheel would be propelled by water striking the top of the wheel rather than the bottom of the wheel, thus generating additional power.

With the exception of the windmill and the tandem harness, most of the technological innovations that lay behind the medieval agricultural revolution were already known to the Carolingians. Only from the mid-eleventh century, however, did these innovations become sufficiently widespread as to have a decisive effect on European agricultural production. Various explanations for this delay have been offered, and climate change must have played some role. Starting in the eighth or ninth century, average temperatures in Europe gradually rose by about 1° or 2°C, making it possible to farm in Greenland and to produce wine in southern England. But although the warming climate benefited northern Europe by drying the soil and lengthening the growing season, higher temperatures and diminishing rainfall hurt Mediterranean agriculture in equal measure. Greater physical security also played a role. Viking, Hungarian, and Muslim attacks were decreasing, and more powerful governments kept better domestic peace than they had been able to do a century before. The fundamental change, however, lay in the growing confidence of entrepreneurial peasants and lords that if they invested labor and money in agricultural improvements, they would profit from the resulting surpluses.

More than anything else, it was the expanding demand for agricultural produce that encouraged peasants and landlords to make productive investments in the land. Behind the growing demand for foodstuffs lay the two fundamental economic factors that drove the high medieval economy forward: a rapidly increasing European population and an increasingly efficient market for goods.

WHAT IMPACT DID THE MEDIEVAL AGRICULTURAL REVOLUTION HAVE ON THE LIVES OF EUROPEANS?

THE MEDIEVAL AGRICULTURAL REVOLUTION   291

MANORIALISM, SERFDOM, AND AGRICULTURAL PRODUCTIVITY

In England, northern France, and western Germany, increasing use of the heavy-wheeled plow between 800 and 1050 coincided with a fundamental change in patterns of peasant settlement. During the early Middle Ages, most free peasant farmers lived on individual plots of land that they farmed with their own resources and for which they paid their landlord some kind of customary rent. Starting in the ninth century, however, many of these individual peasant holdings began to be consolidated into large, common fields that were farmed communally by peasants living in villages. The resulting complex of rents, renders, dues, fines, and fields is sometimes called a *manor*.

In some areas, the impetus for these changes in settlement patterns came from the peasants themselves.

A Tavern Scene. Customers in an upstairs room drink wine from cups and bottles, while the cellarer hands up another cup drawn from the barrels of wine stored below.

Large fields could be farmed more efficiently than small fields. Investment costs were lower: a single plow and a dozen oxen might suffice for an entire village, obviating the need for every farmer to maintain his own plow and plow beasts. Common fields were potentially more productive also, allowing the villagers to experiment with new crops and new crop-rotation systems and to support larger numbers of animals on common pastures. Peasants living together in a village might be able to support a parish church, a communal oven, a blacksmith, a mill, and a tavern. They could also converse and socialize, celebrate, and mourn with their neighbors. In a difficult and demanding natural environment, these were not negligible considerations.

Despite the potential advantages the manorial system offered to peasants, lords played the dominant role in forcing its creation, and it was they who took the greatest benefits from it. It was easier for lords to control and exploit peasants living in villages than peasants living on scattered individual farms. Manorialism also allowed lords to claim a larger share of their peasants' agricultural production. On many manors, the common fields were divided into narrow strips assigned in alternating fashion to individual peasants, for which each peasant landholder paid rent to the lord, but from which each peasant took the profits. In addition to rents, however, most lords also claimed a third to a half of the total acreage in the common fields as their own demesne (pronounced *demean*) land, from which they took all the produce for their own use. To farm this demesne land, manorial lords imposed or increased labor services on peasant farmers, reducing many formerly free peasants to the status of serfs.

Serfs had existed in Europe for centuries, even in areas where the manorial system never took hold. There is no doubt, however, that the development of manorialism considerably increased the incidence of serfdom in northern Europe as compared with Spain, northern Italy, southern France, and central Germany. Unlike free peasants, serfs could not leave their land or their lord without his permission (although in practice, many did so, especially to become town dwellers). Serfs worked for their lords regularly without pay; paid humiliating fines to their lord when they fornicated illicitly, married, or died; and were subject to the jurisdiction of their lord's manorial court. Like slaves, their servile status was heritable; but unlike slaves, their obligations to their lord were fixed by custom, and they were not supposed to be sold apart from the lands they held.

NEW CROP-ROTATION SYSTEMS

From the standpoint of agrarian productivity, the greatest advantage of the manorial system was the fact that it made possible the adoption of new, more efficient crop-rotation systems. For centuries, farmers had known that if they sowed the same crop on the same land year after year, they would eventually exhaust the soil. The traditional solution to this difficulty was to divide one's land, planting half in the fall to harvest in the spring, and leaving the other half to lie fallow. In the dry, thin soils of the Mediterranean, this remained the most common cropping pattern throughout the Middle Ages. In the wet, fertile soils of northern Europe, however, farmers slowly discovered that a three-field crop-rotation system could produce a sustainable increase in overall agricultural production. Under this system, one third of the land would lie fallow, often being used for pasturage, so that the animals' droppings would fertilize the soil; one third would be planted with winter wheat or rye, which was sown in the fall and harvested in the early summer; and one third would be planted with another crop (usually oats or barley, but sometimes legumes or fodder crops such as alfalfa, clover, or vetch) that could be sown in the spring and harvested in the fall. The fields were then rotated over a three-year cycle.

This system immediately increased, from 50 percent to 67 percent, the amount of land under cultivation in any given year. No less important, it also produced higher yields per acre of wheat and rye, particularly if legumes or fodder crops (which replace the nitrogen that wheat and rye leach out of the soil) were a regular part of the crop-rotation pattern. With two separate growing seasons, the system provided some insurance against loss from natural disasters. It also produced new types of food. Oats could be consumed by both humans and horses, while legumes provided a source of protein to balance the major intake of cereal carbohydrates from bread and beer, the two main staples of the peasant diet in northern and central Europe. Additional fodder made it possible to support more and healthier animals, increasing the efficiency of plow beasts, diversifying the economy of the manor and providing an additional source of protein in the human diet through meat and milk. The new crop-rotation system also helped spread labor more evenly over the course of the year, allowing more careful attention to weed control, liming, and fertilizing of the common fields.

SERFDOM AND THE LIMITS OF MANORIALISM

It is important to remember that classic manorialism of the high medieval type, with servile peasants laboring on lordly demesne lands, was never the predominant form for European agriculture. By and large, the manorial system was limited to England, northern France, and western Germany. Even in these areas, moreover, it was beginning to break down by the end of the twelfth century, as lords began to commute labor services into cash payments, to free their serfs (again in return for cash payments), and to live from rents paid in cash rather than from the actual agricultural produce of their estates.

The reasons for the decline of serfdom during the thirteenth century are complex and did not affect all areas of Europe equally. As the European economy became increasingly monetized, many lords simply found it more convenient to collect their revenues directly from their peasants in cash, rather than taking the risks associated with marketing agricultural produce directly. This strategy also had its dangers, however. In the inflationary circumstances of the thirteenth century, lords who could not increase the rents their peasants paid them suffered marked declines in their real incomes, sending many knights and lesser lords into economic crisis. In England and Catalunya, by contrast, which had two of the most thoroughly commercialized agricultural economies in medieval Europe, serfdom lasted longer than almost anywhere else in western Europe. In Austria and Poland, which were far less monetized, serfdom also increased during the

An Eleventh-Century Viking Coin Hoard from Sweden.
The larger coins are Muslim and Byzantine; the smaller silver pennies are European.

WHAT WERE THE MAJOR CAUSES OF URBAN GROWTH DURING THE HIGH MIDDLE AGES?

THE GROWTH OF TOWNS AND COMMERCE   293

thirteenth century, as it did in northern Spain. There is thus no simple correlation between commercialization and the decline of serfdom. In most of Europe, however, the generalization holds: serfs and free peasants became increasingly indistinguishable during the thirteenth century as lords freed serfs in return for cash. Even in France, however, some servile obligations would continue to exist as nagging indignities right down to the French Revolution in 1789. And in central and eastern Europe and Russia, serfdom underwent a resurgence during the later Middle Ages that would carry it into the eighteenth and nineteenth centuries.

THE GROWTH OF TOWNS AND COMMERCE

What were the major causes of urban growth during the High Middle Ages?

This agricultural revolution was the foundation on which the commercial revolution of the High Middle Ages rested. Here too, the groundwork for new developments had been laid in the ninth and tenth centuries. By the year 1000, silver from the Harz Mountains in Saxony was already fueling a triangular trade between England, Flanders, and the expanding cities of the Rhineland that brought raw wool from England to Flanders and wool cloth from Flanders to the Rhineland, whose merchants then distributed it as far away as Italy and Byzantium. Millions of silver pennies were in circulation around the North Sea, where an integrated system of exchange among English, Scandinavian, and Rhenish currencies had developed. English merchants were active in Constantinople and northern Spain, exchanging northern silver for Byzantine silks, Islamic spices, and African gold. Scandinavian merchants and warriors ranged even more widely, establishing cities in Ireland, principalities in Normandy and southern Italy, and trading outposts such as Novgorod and Kiev along the Russian trade routes that ran from the Baltic to the Black Sea (and thence to Constantinople) and to the Caspian Sea (and on into the Abbasid Empire).

To facilitate such investment, Italian merchants developed new forms of commercial partnership contracts; new methods of accounting (including double-entry bookkeeping); and new credit mechanisms, some of which they borrowed from Byzantine and Muslim examples.

COMMERCE

During the eleventh and twelfth centuries, however, the greatest developments in long-distance commerce took place in the burgeoning cities of northern Italy. A series of naval victories by Venetian, Pisan, and Genoese forces gave these cities control over the carrying trade among Constantinople, Alexandria, and the West. The growing prosperity of western European nobles and churchmen created an expanding market for eastern luxury goods, while the improved domestic security of high medieval Europe made it possible for merchants to provide such goods with at least a modicum of security and safety. In the twelfth century, an organized system of fairs emerged in the central French region of Champagne, where Flemish merchants sold cloth to Italians and Italian merchants sold Muslim spices and Byzantine silks to Flemings, French, and Germans. By 1300, however, these fairs were beginning to decline as Italian merchants succeeded in opening up a direct route by sea between Italy and the Atlantic ports of northern Europe. It now became practical to import raw wool directly from England to northern Italy, where towns like Florence could produce and finish wool cloth themselves. As the Italian cloth industry grew, the Flemish cloth industry declined, yet another sign of the increasing extent to which Europe was becoming a unified economy.

Long-distance trade was a risky enterprise. Fortunes could be lost as easily as they could be made. Piracy was commonplace, and the Mediterranean Sea was notoriously dangerous to sailors and their ships. Merchants were often disdained by the landed aristocracy because they could claim no ancient lineages and because they were too obviously concerned with making money. Their courage, however, was undeniable; even in battle, the citizen armies of Milan or Florence often got the better of their aristocratic opponents. Above all, however, Italian success in opening up the new trade routes of the High Middle Ages depended on the willingness of both merchants and nobles to invest substantial sums of money in ships, cargoes, and pack animals. To facilitate such investment, Italian merchants developed new forms of commercial partnership contracts; new methods of accounting (including double-entry bookkeeping); and new credit mechanisms, some of which they borrowed from Byzantine and Muslim examples. Some of these new credit

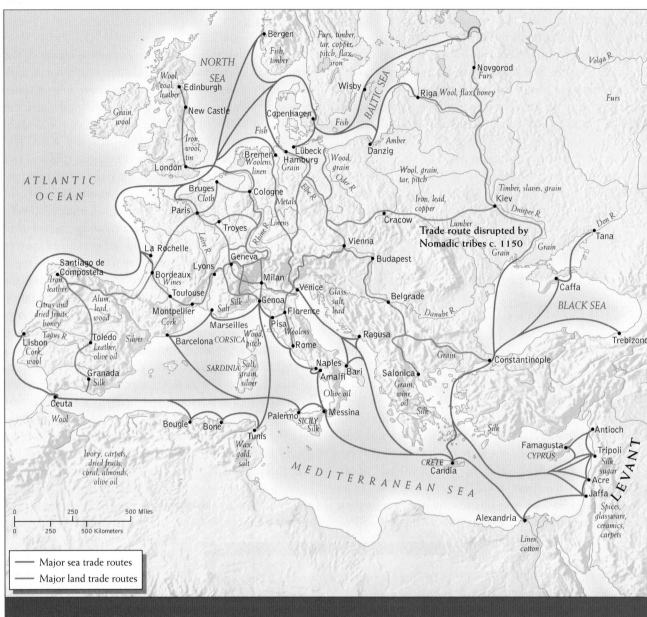

MEDIEVAL TRADE ROUTES

This map details the routes by which long-distance trade moved in and around Europe during the eleventh and twelfth centuries. What was the relationship between trade routes and rivers, and why? Why was the agricultural revolution and the revival of trade crucial to the extension of major trade routes in the west? What factors led to the intense proliferation of trade routes among England, Bruges, and the Rhine Valley? What trade patterns emerge as different regions begin specializing in certain goods?

arrangements ran afoul of the western Christian church, which condemned almost all forms of money-lending as usury. But the demand for capital to fuel the new commercial economy was irresistible, and slowly attitudes began to change. From the thirteenth century on, leading churchmen also began to speak more favorably of merchants. Saint Bonaventura, a thirteenth-century Italian Franciscan, argued, for example, that in

Old Testament times, God had shown special favor to shepherds such as King David; in New Testament times, he had favored fishermen such as Saint Peter; but in modern times, God's favor now went out to merchants such as Saint Francis of Assisi.

It would be misleading, however, to think of the commercial revolution or the urban revolution of the High Middle Ages as principally the result of long-

WHAT WERE THE MAJOR CAUSES OF URBAN GROWTH DURING THE HIGH MIDDLE AGES?

THE GROWTH OF TOWNS AND COMMERCE   295

Medieval Money Lenders and Their Borrowers. As long distance trade expanded in the Middle Ages, merchants developed new methods of financing their voyages. Many of these practices conflicted with the medieval Christian church, which decried these new forms of moneylending as usury. This Italian manuscript depicts the seven vices associated with moneylending.

distance trade. Some towns did receive great stimulus from such trade, and the growth of such major cities as Venice (about 100,000 people in 1300) and Genoa (80,000) would have been impossible without it. But the prosperity of most towns, including such enormous cities as Paris (with a population of 200,000 people in 1300), Florence (100,000), Milan (80,000 to 100,000), and London (60,000 to 80,000), depended primarily on the wealth of their surrounding hinterlands, from which they drew their food supplies, their raw materials, and the bulk of their population. The quickening of economic life in general was the major cause of urban growth during the High Middle Ages. Long-distance trade was but one aspect of this larger economic and commercial transformation of European life.

TOWNS

Towns, both large and small, existed in a symbiotic relationship with the countryside around them, providing markets and manufactured goods while the inhabitants lived off the rural food surplus. Urban areas expanded through the constant immigration of free peasants and escaped serfs in search of a better life. Once towns started to flourish, many of them began to specialize in certain enterprises. Paris and Bologna became the homes of leading universities; Venice,

Genoa, Cologne, and London became centers of long-distance trade; Milan, Florence, Ghent, and Bruges specialized in manufactures. The most important urban industries were those devoted to the making and finishing of wool (and in Venice, cotton) cloth. Most urban manufacturing was done by individual artisans in small, privately owned workshops whose production was regulated by professional associations known as guilds.

Usually only master artisans, who were experts at their trade and ran their own shops, were allowed to be full members of a craft guild. As a result, guilds generally promoted the interests of their richest and most successful members by trying to preserve monopolies and limit competition. To these ends, terms of employment were strictly regulated. If an apprentice or a journeyman (from the French *journée*, meaning "day," or by extension "day's work"—that is, someone who had completed his apprenticeship but still worked for a master craftsman) wished to become a master, he had to produce a "masterpiece" for judging by the masters of the guild. If the market was judged too weak to support additional master craftsmen, even a masterpiece would not secure a craftsman the coveted right to set

A Medieval Cheese Shop. Cheese was an extremely important part of the medieval diet in both town and countryside. This urban cheesemaker's shop opens out onto the street; behind him, his cat guards against rodents.

View of Paris. The city looked this way at the end of the Middle Ages, around 1480. Note the prominence of the Cathedral of Nôtre Dame in the center and the large number of other church spires; note, too, how closely all the buildings are packed behind the walls.

up his own shop; yet without such status, some towns even forbade journeymen to marry. Craft guilds controlled prices and wages, prohibited after-hours work, and formulated detailed regulations governing methods of production and the quality of materials to be used by their members. They also served important social functions as religious associations, benevolent societies, and drinking clubs, looking after their members in times of trouble and supporting the dependents of master craftsmen who died.

Merchants also established guilds, which in some towns became so powerful that membership in a merchant guild became a prerequisite for service in town government. Like the more numerous but less powerful craft guilds, merchant guilds sought to control the local market by restricting competition and enforcing uniform pricing. Often they also controlled admissions to citizenship in the city. By their nature, guilds were exclusionary organizations. Because they were explicitly Christian, they were almost invariably closed to Jews and Muslims. They also significantly restricted the economic opportunities available to ordinary wage earners, and especially to women. Women were not automatically excluded from most guilds, and a few craft guilds were specifically female. Despite the

important role women played as urban wage earners, however, the male-dominated guilds ensured that women would have no influence over the terms and conditions under which they worked or the wages they would be paid for their labor.

To modern eyes, most medieval towns and cities would still have seemed half rural even in 1300. Streets were often unpaved, houses had gardens for raising vegetables, and farm animals were everywhere. In the early twelfth century, the heir to the throne of France was killed when his horse tripped over a pig running loose in the streets of Paris. Sanitary conditions were poor, and the air must often have reeked of excrement, both animal and human. One fourteenth-century Londoner channeled his sewage for months into the basement of his neighbor's house; only when the basement filled and the sewage began to flood the public street was his offense detected. In such a world, disease ran rampant, especially in the overcrowded neighborhoods where the poorest urban dwellers lived. At every level of urban society, however, fertility rates were low and infant mortality high. Most cities sustained their population only through continuing immigration from the countryside. Fire was an omnipresent danger, and economic tensions

> Despite the important role women played as urban wage earners, however, the male-dominated guilds ensured that women would have no influence over the terms and conditions under which they worked or the wages they would be paid for their labor.

How did the First Crusade alter the balance of power between Europe and Byzantium?

BYZANTIUM, ISLAM, AND THE CRUSADES   297

and family rivalries could lead to bloody riots. Yet for all this, urban folk took great pride in their new cities and ways of life. A famous paean to London, for example, written by a twelfth-century resident of the city, boasted of its prosperity, piety, and perfect climate (!) and claimed that except for frequent fires, London's only nuisance was "the immoderate drinking of fools." His pride was echoed in scores of other European cities as their citizens increasingly asserted their distinctive local identities and their communal privileges as merchants, artisans, and self-governing corporations.

BYZANTIUM, ISLAM, AND THE CRUSADES

How did the First Crusade alter the balance of power between Europe and Byzantium?

As the power of the Abbasid caliphate declined during the ninth and tenth centuries, the Byzantine Empire expanded. In the mid-ninth century, Byzantium's position was still precarious. A Muslim fleet had recently captured Sicily and Crete; pagan Slav immigration into the Balkans was rapidly undermining Byzantine control of that region; Muslim pressure on the eastern borders of the empire continued unabated, although the borders themselves remained pretty much where they had been since the early eighth century; and a new enemy

had emerged in the Viking (Rus) raiders and traders who had established themselves along the Russian river systems that fed into the Black and the Caspian Sea. The Rus's most important trading connections were with the Abbasids, with whom they exchanged slaves, honey, wax, and furs for Abbasid silver, Indian spices, and Chinese silks. But the Rus knew their way to Constantinople also. In 860, when the Byzantine emperor and his army were busy on the eastern frontier with the Muslims, a Rus fleet sailed into the Black Sea and sacked Constantinople itself.

THE BYZANTINE REVIVAL

By 1025, however, Byzantium's position had been transformed. After several centuries of missionary inactivity, ninth-century Byzantine missionaries, most famously Saints Cyril and Methodius, converted the Balkan Slavs to Orthodox Christianity, devising for them a written language known as Old Church Slavonic and creating the Cyrillic alphabet, which is still used today in Bulgaria, Serbia, and Russia. Military conquest quickly followed. By 1025, when Emperor Basil II ("the Bulgar-slayer") died, the Byzantines had firmly annexed Greece, Bulgaria, and modern-day Serbia to their empire. They had also established a military and commercial alliance with the western Rus kingdom centered around Kiev, decisively reorienting the Rus toward Constantinople and away from Islam. In 911, about 700 Rus served with the Byzantine fleet in an attack on Muslim Crete. In 945 a commercial treaty was established. In 957, a Kievan Christian princess named Olga (Helga) was lavishly entertained on a state visit to Constantinople. And in 989,

An Eleventh-Century Byzantine Naval Battle. Control over the seas was critical to Byzantine commerce. Here, two galleys prepare to engage in hand-to-hand combat.

the emperor Basil II turned to Vladimir, prince of Kiev, for the troops he needed to win a civil war against his imperial rival, Bardas Phokas, a member of the increasingly powerful nobility from the eastern borders of the empire. In return for Vladimir's help, Basil gave his sister, Anna, in marriage to Vladimir; and Vladimir, along with his people, accepted baptism into the Orthodox church. Russia has remained an Orthodox bastion until the present day.

Between the 930s and the 970s, the Byzantines also launched a series of successful campaigns along their

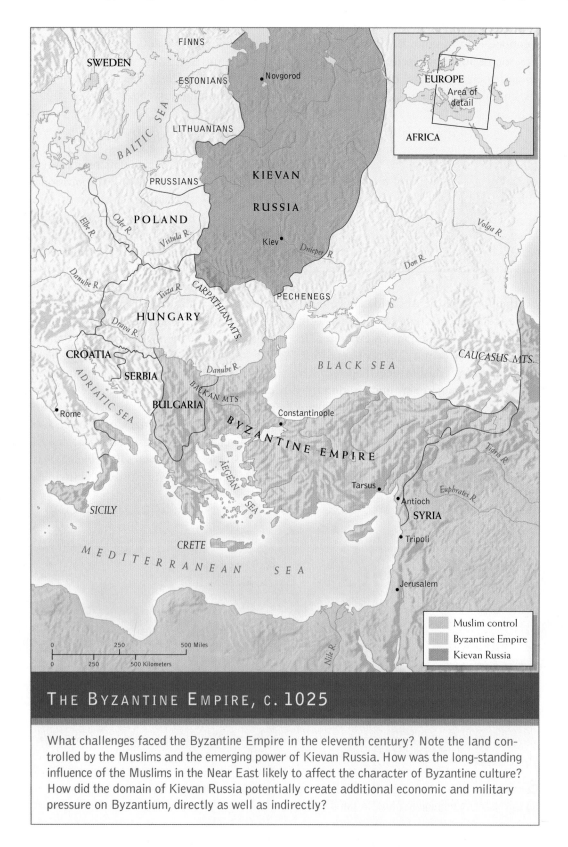

THE BYZANTINE EMPIRE, C. 1025

What challenges faced the Byzantine Empire in the eleventh century? Note the land controlled by the Muslims and the emerging power of Kievan Russia. How was the long-standing influence of the Muslims in the Near East likely to affect the character of Byzantine culture? How did the domain of Kievan Russia potentially create additional economic and military pressure on Byzantium, directly as well as indirectly?

HOW DID THE FIRST CRUSADE ALTER THE BALANCE OF POWER BETWEEN EUROPE AND BYZANTIUM?

BYZANTIUM, ISLAM, AND THE CRUSADES   299

eastern and southeastern frontiers with the Abbasids, reconquering territories that had not been in Byzantine hands since the seventh century. Although most of the peoples of the reconquered territories had remained Christian through three centuries of Islamic rule, the Armenians and the Syrians in particular had their own distinctive Christian traditions that were at odds, both doctrinally and linguistically, with the Greek-speaking church at Constantinople. For an empire that had defined itself for centuries on the basis of its orthodoxy (the word itself means "correct belief"), incorporating such "heretics" threatened the foundations on which the unity of the empire rested.

Even more important, however, the eastern conquests greatly increased the power of the local noble families who led them and profited from them, creating for the first time a center of power within the empire that lay outside the imperial capital at Constantinople. Tensions and rivalries between these eastern noble families and the imperial officials at the capital disturbed Byzantine politics for most of the tenth century. After an attempted coup by the head of one such family, the emperor Basil II (976–1025) savagely suppressed the leading eastern magnate families, and also redirected Byzantine military power westward toward Bulgaria, which he conquered with the assistance of a naval force supplied by the Venetians. But this check on the eastern magnates' ambitions proved only temporary. After Basil's death, the imperial throne passed to a series of aged and incompetent relations. In the resulting power vacuum, noble military families came more and more to dominate the countryside; while at court, tax revenues decreased as imperial expenditures rose. To pay the bills, the emperors debased the Byzantine gold coinage, reducing its value by 50

percent between 1040 and 1080 and undermining Byzantine commerce precisely when Venice, Genoa, and Pisa were consolidating their control over the eastern Mediterranean trade routes. By 1081, when the eastern magnate families triumphed by placing Alexius Comnenus on the imperial throne, the Byzantine Empire had been crippled as a Mediterranean power.

THE INVASION OF THE TURKS

By the late eleventh century, Byzantium faced new threats from several quarters. Venice, Genoa, and Pisa had emerged as the dominant naval powers in the eastern Mediterranean and had to a considerable extent taken over the lucrative trade between Islamic North Africa (including Egypt) and the west. The growing power of Fatimid Egypt was beginning to roll back Byzantine gains along the empire's southeastern frontier with Syria. But most disastrous of all, a new Sunni Muslim power, the Seljuk Turks, had emerged in central Asia and had begun to move into Asia Minor, the very heartland of the Byzantine Empire. When the Turks captured Armenia, the emperor tried to eject them; but the eastern noble families refused their support, and in the decisive battle of Manzikert (1071), the imperial army was annihilated. The way now lay open for the Turks to seize all of Anatolia; at a blow, the wealthiest and most productive part of the Byzantine Empire now fell into Turkish hands. In the same year, another Turkish band captured Jerusalem from the Shiite Fatimids, restoring the Holy City to Sunni control. Within five years, almost all of Syria and Asia Minor lay in Turkish hands. In the west, a rebellion by the Balkan Slavs also erupted around this time, further reducing the already severely depleted treasury of the Byzantine Empire.

By the 1090s, however, Alexius Comnenus had rebuilt the treasury and restored Byzantine control over the Balkans, and was beginning to plan a campaign against the Turks. During the eleventh century, western knights had emerged as the most effective heavily armored cavalry troops in the world. Alexius had confronted such knights in 1085, when he repelled a Norman invasion of Greece. He was anxious to make use of them, however, against the mounted but lightly armored Turks. To recruit a force of heavy cavalry, Alexius sent a request to Pope Urban II, hoping for a contingent of a few thousand troops with which he might be able to roll back Turkish gains in Anatolia. Within a year, however, the pope had set in motion a vast crusading army of 100,000 Westerners to retake the Holy City of Jerusalem for Christendom.

C H R O N O L O G Y

BYZANTINE EMPIRE, 900–1204

Successful campaigns against the Abbasid rulers	930–970
Russia converts to orthodoxy	911–989
Emperor Basil II	976–1025
Turkish invasions (defeat of Manzikert)	1071
Reign of Alexius Comnenus	1081–1118
First Crusade	1095–1099
Fourth Crusade, capture of Constantinople	1204

ADVICE TO THE BYZANTINE EMPEROR, ELEVENTH CENTURY

This anonymous work was addressed to one of the eleventh-century Byzantine emperors. It reflects the author's concern with the indolence of the emperor and the growing power of the nobility on the eastern frontiers of the empire. The problems the author addresses here would culminate in 1081 with the ascension of one of these eastern nobles, Alexius Comnenus, to the imperial throne.

Holy Lord, God has elevated you to the imperial authority and has made you by his grace, as you are called, a god on earth, to do and to act as you will. Let then your acts and your deeds be full of understanding and truth, and may justice dwell in your heart. Look, therefore, and act toward all—toward those who are in a position of authority and toward all others—with an equal eye. And do not evilly coerce some while bestowing benefits on others. . . . But let there be equality for all. . . .

The emperor is the model and example for all, and all men look up to him and imitate his conduct. And if his ways are good, men are eager to follow them quickly; but if they are bad and worthy of blame, men will do the same. Therefore, I beg you, take hold of and adopt the four virtues: courage (I mean that of the soul), and justice, temperance, and wisdom. . . .

I know, Your Majesty, that by nature man is desirous of relaxation. But there has come into fashion a custom not helpful but rather damaging; that the emperor not go abroad into the countries under his rule, both in the East and in the West, but that he spend his time in Constantinople, as if in prison there. If someone had indeed restricted you to a single city, in that case you would have to make an effort to leave that area. But the fact is that you have done this to yourself. What, then, is to be said? Go out into the countries under your rule and into your provinces and see for yourself what injustices the poor suffer and what the tax collectors, whom you dispatch, are doing. Ascertain whether the poor have been wronged, and correct all wrong things. Thus both the provinces of the Byzantines and the lands of the peoples under your rule will know that they have an emperor and lord who rules them. Then you yourself will know the strength of each province and fortress and land, how each is situated, and what damage it suffers and what benefits accrue to it. Then there will arise no rebellion or revolt against your agents, but all the areas under your rule will be at peace.

I realize that your ministers . . . will admonish you that this advice is not sound; they will tell you that, as you advance through your countries and provinces with your army and imperial entourage, you will oppress them. They may even say that, if you leave Byzantium, another will seize the imperial throne in your place. When I have thought of this, I have laughed. For the one left by you in the palace, charged with the direction of affairs . . . will, if he is energetic and adequate, be entirely effective, and he will be ever vigilant and will do whatever should be done.

Deno John Geanakoplos, ed. and trans., *Byzantium: Church, Society and Civilization Seen through Contemporary Eyes* (Chicago, 1984), pp. 20–21.

QUESTIONS FOR ANALYSIS

1. What does the author mean when he addresses the emperor as "a god on earth"?
2. If he is allowed to do as he wills, why should the emperor restrain his desires and arbitrary tendencies? What difference would it make for him to travel through the countries he rules?

HOW DID THE FIRST CRUSADE ALTER THE BALANCE OF POWER BETWEEN EUROPE AND BYZANTIUM?

BYZANTIUM, ISLAM, AND THE CRUSADES   301

THE FIRST CRUSADE

The reasons that Urban's summons met with such a massive response are complex. Urban himself probably saw the crusade as a means for achieving at least four ends. One was to bring the Orthodox church back into communion with the papacy. Relations between the two churches had been ruptured in 1054, when a papal emissary and the Orthodox patriarch of Constantinople had each excommunicated the other. If Urban could succeed in uniting the two churches, he would gain a great victory for the Gregorian program of papal monarchy, one of whose goals was to establish the primacy of the papacy over all other bishops and churches. A second motive was to embarrass Urban's greatest enemy, the German emperor Henry IV. Henry and the papacy had been at war for more than twenty years over their respective claims to supremacy within Christendom. By calling a mighty crusade to retake Jerusalem, Urban probably hoped to establish his own claims as pope to be the rightful leader of western Christian society (see Chapter 9). Third, by sending off a large contingent of fighters, Urban hoped to achieve peace at home. Earlier in the century, a number of French bishops and abbots had supported a peace movement that prohibited attacks on noncombatants (the "Peace of God") and prohibited fighting on certain holy days (the "Truce of God"). At the 1095 ecclesiastical council at Clermont where he announced the First Crusade, Urban also promulgated the first full papal approval of this peace movement. In effect, Urban told the assembled knights that if they wished to fight, they could do so justly for a Christian cause overseas. Finally, the goal of Jerusalem itself genuinely inspired Urban. Jerusalem was regarded by medieval geographers as the center of the earth as well as being the most sacred shrine of the Christian religion because it was Jesus' homeland. To the untutored knights of western Europe, as perhaps to Urban himself (whose family came from the knighthood of southern France), it seemed only right that Christian knights should assist their Lord Christ to recover his own land from the Muslims who had seized it from him.

The response to Urban's call exceeded all expectations. Within a year of the pope's summons, an army of 100,000 men, women, and children, drawn from all over western Europe, was on the march toward Constantinople, where they intended to gather before departing for Jerusalem. As with any large enterprise, the participants' motives for joining the crusade varied. Some hoped to win lands or establish principalities for themselves in the east. Others were drawn simply by the prospect of adventure. Many were dependents of greater men, accompanying their lords because it was their duty to do so. Some may have been motivated by obscure prophecies and apocalyptic fervor. Most probably had no idea how long a journey would be involved or even what direction they would be traveling.

But the dominant motive for going on the First Crusade was religious. Except for a few of the greatest lords—and they mostly Normans from southern Italy—the prospect of winning new lands in the east was both unlikely and undesired. Indeed, one of the greatest challenges facing the Latin (Crusader) kingdom of Jerusalem after 1099 was precisely the fact that crusaders so rarely wanted to stay on in the east. After fulfilling their vows, the vast majority of crusaders went home. The risks of dying on such a journey were high; the costs of embarking on it were enormous. Crusading knights needed a minimum of two years' revenues in hand to finance their journey. To raise such sums, most were forced to mortgage lands and borrow heavily from family, friends, monasteries, and merchants. They then had to find some way to pay back these loans if and when they returned home. On any rational judgment of financial advantage, the crusade was a fool's errand. But it did offer solace to the Christian soul. For centuries pilgrimages had been the most popular type of Christian penance, and the pilgrimage to Jerusalem was considered to be the most sacred and efficacious one of all. Urban II made this point explicit at Clermont, promising that crusaders would be freed from all other penances imposed by the church. Some crusade preachers went even further by promising what became known as a plenary indulgence: that crusaders would be entirely freed from otherworldly punishments in purgatory for all the sins they had committed up to that point in their lives, and that the souls of those who died on crusade would go straight to heaven. The plenary indulgence was a truly extraordinary offer, and crowds flocked to take advantage of it.

Crusade preaching emphasized the vengeance that Christ's soldiers should exact on his enemies in the East. But to some crusaders, it seemed absurd to wait until they arrived in Jerusalem to undertake this aspect of their mission. Muslims might hold Jesus' property at Jerusalem, but Christian theology held Jews responsible for the

> Crusading knights needed a minimum of two years' revenues in hand to finance their journey. To raise such sums, most were forced to mortgage lands and borrow heavily from family, friends, monasteries, and merchants.

CALLS TO CRUSADE, 1074–1100

These documents illustrate how appeals to Europeans to embark on a military expedition to the east developed between 1074 and c. 1100. The first document is a letter addressed by Pope Gregory VII in 1074 to all Christians. The second document, a letter from Pope Gregory to King Henry IV of Germany in 1074, reports in grandiose terms on Gregory's efforts to organize a military expedition to the east and explains his motives for doing so. The third document is an account by Fulcher of Chartres of Pope Urban II's call at the Council of Clermont in 1095. Fulcher is thought to have attended the council. The fourth document, which pretends to be a letter from the Byzantine emperor Alexius Comnenus to Count Robert of Flanders urging him to join a military expedition to the east, was composed for propagandistic purposes at an unknown date between 1088 and 1105. There is no evidence that any of the letter's lurid charges against the Turks were true. Do these letters help explain why Urban's call received so much more of a response than did Gregory's?

POPE GREGORY VII'S CALL TO ASSIST THE GREEKS, MARCH 1074

Gregory, bishop, servant of the servants of God, to all who are willing to defend the Christian faith, greeting and apostolic benediction.

We hereby inform you that the bearer of this letter, on his recent return from across the sea came to Rome to visit us. He repeated what we had heard from many others, that a pagan race had overcome the Christians and, with horrible cruelty, had devastated everything almost to the walls of Constantinople, and were now governing the conquered lands with tyrannical violence, and that they had slain many thousands of Christians as if they were but sheep. If we love God and wish to be recognized as Christians, we should be filled with grief at the misfortune of this great empire and the murder of so many Christians. But simply to grieve is not our whole duty. The example of our Redeemer and the bond of fraternal love demand that we should lay down our lives to liberate them. . . . Know, therefore, that we are trusting in the mercy of God and in the power of his might and that we are striving in all possible ways and making preparations to render aid to the Christian empire as quickly as possible. Therefore, we beseech you by the faith in which you are united through Christ . . . and by the authority of Saint Peter, prince of the apostles, we admonish you that you be moved to proper compassion by the wounds and blood of your brethren and the danger of the aforesaid empire and that, for the sake of Christ, you undertake the difficult task of bearing aid to your brethren [i.e., the Byzantines].

Send messengers to us at once to inform us what God may inspire you to do in this matter.

O. J. Thatcher and E. H. McNeal, eds., *A Sourcebook for Medieval History, Selected Documents Illustrating the History of Europe in the Middle Ages* (New York, 1905), pp. 512–513.

POPE GREGORY VII'S LETTER TO KING HENRY IV, DECEMBER 1074

Gregory . . . to the glorious King Henry, greeting. . . .

Further, I call to your attention that the Christians beyond the seas, a great part of whom are being destroyed by the heathen with unheard-of slaughter and are daily being slain like so many sheep, have humbly sent to beg me to succor these our brethren in whatever ways I can, that the religion of Christ may not utterly perish in our time—which God forbid! I, therefore, smitten with exceeding grief and led even to long for death—for I would rather stake my life for these than reign over the whole earth and neglect them—have succeeded in arousing certain Christian men so that they are eager to risk their lives for their brethren in defense of the law of Christ and to show forth more clearly than the day the nobility of the sons of God. This summons has been readily accepted by Italians and northerners, by divine inspiration as I believe—nay, as I can absolutely assure you—and already fifty thousand men are preparing, if they can have me for their leader and prelate, to take up arms against the enemies of God and push forward even to the sepulcher of the Lord under his supreme leadership.

I am especially moved toward this undertaking because the Church of Constantinople, differing from us on the doctrine of the Holy Spirit, is seeking the fellowship of the Apostolic See [i.e., the papacy], the Armenians are almost entirely estranged from the Catholic faith and almost all the Easterners are waiting to see how the faith of the Apostle Peter will decide among their divergent views. . . .

I beg for your advice and for your help according to your good pleasure. For if it shall please God that I go, I shall leave the Roman Church, under God, in your hands to guard her as a holy mother and to defend her for his honor.

Ephraim Emerton, ed., *The Correspondence of Pope Gregory VII* (New York, 1969), pp. 57–58.

POPE URBAN II'S CALL AT CLERMONT, NOVEMBER 1195

Most beloved brethren: Urged by necessity, I, Urban, by the permission of God chief bishop and prelate over the whole world, have come into these parts as an ambassador with a divine admonition to you, the servants of God. . . .

Although, O sons of God, you have promised more firmly than ever to keep the peace among yourselves and to preserve the rights of the church, there remains still an important work for you to do. Freshly quickened by the divine correction, you must apply the strength of your righteousness to another matter which concerns you as well as God. For your brethren who live in the east are in urgent need of your help, and you must hasten to give them the aid which has often been promised them. For, as most of you have heard, the Turks and Arabs have attacked them and have conquered the territory of Romania [the Byzantine Empire] as far west as the shore of the Mediterranean and the Hellespont, which is called the Arm of Saint George. They have occupied more and more of the lands of those Christians, and have overcome them in seven battles. They have killed and captured many, and have destroyed the churches and devastated the empire.

If you permit them to continue thus for a while with impunity, the faithful of God will be much more widely attacked by them. On this account I, or rather the Lord, beseech you as Christ's heralds to publish this everywhere and to persuade all people of whatever rank, footsoldiers and knights, poor and rich, to carry aid promptly to those Christians and to destroy that vile race from the lands of our friends. I say this to those who are present, but it is meant also for those who are absent. Moreover, Christ commands it.

All who die by the way, whether by land or by sea, or in battle against the pagans, shall have immediate remission of sins. This I grant them through the power of God with which I am invested. O what a disgrace, if such a despised and base race, which worships demons, should conquer a people which has the faith of omnipotent God and is made glorious with the name of Christ! With what reproaches will the Lord overwhelm us if you do not aid those who, with us, profess the Christian religion!

Let those who have been accustomed to wage unjust private warfare against the faithful now go against the infidels and end with victory this war which should have been begun long ago. Let those who for a long time have been robbers now become knights. Let those who have been fighting against their brothers and relatives now fight in a proper way against the barbarians. Let those who have been serving as mercenaries for small pay now obtain the eternal reward. Let those who have been wearing themselves out in both body and soul now work for a double honor. Behold! On this side will be the sorrowful and poor, on that, the rich; on this side, the enemies of the Lord, on that, his friends. Let those who go not put off the journey, but rent their lands and collect money for their expenses; and as soon as winter is over and spring comes, let them eagerly set out on the way with God as their guide.

S. J. Allen and Emilie Amt, eds., *The Crusades: A Reader* (Peterborough, Ont., Canada, 2003), pp. 39–40.

The Spurious Letter of Alexius Comnenus to Count Robert of Flanders, c. 1100

O incomparable Count, great defender of the faith, it is my desire to bring to your attention the extent to which the most holy empire of the Christian Greeks is fiercely beset every day by the Patzinaks and Turks . . . and how massacres and unspeakable murders and outrages against Christians are perpetrated. . . .

For they circumcise Christian boys and youths over the baptismal fonts of Christian [churches] and spill the blood of circumcision right into the baptismal fonts and compel them to urinate over them, afterward leading them violently around the church and forcing them to blaspheme the name of the Holy Trinity. Those who are unwilling they torture in various ways and finally murder. When they capture noble women and their daughters, they abuse them sexually in turns, like animals. Some, while they are wickedly defiling the maidens, place the mothers facing, constraining them to sing evil and lewd songs while they work their evil. . . .

But what next? We pass on to worse yet. They have degraded by sodomizing them men of every age and rank—boys, adolescents, young men, old men, nobles, servants, and, what is worse and more wicked, clerics and monks, and even—alas and for shame! Something which from the beginning of time has never been spoken or heard of—bishops! They have already killed one bishop with this nefarious sin.

They have polluted and ruined the holy places in innumerable ways and threaten even worse things. In the face of all this, who would not weep— Who would not be moved? Who would not shudder? Who would not pray? Nearly the entire territory from Jerusalem to Greece, and all of Greece with its upper regions . . . have all been invaded by them, and hardly anything remains except Constantinople, which they threaten soon to take from us unless we are speedily relieved by the help of God and the faithful Latin Christians. . . .

For the sake of the name of God and the piety of all those who uphold the Christian faith, we therefore implore you to lead here to help us and all Greek Chris-tians every faithful soldier of Christ you can obtain in your lands, great, small or middling, that they might struggle for the salvation of their souls to free the kingdom of the Greeks, just as in past years they have liberated, to some extent, Galicia and other western kingdoms from the yoke of the unbelievers. For although I am emperor, no remedy remains to me . . . and I am reduced to waiting in a single city for the imminent arrival of the Turks. And since I prefer to be subject to you, the Latins, rather than have Constantinople taken by the Turks, you should fight courageously and with all your strength so that you might receive in bliss a glorious and indescribable reward in heaven.

[The letter then goes on to describe the many Christian relics in Constantinople, and the wealth of the city, urging Robert to prevent all this from falling into the hands of the Turks.]

Act therefore while you have time, lest you lose the kingdom of the Christians and, what is worse, the sepulcher of the Lord, and so that you may earn a reward rather than a punishment hereafter. Amen.

John E. Boswell, ed. and trans., *Christianity, Social Tolerance and Homosexuality* (Chicago, 1980), pp. 367–369.

QUESTIONS FOR ANALYSIS

1. Consider the message implicit in Pope Gregory and Urban's call to the Crusades. Why would king and commoner alike join a holy Crusade to unknown and hostile lands?

2. Why do the authors of these letters present the oppression of Greek Christians primarily as a religious, rather than ethnic, problem?

3. Why would you suspect the veracity of the "Letter of Alexius Comnenus to Count Robert" even if it did not have "spurious" in the title?

---

death of Jesus himself. During the course of the eleventh century, Jewish communities had grown up in most of the larger cities of the Rhineland and in many of the smaller towns and cities of northern France. Assaults by bands of crusaders against Jewish communities began in northern France in the spring of 1096 and quickly spread to the Rhineland as the crusaders moved east. Hundreds of Jews were killed in Mainz, Worms, Speyer, and Cologne, and hundreds more were forcibly baptized as the price for escaping death at the hands of crusading knights. Despite the efforts of church authorities to prevent them, attacks on Jews would remain a regular and

How did the First Crusade alter the balance of power between Europe and Byzantium?

Byzantium, Islam, and the Crusades   305

predictable feature of Christian crusading until the thirteenth century.

Surprised by the nature and scale of the western response to his appeal, Alexius Comnenus did his best to move the crusaders quickly through Constantinople and into Asia Minor. Differences in outlook between the western crusaders and the Byzantine emperor quickly became apparent, however. Alexius had little interest in an expedition to Jerusalem, but insisted that the crusaders promise to restore to the empire any territory they captured from the Muslims. To the crusaders, this seemed like treachery—an impression that heightened into certainty when supplies they expected from Constantinople on their journey failed to materialize. From Alexius's standpoint, the crusader army was a threat, not least because it contained within it several of the Norman leaders who had attempted to conquer his empire only ten years earlier. The crusaders, however, saw themselves as on a mission from God. They did not understand the Byzantine emperor's willingness to make alliances with some Muslim rulers

> Despite the efforts of church authorities to prevent them, attacks on Jews would remain a regular and predictable feature of Christian crusading until the thirteenth century.

against other Muslim rulers, and they speedily concluded that the Byzantines were in fact working to undermine the crusading effort, perhaps even supporting the Muslims against them. Such suspicions were unfounded, but they contributed to a growing western conviction that the Byzantine Empire itself was an obstacle to the successful recovery of Jerusalem for Christendom.

Against great odds the First Crusade succeeded. In 1098 the crusaders captured Antioch and with it most of the Syrian coast. At the end of 1099, they took Jerusalem, mercilessly slaughtering its Muslim, Jewish, and Christian inhabitants. Their success stemmed mainly from the fact that the crusaders' Muslim opponents were at that moment internally divided. The Fatimids had recaptured Jerusalem from the Turks just months before the crusaders arrived, and the Turks themselves were at war with each other. But western military tactics, in particular the dominance in the open field of the heavily armored knights, also played an important role in the crusaders' success.

Equally critical was the naval support the First Crusade received from Genoa and Pisa, which hoped that a successful crusade would allow them to control the Indian spice trade that passed through the Red Sea and on to Alexandria in Egypt. In this respect, the First Crusade contributed to the further decline of Byzantine commerce, which was already suffering both from Italian competition in the Mediterranean and from the disruptive impact of the Turkish invasions on the trade routes that had previously connected Constantinople with Baghdad and the Central Asian silk route to China. All these trends were under way before the First Crusade began, but the establishment of the Latin kingdom accelerated them. To that extent, the First Crusade contributed significantly to the changing balance of power between Byzantium and western Europe.

The Later Crusades

The First Crusade had much less of an impact on the balance of power between the Islamic world and Europe. The crusader kingdom was never more than an underpopulated, narrow strip of colonies along the coastline of Syria and Palestine. So long as the crusaders did not control the Red Sea, the main routes of Islamic commerce with India and the Far East were unaffected by the change in Jerusalem's religious allegiance. Nor, for that matter, did the crusaders in any way wish to

A Crusading Knight. The association between knighthood and crusading helped to raise the social status of knights. Here, a mid-thirteenth century crusading knight, dressed head to foot in expensive chain mail, is shown kneeling in prayer.

interfere with the overland caravan routes that led through their new territories. For the Muslims, the loss of Jerusalem was a religious affront much more than an economic one, and it was for religious reasons that they began to plan its recovery. By 1144, most of the crusader principalities in Syria had been recaptured. When Christian warriors led by the king of France and the emperor of Germany came east in the Second Crusade to recoup the losses, they suffered crushing defeats. Not long afterward, Syria and Egypt were united under the great Muslim leader Saladin, who finally recaptured Jerusalem in 1187. In response, the Third Crusade was launched, led by the German emperor Frederick Barbarossa, the French king Philip Augustus, and the English king Richard the Lionheart. This campaign also

failed. Barbarossa drowned in Asia Minor on the way to Jerusalem, and Philip Augustus soon went home. Richard the Lionheart's heroic efforts enabled the Latin kingdom to survive for another century; but even he could not recapture Jerusalem.

The dream, however, did not die. When Innocent III became pope in 1198, his main ambition was to win back Jerusalem. He summoned the Fourth Crusade to that end, but it proved a disaster. Civil war in Germany, combined with war between England and France, severely reduced the number of knights willing to participate; and when the Venetians, who had contracted to transport the crusader army to the Holy Land, discovered that only half the predicted crusaders would arrive and that they would therefore not be properly paid,

THE ROUTES OF THE CRUSADERS, 1096–1204

Compare the routes followed by the first three crusades. Why were they so similar? Why was the route of the Fourth Crusade so different? Why was Genoa so much more important than Venice as an embarkation point for crusaders?

How did the First Crusade alter the balance of power between Europe and Byzantium?

Byzantium, Islam, and the Crusades   307

they diverted the crusade toward a successful attack on Constantinople itself in 1204. The result was an enormous commercial windfall for Venice, but the effective destruction of the Byzantine Empire, which for the next sixty years was divided into Latin-ruled and Greek-ruled provinces. In 1261 the Venetians' rivals, the Genoese, helped a new imperial claimant, Michael VIII Palaeologus, recover the Byzantine throne and, with it, control over Constantinople. But the Byzantine Empire was now reduced to little more than the city itself, leaving both Asia Minor and the Balkans open to their eventual conquest by the Ottoman Turks.

Despite the debacle of the Fourth Crusade, western efforts to recover Jerusalem continued throughout the thirteenth century. Only in 1229, however, when the western Roman emperor Frederick II negotiated a treaty with the Egyptian sultan that returned Jerusalem to Christian control for a period of ten years, did any western leader attempt to achieve this objective directly. Instead, thirteenth-century crusades were aimed mainly at Egypt (1217–1219, 1248–1254) and, in 1270, Tunis. The crusaders' strategic goal was to cut the economic lifelines that supported Muslim control of the Holy Land. In explaining these later crusades, however, it becomes increasingly difficult to disentangle crusade-motivated calculations toward recapturing Jerusalem (which was, in any event, a shattered city with no walls and a tiny population) from the aspirations of Italian merchants to control the Far Eastern trade that ran through Egypt and the gold trade from sub-Saharan Africa that ran through Tunis. The great mercantile city of the thirteenth-century Latin kingdom was Acre, not Jerusalem. Its fall in 1291 marked the end of any further western expeditions (though not of plans for such expeditions) to recover the Holy Land from Islam.

THE CONSEQUENCES OF THE CRUSADES

For Byzantium, the impact of the crusading movement was disastrous. The crusades coincided with, and to some extent caused, a decisive shift in the balance of economic and military power between western Europe and the faltering Byzantine Empire. On the Islamic world, by contrast, the impact of the crusades was much more modest. Trade between Islam and the West continued despite periodic interruptions caused by crusader attacks on Syria, Egypt, and North Africa. The greatest economic gains went to the Italian maritime republics of Venice and Genoa; but Islamic merchants too came to depend increasingly on western markets for their goods. Both sides also gained in military terms: westerners learned new techniques of fortification, and Muslims learned new methods of siege warfare and new respect for the uses of heavy cavalry. Finally, the crusades also helped crystallize both Christian and Islamic doctrines of holy war against the infidel. Neither Christian holy war nor Muslim *jihad* drew much doctrinally from the other. The collision between them, however, deepened the mutual hostility that already separated the Islamic world and Christian Europe.

The impact of the crusades on western Europe is more difficult to assess. From one standpoint, the crusades were an ultimately unsuccessful chapter in a generally successful story of western expansionism during the High Middle Ages. In the Middle East, however, as they did in Greenland and North America, western Europeans overreached themselves. They could not maintain the colonies they established, and they were ultimately forced to withdraw. Nor did the crusades "open up" Europeans to a wider world of which they had previously known nothing. That wider world already existed in 1095, and Europeans were already part of it. Trade with the Islamic world, and beyond it with India and the Far East, did bring enormous prosperity to the Italian maritime republics, especially Genoa and Venice. But these trading links had existed before the crusades and continued after they ended. It is arguable, indeed, that crusading diminished, rather than increased, the economic and cultural exchange between western Europe and the Islamic world that might otherwise have taken place.

CHRONOLOGY

THE CRUSADES

First Crusade (recapture of Jerusalem)	1095–1099
Second Crusade (defeated by Seljuk Turks)	1145–1149
Third Crusade (Frederick Barbarossa and Richard the Lionheart)	1187–1192
Fourth Crusade (sack of Constantinople)	1201–1204
Fifth Crusade (capture of Damietta)	1217–1221
Peace treaty regains Jerusalem	1229–1244
Sixth Crusade (defeat of Louis IX of France)	1248–1254
Seventh Crusade (death of Louis IX of France)	1270

PREPARING TO DEPART ON CRUSADE

Before crusaders departed for the Holy Land, they were obliged to remedy all injustices they might have committed, and to put their affairs in order. This was a religious requirement for anyone setting out on a penitential pilgrimage, but it was also a practical recognition that many crusaders would die on their journey. The human emotions that accompanied such departures are clearly expressed in Jean de Joinville's account of his preparations to depart with King Louis IX of France on the Sixth Crusade (1248–1254).

At Easter, in the year of our Lord 1248, I summoned my men, and all who held fiefs from me, to Joinville. On Easter Eve, when all the people I had summoned had arrived, my son, Jean . . . was born to me by my first wife. . . . We feasted and danced the whole of that week. . . .

On the Friday I said to them: "My friends, I'm soon going overseas and I don't know whether I shall ever return. So will any of you who have a claim to make against me come forward. If I have done you any wrong I will make it good, to each of you in turn, as I have been used to do in the case of those who had any demand to make of me or my people." I dealt with each claim in the way the men on my lands considered right; and in order not to influence their decision I withdrew from the discussion, and afterwards agreed without demur to whatever they recommended.

Since I did not wish to take away with me a single penny to which I had no right, I went to Metz in Lorraine, and mortgaged the greater part of my land. I can assure you that, on the day I left our country to go to the Holy Land, I had in my possession, since my lady mother was still alive, an income of no more than a thousand *livres* from my estates. All the same I went, and took with me nine knights, and two knights-banneret besides myself. I bring these things to your notice so that you may understand that if God, who has never failed me, had not come to my help, I should scarcely have been able to hold out for so long a time as the six years that I remained in the Holy Land. . . .

On the day I left Joinville I sent for the Abbot of Cheminon, who was said to be the wisest and worthiest monk of the Cistercian Order. . . . This same abbot . . . gave me my pilgrim's staff and wallet. I left Joinville immediately after—never to enter my castle again until my return from oversea—on foot, with my legs bare, and in my shirt. Thus attired I went to Blécourt and Saint-Urbain, and to other places where there are holy relics. And all the way . . . I never once let my eyes turn back towards Joinville, for fear my heart might be filled with longing at the thought of my lovely castle and the two children I had left behind.

M. R. B. Shaw, ed. and trans., *Chronicles of the Crusades* (Baltimore, 1963), pp. 192, 195.

QUESTIONS FOR ANALYSIS

1. Feudal lords were allowed in some cases to levy a tax on their lands, on both their own possessions and those of their vassals and peasants. How did Jean de Joinville take care of the people under his jursdiction before leaving on a crusade?

2. How closely did the departing Joinville regulate his estates? As an educated but still rustic western European, what would he think about the lasting effects his departure would have on his estates?

WHAT WAS THE RELATIONSHIP BETWEEN CHIVALRY AND THE CULT OF COURTLY LOVE?

SOCIAL MOBILITY AND SOCIAL INEQUALITY IN HIGH MEDIEVAL EUROPE   309

It would be wrong, however, to end our discussion of the crusades on such a minor note. A drive by western merchants, backed by western military force, to control the trade in spices, silks, and gold by "cutting out the Islamic middleman" is clearly visible in thirteenth-century crusading. This impulse would continue and would eventually lead to the creation of worldwide European mercantile and colonial empires from the sixteenth century on. Nor should we ignore or diminish the lasting influence of the crusading ideal on Europeans' image of themselves. Crusading had dramatic successes in Spain, where between 1100 and 1250 the kings of Castile and Portugal and the crown of Aragon led the reconquest of the Iberian peninsula from Islam. In Iberia particularly, crusading retained its ideological significance until the end of the sixteenth century, providing an important motivation behind the Portuguese and Spanish voyages of discovery during the fifteenth century and the conquest of the Americas during the sixteenth century. Crusading would also continue to color European relations with Islam, and especially with the Ottoman Turks, whose sixteenth-century conquests would bring them to the gates of Vienna and the borders of Italy. Even Napoleon, the last of the western Roman emperors, was not immune to the crusading ideal. He too would lead a successful, but short-lived, reconquest of Jerusalem.

SOCIAL MOBILITY AND SOCIAL INEQUALITY IN HIGH MEDIEVAL EUROPE

What was the relationship between chivalry and the cult of courtly love?

The increasing wealth of high medieval Europe also transformed the social structure of European society. In the tenth century, it was still possible to describe European society as being divided among "those who worked, those who prayed, and those who fought." By 1300, however, such a description no longer bore even a tangential relationship to reality. New commercial and professional elites had emerged in the burgeoning cities of western Europe. By 1300, the wealthiest members of European society were merchants and bankers, not nobles. The greatest noble families affected a disdain for commerce, but nobles too found themselves drawn increasingly into the world of trade, despite their contempt for such "calculators." Nobles still fought, of course; but so too did knights, urban crossbowmen, peasant longbowmen, citizen militias, and peasant levies. Even work had become more complex. By 1300, half the peasants in England farmed plots of land too small to support their families. They survived, and sometimes even prospered, on a shifting combination of farming, wage labor, hunting, gathering, and charity. Such lines as existed between town and countryside were easily crossed. Rural people moved to towns and townspeople moved back to the countryside with regularity and ease. Schools of all sorts had emerged, and the products of those schools—lawyers, doctors, estate administrators, clerks, and government officials—made up a new and growing professional class that further complicated efforts to describe European society in terms of the three orders of workers, prayers, and fighters.

Increasing wealth made European society more complex. Society also became more fluid. The image of fortune's wheel, whose ceaseless turning raised the unimportant to greatness while reducing the great to poverty, was a favorite symbol during the High Middle Ages, and for good reason. A shipwreck, a stolen cargo, a bad investment, or a political miscalculation could ruin even the wealthiest and most powerful families. At the same time, however, poor people with ability and luck could sometimes rise to extraordinary heights.

Fortune's Wheel. From a fourteenth-century French manuscript.

Careers in the church were particularly open to men of talent. Royal service was another route to social advancement. But fortune's wheel also brought men down. Dante Alighieri (*DAHN-tay ahl-eeg-YEE-ree*), a rising man in the government of his native city of Florence, in 1302 was exiled from Florence for life. He wrote his greatest poetry in exile, "tasting the bitter crumbs of other men's bread."

NOBLES AND KNIGHTS

New wealth brought social mobility, but it also created a more highly stratified society, especially among the nobility. In the Carolingian period, the nobility comprised a relatively small number of ancient families of approximately equal social rank who married among themselves. During the tenth and eleventh centuries, however, new families began to establish themselves as territorial lords, rivaling and sometimes surpassing the old Carolingian noble families in power and wealth. Some of these new families were descended from Carolingian officeholders who had taken advantage of the Carolingians' collapse to establish their independence. Others were simply freebooters whose power rested on their control over castles, knights, and manors. Until the twelfth century, the old Carolingian noble families attempted to resist the claims of these new families to noble rank and status. By the end of the thirteenth century, however, a new nobility had emerged in western Europe that included these new families of counts, castle holders, and knights but that also made a series of careful distinctions in rank among dukes, counts, castellans (castle holders), and knights.

Knights were not necessarily nobles in the eleventh century. Knighthood was instead a social order consisting of men of widely varying social rank. Some eleventh-century knights were the sons of great nobles, but others were little more than peasants mounted on horseback and armed with swords. As a specialized warrior group, knights associated with the nobility. A degree of social prestige rubbed off on them from this fact. But the key developments that raised the knights into the ranks of the nobility took place during the twelfth and thirteenth centuries and were directly connected with the growing wealth of medieval European society. As the costs of knightly equipment rose, the number of men who could afford the heavier horses,

stronger swords, and improved armor that mid-thirteenth-century knights required declined dramatically. The style of domestic life expected of knights also became more elaborate and expensive. In 1100, a knight could get by with a woolen surcoat, two horses, and a groom. By 1250, a knight required a string of horses, silk clothing, and a retinue of servants, squires, and grooms. To support such an extravagant lifestyle, a knight needed either a sizable annual fee from his lord or else large estates, a minimum of 1,200 acres. At four pence per acre in rent, 1,200 acres would produce an annual income of twenty pounds per year, the minimum income considered necessary in thirteenth-century England to sustain a man as a knight. By way of comparison, a common laborer, working for wages of around two pence per day, might hope to earn one to two pounds per year.

CHIVALRY AND COURTLY LOVE

As the costs of knighthood increased, so too did its social prestige. From the mid-twelfth century on, the kings and nobles of Europe began to embrace and encourage the knightly code of values known as chivalry, which stressed bravery, loyalty, generosity, skill with weapons, and proper manners as constituent elements in true nobility. *Chivalry* literally means "horsemanship," and mounted combat (whether on the battlefield or in tournaments) would for long remain the defining element in the European nobility's image of itself. First and foremost, however, chivalry was a social ideology that appealed to the knights and nobles of western Europe because it gave them a way of distinguishing themselves from all those other groups in high medieval society—merchants, lawyers, artisans, and prosperous free farmers—who were their rivals in wealth and sometimes in political influence. Although traditionally the nobility had stressed descent from noble ancestors as the key element in social rank, in the socially mobile world of the High Middle Ages many families who lived nobly did not in fact have prestigious ancestors, whereas other families who did have such ancestors no longer had the wealth to maintain an appropriately noble style of life. Of what, then, did nobility consist? Was noble status a matter of birth or was it a result of an individual's own achievements? The amalgamation between knighthood and nobility fostered by chivalry

> As the costs of knightly equipment rose, the number of men who could afford the heavier horses, stronger swords, and improved armor that mid-thirteenth-century knights required declined dramatically.

WHAT WAS THE RELATIONSHIP BETWEEN CHIVALRY AND THE CULT OF COURTLY LOVE?

SOCIAL MOBILITY AND SOCIAL INEQUALITY IN HIGH MEDIEVAL EUROPE   311

offered something to both sides. To the old noble families, it offered assurance that virtue inhered in their blood and that chivalric values were most often to be found in those born to noble parents. To the knights, however, as to the merchants and lawyers who sometimes adopted its language and customs, chivalry offered a way of legitimizing the social positions they had attained through their own loyalty, bravery, and skill.

Chivalry began as the value system of a socially diverse knightly order. By the end of the thirteenth century, however, it had become the ideology of a social class, functioning to demarcate those who were (or aspired to be) noble from those who were (or did) not. These lines of social demarcation were particularly clear on the battlefield, where the chivalric code pertained exclusively to knights. Chivalry obliged a knight to treat a knightly opponent with courtesy and respect, capturing him for ransom rather than killing him and trusting in his prisoner's word (his *parole*) that his ransom would be paid. No such compunctions applied, however, to common soldiers, urban militias, and archers. Under the laws of chivalric war, they could be slaughtered at will by the knights, without any prospect of being captured for ransom.

> Chivalry began as the value system of a socially diverse knightly order. By the end of the thirteenth century, however, it had become the ideology of a social class, functioning to demarcate those who were (or aspired to be) noble from those who were (or did) not.

Closely linked to the ideology of chivalry was the so-called cult of courtly love, which made noble women into objects of veneration for their knightly admirers. Here too, there was an important element of social class. Courtly love was "refined" love, the "courteous" love appropriate to a royal or noble court. But the exponents of courtly love distinguished sharply between noble women, who alone were capable of refined love (and who should therefore be wooed and won through proper manners, poetry, and valiant deeds) and peasant women, on whom such courtliness would be wasted. Noble women were to be courted; but peasant women could be taken by force, if they would not yield willingly to the desires of a nobleman.

To what extent did the new doctrines of courtly love affect the attitudes of noblemen toward noblewomen? The question remains controversial for two reasons. One is that most of our evidence about courtly love comes from literature, and historians differ as to how accurately literature reflects life. The other is that putting women on a pedestal is itself another, albeit gentler, way of constraining women's choices. There can be no question, however, that there was a change in literary attitudes toward the female sex. Until the twelfth century, women were virtually ignored in literature. But within a few decades after 1100, noblewomen were suddenly turned into objects of elaborate veneration by lyric poets and writers of romances.

Although the literature of courtly love was extremely idealistic and somewhat artificial, it expressed the values of a gentler noble culture wherein upper-class women were more respected than before. Moreover, certain royal women in the twelfth and thirteenth centuries actually did rule their states on various

Images of Aristocracy. This early fifteenth-century illustration, from the *Très Riches Heures* commissioned by Jean, Duke of Berry, depicts the leisurely elegance that became such an important feature of medieval aristocratic life.

occasions when their husbands or sons were unable to do so. From 1109 until her death in 1126, Queen Urraca ruled the combined kingdom of León-Castile in Spain. The indomitable Eleanor of Aquitaine (1122?–1204), wife of Henry II, played a crucial role in the government of England when her son Richard I (the Lionheart) went on crusade from 1190 to 1194. The strong-willed Blanche of Castile ruled France extremely well twice in the thirteenth century, once during the minority of her son Louis IX and again when he was off crusading. Queens are not, of course, typical women; and from a modern perspective, high medieval noblewomen were still very constrained. But from the point of view of the past, the High Middle Ages was a time of progress for the women of the upper classes. One striking symbol of this change comes from the history of the game of chess. Before the twelfth century chess was played in the Islamic world; but there the equivalent of the queen was a male figure, the king's chief minister, who could move only diagonally, one square at a time. In twelfth-century Europe, however, this piece was turned into a queen, and sometime before the end of the Middle Ages she began to move all over the board.

POLITICS AND GOVERNMENT

How did government and politics change during the High Middle Ages?

The profound social and economic changes of the High Middle Ages also gave rise to new forms of government and political life. In the early Middle Ages, monarchy was virtually the only form of government western Europeans knew. Towns were small and usually ruled by their bishops or kings. Kingdoms too were small and were thought of as pertaining to a particular people such as the Lombards, the Visigoths, the West Saxons, or the Salian Franks. During the eighth and ninth centuries, most of these ethnic kingdoms disappeared as larger, more powerful, territorially based kingdoms emerged in England and in the Carolingian Empire. In England, the West Saxon monarchy survived the ninth-century Viking invasions to become the sole rulers of a united English kingdom. In Germany also, a single royal dynasty, the Ottonians, emerged during the tenth century as the undisputed kings of the East Frankish realm. In France, Catalunya, and northern Italy,

however, the Carolingians' collapse came near to erasing monarchical power altogether. In the resulting power vacuum, two new structures of political authority slowly emerged in the heartland of the former Carolingian Empire: feudal principalities and self-governing cities.

URBAN GOVERNMENT

Early medieval kings were well aware of the value of towns; and where strong monarchies survived (as, for example, in England and Germany), tenth-century kings were active founders of new towns and cities. In Flanders, Catalunya, and northern Italy, however, where kingship collapsed during the late ninth and tenth centuries, self-governing cities developed during the tenth and eleventh centuries without any close monarchical control. We have spoken already of the general economic factors that led to the growth of cities during the High Middle Ages: the increasing agricultural wealth of the countryside, growing population, and developing networks of local and long-distance trade. These factors brought large numbers of immigrants into the cities. They also attracted the local nobility, many of whom became involved in the burgeoning economic and political life of the city, especially as cities began to extend their control over the surrounding countryside. In northern Italy especially, nobles moved to the cities, where they lived in fortified urban towers surrounded by their knightly retainers, their servants, and their urban supporters just as they would have done in a castle in the countryside. Their presence lent a distinctly aristocratic cast to political life in the towns, but it also introduced a violent culture of honor and vendetta into urban life. Attempts to control noble violence in Italian cities led, in the thirteenth century, to efforts in some towns (such as Florence) to ban nobles from holding governmental office altogether. But the destabilizing effects of such feuds continued, ultimately undermining traditions of urban republican government and paving the way for the emergence, during the later Middle Ages, of such great princely families as the Visconti of Milan and the Medici of Florence, whose dynastic rule made a mockery of the democratic forms of urban political life.

Considering how large the great cities of western Europe became during the twelfth and thirteenth centuries, it is astonishing to realize how informal, even ad hoc, their governmental arrangements were. Where kings or powerful feudal lords continued to rule,

How did government and politics change during the High Middle Ages?

Politics and Government   313

A City on Fire. Once a fire began to spread in a medieval city, women, children, and priests were swiftly evacuated, and servants of the rich would start carrying out their masters' possessions. Here the Swiss city of Bern is shown in flames: although a bucket brigade tried desperately to extinguish the fire with water taken from the town moat, chronicles report that the city was leveled by flames in less than half an hour.

towns and cities often received special charters of liberty that defined their jurisdictional rights and established the basic structures of urban self-government. In northern Europe, these usually involved a mayor and a council elected from among the leading citizens of the town. Elsewhere, for example in Rome, powerful rulers such as the pope resisted all efforts to establish independent city governments. In northern Italy, however, only a few powerful lords—mostly bishops—remained to support or to resist demands for urban self-government. Urban dwellers in Italy therefore had to work out their governmental arrangements for themselves.

In the twelfth century, many north Italian cities entrusted their governments formally to consuls, drawn from among the leading magnates of the city. Often, however, an informal association of citizens known as the "commune" undertook a wide variety of governmental functions side by side with the consuls. Even the communes, however, were distinctly oligarchical in character. As social stratification increased during

> Where kings or powerful feudal lords continued to rule, towns and cities often received special charters of liberty that defined their jurisdictional rights and established the basic structures of urban self-government.

the thirteenth century, many cities found themselves split between a ruling class of magnates and a popular party that felt itself excluded from the interlocking structures of power that controlled city government and the guilds. These tensions were heightened by magnates who sought to mobilize the *populares* against their own factional enemies. To control the resulting violence, cities sometimes turned to an outsider, known as a *podestá*, usually a noble with legal training, who ruled as a virtual dictator for a strictly limited term of office. Others cities adopted the model of Venice and became more formally oligarchical, casting off even the pretence of being a popular republic. By 1300, however, even cities that remained republics in principle were becoming increasingly oligarchical in practice. Terms of office were getting longer, the jurisdictional claims of urban governments were expanding, and traditions of dynastic succession to office were beginning that would lead to the urban principalities of the later Middle Ages.

FEUDALISM AND THE EMERGENCE OF NATIONAL MONARCHIES

What was the relationship between feudalism and the rise of national monarchies?

In theory, of course, Europe remained a continent of kingdoms even during the tenth and eleventh centuries, when monarchical power in France and Italy was at its lowest ebb. In France, the Capetian dynasty succeeded the Carolingians without interruption in 987, keeping alive the memory that all France had once owed allegiance to a single king. In northern Italy, a number of local rulers vied with each other to claim the Carolingians' fallen mantle of royalty for themselves until their claims were finally trumped, after 962, by the newly crowned Ottonian emperors of Germany. In practice, however, neither the Ottonians in Italy nor the Capetians in France were able to control all the territories over which they claimed to rule. By the year 1000, effective political and military power in France lay mostly in the hands of lesser men—dukes, counts, castellans, and knights—whose power rested on their capacity to channel the increasing wealth of the countryside into their own hands. The symbol of their authority was the castle, often little more than a wooden tower set on a hill with a wooden palisade around it. But when manned by a force of mounted knights, even a wooden castle could be a formidable fortification, certainly sufficient to overawe the peasant farmers of an area, and frequently capable of withstanding the attacks of rival lords. From their castles, these counts, castellans, and knights constructed "lordships": self-contained territories within which they exercised not only the property rights of landlords over peasants but also the public rights to mint money, judge legal cases, raise troops, wage war, collect taxes, and impose tolls. By the year 1000, France had become a patchwork kingdom composed of essentially independent territorial principalities ruled by counts or dukes, which were in turn divided into smaller lordships ruled by castellans and knights.

THE PROBLEM OF FEUDALISM

This highly decentralized political system, in which public powers of minting, justice, taxation, and defense were vested in the hands of private lords, is conventionally referred to as feudalism. As a term, *feudalism* is in many ways unsatisfactory, not least because it has been used by historians to mean so many different things. Marxist historians use it to describe an economic system—in Marxist terms, a "mode of production"—in which wealth is overwhelmingly agricultural and cities have not yet formed. Social historians see "feudal society" as characterized by an aristocratic social order bound together by mutual oaths and supported by the labor of serfs attached to manors. Legal historians speak of feudalism as a system of landholding in which lesser men held land from greater men in return for services of various kinds, whereas military historians see feudalism as a method of raising troops, a system whereby kings, dukes, and counts granted land to lesser men in return for specified quotas of knightly military service. Reflecting on this plethora of meanings, some recent historians have suggested we should abandon the term *feudalism* altogether, arguing that because economic, social, and political relations differed so greatly from one area of medieval Europe to another it is misleading to speak of feudalism as any kind of "system" at all.

If, however, we define feudalism as a political system in which public powers are exercised by private lords, then there is general agreement that feudalism took shape first and most fully in tenth- and eleventh-century France, after the Carolingian Empire had disintegrated. From France, the language and customs of feudalism spread to other areas of Europe, changing as they were adapted to the particular social, economic, and political circumstances of different regions and countries. Finally, in the twelfth and thirteenth centuries, feudalism developed into an ideology justifying a hierarchical legal and political order that subordinated knights to counts and counts to kings. In this modified form, feudalism legitimated powerful monarchies and helped lay the groundwork for the emergence of European nation-states.

What then was feudalism? At its simplest level, a "fee" or "fief" (rhymes with *reef*; in Latin, *feudum*) was a kind of contract, in which someone granted something of value—often land but sometimes revenues from tolls or mills, or an annual grant of money—to someone else in return for service of some kind. Frequently there was a degree of inequality in such contracts, particularly if land was involved, because land was regarded as the most valuable gift one person could give to another. When a man accepted land from another in return for promises of service, a degree of subordination by the recipient toward the giver was usually implied. In some areas, the recipient of a fief might therefore become the vassal (from a Celtic word meaning "boy") of the gift

WHAT WAS THE RELATIONSHIP BETWEEN FEUDALISM AND THE RISE OF NATIONAL MONARCHIES?

FEUDALISM AND THE EMERGENCE OF NATIONAL MONARCHIES   315

giver, who thereby became his lord; and their new relationship might be solemnized by an act of homage, whereby the vassal became "the man" (in French, *l'homme*) of his lord in return for his fief. Elsewhere, however, fiefs existed without vassalage, and vassalage existed without homage. The terms themselves matter less than the relationship that arose when one individual held land from another in return for service. It was this relationship that lay at the heart of feudalism as it emerged in the chaos of tenth-century France.

In a world in which central governmental authority had collapsed, these essentially personal relationships of service in return for landholding became an important element in ordering social and political relations among counts, castellans, and knights. At the same time, however, these relationships were entirely unsystematic. Even in northern France, where feudalism pervaded aristocratic life, many castellans and knights held their lands freely, owing no service whatsoever to the count or duke within whose territories their lands lay. Nor were feudal relationships necessarily hierarchical. Counts sometimes held lands from knights; knights frequently held lands from each other, and many landholders held fiefs from a number of different lords. Feudalism in the tenth and eleventh centuries created no feudal pyramids, in which knights held from counts, and counts held from kings in an orderly, hierarchical system of landholding and loyalty. Feudalism of this sort emerged only in the twelfth and thirteenth centuries, when powerful kings began to insist that feudalism *should* be structured in such an orderly way, with kings at the apex of a political and social pyramid.

THE NORMAN CONQUEST OF ENGLAND

Feudalism first emerged as an ordered, hierarchical system of landholding and military service in England, in the peculiar circumstances resulting from the Norman Conquest of 1066. During the tenth and eleventh centuries, England was the wealthiest, most highly centralized, and administratively sophisticated kingdom in western Europe. In 1066, however, Duke William of Normandy, the descendant of Vikings (known as Northmen, hence "Normans") who had settled this northwestern corner of France during the tenth century, laid claim to the English Crown and crossed the Channel to conquer what he had claimed. Fortunately for him the newly installed English king, Harold, had just warded off a Viking attack in the north and thus could not offer resistance at full strength. At the battle of Hastings, Harold and his English troops fought bravely but ultimately could not withstand the onslaught of the fresher Norman troops. As the day waned Harold fell, mortally wounded by a random arrow; his forces fled, and the Normans took the field—and with it, the kingdom of England. Duke William now became King William the Conqueror and set about to exploit his new prize.

William rewarded his Norman followers with extensive grants of English land. As the kingdom's conqueror, however, William could claim with some justice that all the land of England belonged ultimately to him and therefore that all the land in England must be held from him in return for service of some sort. The Norman lords were already accustomed to holding land in return for service in Normandy. In England, however,

The Bayeux Tapestry. Embroidered shortly after the Battle of Hastings, the Bayeux Tapestry is a 231-foot document of the battle and the events leading up to it. Here the Saxon Earl Harold, on a journey to Normandy, takes an oath of loyalty to Duke William of Normandy. By accepting the throne of England a few years later, Harold broke his oath, thus justifying, in Norman eyes, the Norman conquest of England.

feudalism after 1066 was much more highly centralized than it had ever been in Normandy, because in England William could draw on the administrative authority of the English state to enforce his claims to be the feudal lord of the entire country.

As king of England, William also exercised a variety of public rights that did not derive from feudalism at all. In England, only the king could coin money and only the king's money was allowed to circulate. Like their Anglo-Saxon predecessors, William and his sons also collected a national land tax, supervised justice in public courts, and had the sole authority to summon the population of England to arms. The Norman kings retained the Anglo-Saxon officer of local government known as the sheriff to help them administer and enforce their rights. William was also able to insist that all the landholders in England owed loyalty ultimately to the king—even if they did not hold a scrap of land directly from him. William's kingship thus represented a powerful fusion of Carolingian-style traditions of public power with the new feudal structures of power and landholding that had grown up in northern France in the tenth and eleventh centuries.

> William's kingship thus represented a powerful fusion of Carolingian-style traditions of public power with the new feudal structures of power and landholding that had grown up in northern France in the tenth and eleventh centuries.

FEUDAL MONARCHY IN ENGLAND

The history of English government in the two centuries after William is primarily a story of kings tightening up the feudal system to their advantage until they superseded it altogether by creating a strong national monarchy—a process sometimes referred to as "the rise of administrative kingship." The first king to take steps in this direction was the Conqueror's energetic son Henry I (1100–1135). To supervise financial accounting at his court, Henry created a specialized administrative office known as the Exchequer, so called because it used an abacuslike checkered cloth to calculate receipts and expenditures. He strengthened the Anglo-Saxon system of local administration by appointing powerful sheriffs to supervise the counties. He also instituted a system of traveling circuit judges to administer royal justice in the countryside and to act as a check on the sheriffs. Henry's overbearing style of rule was unpopular, and after his death it helped provoke a civil war. But it also brought England many years of domestic peace and prosperity.

THE REIGN OF HENRY II

After the civil wars that marked the reign of King Stephen (1135–1154), the people of England longed for a king who would bring back the good old days of Henry I. They found such a king in Henry's grandson Henry II (1154–1189). Henry II was already the ruler of Normandy, Anjou, Maine, and Aquitaine when he became king of England. As a result, England quickly found itself integrated into the political and cultural world of western France. England, however, was Henry II's richest territory and his only kingdom; for both reasons, it was imperative that he repair the damage done to the country under Stephen.

Henry II restored his grandfather's administrative system with remarkable speed. The Exchequer was up and running again within a year; soon thereafter, royal justices resumed their tours of the countryside. To facilitate their work, Henry II ordered juries of local men to report under oath every murder, arson, robbery, or other major crime that had occurred since the judges' last visit. He also expanded the use of juries to determine the facts in civil cases. These innovations are the origin of our modern system of grand and trial juries. To make it easier for plaintiffs to bring civil suits into the royal courts, Henry also developed a system of "writs," which provided a regularized, inexpensive way for common people to seek justice. They did not always obtain it; but at least they now had a chance to do so. These legal innovations were immensely popular; because they brought many more people into the royal courts (both as plaintiffs and as jurors), they also strengthened people's sense of attachment to the king's government.

To improve the administration of justice, Henry II also tried to reform the operations of the church courts. Here, however, he ran into a buzzsaw of opposition led by the flamboyant archbishop of Canterbury, Thomas Becket. In Henry I's time, criminal cases involving clerics had been tried in the county courts, where sheriffs and church officials presided jointly over them. By Henry II's day, however, a new, independent system of church courts had developed in England and elsewhere in Europe, which claimed the exclusive right to try and sentence clergy accused of committing crimes. Punishment in church courts was generally much milder than in the king's courts; in particular, church courts were

WHAT WAS THE RELATIONSHIP BETWEEN FEUDALISM AND THE RISE OF NATIONAL MONARCHIES?

FEUDALISM AND THE EMERGENCE OF NATIONAL MONARCHIES   317

Martyrdom of Thomas Becket. From a thirteenth-century English psalter. One of the knights has struck Becket so mightily that he has broken his sword.

prohibited from imposing capital penalties, even on clerics who murdered their superiors. This struck Henry II as unjust. In the Constitutions of Clarendon (1164), Henry tried to force the bishops of England to accept his claim that by ancient custom, clerics convicted in church courts of serious crimes should first lose their clerical status and then be handed over to the royal court for sentencing as laymen. Thomas Becket objected to this procedure, declaring that it amounted to "double jeopardy": punishing someone twice for the same crime. Becket and Henry had once been close friends, but Becket's stubborn insistence that Henry's real goal was to undermine the rights of the church shattered the relationship between them. Becket fled to the pope, who was then living in France under the protection of Henry II's enemy, King Louis VII of France. When Becket finally returned to England in 1170, he was murdered almost immediately in Canterbury Cathedral by four of Henry's knights after the king, in an outburst of anger, had rebuked them for

doing nothing to rid him of "this meddlesome priest." Becket was immediately proclaimed a martyr and a saint; Henry was compelled to appear as a pentitent, barefoot and dressed only in a shirt, before Becket's tomb to ask the saint's forgiveness for the rash words that had provoked his murder.

In the long run, however, these dramatic events did not seriously undermine Henry II's relationship either with the papacy or with the English church. Henry was forced to surrender several of his claims, including the right to sentence criminal clerics in royal courts and to restrict appeals from England to the papal court. But he retained the right to nominate clerics to high church offices and to have such elections held in his presence. As a result, the king's candidates were almost always confirmed to the offices for which he nominated them.

The most concrete proof of Henry II's success is that his government worked so well after his death. Henry's son, the swashbuckling Richard I, the "Lionheart," ruled his father's empire for ten years, from 1189 to 1199, but spent only about six months in England because he was otherwise engaged in crusading or defending his possessions on the Continent. Nonetheless, Richard's government became steadily more efficient, owing to the work of capable administrators and officials. The legal system continued to develop, and the country raised two huge sums for Richard by taxation: one to pay for his crusade to the Holy Land, and the other to pay his ransom when he was captured by an enemy on his return. It also steadily supported his wars to defend his French territories against King Philip Augustus of France.

THE REIGN OF JOHN AND THE MAGNA CARTA

Had Richard lived, the map of Europe might look very different today: had he defeated King Philip (as he might well have done), France itself might not exist with anything like its current borders. But Richard was killed in 1199 by a crossbowman while besieging a small castle in southern France. His successor, his brother John (1199–1216), was a much less capable military leader, who quickly lost nearly all of his lands in France. By the end of 1204, King Philip had ousted John from Normandy, Anjou, Brittany, and Maine, leaving only Aquitaine (the inheritance of Eleanor of Aquitaine, Henry II's queen) still in English hands.

John devoted the rest of his reign to raising the money he would need to recover his lost French territories. To

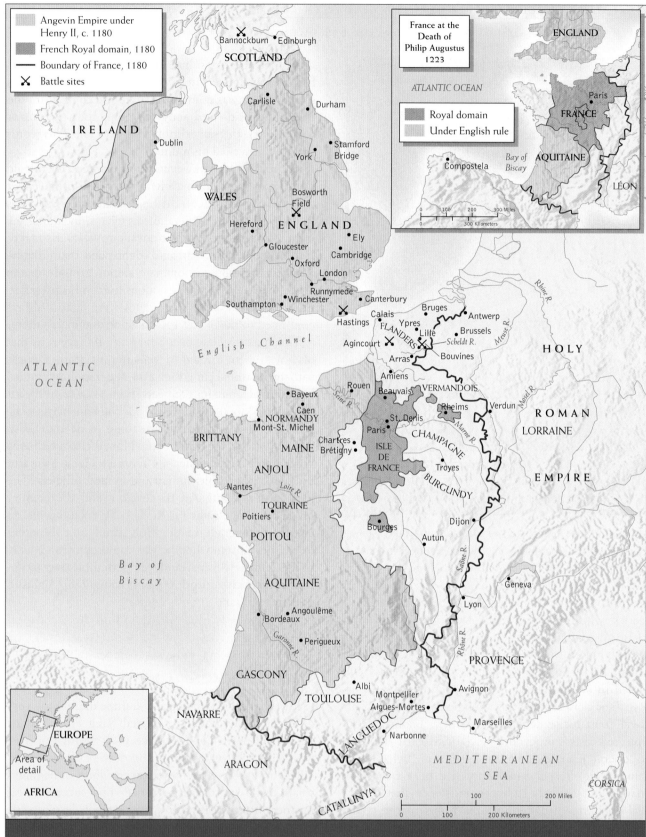

Legend (top left):
- Angevin Empire under Henry II, c. 1180
- French Royal domain, 1180
- Boundary of France, 1180
- ✕ Battle sites

Inset (top right):
France at the Death of Philip Augustus 1223

ATLANTIC OCEAN

- Royal domain
- Under English rule

ENGLAND

Paris
FRANCE
AQUITAINE
LÉON

Bay of Biscay
Compostela

Map labels:

SCOTLAND
✕ Bannockburn · Edinburgh
Carlisle
Durham
IRELAND
Dublin
Stamford Bridge
York
WALES
Bosworth Field ✕
Hereford
ENGLAND
Ely
Gloucester
Cambridge
Oxford
London
Runnymede
Winchester · Canterbury
Southampton
Hastings ✕
Calais
Bruges
Antwerp
Ypres
Brussels
FLANDERS
Lille
Agincourt ✕
Arras
✕ Bouvines
Scheldt R.
HOLY
ATLANTIC OCEAN
English Channel
Amiens
VERMANDOIS
Meuse R.
Rhine R.
Bayeux
Rouen
Beauvais
Rheims
Verdun
ROMAN
Caen
NORMANDY
Seine R.
St. Denis
Moselle R.
Mont-St. Michel
Paris
CHAMPAGNE
LORRAINE
BRITTANY
Chartres
Brétigny
ISLE DE FRANCE
Marne R.
MAINE
Troyes
EMPIRE
ANJOU
BURGUNDY
Nantes
Loire R.
TOURAINE
Poitiers
Bourges
Dijon
POITOU
Autun
Saône R.
Bay of Biscay
Geneva
AQUITAINE
Lyon
Angoulême
Bordeaux
Rhône R.
Perigueux
Garonne R.
PROVENCE
GASCONY
Avignon
Albi
TOULOUSE
Montpellier
Aigues-Mortes
Marseilles
NAVARRE
LANGUEDOC
Narbonne
ARAGON
MEDITERRANEAN SEA
CORSICA
CATALUNYA

Lower left inset:
EUROPE
Area of detail
AFRICA

FRANCE AND ENGLAND, 1180–1223

Consider the vast geographical expanse of Henry II's empire in 1180. What were the primary requirements for holding this empire together? What advantages did the kings of France enjoy in their struggles with Henry and his sons? What did it mean to be French in such a world? Would the wars between the Angevins and the Capetians have encouraged the emergence of national identities within their kingdoms? Why or why not?

WHAT WAS THE RELATIONSHIP BETWEEN FEUDALISM AND THE RISE OF NATIONAL MONARCHIES?

FEUDALISM AND THE EMERGENCE OF NATIONAL MONARCHIES   319

CHRONOLOGY

NOTEWORTHY NORMAN AND ANGEVIN KINGS, 1066–1327

William I (the Conqueror)	1066–1087
Henry I	1100–1135
Stephen	1135–1154
Henry II	1154–1189
Richard I (the Lionheart)	1189–1199
John	1199–1216
Henry III	1216–1272
Edward I	1272–1307
Edward II	1307–1327

do so, he pressed his feudal rights to their limits, demanding massive fines from his nobility and imposing heavy taxes on the country. When John's 1214 military expedition to France met with another crushing defeat by Philip Augustus at the battle of Bouvines, the exasperated magnates of England rebelled. In 1215 they forced John to renounce his extortionate fiscal practices in a great charter of liberties known to posterity as Magna Carta. Because John had relied so heavily on his feudal powers, most of Magna Carta's provisions dealt directly with such matters, insisting that the king must in future respect the traditional rights of his vassals. But Magna Carta also established some important general principles: that taxation could not be raised by the Crown without the consent of the kingdom and that no free man could be punished by the Crown except by the judgment of his equals and by the law of the land. Above all, however, Magna Carta was important as an expression of the principle that the king is bound by the law.

As the American medievalist J. R. Strayer has said, "Magna Carta made arbitrary government difficult, but it did not make centralized government impossible." In the century after its issuance, the progress of centralized government continued apace. In the reign of John's son, Henry III (1216–1272), the nobility vied with the king for control of the government but did so on the assumption that centralized government itself was a good thing. Throughout Henry's reign, administrators continued to perfect more efficient legal and administrative institutions, including a system of central and local courts, and a taxation system that assessed both nobles and commoners in proportion to their wealth.

The last and most famous branch of the medieval English governmental system was Parliament. This gradually emerged as a separate institution in the decades around 1300, above all owing to the wishes of Henry III's son, Edward I (1272–1307). Although Parliament later became a check against unlimited royal power, in its origins Parliament was very much a royal creation, summoned because kings found it useful to consult with their nobles, knights, and townsmen in a single assembly. Edward I called parliaments frequently to raise money to finance his wars in Wales, Scotland, and France. Magna Carta had demanded that no taxation be imposed without the common consent of the realm. Parliament provided an efficient way to secure such consent as well as to inform those present (principally the nobility, but frequently including knightly representatives from the counties and the major towns) why such taxation was necessary. Edward also used parliaments to take advice about pressing concerns, to hear judicial cases involving great men, to review local administration, to hear complaints from the countryside, and to promulgate new laws in response to those complaints. Parliaments were thus political institutions no less than financial and judicial ones. They played an essential role in English government from the fourteenth century on.

FEUDAL MONARCHY IN FRANCE

Administrative kingship developed more slowly in France than in England, but by 1300 it had reached a comparable stage in both countries. During the tenth century, most of the Carolingian institutions of local government in France had collapsed; as a result, the new Capetian Dynasty of French kings (987–1328) had to rebuild such institutions from scratch. For nearly 200 years, it seemed unlikely they would ever be able to do so. As kings of France, the early Capetians ruled directly only a small area around Paris known as the Île-de-France, roughly the size of Vermont. Outside their home territory, the Capetian kings could claim only to be the feudal overlords of the independent counts and dukes who ruled the rest of France. An idea of France survived as a legacy from the Carolingian period; but in all other respects, the Capetians had to reinvent their kingdom.

In many ways the Capetians were fortunate. Quite against the biological odds, they managed to produce sons for 300 years without interruption. They also proved surprisingly long lived: on average, each Capetian king ruled for thirty years. As a result, they avoided both succession disputes and destructive minority governments. They ruled a remarkably rich agricultural territory, which provided them with a steadily increasing source of income. They also acquired significant prestige as protectors of popes fleeing from the German emperors and as the patrons of the University of Paris, which became the leading European center of learning during the twelfth and thirteenth centuries. Beyond all this, however, the Capetians proved to be a shrewd and wily line of kings, who carefully husbanded their strength while their more powerful enemies overreached themselves.

THE GROWTH OF ROYAL POWER IN FRANCE

The steady growth of royal power in France began under Louis VI "the Fat" (1108–1137). It was Louis who consolidated royal control over the Île-de-France by subduing its turbulent robber barons. Once this was accomplished, agriculture and trade could prosper and the intellectual life of Paris began to flourish. Louis's son Louis VII (1137–1180) was thoroughly overshadowed by his rival, King Henry II of England. But he managed nonetheless to increase the resources and the prestige of the French monarchy (at one point Louis was protecting Thomas Becket and Pope Alexander III at the same time). By inciting rebellions by Henry II's sons against their father, he also kept the Angevin Empire in a constant state of discord.

It was Louis VII's son Philip II who finally turned the tide against the Angevins and who marks the true beginning of administrative kingship in France. Like his father, Philip understood that he could not win a direct military confrontation with Henry II or Richard I. King John, however—known to his detractors as "soft sword"—was another matter. To facilitate his succession to his brother's throne, John agreed to do homage to Philip for all his lands in France. Philip then took

advantage of his position as John's feudal overlord to undermine John's control over these territories. When John refused to permit such incursions, Philip declared all John's lands in France to be forfeit to the French crown. A war of conquest quickly followed. By 1204, the richest part of the Angevin territories in France were in Philip's hands.

Philip now had the resources to begin building an effective system of local administration. He had already taken steps to deepen his own administrative control over the Île-de-France. He now extended those lessons to the newly conquered territories of Normandy, Maine, and Anjou. Wisely, he chose to maintain most of the administrative institutions the Angevins had created there. To supervise these territories, however, he appointed new royal officials known as *baillis* with full judicial, administrative, and military authority. Philip drew his *baillis* from among the knights and petty nobles of the Île-de-France and rotated them frequently from region to region. This ensured not only that they would be loyal to Philip but also that they would not develop dangerous connections with the territories they ruled on Philip's behalf. Philip also improved his central administration by adopting stricter systems of financial accounting and record keeping.

The administrative pattern Philip established, of combining local diversity with centralized royal control, would continue to characterize French government for the next 500 years. Philip's son, Louis VIII (1223–1226), would extend it to the newly conquered territories of southern France. His son, Louis IX (1226–1270), would deepen and extend it further. Even more important, however, Louis IX would legitimize it by his own extraordinary devotion to justice at home and crusading abroad. Louis IX became the epitome of thirteenth-century kingship; after his death, he would be canonized by the church as Saint Louis. His successors would draw on the prestige of "good King Louis" for centuries to come.

That prestige came close to being squandered, however, by Saint Louis's ruthless grandson Philip IV, "the Fair" (1285–1314). Philip waged aggressive wars against Flanders in the northeast and the remaining English territories in the southwest. As we will see in Chapter 9, he also sought to undermine papal control over the church in France. To finance these campaigns, his administration became a voracious money-raising machine. Despite his enormous resources, however, Philip could not match the capacity of his enemy, Edward I, to raise cash from his subjects through voluntary taxation. Although Philip experi-

CHRONOLOGY

NOTEWORTHY CAPETIAN KINGS, 987–1328

Hugh Capet	987–996
Louis VI	1108–1137
Louis VII	1137–1180
Philip Augustus	1179–1223
Louis VIII	1223–1226
Louis IX	1226–1270
Philip IV	1285–1314

WHAT WAS THE RELATIONSHIP BETWEEN FEUDALISM AND THE RISE OF NATIONAL MONARCHIES?

FEUDALISM AND THE EMERGENCE OF NATIONAL MONARCHIES   321

King Philip the Fair of France. An author is presenting a copy of his book to the mighty king, enthroned on a dais.

ENGLAND AND FRANCE: COMPARISONS AND CONTRASTS

During the High Middle Ages, both England and France developed effective, centralized administrative monarchies and defined national identities. By 1300, France had become the most formidable national monarchy in Europe. England too was a budding imperial power, with ambitions to dominate the entire British Isles and to maintain its control over southwestern France. Rivalry between these two kingdoms had already led to war in the 1290s; this warfare would continue, off and on, for the next 200 years.

Despite their similarities, however, the two countries had developed very differently during the High Middle Ages. These differences would mark the history of the two kingdoms until the nineteenth century. England, a far smaller country than France, was much more tightly unified. Within England itself (excluding English claims to rule over Wales and Scotland), no regional languages or loyalties threatened the unity of the English kingdom. English nobles could and did rebel against their kings; but in doing so, they could not draw support from regional resentments against the capital. In France, by contrast, regional separatism remained a significant force. Southern France in particular continued to regard itself as an occupied land; but even the Normans chafed at being ruled from Paris. Disaffected French nobles and English invaders would draw support from such regionalism for centuries to come.

The two countries were also governed in quite different ways. In England, the Norman and Angevin kings built their administration on a surviving bedrock of local institutions from the Anglo-Saxon period. They could also rely on local men, and especially local knights, to do much of the work of local government without pay. This made English administration inexpensive; but it also meant that governmental policies had to be popular or else this voluntary work would grind to a halt. English kings were generally careful, therefore, to seek formal consent for their actions from assemblies of nobles, knights, and commoners. As a result, England gradually became a monarchy limited by the requirement that its people must consent to its policies.

The French kings, by contrast, ruled a much larger and richer country, which provided them with sufficient wealth to pay for a bureaucratic, salaried administration at both the central and local levels. Because these officials were royal representatives with no independent

mented with representative assemblies similar to the English Parliament, these Estates General (as they came to be called) never played a role in French government comparable to Parliament in England. There were many reasons for this, but perhaps the most fundamental one was the fact that the French nobility successfully claimed to be exempt from paying direct taxation to the crown. Ever since the Anglo-Saxon period, English monarchs had been powerful enough to ensure that their nobility must pay the taxes to which they consented. The weakness of the early Capetian kings had prevented a similar custom from taking root in France, and even Philip IV found it easier to accept this state of affairs rather than to challenge it. Noble exemptions from taxation would therefore remain a political problem for the French monarchy right on up until the French Revolution of 1789.

standing in local society, they were inclined to obey the king's orders without question. Their role was to control regional separatism, not to foment it. This meant that the Capetian kings had less need to summon the kinds of representative assemblies on which English kings depended for support. As a result, however, the Capetians lacked effective institutional mechanisms for mobilizing public opinion behind them. The early weakness of the Capetian kings also prevented them from requiring their nobility to pay taxes to the crown. In the later Middle Ages, under the pressure of almost constant war, these weaknesses would prove disastrous.

GERMANY

Germany in the High Middle Ages followed a very different pattern. In the year 1050, Germany appeared to be the strongest monarchy in western Europe. Although the country was divided into a number of semi-autonomous duchies, the German emperors had constructed a powerful monarchy on Carolingian-style foundations: a close alliance with the church, a tradition of sacral kingship, and profitable conquests in the Slavic lands to the east. To rule their wide territories—which included Switzerland, eastern France, and most of the Low Countries, as well as claims to northern Italy—the emperors relied heavily on cooperation with the church. The leading royal administrators were archbishops and bishops whom the German emperors appointed and installed in their sacred offices, just as their Carolingian predecessors had done. Even the pope was frequently an imperial appointee. Often, these leading churchmen were members of the imperial family itself, who could counterbalance the strength of the regional dukes. Germany was not so administratively sophisticated as was eleventh-century England, but there was no question about the effectiveness of monarchical authority. It simply rested on other foundations.

THE CONFLICT WITH THE PAPACY

In 1056, however, the emperor Henry III died, leaving as his heir a small boy, the future Henry IV. From this point on, the strength of the monarchy began to unravel. Henry III had installed a new group of reforming clergy at the papal court, whose policies will be discussed more fully in the next chapter. Conflicts between the regents for the boy king Henry IV and the papal reformers began almost immediately. Conflicts also

erupted between the regents (who came from central and southern Germany) and the nobility of Saxony. When Henry IV began to rule on his own, the Saxon conflicts escalated. In 1073, these hostilities erupted into a disastrous and destructive civil war.

Just as the Saxon war ended, however, a new conflict broke out with the papal reformers at Rome. For reasons that will be discussed in the next chapter, the newly elected pope Gregory VII (1073–1085) became convinced that to reform the spiritual life of the church, it was necessary first to free the church from the control of laymen, including the emperor. Henry refused to accept Gregory's attempts to prohibit him from selecting and installing in office his own bishops and abbots and began to plot to remove Gregory from the papacy. Gregory, in turn, allied himself with the Saxon nobility, reigniting the civil war from which Germany had not yet recovered. This time, the war went against Henry; and the dissident nobles, supported by Gregory, began to plot Henry's own deposition. There then followed one of the most dramatic scenes of the Middle Ages. In the depths of winter in 1077 Henry hurried across the Alps to abase himself before Pope Gregory in the north Italian castle of Canossa. As Gregory described the scene in a letter to the German princes, "There on three successive days, standing before the castle gate, laying aside all royal insignia, barefooted and in coarse attire, Henry ceased not with many tears to beseech the apostolic help and comfort." No German ruler, much less a Roman emperor, had ever been so humiliated. The memory would remain etched in German historical consciousness for centuries to come.

The events at Canossa forestalled Henry's deposition, but they did not resolve the war. The struggle between pope and emperor continued until 1122, when Henry's son Henry V finally reached a compromise with the papacy. By then, however, the German nobility had won far more practical independence from the crown than they had had before. After fifty years of nearly constant war, they had also become far more militarized and dangerous. In 1125, when Henry V died childless, they gained further authority by making good on their claims to elect a new ruler regardless of hereditary succession—a principle that would thereafter often lead them to choose the weakest successors or to embroil the country in civil war. The pope's right to crown any new Roman emperor gave him a stake in the selection process also. For obvious reasons, the papacy feared an overly powerful German monarch. Although the popes valued the German emperors as counterweights to the Normans in southern Italy, they

WHAT WAS THE RELATIONSHIP BETWEEN FEUDALISM AND THE RISE OF NATIONAL MONARCHIES?

FEUDALISM AND THE EMERGENCE OF NATIONAL MONARCHIES   323

THE HOLY ROMAN EMPIRE, C. 1200

Are the borders of the Holy Roman Empire defined by rivers, oceans, or mountain ranges? How would you explain this fact? Does the Kingdom of Germany have any such natural borders? Note the position of the Papal States in central Italy. Why would the prospect of a single heir to the Holy Roman Empire and to the Kingdom of Sicily have frightened the popes? Were their fears well founded? Why or why not?

feared them in equal measure. Should the German emperors succeed in ruling northern and central Italy directly, the papacy—on whose spiritual independence the salvation of all Christians depended—risked becoming their puppet. This fear propelled the next century of papal-imperial conflict.

FREDERICK BARBAROSSA AND HENRY VI

A major attempt to stem the tide running against the German monarchy was made by Frederick I (1152–1190), who came from the family of Staufen (or Hohenstaufen, meaning "high Staufen"). Frederick, called "Barbarossa" ("red beard"), reasserted the independent dignity of the empire by calling his realm the "Holy Roman Empire," on the theory that it was a universal empire descending from Rome and blessed by God. At the same time, however, he also tried to rule in cooperation with the German princes, supporting their efforts to bring their own territorial nobles to heel and trusting that the princes would in turn support his attempts to reassert imperial control over the wealthy but increasingly independent cities of northern Italy.

By and large, Frederick made this system work, but at the cost of a lengthy war in Italy and destructive conflict with the papacy. Led by Milan and supported by the papacy, the north Italian cities formed an alliance, the Lombard League, to resist Frederick's claims to rule in Italy. Meanwhile, the princes in Germany were continuing to gather strength, especially by colonizing the rich agricultural lands east of the Elbe. Ultimately, however, Frederick achieved a compromise with both the Lombard League and the papacy, which guaranteed the political independence of the towns in return for large cash payments they would make to the emperor. His 1184 imperial court at Mainz was one of the most splendid occasions of the twelfth century. He secured the princes' approval for his son Henry to succeed him as king and emperor, and he arranged a marriage between Henry and the sister of the Norman king of Sicily. Finally, in 1189, he departed on the Third Crusade and died on his way to the Holy Land.

Barbarossa's careful planning bore fruit in the reign of his son Henry VI. Henry succeeded to his father's throne without difficulty. He enjoyed a huge income from the north Italian towns; and when his wife's brother died suddenly without heirs, he became the king of Sicily also. This was the nightmare the papacy had always feared, for now a single, enormously powerful ruler controlled both northern and southern Italy, leaving the papal lands in central Italy surrounded on all sides. Fortunately for the papacy, however, Henry

VI died in 1197 at the age of thirty-two, leaving as his heir a three-year-old son, the future Frederick II. The new pope, Innocent III (1198–1216), threw all his energy into an attempt to break the links that Barbarossa and Henry VI had forged between Germany, northern Italy, and the kingdom of Sicily. When a civil war erupted in Germany over the succession to the throne, Innocent threw his support back and forth between the two main claimants, hoping to secure some kind of promise from the successful claimant that would return Sicily to the papacy, which claimed to have granted it to the Normans as a fief. When Otto IV, the non-Staufen claimant to the throne, finally appeared to have won a decisive victory, Innocent played his last card. He sent the sixteen-year-old Frederick II north with a small army, never imagining that so small a force, led by so young a man, could ever triumph. Otto, however, threw in his lot with his cousin, King John of England; and when Otto's forces were routed at the battle of Bouvines by King Philip Augustus of France, Frederick II wound up as the new, and undisputed, king of Germany.

FREDERICK II

Frederick II (1216–1250) was one of the most fascinating of all medieval rulers. Having grown up in Sicily, Frederick spoke Arabic as well as Latin, German, French, and Italian. He was a patron of learning who composed a famous treatise on falconry that holds an honored place in the early history of Western observational science. He maintained a menagerie of exotic animals, a troop of Muslim archers, and a harem of veiled and secluded women, all of which traveled with him on his journeys. When Frederick entered a town, the effect was electrifying. But despite this appearance of exoticism, he was also a very conventional medieval ruler who sought to pursue his grandfather's policies of supporting the territorial princes in Germany while enforcing imperial rights in Italy. Much had changed, however, in the two decades of upheaval that had followed the death of the emperor Henry VI. In Germany, the princes had already become so entirely autonomous that there was little Frederick could do except to recognize their privileges. This he proceeded to do; but in exchange, he got them to elect his sons (first Henry, and then Conrad) to succeed him as kings of Germany. Frederick's biggest problems lay in Italy. In northern Italy, the cities of the Lombard League had once again shaken off their obligations to pay taxes to the empire; while in Sicily, the enormously powerful and administra-

FREDERICK II CHANGES
THE HEIGHT OF THE HEAVENS

As a result of the propaganda war that erupted between Frederick II and the papacy during the 1240s, a series of stories began to circulate about Frederick's exotic intellectual and scientific interests: that he had ordered infants to be raised in isolation to discover what language they would naturally speak; that he had had men disemboweled before him to study the processes of digestion; and that he sealed a man up in a cask to die to prove that the soul perished with the body. None of these stories has any basis in fact, but all illustrate the effect the image of Frederick had on his contemporaries.

The following story concerns Frederick's court astrologer, Michael Scot (d. 1236), an influential scholar who translated a number of Aristotelian and astronomical works and commentaries from Arabic to Latin. It is taken from the chronicle of Salimbene de Adam, a Franciscan supporter of the pope in the struggle against Frederick.

The seventh example [of Frederick's idiosyncrasies] was that he once asked Michael Scot to tell him the distance of his palace from heaven. And after Michael gave the answer that seemed correct to him, the Emperor took him away for a few months as if merely on a pleasure trip, commanding his architects and stone masons in the meantime to lower that room of his palace in such a way that no one could detect it. This was done, and when the Emperor returned to his palace with the astrologer, he asked him again how far distant the palace was from heaven. And after he had completed his calculations, Michael Scot answered that either the heavens had risen or the earth had sunk. Then the emperor knew that he was a true astrologer.

I have heard and know many other idiosyncrasies of Frederick, but I keep quiet for the sake of brevity, and because reporting so many of the Emperor's foolish notions is tedious to me.

Joseph Baird, Giuseppe Baglivi, and John Robert Kane, eds. and trans., *The Chronicle of Salimbene de Adam*, Medieval and Renaissance Texts and Studies, vol. 4. (Binghamton, N.Y., 1986), pp. 355–356.

QUESTIONS FOR ANALYSIS

1. This story contains magical and practical elements as well as ridicule. Why was it considered exotic for the emperor to have scientific interests?
2. To discuss the previous questions, you may have considered astrology a science, but if it is not, what would be the value of Frederick's test for the astrologer?

tively sophisticated kingdom created by the Normans had fallen into chaos.

Frederick tackled these problems in order. From 1212 until 1220, Frederick was in Germany, solidifying his relationship with the German nobility and recovering as much Staufen land as he could after twenty years

of war. From 1220 until 1226 he was in Sicily and northern Italy, reestablishing his authority there. From 1227 until 1229 he was on crusade, where he succeeded in recovering Jerusalem through negotiations with the Muslim ruler of Egypt, with whom Frederick spoke Arabic and shared a love of falconry. From 1230

The Emperor Frederick II. He is shown here holding a fleur de lis, as a symbol of rule, with a falcon at his side.

to 1235 he was again in Sicily, restoring his authority after an abortive papal invasion of the territory. From 1235 to 1237 he was in Germany, arguably the high point of his reign. In 1237, however, he overreached himself by asserting his rights as emperor to rule the north Italian cities directly, bypassing their own governmental structures. The result was another Lombard League and another lengthy war, which continued until Frederick's death in 1250. The papacy was a key player in this war, going so far as to excommunicate Frederick from the church and, after his death, forbidding any of his descendants ever again to occupy the thrones of Germany or Sicily. We will never know whether the papacy could have made this claim effective, for in 1254, Frederick's last surviving legitimate son died. With him went the last prospect for the continuation of effective monarchical rule in Germany. Emperors would continue to be elected, but in practice, monarchical authority in Germany was now gravely weakened. Effective political power in Germany would thereafter be divided among several hundred territorial princes whose rivalries would embroil German politics until the end of the nineteenth century.

IBERIA

The Iberian peninsula was even more regionalized than was Germany. In contrast to Germany, however, Spain would emerge from the Middle Ages with the most powerful monarchy in early modern Europe. The key to the strength of the Spanish monarchies of the High Middle Ages lay in their successful reconquest of the peninsula from the Muslims, and in the lands, booty, and plunder these conquests provided. During the High Middle Ages Iberia contained four major Christian kingdoms: the northern mountain state of Navarre, which would always remain comparatively insignificant; Portugal in the west; the combined kingdom of Aragon and Catalunya in the southeast; and Castile in the center. Throughout the twelfth century, Christian armies steadily advanced, culminating in the year 1212 in a major victory by a combined Aragonese–Castilian army over the Muslims at Las Navas de Tolosa. By the end of the thirteenth century all that remained of earlier Muslim domination was the small state of Granada in the extreme south, and Granada survived mostly because it was willing to pay tribute to the Christians. Castile became by far the largest Spanish kingdom in area, but it was balanced in wealth by the more urban and trade-oriented kingdom of Aragon and Catalunya. Wars between Castile and Aragon weakened both kingdoms during the later Middle Ages; but when the marriage of Ferdinand of Aragon and Isabella of Castile joined these two ancient enemies, a united Spanish monarchy was born. In 1492, the Catholic monarchs (as Ferdinand and Isabella were known) captured Granada, the last remaining Muslim territory in Spain. A few months later, Isabella commissioned an Italian adventurer named Christopher Columbus to sail to India by heading west across the Atlantic Ocean. Columbus failed. But his accidental encounter with the American continents would make sixteenth-century Spain the most powerful kingdom in Europe.

CONCLUSION

In the year 1000, Europe was the least powerful, the least prosperous, and the least intellectually sophisticated of the three Western civilizations that had emerged out of the Roman world. By 1300, its position vis-à-vis both the Byzantine and the Islamic worlds had been transformed. This transformation rested on economic foundations: an increasingly efficient agriculture, a growing population, and expanding trade.

CONCLUSION   327

Christian territory, c. 900
Reconquista, c. 900–1150
Reconquista, c. 1150–1250
Muslim holdings, c. 1250

THE RECONQUEST OF IBERIA, 900–1250

Note the position of the Christian kingdoms circa 900 and the progress of the Christian reconquest over the subsequent few centuries. What factors helped shelter and sustain the small Christian kingdoms that survived Islam's initial push? Why did Castile become the largest of the Christian kingdoms as the reconquest progressed? Why did the smaller Aragon and Catalunya maintain important positions as wealthy and significant powers? How did the struggles and successes of Christians in Iberia influence the crusader movement?

These changes produced a dynamic, expansionist, self-confident, and mobile society in which individuals cast off old roles and took on new ones with bewildering speed. No less important, however, were the political and military changes Western Europe underwent during these centuries. By 1100, the heavily armored, mounted knight had emerged as the most formidable military weapon of the day. It was only during the twelfth and thirteenth centuries, however, that European governments developed the administrative and political capacity to control these knights and to direct them toward purposes larger than mere brigandage and extortion.

Until the High Middle Ages, the Western world had known two basic patterns of human government: city-states and empires. City-states were more capable of mobilizing the loyalty of their citizens; as a result, they could sometimes win extraordinary victories against more powerful imperial rivals, as the Greeks did against the Persians. But city-states were frequently divided by internal economic and social rivalries; and in the long run, they were not militarily strong enough to defend themselves against foreign conquerors. Empires, by contrast, could win battles and maintain powerful administrative bureaucracies, but they were generally too far flung and rapacious to inspire deep loyalties among their subjects.

The national monarchies of the High Middle Ages would prove to be the "golden mean" between these extremes. They were large enough to defend themselves, and wealthy enough to develop sophisticated adminis-trative techniques. But they also commanded sufficient citizen participation and loyalty to support them in times of stress when empires would have foundered. By 1300, the kings of England, France, and the Iberian peninsula had largely succeeded in claiming the primary loyalty of their subjects, superseding the claims of locality, region, or even the church. Their victory was not yet complete; and in the later Middle Ages, France in particular would come near to collapse. But in the end, the national monarchies of the High Middle Ages would endure to become the foundations on which the nation-states of modern Europe would be constructed. So important would this historical pedigree become that modern nation-states that did not have a medieval origin would often be compelled to invent one.

KEY TERMS

manorialism	First Crusade	feudalism
serfdom	chivalry	William the Conqueror
guilds	courtly love	Magna Carta

SELECTED READINGS

Abulafia, David. *Frederick II: A Medieval Emperor.* London and New York, 1988. The only reliable biography of Frederick II; it strips away much of the legend that has hitherto surrounded this monarch.

Abulafia, David, ed. *The New Cambridge Medieval History. Volume 5: c. 1198–c. 1300.* Cambridge, 1999. An up-to-date survey, with contributions by more than thirty specialists. Excellent bibliographies.

Amt, Emily, ed. *Women's Lives in Medieval Europe: A Sourcebook.* New York, 1993. An excellent source collection.

Arnold, Benjamin. *Princes and Territories in Medieval Germany.* Cambridge and New York, 1991. The best English-language survey; it correctly avoids portraying the political history of medieval Germany as a story of failure.

Baldwin, John W. *The Government of Philip Augustus.* Berkeley, Calif., and Los Angeles, 1986. A landmark scholarly account, detailed but readable.

Bartlett, Robert. *The Making of Europe: Conquest, Colonization and Cultural Change, 950–1350.* Princeton, N.J., 1993. A wide-ranging examination of the economic, social, and religious expansion of Europe, full of stimulating ideas and insights.

Clanchy, Michael. *England and Its Rulers, 1066–1307,* 3d ed. Oxford and Malden, Mass., 2006. A lively and consistently interesting survey, highly recommended.

Dunbabin, Jean. *France in the Making, 843–1180,* 2d ed. Oxford and New York, 2000. An authoritative survey of the disparate territories that came to make up the medieval French kingdom.

Dyer, Christopher. *Making a Living in the Middle Ages: The People of Britain 850–1520.* New Haven, 2002. A splendid new synthesis that combines social, economic, and archaeological evidence.

Fuhrmann, Horst. *Germany in the High Middle Ages, c. 1050–1200.* Cambridge, 1986. A useful, short account in English of the history of twelfth-century Germany.

Gillingham, John. *The Angevin Empire,* 2d ed. Oxford and New York, 2001. The best treatment by far of its subject, brief but full of ideas.

Hallam, Elizabeth, and Judith Everard. *Capetian France, 987–1328,* 2d ed. New York, 2001. An excellent textbook; a bit dry, but clear and well organized.

Herlihy, David, ed. *The History of Feudalism.* New York, 1970. Collects the texts on which scholarly discussion continues to focus.

Hyde, J. Kenneth. *Society and Politics in Medieval Italy.* New York, 1973. A survey that sets the political history of the Italian city-states in its social context.

Jones, P. J. *The Italian City-State: From Commune to Signoria.* Oxford and New York, 1997. A fundamental reinterpretation, with important revisions to the standard accounts of Hyde and Waley.

Jordan, William C. *Europe in the High Middle Ages: The Penguin History of Europe.* Vol. III. New York and London, 2003. An outstanding new survey, the best since Southern.

Kaeuper, Richard W. *Chivalry and Violence in Medieval Europe.* Oxford and New York, 1999. A darker view of chivalry than Keen's.

Keen, Maurice. *Chivalry.* New Haven, Conn., 1984. Masterful treatment of chivalry from its origins to the sixteenth century, engagingly written.

Lambert of Ardres. *The History of the Counts of Guines and Lords of Ardres.* Trans. Leah Shopkow. Philadelphia, 2000. A tremendously informative chronicle of an important Flemish family, now available in English.

Leyser, Henrietta. *Medieval Women: A Social History of Women in England, 440–1500.* New York, 1995. Although limited to one country, this is the best of the recent surveys treating medieval women.

Lopez, Robert S., and Irving W. Raymond, eds. *Medieval Trade in the Mediterranean World.* New York, 1990. A pathbreaking collection of source material on Italian medieval trade.

Moore, Robert I. *The First European Revolution, c. 970–1215.* Oxford and Cambridge, Mass., 2000. A remarkable description of the ways in which European society was fundamentally reshaped during the eleventh and twelfth centuries.

Otto, Bishop of Freising. *The Deeds of Frederick Barbarossa.* Trans. C. C. Mierow. New York, 1953. A contemporary chronicle interesting enough to read from start to finish.

Reilly, Bernard F. *The Medieval Spains.* New York, 1993. A succinct account that covers the entire Iberian peninsula from 500 to 1500.

Reynolds, Susan. *Fiefs and Vassals: The Medieval Evidence Reinterpreted.* Oxford and New York, 1994. A detailed revisionist account that sees feudalism as the invention of high and late medieval legal thinkers rather than as a description of tenth- and eleventh-century realities.

Richard, Jean. *Saint Louis: Crusader King of France.* Cambridge, 1992. An abridged version of Richard's standard biography of King Louis IX, originally published in French.

Southern, Richard W. *The Making of the Middle Ages.* New Haven, Conn., 1992. A classic work, first published in 1951 but still fresh and exciting.

Stow, Kenneth R. *Alienated Minority: The Jews of Medieval Latin Europe.* Cambridge, Mass., 1992. An excellent survey of a neglected topic.

Suger, Abbot of Saint Denis. *The Deeds of Louis the Fat.* Trans. R. Cusimano and J. Moorhead. Washington, D.C., 1992. A revealing picture of the challenges that faced the early twelfth-century kings of France as they fought to subdue the local nobility of the Île-de-France.

Waley, Daniel. *The Italian City-Republics.* New York, 1969. A classic introduction to the subject.

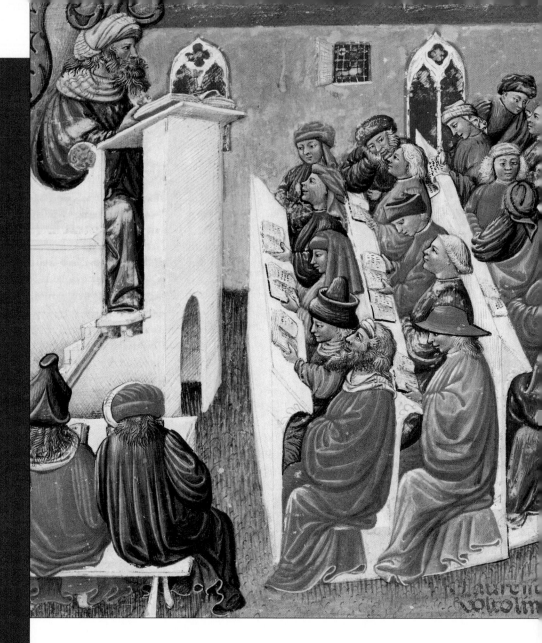

THE HIGH MIDDLE
AGES: RELIGIOUS
AND INTELLECTUAL
DEVELOPMENTS,
1000–1300

THE RELIGIOUS AND INTELLECTUAL CHANGES of the High Middle Ages altered European life profoundly. Indeed, it is not too much to say that the fundamental character of European civilization was permanently transformed by the developments that occurred during these crucial centuries. With respect to religious life, the period witnessed both the emergence of the papacy as the dominant organizational force in western Christianity and a remarkable effort on the part of the church to extend and deepen the influence of Christianity among the laity. Parish churches mushroomed across the landscape, and new monastic and religious orders developed, many of which took as their primary mission the task of ministering to the world outside the monastic cloister. For the first time since the late Roman period, preaching, confession, pilgrimages, and private prayer became central elements in the religious life of European Christians. At the same time, however, these new patterns of Christian piety emphasized the religious and social distinctions between Christians and their non-Christian neighbors. The result was a marked increase in the persecution of minority groups within European society, and the creation of what some historians have called a "persecuting society" in which the identification and oppression of heretics, Jews, gay people, lepers, and Muslims became an essential element in the growing power of both church and state.

The High Middle Ages also witnessed a remarkable revival of intellectual and cultural life. From the mid-twelfth century on, hundreds of new works of classical literature and philosophy, including the entirety of the surviving works of Aristotle, poured into western Europe from the Islamic world and, to a lesser degree, from Byzantium. Even before the stimulus of these new texts, however, European intellectuals had begun to think in new, more rigorous ways about fundamental problems in theology, philosophy, and law. Fueling this intellectual revolution (which is sometimes referred to as the "Renaissance of the Twelfth Century") was the emergence and rapid growth of universities, accompanied by an even more widespread expansion of primary schooling. New literary forms also began to emerge: vernacular lyric poetry, extended allegories, and above all romances. For the first time in centuries it began to be possible to speak of a European reading public.

FOCUS QUESTIONS

• How was the Latin Church reformed?

• How did the Latin Church control popular heresy?

 • How did the recovery of classical learning affect medieval intellectual life?

• What common themes unite the literature, art, and architecture of the High Middle Ages?

In education, thought, and the arts, early medieval Europe had been a backwater, especially in comparison with Byzantium and Islam. By 1300, however, Europe had become the intellectual and artistic leader among these three western civilizations. Europeans now boasted that learning and the arts had come to them from Egypt, Greece, and Rome; and that although they were pygmies who sat on the shoulders of giants, they nonetheless saw farther and more clearly than had the intellectual giants of antiquity on whose shoulders they sat. Such boasts were largely justified. In the High Middle Ages, Europeans built their intellectual and artistic accomplishments on ancient foundations, but they also began to make major contributions of their own.

THE REFORM OF THE CHURCH

How was the Latin Church reformed?

The combined effects of Carolingian collapse; Viking, Muslim, and Hungarian attacks; and the growing power of local noble families were disastrous for the religious life of ninth- and tenth-century Europe. For several centuries, church reformers had sought to improve the religious lives of the laity by strengthening the control that powerful bishops exercised over the local clergy within their dioceses. By the middle of the tenth century, however, that strategy lay in ruins. Many parish churches had been abandoned or destroyed, while those that survived were often regarded as the personal property of some powerful local family, whose responsibility for protecting these churches easily became a license to oppress them. In these circumstances, a parish church frequently became simply a manorial appurtenance, like the lord's mill or oven or forge, which his peasants were obliged to use and from which he took the profits. Even bishoprics fell into the hands of noble families, who appointed relatives to them or sold them as if they were pieces of family property. Monasteries underwent a similar process of privatization. Some became dumping grounds for aristocratic younger sons who might live in the monastery without ever taking monastic vows. Other monasteries had troops of knights thrust on them. Some even had lay abbots. It was all very distant from what Saint Benedict had outlined in his *Rule for Monasteries*.

In the absence of effective kingship, bishops were helpless against such entrenched local power. Nor could the papacy correct the situation. Indeed, as the bishops of Rome, the popes themselves were among the worst examples of the negative impact too much local influence could have on the spiritual standards of the clergy. Most of the tenth-century popes were incompetent or corrupt, the sons or tools of powerful Roman families who sought to control the papacy to rule the city of Rome itself. Some were astonishingly debauched. The worst of them, John XII, became pope in 955 at the age of eighteen through the influence of his family, which had ruled Rome for half a century. Pope John was nearly illiterate and thoroughly licentious. His critics claimed that female pilgrims would not even enter the Lateran Palace for fear that the pope would molest them; and he is reported to have died in the midst of yet another carnal act, either from sheer amorous exertion or else by the sword of a jealous husband who found the pope in bed with his wife. As the guardian of the tombs of Saints Peter and Paul and the spiritual head of western Christendom, the papacy remained a respected institution, even in its tenth-century nadir. But the popes who occupied Saint Peter's chair left a great deal to be desired as moral and spiritual leaders of Western society.

MONASTIC REFORM, 900–1050

The first stirrings of reform emerged in the monasteries of tenth-century Europe, beginning with that of Cluny in Burgundy. Founded in 910 by a pious nobleman, Cluny was a Benedictine house, but with two important constitutional innovations. One was that to keep it free from domination by local noble families or the local bishop, Cluny was placed directly under the protection of the papacy. The second was that it undertook the reform or foundation of a large number of daughter monasteries. Whereas formerly all Benedictine houses had been independent and equal, Cluny established a network of dependent Cluniac houses across Europe, all of which remained subordinate to the mother house at Cluny. By 1049, there were sixty-seven such Cluniac priories (as the daughter monasteries were called), each one performing the same elaborate round of prayer and worship for which Cluny became famous, and each entirely free from the control of local secular or ecclesiastical powers. Under the rule of a series of pious and remarkably long-lived abbots, Cluny became

> Under the rule of a series of pious and remarkably long-lived abbots, Cluny became famous for its high spiritual standards and its carefully ordered liturgical life.

famous for its high spiritual standards and its carefully ordered liturgical life. In the eyes of the Cluniacs, however, their success depended on their absolute freedom from outside interference in their religious life. When Cluny reformed a monastery, therefore, it insisted on two things: first, that the Benedictine vows be strictly enforced on all monks; and second, that the selection of new abbots and priors be accomplished by a free election of the monks, without any buying or selling of the office (a sin known as "simony," after Simon Magus, a magician in the New Testament who tried to buy the power of the Holy Spirit from Jesus' disciples).

Cluniac influence was strongest in France and Italy, where the virtual absence of effective kingship made royally sponsored monastic reforms impossible. Here, and in Lotharingia, pious nobles usually took the lead in promoting monastic reforms. In Germany and England, by contrast, monastic reform emerged during the tenth and eleventh centuries as an essential responsibility of a Christian king. Following Cluniac example, these kings insisted on the strict observance of poverty, chastity, and obedience within the monastery, and instituted elaborate rounds of group liturgical prayer. In contrast to Cluny, however, it was the kings themselves who guaranteed the reformed monasteries' freedom from outside interference, and it was they who appointed the abbots, just as they also appointed the bishops of their kingdoms.

As a result of these parallel movements for monastic reform, monasticism became the dominant spiritual model for tenth- and eleventh-century Latin Christianity. The peaceful, orderly round of the monks' daily worship was seen as mirroring the perfect harmony of heaven; their prayers were regarded as uniquely effec-

tive in preserving a sinful world from the destruction a just God might otherwise wreak on it; and monks themselves were seen as "angelic men," whose personal poverty, chastity, and perfect obedience faithfully reflected the virtues of heaven itself. But monasteries also had an important influence on patterns of piety outside the cloister. For centuries, monasteries had been the repositories and guardians of the relics of departed saints, whose powers were believed to protect the monasteries that housed their earthly bodies. From the tenth century on, however, monasteries increasingly attracted the attentions of pious laypeople, who came seeking miraculous cures from the saint (or saints) whose relics were housed there. The vast majority of such pilgrimages were to local shrines. But regular long-distance pilgrimage routes also began to develop, to such places as Santiago de Compostela in Spain and the Church of Saint Faith in southern France. Traffic also increased to such traditional pilgrimage sites as Rome and Jerusalem. Pilgrimage was one of the important ways in which the new patterns of Christian piety developed in monasteries began to spread to the laity outside the monastic walls.

THE PAPAL REFORM MOVEMENT

From the monasteries, the reform movement began to affect the bishops also. In England, kings appointed a number of reformed monks to bishoprics. In Germany, kings retained nonmonastic bishops but enforced strict requirements of personal holiness on the bishops and abbots whom they appointed to office. With royal encouragement, bishops also began to rebuild and expand their cathedral churches to make them more suitable reflections of divine majesty, in accordance with Cluniac example. The Cluniacs themselves, however, went further, and began to lobby for the reform of the entire church, including bishops, unreformed monasteries, and even the parish clergy. They centered their attacks on simony, but they also demanded that personal poverty and celibacy be enforced on all monks and priests. This last demand was in some ways the most radical. Although a series of fourth- and fifth-century church councils had declared that priests should be celibate, this requirement had been largely ignored thereafter. In the year 1000, the vast majority of the parish priests across Europe were married. Married bishops were rarer, but not unknown. In Brittany, the archbishop of Dol and his wife publicly celebrated the marriage of their daughters, endowing them with lands belonging to the bishopric; in Milan, the archbishops flatly rejected reformers' calls for celibacy, declaring

CHRONOLOGY

REFORM OF THE CHURCH, 900–1215

Monastic reform	900–1050
Cluniac priories	910–1050
Papal reform movement	1049–1122
Pope Leo IX	1049–1054
Pope Gregory VII	1073–1085
Investiture Conflict	1075–1122
Concordat of Worms	1122
Consolidation of the papal monarchy	1100–1216
Concord of Discordant Canons	1140
Reign of Innocent III	1198–1216
Fourth Lateran Council	1215

A MIRACLE OF SAINT FAITH

Although pilgrimages and relics cults had been a part of Christian religious practice for centuries, they became much more central elements in popular piety from the tenth century on. To the monasteries that housed miracle-working relics, pilgrims brought money and spiritual prestige, resulting in competition between monastic houses that sometimes led one house to steal the relics of another. But some critics worried that these newly popular pilgrimage shrines were encouraging idolatry. The author of this account, Bernard of Angers, was one such critic; but in this case he was quickly won over by the evidence of Saint Faith's miracles.

The relics of Saint Faith, a fourth-century martyr, were stolen by the monks of Conques (in southern France) during the ninth century and became famous during the tenth century for their miraculous healing powers. They were housed in the reliquary shown in the accompanying illustration. Bernard's description of his visit to her shrine is a very revealing account of the initially negative impression this ornate reliquary made on him.

It is an ancient custom in all of Auvergne, Rodez, Toulouse and the neighboring regions that the local saint has a statue of gold, silver, or some other metal . . . [that] serves as a reliquary for the head of the saint or for a part of his body. The learned might see in this a superstition and a vestige of the cult of demons, and I myself . . . had the same impression the first time I saw the statue of Saint Gerard . . . resplendent with gold and stones, with an expression so human that the simple people . . . pretend that it winks at pilgrims whose prayers it answers. I admit to my shame that turning to my friend Bernerius and laughing I whispered to him in Latin, "What do you think of the idol? Wouldn't Jupiter or Mars be happy with it?" . . .

Three days later we arrived at St. Faith. . . . We approached [the reliquary] but the crowd was such that we could not prostrate ourselves like so many others already lying on the floor. Unhappy, I remained standing, fixing my view on the image and murmuring this prayer, "St. Faith, you whose relics rest in this sham, come to my assistance on the day of judgment." And this time I looked at my companion . . . because I found it outrageous that all of these rational beings should be praying to a mute and inanimate object. . . .

Later I greatly regretted to have acted so stupidly toward the saint of God. This was because among other miracles Don Adalgerius, at that time dean and later . . . abbot [of Conques] told me a remarkable account of a cleric named Oldaric. One day when the venerable image had to be taken to another place, . . . he restrained the crowd from bringing offerings and he insulted and belittled the image of the saint. . . . The next night, a lady of imposing severity appeared to him: "You," she said, "how dare you insult my image?" Having said this, she flogged her enemy with a staff. . . . He survived only long enough to tell the vision in the morning.

Thus there is no place left for arguing whether the effigy of St. Faith ought to be venerated since it is clear that he who reproached the holy martyr nevertheless retracted his reproach. Nor is it a spurious idol where nefarious rites of sacrifice or of divination are conducted, but rather a pious memorial of a holy virgin, before which great numbers of faithful people decently and eloquently implore her efficacious intercession for their sins.

Bernard of Angers, "The Book of the Miracles of St. Faith," in Patrick J. Geary, ed. and trans., *Readings in Medieval History*, 3d ed. (Peterborough, Ont., Canada, 2003), pp. 333–334 (slightly modified).

QUESTIONS FOR ANALYSIS

1. Why were medieval Europeans well prepared to embrace a cult of relics? Is there any parallel in the modern age? What did medieval men and women hope to obtain from the veneration of relics?
2. What does the belief in the miraculous healing power of relics illustrate about medieval popular piety in general?

that their patron saint, Bishop Ambrose of Milan, had been married and that he had granted his diocese permission to have a married priesthood forever.

In Rome, the papacy remained resolutely unreformed until 1046, when the German emperor Henry III came to Rome, deposed all three of the local Roman nobles who claimed to be pope and appointed in their place his own relative, a German monastic reformer who took the name Pope Leo IX (1049–1054). Leo and his supporters (mostly German, but some Italian)

The Reliquary of Saint Faith, Early Tenth Century.

quickly took control of the papal court and began to promulgate decrees against simony, clerical marriage, and immorality of all sorts throughout the church. To enforce these decrees, Leo and his entourage traveled through France, Italy, Germany, and Hungary, disciplining and deposing clerics who had purchased their positions or who refused to give up their wives (whom the reformers insisted on calling "concubines"). Implicit in Leo's reforming efforts was thus a new vision of the church itself as a hierarchical organization in which priests obeyed bishops and bishops obeyed the pope not only as the spiritual and doctrinal leader of western Christendom but also as the legal and jurisdictional ruler of the entire Christian church.

Leo and the reform popes were able to enforce their decrees only in those areas of Europe where they could count on the support of secular rulers. Among these secular supporters, the most important was of course the emperor Henry III, whose protection insulated the papal reformers from the Roman noble families who would otherwise have deposed them. In 1056, however, Henry III died, leaving a young child as his heir, the future Henry IV. Without their imperial protector, the reformers were now at the mercy of the Roman political factions. When the reigning reform pope died in 1058, the Roman nobles seized their opportunity to install as pope one of their own lackeys. Briefly, it looked as if the entire reform program might be lost. But the reformers rallied outside Rome, and elected their own pope (who took the name Nicholas II). Allying themselves militarily with the Norman rulers of central and southern Italy, they drove the nonreformed pope out of Rome.

In 1059, Pope Nicholas II issued a new decree on papal elections, vesting the right to elect a pope solely with the cardinals, but "saving the rights of the Emperor." The decree is significant for two quite different reasons. First, it represents a milestone in the evolution of the College of Cardinals as a special body within the church. Ever since the tenth century a number of bishops and clerics drawn from churches in and near Rome had taken on an important role as advisers and administrative assistants of the popes. This decree was the first time, however, that the cardinals' powers had been clearly recognized. Thereafter the College of Cardinals took on an increasingly well-defined identity, becoming an important force in creating continuity of papal policy, especially when there was a quick succession of pontiffs. The cardinals still elect the pope today.

The decree was also significant, however, because it opened up a breach between the reform party in Rome and the German imperial court. In the circumstances of 1059, the Electoral Decree was intended to justify the reformers' actions of the previous year and to protect future papal elections from the influence of the Roman aristocracy. But although the decree obviously drew on Cluniac ideals about free elections as an essential element in a reformed church, it was not intended to deprive the German emperor of his traditional role as papal protector. The simple fact was, however, that in 1059 there was no emperor who could play this role; and if the alternative was the return of the Roman nobility and the destruction of the entire reform effort, then even an alliance with the brutal and unreliable Normans seemed preferable. Nonetheless, the Electoral Decree greatly offended the advisers of the young king Henry IV, who saw it as a challenge to the emperors' rights to nominate new popes and who also bitterly resented the reformers' alliance with the Normans, whose designs on imperial territories in central Italy were well known. The resulting hostility between the young king's regents and the papal court poisoned the atmosphere in which King Henry IV grew to maturity.

> Superficially, the issue that divided Gregory and Henry was whether Henry or any other layman could appoint a bishop or abbot and then dress him with the symbols of his spiritual office, a practice known as "lay investiture."

THE INVESTITURE CONFLICT

A new and momentous phase in the history of the reform movement began in 1073 with the election of Pope Gregory VII (1073–1085). Gregory was a Roman whose election was violently supported by a mob of Roman citizens. Gregory was already a well-known reformer with long experience at the papal court. It is likely that he would have been elected by the cardinals anyway, even without the interference of the Roman mob. But the circumstances of his election clearly violated the terms of the 1059 Electoral Decree, and this fact weakened Gregory in his first few years as pope. Henry IV was also anxious for a reconciliation with Rome, not least because between 1073 and 1075 he was involved in a major civil war with his own nobility in Saxony. Both Gregory and Henry began, therefore, by treating one another with great deference. Henry blamed the advisers of his youth for the troubles that had arisen between his own court and Rome and promised to make amends. Gregory, in turn, spoke of pope and emperor as the two eyes of a single, Christian body and promised to leave the church in Henry's care if he, Gregory, should lead (as he briefly hoped to

do) a military expedition eastward against Islam. On the surface, it appeared that the harmonious relations between papacy and empire that had existed under Henry's father had been fully restored.

By the end of 1075, however, relations between the two men were at a breaking point. For the next half century, western Europe would be riven by conflict between the papacy and the empire—a conflict that would permanently alter the relationship between spiritual and temporal authority in western Christendom. Superficially, the issue that divided Gregory and Henry was whether Henry or any other layman could appoint a bishop or abbot and then dress him with the symbols of his spiritual office, a practice known as "lay investiture." In fact, however, the Investiture Conflict raised fundamental issues about the nature of Christian kingship, the relationship between political and religious authority, and the control that popes and kings should exercise over the clergy. Not all these issues were fully resolved by 1122, when a compromise known as the Concordat of Worms (*vuhrms*) finally ended the Investiture Conflict. But the conflict was a turning point nonetheless, because it brought to a permanent end the old Carolingian traditions of sacred kingship and established once and for all the independent jurisdictional authority of the church versus all lay rulers.

Gregory was a devoted church reformer whose goals were the traditional ones of ending simony and clerical marriage. Unlike previous papal reformers, however, Gregory became convinced that these goals could not be achieved until the Cluniac goal of ensuring free elections to all church offices had first been realized. Gregory therefore proceeded to prohibit all clerics from accepting any church office from a layman, declaring this prohibition to be "a truth . . . necessary for salvation." Henry IV flatly refused to accept this decree, not only because it infringed on his own traditional rights as a Carolingian-style king and emperor but also because the bishops and abbots of Germany and northern Italy were critically important to his own ability to rule his kingdoms. Henry proceeded, therefore, to appoint and invest a new archbishop in Milan in defiance of Gregory's prohibition. Gregory responded by reminding Henry that he, Gregory, occupied Saint Peter's chair, and that Henry therefore owed to Gregory the same obedience he owed to Saint Peter, who was the gatekeeper to heaven. To drive the point home, Gregory excommunicated a number of Henry's advisers, including several of the north Italian bishops who had participated in the investiture of the new archbishop of Milan. Henry thereupon renounced his obedience to Gregory, reminding the pope that his election had violated the terms of the 1059 Electoral Decree and calling on him to resign. Gregory responded by excommunicating Henry, along with a large number of German and Italian bishops who were supporting Henry.

In itself, the excommunication of a king was not terribly unusual. Gregory, however, went much further by equating excommunication with deposition, declaring that since Henry was no longer a faithful son of the church, he was therefore no longer the king of Germany. Gregory now called on Henry's subjects to rebel, prompting the Saxon nobility to renew the civil war that had ended only a few months before. In January 1077, Henry was forced to make a humiliating public submission to Pope Gregory at Canossa in the Italian Alps; but when the pope absolved him of his

excommunication, Henry used the opportunity to rally his forces, crush his Saxon opponents, and drive Gregory himself from Rome (see Chapter 8). In 1085, the aged pope died in exile at Salerno, a virtual prisoner of his Norman allies. His last words were reportedly, "I have loved justice and hated iniquity; that is why I die in exile."

By instinct, Pope Gregory was a radical whose confidence in his own rectitude knew no bounds. Early in his career he had been part of the delegation that provoked the 1054 schism with the Byzantine church by demanding that the patriarch of Constantinople acknowledge the primacy of the papacy. As pope, Gregory was convinced that he spoke with Saint Peter's voice and so could not err. When told that his ideas were novel, he replied "The Lord did not say 'I am custom'; the Lord said 'I am truth.'" When it was suggested to him that his policies had brought war, not peace, he replied by citing Scripture: "Cursed be he that shall withhold his sword from blood." His calls for the people of Germany to rise up against their errant king and his sinful bishops were nothing short of revolutionary. Even his admirers referred to him as a Holy Satan, recalling the rebellious angel whose pride had caused his downfall.

Gregory's radical instincts must not obscure, however, his profoundly traditional vision of Christendom. Although the ultimate solution to the Investiture Conflict was to distinguish between "church" and "state" by reserving the symbols of spiritual office to the clergy while permitting laymen to award the symbols of temporal rule, such a distinction was no part of Gregory's own worldview. Indeed, it was precisely because neither Henry nor Gregory could conceive of Christendom as anything other than a thoroughly unified religious and political society that the conflict between them was so intractable. Both Henry and Gregory shared the standard Carolingian presumption that it was the responsibility of earthly rulers to lead their subjects to heaven. They disagreed only about whether the supreme ruler within this unified Christian society should be the emperor or the pope. Neither could imagine a world in which a bishop's

Henry IV and Gregory VII. In the top panel, King Henry appoints Wibert, Archbishop of Milan, to be the new pope, and drives Pope Gregory from Rome. In the lower panel, Pope Gregory is received by the bishops of the Norman kingdom of southern Italy, and then dies in exile. From a twelfth-century German manuscript.

KINGSHIP AS A RELIGIOUS OFFICE: TWO VIEWS

The Investiture Conflict raised fundamental issues concerning the nature of royal authority and the proper relationship between kingship and the church. In a remarkable outpouring of tracts and pamphlets, Europeans continued to debate these questions from a wide variety of perspectives, even after the conflict itself had come to an end. Writing in the early twelfth century, the Anglo-Norman Anonymous presented kings as religious figures who should rule the church as partners with Christ and the bishops. Writing in the 1130s, after the Concordat of Worms, Hugh of Saint Victor sought to distinguish earthly from heavenly power by assigning kings to rule over bodies and the clergy to rule over souls.

THE ANGLO-NORMAN ANONYMOUS

By divine authority and by institution of the holy fathers, kings are ordained in the church of God and are consecrated at the altar with sacred unction and benediction, that they may have the power of ruling the people of the Lord, the Christian people, which is the holy church of God. . . . Therefore kings receive in their consecration the power to rule this church, that they may rule it and strengthen it in judgment and justice and administer it in accordance with the discipline of Christian law; for they reign in the church, which is the kingdom of God, and reign together with Christ, in order that they may rule, protect and defend it. . . . The episcopal order too is instituted and consecrated with sacred unction and benediction, that it also may rule the holy church according to the form of doctrine given to it by God. . . . In this world, then, the priestly authority and the royal power hold the power of sacred government.

Some seek to divide the power in this fashion, saying that the priesthood has the power of ruling souls, the king that of ruling bodies, as if souls could be ruled without bodies and bodies without souls, which cannot be done by any means. For if bodies are well ruled it is necessary that souls are well ruled too and vice versa, since both are ruled for this purpose, that at the resurrection they may both be saved together. . . . Therefore the king is not to be called a layman, for he is the anointed of the Lord, a God through grace, the supreme ruler, supreme shepherd, master, defender and instructor of holy church, lord over his brothers, worthy to be adored by all men, chief and highest prelate. It is not to be said that he is inferior to the bishop because the bishop consecrates him, for it often happens that lesser men consecrate a greater, inferiors their superior, as when the cardinals consecrate a pope.

HUGH OF SAINT VICTOR

There are two lives, one earthly, the other heavenly, one corporeal, the other spiritual. By one the body lives from the soul, by the other the soul lives from God. Each has its own good by which it is invigorated and nourished. . . . Therefore, in each people distributed according to each life, powers were established. Among laymen, to whose zeal and forethought the things that are necessary for earthly life pertain, the power is earthly. Among the clergy, to whose office the goods of the spiritual life belong, the power is divine. The one power is therefore called secular, the other spiritual. . . . The earthly power has as its head the king. The spiritual power has as its head the supreme pontiff. All things that are earthly and made for the earthly life belong to the power of the king. All things that are spiritual and attributed to the spiritual life belong to the power of the supreme pontiff. The spiritual power excels the earthly or secular power in honor and dignity in proportion as the spiritual life is more worthy than the earthly, and the spirit more worthy than the body. For the spiritual power has to institute the earthly power that it may exist, and to judge it if it has not been good. The spiritual power itself was instituted by God in the first place and, when it errs, can be judged by God alone.

Brian Tierny, ed., *The Crisis of Church and State, 1050–1300* (Toronto, 1988), pp. 76–77, 94–95 (slightly revised by R. C. Stacey).

QUESTIONS FOR ANALYSIS

1. How might the comments of the Anglo-Norman Anonymous be used to bolster later medieval arguments of kings who claimed to rule by divine right?
2. Why did Hugh of Saint Victor seek to differentiate religious and secular power?

spiritual office could be separated from the lands and military forces he controlled or in which there could be two entirely separate systems of courts, one dealing with religious matters and controlled by the papacy, the other dealing with secular matters and controlled by kings. Without such a division between the spiritual and the temporal, however, the Investiture Conflict was irresolvable. Neither pope nor emperor was powerful enough to defeat the other; and on some level, all Europe was agreed that both spiritual and temporal authorities were necessary.

The consequences of the Investiture Conflict were thus quite different from what Pope Gregory or King Henry had imagined. On the immediate issue of lay investiture, the Concordat of Worms was a compromise. The German emperor was forbidden to invest prelates with the religious symbols of their office but was allowed to invest them with the symbols of their rights as temporal rulers because the emperor was recognized as their temporal overlord. In practice, the German emperors, like the other kings of western Europe, thus managed to retain a great deal of influence over appointments to bishoprics and abbeys despite allowing the appearance of free elections.

The ultimate consequence of the Investiture Conflict was to create a lasting conceptual distinction between religion and politics in western Europe and to identify the church with religious authority and the state with political authority. Both ideas had been largely absent from western Europe since the fourth-century Constantinian revolution. When the Investiture Conflict began, Henry's principal supporters were his bishops. Gregory's supporters were, for the most part, the Saxon nobility and the other disaffected German princes. In no sense,

therefore, did the Investiture Conflict begin as a "church–state" conflict. By 1122, however, that is what it had become. The Concordat of Worms resolved the papal–imperial conflict by distinguishing between the temporal power of kings and the spiritual power of the clergy. It also firmly identified the bishops as a part of a hierarchical clerical order headed by the pope. The boundaries between temporal and spiritual authority would continue to be subject to controversy in medieval Europe. Should kings or clerics judge clergy who committed secular crimes? Who should rule on the validity of marriages when rights to inherit property were at issue? But these were jurisdictional conflicts that sought to define the boundaries between religion and politics. These conflicts did not challenge the fundamental presumption that such a distinction existed. Therefore, these conflicts were resolvable through law—one reason that the elaboration of legal systems, both ecclesiastical and secular, became such a preoccupation for twelfth- and thirteenth-century western Europe. In this respect also, the Investiture Conflict marks a watershed in European history.

> The Concordat of Worms resolved the papal–imperial conflict by distinguishing between the temporal power of kings and the spiritual power of the clergy. It also firmly identified the bishops as a part of a hierarchical clerical order headed by the pope.

THE CONSOLIDATION OF THE PAPAL MONARCHY

The Concordat of Worms was a compromise, but the Investiture Conflict as a whole was a victory for the papacy. The conflict helped rally the western clergy behind the pope, strengthening the papacy's claim to jurisdictional supremacy over the entire clerical hierarchy. The dramatic struggle also galvanized the European populace.

As one contemporary reported, nothing else was talked about "even in the women's spinning rooms and the artisans' workshops." Pope Gregory and his successors had urged the common people of Europe to reject the authority of simoniac bishops and married priests. Thousands had responded, sometimes with violence. The result was a vastly greater popular interest in religious matters, which the church thereafter would struggle to contain within the bounds of religious orthodoxy.

Like Gregory VII, the popes of the twelfth and thirteenth century were fully committed to establishing the monarchical authority of the papacy over the church. But they were far less impetuous than Gregory had been, choosing instead to pursue their aims by carefully building up the governmental apparatus of the church. Specially commissioned papal officials ("legates") were sent out from Rome to convey and enforce papal commands. Many of these commands arose from the hundreds (and eventually thousands) of legal cases that poured into Rome from litigants seeking justice from the pope. In turn, this growing mass of litigation encouraged the development of an authoritative body of church law by which such cases could be resolved. The key step in this development was taken around 1140 in Bologna by a law teacher named Gratian, whose massive compilation and codification of the decrees of previous popes and church councils (known as the *Decretum* or, more descriptively, as *The Concord of Discordant Canons*) quickly became the standard collection of church, or "canon," law.

Gratian's *Decretum* claimed ecclesiastical jurisdiction for all sorts of cases pertaining not only to the clergy but also to the laity, including such matters as marriage, inheritance, and wills. Although all such cases were supposed to be heard first in local church courts, the popes insisted that they alone could issue dispensations from the strict letter of the law and that the papacy should be the final court of appeals for all canon-law cases. As the power of the papacy and the prestige of the church mounted, cases in canon-law courts and appeals to Rome rapidly increased. By the mid-twelfth century legal expertise had become so important that almost all popes were trained canon lawyers, whereas previously they had usually been monks. Purists decried this development, but it was an inevitable consequence of the growing power and sophistication of the papal monarchy itself.

THE REIGN OF INNOCENT III

By common consent the most capable and successful of all the high medieval popes was Innocent III (1198–1216). Innocent, who was elected at the age of thirty-seven, was one of the youngest and most vigorous individuals ever to be raised to the papacy; more than that, he was expertly trained in theology and had also studied canon law. His major goal was to unify all Christendom under papal hegemony and thereby to bring about the "right order in the world" so fervently desired by Pope Gregory VII. Unlike Gregory, Innocent never questioned the right of kings and princes to rule directly in the secular sphere. But Innocent believed nonetheless that as pope he was obliged to discipline kings whenever they sinned. And he was no less insistent than Gregory VII had been on the obligation of every Christian to obey Saint Peter's representative. As Innocent himself remarked, just "as every knee is bowed to Jesus . . . so all men should obey His Vicar [i.e., the pope]."

To place papal independence on a solid territorial foundation, Innocent consolidated and expanded the papacy's territories in central Italy. For this reason Innocent is often regarded as the founder of the Papal States, of which Vatican City is the last surviving modern remnant.

Innocent sought to implement his goals in many different ways. To place papal independence on a solid territorial foundation, Innocent consolidated and expanded the papacy's territories in central Italy. For this reason Innocent is often regarded as the founder of the Papal States, of which Vatican City is the last surviving modern remnant. In Germany, he engineered the triumph of his own candidate for the imperial office, the emperor Frederick II—a triumph his papal successors would live to regret. Innocent disciplined the French king Philip Augustus for his marital misconduct and forced King John of England to accept Stephen Langton, the pope's own choice, as archbishop of Canterbury. Innocent also compelled John to grant England to the papacy as a fief; and he claimed, with varying degrees of success, a comparable feudal overlordship of Aragon, Sicily, and Hungary. When southern France was threatened by the spread of the Albigensian heresy (to be discussed later), the pope called a crusade to extinguish it by force. He also levied the first income tax on the clergy to support a crusade to the Holy Land.

The crowning achievement of Innocent's pontificate was the summoning of the Fourth Lateran Council to Rome in 1215. This representative assembly of the entire western church defined central dogmas of the faith and made the leadership of the papacy within Christen-

Pope Innocent III. A thirteenth-century fresco from the lower church of Sacro Speco, Subiaco, in Italy.

dom more apparent than ever. The pope was now clearly both disciplining kings and ruling over the church without hindrance.

POPES OF THE THIRTEENTH CENTURY

Innocent's reign was certainly the zenith of the papal monarchy, but it also sowed some of the seeds of future ruin. Innocent himself could administer the Papal States and seek new sources of income without seeming to compromise the spiritual dignity of his office. But future popes who followed his policies had less of his stature and thus began to appear more like ordinary, acquisitive rulers. Moreover, because the Papal States bordered on the kingdom of Sicily, Innocent's successors quickly came into conflict with the neighboring ruler, who was none other than Innocent's protégé Frederick II. Innocent had raised up Frederick, but he could not imagine that Frederick would later become an inveterate opponent of papal power in Italy.

At first these and other problems were not fully apparent. The popes of the thirteenth century continued to enhance their powers and centralize the government of the church. They gradually acquired the right to name candidates for ecclesiastical positions, both high and low, and they asserted control over the curriculum and doctrine taught at the University of Paris. But they also became involved in a protracted political struggle that led to their own demise as temporal powers. This struggle began with the attempt of the popes to destroy Frederick II. To some degree they were acting in self-defense because Frederick threatened their own rule in central Italy. But in combating him they overemployed their spiritual weapons. Instead of merely excommunicating and deposing Frederick, they also called a crusade against him—the first time a crusade was called on a large scale for blatantly political purposes.

After Frederick's death in 1250 a succession of popes made a still worse mistake by renewing and maintaining their crusade against the emperor's heirs, whom they

A GOLIARDIC PARODY OF THE GOSPEL OF MARK, SATIRIZING THE PAPAL COURT

This selection is typical of the parodies of the liturgy and the Bible written by the freewheeling Latin poets of the twelfth century. This particular poem is written in mock biblical verse, and puns on the Christian Gospel of Mark—a mark being a sum of money equal to two thirds of a pound of silver. Like all parodies, it was meant to be humorous, but its accusations—that bribery around the papal court perverted justice—were widespread in twelfth- and thirteenth-century Europe.

Here beginneth the Holy Gospel according to the marks of silver. In those days the Holy Father said unto the Romans: "When the Son of Man shall come unto the seat of our Majesty, first say unto Him: 'Friend, why art Thou come?' but if he continue knocking and give you nothing, then cast Him forth into outer darkness."

And it came to pass that a certain poor priest came to the court of the Lord Pope and cried out, saying, "Do ye at least have pity on me, servants of the Pope, for the hand of poverty hath afflicted me. Verily I am poor and have nothing. I beseech you, therefore, have mercy upon me and pity me." They, however, hearing this were sorely wroth and said unto him, "Friend, may thy poverty go with thee to hell. Get thee behind us, Satan; thou savorest not of money. Amen, Amen we say to thee: thou shalt not enter into the blessings of thy Lord until thou hast given thy last penny."

The poor man went therefore and sold his cloak and his coat and all that he had, and gave unto the cardinals and the treasurers and the papal flunkies. But they said unto him, "And this, what is this among so many?" And they cast him out utterly, and going forth he wept bitterly and would not be comforted.

After this there came to the court a rich priest, exceedingly wealthy, anointed with grease and great with wealth, who had committed murder for the sake of gain.

He first gave unto the treasurer, then he gave unto the flunky, and then he gave unto the cardinals. But they reasoned among themselves, thinking they would receive more. Therefore when the Lord Pope heard that the cardinals and his servants had received many gifts from a priest he was sick, even unto death. But the rich man sent unto him a pallet of gold and silver, and immediately he was made whole.

The Lord Pope called unto him the cardinals and ministers and spake unto them saying: "Beware, brethren, lest any deceive you with vain words. For I have given you an example, so that as I have grasped, so should you grasp also."

Carmina Burana, 21, in *The Wandering Scholars*, 7th ed. trans. Helen Waddell (London, 1934), pp. 150–151 (revised by John E. Boswell).

QUESTIONS FOR ANALYSIS

1. How seriously do you think medieval men and women considered the parodies of the Goliards? For what purpose did the Goliards choose parody over other forms of literature?
2. Do you think that the Goliards were a disruptive force in medieval society? Do they have any modern parallels?

called the "viper brood." To implement this crusade they became preoccupied with raising funds, and they sought and won as their military champion a younger son from the French royal house, Charles of Anjou. But Charles helped the popes only for the purely political motive of acquiring the kingdom of Sicily for himself. Charles won Sicily in 1268 by defeating the last of Frederick II's male heirs. But he then taxed the realm so excessively that the Sicilians revolted in 1282 and offered their crown to the king of Aragon, who had married Frederick II's granddaughter. The king of Aragon accordingly entered the Italian arena and came close to winning Frederick's former kingdom for himself. To prevent such an event, Charles of Anjou and the reigning pope prevailed on the king of France—then Philip III (1270–1285)—to embark on a crusade against Aragon. This crusade was a terrible failure, and Philip III died on it. In the wake of these events Philip's son, Philip IV, resolved to alter the traditional French pro-papal policy. By that time France had become so strong that such a decision was fateful. More than that, by misusing the institution of the crusade and trying to raise increasingly large sums of money to support it, the popes lost much of their spiritual prestige. In 1291 the last crusader outpost in the Holy Land fell without any papal help being offered. Instead, the popes were still trying to salvage their losing crusade against Aragon. Pope Boniface VIII's papal jubilee of 1300, which offered a full crusader's indulgence to anyone who made a pilgrimage to Rome, was a tacit recognition that Rome, not Jerusalem, would henceforth be the central goal of Christian pilgrimage.

DECLINE OF THE PAPAL MONARCHY

The temporal might of the papal monarchy finally collapsed in the reign of Boniface VIII (1294–1303). Not all Boniface's troubles were of his own making. His greatest obstacle was that the national monarchies had gained more of their subjects' loyalties than the papacy could draw on because of the steady growth of royal power and the erosion of papal prestige. Boniface also had the misfortune to succeed a particularly pious, although inept, pope who resigned his office within a year. Since Boniface was entirely lacking in conventional piety or humility, the contrast turned many Christian observers against him. Boniface ruled assertively and presided over the first papal jubilee in Rome in 1300. This was an apparent but, as events would show, hollow demonstration of papal might.

Two disputes with the kings of England and France proved to be Boniface's undoing. The first concerned the clerical taxation that had been initiated by Innocent III.

Although Innocent had levied this tax to support a crusade and had collected it himself, during the course of the thirteenth century the kings of England and France had begun to levy and collect clerical taxes on the pretext that they would use the funds to help the popes on future crusades to the Holy Land or aid in papal crusades against the Hohenstaufens. Then, at the end of the century, the kings started to levy their own war taxes on the clergy without any pretexts at all. Boniface understandably tried to prohibit this step but quickly found that he had lost the support of the English and French clergy. Thus when the kings offered resistance, he had to back down.

Boniface's second dispute was with King Philip IV of France, who deliberately challenged the pope by

Pope Boniface VIII (1294–1303). Boniface commissioned dozens of statues of himself, which were distributed throughout the Papal States. Despite its idealized features, this statue—from the Museo Civico in Bologna—does suggest something of the pope's pugnacious obstinacy.

preparing to try a French bishop for treason, in violation of canon-law protections for the clergy. As in the earlier struggle between Gregory VII and Henry IV of Germany, a bitter propaganda war ensued, but now hardly anyone listened to the pope. Instead, Philip pressed absurd charges of heresy against Boniface and sent his minions to arrest the pope to stand trial. At the papal residence of Anagni in 1303 Boniface, who was in his seventies, was captured and mistreated by Philip's forces. Although the pope was finally rescued by the local citizens, the shock of these events was too much for the old man's strength, and he died a month later. But still Philip pressed his advantage. He forced the new pope, Clement V, not only to justify his attack on Boniface but to thank him publically for his zealous defence of the Catholic faith. Thereafter, any shred of papal independence in regard to the interests of the French monarchy was gone. For the next seventy years, the popes would reside not in Rome, but in Avignon (ab-veb-NYON), on the borders of the kingdom of France; and the papacy would come to be regarded as a virtual pawn of French diplomatic interests.

The humiliating defeat of Pope Boniface VIII at the hands of King Philip of France illustrates the enormous gap that had opened up by 1300 between the rhetoric and the reality of papal power. Although Boniface continued to lay claim to a universal spiritual and temporal authority over Christendom, declaring that kings ruled only through the "will and sufferance" of the church, in fact the papal monarchy now exercised its authority only through the will and sufferance of kings. The growth of nationalism, combined with the increasing sophistication of royal justice, royal taxation, and royal propaganda, had shifted the balance of power in Europe decisively toward the state and away from the church. Europeans were not less religious than they had been before, quite the opposite. But from the later thirteenth century on, pious Christians would look increasingly toward the state, and not toward the papacy, to spearhead campaigns of moral and spiritual improvement within their territories. After 150 years during which the religious nature of royal authority had been steadily undermined, the kings of the later thirteenth century were beginning to restore their sacred luster. This trend would continue throughout the later Middle Ages. It would be shattered, finally, only in the seventeenth century, at the end of a century of religious wars brought on by the Protestant Reformation. Only then would the distinctions between religion and politics established by the Investiture Conflict be fully and firmly established as fundamental principles of European life.

THE OUTBURST OF RELIGIOUS VITALITY

How did the Latin Church control popular heresy?

The papal reform movement spearheaded by Pope Gregory stimulated a European religious revival for two reasons. One was that the campaign to cleanse the church actually achieved a large measure of success: the laity could now respect the clergy more, and many were inspired to join the clergy themselves. According to a reliable estimate, the number of people who joined monastic orders in England increased tenfold between 1066 and 1200, a statistic that does not include the increase in priests. The other reason that the work of Gregory VII in particular helped inspire a revival was that Gregory explicitly called on the laity to help discipline their priests. In letters of great propagandistic power he denounced the sins of "fornicating priests" (including married ones) and urged the laity to drive them from their pulpits or boycott their services. It is not surprising that he touched off something close to a vigilante movement in some parts of Europe. This excitement, taken together with the fact that the papal struggle with Henry IV was really the first European event of universal interest, increased religious commitment immensely. Until about 1050, most western Europeans were Christians in name, but after the Gregorian period Christianity was becoming an ideal and a practice that really began to direct human lives.

CISTERCIANS AND CARTHUSIANS

One of the most visible manifestations of the new piety was the spread of the Cistercian movement in the twelfth century. By around 1100 no form of Benedictine monasticism seemed fully satisfactory to aspirants to holiness who sought great asceticism and, above all, intense "interiority"—unrelenting self-examination and meditative striving toward knowledge of God. The result was the founding of new orders to provide for the fullest expression of monastic idealism. One was the Carthusian order, whose monks were required to live in separate cells, abstain from meat, and fast three days each week on bread, water, and salt. The Carthusians never sought to attract great numbers and therefore remained a small group. But the same was by no means

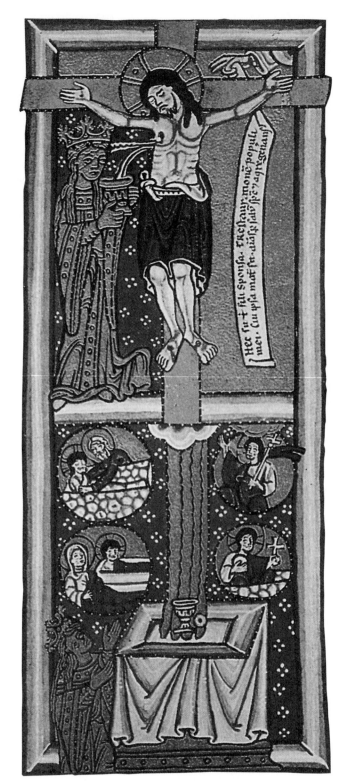

The Mystery of the Mass. In this illustration by the twelfth-century visionary Hildegard of Bingen, the church (shown as a crowned queen, and associated by Hildegard with the Virgin Mary, the queen of heaven) receives the blood of Christ in a communion chalice, while below, the bread and wine of the Mass, which have now become the body and blood of Christ, rest on the altar.

true of the Cistercians. The latter were monks who were first organized around 1100 and who sought to follow the Benedictine rule in the purest and most austere way possible. To avoid worldly temptations, they founded new monasteries in forests and wastelands as far away from civilization as possible. They shunned all unnecessary church decoration and ostentatious utensils, abandoned the Cluniac stress on an elaborate liturgy in favor of more contemplation and private prayer, and seriously committed themselves to hard manual labor. Under the charismatic leadership of Saint Bernard of Clairvaux (1090–1153), a spellbinding preacher, brilliant writer, and the most influential European religious personality of his age, the Cistercian order grew exponentially. There were only 5 houses in 1115 but no less than 343 by 1153. This growth not only meant that many more men were becoming monks but also that many pious lay people were donating funds and lands to support the new monasteries.

At the same time more people were entering or patronizing new monasteries, the nature of religious belief and devotion was also changing. One of many examples was a shift away from the cult of saints to emphasis on the worship of Jesus and veneration of the Virgin Mary. In the new Cistercian order, the veneration of saints' relics was replaced by a concentration on the Eucharist, or sacrament of the Lord's Supper. Of course celebration of the Eucharist had always been an important part of the Christian faith, but only in the twelfth century was it made really central, for only then did theologians fully work out the doctrine of transubstantiation. According to this doctrine, the priest during mass cooperates with God in the performance of a miracle whereby the bread and wine on the altar are changed, or transubstantiated, into the body and blood of Christ. Popular reverence for the Eucharist became so great in the twelfth century that for the first time the practice of elevating the consecrated bread, or host, was initiated so that the whole congregation could see it. The new theology of the Eucharist greatly enhanced the dignity of the priest and encouraged the faithful to meditate on the sufferings of Christ. As a result many developed an intense sense of identification with Christ and tried to imitate his life in different ways.

THE CULT OF THE VIRGIN MARY

Coming a very close second to the renewed worship of Christ in the twelfth century was veneration of the Virgin Mary. This development was more unprecedented because until then the Virgin Mary had been a relatively minor figure in the western church. Exactly why veneration of the Virgin Mary became so pronounced in the twelfth century is not fully clear; but whatever the explanation, in the twelfth century the cult of Mary blossomed throughout all of western Europe. The Cistercians made her their patron saint, Saint Bernard constantly taught about her life and virtues, and practically all the magnificent new cathedrals of the age were dedicated to her: there was Notre Dame ("Our Lady") of Paris, and also a Notre Dame in Chartres, Rheims, Amiens, Rouen, Laon, and many other places. Mary's theological role was that of intercessor with her son for the salvation of human souls. It was held that Mary was the mother of all, an infinite repository of mercy who urged the salvation even of sinners so long as they were loving and ultimately contrite. Numerous

stories circulated about seeming reprobates who were saved because they venerated Mary, who then spoke for them at the hour of death.

The significance of the new cult was manifold. For the first time a woman was given a central and honored place in western Christianity. Theologians still taught that sin had entered the world through Eve, the first woman; but they now counterbalanced this by explaining how the triumph over sin had come through Mary, who gave birth to Christ, the second Adam. Artists and writers who portrayed Mary were also able to concentrate on femininity and scenes of human tenderness and family life, contributing to a general softening of artistic and literary style. But perhaps most important of all, the rise of the cult of Mary was closely associated with a general rise of hopefulness and optimism in the twelfth-century west.

HILDEGARD OF BINGEN

Not only did a woman, Mary, gain a particularly prominent role in the religious cult of the twelfth century but a few living women gained great religious authority. By far the most famous and influential was the German nun and visionary Hildegard of Bingen (1098–1179). Hildegard's descriptions of her religious visions, dictated in freshly original Latin prose, were so compelling that contemporaries had no difficulty in believing that she was directly inspired by God. Consequently when the pope visited Germany he gave her his blessing, and religious and secular leaders sought her advice. Hildegard wrote on a variety of other subjects such as pharmacology and women's medicine. She also composed religious songs whose beauty has been rediscovered in recent times. Visionary though she was, she probably would be surprised to see people today looking for her works in racks of compact discs, where she is often alphabetized as "Bingen" between Beethoven and Brahms.

THE CHALLENGE OF POPULAR HERESY

Sometimes the great religious enthusiasm of the twelfth century went beyond the bounds approved by the church. After Gregory VII had called on the laity to help discipline their clergy it was difficult to control lay enthusiasm. As the twelfth century progressed and the papal monarchy concentrated on strengthening its legal and financial administration, some people began to wonder whether the church, which had once been so inspiring, had not begun to lose sight of its idealistic

Mary and Eve. The correct medieval theological view of women. From Adam's perspective, the naked Eve on his left (Latin: *sinister*) side, takes the apple of sin from the serpent and feeds it to erring mortals while a skeleton waits to carry them to hell. On Adam's right Mary counteracts Eve by feeding a different fruit—the Eucharistic wafer—to the devout.

goals. Another difficulty was that the growing emphasis on the miraculous powers of priests tended to inhibit the religious role of the laity and place it in a distinct position of spiritual inferiority. The result was that in the second half of the twelfth century large-scale movements of popular heresy swept over western Europe for the first time in its history.

The two major twelfth-century heresies were Catharism and Waldensianism. The Cathars, who were strongest in northern Italy and southern France, believed that all matter was created by an evil principle and that holiness required extreme ascetic practices. Some Cathars even argued that there were two gods, one good, the other evil; that the created world was entirely in the power of the evil god; and that spiritual people must seek to escape it. Although such teachings were at variance with Christianity, most Cathar followers believed themselves nonetheless to be Christians. Noblewomen in southern France played a particularly important role in the spread of Catharism, sheltering the sect's wandering preachers and converting their households to the new faith.

By the early fourteenth century, Catharism had been effectively destroyed, but small groups of Waldensians would survive until the seventeenth century, mainly in the mountainous regions of Switzerland and southern Germany.

More typical of twelfth-century religious dissent was Waldensianism, a movement that originated in the French city of Lyons and spread to much of southern France, northern Italy, and Germany. Waldensians were lay folk who wished to imitate the life of Christ and the apostles to the fullest. They therefore translated and studied the Gospels and dedicated themselves to lives of poverty and preaching. Since the earliest Waldensians did not attack any Catholic doctrines, the church hierarchy did not at first interfere with them. Indeed, the Waldensians may have seen themselves initially as a countermovement to Catharism. But the papacy forbade the Waldensians to preach without authorization and condemned them for heresy when they refused to obey. At that point they became more radical and started to create an alternative church, which they maintained offered the only route to salvation.

When Innocent III became pope in 1198 he was faced with a very serious challenge from growing heresies. His two-pronged response was characteristically decisive and fateful for the future of the church. On the one hand, Innocent resolved to crush all disobedience to papal authority, but on the other, he decided to support idealistic religious groups that were willing to accept the authority of the church. Papal monarchy could thus be protected without frustrating all dynamic spirituality within the church.

To suppress Catharism, Innocent authorized the nobles of northern France to launch a crusade against the southern French nobles who had permitted the heresy to flourish within their territories. The "Albigensian Crusade," as this expedition is known, quickly became a war of conquest that led to the dispossession of hundreds of southern landowners by northern invaders. But the crusade did succeed in destroying much of the organizational infrastructure that had supported Catharism. The papacy followed up this success by promoting inquisitorial procedures to root out the remaining heretics. From 1252 on, torture was permitted in such trials. Convicted heretics were sentenced to severe penalties; some were even burned at the stake. Similar procedures were also adopted against the Waldensians, but with less success. By the early fourteenth century, Catharism had been effectively destroyed, but small groups of Waldensians would survive until the seventeenth century, mainly in the mountainous regions of Switzerland and southern Germany.

Another aspect of Innocent's program was to pronounce new religious doctrines enhancing the special status of priests and the ecclesiastical hierarchy. Thus at the Fourth Lateran Council of 1215 he reaffirmed the doctrine that the sacraments administered by the church were the indispensable means of procuring God's grace and that no one could be saved without them. The decrees of the Lateran Council emphasized two sacraments: the Eucharist and penance. The doctrine of transubstantiation was formally defined. All Catholics were required—as they still are—to confess their sins to a priest and then receive the Eucharist at least once a year. The council also promulgated other doctrinal definitions and disciplinary measures that both opposed heresy and asserted the unique dignity of the clergy.

FRANCISCANS AND DOMINICANS

As stated earlier, the other side of Innocent's policy was to support obedient, idealistic movements within the church. The most important of these were the new orders of friars—the Dominicans and the Franciscans. Friars were similar to monks in vowing to follow a rule,

THE CONVERSION OF PETER WALDO

The founder of the Waldensian heresy was a layman, Peter Waldo, who was moved to take up a life of preaching and poverty after hearing the story of Saint Alexis, who had abandoned his family and his wealth to pursue a religious life. Waldo's story bears remarkable similarities to the story of Saint Francis of Assisi a generation or so later. But whereas Saint Francis succeeded in getting his movement recognized by the church, Waldo and his followers were ultimately declared heretical because they refused to accept the church's authority to prohibit them from preaching. Waldo's story illustrates the new spiritual impulses that were influencing laypeople in twelfth-century Europe.

At about this time, in 1173, there was a citizen of Lyons named Peter Waldo, who had made a great deal of money by the evil means of usury. One Sunday he lingered by a crowd that had gathered round a traveling story-teller, and was much struck by his words. He took him home with him, and listened carefully to his story of how St. Alexis had died a holy death in his father's house. Next morning Waldo hastened to the schools of theology to seek advice about his soul. When he had been told of the many ways of coming to God he asked the master whether any of them was more sure and reliable than the rest. The master quoted to him the words of the Lord, "If thou wilt be perfect go sell what thou hast and give it to the poor and thou shalt have treasure in heaven. And come follow me."

Waldo returned to his wife and gave her the choice between having all his movable wealth or his property in land. . . . She was very upset at having to do this and chose the property. From his movable wealth he returned what he had acquired wrongly, conferred a large portion on his two daughters, whom he placed in the order of Fontevrault without his wife's knowledge, and gave a still larger amount to the poor.

At this time a terrible famine was raging through Gaul and Germany. . . . [F]rom May 27 until August 1, Waldo generously distributed bread, soup and meat to anyone who came to him. On the Assumption of the Virgin [August 15] he scattered money among the poor in the streets saying, "You cannot serve two masters, God and Mammon." The people around thought he had gone out of his senses. Then he stood up on a piece of high ground and said, "Friends and fellow-

citizens, I am not mad as you think. . . . I know that many of you disapprove of my having acted so publicly. I have done so both for my own sake and for yours: for my sake, because anybody who sees me with money in future will be able to say that I am mad; for your sake, so that you may learn to place your hopes in God and not in wealth.". . .

1177   Waldo, the citizen of Lyons whom we have already mentioned, who had vowed to God that he would possess neither gold nor silver, and take no thought for the morrow, began to make converts to his opinions. Following his example they gave all they had to the poor, and willingly devoted themselves to poverty. Gradually, both in public and in private they began to inveigh against both their own sins and those of others. . . .

1178   Pope Alexander III held a council at the Lateran palace. . . . The council condemned heresy and all those who fostered and defended heretics. The pope embraced Waldo, and applauded the vows of voluntary poverty which he had taken, but forbade him and his companion to assume the office of preaching except at the request of the priests. They obeyed this instruction for a time, but later they disobeyed, and affronted many, bringing ruin on themselves.

Robert I. Moore, ed. and trans., *The Birth of Popular Heresy* (London, 1975), pp. 111–113 (slightly modified).

QUESTIONS FOR ANALYSIS

1. How does the conversion of Peter Waldo illustrate the kind of psychological tensions facing men and women in the High Middle Ages?

but they differed greatly from monks in their actual conduct. Above all, they did not withdraw from society into monasteries. Instead they imitated the life of Jesus and his apostles, wandering through town and countryside in small groups, preaching and offering spiritual guidance. They also accepted voluntary poverty and begged for their subsistence. In these respects they resembled the Waldensian heretics, but they professed unquestioning obedience to the pope and sought to fight heresy themselves.

The Dominican order, founded by the Spaniard Saint Dominic (1170–1221) and approved by Innocent III in 1216, was particularly dedicated to the fight against heresy and also to the conversion of Jews and Muslims. At first the Dominicans hoped to achieve these ends by preaching and public debate. Hence they became intellectually oriented. Many members of the order gained teaching positions in the infant European universities and contributed much to the development of philosophy and theology. The most influential thinker of the thirteenth century, Saint Thomas Aquinas, was a Dominican who addressed one of his major theological works to converting the "gentiles" (i.e., all non-Christians). The Dominicans always retained their reputation for learning, but they also came to believe that stubborn heretics were best controlled by legal procedures. Accordingly, they became the leading medieval administrators of inquisitorial trials.

In its origins the Franciscan order was quite different from the Dominican, being characterized less by a commitment to doctrine and discipline and more by a sense of emotional fervor. Whereas Saint Dominic and his earliest followers were ordained priests entitled to preach by their office, the founder of the Franciscans, the Italian Saint Francis of Assisi (1182–1226), was a layman who behaved at first remarkably like a social rebel and a heretic. The son of a rich merchant, he became dissatisfied with the materialistic values of his father and resolved to become a servant of the poor. Giving away all his property, he threw off his clothes in public, put on the tattered garb of a beggar, and began without official approval to preach salvation in town squares and to minister to outcasts in the darkest corners of Italian cities.

Saint Francis rigorously imitated the life of Christ and displayed indifference to doctrine, form, and ceremony, except for revering the sacrament of the Eucharist. But he did wish to gain the support of the pope. One day in 1209 he appeared in Rome with a ragged little band of followers to request that Innocent III approve a primitive rule, which was little more than a collection of Gospel precepts. Another pope might have rejected

the layman Francis as a hopelessly unworldly religious anarchist. But Francis was thoroughly willing to profess obedience, and Innocent had the genius to approve Francis's rule and grant him permission to preach. With papal support, the Franciscan order spread, and though it gradually became more civilized, conceding the importance of administrative stability and doctrinal training for all its members, it continued to engage in revivalistic outdoor preaching and to offer a model for "apostolic living" within an orthodox framework. Thus Innocent managed to harness a vital new force that would help maintain a sense of religious enthusiasm within the Church.

Until the end of the thirteenth century both the Franciscans and Dominicans worked closely together

The Earliest Known Portrait of Saint Francis. Dating from the year 1228, this fresco shows the saint without the stigmata, the wounds of Christ's crucifixion he was believed to have miraculously received toward the end of his life.

CHRONOLOGY

EUROPEAN RELIGIOUS REVIVAL, 1100–1300	
Cistercian order established	1098
Cult of the Virgin Mary begins	c. 1100
Catharist heresy emerges	c. 1140
Waldensian heresy emerges	c. 1180
New theology of the Eucharist	c. 1150–1215
Franciscan order established	1209
Fourth Lateran Council	1215
Dominican order established	1216

in Christian society. Fanciful stories of Jewish wealth added an economic element to the developing anti-Semitism of European society as did the fact that across much of thirteenth-century Europe, many Jews made their living as moneylenders.

Throughout the thirteenth century, the church had cooperated with kings in imposing more and more severe restrictions on Jewish life. Starting in the late 1280s, however, kings began to expel their Jewish subjects from their kingdoms altogether: in 1288 from southern Italy, in 1290 from England, and in 1306 from France. Further expulsions followed during the fourteenth century in the Rhineland, and in 1492 from Spain. By 1500, only Italy and Poland still retained any substantial Jewish populations, where they would survive until the Nazi Holocaust during World War II.

with the papal monarchy in a mutually supportive relationship. The popes helped the friars establish themselves throughout Europe and often allowed them to infringe on the duties of parish priests. On their side, the friars combated heresy, helped preach papal crusades, were active in missionary work, and otherwise undertook special missions for the popes. Above all, by the power of their example and by their vigorous preaching, the friars helped maintain religious intensity throughout the thirteenth century.

The success of the Franciscans and the Dominicans in combating the appeal of heretical movements was a great victory for the church, but this success was not sufficient to make the church feel secure in its hold on the people of Europe. Quite the opposite: despite its victories over the Cathars and the Waldensians, the church's inquisitorial processes ground on, discovering heretics even where none in fact existed.

JEWS AND CHRISTIANS

The church also became more and more concerned by the threat it believed that Jews posed to the faith of Christians, despite the fact that persecution and exploitative taxation had made most Jewish communities both smaller and weaker by 1300 than they had been in 1150. Although the church never officially endorsed the wilder flights of popular anti-Semitism, it did little to combat such attitudes either. As a result, by 1300 many ordinary Christians had come to believe that the Jews who lived among them were nothing less than agents of Satan, who routinely crucified Christian children, consumed Christian blood, and profaned the body of Christ in the Eucharist. The failures of organized campaigns to convert Jews to Christianity added to the sense among Christians that there was something demonic about the continuing Jewish presence

Burning of Jews. From a late medieval German manuscript. After the persecutions of the First Crusade, treatment of Jews in western Europe became worse and worse. These Jews were set on by the populace because they were suspected of poisoning wells.

HOW DID THE RECOVERY OF CLASSICAL LEARNING AFFECT MEDIEVAL INTELLECTUAL LIFE?

THE MEDIEVAL INTELLECTUAL REVIVAL   351

THE MEDIEVAL INTELLECTUAL REVIVAL

How did the recovery of classical learning affect medieval intellectual life?

The major intellectual accomplishments of the High Middle Ages were of four related but different sorts: the expansion of primary education and lay literacy, the origin and spread of universities, the acquisition of classical and Muslim knowledge, and the development of new philosophical and theological ideas. Any one of these accomplishments would have earned the High Middle Ages a signal place in the history of Western learning. Taken together, they mark the beginning of an extraordinary era in the intellectual history of Europe that would last until the scientific revolution of the seventeenth century.

THE GROWTH OF SCHOOLS

Around 800 Charlemagne ordered that primary schools be established in every bishopric and monastery in his realm. Although it is doubtful that this command was carried out to the letter, many schools were certainly founded during the Carolingian period. But their continued existence was later endangered by the Viking invasions. Primary education in some monasteries and cathedral towns managed to survive, but until around 1050 the educational opportunities in the European west were meager. Thereafter, however, even contemporaries were struck by the rapidity with which schools sprang up all over Europe. One French monk writing in 1115 stated that when he was growing up around 1075 there was "such a scarcity of teachers that there were almost none in the villages and hardly any in the cities" but that by his maturity there was "a great number of schools," and the study of grammar was "flourishing far and wide." The economic revival, the growth of towns, and the emergence of strong government allowed Europeans to dedicate themselves to basic education as never before.

The high medieval educational boom was more than merely a growth of schools, for the nature of the schools changed, and as time went on so did the curriculum and the clientele. The first basic mutation was

The economic revival, the growth of towns, and the emergence of strong government allowed Europeans to dedicate themselves to basic education as never before.

that monasteries in the twelfth century abandoned their practice of educating outsiders. Earlier, monasteries had taught a few privileged nonmonastic students how to read because there were no other schools for such pupils. But by the twelfth century sufficient alternatives existed. The main centers of European education now became the cathedral schools located in the growing towns. The papal monarchy energetically supported this development by ordering in 1179 that all cathedrals should set aside income for one schoolteacher, who could then instruct all who wished, rich or poor, without fee. The papacy believed correctly that this measure would enlarge the number of well-trained clerics and potential administrators.

At first the cathedral schools existed almost exclusively for the basic training of priests, with a curriculum designed to teach only such literacy as was necessary for performing the basic services of the church. But soon after 1100 the curriculum was broadened as the growth of both ecclesiastical and secular governments created a growing demand for trained officials who had to know more than how to read a few prayers. A thorough knowledge of Latin grammar and composition began to be inculcated, based on the study of classical Roman authors such as Cicero and Virgil. Some schools also began to focus on the study of philosophy, particularly logic, once again relying on classical authors such as Aristotle and Porphyry. This new interest in classical literary and philosophical texts has led scholars to refer to this movement as the Renaissance of the Twelfth Century.

Until about 1200 the students in the urban schools remained predominantly clerical. Even those who hoped to become lawyers or administrators rather than priests usually found it advantageous to take church orders. But afterward more pupils who entered schools were not in the clergy and never intended to be. Some were children of the upper classes, who began to regard literacy as a badge of status. Others were future notaries (men who drew up official documents), estate officials, and merchants who needed some literacy and/or computational skills to advance their own careers. Customarily, the latter groups would not go to cathedral schools but to alternate ones that were more practically oriented. Such schools grew rapidly in the course of the thirteenth century and became completely independent of ecclesiastical control. Not only were their students recruited from the laity but their teachers were usually laymen as well. As time went on instruction ceased to be in Latin, as had hitherto been the case, and was offered in the European vernacular languages instead. But the schools continued to be restricted to males. Some laywomen did become highly educated, but they were taught at home by private tutors.

The rise of lay education was an enormously important development in western European history. As the church lost its monopoly over education, learning became more secular in its orientation and purposes. Laymen could pursue new, nonreligious lines of inquiry; gradually, European culture itself became more independent of religion and of the traditionalism associated with religion, than any other culture in the world. The growth of schools also led to an enormous growth of lay literacy. By 1340 roughly 40 percent of the Florentine population could read; by the later fifteenth century about 40 percent of English men were literate as well. When we consider that literacy around 1050 was almost entirely limited to the clergy and that the literate made up less than 1 percent of the population of western Europe, we can appreciate that an astonishing revolution had taken place. Without it, many of Europe's other accomplishments would have been inconceivable.

THE RISE OF UNIVERSITIES

The emergence of universities was part of the same high medieval educational boom. Originally, universities were institutions that offered instruction in advanced studies that could not be pursued in average cathedral schools: advanced liberal arts and the professional studies of law, medicine, and theology. The earliest Italian university was that of Bologna, an institution that took shape during the course of the twelfth century. Although liberal arts were taught at Bologna, the institution's greatest prominence from the time of its twelfth-century origins until the end of the Middle Ages was as Europe's leading center for the study of law. North of the Alps, the earliest and most prestigious university was that of Paris. The University of Paris started out as a cathedral school like many others, but in the twelfth century it began to become a recognized center of northern intellectual life. One reason for this was that scholars there found the necessary conditions of peace and stability provided by the increasingly strong French kingship; another was that food was plentiful because the area was rich in agricultural produce; third

was that the cathedral school of Paris in the first half of the twelfth century boasted the most charismatic and controversial teacher of the day, Peter Abelard (1079–1142). Abelard, whose intellectual accomplishments we will discuss later, attracted students from all over Europe in droves. According to an apocryphal story told at the time, he was such an exciting teacher that when he was forbidden to teach in French lands because of his controversial views, he climbed a tree and students flocked under it to hear him lecture; when he was then forbidden to teach from the air he started lecturing from a boat and students massed to hear him from the banks. As a result of his reputation, many other teachers settled in Paris and began to offer much more varied and advanced instruction than anything offered in other French cathedral schools. By 1200 the Paris school was evolving into a university that specialized in liberal arts and theology. Around that time Innocent III, who had studied in Paris himself, called the school "the oven that bakes the bread for the entire world."

It should be emphasized that the institution of the university was really a medieval invention. The term *university* originally meant a corporation or guild. All medieval universities were corporations, either of teachers or students, organized like other guilds to protect their interests and rights. But gradually the word *university* came to mean an educational institution with a school of liberal arts and one or more faculties in law, medicine, and theology. Bologna and Paris were established before 1200. During the thirteenth century such famous institutions as Oxford, Cambridge, Montpellier, Salamanca, and Naples were founded or granted formal recognition.

Every university in medieval Europe was patterned after one or the other of two different models. Throughout Italy, Spain, and southern France the standard was generally the University of Bologna, in which the students themselves constituted the corporation. They hired the teachers, paid their salaries, and fined or discharged them for neglect of duty or inefficient instruction. The universities of northern Europe were modeled after Paris, which was a guild not of students but of teachers. It included four faculties—arts, theology, law, and medicine—each headed by a dean. In the great majority of the northern universities arts and theology were the leading branches of study. Before the end of the thirteenth century separate colleges came to be established within the

> The term *university* originally meant a corporation or guild. All medieval universities were corporations, either of teachers or students, organized like other guilds to protect their interests and rights.

How did the Recovery of Classical Learning Affect Medieval Intellectual Life?

The Medieval Intellectual Revival   353

University of Paris. The original college was nothing more than an endowed home for poor students, but eventually the colleges became centers of instruction as well as residences. Although most of these types of colleges have disappeared from the Continent, the universities of Oxford and Cambridge still retain the pattern of federal organization copied from Paris. The colleges of which they are composed are semi-independent educational units.

Most of our modern degrees as well as our modern university organization derive from the medieval system, but actual courses of study have been greatly altered. No curriculum in the Middle Ages included history or anything like the modern social sciences. The medieval student was assumed to know Latin grammar thoroughly before entrance into a university—this he learned in the primary, or "grammar," schools. On admission—limited to males—he was required to spend about four years studying the basic liberal arts, which meant doing advanced work in Latin grammar and rhetoric and mastering the rules of logic. If he passed his examinations he received the preliminary degree of

bachelor of arts (the prototype of our B.A.). To ensure himself a place in professional life he then usually had to devote additional years to the pursuit of an advanced degree, such as master of arts (M.A.), or doctor of laws, medicine, or theology. This was accomplished by reading and commenting on standard ancient works, such as those of Euclid and especially Aristotle. The requirements for the doctor's degrees included more specialized training. Those for the doctorate in theology were particularly arduous: by the end of the Middle Ages the course for the doctorate in theology at the University of Paris had been extended to twelve or thirteen years after the roughly eight years taken for the M.A. Strictly speaking, doctor's degrees, including even that in medicine, conferred only the right to teach. But in practice university degrees of all grades were recognized as standards of attainment and became pathways to nonacademic careers.

Student life in medieval universities was often rowdy. Many students were very immature because it was customary to begin university studies between the ages of twelve and fifteen. Moreover, all university students

Two Medieval Conceptions of Elementary Education. On the left, an illumination from a fourteenth-century manuscript depicts a master of grammar who simultaneously points to the day's lesson and keeps order with a cudgel. Grammar school education is portrayed more gently on the right, a late medieval scene in which a woman personifying the alphabet leads a willing boy into a tower of learning wherein the stories ascend from grammar through logic and rhetoric to the heights of theology.

THE RISE OF THE MEDIEVAL UNIVERSITY

This map shows the distribution and dates of origin of the major universities of medieval Europe. Why were the twelfth- and thirteenth-century universities founded primarily in France, England, and northern Italy? Notice the number and geographical distribution of universities founded in the fourteenth and fifteenth centuries. How would you explain the pattern of these later foundations?

**CENTURY UNIVERSITY
WAS FOUNDED**

- ■ Twelfth century
- ■ Thirteenth century
- □ Fourteenth century
- ■ Fifteenth century
- — Boundaries c. 1500

How did the recovery of classical learning affect medieval intellectual life?

THE MEDIEVAL INTELLECTUAL REVIVAL   355

believed that they constituted an independent and privileged community, apart from that of the local townspeople. Because the latter tried to reap financial profits from the students and the students were naturally boisterous, riots and sometimes pitched battles were frequent between "town" and "gown." But actual study was very intense. Because the greatest emphasis was placed on the value of authority and also because books were prohibitively expensive (they were handwritten on parchment), there was an enormous amount of rote memorization. As students advanced in their disciplines they were also expected to develop their own skills in formal, public disputations. Advanced disputations could become extremely complex and abstract; sometimes they might last for days. The most important fact pertaining to medieval university students was that, after about 1250, there were so many of them. The University of Paris in the thirteenth century numbered about 7,000 students, and Oxford somewhere around 2,000 in any given year. This means that an appreciable proportion of male Europeans who were more than peasants or artisans were gaining at least some education at the higher levels.

THE RECOVERY OF CLASSICAL LEARNING

As the numbers of those educated at all levels vastly increased during the High Middle Ages, so did the quality of learning. This was owing first and foremost to the reacquisition of Greek knowledge and to the absorption of intellectual advances made by the Muslims. Since practically no western Europeans knew Greek or Arabic, works in those languages had to be transmitted by means of Latin translations. But there were very few of these before about 1140: of all the many works of Aristotle only a few logical treatises were available in Latin translations before the middle of the twelfth century. But suddenly an enormous burst of translating activity made almost all of ancient Greek and Arabic scientific knowledge accessible to western Europeans. This activity occurred in Spain and Sicily because Christians there lived in close proximity with Arabic speakers, or Jews who knew Latin and Arabic, either of whom could aid them in their tasks. The result was that by about 1260 almost the entire Aristotelian corpus that is known today was made available in Latin. So also were basic works of such important Greek scientific thinkers as Euclid, Galen, and Ptolemy.

Plato's works were still unknown in Europe, as were the works of the classical Greek poets and dramatists. For the most part, these remained the jealously guarded cultural preserve of Byzantium. But in addition to the thought of the Greeks, Western scholars also became familiar with the accomplishments of the major Islamic philosophers and scientists such as Avicenna and Averroës.

Having acquired the best of Greek and Arabic scientific and speculative thought, Europe was able to build on it and make its own advances. This progress came in different ways. In natural science, westerners could build without much difficulty on this new learning, because it seldom conflicted with the principles of Christianity. One of the most advanced thirteenth-century scientists was the Englishman Robert Grosseteste (GROHS-test; c. 1168–1253), who was so proficient at Greek that he translated all of Aristotle's *Ethics*. He also made very significant theoretical advances in mathematics, astronomy, and optics. He formulated a sophisticated scientific explanation of the rainbow, and he posited the use of lenses for magnification. Grosseteste's leading disciple was Roger Bacon (c. 1214–1294), who is today more famous than his teacher because he seems to have predicted automobiles and flying machines. Bacon in fact had no real interest in machinery, but he did follow up on Grosseteste's work in optics, discussing, for example, further properties of lenses, the rapid speed of light, and the nature of human vision. Grosseteste, Bacon, and some of their followers at the University of Oxford argued that natural knowledge was more certain when it was based on sensory evidence than when it rested on abstract reason. To this degree they can be seen as early forerunners of modern science. But the important qualification remains that they did not perform any real laboratory experiments.

SCHOLASTICISM

The story of the high medieval encounter between Greek and Arabic philosophy and Christian faith is basically the story of the emergence of scholasticism. This word can be, and has been, defined in many ways. In its root meaning *scholasticism* was simply the method of teaching and learning followed in the medieval schools. That meant that it was highly systematic and that it was highly respectful of authority. Yet scholasticism was not

> But suddenly an enormous burst of translating activity made almost all of ancient Greek and Arabic scientific knowledge accessible to western Europeans. This activity occurred in Spain and Sicily because Christians there lived in close proximity with Arabic speakers, or Jews who knew Latin and Arabic, either of whom could aid them in their tasks.

only a method of study: it was a worldview. As such, it taught that there was a fundamental compatibility between the knowledge humans can obtain naturally—that is, by experience or reason—and the teachings imparted by divine revelation. Since medieval scholars believed that the Greeks were the masters of natural knowledge and that all revelation was in the Bible, scholasticism consequently was the theory and practice of reconciling classical philosophy with Christian faith.

PETER ABELARD

One of the most important thinkers who paved the way for scholasticism without yet being fully a scholastic himself was the stormy Peter Abelard, who was active in and around Paris in the first half of the twelfth century. Probably the first western European who consciously sought to forge a career as an intellectual (rather than being merely a cleric who taught on the side or a schoolteacher who had no goal of adding to knowledge), Abelard was so adept at logic that even as a student he easily outshone the experts of his day who had the misfortune to be his teachers. Others might have been tactful about such superiority, but Abelard gloried in openly humiliating his elders in public debate, thereby making himself many enemies. To complicate matters, in 1118 he seduced a brilliant young woman, Heloise, who had been taking private lessons with him. When Heloise became pregnant, Abelard married her (against Heloise's own wishes), but the two decided to keep the marriage secret for the sake of his career. This, however, enraged Heloise's uncle because he thought that Abelard was planning to abandon Heloise; therefore, he took revenge for his family's honor by having Abelard castrated. Seeking refuge as a monk, Abelard soon witnessed his enemies engineer his first conviction for heresy. Still restless and cantankerous, he found no spiritual solace in monasticism and after quarreling and breaking with the monks of two different communities he returned to life in the world by setting himself up as a teacher in Paris from about 1132 to 1141. This was the peak of his career. But in 1141 he again was charged with heresy, now by the highly influential Saint Bernard, and condemned by a church council. Not long afterward the persecuted thinker abjured, and in 1142 he died in retirement.

Abelard told of many of these trials in a letter called *The Story of My Calamities,* one of the first autobiographical accounts written in the West since Saint Augustine's *Confessions.* On first reading, this work appears atypically modern because the author seems to defy the medieval Christian virtue of humility by constantly boasting

Abelard and Heloise. Famous for his colorful personality, Abelard was popular with students but also made many enemies. After getting Heloise, one of his students, pregnant, he was castrated by her uncle and fled to a monastery. Subsequently, he wrote his autobiographical work, *The Story of My Calamities.*

about himself. But Abelard did not write about his calamities in order to boast. Rather, his main intention was to moralize about how he had been justly punished for his lechery by the loss of those parts that had offended and for his intellectual pride by the burning of his writings after his first condemnation. Because Abelard urged intense self-examination and analysis of human motives in an ethical treatise programmatically titled *Know Thyself,* it seems wisest to conclude that he never intended to recommend egotism but rather was one of several prominent twelfth-century thinkers (ironically including his mortal enemy Saint Bernard) who sought to take stock of the human personality by means of personal introspection.

Abelard's greatest contributions to the development of scholasticism were made in his *Sic et Non* (Yes and No) and in a number of original theological works. In the *Sic et Non* Abelard prepared the way for the scholas-

How did the recovery of classical learning affect medieval intellectual life?

The Medieval Intellectual Revival   357

tic method by gathering a collection of statements from the church fathers that spoke for both sides of 150 theological questions. It was once thought that the brash Abelard did this to embarrass authority, but the contrary is true. What Abelard really hoped to do was begin a process of careful study whereby it could be shown that the Bible was infallible and that other authorities, despite any appearances to the contrary, really agreed with each other. Later scholastics would follow his method of studying theology by raising fundamental questions and arraying the answers that had been put forth in authoritative texts. Abelard did not propose any solutions of his own in the *Sic et Non,* but he did start to do this in his original theological writings. In these he proposed to treat theology like a science by studying it as comprehensively as possible and by applying to it the tools of logic, of which he was a master. He did not even shrink from applying logic to the mystery of the Trinity (see below), one of the excesses for which he was condemned. Peter Abelard was one of the first to try to harmonize religion with rationalism and was in this capacity a herald of the scholastic outlook.

> As a member of the Dominican order, Saint Thomas was committed to the principle that faith could be defended by reason.

The Triumph of Scholasticism

Immediately after Abelard's death two further developments prepared the way for mature scholasticism. One was the writing of the *Book of Sentences* between 1155 and 1157 by Abelard's student Peter Lombard. This raised all the most fundamental theological questions in rigorously consequential order, adduced answers from the Bible and Christian authorities on both sides of each question, and then proposed judgments on every case. By the thirteenth century Peter Lombard's work had become a standard text. Once formal schools of theology were established in the universities, all aspirants to the doctorate were required to study and comment on it; it is not surprising that theologians also followed its organizational procedures in their own writings. Thus the full scholastic method was born.

The other basic step in the development of scholasticism was the reacquisition of classical philosophy that occurred after about 1140. Abelard would probably have been glad to draw on the thought of the Greeks, but he could not because few Greek works were yet available in translation. Later theologians, however, could avail themselves fully of the Greeks' knowledge, above all, the works of Aristotle and his Arabic commentators. By around 1250 Aristotle's au-

thority in purely philosophical matters became so great that he was referred to simply as "the Philosopher." Scholastics of the mid-thirteenth century accordingly adhered to Peter Lombard's organizational method but considered Greek and Arabic philosophical authorities as well as purely Christian theological ones. In doing this they tried to construct systems of understanding that most fully harmonized the earlier separate realms of faith and natural knowledge.

The Writings of Saint Thomas Aquinas

By far the greatest accomplishments in this endeavor were made by Saint Thomas Aquinas (1225–1274), the leading scholastic theologian of the University of Paris. As a member of the Dominican order, Saint Thomas was committed to the principle that faith could be defended by reason. More important, he believed that natural knowledge and the study of the created universe were legitimate ways of approaching theological wisdom because "nature" complements "grace." By this he meant to say that because God created the natural world, he can be approached through its terms, even though ultimate certainty about the highest truths can be obtained only through the supernatural revelation of the Bible. Imbued with a deep confidence in the value of human reason and human experience, as well as in his own ability to harmonize Greek philosophy with Christian theology, Thomas was the most serene of saints. In a long career of teaching at the University of Paris and elsewhere he indulged in few controversies and worked quietly on his two great Summaries of theology: the *Summa Contra Gentiles* (Summary against Non-Christians) and the much larger *Summa Theologica* (Summary of Theology). In these he hoped to set the faith on the firmest of foundations.

Saint Thomas's vast Summaries are awesome for their rigorous orderliness and intellectual penetration. He admits in them that there are certain "mysteries of the faith," such as the doctrines of the Trinity and the Incarnation of God in Christ, that cannot be approached by the unaided human intellect; otherwise, he subjects all theological questions to philosophical inquiry. In this, Thomas relied heavily on the work of Aristotle, but he was by no means merely "Aristotle baptized." Instead, he fully subordinated Aristotelianism to basic Christian principles and thereby created his own original philosophical and theological system. Scholars disagree about how far this system

Saint Thomas Aquinas. Portrayed in this fourteenth-century Florentine wall painting, Saint Thomas Aquinas defended studying the natural world through reason as a legitimate way of approaching Christian theology. He outlined his ideas about human reason in the *Summa Contra Gentiles* and the *Summa Theologica*.

diverges from the earlier Christian thought of Saint Augustine, but there seems little doubt that Aquinas placed a higher value on human reason, on human life in this world and on the abilities of humans to participate in their own salvation. Not long after his death Thomas was canonized, for his intellectual accomplishments seemed like miracles. His influence lives on today insofar as he helped inspire confidence in rationalism and human experience. More directly, philosophy in the modern Roman Catholic Church is supposed to be taught according to the Thomistic method, doctrine, and principles.

> It is often thought that medieval thinkers were excessively conservative, but in fact the greatest thinkers of the High Middle Ages were astonishingly receptive to new ideas.

THE PINNACLE OF WESTERN MEDIEVAL THOUGHT

With the achievements of Saint Thomas Aquinas in the mid-thirteenth century, western medieval thought reached its pinnacle. Not coincidentally, other aspects of medieval civilization were reaching their pinnacles at the same time. France was enjoying its ripest period of

peace and prosperity under the rule of (Saint) Louis IX, the University of Paris was defining its basic organizational forms, and the greatest French Gothic cathedrals were being built. Some ardent admirers of medieval culture have fixed on these accomplishments to call the thirteenth the greatest of centuries. Such a judgment, of course, is a matter of taste, and many might respond that life was still too harsh and requirements for religious orthodoxy too restrictive to justify this extreme celebration of the lost past. Whatever our individual judgments, it seems wise to end this section by correcting some false impressions about medieval intellectual life.

It is often thought that medieval thinkers were excessively conservative, but in fact the greatest thinkers of the High Middle Ages were astonishingly receptive to new ideas. As committed Christians they could not allow doubts to be cast on the principles of their faith, but otherwise they were glad to incorporate whatever they could from the Greeks and Arabs. Considering that Aristotelian thought differed radically from any-

WHAT COMMON THEMES UNITE THE LITERATURE, ART, AND ARCHITECTURE OF THE HIGH MIDDLE AGES?

THE BLOSSOMING OF LITERATURE, ART, AND MUSIC   359

thing accepted earlier in its emphasis on rationalism and the fundamental goodness and purposefulness of nature, its rapid acceptance by the scholastics was a philosophical revolution. Another false impression is that scholastic thinkers were greatly constrained by authority. Certainly they revered authority more than we do today, but such scholastics as Saint Thomas did not regard the mere citation of texts—except biblical revelation concerning the mysteries of the faith—as being sufficient to clinch an argument. Rather, the authorities were brought forth to outline the possibilities, but reason and experience then demonstrated the truth. Finally, it is often believed that scholastic thinkers were "antihumanistic," but modern scholars are coming to the opposite conclusion. Scholastics unquestionably gave primacy to the soul over the body and to otherworldly salvation over life in the here and now. But they also exalted the dignity of human nature because they viewed it as a glorious divine creation and they believed in the possibility of a working alliance between themselves and God. Moreover, they had extraordinary faith in the powers of human reason—probably more than we do today.

THE BLOSSOMING OF LITERATURE, ART, AND MUSIC

What common themes unite the literature, art, and architecture of the High Middle Ages?

The literature of the High Middle Ages was varied, lively, and impressive. The revival of grammatical studies in the cathedral schools and universities led to the production of some excellent Latin poetry. The best examples were secular lyrics, especially those written in the twelfth century by a group of poets known as the Goliards. How these poets got their name is uncertain, but it possibly meant "followers of the devil." That would have been appropriate because the Goliards were riotous poets who wrote parodies of the liturgy and burlesques of the Gospels. Their lyrics celebrated the beauties of the changing seasons, the carefree life of the open road, the pleasures of drinking and sport, and especially the joys of love. The authors of these rollicking and satirical songs were mainly wandering students, although some were men of more advanced

years. The names of most are unknown. Their poetry is notable both for its robust vitality and for its clear rejection of Christian asceticism.

VERNACULAR LITERATURE

In addition to Latin, the vernacular languages of French, German, Spanish, and Italian became increasingly popular as media of literary expression. At first, most of the literature in the vernacular languages was written in the form of the heroic epic. Among the leading examples were the French *Song of Roland*, the Norse eddas and sagas, the German *Song of the Nibelungs*, and the Spanish *Poem of the Cid*. Most of these works were composed between 1050 and 1150, although some (such as the *Cid* and the Norse sagas) were not written down until the thirteenth century. These epics portrayed a virile but unpolished warrior society. Blood flowed freely; skulls were cleaved by battle-axes; and heroic warfare, honor, and loyalty were the major themes. If women were mentioned at all, they were subordinate to men. Brides were expected to die for their beloveds, but husbands were free to beat their wives. In one French epic a queen who tried to influence her husband met with a blow to the nose; even though blood flowed she replied, "Many thanks, when it pleases you, you may do it again." Although we find such passages repugnant, the best of the vernacular epics have great literary power despite their unrelentingly masculine focus.

TROUBADOUR POETRY AND COURTLY ROMANCES

In comparison to the epics, an enormous change in both subject matter and style was introduced in twelfth-century France by the troubadour poets and the writers of courtly romances. The origin of their inspiration is debated, but there can be no doubt that they initiated a movement of profound importance for all subsequent Western literature. Their style was far more finely wrought and sophisticated than that of the epic poets; and the most eloquent of their lyrics, which were meant to be sung to music, originated the theme of courtly love. The troubadours idealized women as marvelous beings who could grant intense spiritual and sensual gratification. But because the women they chose to love were usually the wives of powerful lords, they wrote more often of longing than of romantic fulfillment.

In addition to their love lyrics, the troubadours wrote several other kinds of short poems. Some were simply bawdy. In these, love is not mentioned at all, but the poet revels in thoughts of carnality, comparing, for example, riding his horse to riding his mistress. Other troubadour poems treat feats of arms or comment on contemporary political events; a few even meditate on matters of religion. But whatever the subject matter, the best troubadour poems were always clever and innovative. The literary tradition originated by the southern French troubadours was continued by the trouvères in northern France and by the minnesingers in Germany. Thereafter many of their innovations were developed by later lyric poets in all Western languages. Some of their poetic devices were consciously revived in the twentieth century by such literary modernists as Ezra Pound.

An equally important twelfth-century French innovation was the composition of longer narrative poems known as romances, so called because there were written in vernacular, Romance (i.e., deriving from Latin) languages. Romances told engaging stories; they often excelled in portraying character, and their subject matter was usually love and adventure. Some romances elaborated on classical Greek themes, but the most famous were Arthurian. These took their material from the legendary exploits of the British hero King Arthur and his knights. The first great writer of Arthurian romances was the northern Frenchman Chrétien de Troyes (kray-TYAN dub-TWAH), who was active between about 1165 and 1190. Chrétien did much to help create and shape the new form, and he also introduced innovations in subject matter and attitudes. Whereas the troubadours exalted extramarital love, Chrétien was the first to hold forth the ideal of romantic love within marriage. He also described not only the deeds but the thoughts and emotions of his characters.

A generation later, Chrétien's work was continued by the great German poets Wolfram von Eschenbach and Gottfried von Strassburg, perhaps the greatest writers in the German language before the eighteenth century. Wolfram's *Parzival*, a story of love and the search for the Holy Grail, is more subtle, complex, and greater in scope than any other high medieval literary work except Dante's *Divine Comedy*. Like Chrétien, Wolfram believed that true love could be fulfilled only in marriage; and in *Parzival*, for the first time in Western literature since the Greeks, one can see a full psychological development of the hero. Gottfried von Strassburg's *Tristan* is a more somber work that tells of the tragic, adulterous love between Tristan and Isolde. Indeed, it might almost be regarded as the prototype of modern tragic romanticism. Unlike the troubadours, he could see complete fulfillment of love only in death. *Parzival* and *Tristan* have become most famous today in the form of their operatic reconceptions by the nineteenth-century German composer Richard Wagner.

> Whereas the troubadours exalted extramarital love, Chrétien was the first to hold forth the ideal of romantic love within marriage. He also described not only the deeds but the thoughts and emotions of his characters.

Rabbit on the Hunt. Marginal illustrations in medieval manuscripts (this one dates from about 1340) often exhibit ironic humor.

WHAT COMMON THEMES UNITE THE LITERATURE, ART, AND ARCHITECTURE OF THE HIGH MIDDLE AGES?

THE BLOSSOMING OF LITERATURE, ART, AND MUSIC   361

Not all high medieval narratives were so elevated as the romances in either form or substance. A very different new narrative form was the *fabliau*, or verse fable. Although fabliaux derived from the moral animal tales of Aesop, they quickly evolved into short stories that were written less to edify or instruct than to amuse. Often they were very coarse, and sometimes they dealt with sexual relations in a broadly humorous and thoroughly unromantic manner. Many were also strongly anticlerical, making monks and priests the butts of their jokes. They are significant as expressions of growing worldliness and as the first manifestations of the robust realism that was later to be perfected by Boccaccio and Chaucer.

THE DIVINE COMEDY

In a class by itself as the greatest work of medieval literature is Dante Alighieri's *Divine Comedy*. Dante (1265–1321) was active during the early part of his career in the political affairs of his native city of Florence and remained throughout his life intensely connected to that city. Despite his engagement in politics and the fact that he was a layman, he managed to acquire an awesome mastery of the religious, philosophic, and literary knowledge of his time. He not only knew the Bible and the church fathers but—most unusual for a layman—he also absorbed the most recent scholastic theology. In addition, he was thoroughly familiar with Virgil, Cicero, Boethius, and numerous other classical writers and was fully conversant with the poems of the troubadours and the Italian poetry

of his own day. In 1301 he was expelled from Florence after a political upheaval and was forced to live the rest of his life in exile. The *Divine Comedy*, his major work, was written during this final period.

Dante's *Divine Comedy* is a monumental narrative in powerful rhyming Italian verse, which describes the poet's journey through hell, purgatory, and paradise. At the start Dante tells of finding himself in a "dark wood," his metaphor for a deep personal midlife crisis in which he had wandered away from his Christian faith. He is led out of this forest of despair by the Roman poet Virgil, who represents the heights of classical reason and philosophy. Virgil guides Dante on a trip through hell and purgatory; then Dante's deceased beloved, Beatrice, who symbolizes Christian wisdom and blessedness, takes over and guides him through paradise. In the course of this progress from hell to heaven Dante meets both historical personages and his own contemporaries, who explain why they met their several fates. As the poem progresses Dante grows in wisdom and understanding, until finally he returns with new confidence and certainty to his own lost Christian faith.

Every reader finds a different combination of wonder and satisfaction in Dante's magnificent work. Some—especially those who know Italian—marvel at the vigor and inventiveness of Dante's language and images. Others are awed by his subtle complexity and poetic symmetry; others by his array of learning; others by the vitality of his characters and individual stories; and still others by his soaring imagination. The historian finds

The Poet Dante Driven into Exile. On the left Dante is expelled from Florence; on the right he begins work on his great poem, the *Divine Comedy*. From a mid-fifteenth-century Florentine manuscript. (The nearly completed dome of Florence's cathedral can be seen at the far left.)

it particularly remarkable that Dante could sum up the best of medieval learning in such an artistically satisfying manner. Dante stressed the priority of salvation, but he viewed earth as existing for human benefit. He allowed humans free will to choose good and avoid evil and accepted Greek philosophy as authoritative in its own sphere; for example, he called Aristotle "the master of them that know." Above all, his sense of hope and his ultimate faith in humanity—remarkable for a defeated exile—most powerfully expresses the dominant mood of the High Middle Ages and makes Dante one of the two or three most stirringly affirmative writers who ever lived.

ART AND ARCHITECTURE

The closest architectural equivalents of the *Divine Comedy* are the great high medieval Gothic cathedrals, for they too have qualities of vast scope, balance of intricate detail with careful symmetry, soaring height, and affirmative religious grandeur. But before we approach the Gothic style, it is best to introduce it by means of its high medieval predecessor, the style of architecture known as the Romanesque. This style had its origins in the tenth century, but became fully formed in the eleventh and the first half of the twelfth centuries, when the religious reform movement sparked the building of many new monasteries and large churches. The Romanesque style aimed to manifest the majesty of God in stone by rigorously subordinating all architectural details to a uniform system. The essential features of the Romanesque style were the rounded arch, massive stone walls, enormous piers (support columns), small windows, and the predominance of horizontal lines. Together, these features gave Romanesque architecture a sense of stability and permanence. Interiors were plain, but sometimes relieved by mosaics or frescoes in bright colors and—a very important innovation for Christian art—the introduction of sculptural decoration, both within and without. For the first time, full-length human figures appeared on facades. These are usually grave and elongated far beyond natural dimensions, but they have much evocative power and represent the first manifestations of a revived interest in sculpting the human form.

In the course of the twelfth and thirteenth centuries the Romanesque style was supplanted throughout most

The essential features of the Romanesque style were the rounded arch, massive stone walls, enormous piers (support columns), small windows, and the predominance of horizontal lines.

of Europe by the Gothic. Although trained art historians can see how certain traits of the one style led to the development of the other, the appearance of the two styles is distinctively different. In fact, the two seem as different as the epic is different from the romance, an appropriate analogy because the Gothic style emerged in France in the mid-twelfth century exactly when the romance did and because it was far more sophisticated, graceful, and elegant than its predecessor, in the same way that the romance compared with the epic.

Gothic architecture was one of the most intricate of building styles. Its basic elements were the pointed arch, groined and ribbed vaulting, and the flying buttress. These devices made possible a much lighter and loftier construction than could ever have been achieved with the round arch and the engaged pier of the Romanesque. In fact, the Gothic cathedral could be described as a skeletal framework of stone enclosed by enormous windows. Other features included lofty spires; rose windows; delicate tracery in stone; elaborately sculpted facades; multiple columns; and the more frequent use of gargoyles, or representations of mythical monsters, as decorative devices. Ornamentation was generally concentrated on the exterior. But the inside of the Gothic cathedral was never somber or gloomy. The stained-glass windows served not to exclude the light but to glorify it, to catch the rays of sunlight and suffuse them with a richness and warmth of color that nature itself could hardly duplicate even in its happiest moods.

Many people still think of the Gothic cathedral as the expression of purely ascetic otherworldliness, but this estimation is highly inaccurate. Certainly all churches are dedicated to the glory of God and hope for life everlasting, but Gothic ones sometimes included stained-glass scenes of daily life that had no overt religious significance at all. More important, Gothic sculptures of religious figures such as Jesus, the Virgin Mary, and the saints were becoming far more naturalistic than anything hitherto created in the medieval West. So too was the sculptural representation of plant and animal life, which rose to extraordinary levels of botanical and zoological accuracy. Moreover, Gothic architecture was also an expression of the medieval intellectual genius. Each cathedral, with its many symbolic figures, was a kind of encyclopedia of medieval knowledge carved in stone. Finally, Gothic cathedrals were manifestations of urban pride. Always

WHAT COMMON THEMES UNITE THE LITERATURE, ART, AND ARCHITECTURE OF THE HIGH MIDDLE AGES?

THE BLOSSOMING OF LITERATURE, ART, AND MUSIC   363

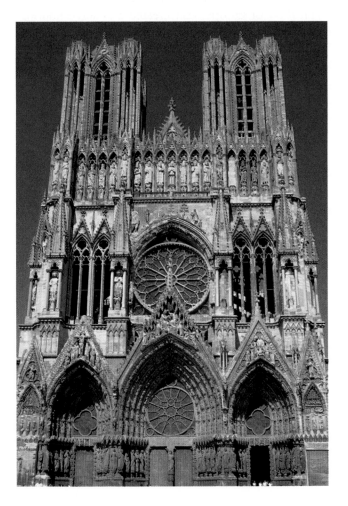

located in the growing medieval cities, they were meant to be both centers of community life and expressions of a town's greatness. When a new cathedral went up the people of the entire community participated in erecting it, and rightfully regarded it as almost their own property.

DRAMA AND MUSIC

Surveys of high medieval accomplishments should not omit drama and music. Our own modern drama descends at least as much from the medieval form as from the classical one. Throughout the medieval period some Latin classical plays were known in manuscript but were never performed. Instead drama was born all over again within the church. In the early Middle Ages certain passages in the liturgy began to be acted out. Then, in the twelfth century, short religious plays in Latin began to be composed for performance inside churches. Rapidly thereafter, these Latin plays were supplemented or supplanted by ones in the vernacular so that the whole congregation could understand them. Around 1200, these started to be performed outside, in front of the church, so that they would not take time away from the services. As soon as that happened, drama entered the everyday world: nonreligious stories were introduced, character portrayal was expanded, and the way was prepared for the Elizabethans and Shakespeare.

Just as drama developed within the liturgy and then moved beyond it, so too did music. Until the High Middle Ages Western music was homophonic—that is, it developed only one melody at a time without any harmonic background. The great high medieval invention was polyphony, the playing or singing of two or more harmonious melodies together. Some experiments along these lines may have begun as early as the tenth century, but the most fundamental breakthrough was achieved at the cathedral of Paris around 1170,

Romanesque and Gothic. Top: West front of the Church of Notre Dame la Grande, Poitiers. Constructed between 1135 and 1145, this typical example of Romanesque architecture emphasizes the repetition of rounded arches and horizontal lines. Bottom: Rheims Cathedral. Built between 1220 and 1299, this High Gothic cathedral places great stress on vertical elements. The gabled portals, pointed arches, and multitude of pinnacles all accentuate the height of this structure.

when the Mass was first sung by two voices weaving together two different melodies in counterpoint. Roughly concurrently, systems of musical notation were also invented. Because performers no longer had to rely on memory, music could become more complex. All the greatness of European music followed from these first steps.

CONCLUSION

For almost 100 years, scholars have spoken of the sweeping intellectual, religious, and cultural changes of the High Middle Ages as constituting the Renaissance of the Twelfth Century. This categorization still seems apt. Like those of the more famous Italian Renaissance of the fourteenth and fifteenth centuries, the intellectual changes of the High Middle Ages were profoundly influenced by the recovery and intensive study of classical texts. But in both periods, the use made of these classical texts was distinctive and unique. Neither of these movements were mere revivals; rather both were creative adaptations of classical ideas to a new and distinctively Christian culture.

Even more so than the Italian Renaissance, however, the twelfth-century renaissance marks the origin of a set of distinctive attitudes and ideas that have characterized western European civilization ever since. Our modern conceptions of love and friendship; our fascination with human motivation and intention; indeed, our very interest in psychology itself, all derive from twelfth-century developments. So too does our emphasis on the essential interiority of Christian piety, our vision that true religion ought to be expressed in practical works of charity in the world, and our presumption that religion and politics are separable spheres of human endeavor and concern. Even our modern impulse to define and persecute minority groups has roots in twelfth- and thirteenth-century efforts to suppress Jews, heretics, and sexual minorities.

Many of the people who made such important contributions to learning, thought, literature, architecture, drama, and music must have intermingled with each other in the Paris of the High Middle Ages. Some of them no doubt prayed together in the cathedral of Notre Dame. The names of the leading scholars are remembered, but the names of most of the others are unknown. Yet taken together they did as much for the civilization of Europe, and created as many enduring monuments, as did their counterparts in ancient Athens. Their names may be forgotten, but their achievements live on still.

KEY TERMS

Cluny

Investiture Conflict

cult of the Virgin Mary

Franciscan order

Dominican order

Peter Abelard

Saint Thomas Aquinas

courtly love

Divine Comedy

Gothic style

SELECTED READINGS

Baldwin, John W. *The Scholastic Culture of the Middle Ages: 1000–1300.* Lexington, Mass., 1971. A fine introduction.

Blumenthal, Uta-Renate. *The Investiture Controversy.* Philadelphia, 1988. A clear review of a complicated subject.

Boswell, John E. *Christianity, Social Tolerance, and Homosexuality: Gay People in Western Europe from the Beginning of the Christian Era to the Fourteenth Century.* Chicago, 1980. A pioneering account, particularly good on twelfth-century poetry.

Chrétien de Troyes. *Arthurian Romances.* Trans. W. W. Kibler. New York, 1991.

Clanchy, Michael T. *Abelard: A Medieval Life.* Oxford and Cambridge, Mass., 1997. A great biography.

Cobban, Alan B. *The Medieval Universities.* London, 1975. The best short treatment in English.

Colish, Marcia. *Medieval Foundations of the Western Intellectual Tradition, 400–1400.* New Haven, Conn., 1997. An encyclopedic and exhaustive work, best used as a reference.

Dante Alighieri. *The Divine Comedy*. Trans. Mark Musa. 3 vols. Baltimore, Md., 1984–1986.

Dronke, Peter. *Women Writers of the Middle Ages*. New York, 1984. A rich literary study.

Gottfried von Strassburg. *Tristan*. Trans. A. T. Hatto. Baltimore, Md., 1960.

Knowles, David. *The Evolution of Medieval Thought*, 2d ed. London, 1988. An authoritative survey, thoroughly revised in the second edition.

Lambert, Malcolm. *Medieval Heresy*, 3d ed. Oxford and Cambridge, 2002. The standard synthesis; deeply learned and fully annotated.

Lawrence, Clifford Hugh. *The Friars: The Impact of the Early Mendicant Movement on Western Society*. London and New York, 1994. The best short introduction to the early history of the Franciscans and the Dominicans.

Lawrence, Clifford Hugh. *Medieval Monasticism: Forms of Religious Life in Western Europe in the Middle Ages*, 3d ed. London and New York, 2000. This edition includes material on the friars drawn from his 1994 book.

Leclerq, Jean. *Bernard of Clairvaux and the Cistercian Spirit*. Kalamazoo, Mich., 1976. An empathetic account by the greatest twentieth-century scholar of Cistercianism.

Leclerq, Jean. *The Love of Learning and the Desire for God*, 3d ed. New York, 1982. A beautiful account of twelfth-century monastic culture, seen from the perspective of Saint Bernard of Clairvaux.

The Letters of Abelard and Heloise. Trans. Betty Radice. London and New York, 1974. Includes Abelard's autobiographical *Story of My Misfortunes*.

Miller, Maureen C. *Power and the Holy in the Age of the Investiture Conflict. A Brief History with Documents*. Boston, 2005. A stimulating approach to the eleventh-century conflicts over temporal and spiritual power, with many newly translated sources.

Morris, Colin. *The Papal Monarchy: The Western Church from 1050 to 1250*. Oxford, 1989. An excellent scholarly survey; part of the Oxford History of the Christian Church series.

Newman, Barbara, ed. *Voice of the Living Light: Hildegard of Bingen and Her World*. Berkeley, Calif., and Los Angeles, 1998. The best introduction to Hildegard's life and work; discusses her roles as abbess, religious thinker, prophet, correspondent, artist, medical writer, composer, dramatist, and poet.

Sheingorn, Pamela, trans. *The Book of Sainte Foy*. Philadelphia, 1995.

Smalley, Beryl. *The Study of the Bible in the Middle Ages*, 3d ed. Oxford, 1983. The standard work, gracefully written yet immensely learned.

Southern, Richard W. *Scholastic Humanism and the Unification of Europe. Vol. 1: Foundations*. Oxford and Cambridge, Mass., 1995. A major reinterpretation of scholasticism and humanism by the foremost historian of both traditions.

Southern, Richard W. *Western Society and the Church in the Middle Ages*. Baltimore, Md., 1970. An insightful interpretation of the interplay between society and religion by one of the greatest historians of the twentieth century.

Swanson, R. N. *The Twelfth-Century Renaissance*. Manchester, UK, 1999. The most accessible and up-to-date survey of the intellectual developments of the twelfth century.

Tierney, Brian. *The Crisis of Church and State, 1050–1300*. Toronto, 1988. An indispensable collection for both teachers and students.

Wakefield, Walter, and Austin P. Evans, eds. and trans. *Heresies of the High Middle Ages*. New York, 1969, 1991. A comprehensive collection of sources, best used in conjunction with Lambert.

Wilhelm, James J., ed. and trans. *Medieval Song: An Anthology of Hymns and Lyrics*. New York, 1971. An excellent collection of sacred and secular poetry that illustrates the connections between them.

Wolfram von Eschenbach. *Parzival*. Trans. H. M. Mustard and C. E. Passage. New York, 1961.

PART IV

FROM MEDIEVAL TO MODERN

FOR MOST OF THE TWENTIETH CENTURY, historians portrayed the Italian Renaissance and the Protestant Reformation as marking a dramatic break in European history, which brought the Middle Ages to an end and ushered in the modern world. To be sure, the sixteenth and seventeenth centuries saw decisive transformations in European life. For the first time, European sailors, soldiers, and merchants forged worldwide trading networks that brought the mineral and agricultural riches of the Western Hemisphere into their Atlantic ports. The Protestant Reformation shattered the religious unity of Europe, and a century of religious wars served only to cement those divisions. Meanwhile, new trends in cultural and intellectual life, many of which had begun in fourteenth- and fifteenth-century Italy, began to spread widely throughout the rest of Europe.

It is increasingly clear, however, that most of the new developments of the sixteenth and seventeenth centuries had deep roots in the later Middle Ages. The voyages that took sixteenth-century Europeans around the globe began in the thirteenth century with the conquest of the "Atlantic Mediterranean." The intensive study of classical Roman and Greek literature that characterized the Italian Renaissance developed out of the classical revival in the twelfth and thirteenth centuries. Even the theological doctrines of the Protestant reformers had roots in the theological controversies of the later Middle Ages. And all these developments took place in the context of continuing cultural and economic exchange between Europe, the Islamic world, and Byzantium.

	POLITICS	SOCIETY AND CULTURE	ECONOMY	INTERNATIONAL RELATIONS
1200	Chingiz (Genghis) Khan rules over Mongol clans (1206–1227)		Silk Road connects Europe with India, China, and Indonesia (1200s) Polo brothers travel to China (1200s)	Mongols conquer southern Russia (1237–1240) Mongols annihilate Hungarian army at River Sajo (1241) Mongol forces withdraw from Europe (1241)
1300	Yuan dynasty in China (1279–1368) Rise of Ottoman Dynasty (1300) Babylonian Captivity of the church (1305–1378)	Civic humanism begins in Italy (1300s) Francesco Petrarch (1304–1374) Giovanni Boccaccio (1313–1375)	Development of mechanical clocks and compasses (1300) Explorers reach Azores and Cape Verde Islands (1300s) Over a tenth of Europe dies during the Great Famine (1316–1322)	
		John Wyclif, Oxford theologian (1330–1384) Geoffrey Chaucer (1340–1400)	Heavy cannons first employed (1330) Silver shortage begins in Europe (1340s)	Hundred Years' War (1337–1453)
	Jacquerie rebellion in France (1358) Ming Dynasty in China (1368–1644) The Great Schism, ended by Council of Constance (1378–1417) Florentine Ciompi uprising (1378) English Peasants' Revolt (1381)	Leonardo Bruni (1370–1444) Jan van Eyck (1380–1441) University of Heidelberg founded (1385)	Onset of the Black Death, from which half of Europe dies (1347)	
			Medici family, originators of modern banking, flourishes (1397–1494)	Poland and Lithuania united (1386) Ottomans defeat Serbian empire at battle of Kosovo (1389)
1400	Italian territorial papacy (1417–1517)	Giovanni Aurispa returns with classical manuscripts (1423) Sandro Botticelli (1445–1510) Neoplatonism in Italy (1450–1600) Leonardo da Vinci (1452–1519)	Portugal establishes Atlantic colonies (1400–1460)	Rise of Grand Duchy of Moscow (1400s) Turks conquer Constantinople (1453) England loses Bordeaux (1453)
	Edward, duke of York dethrones Henry VI after War of the Roses (1461) Reign of Ivan III, the Great, tsar of all Russias (1462–1505) Ferdinand of Aragon marries Isabella of Castille, forming modern Spain (1469)	Desiderius Erasmus (1469–1536) Niccolò Machiavelli, author of *The Prince* (1469–1527) Albrecht Dürer (1471–1528) Sir Thomas More (1478–1535) Raphael (1483–1520)	Invention of movable type; the Gutenberg Bible (1454)	
			Explorers round the Cape of Good Hope (1487) Dias rounds southern tip of Africa (1488)	French monarchy absorbs Burgundy (1477)
		The High Renaissance begins (1490) The Catholic Reformation begins (1490)	Portugal founds slave-based plantation in St. Thomas (1490) Columbus lands in West Indies (1492) Disease kills much of Native American population (1492–1538) Vasco da Gama reaches India (1498)	Christian monarchs expel Jews (1492) and Muslims (1502) from Spain
1500		Roman Inquisition begins (1500) Saint Peter's Basilica erected in Rome (1500–1520) Papacy of Julius II (1503–1513) Saint Francis Xavier, missionary in Asia (1506–1552) Andrea Palladio (1508–1580) John Calvin (1509–1564)	Grain prices in Europe increase fivefold (1500–1650)	
	Reign of Charles V, Holy Roman emperor (1506–1556)			

FROM MEDIEVAL TO MODERN

POLITICS	SOCIETY AND CULTURE	ECONOMY	INTERNATIONAL RELATIONS	
	Papacy of Leo X, son of Lorenzo de Medici (1513–1521)			1513
	Luther posts Ninety-Five Theses (1517)	Portuguese ships reach Spice Islands and China (1515)		
	Emergence of Zwinglianism, Anabaptism, and Calvinism (1520–1550)		Cortes conquers Aztec Empire (1519–1522)	
	Edict of Worms (1521)		Ottomans conquer Syria, Egypt, and Hungary (1510–1540)	
	Peter Brueghel, painter of *Harvesters* and *Massacre of the Innocents* (1525–1569)			
	Baldassare Castiglione's *Book of the Courtier* (1528)		Charles V, Holy Roman emperor, sacks Rome (1527)	
	Michel de Montaigne (1533–1592)			
	Henry VIII becomes head of the Church of England (1533–1534)		Francisco Pizarro topples Incas (1533)	
	Calvin's *Institutes of the Christian Religion* (1536)			
	St. Ignatius Loyola publishes *Spiritual Exercises* (1541)	Rapid inflation marks the Price Revolution (1540s)		
	El Greco, painter of *View of Toledo* (1541–1614)	Silver found in Mexico and Bolivia (1543–1548)		
	Council of Trent (1545–1563)			
	Edmund Spenser, author of *The Faerie Queen* (1552–1599)		Peace of Augsburg (1555)	
Reign of Philip II of Spain (1556–1598)				
Reign of Elizabeth I of England (1558–1603)	First *Roman Index of Prohibited Books* established (1564)			
	William Shakespeare (1564–1616)			
	Papacy of Pius V (1566–1572)		Ottomans defeated by Habsburgs and Venetians at Lepanto (1571)	
	St. Bartholomew's Day massacre (1572)		Philip II annexes Portugal (1580)	
English navy defeats the Spanish Armada (1588)		New World silver production peaks at 10 million ounces per year (1590s)		
Reign of Henry IV, first of the Bourbon Dynasty in France (1589–1610)				
Edict of Nantes (1598)				
Reign of James I, first of the Stuart Dynasty (1603–1625)	John Milton (1608–1674)		Thirty Years' War (1618–1648)	1600
		Spanish economy collapses when silver imports drop (1620–1640)		
	Blaise Pascal (1623–1662)			
Cardinal Richelieu, first minister of France (1624–1642)				
Reign of Charles I of England (1625–1649)			Gustavus Adolphus of Sweden enters Thirty Years' War (1630)	
English Civil War (1642–1649)				
The Fronde, a series of French aristocratic revolts (1648–1653)			Peace of Westphalia (1648)	
Oliver Cromwell rules England (1649–1658)				
Louis XIV of France comes of age (1651)	Thomas Hobbes's *Leviathan* (1651)			
Charles II and the Restoration (1660–1685)				

CHAPTER TEN

THE LATER
MIDDLE AGES,
1300–1500

TEXTBOOK ACCOUNTS OF THE LATER MIDDLE AGES generally make for grim reading. The period is traditionally seen as one of disintegration and crisis, in which the high medieval world collapsed in chaos and violence, producing social and political upheaval, religious disillusionment, and widespread psychological anxiety. During these disastrous centuries, epidemic disease cut the European population in half, crops failed, and the economy shrank. The shortcomings of the church brought a storm of criticism, but few reforms in religious life resulted. Even the weather got worse. It is all enough to make the sensitive reader shudder, turn the page, and pass on to the sunnier atmosphere of the Italian Renaissance, the chapter that usually follows this late medieval litany of disaster, death, and decay.

There can be no doubt that the fourteenth and fifteenth centuries were indeed an age of adversity for Europeans. Famine and plague cut fearful swaths through the populace; war was a recurrent fact of life across most of the continent; the economy shrank; and the papacy spent seventy years in continuous exile from Italy, only to see its prestige decline even further after it returned to Rome. But to characterize these centuries as simply ones of doom and gloom would profoundly misrepresent the courage and resilience that the people of Europe displayed in the face of famine, war, and plague. It would also cause us to miss many of the fundamental transformations that shaped European society for the next 400 years. Despite the challenges it faced, European civilization did not collapse during the later Middle Ages. Instead, this was a period of creativity and innovation that preserved and extended the most enduring features of high medieval European life into the early modern era.

FOCUS QUESTIONS

• How did climate change affect early fourteenth-century Europe?

• What were the economic consequences of the Black Death on Europe?

• To what extent were the social changes of the later Middle Ages a consequence of the plague?

• Why was warfare such a constant feature of late medieval life?

• Why did Russia develop differently from other late medieval European states?

• Why did late medieval efforts to reform the institutions of the Catholic Church fail?

• Were late medieval people disillusioned with their church?

• What accounts for the remarkable creativity of late medieval cultural life?

• How did technological advances affect everyday life?

CHANGES IN THE LAND

How did climate change affect early fourteenth-century Europe?

By 1300, the high medieval expansion of the European economy was reaching its limits. Between 1000 and 1300, the European population tripled in size. To feed its growing numbers of people, Europe transformed itself into a continent of grain fields that stretched, almost unbroken, from Ireland to Poland and on into Ukraine. Even within the agricultural heartlands of western Europe, where wheat, barley, rye, and oats had been grown for centuries, the pressures to produce more grain brought dramatic changes to the landscape that undermined the long-term sustainability of European agriculture. Forests were cleared, marshes drained, and pastureland reduced, all to grow more grain. Expanding urban populations offered lucrative markets for European grain producers, and the increasing size of European ships made the transport of grain more efficient than it had ever been before. But still Europe was barely able to feed itself. By 1300, the continent was reaching the ecological and technological limits of its capacity to support its population.

Until the early fourteenth century, agricultural conditions generally favored the intensive cultivation of the cereal crops on which European civilization increasingly depended. During the twelfth and thirteenth centuries, a gradually warming climate lengthened the growing season in northern Europe, making it possible to grow grain even on thin or boggy soils better suited to pasturing animals or planting fruit trees. Starting in the Arctic at the end of the thirteenth century, however, this warming trend reversed itself, and from the middle of the fourteenth century, the mainland of Europe became progressively colder. This change was not cataclysmic —we are talking about a change of perhaps one to two degrees centigrade in average annual temperatures, spread across 500 years—but it was sufficient to cause substantial changes in rainfall patterns, to shorten growing seasons, and to lessen the productivity of cereal agriculture in northern Europe, especially in marginal areas such as Greenland, where European settlements disappeared entirely during the fifteenth century.

The vulnerability of the European economy to such long-term climate changes was dramatically revealed in 1315, when a great famine struck northern Europe that would last for seven years. Warfare contributed to the suffering, but the root causes of this great famine were climatic. For reasons we do not understand (but which may have to do with massive volcanic explosions in Indonesia darkening the atmosphere with ash), the winters in northern Europe between 1310 and 1330 were exceptionally harsh, and the summers unseasonably cold and wet. Then, starting in 1315, torrential spring and summer rains washed away sown fields, while the cold summer weather prevented the remaining crops from ripening. Europeans could generally ride out a

Peasants Harvesting Grain. Harvesting with sickles was backbreaking work, as this illustration of English serfs working under the direction of a reeve indicates. By the early fourteenth century, Europe had become a continent of grain fields.

WHAT WERE THE ECONOMIC CONSEQUENCES OF THE BLACK DEATH FOR EUROPE?

THE BLACK DEATH AND ITS CONSEQUENCES   373

year or two of such conditions with only modest loss of life. But between 1315 and 1322, these adverse weather conditions were nearly continuous. The result was starvation on a very large scale. Weakened by malnutrition, people and domestic animals also fell victim to epidemic diseases. By 1322, when conditions at last began to improve, 10 to 15 percent of the European population north of the Alps and the Loire had perished. Even after 1322, however, growing conditions did not return entirely to normal. Cold winters continued until 1330. In Italy, floods swept away the bridges of Florence in 1333, and in 1343 a tsunami destroyed the port of Amalfi. Earthquakes and comets added to the sense of alarm and uncertainty.

And then a disaster struck that was so horrifying it seemed to many to portend the end of the world.

THE BLACK DEATH AND ITS CONSEQUENCES

What were the economic consequences of the Black Death for Europe?

The *Black Death* is the name given since the sixteenth century to a deadly illness that spread from Mongolia to China, northern India, the Middle East, and the Crimea during the 1330s and 1340s. By 1346, the disease had reached the Black Sea. From there, in 1347, Genoese galleys brought it, inadvertently, to Sicily and northern Italy. From Italy the plague (as contemporaries called it, from the Latin word *plaga*, "a blow") spread throughout western Europe along the trade routes, first striking the seaports, then moving inland. It moved with astonishing rapidity, advancing about two miles per day during 1348 and 1349 in both summer and winter. By 1350, the plague had reached Scandinavia and northern Russia, from which it then spread southward until it linked up with the earlier waves of infection that had brought it from Central Asia to the Black Sea.

After this initial pandemic outbreak, the Black Death continued

to erupt in local epidemics for the next 300 years. Across most of fifteenth-century Europe, localities could expect a renewed outbreak of plague every decade. Gradually, however, the attacks of plague became less frequent and less deadly. The last European-wide plague outbreak occurred between 1661 and 1669, striking London in 1665 with particular severity. After 1720, however, the Black Death disappeared from western Europe, although it continued to afflict Poland and Russia until the end of the eighteenth century.

Mortality from the Black Death was on an almost unimaginable scale. At least a third, and probably half, the population of Europe died in the initial outbreak of 1347–1350. Thereafter, the population continued to decline. By 1450, the combined effects of plague, famine, and war had reduced the total population of Europe by at least 50 percent, and perhaps by as much as two thirds, from its high point around 1300. The European population did not fully recover to its pre-plague levels until the end of the seventeenth century.

This massive population decline also had dramatic effects on the landscape of Europe. In Germany alone, more than 40,000 villages attested before 1348 had disappeared by 1500. And even when villages survived, the fewer workers forced changes in agricultural practice. Around Paris, for example, more than half the farmland under plow in 1348 had been turned into pastureland by 1450. Elsewhere, abandoned fields and villages reverted to woodland, increasing the forested areas in parts of Europe by as much as one third over their pre-1348 levels. Better crop rotation systems and less intensive exploitation of marginal lands also helped restore the ecological balance of European agriculture in the aftermath of the plague.

Burying Plague Victims at Tournai, 1349. This contemporary illustration shows the dead being buried in wooden coffins. Despite the high mortality rates, survivors strove to bury their dead with dignity whenever possible.

Initial reactions to the Black Death ran the gamut from frenzied panic to supine resignation. Observers quickly realized that the plague was contagious, but how precisely it spread remained a mystery. At the time, most medical experts believed that the plague was spread through bad air and so urged people to flee from stricken areas (thus spreading the disease even faster) or to cover their noses with sweet-smelling

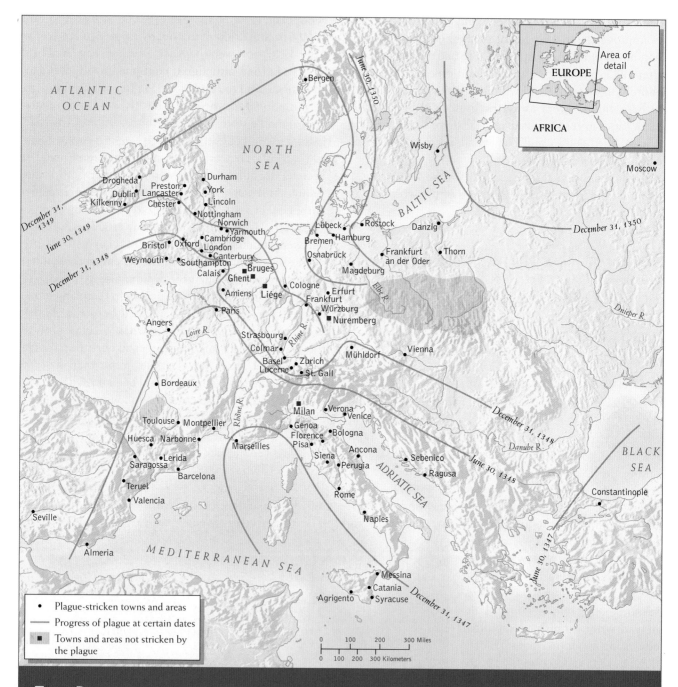

THE PROGRESS OF THE BLACK DEATH, FOURTEENTH CENTURY

Where did the Black Death come from, and where did it enter Europe, generally speaking? Why was the onslaught of the disease so devastating; and what agricultural, economic, and demographic factors helped make Europeans around 1350 so vulnerable to the disease? Note the rapid spread of the Black Death. Would such a rapid advance have been likely during the early Middle Ages or even in the ancient world? How did the growth of towns, trade, and travel contribute to the spread of the Black Death?

WHAT WERE THE ECONOMIC CONSEQUENCES OF THE BLACK DEATH FOR EUROPE?

THE BLACK DEATH AND ITS CONSEQUENCES   375

Plague Doctor Wearing Bird Beak Mask. Sweet-smelling herbs and flowers were placed in the masks' noses to counteract the bad air through which the plague was believed to travel.

flowers to counteract the miasma (as the "bad air" was known). Some people locked themselves in their houses, refusing to admit anyone until the threat had passed. Others did nothing, surrendering themselves to their fate; while still others (or so at least it was alleged by moralists) abandoned themselves to their desires, declaring, "Let us eat, drink, and be merry, for tomorrow we may die."

Others looked for scapegoats. When rumors began to circulate that Jews had caused the plague by poisoning the wells, scores of Jewish communities were attacked and thousands of their inhabitants massacred in the Rhineland, southern France, and Christian Spain. No such attacks on Jews are known from the Muslim areas of Spain or from elsewhere in the Muslim world, despite the fact that these areas suffered from the plague no less than did Christian Europe. Pope Clement VI (1342–1352) tried to halt these attacks, sending letters throughout Europe pointing out that Jews were dying from the plague in the same numbers as were Christians and ordering Christians to protect their Jewish neighbors from violence. But the letters did little good, and by the time they were received much of the damage had already been done.

A Procession of Flagellants, 1349. Participants scourge themselves with whips as they march in procession through Tournai. Their white clothing and black hats are symbols of penance.

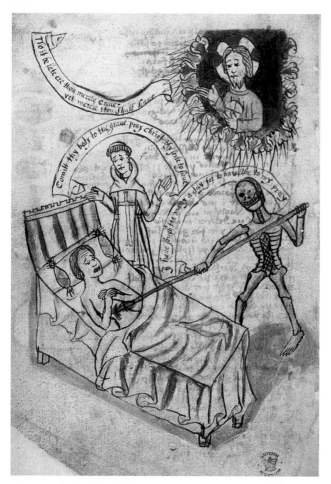

Plague Claims a Victim. An English priest gives the last rites to a bedridden plague victim, as a smiling devil pierces the victim with his spear and Christ looks on from heaven. In some English dioceses, two thirds of the priests died of the plague.

Perhaps the most famous response to the plague was the Flagellant movement, so called from the whips (*flagella*) with which these traveling bands of penitents beat themselves bloody in hopes of appeasing the wrath of God, which had brought the plague down on a sinful world. Such whips were first used in penitential demonstrations around 1260, but the practice was revived and extended in 1348 and 1349, when it seemed to many that the end of the world might be at hand. But the unruly and sometimes hysterical mobs that gathered around the flagellants aroused the concern of both ecclesiastical and secular authorities, and the movement was suppressed by papal order at the end of 1349.

In focusing on the flagellants, however, we should not overlook the vastly larger number of ordinary churchmen who stayed at their posts, ministering to the dead and dying until the plague claimed them too. A few priests may have fled, but where we can count

them, the huge numbers of priests who died in the plague suggest that those who fled were a small and unrepresentative minority. On the whole, the clergy of Christian Europe acquitted themselves with courage in the face of this fearsome disease. There is no evidence to suggest that their response to the plague was contemptible or that it led to religious disillusionment on the part of their parishoners.

WHAT CAUSED THE BLACK DEATH?

Until very recently, most historians were confident that the Black Death was the result of a pandemic outbreak of *Yersinia pestis*, the microbe responsible for bubonic plague and for its even deadlier cousins, pneumonic and septicemic plague. In its bubonic form, *Y. pestis* is carried by fleas that travel on the backs of rats; humans catch it only if they are bitten by an infected flea or rat. Bubonic plague attacks the lymphatic system, producing enormous swellings (*buboes*) of the lymph nodes in the groin, neck, and/or armpit and causing boils and carbuncles to erupt on the skin. Pneumonic plague results when *Y. pestis* infects the lungs, allowing the contagion to spread in the same ways as the common cold. Septicemic plague occurs when an infected flea introduces *Y. pestis* directly into the human bloodstream, causing death within hours, often before any symptoms of the disease can manifest themselves.

This traditional explanation of the Black Death may still be proved to be correct. But doubts about this explanation have arisen in recent years from an entirely unexpected direction. Studies of HIV/AIDS have shown that among European populations only, a genetic mutation (known as the CCR5-delta 32 mutation) occurred 2,000 to 3,000 years ago. This mutation renders people who carry it either entirely or substantially immune to HIV infection by blocking the T receptors through which HIV enters the cells. Like all such mutations, this one was a random occurrence, and it conveyed no particular evolutionary advantage when it first occurred. Approximately 700 years ago, however, and lasting for the next 300 years or so, some epidemic event took place that selected for this particular mutation, driving up its frequency in the overall European populations to about one in ten individuals, but ranging from a low of 4 percent in Sardinia to a high of around 16 percent in Scandinavia and northern Russia.

This epidemic event can only have been the Black Death; and if the CCR5-delta 32 mutation did impart a substantial or complete immunity to the Black Death, then this would also explain why the disease gradually disappeared from Europe, whereas it has continued

WHAT WERE THE ECONOMIC CONSEQUENCES OF THE BLACK DEATH FOR EUROPE?

THE BLACK DEATH AND ITS CONSEQUENCES   377

periodically to ravage other parts of the world into the twentieth century. *Y. pestis*, however, does not enter human cells through the T receptors. How then could this particular genetic mutation have provided an immunity to the Black Death, if indeed the Black Death was caused by *Y. pestis*?

Two possible explanations suggest themselves. First, *Y. pestis* itself may have mutated; although the modern form of the microbe does not enter cells through the T receptors, perhaps the medieval form of the microbe did. The second possibility, however, is that the Black Death was not caused by *Y. pestis* at all; it was caused by an as-yet-unknown infection that could be either bacterial or viral and that we have not yet identified. At the moment, we do not know which of these explanations is correct or, indeed, whether some other explanation entirely will prove to be the answer to the puzzle of what caused the Black Death. Research is continuing but already provides a striking example of the contributions to historical understanding that are emerging from modern microbiology and the genetic sciences.

THE IMPACT ON THE COUNTRYSIDE

The economic and social consequences of the plague were profound. During the plague years of 1348–1350, harvests rotted in the fields, manufacturing ceased, and trade was disrupted. Basic commodities became scarcer and prices rose, prompting efforts by governments to enforce, through legislation, a return to preplague prices and wages. By 1375, however, the new demographic realities were beginning to alter the underlying patterns of the European economy. By 1400, Europe had entered a new economic world.

In the countryside, grain production declined after 1350 from its preplague levels; but the overall population declined much more. With so many fewer mouths to feed and grain relatively more abundant, the price of grain fell; but with many fewer workers competing for employment, wages rose and work became more easily obtainable. With wages high and bread prices low, ordinary people could now afford not only to buy more bread but also to purchase dairy products, meat, fish, fruits, and wine on a more regular basis. As a result, the people of Europe in the later Middle Ages ate a more balanced diet, and were consequently better nourished, than they had been for centuries or than some are today. A recent study of the contents of fifteenth-century rubbish dumps has concluded that the people of Glasgow, Scotland, ate a healthier diet in 1405 than they did in 2005!

A healthier ecological balance between arable land, pastureland, and woodland was also reestablished in the wake of the plague. Faced with declining prices for cereal crops, many small farmers reduced their grain fields and expanded their sheep and cattle herds. By turning arable land into pastureland, they reduced their labor costs, increased the overall profitability of their farms, and improved the fertility of the soil through better manuring. With land so easily available, small farmers were also able to increase the size of their landholdings, which led to further efficiencies of scale. And with the lessened demand for fuel, forests too began to recover and expand.

Great lords were slower to adjust to the changed economic circumstances created by the plague. Some lords responded to rising wage costs by demanding additional unpaid labor from their peasant tenants. In eastern Europe, many peasants were actually forced into serfdom for the first time during the fifteenth century, as lords expanded their grain fields to supply the growing Baltic grain trade. In Castile, Poland, and Germany also, late medieval lords succeeded in imposing new forms of serfdom on the peasantry, which would last

A Cured-Meat Merchant's Shop. Prepared foods, including smoked and cured meats, became increasingly popular and affordable in the later Middle Ages.

until the sixteenth and seventeenth centuries. In Iberia and Italy, even outright slavery became more common after the plague, after nearly disappearing during the twelfth and thirteenth centuries (on the growing late medieval slave trade, see Chapter Eleven).

In France, by contrast, where the peasantry was already relatively freer than in most other European countries by 1300, the later Middle Ages brought few changes in peasant freedom. Rents declined, but lords made up these losses by imposing other fees on them. In England, however, where serfs in 1300 were much more burdened than they were in France, serfdom declined and ultimately disappeared altogether during the later Middle Ages. In the new world of social mobility and economic opportunity created by the plague, English serfs found it relatively easy to vote with their feet, either by moving to the lands of a less demanding lord or by becoming town dwellers. To retain serfs on their estates, English lords were forced to offer them more favorable terms: lower rents, more animals, fewer work requirements, and greater personal freedoms. As a result of such accomodations, serfdom had effectively disappeared from England by the early sixteenth century.

For the unfree peasant farmers of late medieval Europe, the improved economic circumstances of their lives thus did not necessarily lead to greater personal freedom with respect to their lords. Except in England (and to a lesser extent in Catalunya), most serfs were not substantially freer of lordly control in 1500 than they had been before the plague. For free peasants and town dwellers, however, the economic conditions produced by the plague brought significantly increased social mobility and a wealth of new opportunities. The result was a widening gap between the rich and the poor at all levels of rural society, from peasants to the greatest lords.

THE IMPACT ON TOWNS

Towns were especially sensitive barometers of the changing economic climate of the later Middle Ages. After reaching their demographic peak around 1300, some towns were already experiencing declining populations and economic difficulties even before the Black Death struck. The plague, however, made the existing situation very much worse. Overcrowding, combined with the generally unsanitary conditions of medieval urban life, made Europe's cities particularly vulnerable to the plague. But warfare and

local economic crises also contributed significantly to the population declines that afflicted so many late medieval cities. At Florence, for example, the population of the city rebounded quickly from the initial onslaught of the plague. By 1427, however, the population of Florence and its surrounding region had dropped from around 300,000 in 1338 to only about 100,000. At Toulouse in southern France, the population held fairly steady until the end of the fourteenth century, but then dropped from 26,000 to about 8,000 people between 1385 and 1430, largely as a result of devastation caused by the Hundred Years' War. London and Paris, by contrast, suffered only short-term declines as a result of the plague; their population losses to the plague were quickly made up by the large-scale immigration of new workers from the countryside. Many of these new workers were women, whose economic opportunities were greatly enhanced by the urban labor shortages resulting from the plague.

After 1450, however, Europe's towns and cities were once again growing; and by 1500, approximately 20 percent of the European population lived in urban areas, a larger percentage than had been the case two centuries before. Fueling this late-fifteenth-century urban growth was the increasing specialization of the late medieval European economy, made possible by the combined effects of plague and trade. With farmers now under less pressure to produce grain, they were

English Soldiers Setting Fire to St. Lo. When a town fell after a siege, both the town and its inhabitants were at the mercy of the besiegers, who were generally entitled to loot, rape, and plunder at will. The devastation from such attacks could be horrendous.

WHAT WERE THE ECONOMIC CONSEQUENCES OF THE BLACK DEATH FOR EUROPE?

THE BLACK DEATH AND ITS CONSE͞_____

ES 379

Merchants Unloading ͞
From an early-fifteenth͞·
French manuscript.

freer to turn their lands to producing the agricultural products to which their lands were best suited. As a result, more specialized and efficient regional economies began to emerge. Sweden produced butter, which it traded for German and Baltic grain; England produced wool, which it traded for French wine and Italian cloth; Castile produced leather, which it traded for silks, fruits, grain, and spices; and so on in almost endless variety.

Towns with links to these networks of regional exchange benefited particularly from the new economic circumstances of the later Middle Ages. In northern Germany a group of cities and towns under the leadership of Lübeck and Bremen formed the Hanseatic League, whose members transported German and Baltic grain to Scandinavia and eastern England in exchange for dairy products, fish, furs, and (from England) wool and wool cloth. In northern Italy, the enhanced demand for luxury goods brought new wealth not only to the spice- and silk-trading city of Venice but also to the fine cloth producers of Milan and to the bankers and jewelers of Florence. Milan also prospered from its armaments industry, which supplied the warring states of Europe with armor and weapons, while Genoa profited from its trade in bulk goods, especially grain.

Not all late medieval towns prospered—the Flemish cities in particular suffered through a serious economic depression—but on the whole, European urban centers profited from the new economic circumstances created by the plague. Had this not been the case, these cities would not have been able to participate in the remarkable extension of European commercial networks to Africa, Asia, and ultimately the Americas that began in

the fifteenth century and would continue, wi͞ terruption, until the end of the nineteenth͞ (For further discussion of European commerc͞ nization, and conquest during this period, see (͞ Eleven.)

The economic world of the late Middle Ag͞ stimulated the development of new business, acc͞ ing, and banking techniques. New forms of bus͞ partnerships, together with the development of i͞ ance contracts, helped minimize the risks associ͞ with long-distance trading voyages. Double-en͞ bookkeeping, widely used in Italy from the mi͞ fourteenth century on, gave merchants a much clearer

The Banker and His Wife, by Quentin Massys.

debts they owed and the debts that were pic̣... n—and hence of their profits and losses— oven possible before. Banks too altered many thier methods of doing business. The Medici Florence established branches of their bank the major cities of Europe but were careful ...ze these branches so that if one branch failed, ...no longer drag down the rest of the firm with ...ious branch-banking arrangements had done. ...lso experimented with advanced credit tech-... Some even allowed their clients to transfer ...between bank branches without any real money ...ng hands. Such book transfers were at first ...ted only by oral command, but after 1400 they ...d to be carried out by written orders. These were ...arliest ancestors of the modern check.

...OCIAL CHANGE IN THE ...ATER MIDDLE AGES

To what extent were the social changes of the later Middle Ages a consequence of the plague?

Famine, plague, and war put extraordinary pressures on social order in later medieval Europe. It is perhaps surprising that revolutionary changes were avoided. Nonetheless, by 1500 European society was different in important and lasting ways from what it had been 200 years before. Not all of these changes were directly a result of the plague; but the plague's influence can be discerned behind most of them.

REVOLTS AND REBELLIONS

The economic consequences of the plague were ultimately beneficial for those who survived it. But European society did not adjust easily to the new world created by the plague. Between 1350 and 1425, hundreds of popular revolts shook later medieval Europe. In 1358, for example, French peasants in the countryside around Paris rose up against their lords in an orgy of arson, murder, and rape, in a rebellion known as the Jacquerie (by their social superiors, all French peasants were caricatured as being named "Jacques"). In England too, a massive rising of peasants, artisans, and town dwellers (known misleadingly as the Peasants' Revolt) marched on London in 1381, demanding an end to serfdom, fixed rents for landholdings, and the more effec-

tive prosecution of the ongoing war with France. In Florence, workers in the wool cloth industry (known as the Ciompi, pronounced *chee-OM-pee*), beset by high unemployment and frequently cheated by their masters who controlled both the wool industry and the Florentine government, seized control of the city, demanding tax relief, full employment, and political representation in city government. Six weeks later, however, the Ciompi lost their hold on power, and a new government of masters revoked their reform measures.

The local circumstances that lay behind each of these revolts are unique, but certain general features do stand out about these and the hundreds of other similar revolts that occurred during these years. Most important, these revolts were not bread riots. Those who took part in them were not destitute, and their demands were almost never for the necessities of life. Some, like the English Peasants' Revolt and the 1408 rebellion at Lübeck in Germany, were touched off by resistance to new and higher taxes. Others, like the Jacquerie and the revolt of the Ciompi, took place at moments when unpopular governments were weakened by factionalism and military defeat. But as the historian Samuel Cohn Jr. has written, "politics, betrayal, and abuse were the sparks of rebellion, not conditions of misery or increased feudal exactions. It was

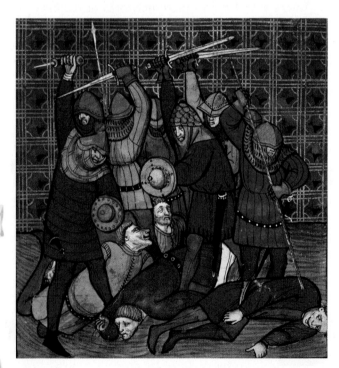

The Suppression of the Jacquerie, 1358. Although their initial attacks caught the lords off guard, the peasant rebels were no match for well-armed soldiers, who suppressed the rebellion with savage brutality.

FROISSART ON THE ENGLISH PEASANTS' REVOLT, 1381

Jean Froissart (1337?–1410?) is best known as the author of a lengthy history of the Hundred Years' War. He was not an eyewitness to the events of the Peasants' Revolt, but he had excellent English connections from whom he presumably derived his information. Froissart's perspective is entirely that of the aristocrats whom he served and with whom he associated. This fact makes his modest sympathy for the rebels of 1381 all the more interesting, particularly compared with his earlier, entirely negative portrayal of the 1358 Jacquerie rebels in France.

While these negotiations and discussions were going on, there occurred in England great disasters and uprisings of the common people, on account of which the country was almost ruined beyond recovery. Never was any land or realm in such great danger as England at that time. It was because of the abundance and prosperity in which the common people then lived that this rebellion broke out, just as in earlier days the Jack Goodmans rose in France and committed many excesses, by which the noble land of France suffered grave injury. . . .

These bad people . . . began to rebel because, they said, they were held too much in subjection, and when the world began there had been no serfs and could not be, unless they had rebelled against their Lord, as Lucifer did against God; but they were not of that stature, being neither angels nor spirits, but men formed in the image of their masters, and they were treated as animals. This was a thing they could no longer endure, wishing rather to be all one and the same; and, if they worked for their masters, they wanted to have wages for it. In these machinations they had been greatly encouraged originally by a crack-brained priest of Kent called John Ball . . . who had the habit on Sundays after mass, when everyone was coming out of church, of going to the cloisters or the graveyard, assembling the people round him and preaching thus:

"Good people, things cannot go right in England and never will, until goods are held in common and there are no more serfs and gentlefolk, but we are all one and the same. In what way are those whom we call lords greater masters than ourselves? How have they deserved it? Why do they hold us in bondage? If we all spring from a single father and mother, Adam and Eve, how can they claim or prove that they are lords more than us, except by making us produce and grow the wealth which they spend? They are clad in velvet and camlet lined with squirrel and ermine, while we go dressed in coarse cloth. They have the wines, the spices, and the good bread: we have the rye, the husks and the straw, and we drink water. They have shelter and ease in their fine manors, and we have hardship and toil, the wind and the rain in the fields. And from us must come, from our labor, the things which keep them in luxury. We are called serfs and beaten if we are slow in our service to them, yet we have no sovereign lord we can complain to, none to hear us and do us justice. Let us go to the King—he is young—and show him how we are oppressed, and tell him that we want things to be changed, or else we will change them ourselves. If we go in good earnest and all together, very many people who are called serfs and are held in subjection will follow us to get their freedom. And when the King sees and hears us, he will remedy the evil, either willingly or otherwise."

These were the kind of things which John Ball usually preached in the villages on Sundays . . . and many of the common people agreed with him.

Geoffrey Brereton, ed. and trans., *Froissart: Chronicles* (London and New York, 1968), pp. 211–213.

QUESTIONS FOR ANALYSIS

1. Why might Froissart have been more sympathetic to the uprising of the common people in England than he was to the French Jacquerie?

the nobles' political failures that led to the Jacquerie: their failure to protect their villagers from assaults by the English or by the regent of France and their collusion with the enemy in warlike pillaging of peasant property." Similarly, it was the failures of English armies in France and the rebels' belief that corruption on the part of those ruling in the name of the fourteen-year-old King Richard II caused the defeats that lay behind the Peasants' Revolt. The same point has been made about the urban rebellions of the period. As Cohn pointed out, "seldom did the revolts of artisans or workers directly attack their employers. Instead, their riots turned on politics. . . . [The revolts were] assaults against the arrogance, violence, and corruption of ruling aristocrats and merchant oligarchies."

Behind the social and political unrest of the period lay, therefore, not poverty and hunger but the growing prosperity and self-confidence that village communities and urban workers felt in the changed economic circumstances that arose from the plague. For the most part, the rebels' hopes that they could fundamentally alter the social and political conditions of their lives were frustrated. Kings, aristocrats, and urban oligarchs sometimes lost their nerve in the middle of an uprising, but they were almost always successful, after a time, in restoring their control and reasserting their dominance. After 1425, the number of such popular rebellions diminished. But they did not end; and this tradition of popular rebellion, established during the the later Middle Ages, would remain an important feature of European life for the next 200 years.

complex and uncertain, at a time when the costs of leading an appropriately noble style of life were continuing to escalate rapidly. As a result, the nobility of later medieval Europe felt themselves to be less secure in their wealth and social standing than they had been before the plague. These insecurities color almost all aspects of late medieval aristocratic life.

Across Europe, most noble families continued to derive the bulk of their revenues from their vast landholdings, just as they had done in the high Middle Ages. But many late medieval lords also tried to increase their nonagricultural sources of income. In Catalunya, Italy, Germany, and England, it was relatively common for nobles to invest in trading ventures. In France and Castile, however, direct involvement in retail commerce was regarded as socially demeaning and was, therefore, avoided by established noble families. Success in commerce could still be a route into the nobility, even in France and Castile. But when successful merchants were "ennobled" by kings or princes, they were expected to abandon their old employments and to adopt an appropriately noble way of life: living in rural castles or urban palaces surrounded by lavish households, embracing the values and conventions of chivalry (including a family coat of arms), and serving their prince at court and in war. Service to a king or great lord was an increasingly important expectation for the late medieval nobility, whose fortunes came to depend heavily on the gifts and favors (including tax exemptions and profitable marriages) that only rulers could bestow.

ARISTOCRATIC LIFE IN THE LATER MIDDLE AGES

Some late medieval lords failed to adapt to the new world created by the plague. As grain prices fell, rents stagnated, and wages for laborers and servants rose, the fortunes of these lords declined significantly. For the most part, however, the later Middle Ages was not a period of aristocratic crisis. Quite the contrary—the great noble families of fifteenth-century Europe were almost certainly wealthier, on average, than their counterparts had been 200 years before. Nor did the plague undermine the dominant position the nobility had established in European society during the high Middle Ages. It did, however, make their world substantially more

A Noble Hunting Party. This fifteenth-century illustration shows an elaborately dressed group of noble men and women setting out to hunt with falcons, accompanied by their servants and their dogs. The castle at Étampes, on the Loire, can be seen in the background.

To what extent were the social changes of the later Middle Ages a consequence of the plague?

Social Change in the Later Middle Ages   383

Nobility remained, however, an uncertain and difficult status to maintain. What made a man or woman noble? In countries where nobility entailed clearly defined legal privileges (such as exemption from taxation or the right to be tried only in special courts), proven descent from noble ancestors, together with a recognized coat of arms, might be sufficient to qualify a family as noble in the eyes of the law. Legal nobility of this sort was, however, a somewhat less exclusive distinction than we might expect it to have been. In fifteenth-century Castile and Navarre, 10 to 15 percent of the total population had claims to be recognized as noble on these terms. In Poland, Hungary, and Scotland, the legally privileged nobility was closer to 5 percent; whereas in England and France, only 1 to 2 percent could plausibly claim the legal privileges of noble status.

Fundamentally, however, nobility was a marker of social rank, expressed and epitomized by an individual's noble style of life. Chivalry, courtliness, political influence, deference from social inferiors, and the ostentatious display of wealth—all combined to constitute a family's honor and hence to mark it off as noble. In practice, however, the lines of social distinction between noble and non-noble families were often fuzzy. The newly wealthy might live like nobles, even though they had no noble ancestors. Men from obscure families might rise through royal service into the ranks of the nobility, while long-established noble families might disappear through failure of heirs or simply their own political miscalculations. Even on the battlefield, the supremacy of the mounted noble knight was being threatened by the growing importance of lower-class soldiers, archers, and artillery experts in late medieval armies. There were even hints of a more radical critique of noble claims to innate social superiority. As the English rebels in 1381 enquired, "When Adam dug and Eve spun, Who then was the gentleman?"

Precisely because nobility was so contestable during the later Middle Ages, those who claimed the status took elaborate measures to assert its exclusivity and social distinctiveness. Late medieval aristocrats hosted lavish banquets, with table decorations forty-six feet high and hundreds of courses served over several days.

They dressed in rich and extravagant clothing: close-fitting doublets and hose with long pointed shoes for men, multilayered silk dresses with ornately festooned headdresses for women. They maintained enormous households (in France around 1400, the Duke of Berry had 400 matched pairs of hunting dogs and 1,000 servants) and took part in elaborately ritualized tournaments and pageants, in which the noble participants pretended to be the chivalric heroes of thirteenth-century romances. Aristocrats also emphasized their cultural taste and refinement by supporting authors and artists and sometimes by becoming accomplished poets themselves. Nobility existed only if it was recognized; and to be recognized, noble status had to be constantly reasserted.

Rulers contributed to this process of noble self-assertion; indeed, they were among its principal supporters and patrons. Kings and princes across Europe competed with each other in founding chivalric orders,

The Duke of Berry's Banquet. Uncle of the mad king Charles VI, the Duke of Berry left politics to his brothers, the Duke of Burgundy and the Duke of Anjou. In return, he received enormous subsidies from the royal government, which he spent on sumptuous buildings, artworks, and feasts. Here, the duke interrupts his feasting to dispense alms to the poor. Some of his famous hunting dogs can be seen dining on scraps from his table.

such as the Knights of the Garter in England and the Order of the Star in France. These orders honored knights who had demonstrated in an extraordinary way the idealized chivalric virtues of knightly prowess, loyalty, bravery, generosity, and courtesy on the battlefield. But although membership in these orders was strictly limited, the virtues they celebrated were seen as characterizing the nobility as a whole. By exalting the nobility as a class, chivalric orders helped cement the links that bound the nobility to their kings and princes. So too did the fees, pensions, offices, and marriages that kings and princes could provide to their noble followers. In a world in which the agricultural revenues of noble estates were declining, such rewards of princely service were critically important to maintaining noble fortunes.

It is easy to dismiss the elaborately performative aspects of late medieval aristocratic life as mere play acting—in the historian Johann Huizinga's words, as "a wholesale attempt to act the vision of a dream." To do so, however, would be a mistake. Late medieval rulers depended on the service—military, diplomatic, and political—that the nobility alone could provide, just as the nobility depended on the offices, revenues, prestige, and social affirmation that could be acquired only through service to a royal or princely court. The alliance that was forged in the fifteenth century between kings and their nobility was a response to these mutual needs and would become one of the most characteristic and enduring features of old regime (*ancien régime*) Europe. In France, this ancien régime alliance between crown and nobility lasted until the French Revolution of 1789. In England and Germany, it would last until the outbreak of World War I.

WAR AND THE DEVELOPMENT OF THE LATE MEDIEVAL STATE

Why was warfare such a constant feature of late medieval life?

The ancien régime alliance between crown and nobility was in part a response to the new social and economic world created by the plague. But it was also a product of war and of the impact of war on the development of the late medieval state. The fourteenth and fifteenth centuries saw almost constant warfare at all levels of European society. To fight these wars, governments claimed new powers to tax their subjects and to control their subjects' lives. Armies became larger and military technology became deadlier. Wars became more destructive and society became more militarized. As a result of these developments, the largest and most successful European states (in particular, the national monarchies of Portugal, Spain, and France) were stronger and more aggressively expansionist by 1500 than they had been two centuries before. In 1500, the impact of these newly powerful states was still felt mainly in Europe. By 1600, however, their impact would be felt around the globe.

ENGLAND, FRANCE, AND THE HUNDRED YEARS' WAR

The Hundred Years' War was the largest, longest, and most wide-ranging military conflict of the later Middle Ages. England and France were its principal protagonists, but at one stage or another almost all of the major European powers became involved in it. Active hostilities between England and France lasted from 1337 until 1453, interrupted by truces of varying lengths. The roots of the conflict, however, reach back into the 1290s, when King Edward I of England attempted to conquer the neighboring kingdom of Scotland, thereby provoking the Scottish kingdom to ally itself with France. And the threat of war continued until 1558, when Calais, the last piece of English-held soil in France, passed into French hands. Arguably, therefore, the Hundred Years' War might more accurately be called "The Two Hundred and Sixty Years' War."

The war had several causes. The most fundamental source of conflict, and the most difficult issue to resolve, was that the kings of England held the duchy of Gascony in southern France as vassals of the French king. In the twelfth and thirteenth centuries, this fact had seemed less of an anomaly. But as the conviction grew in the later Middle Ages that kingdoms were territorial entities, within whose borders only a single king should rule, the English presence in Gascony became more and more intolerable to the French crown. That England also had close commercial links, through the wool trade, with the French king's rebellious subjects in Flanders added further fuel to the fires of Anglo-French hostility. So too did the continuing French alliance with the Scots, who had been resolutely resisting English attempts to conquer their kingdom since the 1290s.

WHY WAS WARFARE SUCH A CONSTANT FEATURE OF LATE MEDIEVAL LIFE?

WAR AND THE DEVELOPMENT OF THE LATE MEDIEVAL STATE 385

Greatly complicating all this, however, was a succession dispute over the French crown itself. In 1328, the last of King Philip IV's three sons died without leaving a son to succeed him. A new dynasty, the Valois, thereupon replaced the Capetians on the throne of France. Only by prohibiting inheritance through women, however, could the Valois kings claim to be the closest heirs to the Capetians. Otherwise, the rightful heir to the throne of France was King Edward III of England, whose mother, Isabella, was the only daughter of King Philip IV of France. In 1328, Edward was only fifteen years old, and he did not protest the succession of his Valois cousins. In 1337, however, when war erupted between France and England over Scotland and Gascony, Edward III responded by claiming to be the rightful king of France—a claim all subsequent English kings would uphold until the eighteenth century.

The Hundred Years' War itself can be divided into three main phases. In the first phase, from 1337 until 1360, the English won a series of startling military victories, most famously at Crécy (1346), Calais (1347), and Poitiers (1356). Although France was richer and more populous than England by a factor of at least three to one, the English political system was more effective in mobilizing the entire population behind the war effort. Taxes poured into King Edward's coffers, enabling him to hire and maintain a professional army of seasoned and well-disciplined soldiers, nobles, and longbowmen. The huge but poorly led feudal armies assembled by King Philip VI of France and his son, King John II, proved no match for the tactical superiority of the smaller English armies on the battlefield. English armies pillaged the French countryside at will; civil wars broke out between individual French lords; and when King John II himself was captured in 1356 at the Battle of Poitiers (*pwah-TYAY*), the French kingdom dissolved into chaos. Mercenary bands of French and English soldiers, known as "Free Companies," roamed the countryside, attacking and looting peasant villages and holding towns to ransom, at a time when France, like the rest of Europe, was struggling to recover from the initial devastation of the Black Death. In 1358, peasant frustration with the inability of both the crown and the French nobility to protect them boiled over in the savage rebellion of the Jacquerie.

In 1360, the Treaty of Bretigny brought the first phase of the war to an end. In return for renouncing his claims to the throne of France, Edward III of England received full sovereignty over a greatly enlarged duchy of Gascony (to be ruled over by Edward's son and heir, the Black Prince) and the promise of a huge ransom for the captive king of France. But the terms of the treaty were never honored by either side. The French crown continued to treat the duke of Gascony as a vassal, and the kings of England never surrendered their claims to be the rightful kings of France. The treaty brought

THE FRENCH SUCCESSION
IN 1328

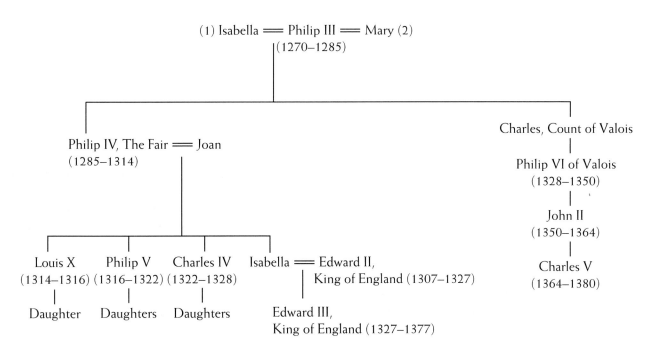

Soldiers Pillage a Parisian House. Looting was an accepted part of late medieval warfare. Here, soldiers are shown ransacking a fine house for valuables. Silver plate and bedding are tossed from the windows, while other soldiers break open a wine barrel. Elaborate rules governed the division of such spoils of war.

sixteen years of peace between France and England, allowing France a breathing space during which to recover from the devastation of war. It also brought England a large influx of cash from King John's ransom. But it did not resolve the underlying issues that had led to the war itself. Instead, a proxy war developed during the 1360s and 1370s, in which English and French troops fought in support of rival claimants to the throne of Castile and hired themselves out as mercenaries in the service of the warring city-states of northern Italy. By 1376, when formal war resumed between England and France, the Hundred Years' War had become a European-wide conflagration.

After 1376, the tides of war quickly shifted in favor of France. In England the Black Prince died, leaving a ten-year-old son, Richard II (1377–1399), to succeed the aging and senile Edward III. Meanwhile, the new king of France, Charles V (1364–1380), used the peace created by the Treaty of Bretigny to his advantage. By imposing a series of new national taxes on the common people of France, King Charles was able to restore order by ridding the countryside of the Free Companies. And by hiring the leader of one of these Free Companies, Bertrand du Guesclin, as the commander of the king's own army, Charles was able to create a professional military that could match the English in discipline and tactics. By 1380, when King Charles V

died, English territories in France had been reduced to small areas around Bordeaux and Calais.

Unlike his father and grandfather, the new king of England, Richard II, had no interest in the French war. In 1394, he even married the French king's daughter. Under Edward III, however, the war had become extremely popular in England, not only as a matter of national honor and security but also as a reliable source of profit for those who fought in it. Richard's failure to prosecute the war therefore undermined his relationship with the country and especially with his nobility. When, in 1399, he attempted to confiscate the inheritance of his cousin, Henry Bolingbroke, Bolingbroke turned the tables, deposed Richard, and seized the throne as King Henry IV (1399–1413), the first of the Lancastrian kings of England.

As a usurper, Henry IV struggled to maintain his authority as king against a series of rebellions. Frequently ill, he was in no position to renew the French war. When his son Henry V succeeded him in 1413, however, the new king immediately began to prepare for renewed war with France. A brilliant diplomat, Henry sealed alliances with both the emperor Sigismund in Germany and with the dissident Duke of Burgundy, who was locked in a struggle with his rivals to control the French royal government, which had been left rudderless by the growing insanity of the French king, Charles VI

WHY WAS WARFARE SUCH A CONSTANT FEATURE OF LATE MEDIEVAL LIFE?

WAR AND THE DEVELOPMENT OF THE LATE MEDIEVAL STATE   387

King Richard II of England.

(1380–1422). When Henry V invaded France in 1415, he therefore faced only the army of the then-dominant faction around the royal court. The Duke of Burgundy stayed home. At Agincourt, Henry V won another crushing victory over a vastly larger, but badly disciplined French military force, just as Edward III had done at Crécy and the Black Prince had done at Poitiers. By 1420, Henry V had conquered most of France north of the Loire. By the Treaty of Troyes, signed in that year, the aged and infirm King Charles VI recognized Henry V as his heir to the throne of France, thus dispossessing his only surviving son, known as "the dauphin," the future King Charles VII.

Unlike Edward III, who used his claim to be king of France largely as a bargaining chip to secure sovereignty over Gascony, Henry V honestly believed himself to be the rightful king of France. His astonishing success in capturing the French kingdom seemed to the people of England to put the stamp of divine approval on that claim, raising English nationalism to new emotional heights. But Henry's successes in France also transformed the nature of the war, from a profitable war of conquest to an extended and expensive military occupation. It thereby sowed the seeds of eventual English defeat.

Henry himself died in 1422, still actively engaged in extending English control south, toward and across the Loire. King Charles VI died only a few months later. The new king of England and France, Henry VI (1422–1461), was an infant when his father died; but under the leadership of his uncle, the Duke of Bedford, English armies continued their slow push southward, while their ally, the Duke of Burgundy, controlled the northeast. The dauphin, meanwhile, withdrew to the extreme southwest of the country. His confidence in his right to the throne of France had been shatttered by his own mother's declaration that he was not the legitimate son of Charles VI. But as time went on, it also seemed increasingly unlikely that English forces would ever succeed in dislodging him from the territories south of the Loire.

This apparent stalemate was broken by the heroic figure of Joan of Arc. In 1429, Joan, an illiterate peasant girl, made her way to the dauphin's court to announce that an angel had told her that the dauphin was the rightful king of France and that she, Joan, should drive the English out of France. It is a mark of the

CHRONOLOGY

THE HUNDRED YEARS' WAR, 1337–1453

Valois Dynasty begins	1328
Edward III claims French throne	1337
Battle of Crécy	1346
Battle of Poitiers	1356
Battle of Agincourt	1415
French Burgundy allies with England	1419–1435
Joan of Arc commands French troops	1429–1430
Capture of Bordeaux ends war	1453

The Murder of the Duke of Burgundy, 1419. This act of treachery, perpetrated by followers of the French dauphin (the future King Charles VII), made the new Duke of Burgundy into an outright military ally of King Henry V of England, paving the way for the English capture of Paris the following year.

hopelessness of Charles's position that she even got a hearing—much less that he then gave her a contingent of troops, with which she promptly lifted the English siege of Orleans. A series of further victories followed, culminating in 1430 when Joan brought Charles to Reims, the traditional coronation site for the French monarchy, where he was crowned king of France. But despite her victories, Joan remained an embarrassment: a peasant leading nobles, a woman leading men, and a commoner who claimed to have been commissioned by God. When, a few months later, the Burgundians captured her in battle and handed her over to the English, King Charles VII did nothing to try to save her. Accused of witchcraft and tried for heresy, Joan was burned to death in the market square at Rouen in 1431.

The French forces whom she inspired, however, continued on the offensive. In 1435, the Duke of Burgundy withdrew from his alliance with England; and when the English king Henry VI proved first to be incompetent and then to be insane, a series of French military victories during the 1440s finally brought the war to an end, with the capture of Bordeaux in 1453. English kings would threaten to renew the war for another century, and Anglo-French hostility would last until the final defeat of Napoleon in 1815. But after 1453, English control over French territory would be limited to the port of Calais, which would finally fall in 1558.

The Hundred Years' War was the most dangerous challenge to its existence that the French kingdom ever faced. The disintegration of that kingdom, first during

the 1350s and 1360s, and again between 1415 and 1435, glaringly revealed the fragility of the bonds that tied the crown to its nobility and Paris to the outlying regions of Burgundy, Brittany, and Gascony. Nonetheless, the monarchy demonstrated remarkable resilience, and in the end the war strengthened the crown's

Joan of Arc. A contemporary sketch, drawn in the margin of the register of the English-controlled Parlement of Paris in 1429.

THE CONDEMNATION OF JOAN OF ARC BY THE UNIVERSITY OF PARIS, 1431

After Joan's capture by the Burgundians, she was handed over to the English, who put her on trial for heresy. Paris was at this date in English hands, so the verdict of the Parisian masters should not be considered unbiased. On the other hand, there is no evidence that it was extracted by force. Learned theologians were not inclined to approve of peasant women who claimed to hear the voices of angels, who dressed in men's clothes, and who led aristocrats into battle. Joan was condemned for heresy and burned at the stake.

You, Joan, have said that, since the age of thirteen, you have experienced revelations and the appearance of angels, of St Catherine and St Margaret, and that you have very often seen them with your bodily eyes, and that they have spoken to you. As for the first point, the clerks of the University of Paris have considered the manner of the said revelations and appearances. . . . Having considered all . . . they have declared that all the things mentioned above are lies, falsenesses, misleading and pernicious things and that such revelations are superstitions, proceeding from wicked and diabolical spirits.

Item: You have said that your king had a sign by which he knew that you were sent by God, for St Michael, accompanied by several angels, some of which having wings, the others crowns, with St Catherine and St Margaret, came to you at the chateau of Chinon. All the company ascended through the floors of the castle until they came to the room of your king, before whom the angel bearing the crown bowed. . . . As for this matter, the clerks say that it is not in the least probable, but it is rather a presumptuous lie, misleading and pernicious, a false statement, derogatory of the dignity of the Church and of the angels. . . .

Item: you have said that, at God's command, you have continually worn men's clothes, and that you have put on a short robe, doublet, shoes attached by points; also that you have had short hair, cut around above the ears, without retaining anything on your person which shows that you are a woman; and that several times you have received the body of Our Lord dressed in this fashion, despite having been admonished to give it up several times, the which you would not do. You have said that you would rather die than abandon the said clothing, if it were not at God's command, and that if you were wearing those clothes and were with the king, and those of your party, it would be one of the greatest benefits for the kingdom of France. You have also said that not for anything would you swear an oath not to wear the said clothing and carry arms any longer. And all these things you say you have done for the good and at the command of God. As for these things, the clerics say that you blaspheme God and hold him in contempt in his sacraments; you transgress Divine Law, Holy Scripture and canon law. You err in the faith. You boast in vanity. You are suspected of idolatry and you have condemned yourself in not wishing to wear clothing suitable to your sex, but you follow the custom of Gentiles and Saracens.

Carolyne Larrington, ed. and trans., *Women and Writing in Medieval Europe* (New York and London, 1995), pp. 183–184.

QUESTIONS FOR ANALYSIS

1. Why was Joan of Arc condemned for heresy?
2. In what ways does Joan of Arc highlight the major characteristics and preoccupations of the intensified popular piety of the later Middle Ages?

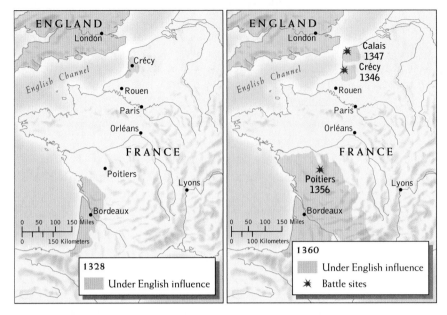

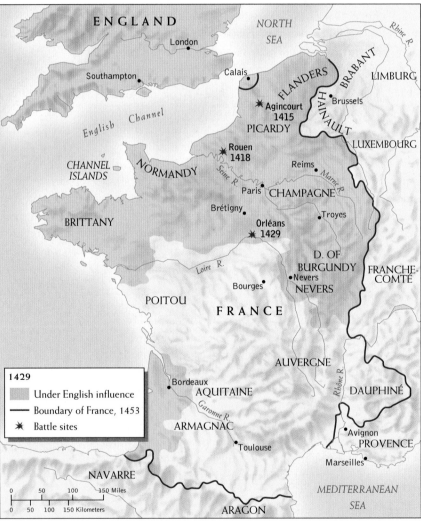

FRANCE DURING THE HUNDRED YEARS' WAR

Here we see three snapshots of the political geography of France during the Hundred Years' War between France and England. In what areas of France did England make its greatest territorial gains before 1360? How and why did this change in the period leading up to 1429? What geographic and strategic advantages did the French monarchy enjoy after 1429 that might help explain its success in recapturing the French kingdom from the English?

WHY WAS WARFARE SUCH A CONSTANT FEATURE OF LATE MEDIEVAL LIFE?

WAR AND THE DEVELOPMENT OF THE LATE MEDIEVAL STATE   391

capacity to rule France. To fight the war successfully, the Valois kings imposed new national taxes that would be the mainstays of French royal finance until 1789. With these new revenues, the Valois were able to create and maintain a standing national army whose size, sophistication, and expensive armaments (including, most important, its artillery) overwhelmed the forces that dissident nobles and regions might bring against it.

Although personally unimpressive, King Charles's victory in the Hundred Years' War laid the foundations on which the power of early modern France would be built. After 1453, the growing power of the French crown became quickly apparent. In 1477, Charles's son, King Louis XI (1461–1483), absorbed the duchy of Burgundy after the last Burgundian duke fell in battle at the hands of the Swiss. In 1485, King Louis XII helped topple King Richard III of England, whose alliance with Brittany had threatened to renew the English war with France. When, a few years later, Louis XII acquired Brittany through marriage, the French kings gained control over the last remaining independent principality within the borders of their kingdom.

The Hundred Years' War also had dramatic effects on the English monarchy. When English armies in France were successful, as they were under Edward III and Henry V, the Crown rode a wave of popularity and the country prospered from the profits of booty and ransoms. When the war turned against the English, however, as it did under Richard II and Henry VI, defeats abroad undermined support for the monarch at home. Of the nine English kings who ruled England between 1307 and 1485, no fewer than five were deposed and murdered by their subjects.

The particular propensity of the English for murdering their kings (a subject of comment across Europe) was a consequence of England's peculiar political system. As we have seen, England was the most tightly governed kingdom in Europe, but the strength of its political system depended on the king's ability to mobilize popular support for his policies through Parliament, while maintaining the support of his nobility through successful wars in Wales, Scotland, and France. This was a delicate task, at which incompetent or tyrannical kings could not succeed. At the same time, however, unsuccessful kingship was even more destablizing in England than it was elsewhere in Europe, because of the power of the English state itself. In France, the nobility could endure the insanity of Charles VI because his government was not powerful enough to threaten them. In England, neither the nobility nor the larger political nation could afford to allow the incompetent kingship of King Henry VI to continue.

King Charles VII of France. The king's bulbous nose, bowed legs, and generally misshapen figure fed rumors that he had been conceived in adultery and so was not the legitimate heir to the throne of France. This portrait, done after his victory over the English, flatters him considerably.

The result was an aristocratic rebellion against Henry VI's government known as the Wars of the Roses, so called (by the nineteenth-century novelist Sir Walter Scott) from the emblems of the two competing factions: the red rose of Henry's family of Lancaster, and the white rose of Henry's cousin, the rival Duke of York. In 1461, after a six-year struggle, Edward, Duke of York finally succeeded in ousting Henry VI. He then ruled successfully until his death in 1483. But when Edward's brother Richard seized the throne from Edward's own young sons, political stability in England collapsed once again. In 1485, Richard III was in turn defeated and killed in the battle of Bosworth Field by the Lancastrian claimant, Henry Tudor, who then resolved the dynastic feud between Lancaster and York by marrying Elizabeth of York, the only surviving child of King Edward IV. As King Henry VII, Henry Tudor systematically eliminated potential rivals for the throne. He avoided expensive foreign wars, asked for little by way of taxation, built up a financial surplus by carefully managing Crown lands, and exercised a tight

King Richard III of England, 1483–1485. Richard deposed his nephews and seized the throne for himself. He was defeated and killed by Henry Tudor (King Henry VII) at Bosworth Field in 1485.

Henry VII. A 1505 portrait by M. Sittow.

(but largely welcome) control over the aristocracy. When he died in 1509 the new Tudor Dynasty was securely established on the throne, and English royal power was fully restored.

Despite the turmoil caused by war and rebellion, late medieval English political life had an essential stability. Local institutions continued to function; Parliament became increasingly important as a point of contact joining Crown, nobility, and local communities; and the political nation itself became steadily larger as prosperity brought new social groups into prominence. Most important, there was never any fundamental challenge to the power of the English state itself. When rebellions broke out, whether led by nobles or peasants, the rebels always sought to control the central government rather than to destroy or break away from it. Despite England's ultimate defeat, the Hundred Years' War strengthened this characteristically English equation between national identity and the power of the state. During the fourteenth and fifteenth centuries, mounting anti-French sentiment contributed to the triumph of English as the national language and to a patriotic vision of England itself as a country uniquely chosen by God. Having lost its continental possessions, England after 1485 became an island nation that looked to the sea as its first line of defense. This too would prove to be an advantage. England in the sixteenth and seventeenth centuries would be well positioned to take advantage of the new world of overseas commerce and colonialism opened up by Columbus's discoveries in the Americas.

GERMANY AND ITALY

Elsewhere, the consequences of late medieval warfare were more uniformly destructive. In Germany, armed conflict among the territorial princes who dominated the country, and between these princes and the German emperors, weakened all the principal combatants significantly. Periodically a powerful emperor would emerge to play a major role on the European scene. But the trend was toward the continuing dissolution of central power in Germany, as princes divided their territories among their heirs and as free cities and local knights strove to shake off the rule of the princes. Between 1350 and 1450, near anarchy prevailed across much of Germany. In the east, however, the rulers of Bavaria, Austria, and Brandenburg were able to strengthen their authority by supporting the efforts of local nobles to subject their peasantry to serfdom and by conquering and colonizing new territories, particularly on the frontier between Prussia and Lithuania.

WHY WAS WARFARE SUCH A CONSTANT FEATURE OF LATE MEDIEVAL LIFE?

WAR AND THE DEVELOPMENT OF THE LATE MEDIEVAL STATE   393

The gains these rulers made during the later Middle Ages would make the Habsburg rulers of Austria and the Hohenzollern rulers of Brandenburg-Prussia the dominant powers in early modern Germany.

In northern and central Italy also, the last half of the fourteenth century was marked by incessant conflict. With the popes living at Avignon from 1309 until 1377, their control over the papal states collapsed. Warfare between city-states erupted throughout the northern half of the peninsula, further complicated by a rash of urban rebellions in the wake of the plague. By around 1400, however, Venice, Milan, and Florence had succeeded in stabilizing their own differing forms of government. Venice was now ruled by an oligarchy of merchants; Milan by a family of despots; and Florence was ruled as a republic, albeit one dominated by the influence of a few wealthy families, especially, after 1434, the Medici banking family. Having settled their internal problems, these three cities then began to expand their territories. By 1454, Venice, Milan, and Florence had subordinated almost all the other northern Italian cities and towns except Genoa, which remained prosperous and independent but gained no new lands. The papacy, meanwhile, now restored to Rome, reasserted its control over central Italy; while in the south, the kingdom of Naples continued to rule unchallenged by the other Italian powers, despite endemic local warfare and persistent maladministration.

A treaty in 1454 brought forty years of peace between these "five great powers." This peace was maintained by a form of "balance of power diplomacy," in which frequently shifting alliances among these five states checked the ambitions of each for further expansion. In 1494, however, a large-scale French invasion of Italy destroyed the diplomatic and military balance between the Italian powers, revealing in the process that the Italian city-states were no match for the powerful national monarchies that had developed during the fifteenth century north of the Alps. French control of the Italian peninsula would be short-lived, however. The ultimate beneficiary of the French invasion of Italy would be the newly united Spanish kingdoms of Aragon and Castile.

THE EMERGENCE OF SPAIN

Spain too had seen incessant strife during the later Middle Ages. Wars between the two principal Spanish kingdoms, Castile and Aragon, had weakened both combatants, while in Castile, a disastrous civil war during the fourteenth century was followed by a period of incompetent kingship and economic hardship during the mid-fifteenth century. In Castile, noble families took advantage of royal weakness to secure greater control over the peasantry on their estates and greater independence from the crown. After 1450, noble factions struggled for control over the Castilian court as feuds between noble families tore the kingdom apart.

The Aragonese crown preserved its authority rather better, benefiting from its alliance with the merchants of Catalunya, who were busily extending their commercial influence throughout the Mediterranean world. After 1458, however, Aragon too fell prey to civil war arising from a succession dispute, in which both France and Castile became involved. By 1469, however, King John had established his son Ferdinand as the unquestioned heir to the throne of Aragon. When, in that year, Ferdinand married Isabella, the heiress to Castile, their union became the basis on which a united Spanish kingdom would eventually be built.

In 1474, Isabella ascended to the throne of Castile; in 1479, Ferdinand became King of Aragon when his father died. Aragon and Castile continued to be ruled as separate kingdoms until 1714; even in contemporary Spain, tensions between the two former kingdoms continue. But the marriage of Ferdinand and Isabella ended the warfare between the kingdoms, and after 1479 the Catholic Monarchs (as Ferdinand and Isabella came to be known) were able to embark on united policies. Vast increases in royal revenues quickly followed. Much of this new revenue was devoted to building up Spanish military forces, which by 1500 were the most powerful in Europe. These forces were first employed to conquer Grenada, the last remaining Muslim principality in Spain, which fell in 1492. A decade later, Spanish armies intervened in Italy, eventually turning all of Italy into a Spanish protectorate. But this new army also played an important role within Spain, providing honorable employment and royal service to the fractious nobles of Castile and Aragon, while overawing any nobles who might be tempted to rebel against the growing power of the Catholic Monarchs.

The conquest of Granada was a turning point for the emerging Spanish monarchy. Both Castile and Aragon had been shaped for centuries by their involvement in the reconquest of Muslim Spain. But the victory of 1492 sealed a vision of Castile in particular as a country uniquely devoted to crusading. That vision of Castile's world mission might not have been so consequential, however, had it not been for the fact that only a few months after the conquest of Granada, Queen Isabella granted three ships to a Genoese adventurer named Christopher Columbus who promised to reach India by sailing westward across the Atlantic Ocean. He failed,

Ferdinand and Isabella Honoring the Virgin. A contemporary Spanish painting in which the royal pair is shown with two of their children in the company of saints from the Dominican order.

of course; but by landing in two new continents, which he claimed for Spain, Columbus extended the Castilian crusading tradition to the New World, with consequences that have lasted to the present day.

The year 1492 also saw the expulsion of the entire Jewish community from Spain, the culmination of a process of Jewish exclusion from Christian Europe that began in the late thirteenth century with the expulsion of the Jewish communities of southern Italy and England, continued with the expulsion of the Jews from France in 1306, and continued during the fourteenth and fifteenth centuries with a series of Jewish expulsions from the towns and cities of the Rhineland. The Spanish expulsion stands out, however, both for the total number of Jews involved (at least 100,000 and possibly as many as 200,000) and because of the rich cultural legacy the Jews of Spain had developed in the 1,000 years during which they had resided on the Iberian Peninsula.

Historians continue to debate why Ferdinand and Isabella ordered this expulsion. Between 1391 and 1420, tens of thousands of Spanish Jews had converted to Catholicism, many as a result of coercion but some from sincere religious conviction. Until around 1450, it seemed possible that these converts (*conversos*) might successfully assimilate into Spanish Christian society. Thereafter, however, the *conversos* became the targets of discriminatory legislation and popular suspicion that they remained secretly Jews. To make proper Christians out of the *conversos*, the Catholic monarchs may have concluded that they needed to remove the "bad influence" posed by the continuing presence of a practicing Jewish community in Spain.

Beyond such practical considerations, however, there may also have been a desire to create a new and explicitly Christian identity for the newly united country over which Ferdinand and Isabella ruled. Spain, per se, did not exist in 1492. Its creation would be the work of centuries, work that continues today. But the need for some common identity that would transcend the rival regional identities of Castilians, Aragonese, and Catalans (not to mention Galicians, Navarrese, Valencians, Basques, and Murcians) may already have been apparent. Certainly it is implied in the title Ferdinand and Isabella took to themselves as the Catholic Monarchs. Like other monarchs in late medieval Europe, Ferdinand and Isabella may have sought to strengthen their emerging nation-state by constructing a newly explicit and exclusively Christian identity for its people and by attaching that new identity to the crown. In such a Christian nation, however, there could be no place for Jews or Muslims.

THE GROWTH OF NATIONAL MONARCHIES

In France, England, Scotland, Portugal, and Spain, the later Middle Ages saw the emergence of markedly more powerful European states than had existed in 1300. But despite the impact of war and plague in reshaping European political life, many of the basic political patterns established during the High Middle Ages endured. Germany and Italy were politically divided by 1300 and remained divided in 1500. England and France, the two most powerful monarchies of the High Middle Ages, remained powerful states in 1500, although the combined kingdoms of Aragon and Castile, together with the kingdom of Portugal, had now emerged as a powerful rival to both. Only the position of Sicily had been fundamentally transformed. Economically exhausted by the demands of its high medieval rulers, Sicily became in the later Middle Ages the impoverished land it has remained until the present day.

WHY DID RUSSIA DEVELOP DIFFERENTLY FROM OTHER LATE MEDIEVAL EUROPEAN STATES?

KIEVAN RUS AND THE RISE OF MUSCOVY   395

Behind these continuities, however, lies one of the most notable developments in later medieval politics: the growing strength of national monarchies. By 1500, the kings of Iberia, England, France, and Scotland were all actively engaged in constructing a sense of national identity among their people and in focusing that identity on themselves. This fusion of nationalism and kingship was a product of the later Middle Ages. Forged by the fires of war and fueled by the growing cultural importance of vernacular languages, this fusion of national identity with kingship produced by 1500 a new type of political organization, the national monarchy, which was stronger and more powerful than anything Europe had seen since the heyday of the Carolingian Empire.

The superiority of these new national monarchies to older forms of political organization such as the empire and the city-state is most clearly visible in Italy. Until 1494, the Italian city-states had appeared to be well governed and powerful. But when the armies of France and Spain invaded the peninsula, the Italian political order collapsed like a house of cards. Germany would suffer the same fate only a few generations later; it would remain a battleground for the competing armies of France and Spain until the end of the seventeenth century.

The new national monarchies were not an unmitigated blessing. They were not only more powerful, they were also more intolerant and exclusionary than their high medieval predecessors, as the expulsion of Jews (and Muslims) from later medieval Europe reveals. But for better or worse, these newly powerful national monarchies would dominate Europe and the wider world for the next 500 years.

KIEVAN RUS AND THE RISE OF MUSCOVY

Why did Russia develop differently from other late medieval European states?

The fourteenth and fifteenth centuries also witnessed the consolidation of the state that would become the dominant power in eastern Europe. Russia, however, developed very differently from the national monarchies of western Europe. Unlike Spain or France or even Germany, Russia by 1500 had taken decisive steps toward becoming the largest multiethnic empire in the Eurasian world.

This development was not inevitable. Had it not been for a combination of late medieval circumstances, one or several east Slavic states might well have developed along the same lines as did the national monarchies of western Europe. As we saw in Chapter Eight, Swedish Vikings (known as Rus) had played a key role in establishing the principality of Kiev in modern-day Ukraine. During the tenth and eleventh centuries, Kiev maintained diplomatic and trading relations with both western Europe and Byzantium. But after 1200, several epoch-making developments combined to separate Russia from western Europe.

The first was the conquest of most of the eastern Slavic states by the Mongols. Commanded by Batu, a grandson of the great Chingiz (Genghis) Khan, the Mongols cut such swaths of devastation through Russia as they advanced westward that, according to one contemporary, "no eye remained open to weep for the dead." In 1240, the Mongols overran Kiev. Two years later they created their own state on the lower Volga River—the khanate of the Golden Horde—which exercised superiority over most of Russia for the following 150 years. During the thirteenth century, the Mongols ruled Russia directly, carrying out censuses, installing their own administrative officials, and requiring the native Russian princes to travel to Mongolia to secure permission from the great khan to rule their territories. After around 1300, however, the Mongols changed course. Rather than rule Russia directly, they instead tolerated the existence of several native Slavic states from which they demanded obedience and regular tribute payments.

THE RISE OF MUSCOVY

Kiev never recovered the dominant position it had enjoyed before the Mongol invasions. The native principality that finally emerged to defeat the Mongols and unify much of Russia was instead the grand duchy of Moscow. Moscow rose to power in the early fourteenth century as a tribute-collecting center for the Mongol khanate. Moscow's alliance with the Mongols did not necessarily protect it from Mongol attacks: the city was destroyed once at the time of the Mongol invasions and again in 1382. But despite these setbacks, Moscow was able, with Mongol support, to absorb the territory of the grand principality of Vladimir and so gradually to become the dominant political power in northeastern Russia.

Moscow also had the advantage of being far removed from the Mongol power base on the lower Volga. Its remote location made Moscow a valuable

THE EXPANSION OF MUSCOVITE RUSSIA TO 1505

The grand duchy of Moscow was the heart of what would soon become the Russian Empire. How did the relative isolation of Moscow compared with Kiev allow for the growth of Muscovite power on the one hand and Moscow's distinctively non-Western culture on the other? Why did the Muscovite Russians identify so closely with the Byzantines, and why did they reserve such pronounced hostility for the West and Latin Christianity? What role did the Kingdom of Poland-Lithuania play in the development of this Russian attitude? How did the natural direction of the expansion of Muscovite power until 1505 help encourage attitudes often at odds with those of western European civilization?

ally for the Mongol khanate, while allowing the grand dukes of Moscow to consolidate their strength without attracting too much attention from the khans. Despite Moscow's remote location, however, the grand duchy maintained commercial contacts with both the Baltic and the Black Sea regions throughout the Mongol

Period. What really distanced Moscow from western Europe was not, therefore, the fact that it was under the thumb of the Mongols. Rather, it was the enormous religious hostility that existed after 1204 between the Orthodox Christian world (to which Moscow adhered) and the Latin Christian world of

WHY DID RUSSIA DEVELOP DIFFERENTLY FROM OTHER LATE MEDIEVAL EUROPEAN STATES?

KIEVAN RUS AND THE RISE OF MUSCOVY   397

Europe. Hostility between these two great branches of Christianity had deep historical roots but became much more pronounced as a result of the Latins' capture of Constantinope, the capital of the Orthodox world, during the Fourth Crusade. During the fourteenth and fiteenth centuries, however, what particularly excited the religious animosity of Moscow toward western European Christianity was the growing strength of the Catholic kingdom of Poland and the fall of Constantinople to the Ottoman Turks in 1453.

THE RIVALRY WITH POLAND

During the High Middle Ages, Poland had been a second-rate power, usually on the defensive against German encroachments. During the fourteenth century, however, Poland's situation changed dramatically, partly because German strength was declining, but above all because the marriage in 1386 of Poland's reigning queen, Jadwiga, to Jagiello, Grand Duke of Lithuania, more than doubled Poland's size, enabling the newly combined kingdom to become a major expanionist state. Even before 1386 Lithuania had begun to carve out an extensive territory stretching from the Baltic Sea into modern-day Belarus and Ukraine. This expansionist momentum increased after its union with Poland. In 1410, at the Battle of Tannenberg, combined Polish and Lithuanian forces inflicted a stunning defeat on the Teutonic Knights, the German military order that ruled neighboring Prussia. Poland-Lithuania then began to push its borders eastward toward Russia. Although many Lithuanian nobles were Orthodox Christians, the established church in Lithuania was Roman Catholic. So too, of course, was the Kingdom of Poland. Thus when Moscow took the offensive against Poland-Lithuania in the late fifteenth century, its campaigns appealed to religious as well as national loyalties. Prolonged warfare ensued, greatly increasing Russian antagonism not only toward Poland-Lithuania but also toward the Latin Christian tradition it represented in the eyes of Muscovites.

MOSCOW AND BYZANTIUM

The growing alienation of Moscow from Latin Christian Europe was further increased by events leading up to the fall of Constantinople to the Turks in 1453. Connections between Byzantium and the Rus went back to the tenth century, when Byzantine missionaries had converted the Kievan Slavs to Orthodox Christianity. Thereafter, the Russian church gradually came to see itself as a special ally of Constantinople in de-fending and maintaining Orthodoxy, an attitude embraced by the Muscovite church also. In 1438, however, Orthodox Church authorities in Constantinople agreed to submit to papal authority and unite with the Latin Christian church, in the hope that this might bring them western military support to withstand the Turks, who were by now knocking at the gates of the besieged city. The Russian church refused to follow Byzantium in this religious submission to Rome, regarding it as a betrayal of Orthodoxy; and when Constantinople fell to the Turks without any help from the west having arrived, Muscovite churchmen regarded the Turkish victory as divine punishment for Constantinople's religious perfidy. After 1453, the Muscovite state declared itself to be the divinely appointed successor to Byzantium, adopting in the process a particularly zealous anti-Catholic ideology, which was reinforced by the military threat from Poland-Lithuania. The Muscovite ruler took the title of *tsar*, which means "caesar," and Russians declared Moscow both "a second Jerusalem" and "the third Rome." "Two Romes have fallen," said a Russian spokesman, "the third is still standing, and a fourth there shall not be."

THE REIGN OF IVAN THE GREAT (1462–1505)

This Byzantine-derived ideology of divine election underlay both the later growth of Russian imperialism and the sacred position ascribed to the rulers of the Muscovite (and later Russian) state. Behind these developments, however, lay also the steadily growing power of the grand dukes of Moscow. Moscow itself achieved effective independence from the Mongols at the end of the fourteenth century, when a rival Mongol ruler named Timur the Lame (Tamurlane) destroyed the Mongal khanate of the Golden Horde. But it was the grand duke Ivan III, known as Ivan the Great, who transformed Moscow into a true imperial power. Declaring himself the White Tsar (and so the legitimate successor to the Mongol Golden Horde), Ivan launched a series of conquests between 1468 and 1485 that annexed, one by one, all the independent Russian principalities that lay between Moscow and the border with Poland-Lithuania. After invading Lithuania in 1492 and 1501, Ivan also succeeded in bringing parts of Belarus and Ukraine under his control. Battles between Russia and Poland-Lithuania would continue for several centuries, but by 1505, when Ivan died, he had established Muscovy as a power to be reckoned with on the European scene.

Ivan the Great.

based empire. As they were for the states of western Europe also, the late Middle Ages were thus a decisive period in the political evolution of the Russian state.

TRIALS FOR THE CHURCH

Why did late medieval efforts to reform the institutions of the Catholic Church fail?

The later Middle Ages were a challenging and difficult period for the institutions of the Catholic Church. Like other large landowners, monasteries suffered from the economic changes brought about by the Black Death. So too did bishops, who confronted the same price scissors (declining revenues and rising costs) as did the secular nobility. No ecclesiastical institution suffered more severe trials, however, than did the late medieval papacy, which endured almost seventy years of continuous exile from Rome—an exile that was followed first by a forty-year schism and then by a protracted battle with reformers who sought to reduce the popes' authority to govern the church.

THE LATE MEDIEVAL PAPACY AND CONCILIARISM

Following the humiliation and death of Pope Boniface VIII (1294–1303) at the hands of King Philip IV of France (see page 343), the late medieval papacy entered into a long period of institutional crisis. After four years of wandering in exile from Rome, the papacy resided continuously from 1309 until 1378 at Avignon, a small papal territory on the southwestern border of France. Here they built up a large and efficient bureaucracy, principally devoted to raising money to fund the reconquest of the papal states in Italy.

When the popes first settled in Avignon, they had not intended to remain there. But Avignon soon proved to have a number of advantages over Rome. It was closer to the major centers of power in fourteenth-century Europe, it was far removed from the tumultuous local politics of Rome and the papal states, and it was safe from the aggressive attentions of the German emperors. All the popes elected during the Avignon period were natives of southern France, as were nearly all the cardinals whom they appointed; for them, Avignon felt like home. As the papal bureaucracy grew in size, it too became more difficult to move. Nor could the wishes of

Under Ivan III, Muscovy evolved rapidly in the direction of political autocracy and imperialism. In 1452, Ivan married the niece of the last Byzantine emperor, giving substance to his claims to be the Orthodox successor to the Byzantine emperors. He would later adopt, as his imperial insignia, the double-headed eagle of Rome. To display his imperial splendor, he also rebuilt his fortified Moscow residence, known as the Kremlin, in magnificent Italian Renaissance style. As tsar, Ivan presented himself as the autocratic ruler not only of Moscow but of all Russians everywhere, and potentially of Belarussians and Ukrainians also.

After Ivan's death, Russian expansionism was principally directed south and east, against the small successor states to the Mongol Golden Horde. From the mid-seventeenth century on, however, Muscovite pressure against Ukraine and Belarus would escalate, leading to the enormous Russian land empire Peter the Great would create in the early eighteenth century. We cannot draw a direct line from Ivan III to Peter the Great. But Peter would appeal to the foundations Ivan laid as justification for his own claims to incorporate both Russians and a wide variety of non-Russian peoples into what would become Europe's largest land-

Why did late medieval efforts to reform the institutions of the Catholic Church fail?

Trials for the Church   399

the king of France be ignored. The French king was the principal secular supporter of the Avignon popes, and he liked having them on the borders of his kingdom, where he could browbeat them as necessary.

But despite Avignon's advantages, the papacy never abandoned the hope of returning to Rome. To do so, however, the popes first had to win back military control over the papal states in central Italy. This effort took decades. To finance these wars, the Avignon popes imposed new taxes and obligations on the churches of France, England, Germany, and Spain. Judicial cases from the church courts also brought large revenues into the papal coffers. More controversially, the Avignon popes also claimed the right to appoint bishops and priests directly to vacant church offices. Such appointments (known as papal provisions) were not necessarily abusive. Although they bypassed the rights of the local clergy to elect their own officials, the men appointed were often of outstanding ability. But all such appointees had to pay large fees to the papacy in return for their appointments, fees that critics declared to be simony (the purchase of church offices for cash).

By these and other measures, the Avignon popes strengthened their administrative control over the church. But this did not make them loved. Clergy and laity alike were alienated by the papacy's insatiable demands for money, and stories quickly spread about the unbridled luxury of the papal court. In fact, most of the Avignon popes were morally upright and personally abstemious; the cash they collected went overwhelmingly to pay the costs of war in central Italy. One, however, Pope Clement VI (1342–1352), was notoriously corrupt and immoral. Clement openly sold spiritual benefits for money, boasted that he would appoint a jackass as bishop if political circumstances warranted, and defended his incessant sexual transgressions by insisting that he fornicated on doctors' orders. His cardinals led equally luxurious and dissolute lives, feasting on exotic birds and drinking from sculptured fountains that spouted the finest wines.

In 1367, Pope Urban V tried to return to Rome but found his way blocked by the troops of King Charles V of France. In 1377, however, Pope Gregory XI succeeded in returning the papacy from Avignon to Rome. But when he died only a year later, disaster struck. Fearful that if the new pope were a Frenchman he might return to Avignon, the Romans rioted, demanding that the cardinals (who were mainly southern

Papal Palace at Avignon. This great palace was begun in 1339 and symbolizes the apparent permanence of the papal residence in Avignon.

French) elect a Roman as the new pope. Fearing for their lives, the cardinals quickly obliged, electing an Italian who took the name Urban VI. Urban, however, immediately began quarreling with the cardinals, revealing what were probably paranoid tendencies. Fearing for their lives once again, the cardinals fled Rome, declared Urban VI's election invalid, and elected as the new pope a French cardinal who took the name Clement VII. Clement and the cardinals then marched on Rome with an army, but they could not dislodge Pope Urban from the city. Urban VI thereupon named a new, entirely Italian college of cardinals, while Clement VII and his cardinals withdrew to Avignon.

The result was the Great Schism, a nearly forty-year period during which the church was ruled first by two and ultimately by three competing popes, each

THE GREAT SCHISM, 1378–1417

During the Great Schism Europe was divided by religious allegiance. What common interests united the supporters of the Avignon pope? The Roman pope? Why did areas like Portugal and Austria find it so difficult to choose which side to support?

WHY DID LATE MEDIEVAL EFFORTS TO REFORM THE INSTITUTIONS OF THE CATHOLIC CHURCH FAIL?

TRIALS FOR THE CHURCH   401

claiming to be the legitimate successor to Saint Peter. Europe's religious allegiances fractured along the lines of political division established by the Hundred Years' War. France, Scotland, Castile, Aragon, and Naples recognized the Avignon pope, while England, Germany, northern Italy, Scandinavia, Bohemia, Poland, and Hungary recognized the Roman pope. Nor was there any obvious way to end this embarrassing state of affairs. Both popes had been elected by the same group of cardinals; and thereafter, whenever one of the popes died, his supporters quickly elected a successor, thus prolonging the Schism. Finally, in 1409, some cardinals from both camps met at Pisa, where they deposed both popes and named a new one. But neither the Roman nor the Avignon pope accepted the council's decisions. As a result, after 1409 there were three rival popes excommunicating each other, instead of only two.

The Great Schism finally ended in 1417 at the Council of Constance, the largest ecclesiastical gathering of the Middle Ages. The council had strong support from several European princes, including King Henry V of England and the emperor Sigismund of Germany, and took care to depose all the other papal claimants before naming its own new pope, an Italian who took the name Martin V. This, however, took three years of effort, and so the council was unable to proceed with its larger goal of reforming the religious life of the church. That task was left for future councils.

The election of Pope Martin V restored the ecclesiastical unity of Europe. It did not, however, end the struggle over how the church should be governed in future. To end the schism, the Council of Constance had declared that supreme authority within the church rested not with the pope, but with itself and all future such general councils. It also ordered that general councils should meet regularly thereafter to oversee the governance and reform of the church.

These conciliar decrees were a revolutionary challenge to the traditions of papal monarchy. It is not surprising that Pope Martin V and his successors did all they could to undermine them. In 1423, when the next required general council met at Siena, Pope Martin sent its representatives back home almost immediately. Constance had specified that a council must meet, but it had not specified for how long that meeting must last! In 1431, however, when the next general council met at Basel, its members immediately took steps to ensure that the pope could not dismiss it. A lengthy struggle for power then ensued, in which the popes and the conciliarists competed for the support of Europe's kings and princes. Finally, in 1449, the Council of Basel dissolved itself in abject failure, bringing to an end this radical experiment in conciliar government over the church and dashing the hopes of those who thought it would lead to a thoroughgoing reform of religious life "in head and members."

THE GROWTH OF NATIONAL CHURCHES

The papacy's victory over the conciliarists was a costly one. To win the support of Europe's kings and princes against the conciliarists, the popes negotiated a series of treaties, known as "concordats," which granted these rulers extensive authority over the churches within their territories. The popes thus secured their own theoretical supremacy over the church at the cost of surrendering their real power to rule it. Under the terms of these concordats, kings now received many of the revenues from local churches that previously had gone to the papacy. They also acquired new powers to appoint candidates to church offices within their kingdoms.

As papal authority over local churches diminished, and the spiritual prestige of the papacy declined, kings and princes became the primary figures toward whom even churchmen looked to reform the religious and moral lives of their people. Many secular rulers responded aggressively to such expectations by closing scandal-ridden monasteries, suppressing heretics, punishing women accused of witchcraft, regulating prostitution, and prohibiting the lower classes from dressing

Joan of Arc drives Prostitutes from Her Army. This illustration, from a 1484 manuscript, tells one of the many legends that grew up around Joan after her death. It also shows the efforts that many late-fifteenth-century rulers made to present themselves as champions of moral reform within their lands.

THE CONCILIARIST CONTROVERSY

The Great Schism produced a fundamental and far-reaching debate about the nature of authority within the church. Arguments for papal supremacy rested on the traditional claims that the popes were the successors of Saint Peter, to whom Jesus Christ had delegated his own authority over the church. Arguments for the supremacy of a general council had been advanced around the University of Paris throughout much of the fourteenth century; but it was only in the circumstances of the schism that these arguments found a wide audience. The documents here trace the history of the controversy, from the declaration of conciliar supremacy at the Council of Constance (Haec Sancta), to the council's efforts to guarantee regular meetings of general councils thereafter (Frequens), to the papal condemnation of appeals to future general councils issued in 1460 (Execrabilis). Note, however, the limitations on Execrabilis. Even this condemnation does not go so far as to actually contradict Haec Sancta. It merely condemns appeals from papal judgment to future general councils that have no specified meeting date. The conciliar ideal was still powerful at the end of the fifteenth century; and in the sixteenth and seventeenth centuries, it would have a profound impact on European political thought about kings.

HAEC SANCTA SYNODUS (1415)

This holy synod of Constance . . . declares that being lawfully assembled in the Holy Spirit, constituting a general council and representing the Catholic Church Militant, it has its power directly from Christ, and that all persons of whatever rank or dignity, even a Pope, are bound to obey it in matters relating to faith and the end of the Schism and the general reformation of the church of God in head and members.

Further, it declares that any person of whatever position, rank, or dignity, even a Pope, who contumaciously refuses to obey the mandates, statutes, ordinances, or regulations enacted or to be enacted by this holy synod, or by any other general council lawfully assembled, relating to the matters aforesaid or to other matters involved with them, shall, unless he repents, be . . . duly punished. . . .

FREQUENS (1417)

The frequent holding of general councils is the best method of cultivating the field of the Lord, for they root out the briars, thorns, and thistles of heresies, errors, and schisms, correct abuses, make crooked things straight, and prepare the Lord's vineyard for fruitfulness and rich fertility. Neglect of general councils sows the seeds of these evils and encourages their growth. This truth is borne in upon us as we recall times past and survey the present.

Therefore by perpetual edict we . . . ordain that henceforth general councils shall be held as follows: the first within the five years immediately following the end of the present council, the second within seven years from the end of the council next after this, and subsequently every ten years forever. . . . Thus there will always be a certain continuity. Either a council will be in session or one will be expected at the end of a fixed period. . . .

R. L. Loomis, ed. and trans., *"Haec Sancta Synodus"* and *"Frequens"* in *The Council of Constance* (New York, 1961), pp. 229, 246–247.

EXECRABILIS (1460)

An execrable abuse, unheard of in earlier times, has sprung up in our period. Some men, imbued with a spirit of rebellion and moved not by a desire for sound decisions but rather by a desire to escape the punishment for sin, suppose that they can appeal from the Pope, Vicar of Jesus Christ; from the Pope, to whom in the person of blessed Peter it was said, "Feed my sheep" and "whatever you bind on earth will be bound in heaven"—from this Pope to a future council. How harmful this is to the Christian republic, as well as how contrary to canon law, anyone who is not ignorant of the law can understand. For . . . who would not consider it ridiculous to appeal to something which does not now exist anywhere nor does anyone know when it will exist? The poor are heavily oppressed by the powerful, offenses remain unpunished, rebellion against the Holy See is encouraged, license for sin is granted, and all ecclesiastical discipline and hierarchical ranking of the Church are turned upside down.

Wishing therefore to expel this deadly poison from the Church of Christ, and concerned with the salvation of the sheep committed to us . . . with the counsel and assent of our venerable brothers, the Cardinals of the Holy Roman Church, together with the counsel and assent of all those prelates who have been trained in canon and civil law who follow our Court, and with our own certain knowledge, we condemn appeals of this kind, reject them as erroneous and abominable, and declare them to be completely null and void. And we lay down that from now on, no one should dare . . . to make such an appeal from our decisions, be they legal or theological, or from any commands at all from us or our successors. . . .

Heiko A. Oberman, Daniel E. Zerfoss, and William J. Courtenay, eds. and trans., *Execrabilis: Defensorum Obedientiae Apostolicae et alia Documenta* (Cambridge, Mass., 1968), pp. 224–227 (with modifications by R. C. Stacey).

QUESTIONS FOR ANALYSIS

1. How might the conciliar movement be seen as a subtle challenge to the authority of the medieval papacy?
2. Why would a pope fear the decisions of a general council?
3. Why was it important to guarantee regular meetings of general church councils?

---

as if they were nobles. By these and other such measures, rulers could present themselves as champions of moral and religious reform while also strengthening their capacity to rule their territories. The result was an increasingly close link between national rulers and the national churches over which they ruled.

Having given away so many of their other revenues, the popes of the late fifteenth century became even more dependent on their own territories in central Italy than their predecessors had been. To build up the Papal States, however, the popes had to rule like other Italian princes: leading armies, jockeying for alliances with other princes, and undermining their oppponents by every possible means. Judged in secular terms, their efforts were by no means a failure. By 1520, the Papal States were one of the better-governed and wealthier principalities in Italy. But such methods did nothing to increase the popes' reputation for piety or to respond to the calls from both clergy and laity for a thoroughgoing reform of religious life. By 1500, disillusionment with the late medieval papacy as a force for spiritual and religious reform within the church was widespread. In the Protestant Reformation, that smoldering tinder would erupt into a European-wide conflagration.

THE PURSUIT OF HOLINESS IN LATE MEDIEVAL PIETY

Were late medieval people disillusioned with their church?

Despite the travails of the institutional church, religious devotion among the laity was more widespread and intense during the later Middle Ages than it had ever been before. The fundamental theme of high medieval preaching, that salvation lay open to any Christian who strove for it, bore fruit during the later Middle Ages in a rapidly multiplying variety of paths that promised to lead the individual believer to God. Some of these paths led their adherents in directions the church declared heretical. For the vast majority of late medieval Christians, however, heresy held no appeal. The church, and especially the sacraments performed by their local parish priests, was the center of their religious lives. To understand late medieval Christianity, we need therefore to start in the parishes.

SACRAMENT, RITUAL, AND SERMON

By 1300, nearly all of Europe was covered by a network of local parish churches within which priests administered the sacraments of the church to the laity. These sacraments—baptism, confirmation, the Mass, confession, marriage, ordination, and extreme unction —were rituals that conveyed the grace and power of God to individual Christian believers. Late medieval piety revolved around them. Baptism initiated the Christian into the life of the church. In the later Middle Ages, it was administered to infants as soon as possible after birth; without baptism, salvation was generally thought to be impossible. Confirmation "confirmed" the promises made on a child's behalf at baptism. Through the priest's ministrations during the Mass (which was celebrated every Sunday and on feast days as well), bread and wine were transubstantiated into the actual body and blood of Christ, which the Christian faithful honored and consumed. Confession of sins to a priest guaranteed their forgiveness by God; but if satisfactory penance for sins were not completed on earth, then it would have to be done after death in purgatory, a nether world between heaven and hell. Marriage was a relatively new sacrament, increasingly emphasized in the later Middle Ages; but still only a minority of Christians would have had their unions solemnized by the church. Ordination conveyed to a priest his special power to bring God's grace to earth through the sacraments, a power that could never be lost, even by a priest who led an immoral life. Extreme unction (or last rites) was administered to a dying person. It ensured the final confession of all sins and so was essential to a good death with the assurance of salvation to come. Like baptism, extreme unction could, in an emergency, be administered by any Christian believer. The other sacraments, however, could be administered only by a properly ordained priest—or, in the case of confirmation and ordination, by a bishop.

This sacramental system was the foundation on which the other practices of late medieval popular piety rested. Pilgrimages, for example, were a form of penance, which could lessen one's time in purgatory. Crusading was a kind of extreme pilgrimage that promised the complete fulfillment of all penances the crusader might owe for all the sins of his (or her) life. Many other pious acts—saying the prayers of the rosary, for example, or giving alms to the poor—could also serve as penance for one's sins as well as constituting good works that would help the believer in his or her journey toward salvation.

But there was more to late medieval piety than simply penance. Like all good works, prayer had other purposes also. The saints generally, and the Virgin Mary in particular, were regarded as powerful intercessors with God. In danger or ill health, believers would pray to such holy figures. Some saints were known for responding to particular ailments; if afflicted with hemorrhoids, for example, one might be well advised to pray to Saint Fiacre. Devotion to the saints might be increased by contact with the relics of a saint, typically pieces of bone or clothing that had belonged to the saint. No relic was more powerful, however, or more central to late medieval piety, than the bread and wine of the Mass, which became, through priestly consecration, the true body and blood of Christ. Believers sometimes attributed astonishing properties to the eucharistic bread of the Mass, feeding it to sick animals or rushing from church to church to see the consecrated bread as many times as possible in a day. Understandably, some of these beliefs and practices, and many alleged relics of the saints, were criticized by church reformers as superstitious. But by and large, these were not practices foisted on an ignorant and credulous laity by a group of clerical con men. They arose and continued because of the deep devotion of laypeople to them, frequently in opposition to the efforts of church reformers to shut them down.

RELIGION AND THE SOCIAL ORDER

Late medieval people understood their religion as a thoroughly integrated part of the social world in which they lived. The church stood literally at the center of their lives. Churchyards were communal meeting places; sometimes they were even the sites of markets. Church buildings were a refuge from attack and a gathering place for village business, whose upkeep and repair was a village responsibility. The church's holidays marked the passage of the year, and the church's bells marked the hours of the day. Understandably, therefore, the holiness of the church tended to be seen as an element in the larger holiness of the community, local or national, of which it was a part.

Not everyone found the conventional practices of late medieval piety spiritually satisfying. Although honored in death, many late medieval saints were distinctly controversial in life; and the lines between a saint and a witch could sometimes be very fine, as Joan of Arc's example reveals. As a child, Saint Catherine of Siena refused altogether to help with the housework and then took over one of the two rooms in her working-class family's house for her prayers, forcing her parents and her dozen siblings into the one remaining room. Julianna of Norwich withdrew from the world into a small cell built next to her local church, where she spent the rest of her life in prayer and contemplation; while Margery Kempe was so moved by the suffering of Jesus on the cross that she would cry hysterically for hours, completely disrupting the Mass and deeply alienating her fellow parishioners.

The extraordinary piety of such individuals could be awe inspiring, but it could also threaten the church's control over religious life and the links that bound individuals to their communities. It could, therefore, be dangerous. Some believers, for example, sought to achieve a mystical union with God through rigorous spiritual exercises; a few of these were ultimately condemned for heresy for declaring that, having succeeded in their mystical quest, they were no longer obliged to obey God's church on earth. And even less radical figures might find themselves treading on dangerous ground, especially if they wrote religious tracts in vernacular languages, so that the laity could more easily read them. Master Eckhart (c. 1260–1327), for example, a German Dominican, taught and wrote in both Latin and German that there was a power or "spark" deep within every human soul wherein God dwelt. By renouncing all sense of self, one could retreat into one's innermost recesses and there find divinity. Eckhart did not recommend ceasing attendance at church—he hardly could have because he preached in churches—but he made it clear that for those seeking to find God, even the sacraments were of lesser importance than the inward journey he described. He also gave the impression to his lay audiences that they might attain godliness largely on their own volition. Church authorities charged him with inciting "ignorant and undisciplined people to wild and dangerous excesses." Although Eckhart pleaded his own doctrinal orthodoxy, some of his teachings were ultimately condemned as heretical.

More safely orthodox was the practical mysticism preached to both monastic and lay audiences during the fifteenth century by such figures as Thomas à Kempis, whose *Imitation of Christ* (c. 1427) did not aim for full mystical union with God but rather for an ongoing sense of divine presence during the conduct of daily life. The *Imitation* taught its readers to be pious Christians while still living actively in the world, emphasizing the importance of the Mass but otherwise stressing inward rather than outward piety and urging believers to meditate on the Bible and to live a simple, moral life. Although written in Latin, the *Imitation* was quickly translated into the leading European vernacular languages. For almost six centuries, it has been more widely read than any other Christian religious work except the Bible.

LOLLARDS AND HUSSITES

For the most part, popular heretical movements were less widespread and less dangerous to the church during the later Middle Ages than they had been in the twelfth and thirteenth centuries. In England and Bohemia, however, heretical movements did pose serious challenges to the established authorities of both church and state. In England, the Lollard heresy began with John Wyclif (c. 1330–1384), an Oxford theologian whose extreme predestinarianism (see page 229) led him to conclude that the sacraments of a corrupt church could not save anyone. He urged the English Crown, therefore, to appropriate ecclesiastical wealth and to replace corrupt priests and bishops with men who would live according to apostolic standards of poverty and piety. Wyclif's followers went even further, presenting themselves as the only true church and dismissing the sacraments of the church as fraudulent attempts to squeeze money from parishioners. In place of the corrupt, official church, Lollard preachers traveled the countryside, bringing with them an English translation of the Bible (which Wyclif himself may have begun) and other vernacular religious literature, which they put directly into the hands of the laity.

Lollardy gained numerous adherents in the last two decades of the fourteenth century, including a group of noble supporters who may have helped fund the movement in its early days. But after the failure of a Lollard uprising in 1414, the movement lost its noble support and went underground. Lollards survived into the sixteenth century, in numbers sufficient to cause occasional alarm to church authorities. But Lollards were never more than a tiny minority movement, which stood in flat opposition to almost everything (including pilgrimages, the sacraments, and religious images) that their neighbors found most satisfying in late medieval religious life.

Wyclif's ideas struck much deeper roots in Bohemia, where they were adopted by Jan Hus (c. 1373–1415), a charismatic preacher at Charles University in Prague who had already been inveighing in well-attended sermons against "the world, the flesh, and the devil." In contrast to the Lollards, however, whose dismissal of the Eucharist cost them much support, Hus emphasized

Title page from the teachings of Jan Hus. An eloquent religous reformer, Jan Hus was burned at the stake in 1415 for heresy. He accused the Catholic church of being corrupt and demanded that the church reform the Eucharist.

there. Rather than being given a fair hearing, Hus was convicted of heresy and burned at the stake.

Hus's supporters in Bohemia quickly raised the banner of open revolt. Nobles took advantage of the situation to seize church lands, while priests, artisans, and peasants rallied together to pursue Hus's goals of religious reform and social justice. Between 1420 and 1424 armies of radical Hussites known as Taborites, lead by a brilliant blind general, Jan Zizka, resoundingly defeated several invading forces of crusading knights sent against them by the papacy. These victories increased the radicalism of the Taborites, inspiring them to heights of apocalyptic fervor. Finally, in 1434 more conservative, aristocratically dominated Hussites overcame the radicals and negotiated a settlement with the church that permitted Utraquism in the Bohemian church alongside Catholic orthodoxy. But Bohemia did not return fully to the Catholic fold until the seventeenth century.

Lollardy and Hussitism exhibit a number of striking similarities. Both began in the universities and then spread to the countryside. Both called for the clergy to live in simplicity and poverty, and both attracted noble support, especially in their early days. Both movements were also strongly nationalistic, employing their own vernacular languages (English and Czech) instead of Latin and identifying themselves with the English or Czech people in opposition to an international, and therefore foreign, official church. They also strongly emphasized the importance of vernacular preaching to the laity. In all these respects, they established patterns that would emerge again in the vastly larger currents of the Protestant Reformation.

the centrality of the Eucharist to Christian piety by demanding that the laity should receive not only the consecrated bread of the Mass but also the consecrated wine, which the late medieval church reserved solely for priests. This demand, known as Utraquism, gained broad popular support among the Bohemian laity and became a rallying symbol for the Hussite movement. Influential nobles also supported Hus, partly out of national pride but partly too in the hope that the reforms Hus demanded in the church might restore to them the revenues they had lost to the church over the previous century. Accordingly, most of Bohemia was behind him when Hus in 1415 agreed to travel to the Council of Constance to defend his views and try to convince the assembled prelates to undertake sweeping reforms of church life. The council had guaranteed Hus's safety, but this assurance was revoked as soon as he arrived

THOUGHT, LITERATURE, AND ART

What accounts for the remarkable creativity of late medieval cultural life?

The hardships of the later Middle Ages might have led intellectual and artistic life to stagnate, but in fact the period was an extremely creative one in thought, literature, and art. In this section we postpone treatment of certain developments most closely related to the early history of the Italian Renaissance but discuss some of the other important intellectual and artistic accomplishments of the fourteenth and fifteenth centuries.

WHAT ACCOUNTS FOR THE REMARKABLE CREATIVITY OF LATE MEDIEVAL CULTURAL LIFE?

THOUGHT, LITERATURE, AND ART   407

THEOLOGY AND PHILOSPHY

During the twelfth and thirteenth centuries, scholastic thinkers like Saint Thomas Aquinas had constructed a picture of a rational, organized, and comprehensible natural world that was structured to lead the inquiring human mind to a knowledge of God and hence to salvation. After 1300, however, confidence in this picture began to ebb. Nominalist thinkers such as the English Franciscan William of Ockham (d. 1349) denied that human reason could prove fundamental theological truths such as the existence of God. Instead, they argued, human knowledge of God, and hence salvation, depended entirely on what God himself had chosen to reveal through scripture. Humans could investigate the natural world but only as a collection of individual entities and interactions. Categories (such as plants or chairs or rocks) were merely human inventions; strictly speaking, they did not exist. And any regularities that were observable in nature existed solely because an all-powerful God actively willed them to continue in this regular way. There was thus no necessary connection between the observable regularities of nature and the unknowable essence of divinity, and no hope of reasoning from the laws of nature to the nature of God. To argue otherwise—to suggest that God *had* to act in accordance with certain natural laws (such as gravity), and that these laws could therefore tell us something about God himself—was an affront to the absolute power and majesty of God.

Nominalism became enormously influential in late medieval universities and had an immense impact on European thought. Ockham's concern about what God might do led his followers to raise some of the seemingly absurd questions for which medieval theology has been mocked—for example, asking whether God can undo the past or whether an infinite number of pure spirits can simultaneously inhabit the same place (the nearest medieval thinkers actually came to asking how many angels can dance on the head of a pin). Nonetheless, the nominalists' insistence on God's omnipotence became one of the basic presuppositions of sixteenth-century Protestantism. The distinction they drew between the rational comprehensibility of the natural world and the incomprehensibility of God encouraged intellectuals to investigate the natural world without reference to supernatural explanations—one of the most important foundations of the modern scientific method. The nominalists' insistence that only individual entities, and not abstract categories, were real and could be studied also helped encourage empiricism: the belief, that is, that knowledge of the world should rest on sense experience rather than abstract reason. This too would be a fundamental building block in the emergence of a modern scientific worldview.

VERNACULAR LITERATURE

Like Ockham's philosophical work, the literature of the later Middle Ages was characterized by an intense concern to describe the world as it is. Such naturalism was not new. High medieval authors such as Wolfram von Eschenbach and Dante had already established the precedents on which their late medieval successors would build. But late medieval authors went much further, especially in describing the foibles and failings of everyday human life. They also pioneered the development of new literary forms for vernacular writing, sometimes in poetry but especially in prose. Most late medieval authors also continued to compose in Latin; but increasingly, the most innovative and ambitious literary work was being written in the vernacular languages of Europe. Behind this development lay three fundamental changes of the later Middle Ages: a growing identification between vernacular languages and nationalism, the continuing spread of lay education, and the emergence of a substantial reading public for vernacular literature. We can see these influences at work in three of the major vernacular authors of the later Middle Ages: Giovanni Boccaccio (1313–1375), Geoffrey Chaucer (c. 1340–1400), and Christine de Pisan (c. 1365–c. 1435).

BOCCACCIO

Boccaccio (*bohk-KAHT-chee-oh*) would deserve an honored place in literary history even for his lesser works, which included courtly romances, pastoral lyrics, and learned treatises. His masterpiece, however, is the *Decameron*, a collection of 100 prose tales, mostly about love, sex, adventure, and trickery, told by a sophisticated party of seven young women and three men temporarily residing in a country villa outside Florence to escape the Black Death. Boccaccio borrowed the outlines of many of these tales from earlier sources, but he transformed them with his own characteristic exuberance and wit.

Boccaccio deliberately wrote in an unaffected, colloquial style, eschewing literary "elegance" to portray men and women exactly as they are. His women are not pallid playthings, distant goddesses, or steadfast virgins but flesh-and-blood creatures with minds and bodies, who interact with men more comfortably and naturally than any women in Western literature had ever done before. His clerics are all too human, much more like other men than they are like angels on earth. His treatment of sexual relations is often graphic, but never demeaning. For all these reasons the *Decameron* is a robust and delightful appreciation of what it means to be human.

CHAUCER

Similar in many ways to Boccaccio as a creator of naturalistic vernacular literature was the Englishman Geoffrey Chaucer (c. 1340–1400). Chaucer was the first major writer whose English can still be read today with relatively little effort. Remarkably, he was both a founder of England's mighty literary tradition and one of the four or five greatest contributors to it: most critics rank him just behind Shakespeare and in a class with Milton, Wordsworth, and Dickens.

Chaucer wrote several highly impressive works, but his masterpiece is unquestionably the *Canterbury Tales*. Like the *Decameron*, this is a collection of stories held together by a frame, in Chaucer's case the device of having a group of people tell stories while on a pilgrimage from London to Canterbury. But there are also differences between the *Decameron* and the *Canterbury Tales*. Chaucer's stories are told in sparkling verse instead of

prose, and they are recounted by people of all different classes—from a chivalric knight to a dedicated university student to a thieving miller with a wart on his nose. Lively women also appear, most memorably the gap-toothed, oft-married Wife of Bath, who knows all "the remedies of love." Each character tells a story that is particularly illustrative of his or her own occupation and outlook on the world. By this device Chaucer was able to create a highly diverse human comedy. His range is greater than Boccaccio's; and although he is no less witty, frank, and lusty than the Italian, he is sometimes more profound.

CHRISTINE DE PISAN

The later Middle Ages saw the emergence of professional authors who made their living with their pens. Significantly, one of the first of these professional *litterati* was a woman, Christine de Pisan (c. 1364–c. 1431). Although born in Italy, Christine spent her adult life in France, where her husband was a member of the king's household. When he died, the widowed Christine turned to writing to support herself and her children. She wrote in a wide variety of literary genres, including treatises on chivalry and warfare that she dedicated to her patron, King Charles VI of France. But she also wrote for a larger and more popular audience. Her

Christine de Pisan. A leading writer of late medieval vernacular prose literature, Christine de Pisan (1365–c.1430) was intent on upholding the dignity of women. She is shown here writing about a gigantic Amazon warrior who could defeat men effortlessly in armed combat.

imaginative tract *The City of Ladies* is an extended defense of the character, nature, and capacities of women against their male detractors, written in the form of an allegory. She also took part in a vigorous pamphlet literature that debated the misogynistic claims made against women in the *Romance of the Rose* (see Chapter Nine). This debate continued for several hundred years and became so famous that it was given a name: the *querelle des femmes*, "the debate over women." Christine was by no means the first female writer of the Middle Ages, but she was the first lay woman to earn a living by her writing.

SCULPTURE AND PAINTING

As naturalism was a dominant trait of late medieval literature, so it was of late medieval art. Already by the thirteenth century Gothic sculptors were paying far more attention than their Romanesque predecessors had to the way plants, animals, and human beings really looked. Whereas early medieval art had emphasized abstract design, the stress was now increasingly on realism: thirteenth-century carvings of leaves and flowers must have been made from direct observation and are clearly recognizable to modern botanists as distinct species. Statues of humans also gradually became more natural and realistic in their portrayals of facial expressions and bodily proportions. By around 1290 the concern for realism had become so great that a sculptor working on a tomb portrait of the German emperor Rudolf of Habsburg allegedly made a hurried return trip to view Rudolf in person, because he had heard that a new wrinkle had appeared on the emperor's face.

> Whereas early medieval art had emphasized abstract design, the stress was now increasingly on realism: thirteenth-century carvings of leaves and flowers must have been made from direct observation and are clearly recognizable to modern botanists as distinct species.

In the next two centuries the trend toward naturalism continued in sculpture and was extended to manuscript illumination and painting. The latter was in certain respects a new art. Wall paintings were common in the Middle Ages and long afterward, especially in the form of *frescoes*, paintings done on wet plaster. But in addition to frescoes, Italian artists in the thirteenth century also began painting pictures on pieces of wood or canvas. These were first done in tempera (pigments mixed with water and natural gums or egg whites), but around 1400 painting in oils was introduced in the European north. These new technical developments created new artistic opportunities. Artists were now able to paint religious scenes on portable altarpieces. They also began painting strikingly sensitive and realistic portraits of their patrons on both wood and canvas.

The most innovative painter of the later Middle Ages was the Florentine Giotto (c. 1267–1337), who brought deep humanity to the religious images he painted on both walls and movable panels. Giotto was preeminently an imitator of nature. Not only do his human beings and animals look more lifelike than those of his predecessors but they seem to do more natural things. When Christ enters Jerusalem on Palm Sunday, boys climb trees to get a better view; when Saint Francis is laid out in death, one onlooker takes the opportunity to see whether the saint had really received Christ's wounds; and when the Virgin's parents, Joachim and Anna, meet after a long separation, they actually embrace and kiss—perhaps the first deeply tender kiss in Western art. Giotto was also the first to conceive of the painted space in fully three-dimensional terms: as one art historian has put it, Giotto's frescoes were the first to "knock a hole into the wall." After Giotto's death a reaction in Italian painting set in. Mid-fourteenth-century artists briefly moved away from naturalism and painted stern, forbidding religious figures who seemed to float in space. But by around 1400 artists came back down to earth and started to build on Giotto's influence in ways that led to the great Italian renaissance in painting.

In the north of Europe painting did not advance impressively beyond manuscript illumination until the early fifteenth century, but then it suddenly came very much into its own. The leading northern European painters were Flemish, first and foremost Jan van Eyck (c. 1380–1441), Roger van der Weyden (c. 1400–1464), and Hans Memling (c. 1430–1494). These three were the greatest early practitioners of painting in oil, a medium that allowed them to engage in brilliant coloring and sharp-focused realism. Van Eyck and van der Weyden excelled at communicating a sense of deep religious piety and portraying minute details of familiar everyday experience. These may at first seem incompatible, but it should be remembered that contemporary manuals of practical mysticism such as the *Imitation of Christ* also sought to link deep piety with everyday existence. Thus it was by no means blasphemous when a Flemish painter portrayed behind a tender Virgin and

The Meeting of Joachim and Anna, by Giotto. Notice how the haloes merge. This aged and infertile couple will soon miraculously have their only child: Mary, the mother of Jesus.

Child a vista of contemporary life with people going about their usual business and a man even urinating against a wall. This union of the sacred and the profane tended to fall apart in the work of Memling, who excelled in either straightforward religious pictures or secular portraits, but it would return in the work of the greatest painters of the Low Countries, Brueghel and Rembrandt.

ADVANCES IN TECHNOLOGY

How did technological advances affect everyday life?

No account of enduring late medieval accomplishments would be complete without mention of certain epoch-making technological advances. Sadly, but probably not unexpectedly, treatment of this subject has to begin with reference to the invention of artillery and firearms. The prevalence of warfare stimulated the development of new weaponry. Gunpowder itself was a Chinese invention, but it was first put to devastating military uses in the late medieval West. Heavy cannons were first employed around 1330. The earliest cannons were so primitive that it often was more dangerous to stand behind than in front of them, but by the middle of the fifteenth century they were greatly improved and began to revolutionize the nature of warfare. In one year, 1453, heavy artillery played a leading role in determining the outcome of two crucial conflicts: the Ottoman Turks used German and Hungarian cannons to breach the defenses of Constantinople—hitherto the most impregnable in Europe—and the French used heavy artillery to take the city of Bordeaux, thereby ending the Hundred Years' War. Cannons thereafter made it difficult for rebellious aristocrats to hole up in their stone castles, and thus they aided in the consolidation of the national monarchies. Placed aboard ships, cannons also enabled European vessels to dominate foreign waters in the subsequent age of overseas expansion. Hand-held firearms, also invented in the fourteenth century, were gradually perfected. Shortly after 1500 the most effective new variety of gun, the musket, allowed foot soldiers to end

A Fifteenth-Century Siege with Cannon. By the mid fifteenth century, cannons were an essential element in siege warfare.

once and for all the earlier military dominance of heavily armored mounted knights. Once lance-bearing cavalries became outmoded and fighting could more easily be carried on by all, the monarchical states that could turn out the largest armies completely subdued internal resistance and dominated the battlefields of Europe.

Other late medieval technological developments were more life enhancing. Eyeglasses, first invented in the 1280s, were perfected in the fourteenth century. These allowed older people to keep on reading when farsightedness would otherwise have stopped them. The great fourteenth-century scholar Petrarch, who boasted excellent sight in his youth, wore spectacles after his sixtieth year and was thus able to complete some of his most important works. Around 1300 the use of the magnetic compass helped ships sail farther away from land and venture out into the Atlantic. One immediate result was the opening of direct sea commerce between Italy and the north. Subsequently, numerous improvements in shipbuilding, map making, and navigational devices enabled Europe to start expanding overseas. In the fourteenth century the Azores and Cape Verde Islands were reached; then, after a long pause caused by Europe's plagues and wars,

the African Cape of Good Hope was rounded in 1488, the West Indies reached in 1492, India reached by the sea route in 1498, and Brazil sighted in 1500. Partly as a result of technology, the world was thus suddenly made much smaller.

Among the most familiar implements of our modern life that were invented by Europeans in the later Middle Ages were clocks and printed books. Mechanical clocks were invented shortly before 1300 and proliferated in the years immediately thereafter. The earliest clocks were too expensive for private purchase, but towns vied with each other to install the most elaborate clocks in their prominent public buildings. The new invention ultimately had two profound effects. One was the further stimulation of European interest in complex machinery of all sorts. This interest had already been awakened by the high medieval proliferation of mills, but clocks ultimately became even more omnipresent than mills because after about 1650 they became quite cheap and were brought into practically every European home. Household clocks served as models of marvelous machines. Equally if not more significant was the fact that clocks began to rationalize the course of European daily affairs.

> The earliest clocks were too expensive for private purchase, but towns vied with each other to install the most elaborate clocks in their prominent public buildings.

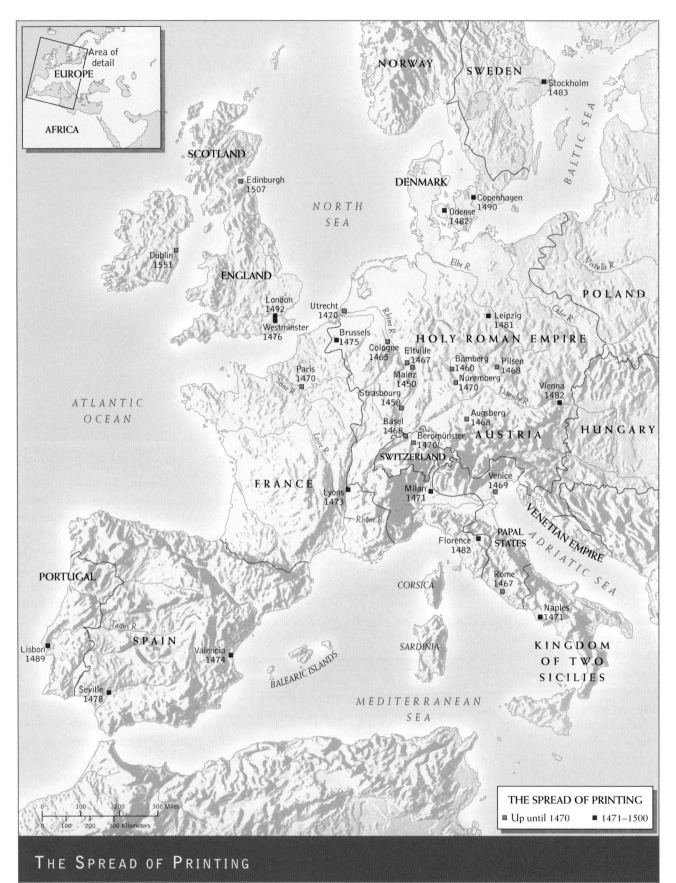

THE SPREAD OF PRINTING

Note how quickly the new technology of printing spread throughout Europe between 1470 and 1500. Where were printing presses most heavily concentrated? Why were there so relatively few printing presses in France, Spain, and England compared with the Low Countries, northern Italy, and Germany? Why were so many printing centers located in river ports?

Devil with Eyeglasses. As spectacles became more common in the later Middle Ages, they were even sported by devils in hell.

Until the advent of clocks in the later Middle Ages time was flexible. Men and women had only a rough idea of how late in the day it was and rose and retired more or less with the sun. In the fourteenth century, however, clocks first started relentlessly striking equal hours through the day and night. Thus they began to regulate work with new precision. People were expected to start and end work "on time" and many came to believe that "time is money." This emphasis on time-keeping brought new efficiencies but also new tensions: Lewis Carroll's white rabbit, who is always looking at his pocket watch and muttering "how late it's getting," is a telling caricature of time-obsessed Western humanity.

The invention of printing with movable type was equally momentous. The major stimulus for this invention was the replacement of parchment by paper as Europe's primary writing material between 1200 and 1400. Parchment, made from the skins of sheep or calves, was extremely expensive: since it was possible to get about only four good parchment leaves from

one animal, it was necessary to slaughter between 200 and 300 sheep or calves to gain enough parchment for a Bible! Paper, made from rags turned into pulp by mills, brought prices down dramatically. Late medieval records show that paper sold at one sixth the price of parchment. Accordingly, it became cheaper to learn how to read and write. With literacy becoming ever more widespread, there was a growing market for still cheaper books, and the invention of printing with movable type around 1450, associated most famously with the Bible produced by Johann Gutenberg in 1454, fully met this demand. By greatly saving labor, the invention made printed books about one fifth as expensive as handwritten ones within about two decades.

As soon as books became easily accessible, literacy increased even more, and book culture became a basic part of the European way of life. After about 1500, Europeans could afford to read and buy books of all sorts—not just religious tracts but instructional manuals, light entertainment, and, by the eighteenth century, newspapers. Printing ensured that ideas would spread quickly and reliably; moreover, revolutionary ideas could no longer be easily extinguished once they were set down in hundreds of copies of books. Thus the greatest religious reformer of the sixteenth century, Martin Luther, gained an immediate following throughout Germany by employing the printing press to run off pamphlets: had printing not been available to him, Luther might have died as Hus did. The spread of books also helped stimulate the growth of cultural nationalism. Before printing, regional dialects in most European countries were often so diverse that people who supposedly spoke the same language often could barely understand each other. After the invention of printing, however, each European country began to develop its own linguistic standards, which were disseminated uniformly by books. The "king's English" was what was printed in London and carried to Yorkshire or Wales. Thus communications were enhanced and governments were able to operate ever more efficiently.

CONCLUSION

Despite economic dislocation and demographic collapse, the later Middle Ages were one of the most creative and inventive periods in the history of western Europe. Why this was so will always remain something of a mystery, until and unless future scholars should unlock the secrets of human creativity itself. What we can see behind the artistic, philosophical, literary, and technological developments of the period, however, is a consistent drive to understand, control, and replicate the workings of the natural world. This fact may offer some clues toward explaining the sources of these developments.

Perhaps most fundamentally, in the later Middle Ages intellectuals broke with the traditional, Neoplatonic vision of nature as a book in which one could read the mind of God. Instead, they came to see the natural world as operating according to its own laws, which were empirically verifiable but which could tell human beings nothing about the God who lay behind them. The resulting sense of the contingency and independence of the natural world was an essential step toward the emergence of a scientific worldview. It also encouraged Europeans to believe that nature itself could be manipulated and directed toward human ends.

Powerful economic and political factors also encouraged the technological inventiveness of the period. Despite the disruptive impact of plague and war, the market for goods was not destroyed. Instead, the resulting labor shortages encouraged European entrepreneurs to experiment with labor-saving technologies and new crops. Incessant warfare encouraged a remarkable burst of military inventiveness. It also enabled more powerful governments to extract a larger percentage of their subjects' wealth through taxation, which they proceeded to invest in ships, cannons, muskets, and

the standing armies that the new weaponry made possible. Increasing per capita wealth produced the capital necessary to invest in mills, factories, clocks, books, and compasses. It also made possible a remarkable increase in the educational level of the European population. Between 1300 and 1500 hundreds and perhaps thousands of new grammar schools were established, and scores of new universities emerged, because parents saw such schools as a reliable route to social advancement for their sons. Women were still excluded from the schools, but increasing numbers of girls were being taught at home, making women an extremely important (perhaps even the dominant) part of the reading public that was emerging in later medieval Europe.

Finally, it may be that dislocation itself promotes innovation, so long as it does not destroy people's confidence in the ultimate improvability of their lives. Europeans suffered enormously from war, plague, and economic crises during the later Middle Ages. But those who survived seized the opportunities their new world presented to them. The confidence they had developed in the High Middle Ages was not destroyed by the travails of the later Middle Ages. By 1500, most Europeans lived more secure lives than their ancestors had 200 years before; and they stood on the verge of an extraordinary new period of expansion and conquest that would take European armies, merchants, and settlers around the globe.

KEY TERMS

Black Death	Master Eckhart	Ivan the Great	William of Ockham
Jacquerie	Hundred Years' War	Boccaccio	
Richard II	Joan of Arc	*Canterbury Tales*	
Avignon	Wars of the Roses	Christine de Pisan	

SELECTED READINGS

Allmand, Christopher T. *The Hundred Years' War: England and France at War, c. 1300–c. 1450.* Cambridge and New York, 1988. Still the best analytic account of the war; after a short narrative, the book is organized topically.

Allmand, Christopher T., ed. *Society at War: The Experience of England and France During the Hundred Years' War.* Edinburgh, 1973. An outstanding collection of documents.

Boccaccio, Giovanni. *The Decameron.* Trans. Mark Musa and P. E. Bondanella. New York, 1977.

Chaucer, Geoffrey. *The Canterbury Tales.* Trans. Nevill Coghill. New York, 1951. A modern English verse translation, lightly annotated.

Cohn, Samuel K., Jr. *Lust for Liberty: The Politics of Social Revolt in Medieval Europe, 1200–1425. Italy, France, and Flanders.* Cambridge, Mass., 2006. An important new account.

Cole, Bruce. *Giotto and Florentine Painting, 1280–1375.* New York, 1976. A clear and stimulating introduction.

Crummey, Robert O. *The Formation of Muscovy, 1304–1613.* New York, 1987. The standard account.

Dobson, R. Barrie. *The Peasants' Revolt of 1381*, 2d ed. London, 1983. A comprehensive source collection, with excellent introductions to the documents and an illuminating discussion of the revolt.

Duffy, Eamon. *The Stripping of the Altars: Traditional Religion in England, 1400–1580.* New Haven, Conn., 1992. The fullest study anywhere of the patterns of fifteenth-century piety at the parish level.

Dyer, Christopher. *Standards of Living in the Later Middle Ages: Social Change in England, c. 1200–1520.* Cambridge and New York, 1989. Detailed but highly rewarding.

Froissart, Jean. *Chronicles.* Trans. Geoffrey Brereton. Baltimore, Md., 1968. A selection from the most famous contemporary account of the Hundred Years' War to about 1400.

Horrox, Rosemary, ed. *The Black Death.* New York, 1994. A fine collection of documents reflecting the impact of the Black Death, especially in England.

Huizinga, Johan. *The Waning of the Middle Ages: A Study of the Forms of Life, Thought, and Art in France and the Netherlands in the Dawn of the Renaissance,* New York, 1924. A classic picture of the "expiring" Middle Ages; a book from whose influence historians are still struggling to escape. Frequently republished, the most recent translation of this work is titled *The Autumn of the Middle Ages.* Trans. Rodney J. Payton and Ulrich Mammitzsch. Chicago, 1996.

John Hus at the Council of Constance. Trans. M. Spinka, New York, 1965. The translation of a Czech chronicle with an expert introduction and appended documents.

Jordan, William Chester. *The Great Famine: Northern Europe in the Early Fourteenth Century.* Princeton, N.J., 1996. An outstanding social and economic study of the disastrous famines that swept northern Europe between 1315 and 1322.

Keen, Maurice, ed. *Medieval Warfare: A History.* Oxford and New York, 1999. The most attractive introduction to this crucially important subject. Lively and well illustrated.

Kempe, Margery. *The Book of Margery Kempe.* Trans. Barry Windeatt. New York, 1985. A fascinating autobiography by an early fifteenth-century Englishwoman who hoped she might be a saint.

Lerner, Robert E. *The Heresy of the Free Spirit in the Later Middle Ages,* 2d ed. Notre Dame, Ind., 1991. A revealing study of a heretical movement that terrified contemporaries, yet hardly existed at all.

Lewis, Peter S. *Later Medieval France: The Polity.* London, 1968. Still fresh and suggestive after forty years. A masterwork.

Memoirs of a Renaissance Pope: The Commentaries of Pius II. Abridged ed. Trans. F. A. Gragg, New York, 1959. Remarkable insights into the mind of a particularly well-educated mid-fifteenth-century pope.

Nicholas, David. *The Transformation of Europe, 1300–1600.* Oxford and New York, 1999. The best textbook presently available.

Oakley, Francis C. *The Western Church in the Later Middle Ages.* Ithaca, N.Y., 1979. The best book by far on the history of conciliarism, the late medieval papacy, Hussitism, and the efforts at institutional reform during this period. On popular piety, see Swanson.

Pernoud, Régine, ed. *Joan of Arc, by Herself and Her Witnesses.* New York, 1966. A collection of contemporary writings about Joan, including the transcripts of her trial.

Shirley, Janet, trans. *A Parisian Journal, 1405–1449.* Oxford, 1968. A marvelous panorama of Parisian life recorded by an eyewitness.

Swanson, R. N. *Religion and Devotion in Europe, c. 1215–c. 1515.* Cambridge and New York, 1995. An excellent study of late medieval popular piety; an excellent complement to Oakley.

Sumption, Jonathan. *The Hundred Years' War.* Vol. 1: *Trial by Battle.* Vol. 2: *Trial by Fire.* Philadelphia, 1999. The first two volumes of a massive narrative history of the war take the story up to 1369.

Vaughan, Richard. *Valois Burgundy.* London, 1975. A summation of the author's four-volume study of the Burgundian dukes.

Ziegler, Philip. *The Black Death.* New York, 1969. A popular account, but reliable and engrossing.

CHAPTER ELEVEN

COMMERCE, CONQUEST, AND COLONIZATION, 1300–1600

BY 1300, THE GREAT EUROPEAN expansion of the High Middle Ages was coming to an end. In Iberia, there would be no further conquests of Muslim territory until 1492, when Granada fell to King Ferdinand and Queen Isabella. In the East, the Crusader kingdoms of Constantinople and Acre collapsed, in 1261 and 1291 respectively. Only the German drive into eastern Europe continued; but by the mid-fourteenth century, it too had been slowed by the rise of a new Baltic state in Lithuania. Internal expansion was also ending, as Europe reached the ecological limits of its resources. Thereafter, the pressure on resources was eased only by the dramatic population losses that resulted during the fourteenth century from the combined effects of famine, plague, and war.

But despite these checks, Europeans in the late Middle Ages did not turn inward. Although land-based conquests slowed, new sea-based empires emerged in the Mediterranean world during the fourteenth and fifteenth centuries, with colonies that extended from the Black Sea to the Canary Islands. New maritime trade routes were opened up through the Strait of Gibraltar, resulting in greater economic integration between the Mediterranean and Atlantic economies and increasing the demand in northwestern Europe for Asian spices and African gold. By the late fifteenth century, Mediterranean mariners and colonists had extended their domination out into the Atlantic, from the Azores in the north to the Canary Islands in the south. Portuguese navigators were also pushing down the west coast of Africa. In 1498 one such expedition would sail all the way around the Cape of Good Hope to India.

The fifteenth-century conquest of the "Atlantic Mediterranean" was the essential preliminary to the dramatic events that began in 1492 with Columbus's attempt to reach China by sailing westward across the Atlantic Ocean and that led, by 1600, to the Spanish and Portuguese conquests of the Americas. Because these events are so familiar, we can easily underestimate their importance. For the native peoples and empires of the Americas, the results of European contact were cataclysmic. By 1600, somewhere between 50 and 90 percent of the indigenous peoples of the

• What impact did the Mongol conquests have on Europe?	• How were the Portuguese able to control Indian Ocean trade?
• Why were slaves so important to Ottoman society?	• What was the impact of New World silver on the European economy?

Americas had perished from disease, massacre, and enslavement. For Europeans, the results of their conquests were less lethal but no less far reaching. By 1300, Europe had eclipsed both Byzantium and the lands of Islam as a Mediterranean power, but outside the Mediterranean and the north Atlantic European power was negligible. By 1600, however, Europe had emerged as the first truly global power in world history, capable of pursuing its imperial ambitions and commercial interests wherever its ships could sail and its guns could reach. Europeans would not achieve full control over the interiors of the African, Asian, and American land masses until the end of the nineteenth century, and their control would last thereafter for less than a century. By 1600, however, European navies ruled the seas, and the world's resources were increasingly being channeled through European hands—patterns that have continued until the present day.

THE MONGOLS

What impact did the Mongol conquests have on Europe?

Trade between the Mediterranean world and the Far East dated back to antiquity, but it was not until the late thirteenth century that Europeans began to establish direct trading connections with India, China, and the Spice Islands of the Indonesian archipelago. For Europeans, these connections would prove profoundly important, although less for their economic significance than for their impact on the European imagination. For the peoples of Asia, however, the appearance of European traders on the Silk Road between Central Asia and China was merely a curiosity. The really consequential event was the rise of the Mongol Empire that made such connections possible.

THE RISE OF THE MONGOL EMPIRE

The Mongols were one of a number of nomadic peoples inhabiting the steppes of Central Asia. Although closely connected with various Turkish-speaking peoples with whom they frequently intermarried, the Mongols spoke their own distinctive language and had their own homeland to the north of the Gobi Desert in present-day Mongolia. Sheep provided them with shelter (in the form of wool tents), clothing, milk, and meat.

Like many nomadic peoples throughout history, the Mongols were highly accomplished cavalry soldiers who supplemented their own pastoralism and craft production by raiding the sedentary peoples to their south. (It was in part to control such raiding from Mongolia that, many centuries before, the Chinese had built the famous Great Wall.) Primarily, however, China defended itself by attempting to ensure that the Mongols remained internally divided and so turned their martial energies most often against each other.

In the late twelfth century, however, a Mongol chief named Temüjin began to unite the various Mongol tribes under his rule. By incorporating the army of each defeated tribe into his own army, Temüjin quickly built up a large military force. In 1206, his supremacy was formally acknowledged by all the Mongols, and he took the title Chingiz (Genghis) Khan—"the oceanic [possibly meaning "universal"] ruler." Chingiz now turned his enormous army against his non-Mongol neighbors. China at this time was divided into three hostile states. In 1209, Chingiz launched an attack on northwestern China; in 1211 he invaded the Chin Empire in north China. At first these attacks were probably looting expeditions rather than deliberate attempts at conquest, but by the 1230s a full-scale Mongol conquest of northern and western China was under way, culminating in 1234 with the fall of the Chin. In 1279, Chingiz's grandson Qubilai (Kublai) Khan completed the conquest of southern (Sung) China, thus reuniting China for the first time in centuries.

Meanwhile, Chingiz turned his forces westward, conquering much of Central Asia and incorporating the important commercial cities of Tashkent, Samarkand, and Bukhara into his expanding empire. When Chingiz died in 1227, he was succeeded by his third son Ögedei (*EHRG-uh-day*), who completed the conquest of the Chin, conquered the lands between the Oxus River and the Caspian Sea and then laid plans for a massive inva-

CHRONOLOGY	
RISE OF THE MONGOL EMPIRE, 1206–1260	
Temujin crowned as Chingiz Khan	1206
Mongols conquer northern China	1234
Mongols conquer southern Russia	1237–1240
Mongol forces withdraw from Europe	1241
Mamluk sultanate halts Mongol advance in Egypt	1260

sion toward the west. Between 1237 and 1240, the Mongol horde (so called from the Turkish word *ordu*, meaning "tent" or "encampment") conquered southern Russia and then launched a two-pronged assault farther west. The smaller of the two Mongol armies swept through Poland toward eastern Germany; the larger army went southwest toward Hungary. In April 1241 the smaller Mongol force met a hastily assembled army of Germans and Poles at the battle of Liegnitz, where

the two sides fought to a bloody standstill. Two days later, the larger Mongol army annihilated the Hungarian army at the River Sajo.

How much farther west the Mongol armies might have pushed will forever remain in doubt, for in December 1241 the Great Khan Ögedei died, and the Mongol forces withdrew from eastern Europe. It took five years before a new great khan could establish himself, and when he died in 1248, the resulting interregnum lasted

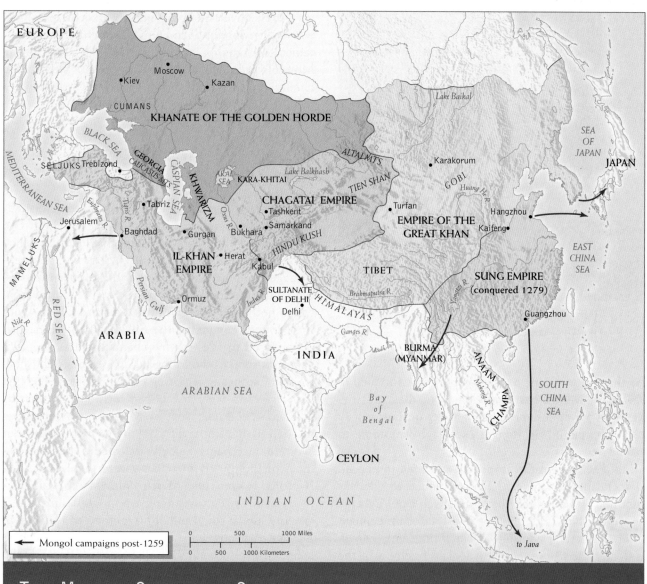

THE MONGOL SUCCESSOR STATES

Consider the breakup of Chingiz Khan's empire after 1259 and the passing similarities its fracture might possess to the disintegration of Alexander's empire, also conquered swiftly and encompassing vast swaths of Europe and Asia. Why did Chingiz Khan's empire splinter? How did the Mongol onslaught against and occupation of major sections of the Arab Muslim world possibly aid the expansion of European civilization and trade into the Mediterranean? At the same time, how did it complicate the situation for the crusader efforts in the Holy Land?

The Head of Timur the Lame. A forensic reconstruction based on his exhumed skull.

for three more years. Mongol conquests continued in Persia, the Middle East, and China; but after 1241 the Mongols never resumed their attacks on Europe. By 1300, the period of Mongol expansion had come to an end.

But the Mongol threat did not suddenly disappear. Descendants of Chingiz Khan continued to rule this enormous land empire (the largest such empire in the history of the world) until the mid-fourteenth century. Later, under the leadership of Timur the Lame (known as Tamerlane to Europeans) it looked briefly as if the Mongol Empire might be reunited. But Timur died in 1405 on his way to invade China; thereafter the various parts of the Mongol Empire fell into the hands of local rulers, including (in Asia Minor) the Ottoman Turks. Mongol cultural influence continued, however, and can be seen in the enormously impressive artwork produced during the fifteenth and sixteenth centuries in Persia and in Mughal India.

The Mongols owed their success to the size, speed, and training of their mounted armies; to the intimi-

dating savagery with which they butchered those who resisted them; and to their ability to adapt the administrative traditions of their subjects to their own purposes. Partly because the Mongols themselves put little store even in their own shamanistic religious traditions, they were also unusually tolerant of the religious beliefs of others—a distinct advantage in controlling an empire that comprised a dizzying array of Buddhist, Christian, and Muslim sects. However, little was distinctively "Mongol" about the way they governed their empire. Except in China, where the Mongol Yuan Dynasty inherited and maintained a complex administrative bureaucracy, the Mongols' rule was relatively unsophisticated, being chiefly directed at securing the steady payment of tribute from their subjects.

EUROPE, THE MONGOLS, AND THE FAR EAST

The Mongols had a keen eye for the commercial advantages their empire could offer them. They took steps to control the caravan routes that led from China through Central Asia to the Black Sea. They also encouraged commercial contacts with European traders, especially through the Iranian city of Tabriz, from which both land and sea routes led on to China. Until the Mongol conquests, the Silk Road to China had been closed to Western merchants and travelers. But almost as soon as the Mongol Empire was established, we find Europeans venturing on these routes. The first such travelers were Franciscan missionaries such as William de Rubruck, sent by King Louis IX of France in 1253 as his ambassador to the Mongol court. But Western merchants quickly followed. The most famous of these early merchants were three Venetians: Niccolo, Maffeo, and Marco Polo. Marco Polo's account of his twenty-year sojourn in China in the service of Qubilai Khan and of his journey home through the Spice Islands, India, and Iran, is one of the most famous travel accounts of all time. Its effect on the imagination of his contemporaries was enormous. For the next two centuries, most of what Europeans knew about the Far East they learned from Marco Polo's *Travels*. Christopher Columbus's copy of this book still survives.

European connections with the western end of the Silk Road would continue until the mid-fourteenth century. The Genoese were especially active in this trade, not least because their rivals, the Venetians, already dominated the Mediterranean trade with Alexandria

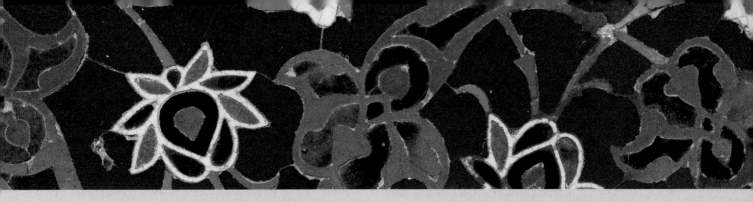

MARCO POLO'S DESCRIPTION OF JAVA

The Venetian merchants Niccolo and Maffeo Polo traveled overland from Constantinople to the court of Qubilai Khan between 1260 and 1269. When they returned a few years later, they brought with them Niccolo's son Marco. A gifted linguist, Marco would remain at the Mongol court until the early 1290s, when he returned to Europe after a journey through Southeast Asia, the Spice Islands, and the Indian Ocean. Marco's account of his travels would shape European images of the Far East for centuries.

Departing from Ziamba, and steering between south and south-east, fifteen hundred miles, you reach an island of very great size, named Java. According to the reports of some well-informed navigators, it is the greatest in the world, and has a compass above three thousand miles. It is under the dominion of one king only, nor do the inhabitants pay tribute to any other power. They are worshipers of idols.

The country abounds with rich commodities. Pepper, nutmegs, spikenard, galangal, cubebs, cloves and all the other valuable spices and drugs, are the produce of the island; which occasion it to be visited by many ships laden with merchandise, that yields to the owners considerable profit.

The quantity of gold collected there exceeds all calculation and belief. From thence it is that . . . merchants . . . have imported, and to this day import, that metal to a great amount, and from thence also is obtained the greatest part of the spices that are distributed throughout the world. That the Great Khan [Qubilai] has not brought the island under subjection to him, must be attributed to the length of the voyage and the dangers of the navigation.

The Travels of Marco Polo, rev. and ed. Manuel Komroff (New York, 1926), pp. 267–268.

QUESTIONS FOR ANALYSIS

1. What effect did Marco Polo's *Travels* have on European images of the Far East?
2. Why did Marco Polo refer to various spices as "rich commodities"? Why were spices so highly valued by Europeans?

and Beirut, through which the bulk of Europe's Far Eastern luxury goods continued to pass. But the Mongols of Iran become progressively more hostile to Westerners as the fourteenth century progressed. By 1344, the Genoese had abandoned Tabriz after attacks on Westerners had made their position there untenable. In 1346, the Mongols of the Golden Horde besieged the Genoese colony at Caffa on the Black Sea. Apart from crippling Genoese commerce in the Black Sea, this siege is memorable chiefly because during it the Black Death was passed from the Mongol army (which had inadvertently brought it from the Gobi Desert, where the disease was endemic) to the Genoese defenders, who returned with it to western Europe, where it proceeded to kill at least one third of the entire European population.

The window of opportunity that made Marco Polo's travels possible was thus relatively short. By the middle of the fourteenth century, hostilities between the various parts of the Mongol Empire were already making travel along the Silk Road perilous. After 1368, when the Mongol (Yuan) Dynasty was overthrown, Westerners were excluded from China altogether, and Mongols were restricted to cavalry service in the Ming imperial armies. The overland trade routes from China to the Black Sea continued to operate; Europeans, however, were no longer able to travel along them. But the new, more integrated commercial world the Mongols created had a lasting impact on Europe, despite the relatively short time during which Europeans themselves were able to participate directly in it. European memories of the Far East would be preserved, and the dream of reestablishing direct connections between Europe and China would survive to influence a new round of European commercial and imperial expansion from the late fifteenth century onward.

THE RISE OF THE OTTOMAN EMPIRE

Why were slaves so important to Ottoman society?

Like the Mongols, the Ottoman Turks were initially a nomadic people whose economy continued to depend on raiding even after they had conquered an extensive empire. The peoples who would become the Ottomans were already established in northwestern Anatolia when the Mongols arrived and were already at least nominally Muslims. But unlike the established Muslim powers in the region, whom the Mongols destroyed, the Ottoman Turks were among the principal beneficiaries of the Mongol conquest. By toppling the Seljuk sultanate and the Abbasid caliphate of Baghdad, the Mongols eliminated the two traditional authorities that had previously kept Turkish border chieftains like the Ottomans in check. Now the Ottomans were free to raid along their soft frontiers with Byzantium unhindered. At the same time, however, they remained far enough away from the centers of Mongol authority to avoid being destroyed themselves.

By toppling the Seljuk sultanate and the Abbasid caliphate of Baghdad, the Mongols eliminated the two traditional authorities that had previously kept Turkish border chieftains like the Ottomans in check.

THE CONQUEST OF CONSTANTINOPLE

By the end of the thirteenth century, the Ottoman Dynasty had established itself as the leading family among the Anatolian border lords. By the mid-fourteenth century, it had solidified its preeminence by capturing a number of important cities. These successes brought the Ottomans to the attention of the Byzantine emperor, who in 1345 hired a contingent of Ottomans as mercenaries. Thus introduced into Europe, the Ottomans quickly made themselves at home. By 1370, they had extended their control all the way to the Danube. In 1389 Ottoman forces defeated the powerful Serbian Empire at the battle of Kosovo, enabling them to consolidate their control over Greece, Bulgaria, and the Balkans.

In 1396 the Ottomans attacked Constantinople, but withdrew to repel a Western crusading force that had been sent against them. In 1402, they attacked Constantinople again, but once more were forced to withdraw, this time to confront a Mongolian invasion of Anatolia. Led by Timur the Lame, the Mongol army captured the Ottoman sultan and destroyed his army; for the next decade it appeared that Ottoman hegemony over Anatolia might be gone forever. By 1413, however, Timur was dead, a new sultan had emerged, and the Ottomans were able to resume their conquests. Ottoman pressure on Constantinople continued during the 1420s and 1430s, producing a steady stream of Byzantine refugees who brought with them to Italy the surviving masterworks of classical Greek literature. But it was not until 1451 that a new sultan, Mehmet II, turned his full attention to the conquest of the imperial city. In 1453, after a brilliantly executed siege, Mehmet succeeded in breaching the city's walls. The Byzantine emperor was killed in the assault, the city itself was thoroughly plundered, and its population was sold into slavery. The Ottomans then settled down to rule their new capital in a style reminiscent of their Byzantine predecessors.

The Ottoman conquest of Constantinople was an enormous psychological shock to Christian Europe, but its economic impact on western Europe was minor. Ottoman control over the former Byzantine Empire did reduce European access to the Black Sea, but the bulk of the Far Eastern luxury trade with Europe had never passed through the Black Sea ports in the first place. Europeans got most of their spices and silks through Venice, which imported them from Alexandria and Beirut. These two cities did not fall to the Ottomans until the 1520s. In no sense, therefore, can the Ottomans be seen as the spur that propelled Portuguese efforts during the late fifteenth century to establish a direct sea route between Europe, India, and the Spice Islands. If anything, the opposite is the case. After the Portuguese established a direct sea route between Europe and India, it was their attempts to exclude Muslims from the Indian Ocean spice trade that helped spur the Ottoman conquests of Syria, Egypt, and Hungary during the 1520s and 1530s. To be sure, these Ottoman conquests had other motives also, including the desire to control the Egypt-

ian grain trade. But by eliminating the merchants who had traditionally dominated the overland spice trade through Beirut and Alexandria, the Ottomans also hoped to redirect this trade through Constantinople, and then up the Danube into western Europe.

The effects of the Ottoman conquest of Constantinople on western Europe were modest. On the Ottomans themselves, however, their conquest was transformative. Vast new wealth poured into Ottoman society, which the Ottomans increased by carefully tending to the industrial and commercial interests of their new capital city. Trade routes were redirected to feed the capital, and the Ottomans became a naval power in the eastern Mediterranean and the Black Sea. As a result, Constantinople's population grew from less than 100,000 in 1453 to more than 500,000 in 1600, making it the largest city in the world outside China.

WAR, SLAVERY, AND SOCIAL ADVANCEMENT

Despite the Ottomans' careful attention to commerce, their empire rested on raiding and conquest. Until the end of the sixteenth century, the Ottoman Empire was therefore on an almost constant war footing. To continue its conquests, the size of the Ottoman army and administration grew exponentially. But this growth drew more and more manpower from the empire. Because the Ottoman army and administration were largely composed of slaves, the demand for more soldiers and administrators could best be met through further conquests that would capture yet more slaves. Further conquests, however, required a still larger army and an even more extensive bureaucracy; and so the cycle continued.

Sultan Mehmet II, "The Conqueror" (1451–1481), by Ottoman Artist Siblizade Ahmed. The sultan's pose and handkerchief are Central Asian conventions in portraiture, but the subdued color and three-quarter profile show the influence of Italian Renaissance portraits. The sultan wears the white turban of a scholar but also wears the thumb ring of an archer, neatly reflecting his combination of scholarly and military attainments.

CHRONOLOGY

RISE OF THE OTTOMAN EMPIRE, 1300–1571

Ottomans become leading Anatolian family	1300
Byzantine emperor hires Ottoman mercenaries	1345
Ottomans enter Europe	1350s
Ottomans defeat Serbian empire	1389
Ottomans conquer Constantinople	1453
Ottomans conquer Syria, Egypt, Hungary	1520s
Battle of Lepanto	1571

Slaves were the backbone of the Ottoman army and administration, as they had been in Mamluk Egypt. But slaves were also critical to the lives of the Ottoman upper class. One of the important measures of status in Ottoman society was the number of slaves in one's household. After 1453, new wealth permitted some Ottoman notables to maintain households in which thousands of slaves attended to their masters' whims. In the sixteenth century, the sultan's household alone numbered more than 20,000 slave attendants, not including his bodyguard and his elite infantry units, both of which were also composed of slaves.

The result was an almost insatiable demand for slaves, especially in Constantinople itself. Many of these slaves were captured in war. Many others were taken from Poland and Ukraine in raids by Crimean slave merchants, who then shipped their captives to the slave markets of Constantinople. But slaves were also recruited (some willingly, some by coercion) from rural areas of the Ottoman Empire itself. Because the vast majority of Ottoman slaves were household servants and administrators rather than laborers, some people willingly accepted enslavement, believing that they would be better off as slaves in Constantinople than as impoverished peasants in the countryside. In the Balkans especially, many people were enslaved as children, handed over by their families to pay the infamous child tax the Ottomans imposed on rural areas too poor to pay a monetary tribute. Although unquestionably a wrenching experience for families, this practice did open up opportunities for social advancement. Special academies were created at Constantinople to train the most able of these enslaved children to act as administrators and soldiers, and some rose to become powerful figures in the Ottoman Empire. Slavery therefore carried relatively little social stigma. Even the sultan himself was most often the son of an enslaved woman.

Because Muslims were not permitted to enslave other Muslims, the vast majority of Ottoman slaves were from Christian families (although many converted to Islam later in life). But because so many of the elite positions within Ottoman government were held by slaves, the paradoxical result of this reliance on slave administrators was that Muslims, including Turks, were effectively excluded from the main avenues of social and political advancement in Ottoman society. Nor was Ottoman society characterized by a powerful hereditary nobility of the sort that dominated contemporary European society. As a result, power in the fifteenth- and sixteenth-century Ottoman Empire was remarkably, perhaps even uniquely, open to men of ability and talent, provided

that such men were slaves and therefore not Muslims by birth. Nor was this pattern of Muslim exclusion limited to government and the army. Commerce and business also remained largely in the hands of non-Muslims, most frequently Greeks, Syrians, and Jews. Jews in particular found in the Ottoman Empire a welcome refuge from the persecutions and expulsions that had characterized Jewish life in late medieval Europe. After their 1492 expulsion from Spain, more than 100,000 Spanish (Sephardic) Jews ultimately immigrated into the Ottoman Empire.

Ottoman Orthodoxy. This Ottoman genealogical chart shows the descent of Sultan Mehmet III (1595–1603) from the Prophet Muhammad (shown veiled).

OTTOMAN JANISSARIES

The following account is from a memoir written by a Christian Serb who was captured as a youth by Sultan Mehmet II the Conqueror, converted to Islam, and then served eight years in the Ottoman janissary corps. In 1463, however, the fortress he was defending for the Sultan was captured by the Hungarians, and the author thereupon returned to Christianity.

Whenever the Turks invade foreign lands and capture their people an imperial scribe follows immediately behind them, and whatever boys there are, he takes them all into the Janissaries and gives five gold pieces for each one and sends them across the sea [to Anatolia]. There are about two thousand of these boys. If, however, the number of them from enemy peoples does not suffice, then he takes from the Christians in every village in his land who have boys, having established what is the most every village can give so that the quota will always be full. And the boys whom he takes in his own land are called *cilik*. Each one of them can leave his property to whomever he wants after his death. And those whom he takes among the enemies are called *pendik*. These latter after their deaths can leave nothing; rather, it goes to the emperor, except that if someone comports himself well and is so deserving that he be freed, he may leave it to whomever he wants. And on the boys who are across the sea the emperor spends nothing; rather, those to whom they are entrusted must maintain them and send them where he orders. Then they take those who are suited for it on ships and there they study and train to skirmish in battle. There the emperor already provides for them and gives them a wage. From there he chooses for his own court those who are trained and then raises their wages.

Konstantin Mihailovic, *Memoirs of a Janissary* (Michigan Slavic Translations 3), trans. Benjamin Stolz (Ann Arbor, Mich., 1975), pp. 157–159.

QUESTIONS FOR ANALYSIS

1. What role did the janissary corps play in the Ottoman Empire?
2. Were the Ottoman incursions into the West a serious threat to the European balance of power?

RELIGIOUS CONFLICTS

The Ottoman sultans were relentlessly orthodox Sunni Muslims, who lent staunch support to the religious and legal pronouncements of the Islamic scholarly schools. In 1516, the Ottomans captured the cities of Medina and Mecca, thus becoming the defenders of the holy sites. Soon after, they captured Jerusalem and Cairo, putting an end to the Mamluk sultanate of Egypt. In 1538 the Ottoman ruler formally adopted the title of caliph, thereby declaring himself to be the legitimate successor of the Prophet Muhammad.

In keeping with Sunni traditions, the Ottomans were also religiously tolerant toward non-Muslims, especially during the fifteenth and sixteenth centuries. They organized the major religious groups of their empire into legally recognized units known as *millets*, permitting them considerable rights of religious self-government. After

1453, however, the Ottomans were particularly careful to protect and promote the authority of the Greek Orthodox patriarch of Constantinople over the Orthodox Christians of their empire. As a result, the Ottomans enjoyed staunch support from their Orthodox Christian subjects during their sixteenth-century wars with the Latin Christians of western Europe. Despite the religious diversity of their empire, the Ottomans' principal religious conflicts were therefore not with their own subjects, but with the Shi'ite Muslim Dynasty that ruled neighboring Persia. Time and again during the sixteenth century, Ottoman expeditions against western Europe had to be abandoned when hostilities erupted with the Persians.

THE OTTOMANS AND EUROPE

During the sixteenth century, the Habsburg rulers of Spain, Germany, and Austria were similarly distracted by their own conflicts with the Catholic kings of France (with whom the Ottomans made an alliance) and with the Protestant princes of Germany, the Netherlands, and England. As a result, the contest between the Ottoman Empire and the Western powers never really lived up to the rhetoric of holy war that both sides employed in their propaganda. In 1396, a Western crusader army was annihilated by the Ottomans at the battle of Nicopolis. In the sixteenth and seventeenth centuries, Ottoman armies several times

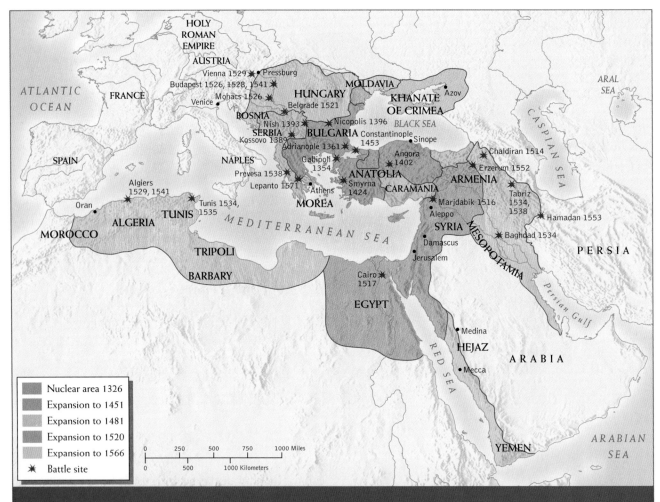

THE GROWTH OF THE OTTOMAN EMPIRE

Consider the patterns of Ottoman expansion revealed in this map. Did the 1453 capture of Constantinople lead to immediate further conquests? Why do you suppose this was? Compare the extent of the Ottoman Empire in 1566 with that of the Byzantine Empire under Justinian (see the map on page 237). How would you account for these similarities? Why didn't the Ottoman Empire continue its rapid expansion after 1566?

besieged Vienna. But despite these dramatic moments, conflicts between the Ottomans and the rulers of western Europe were fought out mainly through pirate raids and naval battles in the Mediterranean. The main result of this contest was thus a steady escalation in the scale and cost of navies. In 1571, when a combined Habsburg and Venetian force defeated the Ottoman fleet at Lepanto, more than 400 ships took part, with both sides deploying naval forces ten times larger than they had possessed half a century before.

Although undeniably a victory for the Habsburgs and their Venetian allies, the battle of Lepanto was far less decisive than is often suggested. The Ottoman navy was speedily rebuilt; by no means did Lepanto put an end to Ottoman influence over the eastern Mediterranean Sea. Nevertheless, after 1571 both Ottoman and Habsburg interests shifted away from their conflict with each other. The Ottomans embarked on a long and costly war with Persia, while the Spanish Habsburgs turned their attention toward their new empire in the Atlantic. By the mid-seventeenth century, when a new round of Ottoman-European conflicts began, the strength of the Ottoman Empire had been sapped by a series of indolent, pleasure-loving sultans and by the tensions that arose within the Ottoman Empire itself as it ceased to expand. The Ottoman Empire would last until 1918; but from the mid-seventeenth century on, it was no longer a serious rival to the global hegemony the European powers were beginning to achieve.

MEDITERRANEAN COLONIALISM

How were the Portuguese able to control Indian Ocean trade?

During the fifteenth century, Europeans focused their colonial and commercial ambitions more and more on the western Mediterranean and the Atlantic world. Although historians have sometimes argued the contrary, this reorientation was not a result of the rising power of the Ottoman Empire. Instead, this westward orientation was the product of two related developments: the growing importance to late medieval Europe of the African gold trade; and the growth of European colonial empires in the western Mediterranean Sea.

SILVER SHORTAGES AND THE SEARCH FOR AFRICAN GOLD

Europeans had been trading for African gold for centuries, mainly through Muslim middlemen who transported this precious metal in caravans from the Niger River area where it was produced to the North African ports of Algiers and Tunis. From the thirteenth century on, Catalan and Genoese merchants maintained colonies in Tunis, where they traded woolen cloth for North African grain and sub-Saharan gold.

What accelerated the late medieval demand for gold, however, was a serious silver shortage that affected the entire European economy during the fourteenth and fifteenth centuries. Silver production in Europe fell markedly during the 1340s and remained at a low level thereafter, as Europeans reached the limits of their technological capacity to extract silver ore from deep mines. This shortfall in silver production was compounded during the fifteenth century by a serious balance-of-payments problem: more European silver was flowing east in the spice trade than could be replaced using existing mining techniques on known silver deposits. Gold currencies represented an obvious alternative for large transactions, and from the thirteenth century on European rulers with access to gold were minting gold coins. But Europe itself had few natural gold reserves. To maintain and expand these gold coinages, new and larger supplies of gold were needed. The most obvious source for this gold was Africa.

MEDITERRANEAN EMPIRES: CATALUNYA, VENICE, AND GENOA

The growing European interest in the African gold trade coincided with the creation of sea-based Mediterranean empires by the Catalans, the Venetians, and the Genoese. During the thirteenth century, the Catalans conquered and colonized a series of western Mediterranean islands, including Majorca, Ibiza, Minorca, Sicily, and Sardinia.

Silver production in Europe fell markedly during the 1340s and remained at a low level thereafter, as Europeans reached the limits of their technological capacity to extract silver ore from deep mines.

Except in Sicily, the pattern of Catalan exploitation was largely the same on all these islands: expropriation or extermination of the native (usually Muslim) population; economic concessions to attract new settlers; and a heavy reliance on slave labor to produce foodstuffs and raw materials for export.

Unlike Catalan colonization efforts, which were mainly carried on by private individuals operating under a crown charter, Venetian colonization was directed by the city's rulers and was focused mainly on the eastern Mediterranean, where the Venetians dominated the trade in spices and silks. The Genoese, by contrast, had more extensive interests in the western Mediterranean world where they traded bulk goods such as cloth, hides, grain, timber, and sugar. Genoese colonies tended to be more informal and family based than Venetian or Catalan colonies, constituting more of a network than an extension of a sovereign empire. They were also more closely integrated into the native societies of North Africa, Spain, and the Black Sea than were the Venetian or the Catalan colonies. Genoese colonies pioneered the production of sugar and sweet Madeira wines in the western Mediterranean, first in Sicily and later in the Atlantic islands off the west coast of Africa. To transport such bulky goods, the Genoese moved away from the oared galleys favored by the Venetians toward larger, fuller-bodied sailing ships that could carry greater volumes of cargo. With further modifications to accommodate the rougher sailing conditions of the Atlantic Ocean, these were the ships that would carry sixteenth-century Europeans around the globe.

> Starting around 1270, however, Italian merchants began to sail through the Strait of Gibraltar and on to the wool-producing regions of England and the Netherlands. This was the essential first step in the extension of Mediterranean patterns of commerce and colonization into the Atlantic Ocean.

FROM THE MEDITERRANEAN TO THE ATLANTIC

Until the late thirteenth century, European maritime commerce had been divided between a Mediterranean and a north Atlantic world. Starting around 1270, however, Italian merchants began to sail through the Strait of Gibraltar and on to the wool-producing regions of England and the Netherlands. This was the essential first step in the extension of Mediterranean patterns of commerce and colonization into the Atlantic Ocean. The second step was the discovery (or possibly rediscovery), during the fourteenth century, of the Atlantic island chains known as the Canaries and the Azores by Genoese sailors. Efforts to colonize the Canary Islands, and to convert and enslave their inhabitants, began almost immediately. But an effective conquest of the Canary Islands did not really begin until the fifteenth century, when it was undertaken by Portugal and completed by Castile. The Canaries, in turn, became the base from which further Portuguese voyages down the west coast of Africa proceeded. They were also the jumping-off point from which Christopher Columbus would sail westward across the Atlantic Ocean in hopes of reaching Asia.

THE TECHNOLOGY OF SHIPS AND NAVIGATION

The European empires of the fifteenth and sixteenth centuries rested on a mastery of the oceans. The Portuguese caravel—the workhorse ship of the fifteenth-century voyages to Africa—was based on ship and sail designs that had been in use among Portuguese fishermen since the thirteenth century. Starting in the 1440s, however, Portuguese shipwrights began building larger caravels of about 50 tons displacement with two masts, each carrying a triangular (lateen) sail. Such ships were capable of sailing against the wind much more effectively than were the older, square-rigged vessels. They also required much smaller crews than did the multi-oared galleys that were still commonly used in the Mediterranean. By the end of the fifteenth century, even larger caravels of around 200 tons were being constructed, with a third mast and a combination of square and lateen sails. Columbus's *Niña* was of this design, having been refitted with two square sails in the Canary Islands to enable it to sail more efficiently before the wind during the Atlantic crossing.

Europeans were also making significant advances in navigation during the fifteenth and sixteenth centuries. Quadrants, which calculated latitude in the Northern Hemisphere by the height of the North Star above the horizon, were in widespread use by the 1450s. As sailors approached the equator, however, the quadrant became less and less useful, and they were forced instead to make use of astrolabes, which reckoned latitude by the height of the sun. Like quadrants, astrolabes

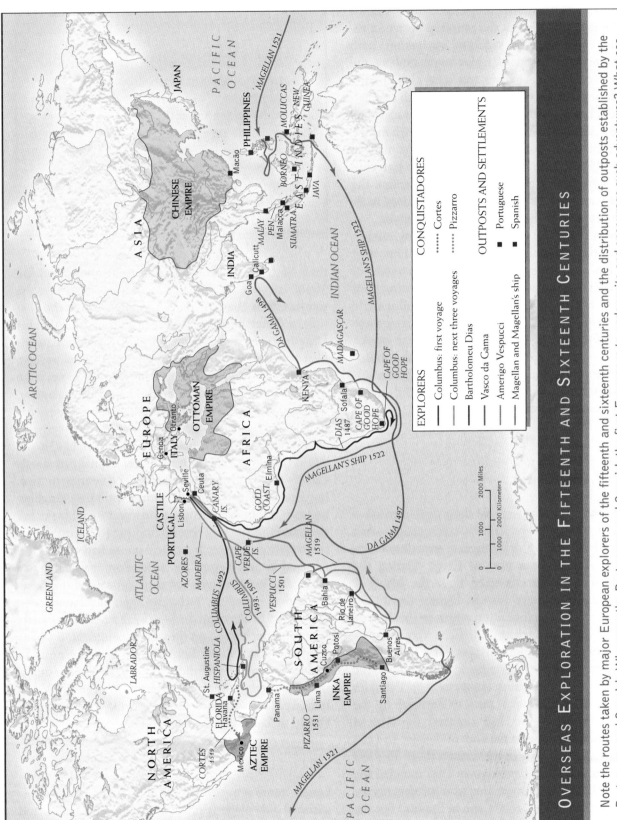

OVERSEAS EXPLORATION IN THE FIFTEENTH AND SIXTEENTH CENTURIES

Note the routes taken by major European explorers of the fifteenth and sixteenth centuries and the distribution of outposts established by the Portuguese and Spanish. Why were the Portuguese and Spanish the first Europeans to underwrite and encourage such adventures? What economic and cultural factors precipitated such efforts? What were the motives for such voyages? How did the establishment of economic outposts in Africa, America, and the East Indies radically alter the balance of power in the Old World, and why? Might the Americas have had to wait even longer for European "discovery" had da Gama found the route around Africa sooner?

had been known in western Europe for centuries. But it was not until the 1480s that the astrolabe became a really useful instrument for seaborne navigation, with the preparation of standard tables sponsored by the Portuguese crown. Compasses too were also coming into more widespread use during the fifteenth century. Longitude, however, remained impossible to calculate accurately until the eighteenth century, when the invention of the marine chronometer finally made it possible to keep accurate time at sea. In the sixteenth century, Europeans sailing east or west across the oceans generally had to rely on their skill at dead reckoning to determine where they were on the globe.

European sailors also benefited from a new interest in maps and navigational charts. Especially important to Atlantic sailors were books known as *rutters* or *routiers*. These contained detailed sailing instructions and descriptions of the coastal landmarks a pilot could expect to encounter on route to a variety of destinations. Mediterranean sailors had had similar books, known as *portolani*, since at least the fourteenth century. In the fifteenth century, however, this tradition was extended to the Atlantic Ocean; by the end of the sixteenth century, rutters spanned the globe.

PORTUGAL, AFRICA, AND THE SEA ROUTE TO INDIA

It was among the Portuguese that these dual interests—the African gold trade and Atlantic colonization—first came together. In 1415, a Portuguese expedition captured the north African port of Ceuta. During the 1420s the Portuguese colonized both the island of Madeira and the Canary Islands. During the 1430s, they extended these colonization efforts to the Azores. By the 1440s they had reached the Cape Verde Islands. In 1444 Portuguese explorers first landed in the area between the Senegal and the Gambia River mouths on the African mainland, where they began to collect cargoes of gold and slaves for export back to Portugal. By the 1470s, Portuguese sailors had rounded the African "bulge" and were exploring the Gulf of Guinea. In 1483 they reached the mouth of the Congo River. In 1488 the Portuguese captain Bartholomeu Dias rounded the southern tip of Africa. Blown around it accidentally by a gale, Dias named the point "Cape of Storms," but the king of Portugal took a more optimistic view of Dias's achievement. He renamed it the Cape of Good Hope and began planning a naval expedition to India. Finally in 1497–1498, Vasco da Gama rounded the cape, and

CHRONOLOGY

PORTUGUESE MARITIME EXPANSION, 1420s–1515

Colonization of Madeira and Canary Islands	1420s
Colonization of the Azores	1430s
Dias rounds the Cape of Good Hope	1488
Da Gama reaches India	1497–1498
Portuguese reach Malacca in Southeast Asia	1511
Portuguese reach Spice Islands	1515

then, with the help of a Muslim navigator named Ibn Majid, crossed the Indian Ocean to Calicutt on the southwestern coast of India, opening up for the first time a direct sea route between Europe and the Far Eastern spice trade. Although da Gama lost half his fleet and one third of his men on his two-year voyage, his cargo of spices was so valuable that his losses were deemed insignificant. His heroism became legendary, and his story became the basis for the Portuguese national epic, the *Lusiads*.

Now master of the quickest route to riches in the world, the king of Portugal swiftly capitalized on da Gama's accomplishment. After 1500, Portuguese trading fleets sailed regularly to India. In 1509, the Portuguese defeated an Ottoman fleet and then blockaded the mouth of the Red Sea, attempting to cut off one of the traditional routes by which spices had traveled to Alexandria and Beirut. By 1510 Portuguese military forces had established a series of forts along the western Indian coastline, including their headquarters at Goa. In 1511 Portuguese ships seized Malacca, a center of the spice trade on the Malay peninsula. By 1515 they had reached the Spice Islands and the coast of China. So completely did the Portuguese now dominate the spice trade that by the 1520s even the Venetians were forced to buy their pepper in the Portuguese capital of Lisbon.

ARTILLERY AND EMPIRE

Larger, more maneuverable ships and improved navigational aids made it possible for the Portuguese and other European mariners to reach Africa, Asia, and the Americas by sea. But fundamentally, these sixteenth-century European commercial empires were a military achievement. As such, they reflected what Europeans had learned in their wars against each other during the fourteenth and fifteenth centuries. Perhaps the most critical military advance of the late Middle Ages was the increasing sophistication of artillery, a development made possible not only by gunpowder, but also by improved metallurgical techniques for casting cannon barrels. By the middle of the fifteenth century, the use of artillery pieces had rendered the stone walls of medieval castles and towns obsolete, a fact brought home in 1453 by the successful French siege of Bordeaux (which brought to an end the Hundred Years' War), and by the Ottoman siege of Constantinople (which brought to an end the Byzantine Empire).

One of the reasons the new ship designs (first caravels, and later the even larger galleons) were so important was that their larger size made it possible to mount more effective artillery pieces on them. Increasingly during the sixteenth century, European naval vessels were conceived as floating artillery platforms, with scores of guns mounted in fixed positions along their sides and swivel guns mounted fore and aft. These guns were vastly expensive, as were the ships that carried them; but for those rulers who could afford to possess them, such ships made it possible to project military power around the world. In 1498, Vasco da Gama became the first Portuguese captain to sail into the Indian Ocean; but the Portuguese did not gain control of that ocean until 1509, when they defeated a combined Ottoman and Indian naval force at the battle of Div. Portuguese trading outposts in Africa and Asia were fortifications, built not only to guard against the attacks of native peoples but also to ward off assaults from other Europeans. Without this essential military component, the European maritime empires of the sixteenth century would not have existed.

> Increasingly during the sixteenth century, European naval vessels were conceived as floating artillery platforms, with scores of guns mounted in fixed positions along their sides and swivel guns mounted fore and aft.

PRINCE HENRY THE NAVIGATOR

Because we know that these fifteenth-century Portuguese expeditions down the African coast did ultimately open up a sea route to India and the Far East, it is tempting to presume that this was their goal from the beginning. It was not. The traditional narrative of these events, which presents exploration as their mission, India as their goal, and Prince Henry the Navigator as the guiding genius behind them, no longer commands the confidence of most historians. Only from the 1480s did India clearly become the goal toward which these voyages were directed. Before the 1480s, Portuguese involvement in Africa was driven instead by much more traditional goals: crusading ambitions against the Muslims of North Africa; the desire to establish direct links with the sources of African gold production south of the Sahara Desert; the desire to colonize the Atlantic islands; the burgeoning market for slaves in Europe and in the Ottoman Empire; and the hope that somewhere in Africa they might find the legendary Prester John, a mythical Christian king whom Europeans believed would be their ally against the Muslims if only they could locate him. In the twelfth and thirteenth centuries, they had sought him in Asia. But from the 1340s on, he was believed to reside in Ethiopia, an expansive term that to most Europeans seems to have meant "somewhere in Africa."

Nor does Prince Henry (whose title, "the Navigator," was not assigned to him until the seventeenth century) seem so central a figure in Portuguese exploration as he was once thought to be. In fact, he directed only eight of the thirty-five Portuguese voyages to Africa between 1419 and his death in 1460; and the stories about his gathering a

A Turkish Brass Cannon of the Fifteenth Century. This eighteen-ton gun fired balls twenty-five inches in diameter.

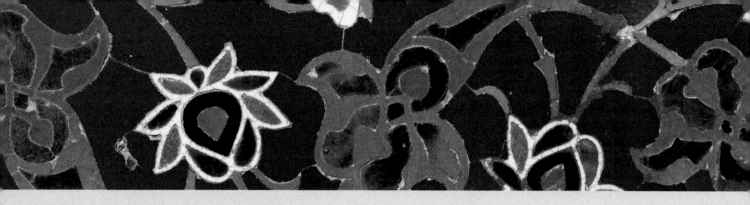

THE LEGEND OF PRESTER JOHN

The Travels of Sir John Mandeville is an almost entirely fictional account of the wonders of the East, written by an English expatriate during the first half of the fourteenth century. Despite the fact that Mandeville (almost certainly a pseudonym) knew almost nothing about the lands he describes, his book became a primary source for European ideas about South and East Asia. Although Mandeville locates the legendary Prester John in Persia, India, or China (his geography is fuzzy, to say the least), by the fifteenth century Europeans were searching for Prester John in Africa.

This emperor Prester John has great lands and has many noble cities and good towns in his realm and many great, large islands. For all the country of India is separated into islands by the great floods that come from Paradise, that divide the land into many parts. And also in the sea he has many islands. . . .

This Prester John has under him many kings and many islands and many varied people of various conditions. And this land is full good and rich, but not so rich as is the land of the Great Khan. For the merchants do not come there so commonly to buy merchandise as they do in the land of the Great Khan, for it is too far to travel to. . . .

[Mandeville then goes on to describe the difficulties of reaching Prester John's lands by sea.]

This emperor Prester John always takes as his wife the daughter of the Great Khan, and the Great Khan in the same way takes to wife the daughter of Prester John. For these two are the greatest lords under the heavens.

In the land of Prester John there are many diverse things, and many precious stones so great and so large that men make them into vessels such as platters, dishes, and cups. And there are many other marvels there that it would be too cumbrous and too long to put into the writing of books. But of the principal islands and of his estate and of his law I shall tell you some part.

This emperor Prester John is Christian and a great part of his country is Christian also, although they do not hold to all the articles of our faith as we do. . . .

And he has under him 72 provinces, and in every province there is a king. And these kings have kings under them, and all are tributaries to Prester John.

And he has in his lordships many great marvels. For in his country is the sea that men call the Gravelly Sea, that is all gravel and sand without any drop of water. And it ebbs and flows in great waves as other seas do, and it is never still. . . . And a three-day journey from that sea there are great mountains out of which flows a great flood that comes out of Paradise. And it is full of precious stones without any drop of water. . . .

He dwells usually in the city of Susa [in Persia]. And there is his principal palace, which is so rich and so noble that no one will believe the report unless he has seen it. And above the chief tower of the palace there are two round pommels of gold and in each of them are two great, large rubies that shine full brightly upon the night. And the principal gates of his palace are of a precious stone that men call sardonyxes [a type of onyx], and the frames and the bars are made of ivory. And the windows of the halls and chambers are of crystal. And the tables upon which men eat, some are made of emeralds, some of amethyst, and some of gold full of precious stones. And the legs that hold up the tables are made of the same precious stones. . . .

Mandeville's Travels, ed. M. C. Seymour (Oxford, 1967), pp. 195–199 (language modernized from Middle English by R. C. Stacey).

QUESTIONS FOR ANALYSIS

1. How persuasive was the myth of Prester John? Would you consider such a myth important enough to serve as a primary motive for European exploration?

Prince Henry the Navigator, by a Fifteenth-Century Portuguese Painter. This portrait is taken from a group portrait of the Portuguese royal family. Although thought to depict Henry, the identification is not certain.

school of navigators and cartographers on the Atlantic coast of Portugal, about his role in designing improved ships and navigational instruments, and about his encouragement of scientific learning generally have all been shown to be false. Henry did play an important role in organizing Portuguese colonization of Madeira, the Canary Islands, and the Azores; and he also pioneered the Portuguese slave trade, first on the Canaries (whose Stone Age population was almost entirely enslaved) and then along the Sene-Gambian coast of Africa. His main goal, however, was to outflank the cross-Saharan African gold trade by intercepting this trade at its source. To this end, he built a series of forts along the African coastline, most famously at Arguim, to which he hoped to divert the cross-Saharan gold caravans. This was also his reason for colonizing the Canary Islands, which he saw as a staging ground for expeditions into the African interior. There is no evidence that he ever dreamed of reaching India by sailing around Africa. Indeed, quite the opposite seems to

be the case. Portuguese progress toward the Cape of Good Hope proceeded much more rapidly in the years after Henry's death than it had during his lifetime. Henry himself was a crusader against Islam, a prince in search of a kingdom, a lord seeking resources to support his followers, and an aspiring merchant who hoped to make a killing in the gold trade but found his main profits in slaving. He was, in all these respects, a man of his time, which is to say, of the fifteenth century. He was not the architect, or even the visionary, of Portugal's sixteenth-century maritime empire.

ATLANTIC COLONIZATION AND THE GROWTH OF SLAVERY

The profits Prince Henry had hoped would come from the African gold trade did not materialize during his lifetime. He therefore had to make his expeditions pay by other means. One of those means was the slave trade. Although slavery in most of western Europe had effectively disappeared by the early twelfth century, slavery continued in Iberia (and to a lesser extent in Italy) throughout the high and late Middle Ages. Until the mid-fifteenth century, however, slavery on the Iberian mainland and in Italy remained very small in scale. The major Mediterranean slave markets of the fourteenth and early fifteenth centuries lay in Muslim lands, and especially in the Ottoman Empire. Relatively few of the slaves who passed through these markets were Africans. Most were European Christians, predominantly Poles, Ukrainians, Greeks, and Bulgarians. Thus the patterns of slavery were not racialized in the late medieval Mediterranean world, except insofar as "primitive" peoples such as the natives of the Canary Islands or of Sardinia were more likely to be regarded as targets for enslavement.

From the mid-fifteenth century on, however, Lisbon began to emerge as a significant market for enslaved Africans. Something on the order of 15,000 to 20,000 Africans were sold in Lisbon during Prince Henry's lifetime, most of them between 1440 and 1460. In the half century after his death, the numbers grew, amounting to perhaps 150,000 African slaves imported into Europe by 1505. For the most part, these slaves were regarded as status symbols—one reason they were so frequently depicted in paintings of the period. Even in the Atlantic colonies—Madeira, the Canaries, and the Azores—the land was worked mainly by European settlers and sharecroppers. Slave labor, if it was employed at all, was generally used only in sugar mills. This meant that on the Azores, which remained a wheat-producing colony, slavery found no real foothold. On Madeira and the Canaries, where sugar became the predominant cash crop during the last quarter of the fifteenth century, some slaves were introduced. But even sugar production did not lead to the widespread introduction of slavery on these islands.

A new style of slave-based sugar plantations began to emerge in Portugal's Atlantic colonies only in the 1460s, starting on the Cape Verde Islands and then extending southward into the Gulf of Guinea. These islands were not populated when the Portuguese began to settle them, and their climate was such as to discourage any large number of Europeans from settling there. They were ideally located, however, to purchase laborers from the slave traders along the nearby West African coast. No comparable system of large-scale, slave-based plantation production had been seen in Europe or Africa since the Roman period. But it was this model of sugar plantations staffed by enslaved Africans that would be exported to the Caribbean islands of the Americas by their Spanish conquerors, with incalculable consequences for Africa, the Americas, and Europe.

EUROPE ENCOUNTERS A NEW WORLD

What was the impact of New World silver on the European economy?

The decision by Spain's rulers to underwrite Columbus's famous voyage was an outgrowth of the progress of these Portuguese ventures. After 1488, when Dias successfully rounded the Cape of Good Hope, it was clear that Portugal would soon dominate the sea lanes leading eastward to Asia. The only alternative for Portugal's Spanish rivals was to finance someone bold enough to try to reach Asia by sailing west. The popular image of Christopher Columbus (1451–1506) as a visionary who struggled to convince hardened ignoramuses that the world was round does not bear up under scrutiny. In fact, the sphericity of the earth had been widely known throughout European society since at least the twelfth century. What made Columbus's scheme seem plausible to King Ferdinand and Queen Isabella was, first, the discovery and colonization of the Canary Islands and the Azores, which had reinforced a view of the Atlantic as being dotted with islands all the way to Japan; and second, the Genoese mariner's own astonishing miscalculation of the actual size of the earth, which convinced him that he could reach Japan and China in about a month's clear sailing westward from the Canary Islands. America was actually rediscovered by Europeans at the end of the fifteenth century as the result of a colossal error in reckoning. Columbus himself never realized his mistake. When he reached the Bahamas and the island of Hispaniola in 1492 after only a month's sailing, he returned to Spain to report that he had indeed reached the outer islands of Asia.

THE DISCOVERY OF A NEW WORLD

Columbus was not the first European to set foot on the American continents. Viking sailors had reached and briefly settled present-day Newfoundland, Labrador, and perhaps New England around the year 1000. But knowledge of these Viking landings had been forgotten or ignored throughout Europe for hundreds of years. In the fifteenth century, even the Scandinavian settlements in Greenland had been abandoned. It would be perverse, therefore, to deny Columbus credit for his accomplishments. Although Columbus himself never accepted the reality of what he had discovered, those who followed him soon did and busily set out to exploit this new world.

Understandably, Columbus brought back no Asian spices from his voyages. He did, however, return with some small samples of gold and a few indigenous people, whose existence gave promise of entire tribes that might be "saved" (by conversion to Christianity) and enslaved by Europeans. This provided sufficient incentive for the Spanish monarchs to finance three more expeditions by Columbus and many more by others. Soon the mainland was discovered as well as further islands, and the conclusion quickly became inescapable that a new world had indeed been found. Awareness of this new world was most widely publicized by the Italian geographer Amerigo Vespucci. Though he may not have deserved this honor, the continents of the Western Hemisphere became known thereafter as "America" after Vespucci's first name.

WHAT WAS THE IMPACT OF NEW WORLD SILVER ON THE EUROPEAN ECONOMY?

EUROPE ENCOUNTERS A NEW WORLD   435

The realization that this was indeed a new world was at first a disappointment to the Spanish, for with a major land mass lying between Europe and Asia, Spain could not hope to beat Portugal in the race for Asian spices. Any remaining doubt that not one, but two vast oceans separated Europe from Asia was completely removed in 1513, when Vasco Núñez de Balboa first viewed the Pacific Ocean from the Isthmus of Panama. Not entirely admitting defeat, Ferdinand and Isabella's grandson, the Holy Roman emperor Charles V, accepted Ferdinand Magellan's offer in 1519 to see whether a route to Asia could be found by sailing around South America. But Magellan's voyage demonstrated beyond question that the globe was simply too large for any such plan to be feasible. Of the five ships that left Spain under Magellan's command, only one returned three years later, having been forced to circumnavigate the globe. Out of a crew of 265 sailors, only eighteen survived. Most had died from scurvy or starvation; Magellan himself had been killed in a skirmish with native peoples in the Philippines. This fiasco brought to an end all hope of discovering an easy southwest passage to Asia. The dream of a northwest passage survived, however, and continued to motivate European explorers of North America until the nineteenth century.

THE SPANISH CONQUEST OF AMERICA

Although the discovery of this new continent was initially a disappointment to the Spanish, it quickly became clear that the New World had great wealth of its own. From the start, Columbus's gold samples, in themselves rather paltry, had nurtured hopes that somewhere in America gold might lie piled in ingots, ready to enrich whatever European adventurer discovered them. Rumor fed rumor, until a few freelance Spanish soldiers really did strike it rich beyond their most avaricious imaginings. Between 1519 and 1521, the *conquistador* (Spanish for "conqueror") Hernando Cortés, with a force of 600 Europeans but with the assistance of thousands of the Aztecs' unhappy subjects,

Spanish Conquistadors in Mexico. This sixteenth-century drawing of conquistadors massacring Mexican natives emphasizes the advantages that plate armor and steel swords gave to the Spanish soldiers.

overthrew the Aztec Empire of Mexico and carried off its rulers' fabulous wealth. Then in 1533 another conquistador, Francisco Pizarro, this time with only 180 men, toppled the highly centralized South American empire of the Inkas and carried off its great stores of gold and silver. Cortés and Pizarro had the advantage of some cannons and a few horses (both unknown to the native peoples of the Americas), but they achieved their victories primarily by sheer audacity, courage, and treachery. They were aided also by the unwillingness of the indigenous peoples whom the Aztecs and the Inkas had subjected to fight on behalf of their oppressors. Little did the Spaniards' erstwhile allies know how much worse their new conquerors would soon prove to be.

THE PROFITS OF EMPIRE IN THE NEW WORLD

Cortés and Pizarro were plunderers who captured in one fell swoop hoards of gold and silver that had been accumulated for centuries by the native civilizations of Mexico and Peru. Already, however, a search had begun for the sources of these precious metals. The first gold deposits were discovered in Hispaniola, where surface mines were speedily established using native laborers who died in appalling numbers from disease, brutality, and overwork. Of the approximately 1 million native people who lived on Hispaniola in 1492, only 100,000 survived by 1510. By 1538, their numbers were down to 500.

With the loss of so many workers, the Hispaniola mines became uneconomical to operate, and the European colonists turned instead to cattle raising and sugar production. Modeling their sugarcane plantations on those of the Cape Verde Islands and St. Thomas in the Gulf of Guinea, colonists imported African slaves to labor in the new industry. Sugar production was by its nature a highly capital-intensive undertaking. The need to import slave labor added further to its costs, guaranteeing that control over the sugar industry would fall into the hands of a few extremely wealthy planters and financiers.

Despite the importance of sugar production on the Caribbean islands and of cattle ranching on the Mexican mainland, mining shaped the Spanish colonies of Central and South America most fundamentally. Gold was the lure that had initially drawn the Spanish conquerors to the New World, but silver became their most lucrative export. Between 1543 and 1548, vast sil-

ver deposits were discovered north of Mexico City and at Potosí in Bolivia. Even before the discovery of these deposits, the Spanish crown had taken steps to assume direct governmental control over its Central and South American colonies. It was therefore to the Spanish crown that the profits from these astonishingly productive mines accrued. Potosí quickly became the most important mining town in the world. By 1570, it numbered 120,000 inhabitants, despite being located at an altitude of 15,000 feet where the temperature never climbs above 59 degrees Fahrenheit. As in Hispaniola, enslaved native laborers died by the tens of thousands in these mines and in the disease-infested boom towns that surrounded them.

New mining techniques (in particular, the mercury-amalgamation process, introduced into Mexico in 1555 and Potosí in 1571) made it possible to produce even greater quantities of silver, at the cost of even greater mortality among the native laborers. Between 1571 and 1586, silver production at Potosí quadrupled, reaching a peak in the 1590s, when 10 million ounces of silver per year were arriving in Spain from the Americas. In the 1540s, the corresponding figure was only 1.5 million ounces. In the peak years of domestic European silver production, between 1525 and 1535, only about 3 million ounces of silver per year were being produced, and this figure dropped steadily from about 1550 on. Europe's silver shortage came triumphantly to an end during the sixteenth century, but the silver that now circulated there came almost entirely from the New World.

This massive infusion of silver into the European economy accelerated an inflation that had begun already in the later fifteenth century. Initially, this inflation was driven by the renewed growth of the European

CHRONOLOGY

ENCOUNTERING THE NEW WORLD, C. 1000–1545

Vikings settle Newfoundland	c. 1000
Columbus reaches Hispaniola	1492
Balboa reaches Pacific Ocean	1513
Magellan's fleet sails around the world	1519–1522
Cortés conquers the Aztecs	1521
Pizarro conquers the Inkas	1533
Potosí silver deposits discovered	1545

ENSLAVED NATIVE LABORERS AT POTOSÍ

Since the Spanish crown received one fifth of all the revenues from mines (as well as maintaining a monopoly over the mercury used to refine the silver ore into silver), it had an important stake in ensuring the productivity of the mines. To this end, the crown granted colonial mine owners the right to conscript native peoples to work in the mines. This account from about 1620 describes the conditions under which these forced native laborers worked. It is not surprising that mortality rates among such laborers were horrendous.

According to His Majesty's warrant, the mine owners on this massive range [at Potosí] have a right to the conscripted labor of 13,300 Indians in the working and exploitation of the mines, both those which have been discovered, those now discovered, and those which shall be discovered. It is the duty of the *Corregidor* (municipal governor) of Potosí to have them rounded up and to see that they come in from all the provinces between Cuzco . . . and as far as the frontiers of Tarija and Tomina. . . .

The conscripted Indians go up every Monday morning to the . . . foot of the range; the *Corregidor* arrives with all the provincial captains or chiefs who have charge of the Indians assigned him for his miner or smelter; that keeps him busy till 1 P.M., by which time the Indians are already turned over to these mine and smelter owners.

After each has eaten his ration, they climb up the hill, each to his mine, and go in, staying there from that hour until Saturday evening without coming out of the mine; their wives bring them food, but they stay constantly underground, excavating and carrying out the ore from which they get the silver. They all have tallow candles, lighted day and night; that is the light they work with, for as they are underground, they have need for it all the time. . . .

These Indians have different functions in the handling of the silver ore; some break it up with bar or pick, and dig down in, following the vein in the mine; others bring it up; others up above keep separating the good and the poor in piles; others are occupied in taking it down from the range to the mills on herds of llamas; every day they bring up more than 8,000 of these native beasts of burden for this task. These teamsters who carry the metal are not conscripted, but are hired.

Antonio Vázquez de Espinosa, *Compendium and Description of the West Indies*, trans. Charles Upson Clark (Washington, D.C.,1968), p. 62.

QUESTIONS FOR ANALYSIS

1. What was the human cost of the Potosí silver mine?

population, an expanding economy, and a relatively fixed supply of food. From the 1540s on, however, inflation was largely the product of the greatly increased supply of silver that was now entering the European economy. The result was what historians have termed "the Price Revolution." Although the effects of this inflation were felt throughout the European continent, Spain was affected with particular severity. Between

1500 and 1560, Spanish prices doubled; between 1560 and 1600, they doubled again. Such exceptionally high prices in turn undermined the competitiveness of Spanish industries. When the flow of New World silver to Spain slowed dramatically during the 1620s and 1630s, the Spanish economy collapsed.

After 1600, lessening quantities of New World silver entered the European economy, but prices continued to rise, albeit more slowly than before. By 1650, the price of grain within Europe had risen to five or six times its level in 1500, producing social dislocation and widespread misery for many of Europe's poorest inhabitants. In England, the period between about 1590 and 1610 was probably the most desperate the country had experienced for 300 years. As the population rose and wages fell, living standards dropped dramatically. If we compute living standards by dividing the price of an average basket of food by the average daily wage of a building laborer, then standards of living were lower in England in 1600 than they had been even in the terrible years of the early fourteenth century. It is no wonder, then, that so many Europeans found emigration to the Americas a tempting prospect. We may wonder, indeed, what might have happened in seventeenth-century Europe had the new world of the Americas not existed as an outlet for Europe's growing population.

CONCLUSION

By 1600, colonization and overseas conquest had profoundly changed both Europe and the wider world. The emergence during the sixteenth century of Portugal and Spain as Europe's leading long-distance traders permanently moved the center of gravity of European economic power away from Italy and the Mediterranean toward the Atlantic. Deprived of its role as the principal conduit for the spice trade, Venice gradually declined. The Genoese moved increasingly into the world of finance, backing the commercial ventures of others, particularly of Spain. By contrast, the Atlantic ports of Spain and Portugal bustled with vessels and shone with wealth. By the mid-seventeenth century, however, economic predominance was passing to the north Atlantic states of England, Holland, and France. Spain and Portugal would retain their American colonies until the nineteenth century. But from the seventeenth century on, it would be the Dutch, the French, and especially the English who would establish new European empires in North America, Asia, Africa, and Australia. By and large, these new empires would last until the World War II.

KEY TERMS

Chingiz Khan	gunpowder	Prince Henry the Navigator	New World silver
Marco Polo	Canary Islands		Aztecs
Timur the Lame	caravels	Christopher Columbus	Inkas
Ottoman Janissaries	astrolabe	conquistador	

SELECTED READINGS

Abu-Lughod, Janet L. *Before European Hegemony: The World System A.D. 1250–1350.* Oxford and New York, 1989. A study of the trading links among Europe, the Middle East, India, and China, with special attention to the role of the Mongol Empire; extensive bibliography.

Allsen, Thomas T. *Culture and Conquest in Mongol Eurasia.* Cambridge and New York, 2001. A synthesis of the author's earlier studies, emphasizing Mongol involvement in the cultural and commercial exchanges that linked China, Central Asia, and Europe.

Amitai-Preiss, Reuven, and David O. Morgan, eds. *The Mongol Empire and Its Legacy.* Leiden, 1999. A collection of essays that represents some of the new trends in Mongol studies.

The Book of Prophecies, Edited by Christopher Columbus. Trans. Blair Sullivan, ed. Roberto Rusconi. Berkeley and Los Angeles, 1996. After his third voyage, from which Columbus was returned to Spain in chains, he compiled a book of quotations from various sources, selected to emphasize the millenarian implications of his discoveries; a fascinating insight into the mind of the explorer.

Christian, David. *A History of Russia, Central Asia and Mongolia*. Volume 1: *Inner Eurasia from Prehistory to the Mongol Empire*. Oxford, 1998. The authoritative English-language work on the subject.

Coles, Paul. *The Ottoman Impact on Europe*. London, 1968. An excellent introductory text, still valuable despite its age.

Fernández-Armesto, Felipe. *Before Columbus: Exploration and Colonisation from the Mediterranean to the Atlantic, 1229–1492*. London, 1987. An indispensible study of the medieval background to the sixteenth-century European colonial empires.

Fernández-Armesto, Felipe. *Columbus*. Oxford and New York, 1991. An excellent biography that stresses the millenarian ideas that underlay Columbus's thinking. A good book to read after Phillips and Phillips.

Flint, Valerie I. J. *The Imaginative Landscape of Christopher Columbus*. Princeton, N.J., 1992. A short, suggestive analysis of the intellectual influences that shaped Columbus's geographical ideas.

The Four Voyages: Christopher Columbus. Trans. J. M. Cohen. New York, 1992. Columbus's own self-serving account of his four voyages to the Indies.

Goffman, Daniel. *The Ottoman Empire and Early Modern Europe*. Cambridge and New York, 2002. A revisionist account that presents the Ottoman Empire as a European state.

The History and the Life of Chinggis Khan: The Secret History of the Mongols. Trans. Urgunge Onon. Leiden, 1997. A newer version of *The Secret History*, now the standard English version of this important Mongol source.

Inalcik, Halil. *The Ottoman Empire: The Classical Age, 1300-1600*. London, 1973. The standard history by the dean of Turkish historians.

Inalcik, Halil, ed. *An Economic and Social History of the Ottoman Empire, 1300–1914*. Cambridge, 1994. An important collection of essays, spanning the full range of Ottoman history.

Jackson, Peter. *The Mongols and the West, 1221–1410*. Harlow, UK, 2005. A well-written survey that emphasizes the interactions among the Mongol, Latin Christian, and Muslim worlds.

Kafadar, Cemal. *Between Two Worlds: The Construction of the Ottoman State*. Berkeley, Calif., and Los Angeles, 1995. An important study of Ottoman origins in the border regions between Byzantium, the Seljuk Turks, and the Mongols.

Larner, John. *Marco Polo and the Discovery of the World*. New Haven, Conn., 1999. A study of the influence of Marco Polo's *Travels* on Europeans.

Morgan, David. *The Mongols*, 2d ed. Oxford, 2007. An accessible introduction to Mongol history and its sources, written by a noted expert on medieval Persia.

Parker, Geoffrey. *The Military Revolution: Military Innovation and the Rise of the West (1500–1800)*, 2d ed. Cambridge and New York, 1996. A work of fundamental importance for understanding the global dominance achieved by early modern Europeans.

Phillips, J. R. S. *The Medieval Expansion of Europe*, 2d ed. Oxford, 1998. An outstanding study of the thirteenth- and fourteenth-century background to the fifteenth-century expansion of Europe. Important synthetic treatment of European relations with the Mongols, China, Africa, and North America. The second edition includes a new introduction and a bibliographical essay; the text is the same as in the first edition (1988).

Phillips, William D., Jr., and Carla R. Phillips. *The Worlds of Christopher Columbus*. Cambridge and New York, 1991. The first book to read on Columbus: accessible, engaging, and scholarly. Then read Fernández-Armesto's biography.

Ratchnevsky, Paul. *Genghis Khan: His Life and Legacy*. Trans. Thomas Nivison Haining. Oxford, 1991. An English translation and abridgment of a book first published in German in 1983. The author was one of the greatest Mongol historians of his generation.

Rossabi, M. *Khubilai Khan: His Life and Times*. Berkeley, Calif., 1988. The standard English biography.

Russell, Peter. *Prince Henry "The Navigator": A Life*. New Haven, Conn., 2000. A masterly biography by a great historian who has spent a lifetime on the subject. The only book one now needs to read on Prince Henry.

Saunders, J. J. *The History of the Mongol Conquests*. London, 1971. Still the standard English-language introduction; somewhat more positive about the Mongols' accomplishments than is Morgan.

Scammell, Geoffrey V. *The First Imperial Age: European Overseas Expansion, 1400–1715*. London, 1989. A useful introductory survey, with a particular focus on English and French colonization.

The Secret History of the Mongols. Trans. F. W. Cleaves. Cambridge, Mass., 1982.

The Secret History of the Mongols and Other Pieces. Trans. Arthur Waley. London, 1963. The later Chinese abridgment of the Mongol original.

The Travels of Marco Polo, trans. R. E. Latham. Baltimore, Md., 1958. The most accessible edition of this remarkably interesting work.

CHAPTER TWELVE

THE CIVILIZATION
OF THE RENAISSANCE,
C. 1350–1550

THE PREVALENT MODERN NOTION that a "Renaissance period" followed western Europe's Middle Ages was first expressed by numerous Italian writers who lived between 1350 and 1550. According to them, 1,000 years of unrelieved darkness had intervened between the Roman era and their own times. During these dark ages the muses of art and literature had fled Europe before the onslaught of barbarism and ignorance. Almost miraculously, however, in the fourteenth century the muses suddenly returned, and Italians happily collaborated with them to bring forth a glorious "renaissance of the arts."

Ever since this periodization was advanced, historians have taken for granted the existence of some sort of renaissance intervening between medieval and modern times. Indeed, from the late eighteenth to the early twentieth centuries many scholars went so far as to argue that the Renaissance was not just an epoch in the history of learning and culture but that a unique Renaissance spirit transformed all aspects of European life—political, economic, and religious as well as intellectual and artistic. Today, however, most experts no longer accept this characterization because they find it impossible to locate any truly distinctive "Renaissance" politics, economics, or religion. Instead, most scholars reserve the term *Renaissance* to describe certain trends in thought, literature, and the arts that emerged in Italy from roughly 1350 to 1550 and then spread to northern Europe during the sixteenth century. That is the approach that we follow here: accordingly, when we refer to a "Renaissance" period in this chapter, we mean to limit ourselves to an epoch in intellectual and cultural history.

FOCUS QUESTIONS

- How did the Italian Renaissance culture differ from the culture of the High Middle Ages?

- Why did the Renaissance occur in Italy?

- What were the principal characteristics of Italian Renaissance art?

- Why did the Renaissance decline around 1550?

- How did the northern and Italian Renaissances differ from one another?

THE RENAISSANCE AND THE MIDDLE AGES

How did Italian Renaissance culture differ from the culture of the High Middle Ages?

Granted this restriction, some further qualifications are still necessary. Since the word *renaissance* literally means "rebirth," it is sometimes thought that after about 1350 certain Italians who were newly cognizant of Greek and Roman cultural accomplishments initiated a rebirth of classical culture after a long period during which that culture had been essentially dead. In fact, however, the High Middle Ages witnessed no "death" of classical learning. Saint Thomas Aquinas considered Aristotle to be "the Philosopher;" Dante revered Virgil. Similar examples could be cited almost without limit. It would be equally false to contrast an imaginary Renaissance paganism with a medieval age of faith because, however much most Renaissance personalities loved the classics, none saw classicism as superseding Christianity. And finally, all discussions of the Renaissance must be qualified by the fact that there was no single Renaissance position on anything. Renaissance thinkers and artists were enormously diverse in their attitudes, achievements, and approaches. As we assess their accomplishments, we need to beware not to force them into too narrow a mold.

In the twelfth and thirteenth centuries Greek scientific and philosophical treatises became available to western Europeans in Latin translations through Islam, but none of the great Greek literary masterpieces and practically none of the major works of Plato were yet known.

RENAISSANCE CLASSICISM

Nonetheless, in the realms of thought, literature, and the arts, we can certainly find distinguishing traits that make the concept of a "Renaissance" meaningful for intellectual and cultural history. First, regarding knowledge of the classics, there was a significant quantitative difference between the learning of the Middle Ages and that of the Renaissance. Medieval scholars knew many Roman authors, such as Virgil, Ovid, and Cicero, but during the Renaissance the works of others such as Livy, Tacitus, and Lucretius were rediscovered and made familiar. Equally if not more important was the Renaissance recovery of the literature of classical Greece from Byzantium. In the twelfth and thirteenth

centuries Greek scientific and philosophical treatises became available to western Europeans in Latin translations through Islam, but none of the great Greek literary masterpieces and practically none of the major works of Plato were yet known. Nor could more than a handful of medieval Westerners read the Greek language. During the Renaissance, on the other hand, large numbers of Western scholars learned Greek and mastered almost the entire Greek literary heritage that is known today.

Second, Renaissance thinkers not only knew many more classical texts than their medieval counterparts but they used them in new ways. Whereas medieval writers presumed that their ancient sources would complement and confirm their own Christian assumptions, Renaissance writers were more aware of the conceptual and chronological gap that separated their own world from that of their classical sources. At the same time, however, the structural similarities between the ancient city-states and those of Renaissance Italy encouraged Italian thinkers in particular to find in these ancient sources models of thought and action directly applicable to their own day. This firm determination to learn from classical antiquity was even more pronounced in the realms of architecture and art, areas in which classical models contributed most strikingly to the creation of fully distinct Renaissance styles.

Third, although Renaissance culture was by no means pagan, it was more worldly and overtly materialistic in its orientation than was the culture of the twelfth and thirteenth centuries. The evolution of the Italian city-states created a supportive environment for attitudes that stressed the importance of the urban political arena and of living well in this world. Such ideals helped create a culture that was increasingly nonecclesiastical. The relative weakness of the church in Italy also contributed to the more secular culture that emerged there. Italian bishoprics were small and for the most part poorly endowed. Italian universities were also largely independent of ecclesiastical supervision and control. Even the papacy was severely limited in its ability to intervene in the cultural life of the Italian city-states, not least because the papacy's role as a political rival in central Italy compromised its moral authority as an arbiter of cultural and religious values. All these factors helped create a space within which the worldly, materialistic culture of the Renaissance could emerge effectively untrammeled by ecclesiastical opposition.

RENAISSANCE HUMANISM

One word above all comes closest to summing up the most common and basic Renaissance intellectual ideals—namely *humanism*. Renaissance humanism was a program of studies that aimed to replace the thirteenth- and fourteenth-century scholastic emphasis on logic and metaphysics with the study of language, literature, rhetoric, history, and ethics. The humanists always preferred ancient literature; although some (notably Francesco Petrarch and Leon Batista Alberti) wrote in both Latin and the vernacular, most humanists regarded vernacular literature as at best a diversion for the uneducated. Serious scholarship and literature could be written only in Latin or Greek. That Latin, moreover, had to be the Latin of Cicero and Virgil. Renaissance humanists were self-conscious elitists who condemned the living Latin of their scholastic contemporaries as a barbarous departure from ancient (and therefore correct) standards of Latin style. Despite their belief that they were thereby reviving the study of the classics, the humanists' position was thus inherently ironic. By insisting on ancient standards of Latin grammar, syntax, and word choice, the humanists of the Renaissance succeeded ultimately in turning Latin into a fossilized language that thereafter ceased to evolve. They thus contributed, quite unwittingly, to the ultimate triumph of the European vernaculars as the primary languages of intellectual and cultural life.

Humanists were convinced that their own educational program—which placed the study of Latin language and literature at the core of the curriculum and then encouraged students to go on to Greek—was the best way to produce virtuous citizens and able public officials. Their elitism was to this extent intensely practical and directly connected to the political life of the city-states in which they lived. Because women were excluded from Italian political life, the education of women was therefore of little concern to most humanists, although some aristocratic women did acquire humanist training. As more and more fifteenth-century city-states fell into the hands of princes, however, the humanist educational curriculum lost its immediate connection to the republican ideals of Italian political life. Nevertheless, humanists never lost their conviction that the study

> By insisting on ancient standards of Latin grammar, syntax, and word choice, the humanists of the Renaissance succeeded ultimately in turning Latin into a fossilized language that thereafter ceased to evolve.

of the "humanities" (as the humanist curriculum came to be known) was the best way to produce leaders for European society.

THE RENAISSANCE IN ITALY

Why did the Renaissance occur in Italy?

Although the Renaissance eventually became a Europe-wide intellectual and artistic movement, it developed first and most distinctively in fourteenth- and fifteenth-century Italy. Understanding why this was so is important not only to explaining the origins of this movement but also to understanding its fundamental characteristics.

THE ORIGINS OF THE ITALIAN RENAISSANCE

The Renaissance originated in Italy for several reasons. The most fundamental reason was that Italy in the later Middle Ages was the most advanced urban society in all of Europe. Unlike aristocrats north of the Alps, Italian aristocrats customarily lived in urban centers rather than in rural castles and consequently became fully involved in urban public affairs. Moreover, since the Italian aristocracy built its palaces in the cities, the aristocratic class was less sharply set off from the class of rich merchants than in the north. Hence, whereas in France or Germany most aristocrats lived on the income from their landed estates while rich town dwellers (*bourgeois*) gained their living from trade, in Italy so many town-dwelling aristocrats engaged in banking or mercantile enterprises and so many rich mercantile families imitated the manners of the aristocracy that by the fourteenth and fifteenth centuries the aristocracy and upper bourgeoisie were becoming virtually indistinguishable. The noted Florentine family of the Medici (*MEH-dih-chee*), for example, emerged as a family of physicians (as the name suggests), made its fortune in banking and commerce, and rose into the aristocracy in the fifteenth century. The results of these developments for the history of education are obvious: not only was there a great demand for education in the skills of reading and counting

THE HUMANISTS' EDUCATIONAL PROGRAM

These three selections illustrate the confidence of civic humanists such as Vergerius, Bruni, and Alberti that their elite educational program would be of supreme value to the state as well as to the individual students who pursued it. Not everyone agreed with the humanists' claims, however, and a good deal of self-promotion lies behind them.

VERGERIUS ON LIBERAL STUDIES

We call those studies *liberal* which are worthy of a free man; those studies by which we attain and practice virtue and wisdom; that education which calls forth, trains, and develops those highest gifts of body and of mind which ennoble men, and which are rightly judged to rank next in dignity to virtue only. . . . It is, then, of the highest importance that even from infancy this aim, this effort, should constantly be kept alive in growing minds. For . . . we shall not have attained wisdom in our later years unless in our earliest we have sincerely entered on its search. [P. P. Vergerius (1370–1444), *"Concerning Excellent Traits."*]

ALBERTI ON THE IMPORTANCE OF LITERATURE

Letters are indeed so important that without them one would be considered nothing but a rustic, no matter how much a gentlemen [he may be by birth]. I'd much rather see a young nobleman with a book than with a falcon in his hand. . . .

Be diligent, then, you young people, in your studies. Do all you can to learn about the events of the past that are worthy of memory. Try to understand all the useful things that have been passed on to you. Feed your minds on good maxims. Learn the delights of embellishing your souls with good morals. Strive to be kind and considerate [of others] when conducting civil business. Get to know those things human and divine that have been put at your disposal in books for good reason. Nowhere [else] will you find . . . the elegance of a verse of Homer, or Virgil, or of some other excellent poet. You will find no field so delightful or flowering as in one of the orations of Demosthenes, Cicero, Livy, Xenophon, and other such pleasant and perfect orators. No effort is more fully compensated . . . as the constant reading and rereading of good things. From such reading you will rise rich in good maxims and good arguments, strong in your ability to persuade others and get them to listen to you; among the citizens you will willingly be heard, admired, praised, and loved. [Leon Battista Alberti (1404–1472), *"On the Family."*]

BRUNI ON THE HUMANIST CURRICULUM

The foundations of all true learning must be laid in the sound and thorough knowledge of Latin: which implies study marked by a broad spirit, accurate scholarship, and careful attention to details. Unless this solid basis be secured it is useless to attempt to rear an enduring edifice. Without it the great monuments of literature are unintelligible, and the art of composition impossible. To attain this essential knowledge we must never relax our careful attention to the grammar of the language, but perpetually confirm and extend our acquaintance with it until it is thoroughly our own. . . .

But the wider question now confronts us, that of the subject matter of our studies, that which I have already called the realities of fact and principle, as distinct from literary form. . . . First among such studies I place History: a subject which must not on any account be neglected by one who aspires to true cultivation. . . . For the careful study of the past enlarges our foresight in contemporary affairs and affords to citizens and to monarchs lessons . . . in the ordering of public policy. From History, also, we draw our store of examples of moral precepts. . . .

The great Orators of antiquity must by all means be included. Nowhere do we find the virtues more warmly extolled, the vices so fiercely decried. From them we may learn, also, how to express consolation, encouragement, dissuasion or advice. . . .

Familiarity with the great poets of antiquity is essential to any claim to true education. For in their writings we find deep speculations upon Nature, and upon the Causes and Origins of things, which must carry weight with us both from their antiquity and from their authorship. . . .

Proficiency in literary form, not accompanied by broad acquaintance with facts and truths, is a barren attainment; whilst information, however vast, which lacks all grace of expression would seem to be put under a bushel or partly thrown away. . . . Where, however, this double capacity exists—breadth of learning and grace of style—we allow the highest title to distinction and to abiding fame. . . . [Leonardo Bruni (1369–1444), *"Concerning the Study of Literature."*]

Vergerius and Bruni: William Harrison Woodward, ed., *Vittorino da Feltre and Other Humanist Educators* (London:, 1897), pp. 96–110, 124–129, 132–133. Alberti: Eric Cochrane and Julius Kirshner, eds., *University of Chicago Readings in Western Civilization*, Vol. 5: *The Renaissance* (Chicago, 1986), pp. 81–82.

QUESTIONS FOR ANALYSIS

1. Why did the Italian Renaissance produce such a strong spirit of civic humanism?
2. Do you think that Socrates' and Cicero's perceptions of virtue were identical to those of Vergerius and Bruni? Were Renaissance virutes and classical virtues one and the same thing?
3. Why did humanists such as Leonardo Bruni consider the study of history essential to a full education?

necessary to become a successful merchant but the richest and most prominent families sought above all to find teachers who would impart to their sons the knowledge and skills necessary to argue well in the public arena. Consequently, Italy produced a large number of lay educators, many of whom not only taught students but also demonstrated their learning by producing political and ethical treatises and works of literature. Italian schools created the best-educated upper-class public in all of Europe, along with a considerable number of wealthy patrons who were ready to invest in the cultivation of new ideas and new forms of literary and artistic expression.

A second reason why late medieval Italy was the birthplace of an intellectual and artistic renaissance lay in the fact that it had a far greater sense of rapport with the classical past than any other territory in western Europe. Ancient Roman monuments were omnipresent throughout the peninsula, and classical Latin literature referred to cities and sites that Renaissance Italians recognized as their own. Italians were particularly intent on reappropriating their classical heritage in the fourteenth and fifteenth centuries because they were also seeking to establish an independent cultural identity in opposition to a scholasticism most closely associated with France. Not only did the removal of the papacy to Avignon for most of the fourteenth century and then the

Great Schism from 1378 to 1417 heighten antagonisms between Italy and France but, during the fourteenth century, an intellectual reaction against scholasticism on all fronts encouraged Italians to prefer the intellectual alternatives offered by classical literary sources. As Roman literature and learning took root in Italy, so too did Roman art and architecture, for Roman models could help Italians create a splendid artistic alternative to French Gothicism just as Roman learning offered an intellectual alternative to French scholasticism.

Finally, the Italian Renaissance could not have occurred without the underpinning of Italian wealth. The Italian economy as a whole was probably more prosperous in the thirteenth century than it was in the fourteenth and fifteenth. But late medieval Italy was wealthier in comparison with the rest of Europe than it had been before, a fact that meant that Italian writers and artists were more likely to stay at home than to seek employment abroad. In late medieval Italy, intensive investment in culture arose both from an intensification of urban pride and the concentration of per capita wealth. During the fourteenth century, cities themselves were the primary patrons of art and learning. During the fifteenth century, however, when most Italian city-states succumbed to the hereditary rule of noble families, patronage was monopolized by the princely aristocracy. Among these great princes were

Pope Julius II, by Raphael. The acorns at the top of the throne posts are visual puns for the pope's family name, della Rovere ("of the oak").

the popes in Rome, who based their strength on temporal control of the Papal States. The most worldly of the Renaissance popes—Alexander VI (1492–1503); Julius II (1503–1513); and Leo X (1513–1521), son of the Florentine ruler Lorenzo de' Medici—employed the greatest artists of the day and for a few decades made Rome the artistic capital of Western Europe.

THE ITALIAN RENAISSANCE: LITERATURE AND THOUGHT

In surveying the accomplishments of Italian Renaissance scholars and writers it is natural to begin with the work of Petrarch (Francesco Petrarca, 1304–1374), the "father of Renaissance humanism." Petrarch was a deeply committed Catholic who believed that scholasticism was entirely misguided because it concentrated on abstract speculation rather than on teaching people how to live virtuously and attain salvation. Petrarch thought that the Christian writer must instead cultivate literary eloquence so that he could inspire people to do good. For him the best models of eloquence were to be found in the classical texts of Latin literature, which were doubly valuable because they were also

filled with ethical wisdom. Petrarch dedicated himself, therefore, to rediscovering such texts and to writing his own poems and moral treatises in a Latin style modeled on classical authors. But Petrarch was also a remarkable vernacular poet. The Italian sonnets—later called Petrarchan sonnets—that he wrote for his beloved Laura in the chivalrous style of the troubadours were widely imitated and admired throughout the Renaissance period, and continue to be read today.

Because he was a very traditional Christian, Petrarch's ultimate ideal for human conduct was the solitary life of contemplation and asceticism. But from about 1400 to 1450, subsequent Italian thinkers and scholars, located mainly in Florence, developed a different vision customarily called civic humanism. Civic humanists such as the Florentines Leonardo Bruni (c. 1370–1444) and Leon Battista Alberti (1404–1472) agreed with Petrarch on the need for eloquence and the value of classical literature, but they also taught that man's nature equipped him for action, for usefulness to his family and society, and for serving the state—ideally a republican city-state after the classical or contemporary Florentine model. In their view ambition and the quest for glory were noble impulses that ought to be encouraged. They refused to condemn the striving for material possessions, for they argued that the history of human progress is inseparable from our success in mastering the earth and its resources.

Perhaps the most famous of the civic humanists' writings is Alberti's *On the Family* (1443), in which he argued that the nuclear family was instituted by nature for the well-being of humanity. Within this framework, however, Alberti consigned women to purely domestic roles, asserting that "man [is] by nature more energetic and industrious," and that woman was created "to increase and continue generations, and to nourish and preserve those already born." Although such dismissals of women's intellectual abilities were fiercely resisted by a few notable women humanists, for the most part Italian Renaissance humanism was characterized by a pervasive denigration of women—a denigration expressed also in the works of classical literature that the humanists so much admired.

THE EMERGENCE OF TEXTUAL SCHOLARSHIP

The civic humanists also went far beyond Petrarch in their knowledge of classical (and especially Greek) literature and philosophy. In this they were aided by a number of Byzantine scholars who had migrated to

SOME RENAISSANCE ATTITUDES TOWARD WOMEN

Italian society in the fourteenth and fifteenth centuries was characterized by marriage patterns in which men in their late twenties or thirties customarily married women in their mid- to late teens. This demographic fact probably contributed to the widely shared belief in this period that wives were essentially children, who could not be trusted with important matters and who were best trained by being beaten. Renaissance humanism did little to change such attitudes. In some cases, it even reinforced them.

After my wife had been settled in my house a few days, and after her first pangs of longing for her mother and family had begun to fade, I took her by the hand and showed her around the whole house. I explained that the loft was the place for grain and that the stores of wine and wood were kept in the cellar. I showed her where things needed for the table were kept, and so on, through the whole house. At the end there were no household goods of which my wife had not learned both the place and the purpose. . . .

Only my books and records and those of my ancestors did I determine to keep well sealed. . . . These my wife not only could not read, she could not even lay hands on them. I kept my records at all times . . . locked up and arranged in order in my study, almost like sacred and religious objects. I never gave my wife permission to enter that place, with me or alone. . . .

[Husbands] who take counsel with their wives . . . are madmen if they think true prudence or good counsel lies in the female brain. . . . For this very reason I have always tried carefully not to let any secret of mine be known to a woman. I did not doubt that my wife was most loving, and more discreet and modest in her ways than any, but I still considered it safer to have her unable, and not merely unwilling, to harm me. . . . Furthermore, I made it a rule never to speak with her of anything but household matters or questions of conduct, or of the children.

Leon Battista Alberti, "On the Family," in *The Family in Renaissance Florence,* trans. and ed. Renée N. Watkins. (Columbia, S.C., 1969), pp. 208–213, as abridged in Julie O'Faolain and Lauro Martines, eds., *Not in God's Image: Women in History from the Greeks to the Victorians* (New York, 1973), pp. 187–188.

QUESTIONS FOR ANALYSIS

1. For what reasons did Leon Battista Alberti argue that his wife should have no access to his books or records?
2. Would you expect Renaissance attitudes toward women to have been more liberal and more modern? Did Alberti's comments refer to Italian society as a whole or merely to a small segment of it?

Italy in the first half of the fifteenth century and gave instruction in the Greek language. Italian scholars also traveled to Constantinople and other Eastern cities in search of Greek masterpieces hitherto unknown in the West. In 1423 one Italian, Giovanni Aurispa, alone brought back 238 manuscript books, including works of Sophocles, Euripides, and Thucydides, which were quickly translated into Latin, not word for word, but sense for sense to preserve the literary force of the original. By 1500, most of the Greek classics, including the writings of Plato, the dramatists, and the historians, were available to western Europe.

Related in his textual interests to the civic humanists, but by no means a full adherent of their movement, was the atypical yet highly influential Renaissance thinker Lorenzo Valla (1407–1457). Born in Rome and active primarily as a secretary in the service of the king of Naples, Valla had no allegiance to the republican ideals of the Florentine civic humanists. Instead, he used his skills in grammar, rhetoric, and the painstaking analysis of Greek and Latin texts to show how the thorough study of language could discredit old verities. Most remarkable in this regard was Valla's brilliant demonstration that the Donation of Constantine was a medieval forgery. Whereas papal propagandists had argued that the papacy's rights to temporal rule in western Europe derived from this charter purportedly granted by the emperor Constantine in the fourth century, Valla proved that the charter was full of nonclassical Latin usages and anachronistic terms. Hence he concluded that the "Donation" was the work of a medieval forger whose "monstrous impudence" was exposed by the "stupidity of his language." This demonstration not only discredited a prize specimen of "medieval ignorance" but, more important, introduced the concept of anachronism into all subsequent textual study and historical thought. In his *Notes on the New Testament* he also applied his expert knowledge of Greek to elucidating the true meaning of Saint Paul's letters, which he believed had been obscured by Saint Jerome's Latin Vulgate translation. This work was to prove an important link between Italian Renaissance scholarship and the subsequent Christian humanism of the north.

RENAISSANCE NEOPLATONISM

From about 1450 until about 1600 Italian thought was dominated by a school of Neoplatonists who sought to blend the ideas of Plato, Plotinus, and various strands of ancient mysticism with Christianity. Foremost among these were Marsilio Ficino (1433–1499) and Giovanni Pico della Mirandola (1463–1494), both of whom were members of the Platonic Academy founded by Cosimo de' Medici in Florence. The academy was a loosely organized society of scholars who met to hear readings and lectures. Their hero was Plato: sometimes they celebrated Plato's birthday by holding a banquet in his honor, after which everybody gave speeches as if they were characters in a Platonic dialogue. From the standpoint of posterity, Ficino's greatest achievement was his translation of Plato's works into Latin, which made them widely available to western Europeans for the first time. Ficino himself, however, regarded his *Hermetic Corpus*, a collection of passages drawn from a number of

Pico della Mirandola. When the young nobleman Pico arrived in Florence at age nineteen he was said to have been "of beauteous feature and shape." This contemporary portrait may have been done by the great Florentine painter Botticelli.

ancient mystical writings including the Hebrew Kabbalah, as his greatest contribution to learning.

It is debatable whether Ficino's own philosophy should be called humanist because he moved away from ethics to metaphysics and taught that the individual should look primarily to the hereafter. In Ficino's opinion, "the immortal soul is always miserable in its mortal body." The same issue arises with respect to Ficino's disciple Giovanni Pico della Mirandola. Pico was certainly not a civic humanist because he saw little worth in mundane public affairs. He also fully shared his teacher's penchant for extracting and combining snippets taken out of context from ancient mystical tracts. But he did also believe—and so argued in his famous *Oration on the Dignity of Man*—that there is "nothing more wonderful than man" because he believed that man is endowed with the capacity to achieve union with God if he so wills.

MACHIAVELLI

Hardly any of the Italian thinkers between Petrarch and Pico were really original: their greatness lay mostly in their manner of expression, their scholarship, and their popularization of different themes of ancient thought. The same, however, cannot be said of Renaissance Italy's greatest political philosopher, the Florentine Niccolò Machiavelli (*mah-kee-uh-VEHL-ee*, 1469–1527). Machiavelli's writings reflect the unstable condition of Italy in his time. At the end of the fifteenth century Italy had become the cockpit of international struggles. Both France and Spain had invaded the peninsula and were competing for the allegiance of the Italian city-states, which in turn were torn by internal dissension. In 1498 Machiavelli became a prominent official in the government of the Florentine republic, set up four years earlier when the French invasion had led to the expulsion of the Medici. His duties largely involved diplomatic missions to other Italian city-states. While in Rome he became fascinated with the attempt of Cesare Borgia, son of Pope Alexander VI, to create his own principality in central Italy. He noted with approval Cesare's ruthlessness and shrewdness and his complete subordination of personal morality to political ends. In 1512 the Medici returned to overthrow the republic of Florence, and Machiavelli was deprived of his position. Disappointed and embittered, he spent the remainder of his life at his country estate, devoting his time to writing.

Machiavelli remains a controversial figure even today. Some modern scholars see him as an amoral theorist of realpolitik, disdainful of morality and Christian piety, caring nothing about the proper purposes of political life, but interested solely in the acquisition and exercise of power as an end in itself. Others see him as an Italian patriot, who viewed princely tyranny as the only way to liberate Italy from its foreign conquerors. Still others see him as a follower of Saint Augustine of Hippo, who understood that in a fallen world populated by sinful people, a ruler's good intentions do not guarantee that his policies will have good results. Instead, Machiavelli insisted that a prince's actions must be judged by their consequences and not by their intrinsic moral quality. Human beings, Machiavelli argued, "are ungrateful, fickle, and deceitful, eager to avoid dangers, and avid for gain." This being so, "the necessity of preserving the state will often compel a prince to take actions which are opposed to loyalty, charity, humanity, and religion. . . . So far as he is able, a prince should stick to the path of good but, if the necessity arises, he should know how to follow evil."

In the political chaos of early sixteenth-century Italy, Machiavelli saw a ruthless prince such as Borgia as the only hope for revitalizing the spirit of independence among his contemporaries, and so making them fit, once again, for republican self-rule.

The puzzle is heightened by the fact that, on the surface, Machiavelli's two great works of political analysis appear to contradict each other. In his *Discourses on Livy* he praised the ancient Roman republic as a model for his own contemporaries, lauding constitutional government, equality among the citizens of a republic, political independence for city-states, and the subordination of religion to the service of the state. There is little doubt, therefore, that Machiavelli was a committed republican, who believed in the free city-state as the ideal form of human government. But Machiavelli also wrote *The Prince*, "a handbook for tyrants" in the eyes of his critics, and he dedicated this work to Lorenzo, son of Piero de' Medici, whose family had overthrown the Florentine republic that Machiavelli himself had served.

Because *The Prince* has been so much more widely read than the *Discourses*, interpretations of Machiavelli's political thought have often mistaken the admiration he expressed in *The Prince* for Cesare Borgia as an endorsement of princely tyranny for its own sake. Machiavelli's real position was quite different. In the political chaos of early sixteenth-century Italy, Machiavelli saw a ruthless prince such as Borgia as the only hope for revitalizing the spirit of independence among his contemporaries, and so making them fit, once again, for republican self-rule. However dark his vision of human nature, Machiavelli never ceased to hope that his Italian contemporaries would rise up, expel their French and Spanish conquerors, and restore their ancient traditions of republican liberty and equality. Princes such as Borgia were necessary steps toward that end, but for Machiavelli their rule was not the ideal form of government for humankind. In Italy's sunken political situation, however, a princely state was the best form of government toward which Machiavelli's downtrodden contemporaries could aspire.

THE IDEAL OF THE COURTIER

Far more congenial to contemporary tastes than the shocking political theories of Machiavelli were the guidelines for proper aristocratic conduct offered in *The Book of the Courtier* (1528) by the diplomat and count Baldassare Castiglione. This cleverly written forerunner of modern handbooks of etiquette stands in sharp contrast to the earlier civic humanist treatises of Bruni and Alberti. Whereas they taught the sober republican

MACHIAVELLI'S ITALIAN PATRIOTISM

These passages are from the concluding chapter to Machiavelli's treatise The Prince. *Like the book itself, they are addressed to Lorenzo, the son of Piero de' Medici.*

Reflecting on the matters set forth above and considering within myself whether the times were propitious in Italy at present to honor a new prince and whether there is at hand the matter suitable for a prudent and virtuous leader to mold in a new form, giving honor to himself and benefit to the citizens of the country, I have arrived at the opinion that all circumstances now favor such a prince, and I cannot think of a time more propitious for him than the present. If, as I said, it was necessary in order to make apparent the virtue of Moses, that the people of Israel should be enslaved in Egypt, and that the Persians should be oppressed by the Medes to provide an opportunity to illustrate the greatness and the spirit of Cyrus, and that the Athenians should be scattered in order to show the excellence of Theseus, thus at the present time, in order to reveal the valor of an Italian spirit it was essential that Italy should fall to her present low estate, more enslaved than the Hebrews, more servile than the Persians, more disunited than the Athenians, leaderless and lawless, beaten, despoiled, lacerated, overrun and crushed under every kind of misfortune. . . . So Italy now, left almost lifeless, awaits the coming of one who will heal her wounds, putting an end to the sacking and looting in Lombardy and the spoliation and extortions in the Realm of Naples and Tuscany, and cleanse her sores that have been so long festering. Behold how she prays God to send her some one to redeem her from the cruelty and insolence of the barbarians. See how she is ready and willing to follow any banner so long as there be some one to take it up. Nor has she at present any hope of finding her redeemer save only in your illustrious house [the Medici] which has been so highly exalted both by its own merits and by fortune and which has been favored by God and the church, of which it is now ruler. . . .

This opportunity, therefore, should not be allowed to pass, and Italy, after such a long wait, must be allowed to behold her redeemer. I cannot describe the joy with which he will be received in all these provinces which have suffered so much from the foreign deluge, nor with what thirst for vengeance, nor with what firm devotion, what solemn delight, what tears! What gates could be closed to him, what people could deny him obedience, what envy could withstand him, what Italian could withhold allegiance from him? THIS BARBARIAN OCCUPATION STINKS IN THE NOSTRILS OF ALL OF US. Let your illustrious house then take up this cause with the spirit and the hope with which one undertakes a truly just enterprise. . . .

Niccolò Machiavelli, *The Prince*, trans. and ed. Thomas G. Bergin (Arlington Heights, Ill:, 1947), pp. 75–76, 78.

QUESTIONS FOR ANALYSIS

1. Why did Machiavelli argue that Italy needed the type of prince he had outlined in his book *The Prince*?
2. According to Machiavelli, what was wrong with the Italy of his own day?
3. Did Machiavelli espouse the cause of Italian nationalism or the banner of a strong prince like Lorenzo de' Medici? Or were his visions of patriotism and leadership concurrent?

virtues of strenuous service in behalf of city-state and family, Castiglione, writing in an Italy dominated by magnificent princely courts, taught how to attain the elegant and seemingly effortless qualities necessary for acting like a true gentleman. More than anyone else, Castiglione popularized the ideal of the "Renaissance man": one who is accomplished in many different pursuits and is also brave, witty, and "courteous," meaning civilized and learned. Unlike Alberti, Castiglione said nothing about women's role in "hearth and home" but stressed instead the ways in which court ladies could be "gracious entertainers." Widely read throughout Europe for over a century after its publication, Castiglione's *Courtier* spread Italian ideals of civility to princely courts north of the Alps, resulting in the ever-greater patronage of art and literature by the European aristocracy.

Sixteenth-century Italians were also highly accomplished creators of imaginative prose and verse. Machiavelli himself wrote a delightful short story, "Belfagor," and an engagingly bawdy play, *Mandragola*; the great artist Michelangelo wrote many moving sonnets; and Ludovico Ariosto (1474–1533), the most eminent of sixteenth-century Italian epic poets, wrote a lengthy verse narrative called *Orlando Furioso* (The madness of Roland). Although based on the medieval Charlemagne cycle, this work differed radically from any of the medieval epics because it introduced elements of lyrical fantasy and, above all, because it was totally devoid of heroic idealism. Ariosto wrote to make readers laugh and to charm them with descriptions of the quiet splendor of nature and the passions of love. His work embodies the disillusionment of the late Renaissance, the loss of hope and faith, and the tendency to seek consolation in the pursuit of pleasure and aesthetic delight.

THE ITALIAN RENAISSANCE: PAINTING, SCULPTURE, AND ARCHITECTURE

What were the principal characteristics of Italian Renaissance art?

Despite numerous intellectual and literary advances, the longest-lived achievements of the Italian Renaissance were made in the realm of art. Of all the arts, painting was undoubtedly supreme. We have already

seen the artistic genius of Giotto around 1300, but it was not until the fifteenth century that Italian painting began to come fully of age. One reason for this was that in the early fifteenth century the laws of linear perspective were discovered and first employed to give the fullest sense of three dimensions. Fifteenth-century artists also experimented with effects of light and shade (*chiaroscuro*) and for the first time carefully studied the anatomy and proportions of the human body. By the fifteenth century, too, increasing private wealth and the growth of lay patronage had opened the domain of art to a variety of nonreligious themes and subjects. Even subject matter from biblical history was now frequently infused with nonreligious themes. Artists sought to paint portraits that revealed the hidden mysteries of the soul. Paintings intended to appeal primarily to the intellect were paralleled by others whose main purpose was to delight the eye with gorgeous color and beauty of form. The introduction

The Impact of Perspective. Masaccio's painting *The Trinity with the Virgin* illustrates the startling sense of depth made possible by the rules of perspective.

of painting in oil, probably from Flanders, also characterized fifteenth-century painting. The use of the new technique doubtless had much to do with the artistic advance of this period. Because oil does not dry as quickly as fresco pigment, the painter could now work more slowly, taking time with the more difficult parts of the picture and making corrections if necessary as he or she went along.

RENAISSANCE PAINTING IN FLORENCE

The majority of the great painters of the fifteenth century were Florentines. First among them was the precocious Masaccio (1401–1428), known to his contemporaries as "Giotto reborn." Although he died at the age of twenty-seven, Masaccio inspired the work of Italian painters for a hundred years. Masaccio's greatness as a painter is based on his success in "imitating nature," which became a primary value in Renaissance painting. To achieve this effect he employed perspective, perhaps most dramatically in his fresco of the Trinity; he also used chiaroscuro with originality, leading to strikingly dramatic effects.

Masaccio's best-known successor was the Florentine Sandro Botticelli (1445–1510), who depicted both classical and Christian subjects. Botticelli's work excels in linear rhythms and sensuous depiction of natural detail. He is most famous for paintings that portray figures from classical mythology without any overtly Christian frame of reference. His *Allegory of Spring* and *Birth of Venus* employ a style greatly indebted to Roman depictions of gods, goddesses, zephyrs, and muses moving gracefully in natural settings. Consequently, these works were once understood as the expression of Renaissance paganism at its fullest, a celebration of earthly delights breaking sharply with Christian asceticism. More recently, however, scholars have preferred to view them as allegories fully compatible with Christian teachings. According to this interpretation, Botticelli was addressing himself to learned aristocratic viewers, well versed in the Neoplatonic theories of Ficino, which considered ancient gods and goddesses to represent various Christian virtues. Venus, for example, might have stood for a species of chaste love. Although Botticelli's great "classical" works remain cryptic, two points remain certain: any viewer is free to enjoy them on their naturalistic sensuous level,

Birth of Venus, **by Botticelli.** Botticelli was a mystic as well as a lover of beauty, and this painting is most often interpreted as a Neoplatonic allegory.

and Botticelli had surely not broken with Christianity, since he painted frescoes for the pope in Rome at just the same time.

LEONARDO DA VINCI

Perhaps the greatest of the Florentine artists was Leonardo da Vinci (1452–1519), one of the most versatile geniuses who ever lived. Leonardo personified the Renaissance man: he was a painter, architect, musician, mathematician, engineer, and inventor. The illegitimate son of a notary and a peasant woman, Leonardo set up an artist's shop in Florence by the time he was twenty-five and gained the patronage of the Medici ruler of the city, Lorenzo the Magnificent. But if Leonardo had any weakness, it was his slowness in working and difficulty in finishing anything. This naturally displeased Lorenzo and other Florentine patrons, who thought an artist was little more than an artisan, commissioned to produce a certain piece of work of a certain size for a certain price on a certain date. Leonardo, however, strongly objected to this view because he considered himself to be no menial craftsman

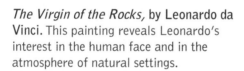

The Virgin of the Rocks, by **Leonardo da Vinci.** This painting reveals Leonardo's interest in the human face and in the atmosphere of natural settings.

The Last Supper, by Leonardo da Vinci.

but an inspired creator. Therefore in 1482 he left Florence for the Sforza court of Milan where he was given freer rein in structuring his time and work. He remained there until the French invaded Milan in 1499; after that he wandered about Italy, finally accepting the patronage of the French king, Francis I, under whose auspices Leonardo lived and worked in France until his death.

The paintings of Leonardo da Vinci began what is known as the High Renaissance in Italy. His approach to painting was that it should be the most accurate possible imitation of nature. Leonardo was like a naturalist, basing his work on his own detailed observations of a blade of grass, the wing of a bird, a waterfall. He obtained human corpses for dissection and reconstructed in drawing the minutest features of anatomy, which knowledge he carried over to his paintings. Leonardo worshiped nature and was convinced of the essential divinity in all living things. It is not surprising, therefore, that he was a vegetarian and that he went to the marketplace to buy caged birds, which he released to their native habitat.

It is generally agreed that Leonardo's masterpieces are *The Virgin of the Rocks* (which exists in two versions), *The Last Supper*, and his portraits of the Mona Lisa and Ginevra da Benci. *The Virgin of the Rocks* typifies not only his marvelous technical skill but also his passion for science and his belief in the universe as a well-ordered place. The figures are arranged geometrically, with every rock and plant depicted in accurate detail. *The Last Supper*, painted on the walls of the refectory of Santa Maria delle Grazie in Milan, is a study of psychological reactions. A serene Christ, resigned to his terrible fate, has just announced to his disciples that one of them will betray him. The artist succeeds in portraying the mingled emotions of surprise, horror, and guilt in the faces of the disciples as they gradually perceive the meaning

of their master's statement. The third and fourth of Leonardo's major triumphs, the *Mona Lisa* and *Ginevra da Benci*, reflect a similar interest in the varied moods of the human soul.

THE VENETIAN SCHOOL

The beginning of the High Renaissance around 1490 also witnessed the rise of the so-called Venetian school, the major members of which were Giovanni Bellini (c. 1430–1516), Giorgione (1478–1510), and Titian (c. 1490–1576). The work of all these men reflected the luxurious, pleasure-loving life of the thriving commercial city of Venice. Most Venetian painters showed little of the Florentine school's concerns with philosophical and psychological issues. Their aim was to appeal to the senses by painting idyllic landscapes and sumptuous portraits of the rich and powerful. In the subordination of form and meaning to color and elegance they mirrored the sumptuous tastes of the wealthy merchants for whom they were created.

Doge Francesco Venier (1555), by Titian. Titian served as the official painter of the Venetian Republic for sixty years. This superb portrait of Venice's ruler shows Titian's mastery of light and color.

PAINTING IN ROME

High Renaissance painting reached its peak in the first half of the sixteenth century. During this period, Rome became the major artistic center of the Italian peninsula, although the traditions of the Florentine school still exerted a potent influence.

RAPHAEL

Among the eminent painters of this period was Raphael (1483–1520), a native of Urbino, and perhaps the most beloved artist of the entire Renaissance. The lasting appeal of his style is due primarily to his ennobling portrayals of human beings as temperate, wise, and dignified creatures. Although Raphael was influenced by Leonardo, he cultivated a much more symbolical or allegorical approach to his painting. His *Disputà* illustrated the relationship between the church in heaven and the church on earth. In a worldly setting against a brilliant sky, theologians debate the meaning of the Eucharist, while in the clouds above, saints and the Trinity repose in the possession of a holy mystery. Raphael's *School of Athens* depicts the harmony between Platonism and Aristotelianism. Plato (painted as a portrait of Leonardo) is shown pointing upward to emphasize the spiritual basis of his world of Ideas, while Aristotle stretches a hand forward to exemplify his claim that the created world embodies these same principles in physical form. Raphael is noted also for his portraits and Madonnas. To the latter, especially, he gave a softness and warmth that seemed to endow them with a sweetness and piety quite different from Leonardo's enigmatic and somewhat distant Madonnas.

MICHELANGELO

The last towering figure of the High Renaissance was Michelangelo (1475–1564), a native of Florence. If Leonardo was a naturalist, Michelangelo was an idealist; where the former sought to recapture and interpret fleeting natural phenomena, Michelangelo, who

School of Athens, by Raphael.

The Creation of Adam, by Michelangelo (1475–1564). One of a series of frescoes on the ceiling of the Sistine Chapel in Rome. Inquiring into the nature of humanity, it represents Renaissance affirmativeness at its height.

embraced Neoplatonism as a philosophy, was more concerned with expressing enduring, abstract truths. Michelangelo was a painter, sculptor, architect, and poet—and he expressed himself in all these forms with a similar power and in a similar manner. At the center of all of his paintings is the male figure, which is always powerful, colossal, magnificent. If humanity, embodied in the male body, lay at the center of Italian Renaissance culture, then Michelangelo, who depicted the male figure without cease, is the supreme Renaissance artist.

Michelangelo's greatest achievements in painting appear in a single location—the Sistine Chapel in Rome—yet they are products of two different periods in the artist's life and consequently exemplify two different artistic styles and outlooks on the human condition. More famous are the sublime frescoes Michelangelo painted on the ceiling of the Sistine Chapel from 1508 to 1512, depicting scenes from the book of Genesis. All the panels in this series, including *God Dividing the Light from Darkness, The Creation of Adam,* and *The Flood,* exemplify the young artist's commitment to classical Greek aesthetic principles of harmony, solidity, and dignified restraint. Correspondingly, all exude a sense of sublime affirmation regarding the Creation and the heroic qualities of humankind. But a quarter of a century later, when Michelangelo returned to work in the Sistine Chapel, both his style and mood had changed dramatically. In the enormous *Last Judgment,* a fresco done for the Sistine Chapel's altar wall in 1536, Michelangelo repudiated classical restraint and substituted a style that emphasized tension and distortion to communicate the older man's pessimistic conception of a humanity wracked by fear and bowed by guilt.

SCULPTURE

In the realm of sculpture the Italian Renaissance took a great step forward by creating statues that were no longer carved as parts of columns or doorways on church buildings or as effigies on tombs. Instead, Italian sculptors for the first time since antiquity carved free-standing statues "in the round." By freeing sculpture from its bondage to architecture, the High Renaissance reestablished sculpture as a separate and potentially secular art form.

DONATELLO

The first great master of Renaissance sculpture was Donatello (c. 1386–1466). His bronze statue of David triumphant over the head of the slain Goliath, the first free-standing nude since antiquity, imitated classical sculpture not just in the depiction of a nude body but also in the subject's posture of resting his weight on one leg. Yet this David is clearly a lithe adolescent rather than a muscular Greek athlete. Later in his career, Donatello more consciously imitated ancient statuary in his commanding portrayal of the proud warrior Gattamelata—the first monumental equestrian statue in bronze executed in the West since the time of the Romans.

MICHELANGELO

Certainly the greatest sculptor of the Italian Renaissance—indeed, probably the greatest sculptor of all time—was Michelangelo. Believing with Leonardo that the artist was an inspired creator, Michelangelo regarded sculpture as the most exalted of the arts because it allowed the artist to imitate God most fully in re-creating human forms. Furthermore, in Michelangelo's view the most God-like sculptor disdained slavish naturalism, for anyone could make a plaster cast of a human figure, but only an inspired creative genius could endow his sculpted figures with a sense of life. Accordingly, Michelangelo subordinated naturalism to the force of his imagination and sought restlessly to express his ideals in ever more arresting forms.

Like his painting, Michelangelo's sculpture followed a course from classicism to mannerism—that is, from

David, by Donatello (c. 1386–1466). The first free-standing nude statue executed in the West since antiquity.

harmonious modeling to dramatic distortion. The sculptor's most distinguished early work, his *David,* executed in 1501, is surely his most perfect classical statue. Choosing, like Donatello, to depict a male nude, Michelangelo conceived of his own *David* as a public expression of Florentine civic ideals and hence as heroic rather than merely graceful. To this end he worked in marble—the "noblest" sculptural medium—and created a figure twice as large as life. By sculpting a serenely confident young man at the peak of physical fitness, Michelangelo celebrated the Florentine republic's own fortitude in resisting tyrants and upholding

***David,* by Michelangelo.** Over thirteen feet high, this serenely self-confident affirmation of the beauty of the human form was placed prominently by the Florentine government in front of Florence's city hall to proclaim the city's humanistic values.

***The Descent from the Cross,* by Michelangelo.** This portrayal of tragedy was made by the sculptor for his own tomb. Note the distortion for effect exemplified by the elongated body and left arm of the figure of Christ. The figure in the rear is Nicodemus, but was probably intended to represent Michelangelo himself.

ideals of civic justice. The serenity seen in *David* was no longer prominent in the works of Michelangelo's middle period; rather, in a work such as his *Moses* of about 1515, the sculptor had begun to explore the use of anatomical distortion to create effects of emotional intensity—in this case, the biblical prophet's righteous rage. While such statues remained awesomely heroic, as Michelangelo's life drew to a close he experimented more and more with exaggerated stylistic mannerisms for the purpose of communicating moods of brooding pensiveness or outright pathos. The culmination of this trend in Michelangelo's statuary is his unfinished

but intensely moving *Descent from the Cross*, a depiction of an old man resembling the sculptor himself grieving over the distorted, slumping body of the dead Christ.

ARCHITECTURE

To a much greater extent than either sculpture or painting, Renaissance architecture had its roots in the past. The new building style was a compound of elements derived from the Middle Ages and from antiquity. It was not the Gothic, however, a style that had never found a congenial soil in Italy, but the Italian Romanesque that

The Villa Rotonda, by Palladio. A highly influential Renaissance private dwelling near Vicenza.

provided the medieval basis for the architecture of the Italian Renaissance. The great architects of the Renaissance generally adopted their building plans from Romanesque churches, some of which they believed, mistakenly, to be Roman rather than medieval. They also copied their decorative devices from the ruins of ancient Rome. The result was an architecture based on the cruciform floor plan of transept and nave, but embodying the decorative features of the column and arch or the column and lintel, the colonnade, and frequently the dome. Renaissance architecture also emphasized geometrical proportion because Italian

builders, under the influence of Neoplatonism, concluded that certain mathematical ratios reflect the harmony of the universe. A fine example of Renaissance architecture is St. Peter's Basilica in Rome, built under the patronage of popes Julius II and Leo X and designed by some of the most celebrated architects of the time, including Donato Bramante (c. 1444–1514) and Michelangelo. Equally impressive are the artfully proportioned aristocratic country houses designed by the northern Italian architect Andrea Palladio (1508–1580), who created secular miniatures of ancient temples such as the Roman Pantheon to glorify the aristocrats who dwelled within them.

CHRONOLOGY

LIVES OF ITALIAN RENAISSANCE SCHOLARS AND ARTISTS	
Petrarch	1304–1374
Leon Battista Alberti	1404–1472
Giovanni Pico della Mirandola	1463–1494
Niccolò Machiavelli	1469–1527
Leonardo da Vinci	1452–1519
Titian	c. 1490–1576
Raphael	1483–1520
Michelangelo	1475–1564

THE WANING OF THE ITALIAN RENAISSANCE

Why did the Renaissance decline around 1550?

Around 1550 the Renaissance in Italy began to decline. The causes of this decline were varied. The French invasion of 1494 and the incessant warfare that ensued was one of the major factors. The French king Charles VIII viewed Italy as an attractive target for his expansive dynastic ambitions. In 1494 he led an army of 30,000 well-trained troops across the Alps to press his claims to the Duchy of Milan and the Kingdom of Naples. Florence swiftly capitulated; within less than a year the French had promenaded down the peninsula and conquered Naples. By so doing, however, they aroused the suspicions of the rulers of Spain, who feared an attack on their own territory of Sicily. An alliance among Spain, the Papal States, the Holy Roman Empire, Milan, and Venice finally forced Charles to withdraw from Italy. But the respite was brief. Charles's successor, Louis XII, launched a second invasion, and from 1499 until 1529 warfare in Italy was virtually uninterrupted. Alliances and counteralliances followed each other in bewildering succession, but they managed only to prolong the hostilities. The French won a great victory at Marignano in 1515, but they were decisively defeated by the Spanish at Pavia in 1525. The worst disaster came in 1527 when rampaging troops under the command of the Spanish ruler and Holy Roman emperor Charles V sacked the city of Rome, causing enormous destruction. Only in 1529 did Charles V finally manage to gain control over most of the Italian peninsula, putting an end to the fighting for a time. Once triumphant, Charles retained two of the largest portions of Italy for Spain—the Duchy of Milan and the Kingdom of Naples—and installed favored princes as the rulers of almost all the other Italian political entities except for Venice and the Papal States. These protégés of the Spanish crown continued to preside over their own courts, to patronize the arts, and to adorn their cities with luxurious buildings; but they were puppets of a foreign power and unable to inspire their retinues with a sense of vigorous cultural independence.

To these political disasters was added a waning of Italian prosperity. Italy's virtual monopoly of trade with Asia in the fifteenth century had been one of the chief economic supports for Italian Renaissance culture, but the gradual shifting of trade routes from the Mediterranean to the Atlantic region, following the overseas discoveries of around 1500, slowly but surely cost Italy its supremacy as the center of European trade. Warfare also contributed to Italy's economic hardships, as did Spanish financial exactions in Milan and Naples. As Italian wealth diminished,

there was less and less of a surplus to support artistic endeavors.

A final cause of the decline of the Italian Renaissance was the Counter-Reformation. During the sixteenth century the Roman church sought increasingly to exercise firm control over thought and art as part of a campaign to combat worldliness and the spread of Protestantism. In 1542 the Roman Inquisition was established; in 1564 the first Roman Index of Prohibited Books was published. Even Michelangelo's great *Last Judgment* in the Sistine Chapel was criticized for showing too many naked bodies. Therefore, Pope Paul IV ordered a second-rate artist to paint in clothing wherever possible. (The unfortunate artist was afterward known as the "underwear maker.") Although this incident may appear merely grotesquely humorous, the determination of ecclesiastical censors to enforce doctrinal uniformity could lead to death, as in the case of the unfortunate Neoplatonic philosopher Giordano Bruno, whose insistence that there may be more than one world (in contravention of the biblical book of Genesis) resulted in his being burned at the stake by the Roman Inquisition in 1600.

> Galileo was not willing to die for his beliefs, but after he publicly retracted his view that the earth revolves around the sun he supposedly whispered, "despite everything, it still moves."

The most notorious example of inquisitorial censorship of intellectual speculation was the disciplining of the great scientist Galileo, whose achievements we will discuss in more detail in Chapter Sixteen. In 1616 the Holy Office in Rome condemned the new astronomical theory that the earth moves around the sun as "foolish, absurd, philosophically false, and formally heretical." When Galileo published a brilliant defense of the heliocentric system in 1632 the Inquisition ordered Galileo to recant his "errors" and sentenced him to house arrest for the duration of his life. Galileo was not willing to die for his beliefs, but after he publicly retracted his view that the earth revolves around the sun he supposedly whispered, "despite everything, it still moves." It is not surprising that the great astronomical discoveries of the next generation were made in northern Europe, not in Italy.

Cultural and artistic achievement was by no means extinguished in Italy after the middle of the sixteenth century. On the contrary, impressive new artistic styles were cultivated between about 1540 and 1600 by painters who drew on traits found in the later work of Raphael and Michelangelo. In the seventeenth cen-

THE STATES OF ITALY DURING THE RENAISSANCE, c. 1494

Note the political divisions of Italy on the eve of the French invasion in 1494. Contemporary observers often described Italy as being divided among five great powers: Milan, Venice, Florence, the Papal States, and the Kingdom of Naples. Which of these powers were most interested in expanding their territory? Which neighboring territories would be most threatened by such attempts at expansion? Why did Florence and the Papal States so often find themselves in conflict with each other?

tury came the dazzling Baroque style, which was born in Rome under ecclesiastical auspices. Similarly, Italian music registered enormous accomplishments virtually without interruption from the sixteenth to the twentieth century. But as Renaissance culture spread from Italy to the rest of Europe, the cultural dominance of the Italians began to wane, and the focus of European high culture shifted toward the princely courts of Spain, France, England, Germany, and Poland.

THE RENAISSANCE IN THE NORTH

How did the northern and Italian Renaissances differ from one another?

Contacts between Italy and northern Europe continued throughout the fourteenth and fifteenth centuries. Italian merchants and financiers were familiar figures at northern courts; students from all over Europe studied at Italian universities such as Bologna or Padua; authors (including Chaucer) and their works traveled to and from Italy; and northern soldiers were frequent participants in Italian wars. Only at the end of the fifteenth century, however, did the new currents of Italian Renaissance learning begin to take firm hold in Spain and northern Europe.

A variety of explanations have been offered for this delay. Northern European intellectual life in the late Middle Ages was dominated by universities such as Paris, Oxford, and Charles University in Prague, whose curricula focused on the study of philosophical logic and Christian theology. This approach left little room for the study of classical literature. In Italy, by contrast, universities were more often professional schools for law and medicine, and universities themselves exercised much less influence over intellectual life. As a result, a more secular, urban-oriented educational tradition took shape in Italy, within which Renaissance humanism was able to develop. Even in the sixteenth century, northern scholars influenced by Italian Renaissance ideals usually worked outside the university system under the patronage of kings and princes.

Before the sixteenth century, northern rulers were also less interested in patronizing artists and intellectuals than were the city-states and princes of Italy. In Italy, such patronage was an important arena for competition between political rivals. In northern Europe, political units were larger and political rivals were fewer. It was therefore more difficult to use art for political purposes in a kingdom than it was in a city-state. In Florence, a statue erected in a central square would be seen by nearly all the city's residents. In Paris, such a

statue would be seen only by a tiny minority of the French king's subjects. Only in the sixteenth century, as northern nobles began to spend more time in residence at the royal court, could kings be reasonably certain that their patronage of artists and intellectuals would be noticed by those whom they were trying to impress.

CHRISTIAN HUMANISM AND THE NORTHERN RENAISSANCE

The northern Renaissance was the product of the grafting of certain Italian Renaissance ideals onto pre-existing northern traditions. This can be seen very clearly in the case of the most prominent northern Renaissance intellectual movement, Christian humanism. Although they shared the Italian humanists' contempt for scholasticism, northern Christian humanists more often looked for ethical guidance from biblical and religious precepts rather than from Cicero or Virgil. Like their Italian counterparts, they sought wisdom from antiquity, but the antiquity they had in mind was Christian rather than classical—the antiquity, that is, of the New Testament and the early church fathers. Similarly, northern Renaissance artists were inspired by the accomplishments of Italian masters to learn classical techniques. But northern artists depicted classical subject matter far less frequently than did the Italians and almost never portrayed completely nude human figures.

> Although they shared the Italian humanists' contempt for scholasticism, northern Christian humanists more often looked for ethical guidance from biblical and religious precepts rather than from Cicero or Virgil.

DESIDERIUS ERASMUS

Any discussion of northern Renaissance accomplishments in the realm of thought and literary expression must begin with the career of Desiderius Erasmus (c. 1469–1536), the "prince of the Christian humanists." The illegitimate son of a priest, Erasmus was born near Rotterdam in Holland but later, as a result of his wide travels, became in effect a citizen of all northern Europe. Forced into a monastery against his will when he was a teenager, the young Erasmus found there little religion or formal instruction of any kind but plenty of freedom to read what he liked. He devoured all the classics he could get his hands on and the writings of many of the church fathers. When he was

How did the northern and Italian Renaissances differ from one another?

THE RENAISSANCE IN THE NORTH   463

Erasmus, by Hans Holbein the Younger (1497–1543).
This portrait is generally regarded as the most telling visual characterization of the prince of the Christian humanists.

about thirty years of age, he obtained permission to leave the monastery and enroll in the University of Paris, where he completed the requirements for the degree of bachelor of divinity. But Erasmus subsequently rebelled against what he considered the arid learning of Parisian scholasticism. Nor did he ever serve actively as a priest. Instead he made his living from teaching, writing, and the proceeds of various ecclesiastical offices that required no spiritual duties of him. Ever on the lookout for new patrons, he traveled often to England, stayed once for three years in Italy, and resided in several different cities in Germany and the Netherlands before settling finally toward the end of his life in Basel, Switzerland. By means of a voluminous correspondence that he kept up with learned friends he made wherever he went, Erasmus became the leader of a northern European humanist coterie. And through the popularity of his numerous publications, he became the arbiter of northern European cultural tastes during his lifetime.

Erasmus's many-sided intellectual activity may best be appraised from two different points of view: the literary and the doctrinal. As a Latin prose stylist, Erasmus was unequaled since the days of Cicero. Extraordinarily learned and witty, he reveled in tailoring his mode of discourse to fit his subject, creating dazzling verbal effects and coining puns that took on added meaning if the reader knew Greek as well as Latin. Above all, Erasmus excelled in the deft use of irony, poking fun at all and sundry, including himself. For example, in his *Colloquies* (from the Latin for "discussions") he had a fictional character lament the evil signs of the times thus: "kings make war, priests strive to line their pockets, theologians invent syllogisms, monks roam outside their cloisters, the commons riot, and Erasmus writes colloquies."

But although Erasmus's urbane Latin style and wit earned him a wide audience for purely literary reasons, he intended everything he wrote to promote what he called the "philosophy of Christ." Erasmus believed that the entire society of his day was caught up in corruption and immorality because people had lost sight of the simple teachings of the Gospels. Accordingly, he offered to his contemporaries three different categories of publication: clever satires meant to show people the error of their ways, serious moral treatises meant to offer guidance toward proper Christian behavior, and scholarly editions of basic Christian texts.

In the first category belong the works of Erasmus that are still most widely read today—*The Praise of Folly* (1509), in which he pilloried scholastic pedantry and dogmatism as well as the ignorance and superstitious credulity of the masses; and the *Colloquies* (1518), in which he held up contemporary religious practices for examination in a more serious but still pervasively ironic tone. In such works Erasmus let fictional characters do the talking; hence his own views can be determined only by inference. But in his second mode Erasmus did not hesitate to speak clearly in his own voice. The most prominent treatises in this second genre are the quietly eloquent *Handbook of the Christian Knight* (1503), which urged the laity to pursue lives of serene inward piety, and the *Complaint of Peace* (1517), which pleaded movingly for Christian pacifism. Erasmus's pacifism was one of his most deeply held values, and he returned to it again and again in his published works.

Despite the success of his literary works, Erasmus considered his textual scholarship his greatest achievement. Revering the authority of the early Latin fathers Augustine, Jerome, and Ambrose, he brought out reliable editions of all their works. He also used his extraordinary command of Latin and Greek to produce a more accurate edition of the New Testament. After reading Lorenzo Valla's *Notes on the New Testament* in 1504, Erasmus became convinced that nothing was more imperative than divesting the New Testament of the myriad errors in transcription and translation that had piled up during the Middle Ages, for no one could be a good Christian without being certain of exactly what Christ's message really was. Hence he spent ten years studying and comparing all the best early Greek biblical manuscripts he could find in order to establish an authoritative text. When it finally appeared in 1516, Erasmus's Greek New Testament, published together with explanatory notes and his own new Latin translation, was one of the most important landmarks of biblical scholarship of all time. In the hands of Martin Luther, it would play a critical role in the early stages of the Protestant Reformation.

SIR THOMAS MORE

One of Erasmus's closest friends, and a close second to him in distinction among the ranks of the Christian humanists, was the Englishman Sir Thomas More (1478–1535). Following a successful career as a lawyer and as speaker of the House of Commons, in 1529 More was appointed lord chancellor of England. He was not long in this position, however, before he incurred the wrath of King Henry VIII. More, who was loyal to Catholic universalism, opposed the king's design to establish a national church under royal control. Finally, in 1534, when More refused to take an oath acknowledging Henry as head of the Church of England, he was thrown into the Tower of London, and a year later met his death on the scaffold as a Catholic martyr. Much earlier, however, in 1516, long before More had any inkling of how his life was to end, he published the one work for which he will ever be best remembered, *Utopia*. Purporting to describe an ideal community on an imaginary island, the book is really an Erasmian critique of the glaring abuses of the time—poverty undeserved and wealth unearned, drastic punishments, religious persecution, and the senseless slaughter of war. The inhabitants of Utopia hold all their goods in common, work only six hours a day so that all may have leisure for intellectual pursuits, and practice the natural virtues of wisdom, moderation, fortitude, and justice. Iron is the precious metal "because it is useful," war and monasticism do not exist, and toleration is granted to all who recognize the

Sir Thomas More, by Hans Holbein the Younger.

existence of God and the immortality of the soul. Although More advanced no explicit arguments in his *Utopia* in favor of Christianity, he clearly meant to imply that if the Utopians could manage their society so well without the benefit of Christian revelation, Europeans who knew the Gospels ought to be able to do even better.

ULRICH VON HUTTEN

Whereas Erasmus and More were basically conciliatory in their temperaments and preferred to express themselves by means of wry understatement, Erasmus's German disciple Ulrich von Hutten (1488–1523) was of a much more combative disposition. Dedicated to the cause of German cultural nationalism, von Hutten spoke up truculently to defend the "proud and free" German people against foreigners. But his chief claim to fame was his collaboration with another German humanist, Crotus Rubianus, in the authorship of the *Letters of Obscure Men* (1515), one of the most stinging satires in the history of literature. This was written as part of a propaganda war in favor of a scholar named Johann Reuchlin who wished to pursue his study of

HOW DID THE NORTHERN AND ITALIAN RENAISSANCES DIFFER FROM ONE ANOTHER?

THE RENAISSANCE IN THE NORTH   465

Hebrew writings—above all, the Talmud. When scholastic theologians and the German inquisitor general tried to have all Hebrew books in Germany destroyed, Reuchlin and his party strongly opposed the move. After a while it became apparent that direct argument was accomplishing nothing, so Reuchlin's supporters resorted to ridicule. Von Hutten and Rubianus published a series of letters, written in intentionally bad Latin, purportedly by some of Reuchlin's scholastic opponents from the University of Cologne. These opponents, given such ridiculous names as Goatmilker, Baldpate, and Dungspreader, were shown to be learned fools who paraded absurd religious literalism or grotesque erudition. Heinrich Sheep's-mouth, for example, the supposed writer of one of the letters, professed to be worried that he had sinned grievously by eating on Friday an egg that contained the embryo of a chick. The author of another boasted of his "brilliant discovery" that Julius Caesar could not have written Latin histories because he was too busy with his military exploits ever to have learned Latin. Although immediately banned by the church, the letters circulated nonetheless and were widely read, giving ever more currency to the Erasmian proposition that scholastic theology and external religious observances had to be set aside in favor of the most earnest dedication to the simple teachings of the Gospels.

Most Christian humanists tried to remain within the Catholic fold while still espousing their ideal of nonritualistic inward piety. But as time went on, the leaders of Catholicism grew less and less tolerant because lines were hardening in the war with Protestantism.

THE DECLINE OF CHRISTIAN HUMANISM

With Erasmus, More, and von Hutten the list of energetic and eloquent Christian humanists is by no means exhausted, for the Englishman John Colet (c. 1467–1519), the Frenchman Jacques Lefèvre d'Étaples (c. 1455–1536), and the Spaniards Cardinal Francisco Ximénez de Cisneros (1436–1517) and Juan Luís Víves (1492–1540) all made signal contributions to the collective enterprise of editing biblical and early Christian texts and expounding Gospel morality. But despite a host of achievements, the Christian humanist movement, which possessed such an extraordinary degree of international solidarity and vigor from about 1500 to 1525, was thrown into disarray by the rise of Protestantism and subsequently lost its momentum.

The irony here is obvious, for the Christian humanists' emphasis on the literal truth of the Gospels and their devastating criticisms of clerical corruption and religious ceremonialism certainly helped pave the way for the Protestant Reformation initiated by Martin Luther in 1517. But, as we will see in Chapter Thirteen, very few of the older generation of Christian humanists were willing to join Luther in rejecting the fundamental principles on which Catholicism was based, and the few who did became such ardent Protestants that they lost the sense of quiet irony that had been a hallmark of Christian humanist expression. Most Christian humanists tried to remain within the Catholic fold while still espousing their ideal of nonritualistic inward piety. But as time went on, the leaders of Catholicism grew less and less tolerant because lines were hardening in the war with Protestantism. Hence any internal criticism of Catholic religious practices seemed like giving covert aid to the enemy. Erasmus himself, who remained a Catholic, died early enough to escape opprobrium, but several of his less fortunate followers lived on to suffer as victims of the Inquisition.

LITERATURE, ART, AND MUSIC IN THE NORTHERN RENAISSANCE

Yet if Christian humanism faded rapidly after about 1525, the northern Renaissance continued to flourish throughout the sixteenth century in literature and art. In France, Pierre de Ronsard (c. 1524–1585) and Joachim du Bellay (c. 1522–1560) wrote elegant sonnets in the style of Petrarch, and in England the poets Sir Philip Sidney (1554–1586) and Edmund Spenser (c. 1552–1599) drew impressively on Italian literary innovations. Indeed, Spenser's *Faerie Queene*, a long chivalric romance written in the manner of Ariosto's *Orlando Furioso*, communicates as well as any Italian work the gorgeous sensuousness typical of Italian Renaissance culture.

RABELAIS

More original than any of the aforementioned poets was the French prose satirist François Rabelais (*ra-beh-LAY*, c. 1494–1553), probably the best loved of all the great European creative writers of the sixteenth century. Like Erasmus, whom he greatly admired, Rabelais began his career in the clergy, but soon after taking holy orders he left his cloister to study medicine. As a practicing physician Rabelais interspersed his professional activities with literary endeavors, composing almanacs, satires against quacks and astrologers, and burlesques of popular superstitions. But by far his most enduring work was his five volumes of "chronicles" published under the collective title *Gargantua and Pantagruel*.

Rabelais's account of the adventures of Gargantua and Pantagruel, originally the names of legendary medieval giants noted for their fabulous size and gross appetites, served as a vehicle for his lusty humor and his penchant for exuberant narrative as well as for the expression of his philosophy of naturalism. To some degree, Rabelais drew on the precedents of Christian humanism. Thus, like Erasmus, he satirized religious ceremonialism, ridiculed scholasticism, scoffed at superstitions, and pilloried every form of bigotry. But unlike Erasmus, who wrote in a highly cultivated classical Latin style comprehensible to only the most learned readers, Rabelais chose to address a far wider audience by writing in an extremely down-to-earth French loaded with the crudest vulgarities. Likewise, Rabelais wanted to avoid seeming in any way preachy and therefore eschewed all suggestions of moralism in favor of giving the impression that he wished merely to offer his readers some rollicking good fun. Yet, aside from the critical satire in *Gargantua and Pantagruel*, there runs through all five volumes a common theme of glorifying the human and the natural. For Rabelais, whose robust giants were really life-loving human beings writ very large, every instinct of humanity was healthy, provided it was not directed toward tyranny over others. Thus in his ideal community, the utopian "abbey of Thélème," there was no repressiveness whatsoever, but only a congenial environment for the pursuit of life-affirming, natural human attainments, guided by the single rule of "love and do what thou wouldst."

ARCHITECTURE

Just as Rabelais recounted stories of medieval giants to affirm Renaissance values, so French architects who constructed such splendid Loire châteaux as Amboise,

Chambord. Built in the early sixteenth century by an Italian architect in the service of King Francis I of France, this magnificent Loire Valley château combines Gothic and Renaissance architectural traits.

HOW DID THE NORTHERN AND ITALIAN RENAISSANCES DIFFER FROM ONE ANOTHER?

THE RENAISSANCE IN THE NORTH   467

Chenonceaux, and Chambord combined elements of the late medieval French flamboyant Gothic style with an up-to-date emphasis on classical horizontality to produce some of the most impressively distinctive architectural landmarks ever constructed in France. Yet much closer architectural imitation of Italian models occurred in France as well, for just as Ronsard and du Bellay modeled their poetic style very closely on Petrarch, so Pierre Lescot, the French architect who began work on the new royal palace of the Louvre in Paris in 1546, hewed closely to the classicism of Italian Renaissance masters in constructing a facade that emphasized classical pilasters and pediments.

PAINTING

Northern Renaissance painting is another realm in which we can discern links between thought and art. Certainly the most moving visual embodiments of the ideals of Christian humanism were conceived by the foremost of northern Renaissance artists, the German Albrecht Dürer (1471–1528). Dürer (*DOOR-er*) was the first northerner to master Italian Renaissance techniques of proportion, perspective, and modeling. Dürer also shared with contemporary Italians a fascination with reproducing the manifold works of nature down to the minutest details and a penchant for displaying the human nude in various postures. But whereas Michelangelo portrayed his *David* or *Adam* entirely without covering, Dürer's nudes are seldom lacking their fig leaves, in deference to more restrained northern traditions. Moreover, Dürer consistently refrained from abandoning himself to the pure classicism and sumptuousness of much Italian Renaissance art because he was inspired primarily by the more traditionally Christian ideals of Erasmus. Thus Dürer's serenely radiant engraving of Saint Jerome expresses the sense of accomplishment that Erasmus or any other contemporary Christian humanist may have had while working quietly in his study; and his *Four Apostles* intones a solemn hymn to the dignity and penetrating insight of Dürer's favorite New Testament authors, Saints Paul, John, Peter, and Mark.

Dürer would have loved nothing more than to have immortalized Erasmus in a major painted portrait, but circumstances prevented him from doing this because the paths of the two men crossed only once, and after Dürer started sketching his hero on that occasion his work was interrupted by Erasmus's press of business.

Saint Jerome in His Study, by Dürer. Saint Jerome, a hero to both Dürer and Erasmus, represents inspired Christian scholarship. Note how the scene exudes contentment, even down to the sleeping lion, which seems rather like an overgrown tabby cat.

Instead, the accomplishment of capturing Erasmus's pensive spirit in oils was left to another great northern Renaissance artist, the German Hans Holbein the Younger (1497–1543; see p. 463). As good fortune would have it, during a stay in England, Holbein also painted an extraordinarily acute portrait of Erasmus's friend and kindred spirit Sir Thomas More, which enables us to see clearly why a contemporary called More "a man of . . . sad gravity; a man for all seasons" (see p. 464). These two portraits in and of themselves point out a major difference between medieval and Renaissance culture. Whereas the Middle Ages produced no convincing naturalistic likenesses of any leading intellectual figures, Renaissance culture's greater commitment to capturing the essence of human individuality created the environment in which Holbein was able to make Erasmus and More come to life.

MUSIC

Music in western Europe in the fifteenth and sixteenth centuries reached such a high point of development that it constitutes, together with painting and sculpture, one of the most brilliant aspects of Renaissance endeavor. The musical theory of the Renaissance was driven largely by the humanist-inspired but largely fruitless effort to recover and imitate classical musical forms and modes. Musical practice, however, showed much more continuity with medieval musical traditions of number and proportion. At the same time, however, a new expressiveness emerges in Renaissance music, along with a new emphasis on coloration and emotional quality. New musical instruments were also developed, including the lute, the viol, the violin, and a variety of woodwind and keyboard instruments including the harpsichord. New musical forms also emerged: madrigals, motets, and, at the end of the sixteenth century, a new Italian form, the opera. As earlier, musical leadership came from men trained in the service of the church. But the distinction between sacred and profane music was becoming less sharp, and most composers did not restrict their activities to a single field. Music was no longer regarded merely as a diversion or an adjunct to worship but came into its own as a serious independent art.

The madrigals, ballads, and other songs composed by the ars nova musicians testify to a rich fourteenth-century tradition of secular music, but the greatest achievement of the period was a highly complicated yet delicate contrapuntal style adapted for ecclesiastical motets.

During the fourteenth century, before or in the early Renaissance period, a musical movement called *ars nova* ("new art") flourished in Italy and France. Its outstanding composers were Francesco Landini (c. 1325–1397) and Guillaume de Machaut (c. 1300–1377). The madrigals, ballads, and other songs composed by the ars nova musicians testify to a rich fourteenth-century tradition of secular music, but the greatest achievement of the period was a highly complicated yet delicate contrapuntal style adapted for ecclesiastical motets. Machaut, moreover, was the first known composer to provide a polyphonic version of the major sections of the Mass.

The fifteenth century ushered in a synthesis of French, Flemish, and Italian elements in the ducal court of Burgundy. This music was melodious and gentle, but in the second half of the century it hardened a little as northern Flemish elements gained in importance. As the sixteenth century opened, Franco-Flemish composers appeared in every important court and cathedral all over Europe, gradually establishing regional-national schools, usually in attractive combinations of Flemish with German, Spanish, and Italian musical cultures. The various genres thus created show a close affinity with Renaissance art and poetry. In the second half of the sixteenth century the leaders of the nationalized Franco-Flemish style were the Fleming Roland de Lassus (1532–1594), the most versatile composer of the age, and the Italian Giovanni Pierluigi da Palestrina (c. 1525–1594), who specialized in highly intricate polyphonic choral music written for Catholic church services under the patronage of the popes in Rome. Music also flourished in sixteenth-century England, where the Tudor monarchs Henry VIII and Elizabeth I were active patrons of the arts. Not only did the Italian madrigal, imported toward the end of the sixteenth century, take on remarkable new life in England, but songs and instrumental music of an original cast anticipated future developments on the Continent. In William Byrd (1543–1623), English music produced a master fully the equal of the great Flemish and Italian composers of the Renaissance period. The general level of musical proficiency seems to have been higher in Queen Elizabeth's day than in ours: the singing of part-songs was a popular pastime in homes

and at informal social gatherings, and the ability to read a part at sight was expected of the educated elite.

Although accomplishments in counterpoint were already very advanced in the Renaissance period, our modern harmonic system was still in its infancy, and thus there remained much room for experimentation. At the same time we should realize that the music of the Renaissance constitutes not merely a stage in evolution but a magnificent achievement in itself, with masters who rank among the greatest of all time. The composers Lassus, Palestrina, and Byrd are as truly representative of the artistic triumph of the Renaissance as are the painters Leonardo, Raphael, and Michelangelo. Their heritage, long neglected, has within recent years begun to be appreciated, and is now gaining in popularity as interested groups of musicians devote themselves to its revival.

CONCLUSION

The contrasts between the Italian and the northern Renaissance are real, but they must not be exaggerated. The intellectuals of Renaissance Italy were formed in a more secular, more urban educational environment than were the northerners, but they were no less fervent in their Christianity. Petrarch's criticism of scholasticism was not that it was too Christian but, rather, that it was not Christian enough. Petrarch opposed the emotional aridity and stylistic inelegance of scholasticism because he believed they threatened the salvation of Christians. Much the same point might be made about Lorenzo Valla. His critique of the tempo-

ral claims of the papacy sprang not only from the conclusions of his textual scholarship but also from a firm Christian piety. The Platonic Academy might honor Plato as if he were a saint of the church, but these men approached Plato's works in the same spirit with which thirteenth-century scholastic theologians had approached the works of Aristotle. As committed Christians, they were convinced that the conclusions reached by the greatest philosophical minds of classical antiquity must be compatible with Christian truth. It was the task of Christian intellectuals to reveal this compatibility and, by so doing, to strengthen the one true faith.

In considering the contrasts between "civic" and "Christian" humanism, we must also keep in mind the enormous diversity of Renaissance thought. Machiavelli is no more typical an Italian Renaissance thinker than is Ficino, Alberti, or Bruno. In comparing Italian thinkers with northern thinkers, we must therefore be careful to compare like with like. Too often, scholars overdraw the contrasts between Renaissance thought in Italy and northern Europe by choosing Machiavelli, for example, to represent all of Italian humanism and Erasmus to represent northern humanism. Two more different figures can hardly be imagined; but their differences have much more to do with their contrasting presuppositions about human nature than with their allegiances to Italian or northern humanism. A very different picture emerges if we compare, for example, John Colet as a representative of northern humanism with Marsilio Ficino as a representative of Italian humanism or if we compare Petrarch with Sir Thomas More.

Nor should we overdraw the contrasts between the Renaissance and the High Middle Ages. Both Italian and northern humanists shared an optimistic view of human nature as improvable despite the consequences of Adam and Eve's disobedience; but none was more optimistic on this score than was Saint Thomas Aquinas. Both groups emphasized the importance of personal introspection and self-examination; but none took this injunction more seriously than did the Cistercian thinkers of the twelfth century. And finally, both groups shared a belief that the exhortations of intellectuals would lift everyone's morals and conduct them to new heights of virtue. In this regard, High Renaissance intellectual life has a kind of naive optimism that contrasts sharply with the darker, more psychologically complex world of the Middle Ages and with the Reformation era that was about to begin.

KEY TERMS

humanism	*The Prince*	Raphael	Utopia
Medici	Baldassare Castiglione	Michelangelo	Rabelais
Petrarch	Leonardo da Vinci	Erasmus	

SELECTED READINGS

Alberti, Leon Battista. *The Family in Renaissance Florence (Della Famiglia).* Trans. Renée Neu Watkins. Columbia, S.C., 1969.

Baxandall, Michael. *Painting and Experience in Fifteenth Century Italy.* Oxford, 1972. A classic study of the perceptual world of the Renaissance.

Brucker, Gene. *Florence, the Golden Age, 1138–1737.* Berkeley and Los Angeles, 1998. The standard account by a master historian.

Bruni, Leonardo. *The Humanism of Leonardo Bruni: Selected Texts.* Trans. Gordon Griffiths, James Hankins, and David Thompson. Binghamton, N.Y., 1987. Excellent translations, with introductions, to the Latin works of a key Renaissance humanist.

Burke, Peter. *The Renaissance.* New York, 1997. A brief introduction by an influential modern historian.

Burkhardt, Jacob. *The Civilization of the Renaissance in Italy.* Many editions. The nineteenth-century work that first crystallized an image of the Italian Renaissance with which scholars have been wrestling ever since.

Cassirer, Ernst, et al., eds. *The Renaissance Philosophy of Man.* Chicago, 1948. Important original works by Petrarch, Ficino, and Pico della Mirandola, among others.

Castiglione, Baldassare. *The Book of the Courtier.* Many editions. The translations by C. S. Singleton (New York, 1959) and by George Bull (New York, 1967) are both excellent.

Cellini, Benvenuto. *Autobiography.* Trans. George Bull. Baltimore, 1956. This Florentine goldsmith (1500–1571) is the source for many of the most famous stories about the artists of the Florentine Renaissance.

Cochrane, Eric, and Julius Kirshner, eds. *The Renaissance.* Chicago, 1986. An outstanding collection, from the University of Chicago Readings in Western Civilization series.

Erasmus, Desiderius. *The Praise of Folly.* Trans. J. Wilson. Ann Arbor, Mich., 1958.

Fox, Alistair. *Thomas More: History and Providence.* Oxford, 1982. A balanced account of a man too easily idealized.

Grafton, Anthony, and Lisa Jardine. *From Humanism to the Humanities: Education and the Liberal Arts in Fifteenth- and Sixteenth-Century Europe.* London, 1986. An influential account that presents Renaissance humanism as the elitist cultural program of a self-interested group of pedagogues.

Grendler, Paul, ed. *Encyclopedia of the Renaissance.* New York, 1999. A valuable reference work.

Hale, John R. *The Civilization of Europe in the Renaissance.* New York, 1993. A synthetic volume summarizing the life's work of a major Renaissance historian.

Hankins, James. *Plato in the Italian Renaissance.* Leiden and New York, 1990. A definitive study of the reception and influence of Plato on Renaissance intellectuals.

Hankins, James, ed. *Renaissance Civic Humanism: Reappraisals and Reflections.* Cambridge and New York, 2000. An excellent collection of scholarly essays reassessing republicanism in the Renaissance.

Jardine, Lisa. *Worldly Goods.* London, 1996. A revisionist account that emphasizes the acquisitive materialism of Italian Renaissance society and culture.

Kanter, Laurence, Hilliard T. Goldfarb, and James Hankins. *Botticelli's Witness: Changing Style in a Changing Florence.* Boston, 1997. This catalog for an exhibit of Botticelli's works, at the Gardner Museum in Boston, offers an excellent introduction to the painter and his world.

King, Margaret L. *Women of the Renaissance.* Chicago, 1991. Deals with women in all walks of life and in a variety of roles.

Kristeller, Paul O. *Eight Philosophers of the Italian Renaissance.* Stanford, 1964. An admirably clear and accurate account that fully appreciates the connections between medieval and Renaissance thought.

Kristeller, Paul O. *Renaissance Thought: The Classic, Scholastic, and Humanistic Strains.* New York, 1961. Very helpful in defining the main trends of Renaissance thought.

Lane, Frederic C. *Venice: A Maritime Republic.* Baltimore, 1973. An authoritative account.

Machiavelli, Niccolò. *The Discourses* and *The Prince.* Many editions. These two books must be read together if one is to understand Machiavelli's political ideas properly.

Martines, Lauro. *Power and Imagination: City-States in Renaissance Italy.* New York, 1979. Insightful account of the connections among politics, society, culture, and art.

More, Thomas. *Utopia.* Many editions.

Murray, Linda. *High Renaissance and Mannerism.* London, 1985. The place to start for fifteenth- and sixteenth-century Italian art.

Olson, Roberta, *Italian Renaissance Sculpture,* New York, 1992. The most accessible introduction to the subject.

Perkins, Leeman L. *Music in the Age of the Renaissance.* New York, 1999. A massive new study that nonetheless needs to be read in conjunction with Reese.

Rabelais, François. *Gargantua and Pantagruel.* Trans. J. M. Cohen. Baltimore, Md., 1955. A robust modern translation.

Reese, Gustave. *Music in the Renaissance,* rev. ed. New York, 1959. A great book; still authoritative, despite the more recent work by Perkins, which supplements but does not replace it.

Rice, Eugene F., Jr., and Anthony Grafton. *The Foundations of Early Modern Europe, 1460–1559,* 2d ed. New York, 1994. The best textbook account of its period.

Rowland, Ingrid D. *The Culture of the High Renaissance: Ancients and Moderns in Sixteenth-Century Rome.* Cambridge and New York, 2000. Beautifully written examination of the social, intellectual, and economic foundations of the Renaissance in Rome.

RULERS OF PRINCIPAL STATES

THE CAROLINGIAN DYNASTY

Pepin of Heristal, Mayor of the Palace, 687–714
Charles Martel, Mayor of the Palace, 715–741
Pepin III, Mayor of the Palace, 741–751; King, 751–768
Charlemagne, King, 768–814; Emperor, 800–814
Louis the Pious, Emperor, 814–840

WEST FRANCIA
Charles the Bald, King, 840–877; Emperor, 875–877
Louis II, King, 877–879
Louis III, King, 879–882
Carloman, King, 879–884

MIDDLE KINGDOMS
Lothair, Emperor, 840–855
Louis (Italy), Emperor, 855–875
Charles (Provence), King, 855–863
Lothair II (Lorraine), King, 855–869

EAST FRANCIA
Ludwig, King, 840–876
Carloman, King, 876–880
Ludwig, King, 876–882
Charles the Fat, Emperor, 876–887

HOLY ROMAN EMPERORS

SAXON DYNASTY
Otto I, 962–973
Otto II, 973–983
Otto III, 983–1002
Henry II, 1002–1024

FRANCONIAN DYNASTY
Conrad II, 1024–1039
Henry III, 1039–1056
Henry IV, 1056–1106
Henry V, 1106–1125
Lothair II (Saxony), 1125–1137

HOHENSTAUFEN DYNASTY
Conrad III, 1138–1152
Frederick I (Barbarossa), 1152–1190
Henry VI, 1190–1197
Philip of Swabia, 1198–1208 } Rivals
Otto IV (Welf), 1198–1215
Frederick II, 1220–1250
Conrad IV, 1250–1254

INTERREGNUM, 1254–1273

EMPERORS FROM VARIOUS DYNASTIES
Rudolf I (Habsburg), 1273–1291
Adolf (Nassau), 1292–1298
Albert I (Habsburg), 1298–1308
Henry VII (Luxemburg), 1308–1313
Ludwig IV (Wittelsbach), 1314–1347
Charles IV (Luxemburg), 1347–1378
Wenceslas (Luxemburg), 1378–1400
Rupert (Wittelsbach), 1400–1410
Sigismund (Luxemburg), 1410–1437

HABSBURG DYNASTY
Albert II, 1438–1439
Frederick III, 1440–1493
Maximilian I, 1493–1519
Charles V, 1519–1556
Ferdinand I, 1556–1564
Maximilian II, 1564–1576
Rudolf II, 1576–1612

Matthias, 1612–1619
Ferdinand II, 1619–1637
Ferdinand III, 1637–1657
Leopold I, 1658–1705
Joseph I, 1705–1711
Charles VI, 1711–1740

Charles VII (not a Habsburg), 1742–1745
Francis I, 1745–1765
Joseph II, 1765–1790
Leopold II, 1790–1792
Francis II, 1792–1806

RULERS OF FRANCE FROM HUGH CAPET

CAPETIAN DYNASTY
Hugh Capet, 987–996
Robert II, 996–1031
Henry I, 1031–1060
Philip I, 1060–1108
Louis VI, 1108–1137
Louis VII, 1137–1180
Philip II (Augustus), 1180–1223
Louis VIII, 1223–1226
Louis IX (St. Louis), 1226–1270
Philip III, 1270–1285
Philip IV, 1285–1314
Louis X, 1314–1316
Philip V, 1316–1322
Charles IV, 1322–1328

VALOIS DYNASTY
Philip VI, 1328–1350
John, 1350–1364
Charles V, 1364–1380
Charles VI, 1380–1422
Charles VII, 1422–1461
Louis XI, 1461–1483
Charles VIII, 1483–1498
Louis XII, 1498–1515
Francis I, 1515–1547

Henry II, 1547–1559
Francis II, 1559–1560
Charles IX, 1560–1574
Henry III, 1574–1589

BOURBON DYNASTY
Henry IV, 1589–1610
Louis XIII, 1610–1643
Louis XIV, 1643–1715
Louis XV, 1715–1774
Louis XVI, 1774–1792

AFTER 1792
First Republic, 1792–1799
Napoleon Bonaparte, First Consul, 1799–1804
Napoleon I, Emperor, 1804–1814
Louis XVIII (Bourbon dynasty), 1814–1824
Charles X (Bourbon dynasty), 1824–1830
Louis Philippe, 1830–1848
Second Republic, 1848–1852
Napoleon III, Emperor, 1852–1870
Third Republic, 1870–1940
Péain regime, 1940–1944
Provisional government, 1944–1946
Fourth Republic, 1946–1958
Fifth Republic, 1958–

RULERS OF ENGLAND

ANGLO-SAXON DYNASTY
Alfred the Great, 871–899
Edward the Elder, 899–924
Ethelstan, 924–939
Edmund I, 939–946
Edred, 946–955
Edwy, 955–959
Edgar, 959–975
Edward the Martyr, 975–978
Ethelred the Unready, 978–1016

Canute, 1016–1035 (Danish Nationality)
Harold I, 1035–1040
Hardicanute, 1040–1042
Edward the Confessor, 1042–1066
Harold II, 1066

HOUSE OF NORMANDY
William I (the Conqueror), 1066–1087
William II, 1087–1100

Henry I, 1100–1135
Stephen, 1135–1154

HOUSE OF PLANTAGENET
Henry II, 1154–1189
Richard I, 1189–1199
John, 1199–1216
Henry III, 1216–1272
Edward I, 1272–1307
Edward II, 1307–1327
Edward III, 1327–1377
Richard II, 1377–1399

HOUSE OF LANCASTER
Henry IV, 1399–1413
HenryV, 1413–1422
Henry VI, 1422–1461

HOUSE OF YORK
Edward IV, 1461–1483
Edward V, 1483
Richard III, 1483–1485

HOUSE OF TUDOR
Henry VII, 1485–1509
Henry VIII, 1509–1547
Edward VI, 1547–1553
Mary, 1553–1558
Elizabeth I, 1558–1603

HOUSE OF STUART
James I, 1603–1625
Charles I, 1625–1649

COMMONWEALTH AND PROTECTORATE, 1649–1659

HOUSE OF STUART RESTORED
Charles II, 1660–1685
James II, 1685–1688
William III and Mary II, 1689–1694
William III alone, 1694–1702
Anne, 1702–1714

HOUSE OF HANOVER
George I, 1714–1727
George II, 1727–1760
George III, 1760–1820
George IV, 1820–1830
William IV, 1830–1837
Victoria, 1837–1901

HOUSE OF SAXE-COBURG-GOTHA
Edward VII, 1901–1910
George V, 1910–1917

HOUSE OF WINDSOR
George V, 1917–1936
Edward VIII, 1936
George VI, 1936–1952
Elizabeth II, 1952–

RULERS OF AUSTRIA AND AUSTRIA-HUNGARY

*Maximilian I (Archduke), 1493–1519
*Charles V, 1519–1556
*Ferdinand I, 1556–1564
*Maximilian II, 1564–1576
*Rudolf II, 1576–1612
*Matthias, 1612–1619
*Ferdinand II, 1619–1637
*Ferdinand III, 1637–1657
*Leopold I, 1658–1705
*Joseph I, 1705–1711
*Charles VI, 1711–1740
Maria Theresa, 1740–1780

*also bore title of Holy Roman Emperor

*Joseph II, 1780–1790
*Leopold II, 1790–1792
*Francis II, 1792–1835 (Emperor of Austria as Francis I after 1804)
Ferdinand I, 1835–1848
Francis Joseph, 1848–1916 (after 1867 Emperor of Austria and King of Hungary)
Charles I, 1916–1918 (Emperor of Austria and King of Hungary)
Republic of Austria, 1918–1938 (dictatorship after 1934)
Republic restored, under Allied occupation, 1945–1956
Free Republic, 1956–

RULERS OF PRUSSIA AND GERMANY

*Frederick I, 1701–1713
*Frederick William I, 1713–1740
*Frederick II (the Great), 1740–1786
*Frederick William II, 1786–1797
*Frederick William III,1797–1840
*Frederick William IV, 1840–1861
*William I, 1861–1888 (German Emperor after 1871)
Frederick III, 1888

*Kings of Prussia

*William II, 1888–1918
Weimar Republic, 1918–1933
Third Reich (Nazi Dictatorship), 1933–1945
Allied occupation, 1945–1952
Division into Federal Republic of Germany in west and
    German Democratic Republic in east, 1949–1991
Federal Republic of Germany (united), 1991–

RULERS OF RUSSIA

Ivan III, 1462–1505
Vasily III, 1505–1533
Ivan IV, 1533–1584
Theodore I, 1534–1598
Boris Godunov, 1598–1605
Theodore II,1605
Vasily IV, 1606–1610
Michael, 1613–1645
Alexius, 1645–1676
Theodore III, 1676–1682
Ivan V and Peter I, 1682–1689
Peter I (the Great), 1689–1725
Catherine I, 1725–1727
Peter II, 1727–1730

Anna, 1730–1740
Ivan VI, 1740–1741
Ellzabeth, 1741–1762
Peter III, 1762
Catherine II (the Great), 1762–1796
Paul, 1796–1801
Alexander I,1801–1825
Nicholas I, 1825–1855
Alexander II,1855–1881
Alexander III, 1881–1894
Nicholas II, 1894–1917
Soviet Republic, 1917–1991
Russian Federation, 1991–

RULERS OF SPAIN

Ferdinand { and Isabella, 1479–1504
{ and Philip I, 1504–1506
{ and Charles I, 1506–1516
Charles I (Holy Roman Emperor Charles V), 1516–1556
Philip II, 1556–1598
Philip III, 1598–1621
Philip IV, 1621–1665
Charles II, 1665–1700
Philip V, 1700–1746
Ferdinand VI, 1746–1759
Charles III, 1759–1788
Charles IV, 1788–1808

Ferdinand VII, 1808
Joseph Bonaparte, 1808–1813
Ferdinand VII (restored), 1814–1833
Isabella II, 1833–1868
Republic, 1868–1870
Amadeo, 1870–1873
Republic, 1873–1874
Alfonso XII, 1874–1885
Alfonso XIII, 1886–1931
Republic, 1931–1939
Fascist Dictatorship, 1939–1975
Juan Carlos I, 1975–

RULERS OF ITALY

Victor Emmanuel II, 1861–1878
Humbert I, 1878–1900
Victor Emmanuel III, 1900–1946

Fascist Dictatorship, 1922-1943 (maintained in northern
  Italy until 1945)
Humbert II, May 9–June 13, 1946
Republic, 1946–

PROMINENT POPES

Silvester I, 314–335
Leo I, 440–461
Gelasius I, 492–496
Gregory I, 590–604
Nicholas I, 858–867
Silvester II, 999–1003
Leo IX, 1049–1054
Nicholas II, 1058–1061
Gregory VII, 1073–1085
Urban II, 1088–1099
Paschal II, 1099–1118
Alexander III, 1159–1181
Innocent III, 1198–1216
Gregory IX, 1227–1241
Innocent IV, 1243–1254
Boniface VIII, 1294–1303
John XXII, 1316–1334
Nicholas V, 1447–1455
Pius II, 1458–1464

Alexander VI, 1492–1503
Julius II, 1503–1513
Leo X, 1513–1521
Paul III, 1534–1549
Paul IV, 1555–1559
Sixtus V, 1585–1590
Urban VIII, 1623–1644
Gregory XVI, 1831–1846
Pius IX, 1846–1878
Leo XIII, 1878–1903
Pius X, 1903–1914
Benedict XV, 1914–1922
Pius XI, 1922–1939
Pius XII, 1939–1958
John XXIII, 1958–1963
Paul VI, 1963–1978
John Paul I, 1978
John Paul II, 1978–2005
Benedict XVI 2005–

GLOSSARY

Peter Abelard (1079–1142)   Famed French theologian, logician, and university lecturer.

abolition of feudalism   The end of the feudal system in France, which was brought about by the popular revolts of 1789. Louis XVI and other nobles established the National Assembly, which abolished all forms of privilege, such as the church tax on harvests, the labor requirement of peasants (known as the corvee), the nobility's hunting privileges, and a variety of tax exemptions and monopolies.

absolutism   Form of government in which one body, usually the monarch, controls the right to make war, tax, judge, and coin money. The term was often used to refer to the state monarchies in seventeenth- and eighteenth-century Europe.

abstract expressionism   The mid-twentieth-century school of art based in New York that included Jackson Pollock, Willem de Kooning, and Franz Kline. It emphasized form, color, gesture, and feeling instead of figurative subjects.

acid rain   Precipitation laced with heavy doses of sulfur, mainly from coal-fired plants.

African National Congress (ANC)   Multiracial organization founded in 1912 whose goal was to end racial discrimination in South Africa.

Afrikaners   Descendants of the original Dutch settlers of South Africa; formerly referred to as Boers.

AIDS   Acquired immune deficiency syndrome. AIDS first appeared in the 1970s and has developed into a global health catastrophe; it is spreading most quickly in developing nations in Africa and Asia.

Akhenaten   The fourteenth-century B.C.E. pharaoh who developed a sun-oriented religion and ultimately damaged Egypt's position in the ancient world.

Alexander (356–323 B.C.E.)   The Macedonian general who conquered northwest Asia Minor, and Persia, and built an empire that stretched as far east as the Indus River.

Algerian War   The war in the 1950s and 1960s between France and Algerians seeking independence. Led by the National Liberation Front (FLN), guerrillas fought the French army in the mountains and desert of Algeria. The FLN also initiated a campaign of bombing and terrorism in Algerian cities that led French soldiers to torture Algerians and attract world attention and international scandal.

Allied Powers   The World War I coalition of Great Britain, Ireland, Belgium, France, Italy, Russia, Portugal, Greece, Serbia, Montenegro, Albania, and Romania.

al Qaeda   The radical Islamic organization founded in the late 1980s by former *mujahedin* who had fought against the Soviet Union in Afghanistan. Al Qaeda carried out the 9/11 terrorist attacks and is responsible as well for attacks in Africa, Southeast Asia, Europe, and the Middle East.

Americanization   The fear of many Europeans from the 1920s and on that U.S. cultural products, such as film, television, and music exerted too much influence. Many of the criticisms centered on America's emphasis on mass production and organization. The fears about Americanization were not limited to culture. They extended to corporations, business techniques, global trade, and marketing.

Amnesty International   Nongovernmental organization formed in 1961 to defend "prisoners of conscience"—those detained for their beliefs, color, sex, ethnic origin, language, or religion.

Anabaptists   Swiss Protestant movement that began in 1521 and insisted that only adults could be baptized Christians. The movement's first generation, who had been baptized as infants according to Catholic practice, was "re-baptized," hence the name.

anarchism   The social and political movement that began in the mid-nineteenth century and advocated the destruction of the state through violence and terrorism.

Apartheid   The racial segregation policy of the Afrikaner-dominated South African government. Legislated in 1948 by the Afrikaner National Party, it existed in South Africa for many years.

appeasement   The policy pursued by Western governments in the face of German, Italian, and Japanese aggression leading up to World War II. The policy, which attempted to accommodate and negotiate peace with the aggressive nations, was based on the belief that another global war like World War I was unimaginable, a belief that Germany and its allies had been mistreated by the terms of the Treaty of Versailles, and a fear that fascist Germany and its allies protected the West from the spread of Soviet Communism.

aqueducts   Engineering system that brought water from the mountains down to Roman cities.

Saint Thomas Aquinas (1225–1274)   Italian Dominican monk and theologian whose intellectual style encouraged the study of ancient philosophers and science as complementary to theology.

Arians   The fourth-century followers of a priest named Arius, who rejected the idea that Christ could be equal with God.

Aristotelian   The system of thought based on the ideas of the Greek philosopher Aristotle. Aristotelian ideas distinguished between the works of humans and those of nature and posited that as God's creation, nature belonged to a different, higher order.

Asiatic Society   A cultural organization founded in 1784 by British Orientalists who lauded native culture but believed in colonial rule.

Assyrians   A Semitic-speaking people that emerged around 2400 B.C.E. in northern Mesopotamia. Their highly militarized empire dominated Near-Eastern politics for close to two thousand years.

astrolabe   An ancient navigational instrument, thought to have been invented in 150 B.C.E., that was used to find latitude while at sea.

Atlantic system   A system of trade and expansion that linked Europe, Africa, and the Americas. It emerged in the sixteenth century in the wake of European voyages across the Atlantic Ocean.

Saint Augustine (c. 354–397)   One of the most influential Christian theologians of all time, Saint Augustine described his conversion in his autobiographical *Confessions* and formulated new aspects of Christian theology in *On the City of God*.

Augustus (63 B.C.E.–14 C.E.)   The grandnephew and adopted son of Julius Caesar and first emperor of the Roman empire.

Auschwitz-Birkenau   The Nazi concentration camp in Poland that was designed to systematically murder Jews and gypsies. Between 1942 and 1944 over one million people were killed in Auschwitz-Birkenau.

Austro-Hungarian empire   The dual monarchy established by the Habsburg family in 1867; it collapsed at the end of World War I.

authoritarianism   A centralized and dictatorial form of government, proclaimed by its adherents to be superior to parliamentary democracy and especially effective at mobilizing the masses. Authoritarianism was prominent in the 1930s.

Avignon   City on the southeastern border of France. Between 305 and 378 it was the seat of the papacy.

Aztecs   Native American people of central Mexico; their empire was conquered by the Spanish in the sixteenth century.

baby boom (1950s)   The post–World War II upswing in U.S. birth rates; it reversed a century of decline.

Francis Bacon (1561–1626)   British philosopher and scientist who pioneered the scientific method and inductive reasoning. In other words, he argued that thinkers should amass observations and then make general observations or theories.

Baghdad Pact (1955)   The Middle Eastern military alliance among countries friendly with America who were also willing to align themselves with the Western countries against the Soviet Union.

balance of power   Initated by the League of Augsburg in 1689, a new diplomatic goal emerged in western and central Europe to preserve a balance of power to prevent any single country from becoming so powerful as to threaten the position of the other major powers within the European state system.

Balfour Declaration   A letter dated November 2, 1917, by Lord Arthur J. Balfour, British Foreign Secretary, that promised a homeland for the Jews in Palestine.

Baroque   An ornate style of art and music associated with the Counter Reformation (from the French word for "irregularly shaped pearl").

Battle of the Marne   A major World War I battle in September 1914, which stifled German advancement in France and led to protracted trench warfare on the western front.

Bay of Pigs (1961)   The unsuccessful invasion of Cuba by Cuban exiles, supported by the U.S. government. The rebels intended to incite an insurrection in Cuba and overthrow the Communist regime of Fidel Castro.

Beer Hall Putsch (1923)   The Nazi invasion of a meeting of Bavarian leaders and supporters in a Munich beer hall; Adolf Hitler was imprisoned for a year after the incident.

Saint Benedict of Nursia (c. 480–c. 547)   Considered the father of western monasticism, Saint Benedict created the Benedictine rule that became the guide for nearly all western monks. Monks were required to follow the rules laid down by Saint Benedict: poverty, sexual chastity, obedience, labor, and religious devotion.

Berlin Airlift (1948)   The supply of vital necessities to West Berlin by air transport primarily under U.S. auspices. It was initiated in response to a blockade of the city that had been instituted by the Soviet Union to force the Allies to abandon West Berlin.

Berlin blockade   From June 1948 until May 1949, the Soviets cut all road, train, and river access from the Western zone of Germany to West Berlin. Unwilling to cede control of their portion of the capital, France, Britain, and the United States airlifted supplies over Soviet territory to the Western zone of Berlin.

Berlin Wall   The wall built in 1961 by East German Communists to prevent citizens of East Germany from fleeing to West Germany; it was torn down in 1989.

Bill of Rights   The first ten amendments to the U.S. Constitution; it was ratified in 1791.

Otto von Bismarck (1815–1890)   The prime minister of Prussia and later the first chancellor of Germany, Bismarck helped consolidate the German people's economic and military power.

Black Death   The epidemic of bubonic plague that ravaged Europe, East Asia, and North Africa in the fourteenth century, killing one-third of the European population.

Black Jacobins   A nickname for the rebels in Saint Domingue, including Toussaint L'Ouverture, a former slave who in 1791 led the slaves of this French colony in the largest and most successful slave insurrection.

Black Panthers   A radical African American group that came together in the 1960s; the Black Panthers advocated black separatism and pan-Africanism.

Blackshirts   The troops of Mussolini's fascist regime; the squads received money from Italian landowners to attack socialist leaders.

Black Tuesday (October 24, 1929)   The day on which the U.S. stock market crashed, plunging the U.S. and international trading systems into crisis and leading the world into the "Great Depression."

Blitzkreig   The German "lightning war" strategy used during World War II; the Germans invaded Poland, France, Russia, and other countries with fast-moving well-coordinated attacks using aircraft, tanks and other armored vehicles, followed by infantry.

Bloody Sunday   On Sunday, January 22, 1905, the Russian tsar's guards killed 130 demonstrators who were protesting the tsar's mistreatment of workers and the middle class.

Giovanni Boccaccio (1313–1375)   Italian prose writer famed for his *Decameron*, one hundred short stories about the human condition, mostly from a comic or cynical point of view.

Boer War   Conflict between British and ethnically European Afrikaners in South Africa, 1898–1902, with terrible casualties on both sides.

Simon de Bolivar (1783–1830)   Venezuelan-born general called "The Liberator" for his assistance in helping Bolivia, Panama, Colombia, Ecuador, Peru, and Venezuela win independence from Spain.

Bolsheviks   Former members of the Russian Social Democratic Party who advocated the destruction of capitalist political and economic institutions and started the Russian Revolution. In 1918 the Bolsheviks changed their name to the Russian Communist Party.

Napoleon Bonaparte (1769–1821)   Corsican-born French general who seized power and ruled as dictator 1799–1814. After successful conquest of much of Europe, he was defeated by Russian and Prussian forces and died in exile.

bourgeoisie   The French term for the middle class, which emerged in Europe during the Middle Ages. The Bourgeoisie sought to be recognized not by birth or title, but by capital and property.

Boxer Rebellion (1899–1900)   Chinese peasant movement that opposed foreign influence, especially that of Christian missionaries; it was finally put down after the Boxers were defeated by a foreign army comprised mostly of Japanese, Russian, British, French, and American soldiers.

British Commonwealth of Nations   Formed in 1926, the Commonwealth conferred "dominion status" on Britain's white settler colonies in Canada, Australia, and New Zealand.

Brownshirts   Troops of young German men who dedicated themselves to the Nazi cause in the early 1930s by holding street marches, mass rallies, and confrontations. They engaged in beatings of Jews and anyone who opposed the Nazis.

bubonic plague   An acute infectious disease caused by a bacterium that is transmitted to humans by fleas from infected rats. It ravaged Europe and parts of Asia in the fourteenth century. Sometimes referred to as the "black death."

Julius Caesar (100–44 B.C.E.)   The Roman general who conquered the Gauls, invaded Britain, and expanded Rome's territory in Asia Minor. He became the dictator of Rome in 46 B.C.E. and was murdered by Brutus and Cassius, which led to the rise of Augustus and the end of the Roman republic.

caliphs   Rulers of the Islamic community who claimed descent from Muhammad.

John Calvin (1509–1564)   French-born Protestant theologian who stressed the predestination of all human beings according to God's will.

Canary Islands   Islands off the western coast of Africa conquered by Portugal and Spain in the mid-1400s. Used to supply expeditions around the African coast and across the Atlantic.

Canterbury Tales   Middle English verse stories by Geoffrey Chaucer (c.1340–1400) that reflect different classes and experiences in late medieval England.

caravans   Companies of men who transported and traded goods along overland routes in North Africa and central Asia; large caravans consisted of 600 to 1,000 camels and as many as 400 men.

caravels   Sailing vessels suited for nosing in and out of estuaries and navigating in waters with unpredictable currents and winds.

Carthage   A great maritime empire that rivaled Rome; at its height, it stretched across the northern coast of Africa from modern-day Tunisia to the Strait of Gibraltar. Carthage fought against Rome in the Punic Wars that began in 264 B.C.E. The wars ended with the destruction of Carthage in 146 B.C.E.

Cassiodorus (490–583)   Author of the *Institutes*, which instructed medieval readers on the essential works of literature a monk should know before moving on to more intensive study of theology and the Bible.

caste system   A hierarchical system of organizing people and distributing labor, often based on heredity or regional origin.

Baldassare Castiglione (1478–1529)   Author of *The Book of the Courtier*, a popular treatise on upper-class social graces.

Catherine the Great (1729–1796)   German-born empress of Russia who maintained an absolutist feudal system but encouraged Enlightenment philosophy and the arts at court.

Catholicism   Branch of Christianity headed by the pope.

Camillo Benso di Cavour (1810–1861)   Anti-papist Italian leader who led the initial stages of revolution against the Habsburgs.

Central Powers   The World War I alliance between Germany, Austro-Hungary, Bulgaria, and Turkey.

Charlemagne (742–814)   Frankish ruler 767–813 who consolidated much of western Europe by adding Lombardy and Saxony to the Frankish kingdoms. With a strong sense of divine purpose, he forced the Christian conversion of pagan peoples and sponsored arts and learning at court. In 800 he became the first Roman emperor in the west since the 5th century.

Chartist movement (1834–1848)   Mass democratic movement to pass the Peoples' Charter in Britain, granting male suffrage, secret ballot, equal electoral districts, and annual Parliaments, and absolving the requirement of property ownership for members of Parliament.

Chernobyl (1986)   Site of the world's worst nuclear power accident; in Ukraine, formerly part of the Soviet Union.

chivalry   From the word for "horsemanship"; an aristocratic ideology originating with the knights of eleventh-century Europe that encouraged military prowess and social graces.

Christine de Pisan (c. 1364–c. 1431)   Born in Italy and spending her adult life in France, Pisan was the first lay woman to earn her living by her writing. While she wrote treatises on chivalry and warfare, she also wrote popular literature such as *The City of Ladies* and pamphlets debating the misogynistic claims made against women.

Winston Churchill (1874–1965)   The British prime minister who led the country during World War II. He also coined the phrase "Iron Curtain" in a speech at Westminster College in 1946.

Church of England   Founded by Henry VIII in the 1530s after his excommunication from the Catholic Church by Pope Clement VII, it is the established form of Christianity in England.

Cicero (106–43 B.C.E.)   The most famous Stoic philosopher and orator of Rome.

Civil Constitution of the Clergy   Issued by the French National Assembly in 1789, the Civil Constitution of the Clergy provided that all bishops and priests should be subject to the authority of the state. Their salaries were to be paid out of the public treasury, and they were required to swear allegiance to the new state, making it clear they served France rather than Rome. The Assembly's aim was to make the Catholic Church of France a truly national and civil institution.

Civil Rights Act (1964)   U.S. legislation that banned segregation in public facilities, outlawed racial discrimination in employment, and marked an important step in correcting legal inequality.

Civil War (1861–1865)   Conflict between the northern and southern states of America that cost over 600,000 lives; this struggle led to the abolition of slavery in the United States.

Cluny   A Benedictine monastery, founded in 910, whose reform ideology tried to separate its network of religious houses from control by lay people.

Cold War (1945–1990)   Ideological conflict in which the U.S.S.R. and Eastern Europe opposed the United States and Western Europe.

collectivization   The process under Stalin in the 1920s and 1930s where peasants were forced to give up private farmland and join collective farms, which were supported by the state.

Colons   French settler population in Algeria that ran the colonial government between 1830 and 1962.

Christopher Columbus (1451–1506)   The Italian sailor who persuaded King Ferdinand and Queen Isabella of Spain to fund his expedition across the Atlantic to discover a new trade route to Asia. He miscalculated the size of the Earth and rather than landing in China or Japan, Columbus reached the Bahamas and the island of Hispaniola in 1492.

Committee of Public Safety   Political body during the French Revolution that was controlled by the Jacobins, who enforced party rule by executing thousands during the Reign of Terror, September 1793–July 1794.

The Communist Manifesto **(1818–1883)**   Radical pamphlet by Karl Marx that predicted the downfall of the capitalist system and its replacement by a system that operated in the interests of the working class (proletariat).

Compromise of 1867   Agreement between the Habsburgs and the peoples living in Hungarian parts of the empire that the Habsburg state would be officially known as the Austro-Hungarian Empire.

concession areas   Territories, usually ports, established by the 1842 Treaty of Nanjing, where Chinese emperors allowed European merchants to trade and European people to settle.

Congo Independent State   Large colonial state in Africa created by Leopold II, king of Belgium, during the 1880s, and ruled by him alone. After reports of mass slaughter and enslavement, the Belgian parliament took the land and formed a Belgian colony.

Congress of Vienna (1814–1815) and Restoration   International conference to reorganize Europe after the downfall of Napoleon. European monarchies agreed to respect each other's borders and to cooperate in guarding against future revolutions and war.

conquistador   Spanish term for "conqueror," applied to European leaders of campaigns against indigenous peoples in central and southern America.

conservativism   Reactionary mode of thinking that held that tradition, including hereditary monarchy, would dispel the divisive ideas of the Enlightenment.

Constantinople   Former capital of the Byzantine empire, eventually renamed Istanbul after its conquest by the Ottomans in 1453.

Constitutional Convention (1787)   Meeting to formulate the Constitution of the United States of America.

Nicholas Copernicus (1473–1543)   Polish astronomer who advanced the radical idea that the earth moved around the sun in *De Revolutionibus*.

Corn Laws   Laws that imposed tariffs on grain imported to Great Britain, intended to protect British farming interests. The Corn Laws were abolished in 1846 as part of a British movement in favor of free trade.

Council of Trent   Intermittent meeting of Catholic leaders (1545–1563) that reaffirmed Catholic doctrine against Protestant criticisms while also reforming the church.

Counter Reformation Movement   To counter the spread of the Reformation, the Counter Reformation was initiated by the Catholic Church at the Council of Trent in 1545.

coup d'état   Overthrow of established state by a group of conspirators, usually from the military.

courtly love   Codes of refined romantic behavior between men and women of high station.

courtly romances   Long narrative poems written in vernacular languages based on myths and legends but expressing ideals of medieval aristocratic conduct.

creoles   Persons of European descent who were born in the West Indies or Spanish America.

Crimean War (1854–1856)   War waged by Russia against Great Britain and France. Spurred by Russia's encroachment on Ottoman territories, the conflict revealed Russia's military weakness when Russian forces fell to British and French troops.

Oliver Cromwell (1599–1658)   Puritan leader of the Parliamentary army that defeated the royalist forces in the English Civil War. After the 1649 execution of King Charles I and dispersion of Parliament, Cromwell ruled as self-styled Lord Protector from 1653 until his death.

Crusades (1096 to 1291) Series of wars undertaken to free Jerusalem and the Holy Lands from Muslim control.

Cuban Missile Crisis (1962) Diplomatic standoff between the United States and the Soviet Union that was provoked by the Soviet Union's attempt to base nuclear missiles in Cuba; it brought the world closer to nuclear war than ever before or since.

cult of domesticity Concept associated with Victorian England that idealized women as nurturing wives and mothers.

cult of the Virgin Mary A surge in veneration of the mother of Jesus beginning in the twelfth century that seemed to portend a change in how women were regarded as religious and moral beings.

cuneiform One of the earliest writing systems, beginning around 3500 B.C.E., it was the Mesopotamian form of writing on clay tablets using a stylus.

Cyrus (c.585–529 B.C.E.) The ruler of the Persians from circa 559 B.C.E. until 529 B.C.E.

Charles Darwin (1809–1882) British naturalist who wrote *Origin of the Species* and developed the theory of natural selection to explain the evolution of organisms.

David King of the Hebrews from around 1000 B.C.E. to 973 B.C.E. David united Israel and made Jerusalem his capital.

Leonardo da Vinci (1452–1519) Florentine painter, architect, musician, and inventor whose breadth of interests typifies Renaissance ideals.

D-Day (June 6, 1944) Date of the Allied invasion of Normandy under General Dwight Eisenhower to liberate Western Europe from German occupation.

Decembrists Russian army officers who were influenced by events in France and formed secret societies that espoused liberal governance. They were put down by Nicholas I in December 1825.

Declaration of Independence Historic U.S. document stating the principles of government on which America was founded.

Declaration of the Rights of Man and of the Citizen (1789) French charter of liberties formulated by the National Assembly that marked the end of dynastic and aristocratic rule. The seventeen articles later became the preamble to the new constitution, which the Assembly finished in 1791.

Olympe de Gouges (1745–1793) French political radical and feminist whose *Declaration of the Rights of Women* demanded an equal place for women in the new French republic.

Dhimmis "Peoples of the Book"; i.e., Jews and Christians, who were given a protected but subordinate place in Muslim society.

Charles Dickens (1812–1870) Hugely popular English novelist whose fiction exposed urban crime, poverty, and injustice but maintained Victorian domestic ideals.

Dien Bien Phu (1954) Defining battle in the war between French colonialists and the Viet Minh that secured North Vietnam for Ho Chi Minh and his army and left the south to form its own government to be supported by France and the United States.

Diet of Worms Examination of Luther by a church council in 1521. The council condemned him, and Luther was rescued by Frederick of Saxony.

Directory Temporary military committee that took over the affairs of the state of France in 1795 from the radicals and held control until the coup of Napoleon Bonaparte.

Discourse on Method Philosophical treatise by René Descartes (1596–1650) proposing that the path to knowledge was through logical speculation, beginning with one's own self: "I think, therefore I am."

Divine Comedy Italian verse narrative by Dante Alighieri (1265–1321); its complex themes exemplify the concerns of medieval learning.

DNA (deoxyribonucleic acid) Discovered by James Watson and Francis Crick in 1953, DNA contains an organism's genetic information and hereditary characteristics.

Dominican Order Founded by the Spaniard Saint Dominic (1170–1221) and approved by Innocent III in 1216, the order was dedicated to the fight against heresy and the conversion of Jews and Muslims. Many members of the order gained teaching positions in the infant European universities and contributed much to the development of philosophy and theology. The Dominicans always retained their reputation for learning, but they also came to believe that stubborn heretics were best controlled by legal procedures. Accordingly, they became the leading medieval administrators of inquisitorial trials.

Dominion in the British Commonwealth Canadian promise to keep up their fealty to the British crown, even after their independence in 1867. Later applied to Australia and New Zealand.

Don Quixote Comical adventure by Spanish writer Miguel de Cervantes (1547–1616) that mocks chivalric ideas.

Dreyfus Affair The 1894 French scandal surrounding accusations that a Jewish captain, Alfred Dreyfus, sold military secrets to the Germans. Convicted, Dreyfus was sentenced to life in prison. However, after public outcry, it was revealed that the trial documents were forgeries and Dreyfus was released.

Il Duce Term designating the fascist Italian leader Benito Mussolini.

Duma The Russian parliament.

Dunkirk The French port on the English Channel where the British and French forces retreated after sustaining heavy losses against the German military. Between May 27 and June 4, 1940, the Royal Navy evacuated over three hundred thousand troops using commercial and pleasure boats.

Earth Summit (1992) Meeting in Rio de Janeiro between many of the world's governments in an effort to address international environmental problems.

Eastern Front Battlefront between Berlin and Moscow during World War I and World War II.

East India Company (1600–1858) British charter company created to outperform Portuguese and Spanish traders in the Far East; in the eighteenth century the company became, in effect, the ruler of a large part of India. There was also a Dutch East India Company.

Edict of Nantes (1598) Edict issued by Henry IV to end the French Wars of Religion. The edict declared France a Catholic country, but tolerated some Protestant worship.

Eiffel Tower   Named after its creator, Gustave Eiffel, the tower was completed in 1889 for the Paris Exposition. This steel monument was twice the height of any other building at the time.

Albert Einstein (1879–1955)   German physicist who developed the theory of relativity, which states that space and motion are relative to each other instead of being absolute.

Elizabeth I (1533–1603)   Protestant daughter of Henry VIII, Queen of England 1558–1603. During her long reign, the doctrines and services of the Church of England were defined and the Spanish Armada was defeated.

Enabling Act (1933)   Emergency act passed by the *Reichstag* (German parliament) that helped transform Hitler from Germany's chancellor, or prime minister, into a dictator, following the suspicious burning of the *Reichstag* building and a suspension of civil liberties.

enclosure   Long process of privatizing what had been public agricultural land in the eighteenth century that changed the nature of economic activity in England.

The *Encyclopedia*   Joint venture of French *philosophe* writers, helmed by Denis Diderot (1713–1784), which proposed to summarize all modern knowledge.

Endeavor   Ship of Captain James Cook, whose widely celebrated voyages to the South Pacific at the end of the eighteenth century supplied Europe with information about the plants, birds, landscapes, and people of this uncharted territory.

Friedrich Engels (1820–1895)   German social and political philosopher who collaborated with Karl Marx on many publications.

English Navigation Act of 1651   Act stipulating that only English ships could carry goods between the mother country and its colonies.

Enlightenment   Intellectual movement stressing natural laws and classifications in nature, in eighteenth-century Europe.

Epicureanism   Greek philosophy that emphasized the individual, denied the existence of spiritual forces, and proposed that the highest good is pleasure.

Desiderius Erasmus (c. 1469–1536)   Dutch-born scholar and social commentator who proclaimed his humanist views in lively treatises like *In Praise of Folly* and the *Colloquies*.

Estates-General   French quasi-parliamentary body called in 1789 to deal with the financial problems that afflicted France at the time. It had not met since 1614.

Etruscans   Non-Indo-European-speaking settlers of the Italian peninsula who dominated the region from the late Bronze Age until the rise of the Romans in the sixth century B.C.E.

Euclid   Hellenistic mathematician whose book *Elements of Geometry* was the basis of modern geometry.

eugenics   Term, meaning "good birth," referring to the project of "breeding" a superior human race. It was popularly championed by scientists, politicians, and social critics in the late nineteenth and early twentieth centuries.

Eurasia   The combined area of Europe and Asia.

European Union (EU)   An international political body that was organized after World War II to reconcile Germany and the rest of Europe as well as to forge closer industrial cooperation. Over time, member states of the EU have relinquished some of their sovereignty, and cooperation has evolved into a community with a single currency, the euro, and a common European parliament.

Exclusion Act of 1882   U.S. congressional act prohibiting nearly all immigration from China to the United States; fueled by animosity toward Chinese workers in the American West.

existentialism   The philosophy that arose out of World War II and emphasized the human condition. Led by Jean Paul Sartre and Albert Camus, existentialists encouraged humans to take responsibility for their own decisions and dilemmas.

fall of the Bastille   On July 14, 1789, the sans culottes, led by the electors of Paris, stormed the Bastille, an ancient fortress, in search of weapons to protect themselves from Louis XVI's troops rumored to be heading toward the city. The fall of the Bastille was the first popular revolt in the French Revolution.

Fascism   The doctrine founded by Benito Mussolini. It emphasized three main ideas: statism ("nothing above the state, nothing outside the state, nothing against the state"), nationalism, and militarism.

Fascists   Radical right-wing group of the disaffected that formed around Mussolini in 1919 and a few years later came to power in Italy.

February Revolution (1917)   The first of two uprisings of the Russian Revolution, which led to the end of the Romanov dynasty.

Federal Deposit Insurance Corporation (FDIC)   Created in 1933 to guarantee all bank deposits up to $2,000 as part of the New Deal in the United States.

Federalists   Supporters of the ratification of the U.S. Constitution, which was written to replace the Articles of Confederation.

Federal Republic of Germany (1949–1990)   Country formed of the areas occupied by the Allies after World War II. Also known as West Germany, this country experienced rapid demilitarization, democratization, and integration into the world economy.

Federal Reserve Act (1913)   U.S. legislation that created a series of boards to monitor the supply and demand of the nation's money.

The *Feminine Mystique*   Groundbreaking book by feminist Betty Friedan (b. 1921), which tried to define "femininity" and explored how women internalized those definitions.

Fertile Crescent   An area of fertile land in what is now Syria, Israel, Turkey, eastern Iraq, and western Iran that was able to sustain settlements due to its wetter climate and abundant natural food resources. Some of the earliest known civilizations emerged there between 9000 and 4500 B.C.E.

feudalism   A loose term reflecting the political and economic situation in eleventh- and twelfth-century Europe. In this system, lords were owed agricultural labor and military service by their serfs, and in turn owed allegiance to more powerful lords and kings.

First Crusade (1095–1099)   Forces were sent by Pope Urban II to assist Byzantine emperor Alexius Comnenus in fighting Turkish forces in Anatolia. The struggle to recapture Jerusalem for western Christianity was eventually successful. This crusade prompted attacks against Jews throughout Europe and resulted in six subsequent military campaigns to the Holy Land.

First World War A total war from August 1914 to November 1918, involving the armies of Britain, France, and Russia (the Allies) against Germany, Austria-Hungary, and the Ottoman empire (the Central Powers). Italy joined the Allies in 1915, and the United States joined them in 1917, helping to tip the balance in favor of the Allies, who also drew upon the populations and material of their colonial possessions. Also known as the Great War.

Five-Year Plan Soviet effort launched under Stalin in 1928 to replace the market with a state-owned and state-managed economy in order to promote rapid economic development over a five-year period and thereby "catch and overtake" the leading capitalist countries. The First Five-Year Plan was followed by the Second Five-Year Plan (1933–1937), and so on, until the collapse of the Soviet Union in 1991.

Flagellants European social group that came into existence during the bubonic plague in the fourteenth century; they believed that the plague was caused by the wrath of God and chose to beat and mutilate themselves as a form of religious penance.

Franciscan order Order of monks established in 1209 by Saint Francis of Assisi (1182–1226); its members strove to imitate the life and example of Jesus.

Frankfurt Assembly An 1848 gathering of delegates from all German states that attempted to unify them into one nation. The liberal agenda and squabbling over whose plan for the nation was best led to the failure of the gathering.

Franz Ferdinand (1863–1914) Archduke of Austria and heir to the Austro-Hungarian empire; his assassination led to the beginning of World War I.

Frederick the Great (1740–1786) Prussian ruler who engaged the nobility in maintaining a strong military and bureaucracy, and led Prussian armies to notable military victories. He also encouraged Enlightenment rationalism and artistic endeavors.

French new wave A group of filmmakers in the 1950s and 1960s that emphasized naturalistic and unsentimental portrayals of ordinary life. Famous new wave directors included Francois Truffaut (1932–1984), Jean-Luc Godard (b. 1930), and Eric Rohmer (b. 1920).

French Revolution of 1830 The French popular revolt against King Charles's July Ordinances of 1830, which dissolved the French Chamber of Deputies and restricted suffrage to exclude almost everyone except the nobility. After several days of violence, Charles abdicated the throne and was replaced by a constitutional monarch, King Louis Philippe.

French Revolution of 1848 Brief uprising caused by economic grievances; it was violently quelled by the government.

Sigmund Freud (1865–1939) The Austrian physician who founded the discipline of psychoanalysis and suggested that human behavior was largely motivated by unconscious and irrational forces.

Front de Libération Nationale (FLN)/Algerian Revolutionary National Liberation Front An anti-colonial, nationalist party that waged an eight-year war, beginning in 1954, against French troops for Algerian independence; the war forced nearly all of the 1 million French colonists to leave.

Galileo Galilei (1564–1642) Italian physicist and inventor. The implications of his ideas raised the ire of the Catholic Church, and he was forced to retract most of his findings.

Mohandas K. (Mahatma) Gandhi (1869–1948) The Indian leader who advocated nonviolent noncooperation and helped win home rule for India in 1947.

Giuseppe Garibaldi (1807–1882) Italian revolutionary leader who led the fight to free Sicily and Naples from the Habsburg empire; the lands were then peaceably annexed by Sardinia.

garrisons Military bases inside cities that were often used for political purposes, such as protecting the rulers and putting down domestic revolt or enforcing colonial rule.

Gaul The region of the Roman empire that is modern Belgium, Germany west of the Rhine, and France.

Gdansk shipyard Site of mass strikes in Poland that led to the formation in 1980 of the first independent trade union, Solidarity, in the Communist bloc.

Geneva Peace Conference (1954) International conference to restore peace in Korea and Indochina. The chief participants were the United States, the Soviet Union, Great Britain, France, the People's Republic of China, North Korea, South Korea, Vietnam, the Viet Minh party, Laos, and Cambodia. The conference resulted in the division of North and South Vietnam.

German Democratic Republic Nation founded from the Soviet zone of occupation of Germany after World War II; also known as East Germany.

German Social Democratic Party Founded in 1875, it was the most powerful Socialist party in Europe before 1917.

Gilgamesh The hero of the Sumerian epic, which was recorded in written form around 2000 B.C.E. Gilgamesh was a powerful ruler who, along with his friend Enkidu, battled monsters and gods and searched for immortality.

Girondins Liberal revolutionary group that supported the creation of a constitutional monarchy during the early stages of the French Revolution.

globalization The term used to describe political, social, and economic networks that span the globe. These global exchanges are not limited by nation states and often rely on new technologies, international laws, and economic imperatives.

Arthur de Gobineau (1816–1882) French writer whose pseudoscientific, racist ideology provided a rationale for European imperialism.

Gold Coast Name that European mariners and merchants gave to that part of West Equatorial Africa from which gold and slaves were exported. Originally controlled by the Portuguese, this area later became the British colony of the Gold Coast.

Gothic style Period of graceful architecture emerging after the Romanesque style in twelfth- and thirteenth-century France. The style is characterized by pointed arches, delicate decoration, and large windows.

Great Depression Period following the U.S. stock market crash on October 29, 1929, and ending in 1941 with America's entry into World War II.

great divide Refers to the division between economically developed nations and less developed nations.

Great East Asia Co-Prosperity Sphere   Term used by the Japanese during the 1930s and 1940s to refer to Hong Kong, Singapore, Malaya, Burma, and other states that they seized during their run for expansion.

Great Terror   The systematic murder of nearly a million people and the deportation of another million and a half to labor camps by Stalin's regime during 1937 in an attempt to consolidate power and remove perceived enemies.

The Great War (1914–1918)   World War I.

Greek Civil War (1821–1827)   Conflict between Greek Christians and Muslim Ottomans.

Pope Gregory I (540?–604)   Roman Catholic Pope 590–604. Used his political influence and theological teachings to separate the western Latin from the eastern Greek church. He also encouraged the Benedictine monastic movement and missionary expeditions.

Guerrillas   Portuguese and Spanish peasant bands who resisted the revolutionary and expansion efforts of Napoleon; after the French word for war, *guerre.*

Guernica   The Basque town bombed by German planes in April 1937 during the Spanish Civil War. It is also the subject of Pablo Picasso's famous painting from the same year.

guest workers   Migrants looking for temporary employment.

guilds   Professional organizations in commercial towns that regulated the business conditions and privileges of those practicing a particular craft.

gulag   The vast system of forced labor camps under the Soviet regime; it originated in 1919 in a small monastery near the Arctic Circle and spread throughout the Soviet Union and to other Soviet-style socialist countries. Penal labor was required of both ordinary criminals and those accused of political crimes (counterrevolution, anti-Soviet agitation).

Gulf War (1991)   Armed conflict between Iraq and a coalition of thirty-two nations, including the United States, Britain, Egypt, France, and Saudi Arabia. The seeds of the war were planted with Iraq's invasion of Kuwait on August 2, 1990.

gunpowder   An explosive mixture of nitrates, sulfur, and charcoal that can be used in firearms. The use of gunpowder transformed warfare in the late middle ages and played a major role in the creation of European empires in Africa and the Americas.

Habsburg empire   Ruling house of Austria, which once ruled the Netherlands, Spain, and Central Europe but came to settle in lands along the Danube River. It played a prominent role in European affairs for many centuries. In 1867, the Habsburg empire was reorganized into the Austro-Hungarian Dual Monarchy, and in 1918 it collapsed.

Hadith   Sayings attributed to the Prophet Muhammad and his early converts. Used to guide the behavior of Muslim peoples.

Hagia Sophia   The largest house of worship in all of Christendom, located in Constantinople and built by the emperor Justinian. When Constantinople fell to Ottoman forces in 1453, it was turned into a mosque.

Hajj   The pilgrimage to Mecca; an obligation for Muslims.

Hammurabi   The ruler of Babylon from 1792 to 1750 B.C.E. Hammurabi issued a collection of laws that were greatly influential in the Near East for centuries.

harem   Secluded women's quarters in Muslim households.

Harlem Renaissance   Cultural movement in the 1920s that was based in Harlem, a part of New York City where a large African American population resided. The movement gave voice to black novelists, poets, painters, and musicians, many of whom used their art to protest racial subordination; also referred to as the "New Negro Movement."

heliocentric   The sun-centered view of the planetary system, which displaced the Earth from the center of the universe.

Henry VIII (1491–1547)   Oft-married English monarch who broke with the Roman Catholic church when the pope refused to grant him an annulment. The resulting modified version of Christianity became the Church of England, or Anglicanism.

Henry of Navarre (1553–1610)   Crowned King Henry IV of France, he renounced his Protestantism but granted limited toleration to Huguenots (French Protestants) with the 1598 Edict of Nantes.

Prince Henry the Navigator (1394–1460)   Portuguese noble who encouraged conquest of western Africa and trade in gold and slaves.

hero cults   Important ancient Greek families would claim that an impressive Mycenean tomb was that of their own famous ancestor and would practice sacrifices and other observances to strengthen their claim. This devotion could extend to their followers, and eventually whole communities would identify with such local heroes.

Hiroshima   Japanese port devastated by an atomic bomb on August 6, 1945.

Adolf Hitler (1889–1945)   The author of *Mein Kampf* and leader of the Nazis. Hitler and his Nazi regime started World War II and orchestrated the systematic murder of over five million Jews.

Hittites   An Indo-European-speaking people that migrated into Anatolia (now Turkey) around the beginning of the second millennium B.C.E.

Ho Chi Minh (1890–1969)   The Vietnamese communist resistance leader who drove the French out of Vietnam and controlled North Vietnam after the Geneva Accords divided the region into four countries.

Holy Roman Empire   The collection of lands in central and western Europe ruled over by the kings of Germany (and later Austria) from the twelfth century until 1806.

Holy Russia   Name applied to Muscovy, and then to the Russian empire, by Slavic Eastern Orthodox clerics who were appalled by the Muslim conquest in 1453 of Constantinople (the capital of Byzantium and of Eastern Christianity), and who were hopeful that Russia would become the new protector of the faith.

home charges   Fees India was forced to pay to Britain as its colonial master; these fees included interest on railroad loans, salaries to colonial officers, and the maintenance of imperial troops outside India.

Homo sapiens   Term defined by Linnaeus in 1737 and commonly used to refer to fully modern human beings.

hoplite A Greek foot soldier armed with a spear or short sword and protected by a large round shield (a hopla). In battle, hoplites stood shoulder to shoulder in a close formation called a phalanx.

Huguenots French Protestants who endured severe persecution in the sixteenth and seventeenth centuries.

Human Comedy Masterpiece of French novelist Honoré de Balzac (1799–1850) that criticized materialist values.

humanism Medieval program of study built around the seven liberal arts: grammer, logic, rhetoric, arithmetic, music, geometry, and astronomy.

human rights The belief that all people have the right to legal equality, freedom of religion and speech, and the right to participate in government. Human rights laws prohibit torture, cruel punishment, and slavery.

Hundred Years' War (1337–1453) Long conflict, fought mostly on French soil, between England and France, centering on English claims to the throne of France.

Saddam Hussein (b. 1937) The former dictator of Iraq who invaded Iran in 1980 and started the eight-year-long Iran-Iraq War; invaded Kuwait in 1990, which caused the Gulf War of 1991; and was overthrown when the United States invaded Iraq in 2003. Involved in Iraqi politics since the mid-1960s, Hussein became the official head of state in 1979.

Il-khanate Mongol-founded dynasty in thirteenth-century Persia.

Imam Muslim religious leader and also a politico-religious descendant of Ali; believed by some to have a special relationship with Allah.

Imhotep The chief adviser to the Pharaoh Djoser, who ruled in the 27th century B.C.E. Often considered to be the first architect, Imhotep designed tombs and other structures to express the power of the Egyptian pharaohs.

Indian National Congress Formed in 1885, this political party was deeply committed to constitutional methods, industrialization, and cultural nationalism.

Indian Rebellion of 1857 The uprising began near Delhi, when the military disciplined a regiment of Indian soldiers employed by the British for refusing to use rifle cartridges greased with pork fat—unacceptable to either Hindus or Muslims. Rebels attacked law courts and burned tax rolls, protesting debt and corruption. The mutiny spread through large areas of northwest India before being violently suppressed by British troops.

Indo-Europeans A group of people that spoke variations of the same language and moved into the Near East and Mediterranean shortly after 2000 B.C.E.

indulgences Remissions of the penances owed by Catholics as part of the process by which their sins are forgiven.

Inkas The highly centralized South American empire that was toppled by the Spanish conquistador Francisco Pizarro in 1533.

Inquisition Tribunal of the Roman Catholic Church that aimed to enforce religious orthodoxy and conformity.

International Monetary Fund (IMF) Established in 1945 to promote the health of the world economy, the IMF is a specialized agency of the United Nations.

intifada Uprising in the Palestinian occupied territories from 1987 to 1993, in protest against the Israeli occupation and politics. The Oslo Agreement (1993) helped to reduce the tension between the two sides and the Intifada all but ceased by the end of 1993. In early 2000, the Intifada resumed.

Investiture Conflict A disagreement between Pope Gregory VII and Emperor Henry IV of Germany that tested the power of kings over church matters. After years of diplomatic and military hostility, it was settled by the Concordat of Worms in 1122.

invisible hand Described in Adam Smith's *The Wealth of Nations*, the idea that the operations of a free market would produce economic efficiency and economic benefits for all.

Irish home rule The late-nineteenth- and early-twentieth-century movement, led by Sinn Fein (established 1905), for Irish self-government.

Irish potato famine Period of agricultural blight from 1845 to 1849 whose devastating results prompted a mass emigration to America.

Iron Curtain Term coined by Winston Churchill in 1946 to refer to the division of Western Europe, under American influence, from Eastern Europe, under the domination of the Soviet Union.

Ivan the Great (1440–1505) Emperor of Russia who annexed neighboring territories and began Russia's career as a European power.

Jacobins Radical French political group that came into existence during the French Revolution, executed the French king, and sought to remake French culture.

Jacquerie Violent 1358 peasant uprising in northern France, incited by disease, war, and taxes.

James I (1566–1625) Monarch of Scotland and England from 1603 to 1625. He oversaw the English vernacular translation of the Bible known by his name.

Janissaries Corps of enslaved soldiers recruited as children from the Christian provinces of the Ottoman empire and brought up with intense loyalty to the Ottoman state and its sultan. The sultan used these forces to curb local autonomy and to serve as his personal bodyguards.

Jesuits Religious order founded in 1540 by Ignatius Loyola to counter the inroads of the Protestant Reformation; the Jesuits were active in politics, education, and missionary work.

Jihad A struggle and, if need be, a holy war toward the advancement of the cause of Islam.

Joan of Arc (c. 1412–1431) French teenager, supposedly divinely inspired, who led forces against the English during the Hundred Years' War. Burned at the stake for heresy by the English and later made a Catholic saint.

Justinian (527–565) Emperor of eastern Rome. Justinian codified Roman law in the Corpus Juris Civilis and tried to reunify the eastern and western halves of the old Roman empire.

Das Kapital (Capital) The 1867 book by Karl Marx that outlined the theory behind historical materialism and attacked the socioeconomic inequities of capitalism. Mixing economic theory and revolutionary politics, the book became the preeminent socialist critique of capitalism.

Johannes Kepler (1571–1601)   Mathematician and astronomer who elaborated on and corrected Copernicus's theory and is chiefly remembered for his discovery of the three laws of planetary motion that bear his name.

Keynesian Revolution   Post-Depression economic ideas developed by the British economist John Maynard Keynes, wherein the state took a greater role in managing the economy, stimulating it by increasing the money supply and creating jobs.

KGB   Soviet political police and spy agency, first formed as the Cheka not long after the Bolshevik coup in October 1917. It grew to more than 750,000 operatives with military rank by the 1980s.

Chingiz Khan (c. 1167–1227)   Title taken by Mongol chief Temujin meaning "The Oceanic Ruler." Began dynasty that conquered much of southern Asia.

Khanate   Major political unit of the vast Mongol empire. There were four Khanates, including the Yuan empire in China, forged by Chingiz Khan's grandson Kubilai in the 13th century.

Nikita Khrushchev (1894–1971)   Leader of the Soviet Union during the Cuban Missile Crisis, Khrushchev had quickly reached power soon after Stalin's death in 1953. His reforms and criticisms of the excesses of the Stalin regime led to his fall from power in 1964.

Kremlin   Once synonymous with the Soviet government, it refers to Moscow's walled city center.

Kristallnacht   The Nazi destruction of seventy-five hundred Jewish stores and two hundred synagogues on November 9, 1938.

kulaks   Originally a pejorative term used to designate better-off peasants, it was used in the late 1920s and early 1930s to refer to any peasant, rich or poor, perceived as an opponent of the Soviet regime. Russian for "fist."

Labour Party   Founded in Britain in 1900, this party represented workers and was based on socialist principles.

League of Nations   International organization founded after World War I to solve international disputes through arbitration; it was dissolved in 1946 and transferred its assets to the United Nations.

Vladimir Lenin (1870–1924)   Leader of the Bolshevik Revolution in Russia (1917) and the first leader of the Soviet Union.

Leonardo da Vinci (1452–1519)   The ultimate Renaissance man, Leonardo was a painter, architect, musician, mathematician, engineer, and inventor. He set up an artist's shop in Florence by the time he was twenty-five and gained the patronage of the Medici ruler of the city, Lorenzo the Magnificent.

Leopold II (1835–1909)   Belgian king who sponsored colonizing expeditions into Africa.

Leviathan   A book by Thomas Hobbes (1588–1679) that recommended a ruler have unrestricted power.

liberalism   Political and social theory that advocates representative government, free trade, and freedom of speech and religion.

lithograph   Art form that involves putting writing or design on stone and producing printed impressions.

Long March (1934–1935)   Trek of over 10,000 kilometers by Mao Zedong and his Communist followers to establish a new base of operations.

lord   Privileged landowner who exercised authority over the people who lived on his land.

lost generation   Refers to the 17 million former members of the Red Guard and other Chinese youth who were denied education from the late 1960s to the mid-1970s as part of the Chinese government's attempt to forestall political disruptions.

Louis XIV (1638–1715)   The "Sun King," known for his opulent court and absolutist political style.

Louis XVI (1754–1793)   Well-meaning but ineffectual king of France, finally deposed and executed with his family by revolutionaries.

Luftwaffe   Literally "air weapon," this is the name of the German air force, which was founded during World War I, disbanded in 1945, and reestablished when West Germany joined NATO in 1950.

Lusitania   The passenger liner that was secretly carrying war supplies and was sunk by a German U-boat (submarine) on May 7, 1915.

Martin Luther (1483–1546)   A German monk who led the Reformation movement. At the center of his ideas is the doctrine, "justification by faith alone," which challenged many of the medieval practices of the Catholic Church and led to the religious wars between Protestants and Catholics.

Lutheranism   Branch of Protestantism that followed Martin Luther's (1483–1546) rejection of the Roman Catholic "doctrine of works."

lycées   System of high schools instituted by Napoleon as part of his domestic reform campaign.

madrassas   Muslim schools devoted to the study of the Quran and Islam.

Magna Carta   "Great Charter" of 1215 signed by King John of England, which limited the king's fiscal powers and is seen as a landmark in the political evolution of the West.

Moses Maimonides (1135–1204)   Spanish-born Jewish scholar, physician, and scriptural commentator.

mandate system   Administered by the League of Nations after the Treaty of Versailles, the mandate system legitimized Europe's dominance of territories in the Middle East, Africa, and the Pacific. Mandate territories were divided into groups based on location and their "level of development."

Nelson Mandela (b. 1918)   The South African opponent of *apartheid* who led the African National Congress and was imprisoned from 1962 until 1990. After his release from prison, he worked with Prime Minister Frederik Willem De Klerk to establish majority rule. Mandela became the first black president of South Africa in 1994.

Manhattan Project   The secret U.S. government research project in Los Alamos, New Mexico, to develop the first nuclear bomb. The first test of a nuclear bomb was near Los Alamos on July 16, 1945.

manorialism   System common to England, northern France, and Germany in the Middle Ages of communal peasant farming under the protection of a landholding lord.

Mao Zedong (1893–1976) The leader of the Chinese Revolution who defeated the Nationalists in 1949 and established the Communist regime in China.

Marshall Plan Economic aid package given to Europe after World War II in hopes of a rapid period of reconstruction and economic gain and to secure the countries from a Communist takeover.

Master Eckhart (c. 1260–1327) Dominican monk who preached an introspective and charismatic version of Christian piety.

Karl Marx (1818–1883) German philosopher and economist who believed that a revolution of the working classes would overthrow the capitalist order and create a classless society. Author of *Das Kapital* and *The Communist Manifesto*.

Maxim gun Invented in 1885 by an American, Hiram Maxim, the Maxim gun was the first portable machine gun. Quickly adopted by the majority of European armies and capable of firing 500 rounds per minute, it played a major role in the imperial conquests of the African continent.

Mayans Native American peoples whose culturally and politically sophisticated empire encompassed lands in present-day Mexico and Guatemala.

Giuseppe Mazzini (1805–1872) Founder of Young Italy and an ideological leader of the Italian Nationalist movement.

Mecca Major commercial city of the Arabian peninsula in the sixth century C.E., at which time the founder of Islam, Muhammad, was born and achieved prominence. From the earliest days of the spread of Islam, the city was the destination of the chief religious pilgrimage for Muslims, and it is now considered the holiest site in the Islamic world.

Medici Dynasty of Florentine bankers and politicians known for their patronage of the arts.

Meiji empire Empire created under the leadership of Mutsuhito, emperor of Japan from 1868 until 1912. During the Meiji period Japan became a world industrial and naval power.

Menander (342 B.C.E.?–292 B.C.E.) Ancient Greek dramatist who wrote over 100 plays, many of which were standards of Western literature for hundreds of years. Only one complete surviving play is known, *The Grouch*, which was rediscovered in 1957.

mercantilism A popular Western belief between 1600 and 1800 that a country's wealth and power was based on a favorable balance of trade (more exports and fewer imports) and the accumulation of precious metals.

Michelangelo (1475–1564) Virtuoso artist, best known for the Sistine Chapel ceiling in Rome and his sculptures *David* and *Pieta*.

John Stuart Mill (1806–1873) English radical philosopher whose writings advocated aspects of socialism and civil liberties.

Slobodan Milosevic (b. 1941) The Serbian nationalist politician who took control of the Serb government and orchestrated the genocide of thousands of Croatians, Bosnian Muslims, Albanians, and Kosovars. After ten years of war, he was ousted by a popular revolt in 2000.

Minoans A sea empire that flourished on Crete and in the Aegean Basin from 1900 B.C.E. until the middle of the second millennium B.C.E.

modernism The series of artistic movements, manifestos, innovations, and experiments that redefined art in the first half of the twentieth century. Modernism rejected history and tradition in favor of expressive and experimental freedom.

Michel de Montaigne (1533–1592) French philosopher known for his *Essays*.

mosque Place of worship for the people of Islam.

Wolfgang Amadeus Mozart (1756–1791) Austrian child prodigy and composer of instrumental music and operas.

Muhammad (570–632 C.E.) The founder of Islam, he claimed to be the prophet whom God (Allah) had chosen for his final revelation to mankind.

Mullahs Iranian religious leaders who led the opposition movement against the shah and denounced the depravity of late-twentieth-century American materialism and secularism.

multinational corporations Corporations based in many different countries that have global investment, trading, and distribution goals.

Muslim Brotherhood Egyptian organization founded in 1938 by Hassan al-Banna. It attacked liberal democracy as a façade for middle-class, business, and landowning interests and fought for a return to a purified form of Islam.

Muslim League National Muslim party of India.

Benito Mussolini (1883–1945) The Italian founder of the Fascist party who came to power in Italy in 1922 and allied himself with Hitler and the Nazis during World War II.

Mutiny of 1857 Uprising of Indian soldiers against the ruling British, sometimes called the Sepoy Rebellion.

Mycenaens The ancient Greek civilization that settled in Greece during the second millennium B.C.E. and organized around powerful citadels.

Nagasaki Second Japanese city on which the United States dropped an atomic bomb. The attack took place on August 9, 1945; the Japanese surrendered shortly thereafter, ending World War II.

Napoleonic Code Legal code drafted by Napoleon in 1804; it distilled different legal traditions to create one uniform law. The code confirmed the abolition of feudal privileges of all kinds and set the conditions for exercising property rights.

National Assembly of France Governing body of France that succeeded the Estates-General in 1789 during the French Revolution. It was composed of, and defined by, the delegates of the Third Estate.

National Association for the Advancement of Colored People (NAACP) Founded in 1910, this U.S. civil rights organization was dedicated to ending inequality and segregation for black Americans.

nationalism Movement to unify a country based on a people's common history and social traditions.

NATO The North Atlantic Treaty Organization, which was a 1949 agreement between the United States, Canada, Great Britain, and 8 European countries that declared that an armed attack against any one of the members would be regarded as an attack against all. Other European countries have since joined.

"navvies"   Slang for laborers who built railroads and canals.

Nazi Party   Founded in the early 1920s, the National Socialist German Workers' Party (NDSAP) gained control over Germany under the leadership of Adolf Hitler in 1933 and continued in power until Germany was defeated in 1945.

Nazism   The National Socialist Workers Party led by Adolf Hitler which advocated a violent anti-Semitic, anti-Marxist, pan-German ideology.

Nefertiti   The wife of Akhenaten, the fourteenth-century B.C.E. Egyptian pharaoh.

Neolithic   The "New" Stone Age, which began around 11,000 B.C.E., saw new technological and social developments, including managed food production, the beginnings of semipermanent and permanent settlements, and the rapid intensification of trade.

New Deal   President Franklin Delano Roosevelt's package of government reforms that were enacted during the 1930s to provide jobs for the unemployed, social welfare programs for the poor, and security to the financial markets.

new imperialism   Expansion of colonial power by Western European nations, especially in Asia, in the last three decades of the nineteenth century.

Isaac Newton (1642–1727)   One of the foremost scientists of all time, Newton was an English mathematician and physicist; he is noted for his development of calculus, work on the properties of light, and theory of gravitation.

New World silver   The most lucrative export from the Spanish colonies in Central and South America was silver. The massive infusion of New World Silver into the sixteenth-century European economy accelerated inflation and eventually caused the collapse of the Spanish economy and widespread misery for the rest of Europe's poorest inhabitants who could not afford the rising prices of goods.

Nicholas I (1796–1855)   Russian tsar who executed the leaders of the 1825 December Revolution and pursued an absolutist reign.

Tsar Nicholas II (1868–1918)   The last Russian tsar, who abdicated the throne in 1917. He and his family were executed by the Bolsheviks on July 17, 1918.

Nicomachean Ethics   The treatise on moral philosophy by Aristotle, which teaches that the highest good consists of the harmonious functioning of the individual human mind and body.

Friedrich Nietzsche (1844–1900)   The German philosopher who denied the possibility of knowing absolute "truth" or "reality," since all knowledge comes filtered through linguistic, scientific, or artistic systems of representation. He also criticized Judeo-Christian morality for instilling a repressive conformity that drained civilization of its vitality.

Non-governmental organizations (NGOs)   Private organizations like the Red Cross that play a large role in international affairs.

North American Free Trade Agreement (NAFTA)   Treaty negotiated in the early 1990s to promote free trade among Canada, the United States, and Mexico.

Novum Organum   Work by English statesman and scientist Francis Bacon (1561–1626) that advanced a philosophy of study through observation.

October Revolution   The October 1917 uprising in Russia led by Lenin and the Bolsheviks to overthrow the provisional Russian government, withdraw Russia from the First World War, and establish a one-party Bolshevik state.

OPEC (Organization of Petroleum Exporting Countries)   Organization created in 1960 by oil-producing countries in the Middle East, South America, and Africa to regulate the production and pricing of crude oil.

Operation Barbarossa   The codename for Hitler's invasion of the Soviet Union.

Opium Wars (1839–1842)   War fought between the British and Qing China to protect British trade in opium; resulted in the ceding of Hong Kong to the British.

oracle at Delphi   Dating to 1400 B.C.E., the oracle was the most important shrine in ancient Greece. A priestess of Apollo who attended the shrine was believed to be able to predict the future. The shrine ceased to function in the fourth century C.E.

Ottoman slavery   Social system of using slave labor for domestic, administrative, and military work that permitted social advancement and religious diversity within the Muslim empire.

Pan-African Conference   1900 assembly in London which sought to draw attention to the sovereignty of African people and their mistreatment by colonial powers.

pan-Slavism   Cultural movement that sought to unite native Slavic peoples within the Russian and Habsburg empires.

papal   Of, relating to, or issued by a pope.

Patria   Latin, meaning "fatherland."

patricians   The uppermost elite class of ancient Rome.

Paul   One of the twelve apostles of Jesus, Paul spread Christianity throughout the Near East and Greece.

Peace of Paris   The 1919 Paris Peace Conference established the terms to end World War I. Great Britain, France, Italy, and the United States signed five treaties with each of the defeated nations: Germany, Austria, Hungary, Turkey, and Bulgaria. The settlement is notable for the territory that Germany had to give up, including large parts of Prussia to the new state of Poland, and Alsace and Lorraine to France; the disarming of Germany; and the "war guilt" provision, which required Germany and its allies to pay massive reparations to the victors.

Pearl Harbor   The American Navy base in Hawaii that was bombed by the Japanese on December 7, 1941, which brought the United States into World War II.

Peloponnesian War   The ancient Greek war between Sparta and Athens that began in 431 B.C.E. and ended with the destruction of the Athenian fleet in 404 B.C.E.

People's Charter   An action of the Chartist Movement (1839–1848); between 1839 and 1842 over 3 million British signed this document calling for universal suffrage for adult males, the secret ballot, electoral districts, and annual parliamentary elections.

perestroika   Introduced by Soviet leader Mikhail Gorbachev in June 1987, *Perestroika* was the name given to economic and political reforms begun earlier in his tenure. It restructured the state bureaucracy, reduced the privileges of the political elite, and instituted a shift from the centrally planned economy to a mixed economy, combining planning with the operation of market forces.

Pericles The fifth-century B.C.E. Athenian leader who served as strategos for thirty years and pushed through reforms to make Athens more democratic by giving every citizen the right to propose and amend legislation and making it easier for citizens to participate in the assembly and the great appeals court of Athens by paying an average day's wage for attendance.

Peterloo Massacre (1819) The killing of 11 and wounding of 460 following a peaceful demonstration for political reform by workers in Manchester, England.

Peter the Great (1672–1725) Energetic tsar who transformed Russia into a leading European country by centralizing government, modernizing the army, creating a navy, and reforming education and the economy.

Francesco Petrarch (1304–1374) Italian scholar and writer who revived interest in classical writing styles and was famed for his love sonnets.

Pharisees A group of Jewish teachers and preachers that emerged in the third century B.C.E. and insisted that all of Yahweh's (God's) commandments were binding on all Jews.

Philip II (382–336 B.C.E.) The Macedonian king who consolidated the southern Balkans and the Greek city-states; he was the father of Alexander.

Phoenicians The semitic-speaking residents of present-day Lebanon from around 1200 to 800 B.C.E. The Phoenician cities were centers for trade throughout the Mediterranean.

Plato's *Republic* The first systematic treatment of political philosophy ever written, it argued for an elitist state in which most people would be governed by intellectually superior "philosopher-kings."

plebians The citizen population of ancient Rome that included farmers, merchants, and the urban poor; plebians comprised the majority of the population.

plebiscite A common tool of authoritarian leaders where they put a question directly to popular vote. This allows the head of state to bypass politicians or legislative bodies who might disagree with him—as well as permitting local officials to tamper with ballot boxes. For example, in 1802, Napoleon was proclaimed consul for life by a plebiscite.

Plotinus (204–270 C.E.) The neo-Platonist philosopher who taught that everything that exists proceeds from the divine and that the highest goal of life should be the mystic reunion of the soul with the divine, which can be achieved through contemplation and asceticism.

polis One of the major political innovations of the ancient Greeks was the Polis, or city-state. They were independent social and political structures, organized around an urban center, containing markets, meeting places, and a temple; they controlled a limited amount of the surrounding territory.

Marco Polo (1254–1324) Venetian merchant who traveled through Asia for twenty years and published his observations in a widely read memoir, *Travels*.

Populists Members of a political movement that supported U.S. farmers in late nineteenth-century America. The term is often used generically to refer to political groups who appeal to the mass of the population.

potato famine (1845–1850) Severe famine in Ireland that led to the migration of large numbers of Irish to the United States.

Prague Spring A period of political liberalization in Czechoslovakia between January and August 1968 that was initiated by Alexander Dubĉek, the Czech leader. This period of expanding freedom and openness in this Eastern bloc nation ended on August 20, when the USSR and Warsaw Pact countries invaded with 200,000 troops and 5,000 tanks.

The Praise of Folly 1511 satire by Erasmus that attacked the corruption of the papacy.

pre-Socratics A group of philosophers on the Greek island of Miletus, including Thales, Anaximander, and Anaximenes, who raised questions about the relationship between the natural world, the gods, and humans, and formulated rational theories to explain the physical universe they observed.

Primitivism Movement in Western art forms in the late nineteenth and early twentieth centuries that used the so-called primitive art forms of Africa, Oceania, and pre-Columbian America to inspire a break with the established art world.

The Prince Influential treatise by Niccolo Machiavelli (1469–1527) that attempts to lay out methods to secure and maintain political power.

Protestantism Division of Christianity that emerged in sixteenth-century western Europe at the time of the Reformation. It focused on individual spiritual needs and rejected the social authority of the papacy and the Catholic clergy.

Ptolemy (c. 85–165 C.E.) One of the most influential ancient Greeks; he was a leading astronomer, mathematician, and geographer who lived his entire life in Alexandria and helped to transform that city into a center of scientific study and scholarship.

puppet states Governments that have little power in the international arena and follow the dictates of their more powerful neighbors or patrons.

Puritans Seventeenth-century reform group of the Church of England; also known as dissenters or nonconformists.

Qur'an (often *Koran*) Islam's holy book, comprised of Allah's revelations.

Sayyid Qutb (1906–1966) The Egyptian critic who became one of the most important intellectual leaders of the Muslim Brotherhood and whose writings are often cited as philosophical inspiration for Osama bin Laden and other Islamic radicals.

François Rabelais (c. 1494?–1553) French humanist satirist best known for his crudely comic *Gargantua and Pantagruel*, in which he espouses the "eat, drink, and be merry" lifestyle. Originally a novice in the Franciscan order, later a Benedictine monk who left the order to study medicine, Rabelais spent time in hiding for fear of being labeled a heretic, and some of his books were banned.

radicals Widely used term in nineteenth-century Europe that referred to those individuals and political organizations that favored the total reconfiguration of Europe's old state system.

Raj Term referring to the British crown's administration of India following the end of the East India Company's rule after the Indian Mutiny of 1857.

Ramadan Ninth month of the Muslim year, during which all Muslims must fast during daylight hours.

Raphael (1483–1520)   Italian painter noted for his warmly human treatment of religious subjects, particularly his Madonnas and large-figure compositions in the Vatican in Rome.

realism   Artistic and literary style which sought to portray common situations as they would appear in reality.

Realpolitik   Political strategy advancing power for its own sake.

reason   According to thinkers like Descartes, reason is a subjective faculty, or unaided ability, to form concepts.

Rebellion of 1857   Indian rebellion against the English East India Company to bring religious purification, an egalitarian society, and local and communal solidarity without the interference of British rule.

Reds   The Bolsheviks.

Reformation   Religious and political movement in sixteenth-century Europe that led to the breakaway of Protestant groups from the Catholic Church; notable figures include Martin Luther and John Calvin.

Reich   A term for the German state. The first Reich corresponded to the Holy Roman Empire (9th century to 1806), the second Reich was from 1871 to 1919, and the third Reich lasted from 1933 through May 1945.

Reign of Terror   Campaign at the height of the French Revolution (1793–1794) in which violence, including systematic executions of opponents of the Revolution, was used to purge France of its "enemies" and to extend the Revolution beyond its borders; radicals executed as many as 40,000 persons who were judged enemies of the state.

Religious Peace of Augsburg   1555 settlement between factions within the Holy Roman Empire that stated a territory would follow the religion of its ruler, whether Catholic or Protestant.

Renaissance   Term meaning "rebirth" that historians use to refer to the expanded cultural production of European nations between 1300 and 1600.

Restoration period (1815–1848)   European movement after the defeat of Napoleon to restore Europe to its pre-French revolutionary status and to prevent radical movements from arising.

Richard II (1367–1400)   King of England (r. 1377–1399), chiefly remembered for his successful resolution of the Peasants' Rebellion (1381) and as a vacillating, yet tyrannical monarch. He was deposed by his cousin Henry Bolingbroke (Henry IV) and assassinated.

Cardinal Richelieu (1585–1642)   First minister to French King Louis XIII, who centralized political power and deprived the Huguenots of many rights.

Rights of Man   A declaration by the French National Assembly in 1789 that declared property to be a natural right, along with liberty, security, and "resistance to oppression." It declared freedom of speech, religious toleration, and liberty of the press inviolable. All citizens were to be treated equally before the law. No one was to be imprisoned or punished without due process of law. Sovereignty resided in the people, who could depose officers of the government if they abused their powers.

Rembrandt Van Rijn (1606–1669)   A Dutch painter famous for his portraits, Biblical scenes, and imaginative experiments with light and shading.

Romanticism   Beginning in Germany and England in the late 18th century and continuing up to the end of the 19th century, a movement in art, music, and literature that countered the rationalism of the Enlightenment by stressing a highly emotional response to nature.

Jean-Jacques Rousseau (1718–1778)   Philosopher and radical political theorist whose *Social Contract* attacked privilege and inequality. One of the primary principles of Rousseau's political philosophy is that politics and morality should not be separated.

Russification   Programs designed to assimilate people of over 146 dialects into the Russian empire by the tsars in the late 19th century.

Rwanda   A former Belgian colony in central Africa that has been torn by ethnic violence between the Hutus and the Tutsis since before the country's independence in 1962.

Saint Bartholomew's Day Massacre   Massacre of French Protestants (Huguenots) by Catholic crowds that began in Paris on August 24, 1572, spreading to other parts of France and continuing into October of that year. More than 70,000 were killed.

St. Domingue   Former French Caribbean colony and site of a slave rebellion in 1791, which embroiled English and French forces until 1804, when St. Domingue was declared the independent nation of Haiti.

salons   Informal gatherings of intellectuals and aristocrats that allowed discourse about Enlightenment ideas.

Santa Sophia   The Byzantine church in Constantinople, constructed by emperor Justinian I in the sixth century, and famous for its dome, which rested on the keystones of four great arches.

Sappho (c. 620–c. 550 B.C.E.)   One of the most famous Greek lyric poets, she wrote beautiful poetry about romantic longing and sexual lust, sometimes about men, but more often about women.

Sargon (r. 2334–2279 B.C.E.)   The Akkadian leader who unified Mesopotamia.

Schlieffen Plan   Devised by Count Alfred von Schlieffen in 1905 and put into operation on August 2, 1914, the Schlieffen Plan required France to be attacked first through Belgium and a quick victory to be secured so that the German army could fight Russia on the Eastern Front.

scientific societies   Organizations that emerged in the seventeenth century to promote the improvement of scientific knowledge, experiments, and collaboration by scientists and philosophers.

Scramble for Africa   European rush to colonize parts of Africa at the end of the nineteenth century.

second industrial revolution   The technological developments in the last third of the nineteenth century, which included new techniques for refining and producing steel; increased availability of electricity for industrial, commercial, and domestic use; advances in chemical manufacturing; and the creation of the internal combustion engine.

Second World   Term invented during the cold war to refer to the Communist countries, as opposed to the West (or First World) and the former colonies (or Third World).

Second World War   Worldwide war that began in September 1939 in Europe, and even earlier in Asia (1930s), and that pitted Britain, the United States, and especially the Soviet Union (the Allies) against Nazi Germany, Italy, and Japan (the Axis).

Seleucus (d. 280 B.C.E.) The Macedonian general who ruled the Asian territory of Alexander the Great's empire and founded Greek colonies such as Antioch and Selsucia.

Semitic The Semitic language family has the longest recorded history of any linguistic group and is the root language for most of the languages of the Middle and Near East. Ancient Semitic languages include the language of the ancient Babylonians and Assyrians, Phoenician, the classical form of Hebrew, early dialects of Aramaic, and the classical Arabic of the *Quran*.

sepoys Hindu and Muslim recruits of the East India Company's military force.

serfdom Slavery-like system of customs and laws whereby peasants were kept poor and stationary by their manor lords; it had spread throughout the West by the 10th century and its peak was the Middle Ages.

Seven Years War (1756–1763) Worldwide war that ended when Prussia defeated Austria, establishing itself as a European power, and when Britain gained control of India and many of France's colonies through the Treaty of Paris. It is known as the French and Indian War in the United States.

Shah Traditional title of Persian rulers.

William Shakespeare (1564–1616) The greatest Elizabethan playwright, Shakespeare worked as actor before becoming a dramatist. The author of *Hamlet, King Lear,* and *Much Ado About Nothing* wrote nearly 40 plays and over 150 sonnets.

Shiism One of the two main branches of Islam. Shiites recognize Ali, the fourth caliph, and his descendants as rightful rulers of the Islamic world; practiced in the Safavid empire.

Shiites An often-persecuted minority religious party within Islam that insists only descendants of Ali can have any authority over the Muslim community. Today, Shiites rule Iran and are numerous in Iraq but make up only 10 percent of the worldwide population of Islam.

Silicon Valley Valley between California's San Francisco and San Jose, known for its innovative computer and high-technology industry.

Sinn Féin The Irish revolutionary organization that formed in 1900 to fight for Irish independence.

Sino-Japanese War (1894–1895) Conflict over the control of Korea in which China was forced to cede the province of Taiwan to Japan.

Adam Smith (1723–1790) Scottish economist and philosopher who proposed that individual self-interest naturally promoted a healthy national economy. He became famous for his influential book, *The Wealth of Nations* (1776).

Social Darwinism Belief that Charles Darwin's theory of natural selection (evolution) was applicable to human societies and justified the right of the ruling classes or countries to dominate the weak.

social democracy The belief that democracy and social welfare go hand in hand, and that diminishing the sharp inequalities of class society is crucial to fortifying democratic culture.

socialism Political ideology that calls for a classless society with collective ownership of all property.

Social Security Act (1935) New Deal act that instituted old-age pensions and insurance for the unemployed in the United States.

the Social Question In the wake of the Industrial Revolution and rapid urbanization, topics such as criminality, water supply, sewers, prostitution, tuberculosis and cholera, alcoholism, wet nursing, wages, and unemployment were studied by political leaders, social scientists, and public health officials throughout Europe and collectively referred to as the "Social Question." Reformers and politicians believed that these issues needed to be addressed to avoid popular revolts in Europe's cities.

Society of Jesus Also called the Jesuit order, a group of priests influenced by military discipline. The society was founded by Saint Ignatius of Loyola (1491–1556) and is still very active in the field of education.

Socrates (469–399 B.C.E.) The ancient Greek philosopher who emphasized the reexamination of all inherited assumptions and tried to base his philosophical speculations on sound definitions of words. He also wished to advance to a new system of truth by examining ethics rather than by studying the physical world.

Solidarity The communist bloc's first independent trade union; it was established in Poland at the Gdansk shipyard in 1980.

Solon (d. 559 B.C.E.) Elected archon in 594 B.C.E., this ancient Greek aristocrat enacted a series of political and economic reforms that made Athenian democracy possible.

Aleksandr Solzhenitsyn (b. 1918) This Soviet novelist was a critic of the Soviet regime and wrote *The Gulag Archipelago*, which was published in 1974.

Sophists Ancient Greek professional teachers who taught that sense perception was the source of all knowledge and that only particular truths could be valid for the individual knower.

South African War (1899–1902) Often called the Boer War, this conflict between the British and Dutch colonists of South Africa resulted in bringing two Afrikaner republics under the control of the British.

Soviet bloc International alliance that included the East European countries of the Warsaw Pact as well as the Soviet Union, but also came to include Cuba.

Spanish-American War (1898) War between the United States and Spain in Cuba, Puerto Rico, and the Philippines. It ended with a treaty in which the United States took over the Philippines, Guam, and Puerto Rico; Cuba won partial independence.

Spanish Armada Supposedly invincible fleet of warships sent against England by Philip II of Spain in 1588, but routed by the English and bad weather in the English Channel.

Spartiate A full citizen of Sparta who was a professional soldier of the hoplite phalanx.

spinning jenny Invention of James Hargreaves (c. 1720–1774) that revolutionized the British textile industry.

S.S. (*Schutzstaffel*) Formed in 1925 to serve as Hitler's personal security force and to guard Nazi party (NDSAP) meetings, the SS were notorious for their participation in carrying out Nazi policies.

Joseph Stalin (1879–1953) The Bolshevik leader who succeeded Lenin as the leader of the Soviet Union in 1924 and ruled until his death.

Strategic Defense Initiative (Stars Wars)   Master plan initiated by President Ronald Reagan that envisioned the deployment of satellites and space missiles to insulate the United States from nuclear bombs missiles.

Stoicism   The ancient Greek and Roman philosophy that held that the cosmos is an ordered whole in which all contradictions are resolved for ultimate good. Everything that happens is rigidly determined in accordance with rational purpose, and no individual is master of his or her fate. Founded in the fourth century B.C.E. and still popular well into the fifth century C.E.

Suez Canal   Built in 1869 across the Isthmus of Suez to connect the Mediterranean Sea with the Red Sea and to lower the costs of international trade.

Sufism   Emotional and mystical form of Islam that appealed to the common people.

sultan   An Islamic political leader. In the Ottoman empire, the sultan combined a warrior ethos with an unwavering devotion to Islam.

Sumerians   The civilization and people that arose in southern Mesopotamia (modern Iraq and Kuwait) around 4000 B.C.E. and developed one of the first written languages.

Sunnis   Orthodox Islam, as opposed to Shiite Islam.

supranational organizations   International organizations such as NGOs, the World Bank, and the IMF.

survival of the fittest   A main concept of Charles Darwin's theory of natural selection (evolution), which holds that as animal populations grow and resources become scarce, a struggle for existence arises, the outcome of which is that only the "fittest" survive.

sweatshops   Textile factories with poor pay and work conditions.

Syndicalism   Late-nineteenth-century organization of workplace associations that included unskilled labor.

tabula rasa   Term used by John Locke (1632–1704) to describe man's mind before he acquired ideas as a result of experience; Latin for "clean slate."

Testament of Youth   The memoir by Vera Brittain about the home front and the changing social norms during World War I.

tetrarchy   Diocletian's political reform, which divided the Roman empire into two halves ruled by two rulers and two lieutenants.

Third Estate   Delegates from the common class to the Estates General, the French legislature, whose refusal to capitulate to the nobility and clergy in 1789 led to the Revolution.

Third Reich   The German state from 1933 to 1945 under Adolf Hitler and the Nazi party.

Third World   Nations—mostly in Asia, Latin America, and Africa—that are not highly industrialized and developed.

Thirty Years' War (1618–1648)   Beginning as a conflict between Protestants and Catholics in Germany, it escalated into a general European war fought in Germany by Sweden, France, and the Holy Roman Empire.

The Three Estates   Eighteenth-century French society was divided into three estates. An individual's status determined his or her legal rights, taxes, and so on. The First Estate was the clergy; the Second was the nobility; and the Third Estate included everyone from wealthy merchants to poor peasants.

Tiananmen Square   Largest public square in the world, located in Beijing, the site of the Chinese pro-democracy movement in 1989 that resulted in the killing of as many as 1,000 protesters by the Chinese army.

Timur the Lame (1336–1405)   Mongol ruler who was the last leader of the Khans' south Asian empire. Also known as Tamerlane.

total war   All-out war involving civilian populations as well as military forces, often used in reference to World War II.

Treaty of Brest-Litovsk (1918)   Separate peace between imperial Germany and the new Bolshevik regime in Russia. The treaty acknowledged the German victory on the Eastern Front and withdrew Russia from the war.

Treaty of Nanjing (1842)   Treaty between China and Britain following the Opium War; it called for indemnities, the opening of new ports, and the cession of Hong Kong to the British.

Treaty of Utrecht (1713)   Resolution to the War of Spanish Succession that redistributed territory among the warring nations of Europe and encouraged England's colonial conquests.

Treaty of Versailles   Signed on June 28, 1919, this peace settlement ended World War I and required Germany to surrender a large part of its most valuable territories and to pay huge reparations to the Allies.

trench warfare   The twenty-five thousand miles of holes and ditches that stretched across the Western Front during World War I and where most of the fighting took place.

Triangular trade   The eighteenth-century commercial Atlantic shipping pattern that took rum from New England to Africa, traded it for slaves taken to the West Indies, and brought sugar back to New England to be processed into rum.

Tripartite Pact (1940)   A pact that stated that the countries of Germany, Italy, and Japan would act together in all future military ventures.

Triple Entente   Alliance developed before World War I that eventually included Britain, France, and Russia.

Truman Doctrine (1947)   Declaration promising U.S. economic and military intervention, whenever and wherever needed, for the sake of preventing further communist expansion.

Truth and Reconciliation Commission   Quasi-judicial body established after the overthrow of the apartheid system in South Africa and the election of Nelson Mandela as the country's first black president in 1994. The commission was to take evidence about the crimes committed during the apartheid years. Those who showed remorse could appeal for clemency. The South African leaders believed that an airing of the grievances from this period would promote racial harmony and reconciliation.

tsar   Russian translation, similar to the German *kaiser*, of the Roman title "caesar" (emperor), a title claimed by the rulers of medieval Muscovy and then the Russian empire.

Mary Tudor (1516–1558)   Catholic daughter of Henry VIII who reinstituted Catholicism in England when she acceded to the throne; she was called "Bloody Mary" for her violent suppression of Protestants during her five-year reign.

Two Treatises on Government   Published in 1690, this work by John Locke (1632–1704) defended humans' right to freedom against absolutist ideas and served as one of the underpinnings of the U.S. Constitution.

Ubaid This culture flourished in Mesopotamia between 5500 and 4000 B.C.E., characterized by large village settlements and the first temples built in that area. A precursor to the Sumerians and the development of "urban" civilizations.

UFA The German film company that produced films by expressionist directors like F. W. Murnau and Fritz Lang during the 1920s. Under Hitler, it was controlled by the state and began turning out Nazi propaganda.

Universal Declaration of Human Rights (1948) United Nations declaration that laid out the rights to which all human beings were entitled.

Utopia Humanist social critique by English statesman Thomas More (1478–1535).

utopian socialism The most visionary of all Restoration-era movements, Utopian socialists, like Charles Fourier, dreamt of transforming states, workplaces, and human relations, and proposed actual plans to do so.

velvet revolutions The peaceful political revolutions throughout Eastern Europe in 1989.

Versailles Splendid palace outside Paris where Louis XIV and his nobles resided.

Versailles Conference (1919) Peace conference between the victors of World War I; resulted in the Treaty of Versailles, which forced Germany to pay reparations and to give up its colonies to the victors.

Queen Victoria (1819–1901) Influential monarch who reigned from 1837 to her death; she presided over the expansion of the British empire as well as the evolution of English politics and social and economic reforms.

Viet Cong Vietnamese communist group formed in 1954; committed to overthrowing the government of South Vietnam and reunifying North and South Vietnam.

A Vindication of the Rights of Woman Noted work of Mary Wollstonecraft (1759–1797), English republican who applied Enlightenment political ideas to issues of gender.

Virgil (70–19 B.C.E.) One of the most influential Roman authors, his surviving works include the Eclogues and the Roman epic poem, the Aeneid.

Visigoths The German "barbarians" who sacked Rome in 410.

Voltaire Pseudonym of French philosopher and satirist Francois Marie Arouet (1694–1797), who championed the cause of human dignity against state and church oppression. Noted Deist and author of Candide.

Voting Rights Act (1965) Law that granted universal suffrage in the United States.

Wars of the Roses Fifteenth-century conflict between the English dynastic houses of Lancaster and York (each symbolized in heraldry by the rose), ultimately won by Lancastrian Henry VII.

Warsaw Pact (1955–1991) Military alliance between the U.S.S.R. and other Communist states that was established as a response to the creation of the NATO alliance.

James Watt (1736–1819) Scottish inventor and scientist who developed the steam engine.

The Wealth of Nations 1776 treatise by Adam Smith, whose laissez-faire ideas predicted the economic boom of the Industrial Revolution.

Weimar Republic The government of Germany between 1919 and the rise of Hitler and the Nazi party.

Western Front Military front that stretched from the English Channel through Belgium and France to the Alps during World War I.

Whites Refers to the "counterrevolutionaries" of the Bolshevik Revolution (1918–1921) who fought the Bolsheviks (the "Reds"); included former supporters of the tsar, Social Democrats, and large independent peasant armies.

William and Mary (1650–1702 and 1662–1694) Dutch noble couple who supplanted the deposed Catholic King James II in 1688 as monarchs of England.

William of Ockham (d. 1349) An English Franciscan monk, Ockham denied that human reason could prove fundamental theological truths such as the existence of God. He argued that there was no necessary connection between the observable laws of nature and the unknowable essence of divinity, and no hope of reason from the laws of nature to the nature of God. Ockham's ideas encouraged intellectuals to investigate the natural world without reference to the supernatural and encouraged empiricism.

William the Conqueror (1027–1087) Duke of French Normandy who crossed the English Channel and defeated Harold for the English throne in 1066. Imposed a centralized feudal system on England and introduced French as the official language.

woman suffrage The movement to win legal and political rights, including the right to vote for all women.

Works Progress Administration (WPA) New Deal program instituted in 1935 that put nearly 3 million people to work building roads, bridges, airports, and post offices.

World Bank International agency established in 1944 to provide economic assistance to war-torn and poor countries. Its formal title is the International Bank for Reconstruction and Development.

Yalta Accords Meeting between President Franklin D. Roosevelt, Prime Minister Winston Churchill, and Premier Josef Stalin that occurred in the Crimea in 1945 to to prepare for the postwar order.

yellow press Newspapers that sought increased circulation by featuring sensationalist reporting that appealed to the masses.

Boris Yeltsin (1931–2007) The President of Russia who led the country after the disintegration of the Soviet Union in 1991.

Young Turks The 1908 Turkish nationalist movement to depose Sultan Abdul Hamid II.

Yugoslavia The Eastern European country that broke apart after the fall of the Soviet Union. Driven by nationalism and ethnic rivalries, the former Yugoslavia divided into six countries: Bosnia-Herzegovina, Croatia, Macedonia, Montenegro, Serbia, and Slovenia.

Zionism Formally founded in 1897, a political movement holding that the Jewish people constitute a nation and are entitled to a national homeland, originally advocating the reestablishment of a Jewish homeland in Palestine.

Zoroastrians   Founded by Zoroaster around 600 B.C.E., this Persian religion urged people to be truthful, to help each other, and to practice hospitality. Those who did would be rewarded in an afterlife after a "judgment day."

Zulus   African tribe that, under Shaka, created a ruthless warrior state in southern Africa in the early 1800s.

Ulrich Zwingli (1484–1531)   A former Catholic priest from Zurich, Zwingli joined Luther and Calvin in attacking the authority of the Catholic Church. Zwingli's reforms resembled those of Luther's except that Zwingli believed that the Eucharist conferred no grace at all. At his peak, Zwingli converted much of northern Switzerland. After Zwingli's death in a battle with Catholic forces, most of his supporters began following John Calvin.

TEXT CREDITS

PHOTO CREDITS

Part I: **2–3**: *King Tutankhamen fighting the Nubians* (Giraudon/Art Resource, NY)

Chapter 1: **6**: *An Egyptian Scribe* (The Louvre, Paris. Photo: Giraudon/Art Resource, NY); **8**: Science Museum, Minnesota; **9** (**top**): Joerg Carstensen/epa/Corbis; **9** (**bottom**): The Bridgeman Art Library; **13** (**top**): © Richard Nowitz Photos; **13** (**bottom**): Himer Fotoarchiv; **16**: © 2003 Nik Wheeler; **17** (**left**): Copyright by the Ashmolean Museum, Oxford; **17** (**right**): Courtesy of the British Museum; **19, 20, 30, 43, 45**: *A Sumerian Banquet* (Bettmann/Corbis); **22**: Courtesy of the Oriental Institute of the University of Chicago; **23** (**top**): From *The Origins of War*, by Arthur Ferrill, published by Thames and Hudson, Inc., New York; **23** (**bottom**): British Museum; **24** (**left**): Iraq Museum, Baghdad, Iraq. Photo: Scala/Art Resource, NY; **24** (**right**): University of Pennsylvania Museum; **25, 27**: Hirmer Fotoarchiv; **28**: The Nelson-Atkins Museum of Art, Kansas City, Missouri (Purchase: Nelson Trust); **29**: Hirmer Fotoarchiv; **31**: The Louvre, Paris. Photo: Herve Lewandowski, Réunion des Musées Nationaux/Art Resource, NY; **35** (**top**): Copyright Jurgen Liepe, Berlin; **35** (**bottom**): Bettmann/Corbis; **36**: *Ancient Civilizations*, 2/e by Scarre/Fagan, © 2003 Reprinted by permission of Pearson Education, Inc., Upper Saddle River, NJ; **37**: Roger Wood/Corbis; **38**: Charles & Josette Lenars/Corbis; **39**: Archivo Iconografico, S.A./Corbis; **41**: Excavations of The Metropolitan Museum of Art, 1929; Rogers Fund, 1930. (30.3.31) Photograph © 1978 The Metropolitan Museum of Art; **42** (**left**): British Museum. Photo: HIP/Art Resource, NY; **42** (**right**): British Museum. Photo: HIP/Art Resource, NY; **44**: Egyptian Museum, Cairo; **46**: The Louvre, Paris/Bridgeman Art Library

Chapter 2: **48**: *Egyptian Slaves at Work* (Egyptian expedition of The Metropolitan Museum of Art, Rogers Fund, 1930 (30.3.77) Photograph © The Metropolitan Museum of Art; **53**: British Museum, London. Photo: Erich Lessing/Art Resource, NY; **56** (**top**): Erich Lessing/Art Resource, NY; **56** (**bottom**): Jose Fuste Raga/Corbis; **57**: Courtesy Museum of Fine Arts, Boston; **58** (**top**): Eric Lessing/Art Resource, NY; **58** (**bottom**): Staaliche Museen zu Berlin—Bildarchiv Preussischer Kulturbesitz/Art Resource, NY; **59, 62, 76, 81**: detail of *Procession Road* (Vorderasiatisches Museum, Staatliche Museen zu Berlin. Photo: Bildarchiv Preussischer Kulturbesitz/Art Resource, NY; **60**: Boltin Picture Library; **61**: British Museum/Art Resource, NY; **63**: Wolfgang Kaehler/Corbis; **64**: Gian Berto Vanni/Corbis; **65** (**top**): Martin A. Ryerson Collection, 1992.4914. Photograph © 1997, The Art Institute of Chicago. All rights reserved; **65** (**bottom**): Boltin Pic-

ture Library; **66** (**top**): Scala/Art Resource, NY; **66** (**bottom**): Gianni Dagli Orti/Corbis; **67**: Gianni Dagli Orti/Corbis; **70**: Erich Lessing/Art Resource, NY; **72**: *Ancient Civilizations*, 2/e by Scarre/Fagan, © 2003. Reprinted by permission of Pearson Education, Inc., Upper Saddle River, NJ; **78**: Courtesy Zev Radovan (www.bibleandpictures.com); **79**: *Assyrian Winged Human-Headed Bull* (Courtesy of The Oriental Institute of The University of Chicago); **82**: British Museum, London. Photo: Erich Lessing/Art Resource, NY; **84**: *Assurbanipal Feasting with His Wife in a Garden* (Courtesy of The Oriental Institute, The University of Chicago); **85**: American Numismatic Society; **88**: British Museum/Bridgeman Art Library; **91**: Courtesy Zev Radovan (www.bibleandpictures.com); **92**: Staatliche Museen zu Berlin. Photo: Bildarchiv Preussischer Kulturbesitz/Art Resource, NY

Part II: **96–97**: *Battle of Issus* (Scala/Art Resource, NY)

Chapter 3: **100**: *The School of Plato* (Scala/Art Resource, NY); **102**: Art Resource, NY; **104, 110, 132**: *A symposium-a festive meal.* 4th century B.C.E. (Kunsthistorisches Museum, Vienna, Austria. Photo: Erich Lessing/Art Resource, NY); **108**: Hirmer Fotoarchiv; **109** (**top**): Réunion des Musées Nationaux/Art Resource, NY; **109** (**bottom**): British Museum, London. Photo: HIP/Art Resource, NY; **113** (**left**): Bridgeman Art Library; **113** (**right**): American School of Classical Studies at Athens: Agora Excavations; **114**: Naples National Museum, Photo: Gianni Dagli Orti/Corbis; **119**: Museo Archeologico Nazionale, Naples, Italy. Photo: Scala/Art Resource, NY; **121**: Réunion des Musées Nationaux/Art Resource, NY; **122**: Scala/Art Resource, NY; **123** (**top**): George Brockway/The Warder Collection, NY; **123** (**bottom**): Vanni/Art Resource, NY; **124** (**left**): Hartwig Koppermann; **124** (**center**): Réunion des Musées Nationaux/Art Resource, NY; **124** (**right**): Nimatallah/Art Resource, NY; **125** (**top**): Royal Ontario Museum; **125** (**bottom**): Réunion des Musées Nationaux/Art Resource, NY; **126** (**top**): British Museum. Photo: HIP/Art Resource, NY; **126** (**bottom**): Museo Nazionale Romano; **128**: Photo: Paul Lipke/Trireme Trust, Montague, MA; **131**: Erich Lessing/Art Resource, NY; **134**: Deutschen Archaologischen

Chapter 4: **136**: *The colossal statue of the Nile River* (Scala/Art Resource, NY); **140**: Scala/Art Resource, NY; **141**: Kunsthistorisches Museum, Vienna; **143**: Vanni Dagli Orti/Corbis; **144** (**top**): Gianni Dagli Orti/Corbis; **145, 155, 156**: *Dionysus Anaploga.* Floor mosaic. 1st century C.E. Corinth, Greece (Vanni/Art Resource, NY); **146**: Museo Archeologico Nationale,

Naples. Photo: Erich Lessing/Art Resource, NY; 148: British Museum, London. Photo: © British Museum/Art Resource, NY; 150 (left): British Museum, London; 150 (right): Muenzkabinett Staatliche zu Berlin. Photo: Bildarchiv Preussischer Kulturbesitz/Art Resource, NY; 152: Historical District Museum, Vraca, Bulgaria. Photo: Erich Lessing/Art Resource, NY; 157 (top): The Metropolitan Museum of Art, Fletcher Fund, 1954. (54.3.3) Photograph © 1982 The Metropolitan Museum of Art; 157 (bottom left): Erdmut Lerner; 157 (bottom right): University Prints; 158 (top): The Metropolitan Museum of Art, Rogers Fund, 1909. (09.39) Photograph © 1977 The Metropolitan Museum of Art; 158 (bottom): Scala/Art Resource, NY; 159 (left): Giraudon/Art Resource, NY; 159 (right): Nimatallah/Art Resource, NY; 160: Verulamium Museum, St. Albans, UK. Photo Bridgeman Art Library

Chapter 5: 164: *Portrait of Pasquio Proculo and his wife* (Alinari/Art Resource, NY); 166: *Sarcophagus and lid with husband and wife.* Italic, Etruscan, Late Classical or Early Hellenistic Period, about 330–300 B.C.; Findspot and Place of Manufacture: Italy, Lazio, Vulci; marble, 93.3 cm high x 117.4 cm width x 213.8 cm length; Museum of Fine Arts, Boston, Gift of Mrs. Gardner Brewer, 86.145a–b. Photograph © 2004 Museum of Fine Arts, Boston; 167: Musei Capitolini, Rome, Italy; Photo: Scala/Art Resource, NY; 169, 179, 186, 191: Mosaic in red tesserae. 2nd century C.E. Corinth, Greece. Photo: Vanni/Art Resource, NY; 172: Scala/Art Resource, NY; 173: British Museum, London; 174: American Numismatic Society; 177: Scala/Art Resource, NY; 178: British Museum. Photo: HIP/Art Resource, NY; 182 (top): American Numismatic Society; 182 (bottom): Scala/Art Resource, NY; 183: Scala/Art Resource, NY; 185: Vanni/Art Resource, NY; 189: Scala/Art Resource, NY; 190: British Museum. Photo: HIP/Art Resource, NY; 192 (top): Scala/Art Resource, NY; 192 (bottom): Vanni/Art Resource; 193: Scala/Art Resource, NY; 194 (left): British Museum. Photo: HIP/Art Resource, NY; 194 (right): British Museum. Photo: HIP/Art Resource, NY; 196: British Museum, London; 197: Gift of Martin A. Ryerson, 1922.4883. Photograph © 1997, The Art Institute of Chicago. All rights reserved; 198: Scala/Art Resource, NY

Chapter 6: 202: *Constantine IV with his brothers Heraclius and Tiberius Conceding Privileges of the Church of Ravenna to Reparato who is protected by Archbishop Mauro* (Alinari/Art Resource, NY); 204: The Warder Collection, NY; 206: The Warder Collection, NY; 207: Scala/Art Resource, NY; 209: Scala/Art Resource, NY; 211 (top): Scala/Art Resource, NY; 211 (bottom): The Louvre, Paris. Photo: Erich Lessing/Art Resource, NY; 213: British Museum, London; 214, 221, 227: *Mausoleum of Galla Placidia, Ravenna, Italy* (Photo: Scala/Art Resource, NY); 217: Scala/Art Resource, NY; 219: The Louvre, Paris. Photo: Herve Lewandowski, RMN/Art Resource, NY; 220: Scala/Art Resource; 225: British Museum, London. Photo: HIP/Art Resource, NY; 229: By permission of the Houghton Library, Harvard University; 230: Scala/Art Resource, NY; 232: Biblioteca Medicea Laurenziana, Florence; 233: The Warder Collection, NY; 235 (top): Scala/Art Resource, NY; 235 (bottom): Scala/Art Resource, NY

Part III: 240–241: Anonymous, 15th century. *The Death of Charlemagne.* Vincent de Beauvais, Le Miroir Historical. Ms. 722/1196, fol. 113 v. French, 15th c. (Photo: Giraudon/Art Resource, NY

Chapter 7: 244: *Muslim Pilgrims on Their Way to Mecca* (Bibliothèque Nationale de France, Paris); 247: Werner Forman/Art Resource, NY; 248: Scala/Art Resource, NY; 250, 257, 265, 278: *Inlaid marble floor, Byzantine.* (Mosaic Museum, Istanbul, Turkey. Photo: Werner Forman/Art Resource, NY); 251: The Art Archive/Dagli Orti; 252: Vanni/Art Resource, NY; 253: The Art Archive/HarperCollins Publishers; 254 (left): Scala/Art Resource, NY; 254 (right): Scala/Art Resource, NY; 259 (left): Khaled al-Hariri/Reuters/Corbis; 259 (right): Courtesy Christian and Kathleen Destoop; 261: cliché Bibliothèque Nationale de France, Paris; 263: Giraudon/Art Resource, NY; 264: Bildarchiv Preussischer Kulturbesitz/Art Resource, NY; 266: Bildarchiv Preussischer Kulturbesitz/Art Resource, NY; 268: cliché Bibliothèque Nationale de France, Paris; 269 (left): British Museum/Art Resource, NY; 269 (right): British Museum/Art Resource, NY; 270: The Pierpont Morgan Library/Art Resource, NY; 272: Kunsthistorisches Museum, Vienna; 274: The Art Archive/Biblioteca del duomo Moderna/Dagli Orti (A); 276: Vatican Library: MS Reg. Ret. 762, fol. 82r, written at Tours 800 A.D. (detail); 279: British Museum. Photo: HIP/Art Resource, NY; 281: Kunsthistorisches Museum, Vienna

Chapter 8: 286: Limbourg Brothers (15th century C.E.). *June. Tres Riches Heures du Duc De Berry,* (Palace and Ste. Chapelle in background). (Giraudon/Art Resource, NY); 289 (top): The Art Archive/Biblioteca Nazionale Marciana, Venice/Dagli Orti (A); 289 (bottom): Biblioteca Riccardiana, Florence, Manuscript Ricc. 492 c. 18, with the permission of the Ministero per I Beni Culturali e Ambientali; 290 (top): British Library/Art Resource, NY; 290 (center): British Library/Art Resource, NY; 290 (bottom): British Library/Art Resource, NY; 291: British Library. Photo: HIP/Art Resource, NY; 292: Statens Historiska Museet, Stockholm. Photo: Werner Forman/Art Resource, NY; 295 (top): The Art Archive/British Library; 295 (bottom): Oesterreichische Nationalbibliothek, Vienna. Photo: Alinari/Art Resource, NY; 296, 300, 302, 308, 325: *View of Paris* (cliché Bibliothèque National de France, Paris); 297: Biblioteca Marciana, Venice. Photo: Werner Forman/Art Resource, NY; 305: British Library. Photo: HIP/Art Resource, NY; 309: Bibliotheque Municipale, Rouen, France. Photo: Giraudon/Art Resource, NY; 311: Art Resource, NY; 313: Diebold Schilling, Official Bernese Chronicle, vol. 1, Burgerbibliothek, Berne, Ms. h.h.I.1, 289; 315: Musee de la Tapisserie, Bayeux, France. Photo: Erich Lessing/Art Resource, NY; 317: The Walters Art Gallery, Baltimore; 321: cliché Bibliothèque Nationale de France, Paris; 326: Biblioteca Apostolica Vaticana, The Vatican, Italy. Photo: Bridgeman Art Library

Chapter 9: 330: *A Lecture Class in a Medieval University* (Bettmann/Corbis); 334, 338, 342, 348: 12th century sleeve of the Dalmatic (detail) (Kunsthistorisches Museum, Vienna, Austria. Photo: Erich Lessing/Art Resource, NY); 335: Treasury, Abbey Ste. Foy, Conques, France. Photo: Giraudon/Art Resource, NY; 337: Thüringer Universität-und Landesbibliothek, Jena, Ms. Bos. Q. 6, fol. 79r; 341: Bettmann/Corbis; 343: Bettmann/Corbis; 345: Copyright Otto Muller Verlag, Salzburg, Austria; 346: Bayerische Staatsbibliothek, München; 349: Scala/Art Resource, NY; 350: Bayerische Staatsbibliothek, München; 353 (both): cliché Bibliothèque Nationale de France, Paris; 356: Giraudon/Art Resource, NY; 358: Alinari Archives/Corbis; 360: The

Bodleian Library, Oxford: MS Bodley. 264, fol. 81v (detail); 361: cliché Bibliothèque Nationale de France, Paris; 363 (both): Richard List/Corbis

Part IV 366–367: *A Portuguese galleon* (National Maritime Museum, London)

Chapter 10: 370: *Les Grandes Chroniques de France* (Erich Lessing/Art Resource, NY); **372:** British Museum. Photo: Snark/Art Resource, NY; **373:** Bibliotheque Royale Albert I, Brussels. Photo: Snark/Art Resource, NY; **375 (top):** Bibliotheque Nationale, Paris. Photo: Archives Charmet/Bridgeman Art Library; **375 (bottom):** Ann Ronan Picture Library, London. Photo: HIP/Art Resource, NY; **376:** British Library. Photo: HIP/Art Resource, NY; **377:** Bibliothèque Nationale, Paris. Photo: Snark/Art Resource, NY; **378:** Bibliotheque Municipale, Besancon, France. Photo: Erich Lessing/Art Resource, NY; **379 (top):** Bibliotheque Nationale, Paris. Photo: Giraudon/Art Resource, NY; **379 (bottom):** Réunion des Musées Nationaux/Art Resource, NY; **380:** British Library. Photo: HIP/Art Resource, NY; **381, 389, 402:** detail from *The Plague of a Murrain Among the Cattle, c. 1250* (The Pierpont Morgan Library, New York. Photo: The Pierpont Morgan Library/Art Resource, NY); **382:** Musee Conde, Chantilly, France. Photo: Réunion des Musées Nationaux/Art Resource, NY; **383:** Musee Conde, Chantilly, France. Photo: Réunion des Musées Nationaux/Art Resource, NY; **386:** British Library. Photo: HIP/Art Resource, NY; **387:** Westminster Abbey, London. Photo: Bridgeman Art Library; **388 (top):** Bibliotheque Nationale, Paris. Photo: Snark/Art Resource, NY; **388 (bottom):** Archives Nationales, Paris. Photo: Réunion des Musées Nationaux/Art Resource, NY; **391:** The Louvre, Paris. Photo: Erich Lessing/Art Resource, NY; **392 (left):** King's College, Cambridge. Photo: Bildarchiv Preussischer Kulturbesitz/Art Resource, NY; **392 (right):** National Portrait Gallery, London; **394:** Art Archive/ Museo del Prado, Madrid; **398:** Vova Pomortzeff/Alamy; **399:** Giraudon/

Bridgeman Art Library; **401:** Bibliotheque Nationale, Paris. Photo: Bildarchiv Preussischer Kulturbesitz/Art Resource, NY; **406:** The Art Archive/British Library; **408:** By permission of the British Library; **410:** Scrovegni Chapel, Padua, Italy. Photo: Scala/Art Resource, NY; **411:** Bibliothèque Royale Albert I, Brussels; **413:** © Bibliotheque Royale Albert I, Brussels, ms. 11209, fol. 3 recto

Chapter 11: 416: *Army of Suleiman the Magnificent conquering Europe* (The Art Archive/Topkapi Museum, Istanbul/Dagli Orti); **420:** John Massey Stewart Picture Library; **421, 425, 432, 437:** *Persian panel of mosaic tilework, 14th–15th century* (Victoria & Albert Museum, London. Photo: Victoria & Albert Museum/Art Resource, NY); **423:** Werner Forman Archive/Topkapi Palace Library, Istanbul/Art Resource, NY; **424:** Mansell/TimePix/Getty Images; **431:** Royal Armouries Museum; **433:** José Pessoa, Arquivo Nacional de Fotografia, Instituto Português de Museus; **435:** The Art Archive/Biblioteca Nacional de Madrid/Dagli Orti.

Chapter 12: 440: *The School of Athens*, by Raphael (Scala/Art Resource, NY); **444, 447, 450:** detail from *Ceiling of Sala di Giove* (Palazzo Farnese, Caprarola, Italy. Photo: Scala/Art Resource, NY); **446:** Art Resource, NY; **448:** Réunion des Musées Nationaux /Art Resource, NY; **451:** Erich Lessing/Art Resource, NY; **452:** Erich Lessing/Art Resource, NY; **453 (top):** Réunion des Musées Nationaux /Art Resource, NY; **453 (bottom):** Scala/Art Resource, NY; **454:** Thyssen-Bornemisza Collection, Madrid, Spain/Art Resource, NY; **455:** Scala/Art Resource, NY; **456:** Scala/Art Resource, NY; **457:** Nimatallah/Art Resource, NY; **458 (left):** Scala/Art Resource, NY; **458 (right):** Erich Lessing/Art Resource, NY; **459:** Sandro Vannini/Corbis; **463:** © Frick Collection, New York; **464:** Réunion des Musées Nationaux /Art Resource, NY; **466:** Vanni/Art Resource, NY; **467:** Bildarchiv Preussischer Kulturbesitz/Art Resource, NY;

INDEX